The Editors

V. A. KOLVE is the author of *The Play Called Corpus Christi*, a study of medieval drama, and of *Chaucer and the Imagery of Narrative: The First Five Canterbury Tales*. He has taught at Oxford, Stanford, the University of Virginia, and most recently at UCLA, as Foundation Professor of English (now Emeritus). He has served as president of the New Chaucer Society and of the Medieval Academy of America.

GLENDING OLSON, Professor Emeritus of English at Cleveland State University, is the author of *Literature as Recreation in the Later Middle Ages* and of many articles on Chaucer and medieval literary theory. He has held NEH and Guggenheim fellowships.

W. W. NORTON & COMPANY, INC.
Also Publishes

ENGLISH RENAISSANCE DRAMA: A NORTON ANTHOLOGY
edited by David Bevington et al.

THE NORTON ANTHOLOGY OF AFRICAN AMERICAN LITERATURE
edited by Henry Louis Gates Jr. and Nellie Y. McKay et al.

THE NORTON ANTHOLOGY OF AMERICAN LITERATURE
edited by Nina Baym et al.

THE NORTON ANTHOLOGY OF CHILDREN'S LITERATURE
edited by Jack Zipes et al.

THE NORTON ANTHOLOGY OF DRAMA
edited by J. Ellen Gainor, Stanton B. Garner Jr., and Martin Puchner

THE NORTON ANTHOLOGY OF ENGLISH LITERATURE
edited by M. H. Abrams and Stephen Greenblatt et al.

THE NORTON ANTHOLOGY OF LITERATURE BY WOMEN
edited by Sandra M. Gilbert and Susan Gubar

THE NORTON ANTHOLOGY OF MODERN AND CONTEMPORARY POETRY
edited by Jahan Ramazani, Richard Ellmann, and Robert O'Clair

THE NORTON ANTHOLOGY OF POETRY
edited by Margaret Ferguson, Mary Jo Salter, and Jon Stallworthy

THE NORTON ANTHOLOGY OF SHORT FICTION
edited by R. V. Cassill and Richard Bausch

THE NORTON ANTHOLOGY OF THEORY AND CRITICISM
edited by Vincent B. Leitch et al.

THE NORTON ANTHOLOGY OF WORLD LITERATURE
edited by Sarah Lawall et al.

THE NORTON FACSIMILE OF THE FIRST FOLIO OF SHAKESPEARE
prepared by Charlton Hinman

THE NORTON INTRODUCTION TO LITERATURE
edited by Alison Booth and Kelly J. Mays

THE NORTON READER
edited by Linda H. Peterson and John C. Brereton

THE NORTON SAMPLER
edited by Thomas Cooley

THE NORTON SHAKESPEARE, BASED ON THE OXFORD EDITION
edited by Stephen Greenblatt et al.

For a complete list of Norton Critical Editions, visit
www.wwnorton.com/college/English/nce_home.htm

A NORTON CRITICAL EDITION

Geoffrey Chaucer
THE CANTERBURY TALES
FIFTEEN TALES AND THE
GENERAL PROLOGUE

AUTHORITATIVE TEXT

SOURCES AND BACKGROUNDS

CRITICISM

SECOND EDITION

Selected and Edited by

V. A. KOLVE

THE UNIVERSITY OF CALIFORNIA AT
LOS ANGELES

GLENDING OLSON

CLEVELAND STATE UNIVERSITY

W • W • NORTON & COMPANY • *New York* • *London*

W. W. Norton & Company has been independent since its founding in 1923, when William Warder Norton and Mary D. Herter Norton first published lectures delivered at the People's Institute, the adult education division of New York City's Cooper Union. The Nortons soon expanded their program beyond the Institute, publishing books by celebrated academics from America and abroad. By midcentury, the two major pillars of Norton's publishing program—trade books and college texts—were firmly established. In the 1950s, the Norton family transferred control of the company to its employees, and today—with a staff of four hundred and a comparable number of trade, college, and professional titles published each year—W. W. Norton & Company stands as the largest and oldest publishing house owned wholly by its employees.

The text of this book is composed in Fairfield Medium with the display set in Bernhard Modern.
Composition by PennSet, Inc.
Manufacturing by the Courier Companies—Westford Division.
Production Manager: Ben Reynolds.

Library of Congress Cataloging-in-Publication Data

Chaucer, Geoffrey, d. 1400.
[Canterbury tales. Selections]
The Canterbury tales : fifteen tales and the general prologue : authoritative texts, sources and backgrounds, criticism / selected and edited by V. A. Kolve, Glending Olson.
    p. cm. — (A Norton critical edition)
Includes bibliographical references.

ISBN 0-393-92587-0 (pbk.)

1. Christian pilgrims and pilgrimages—Poetry. 2. Storytelling—Poetry. 3. Tales, Medieval. I. Kolve, V. A. II. Olson, Glending. III. Title. IV. Series.

PR1867.K65 2005
821'.1—dc22

                                                          2004063642

W. W. Norton & Company, Inc., 500 Fifth Avenue, New York, N.Y. 10110-0017
www.wwnorton.com

W. W. Norton & Company Ltd., Castle House,
75/76 Wells Street, London W1T 3QT

3 4 5 6 7 8 9 0

for
Robert and Sarah Dugenske
and
Justin and Matthew Kash

whose student days are still ahead

Contents

Preface   xi
Chaucer's Language   xv

Selections from *The Canterbury Tales*

The General Prologue   3
The Knight's Tale   23
The Miller's Prologue and Tale   71
The Reeve's Prologue and Tale   88
The Cook's Prologue and Tale   99
The Wife of Bath's Prologue and Tale   102
The Friar's Prologue and Tale   131
The Summoner's Prologue and Tale   140
The Clerk's Prologue and Tale   154
The Merchant's Prologue and Tale   185
The Franklin's Prologue and Tale   212
The Pardoner's Prologue and Tale   233
The Prioress's Prologue and Tale   248
The Prologue and Tale of Sir Thopas   255
From The Prologue and Tale of Melibee   261
The Nun's Priest's Prologue and Tale   269
The Manciple's Prologue and Tale   285
From The Parson's Prologue and Tale   293
Chaucer's Retraction   306

Sources and Backgrounds

THE GENERAL PROLOGUE   311
Giovanni Boccaccio • From the *Decameron*, First Day,
    Introduction   312
Giovanni Boccaccio • From the *Decameron*, Tenth Day,
    Conclusion   325
St. Augustine • [Human Life as a Pilgrimage]   326
Sir William Thorpe • [On Pilgrimage]   327
Thomas Wimbledon • [On the Estates]   333
William Langland • [On Monks]   335
John Gower • [On Monks]   337
Wycliffite Estates Criticism   339
THE MILLER'S PROLOGUE AND TALE   341
The Three Guests of Heile of Bersele   341
THE REEVE'S PROLOGUE AND TALE   344
The Miller and the Two Clerics   344

THE WIFE OF BATH'S PROLOGUE AND TALE 348
  Jean de Meun • From the *Romance of the Rose* 348
  Theophrastus • From *The Golden Book on Marriage* 357
  St. Jerome • From *Against Jovinian* 359
  Walter Map • From *The Letter of Valerius to Ruffinus,*
    against Marriage 373
  From the Gospel According to St. John 379
  From St. Paul to the Corinthians 1 380
  From St. Paul to the Ephesians 383
  From St. Paul to Timothy 1 384
  From St. Paul to Timothy 2 385
  John Gower • The Tale of Florent 386
THE FRIAR'S PROLOGUE AND TALE 397
  Robert Rypon • A Greedy Bailiff 397
THE CLERK'S PROLOGUE AND TALE 399
  Giovanni Boccaccio • From the *Decameron*, Tenth Day,
    Tenth Tale 399
  Francis Petrarch • The Story of Griselda 407
  Francis Petrarch • [Two Letters to Boccaccio] 417
  From *Le Ménagier de Paris* 420
THE MERCHANT'S PROLOGUE AND TALE 422
  The Woman and the Pear-Tree 422
THE FRANKLIN'S PROLOGUE AND TALE 424
  Giovanni Boccaccio • From the *Decameron*, Tenth Day,
    Fifth Tale 424
  Bartholomaeus Anglicus • [On Love and Marriage] 428
THE PARDONER'S PROLOGUE AND TALE 431
  Jean de Meun • From *The Romance of the Rose* 431
  The Hermit, Death, and the Robbers 436
  Thomas of Cantimpré • From *Liber de Apibus* 438
THE PRIORESS'S PROLOGUE AND TALE 439
  The Story of the *Alma Redemptoris Mater* 439
  A Miracle of Our Lady 445
  Alma Redemptoris Mater 448
  Pope Gregory X • [On Christian Mistreatment of Jews] 449
THE PROLOGUE AND TALE OF SIR THOPAS 451
  From *Guy of Warwick* 451
THE NUN'S PRIEST'S PROLOGUE AND TALE 455
  William Caxton • From *Aesop's Fables* 455
  Marie de France • The Cock and the Fox 456
  From *Le Roman de Renart*, Branch 2 457
  Macrobius • [On Dreams] 461
  Geoffrey of Vinsauf • [Lament on the Death of
    Richard I] 463
  Bartholomaeus Anglicus • [On the Cock] 464
THE MANCIPLE'S PROLOGUE AND TALE 466
  Ovid • [The Story of Phoebus and Coronis] 466
  John Gower • The Tale of Phoebus and Cornide 468

Criticism

F. R. H. Du Boulay • The Historical Chaucer 473

Arthur W. Hoffman • Chaucer's Prologue to Pilgrimage:
The Two Voices 492

E. Talbot Donaldson • Chaucer the Pilgrim 503

Barbara Nolan • "A Poet Ther Was": Chaucer's Voices
in the General Prologue to The Canterbury Tales 511

George Lyman Kittredge • [The Dramatic Principle of the
Canterbury Tales] 534

George Lyman Kittredge • [The Marriage Group] 539

Lee Patterson • From The Parson's Tale and the Quitting
of the Canterbury Tales 546

Paul Strohm • From Social Chaucer:
"A Mixed Commonwealth of Style" 556

Carolyn Dinshaw • Eunuch Hermeneutics 566

Geoffrey Chaucer: A Chronology 587

Selected Bibliography 589

Preface

The first part of this edition of *The Canterbury Tales: Fifteen Tales and the General Prologue*—the glossed Chaucer text—is addressed specifically to students making their first acquaintance with Chaucer in his own language, and it takes nothing for granted. All difficult words and constructions are translated, in glosses at the margins of the page or in footnotes at the bottom when longer explanations are required. Because we hope the book will serve introductory courses in literature as well as more specialized courses in medieval studies, the glossing is complete for each of the tales. They may be assigned in any number and in any sequence. We have selected tales generally considered among Chaucer's finest, and whenever possible we have included from Chaucer's framing story passages that locate each tale in its immediate dramatic context.

The glossing is frankly pedagogic, intended to help the student understand Chaucer in the original language rather than to provide a steadily idiomatic modern translation. *Thou*-forms of the verb, for instance, are glossed as such, though a modern translation would express them as *you*. Verbs are glossed in their exact tense, though medieval texts often shift between past and present forms in ways modern English declares ungrammatical. The glosses sometimes provide both a cognate word (which can help fix the original in mind) and a synonym that better conveys its contextual meaning. The glossing, more extensive than that in most modern editions, is intended not only to explain unfamiliar words but to confirm students' likely guesses about more recognizable ones. Chaucer's language is not so far removed from modern English that translation need be the aim of anyone's study. The poet can be understood in his own voice from the beginning.

The text is likewise conservative and pedagogic. This has not seemed to us an appropriate occasion to attempt a radically new edition of Chaucer's text, even if there were general agreement concerning the shape such an edition should take. Although some eighty-two manuscripts of the *Canterbury Tales* survive, in full or in fragment, none is in Chaucer's own hand and none possesses his final authority. He died before the work was complete, and what has come down to us is, in even its earliest examples, scribal and implicitly editorial. Since we have neither autograph nor archetype, Chaucer's "original text" is in fact irrecoverable—and for editors attempting a definitive edition, as for critics specially concerned with Chaucerian metrics and stylistics, that is a great frustration. But the best manuscripts of the *Canter-*

bury Tales are, on the whole, very good, and the variations between them, word by word, reasonably few and only seldom of substantive importance. In the present case, we have used Skeat's landmark edition as our copy-text; for many specific readings we have consulted facsimile editions of the Ellesmere and Hengwrt manuscripts, the editions of Manly & Rickert, Robinson, Baugh, Donaldson, Pratt, Fisher, and the *Riverside Chaucer*, 3d ed., under the general editorship of Larry D. Benson. Skeat lightly normalized the spelling in the manuscripts, a feature we have retained as a convenience for beginning students, along with his use of a hyphen after the *y*-prefix in past participles. Our most systematic change has been to repunctuate the text, for the sake of clarity and in accordance with both medieval and contemporary usage. In matters of punctuation, less has seemed to us more. Finally, for ease of cross-reference, we have numbered the lines of each tale to accord with the standard numbering in the most widely used complete editions of Chaucer's poetry.

The second part of this book offers a collection of documents of various kinds—sources, analogues, or other medieval writings—which represent ways in which Chaucer or his first audiences might have known these stories from elsewhere or ways in which they might have thought about certain aspects of their meaning. Such documents can help students think in historically relevant ways about what Chaucer is most concerned with in these tales. In such study, they will find the differences at least as revealing as the similarities, for the differences help identify choices made, emphases added, roads taken and not taken.

To that end we have worked with a more generous definition of the relevant than do the two most important collections of sources and analogues of the *Canterbury Tales*.[1] We have brought together writings that cast an interesting and suggestive light on the tales included here and have made those writings accessible to students. Some of the translations that follow have been made specially for this volume; certain others, though previously published, have been difficult to come by and seem worth reprinting here. We have not glossed the Middle English writings in this section as extensively as we have the Chaucer texts, but even here we take for granted only a beginner's knowledge of Chaucer's language; a good deal of help is provided. Again, we have normalized certain features of these texts, substituting the appropriate modern letters for Middle English letters no longer current, regularizing *u/v* and *i/j*, eliminating certain scribal idiosyncracies, and modernizing punctuation and capitalization. We hope that both the new translations and the gathering together of what has been widely scattered or out of print will prove welcome, to teacher and student alike.

---

1. *Sources and Analogues of Chaucer's Canterbury Tales*, ed. W. F. Bryan and Germaine Dempster (1941; New York: Humanities P, 1958); *Sources and Analogues of The Canterbury Tales, Vol. I*, ed. Robert M. Correale and Mary Hamel (Cambridge: D. S. Brewer, 2002). At the time of our writing Volume II has not yet appeared but is promised soon. The new *Sources and Analogues* volumes contain texts in their original languages with facing page translations, along with extensive introductions surveying the relation of each tale to its analogues and antecedents.

For reasons of space we have not been able to offer source and background material for every tale included in this edition. Students interested in exploring the relationship of the *Knight's Tale* to its source, Boccaccio's *Teseida*, may find a complete text with English translation in *Theseid of the Nuptials of Emilia*, trans. Vincenzo Traversa (New York: Peter Lang, 2002). There is also a full translation by Bernadette Marie McCoy, *The Book of Theseus* (Sea Cliff, NJ: Teesdale Publishing Associates, 1974), and extensive selections are translated in Nicholas Havely, *Chaucer's Boccaccio* (Cambridge: D. S. Brewer, 1980). A text and translation of the principal analogue to the *Summoner's Tale*, Jacques de Baisieux's *Tale of the Priest's Bladder*, appears in *The Literary Context of Chaucer's Fabliaux*, ed. and trans. Larry D. Benson and Theodore M. Andersson (Indianapolis: Bobbs-Merrill, 1971). No clear analogues exist for the *Cook's Tale*: see the discussion by John Scattergood in Correale and Hamel, *Sources and Analogues of The Canterbury Tales, Vol. I.* For the other tales included here in their entirety we present at least one important source or close analogue, and for certain of Chaucer's richest and most widely discussed—the *General Prologue*, the *Wife of Bath's Tale*, the *Clerk's Tale*, the *Prioress's Tale*—we have tried to provide substantial contextual material.

The third part of the book brings together an updated selection of critical essays on Chaucer. Instead of trying to select a single definitive essay on each tale—beyond the scope of this book, and a difficult if not impossible task—we have chosen historically influential studies that treat the broader critical questions, questions that arise whether one is considering the stories individually or collectively. Hence Hoffman on the double focus, sacred and secular, of the pilgrimage; hence Donaldson on Chaucer the pilgrim, and Nolan on the governing voices of the *Canterbury Tales*; hence two excerpts from Kittredge's seminal work on Chaucer's psychological realism, one on the dramatic appropriateness of tale to teller and one on the dynamics of the "marriage group"; hence Patterson and Strohm on the literary and social implications of the collection's multivocal structure; hence Dinshaw on sexuality, gender, and interpretation. Preceding all these is a biographical essay by the historian F. R. H. Du Boulay that not only sets out the essential facts of Chaucer's life but evokes something of the social and intellectual environment in which he wrote. It can usefully serve as an introduction to this volume as a whole. In the Selected Bibliography at the back of this Norton Critical Edition, we offer suggestions for further reading, tale by tale as well as in Chaucer scholarship more generally.

We offer this expanded selection of fifteen *Canterbury Tales* and the Prologue that introduces them as exemplifying Chaucer's highest achievement in the art of story. His is a Gothic art, full of variety and contradiction, tension and transcendence, an art that dared to look at human life under so many guises and from so many points of view that it lays convincing claim, even in the twenty-first century, to having seen life whole.

In the making of the first edition of this book, the editors received the able assistance of Betsy Bowden, Thomas Cannon, Jr., Raymond Cormier, Rosa DelVecchio, Julie Bates Dock, Mary Dugan, Rita Hammond, Betty Hanson-Smith, and Jeanne Vanecko. Carol Stiles Bemis and Marian Johnson at W. W. Norton provided their careful and cooperative editorial work. For this expanded edition, we gratefully acknowledge the contributions of Jane Dugan, Christina Fitzgerald, and Toni K. Thayer. We thank Carol Bemis again, along with Brian Baker and Katharine Ings, all at Norton, for their attentive and collegial help.

Chaucer's Language

There are many differences between Chaucer's Middle English and modern English, but they are minor enough that a student can learn to adjust to them in a fairly short time. We have sketched below just a few of the principal differences. For fuller treatments see the section on language in the bibliography.

I. Pronunciation

The chief difference between Middle English (ME) and modern English (NE) is in pronunciation. The best way to learn ME is to hear it spoken, by a teacher or on records or tapes. For some good readings of Chaucer in ME see the entries on the Chaucer Studio Recordings and the Norton *Media Companion* in the Special Resources section of the Bibliography. The discussion below will pinpoint the principal sound differences, but it takes practice—listening and reading aloud—to develop a good ME pronunciation.

A. Vowels

ME distinguished between long and short vowels, whereas NE does not, even though it takes longer to say the vowel of "bad" than of "bat." In addition, ME long vowels underwent, over an extended period of time, a change known as the Great Vowel Shift, in which they systematically acquired new sound values. The beginning student can best cope with these differences by working backward from NE pronunciation and spelling, a procedure that will ensure reasonable though not perfect accuracy in ME pronunciation. Accordingly, in the following table of sounds, we have indicated not only Chaucer's spelling and pronunciation (both in International Phonetic Alphabet symbols and in NE equivalents) but also how the vowel sounds have evolved in NE.

Two further aspects of the pronunciation of vowels may be considered in connection with Chaucer's principles of versification. Although scholars are not in complete agreement about the nature of Chaucer's metrics, most assume that his lines are basically iambic pentameter with a good deal of metrical variation. Vowels occurring in combination should all be pronounced, as the meter often makes clear:

And plĕsaŭnt wás hĭs absŏlúcĭoún

More complex is the question of final *e*. Originally there was no such thing as "silent *e*" in English: the final *e* in ME words often represents a reduction of more distinctive Old English inflections. By Chaucer's time it is likely that in normal speech the final *e* was silent, but in his poetry it is frequently pronounced, with the schwa sound [ə] that we use in unstressed syllables such as those at the end of *sofa* and the beginning of *about*. Always pronounce final *e* at the end of lines, and within lines pronounce it or not depending on the requirements of the meter. In the following example the final *e*'s that should be pronounced are italicized:

> Wel coude he sitte on hors, and faire ryde,
> He coude songes make and wel endyte

As these instances indicate, final *e* is usually not pronounced when it appears before words beginning with vowels or weakly pronounced *h*'s.

B. Consonants

ME consonants are pronounced as in NE, with some exceptions:

1. In general, pronounce all consonants in clusters: *g* and *k* before *n* (*gnawe, knife*), although *gn* in French borrowings (*digne, signe*) is [n]; *w* before *r* (*write, wroth*); *l* before *f, v, k, m* (*half* or *halve, folk, palmer*); *ng* is usually pronounced [ŋg], the consonant cluster in *finger* rather than *singer*.

2. *gh* is pronounced with the guttural sound in German *ich*. There is no comparable sound in NE, except for *loch* when pronounced with a heavy Scots accent.

3. *ch* is always pronounced [č], as in NE *church*.

4. *r* should be trilled.

5. *h* is not pronounced at the beginning of words borrowed from French (*honour, hostelrye*); at the beginning of short ME words like *he, his, hit, him, hem*, it is also silent or only weakly pronounced.

6. Final *s* should not be voiced to [z] in stressed positions. At the end of lines Chaucer rhymes *was* with *glas* and *cas, is* with *this*.

II. Morphology

NOUNS: The usual ending for plural and genitive singular forms is *-es*, sometimes *-is*, generally pronounced as a separate syllable. The plural ending *-en* is more common than in NE: e.g., *eyen* instead of *eyes*.

PERSONAL PRONOUNS: Second-person pronouns have both singular forms—*thou, thy* or *thyn, the(e)*—and plural forms—*ye, youre, you* or *yow*. The latter set can be used with singular meaning in some cases.

The third-person singular neuter pronoun may be spelled *it* or *hit*; the possessive case of *it* is *his*, not *its*, which did not enter the language until the Renaissance.

CHAUCER'S SPELLING	EXAMPLES	ME PRONUNCIATION	EVOLUTION IN NE
VOWELS			
a	*after, at*	[a], as in NE *top*	usually becomes [æ], as in NE *after, at*
a, aa	*take, caas*	[a:], as in NE *father*	becomes [e], as in NE *take, case*
e	*best, hem*	[ɛ], as in NE *best*	no change
e, ee	*heeth, ese, see*	[ɛ:], as in NE *bed*	becomes [i], spelled *ea*, as in NE *heath, ease, sea*
e, ee	*swete, be, see*	[e:], as in NE *take*	becomes [i], spelled *e* or *ee*, as in NE *sweet, be, see*
i, y	*hit, in*	[ɪ], as in NE *hit, in*	no change
i, y	*I, ride*	[i:], as in NE *seed*	becomes [ai], as in NE *I, ride*
o	*of, oxe*	[ɔ], as in NE *long*	usually becomes [ə] or [a], as in NE *of, ox*
o, oo	*go, hope, so*	[ɔ:], as in NE *law*	becomes [o], as in NE *go, hope, so*
o, oo	*roote, to, good*	[o:], as in NE *note*	becomes [u] or [ʊ], as in NE *root, to, good*
u, o¹	*up, but, come*	[ʊ], as in NE *put*	usually becomes [ə], as in NE *up, but, come*
ou, ow	*hous, town*	[u:], as in NE *to*	becomes [au], as in NE *house, town*
u, eu, ew	*vertu, salewe*	[y], as in Fr. *tu²*	no NE equivalent
DIPHTHONGS			
ai, ay, ei, ey	*day, sayn, they*	[æɪ], somewhere between NE *hay* and *high*	becomes [e], as in NE *day, say, they*
au, aw	*cause, draw*	[aʊ], as in NE *out*	becomes [ɔ], as in NE *cause, draw*
eu, ew³	*newe, reule*	[ɪu], close to NE *few*	becomes [ɪu] or [u], as in NE *few, rule*
oi, oy	*joye, point*	[ɔɪ], as in NE *joy*	no change
ou, ow	*thought, bowe*	[ɔʊ], a glide between the vowels of NE *law* and *put*	becomes [ɔ] or [o], as in NE *thought, bow*

1. A few words with the short [ʊ] sound in ME are spelled with *o* instead of *u*: *some* (NE *son*), *somne* (NE *sun*), *come, love, some*. These words were originally spelled with *u* in Old English; the *o* spelling is an orthographic change only.
2. This sound occurs only in a few words recently borrowed from French.
3. A few words—the most familiar are *fewe, lewed, shew, shrewe*—should be pronounced [ɛu] instead of [ɪu].

Chaucer's third-person plural forms are notably different from those in NE. *They, their,* and *them* are Scandinavian borrowings, which were assimilated into the language at different times in different ME dialects. Chaucer uses the nominative *thei* but retains the native forms for possessive and accusative case: *hir(e)* or *her(e)* instead of *their, hem* instead of *them.*

RELATIVE PRONOUNS: Chaucer uses *which, that,* or *which that* instead of *who* and *whom* when referring to human beings, as in "But I, that am exiled" and "a wyf, / Whiche that he lovede."

VERBS: The old infinitive form in *-en* appears frequently in Chaucer, but not consistently. For example, in the opening sentence of the *General Prologue* the infinitive of *seek* appears both as *to seken* and *to seke*.

The past participle is usually prefixed by *y-*, as in *hadde y-ronne.*
Verbs are inflected in the present tense as follows:

> *Indicative*—Singular: 1. *take* 2. *takest* 3. *taketh*
>   Plural (all persons): *take(n)*

> *Subjunctive*—Singular: *take*
>   Plural: *take(n)*

As in NE, ME verbs form past tense either by adding *-ed* or by a sound change within the word (e.g., *speke, spak*); the only difference is that some ME verbs that use a sound change have since shifted to the *-ed* form: in Chaucer the past tense of *shape*, for example, is *shop* rather than *shaped*.

ADVERBS: In addition to using *-ly* and *-liche*, Chaucer also uses the suffix *-e* to form adverbs, as in "ful loude he song."

III. Syntax

Chaucer's ME is more flexible in word order than NE, and he uses syntactic patterns no longer common today. Among the most frequent are:

object—subject—verb	But Cristes lore, and his apostles twelve, / He taughte
object—verb—subject	A Yeman hadde he
complement—subject—verb	Curteys he was
complement—verb—subject	Short was his gowne
verb—subject—object	Thus hath this pitous day a blisful ende
subject—auxiliary—object—verb	I have thy feith and thy benignitee . . . assayed

Other features of Chaucer's syntax also differ from standard NE practice. Often he shifts tense within a sentence:

> And doun he *kneleth*, and with humble chere
> And herte soor, he *seyde* as ye shul here . . .

The relative pronoun may be omitted:

> With him ther was dwellinge a poure scoler,
> Hadde lerned art . . .

As in spoken English, grammatical construction may shift in mid-sentence, or the subject may be repeated:

> The reule of Seint Maure, or of Seint Beneit,
> By cause that it was old and somdel streit,
> This ilke monk leet olde thinges pace . . .

> Upon that oother syde Palamon,
> Whan that he wiste Arcite was agon,
> Swich sorwe he maketh . . .

Negation is handled on the principle that if one negative element in a sentence creates denial, further negative elements make the denial even more emphatic. Hence one can find double, triple, and even quadruple negatives in Chaucer:

> He *nevere* yet *no* vileinye *ne* sayde
> In al his lyf, unto *no* maner wight.

Finally, Chaucer uses some verbs in impersonal constructions that have since become personal. *"Me thinketh it"* means "I think" (cf. "It seems to me"). Sometimes the "it" in such constructions is omitted: *"hym liste* ryde so" = "it pleased him to ride in that way."

Selections from
THE CANTERBURY TALES

The Canterbury Tales

The General Prologue

Whan that Aprill with his shoures sote°	*sweet showers*
The droghte° of Marche hath perced to the rote,°	*dryness / root*
And bathed every veyne° in swich licour,°	*vein / such moisture*
Of which vertu° engendred is the flour;	*By power of which*
5 Whan Zephirus° eek with his swete breeth	*the west wind*
Inspired° hath in every holt° and heeth°	*Breathed into / wood / heath*
The tendre croppes,° and the yonge sonne	*sprouts*
Hath in the Ram his halfe cours y-ronne;[1]	
And smale fowles° maken melodye,	*birds*
10 That slepen al the night with open yë°—	*eye(s)*
So priketh hem Nature in hir corages[2]—	
Than longen° folk to goon° on pilgrimages,	*Then long / go*
And palmeres for to seken straunge strondes,[3]	
To ferne halwes,° couthe° in sondry londes;	*far-off shrines / known*
15 And specially, from every shires ende	
Of Engelond to Caunterbury they wende,	
The holy blisful martir[4] for to seke,°	*seek*
That hem hath holpen,° whan that they were seke.°	*helped / sick*
Bifel° that, in that seson on a day,	*It befell*
20 In Southwerk at the Tabard° as I lay°	*(an inn) / lodged*
Redy to wenden° on my pilgrimage	*depart*
To Caunterbury with ful devout corage,°	*heart*
At night was come into that hostelrye°	*inn*
Wel nyne and twenty in a companye	
25 Of sondry folk, by aventure° y-falle°	*chance / fallen*
In felawshipe, and pilgrims were they alle,	
That toward Caunterbury wolden° ryde.	*wished to*
The chambres° and the stables weren wyde,°	*bedrooms / spacious*
And wel we weren esed° atte beste.°	*made comfortable / in the best (ways)*
30 And shortly, whan the sonne was to° reste,	*at*
So hadde I spoken with hem everichon°	*every one*

---

1. Has run his half-course in the Ram; i.e., has passed through half the zodiacal sign of Aries (the Ram), a course completed on April 11. A rhetorically decorative way of indicating the time of year.
2. Nature so spurs them in their hearts.
3. And pilgrims to seek foreign shores.
4. Thomas Becket, archbishop of Canterbury, murdered in 1170 and canonized shortly thereafter. The place of his martyrdom was the greatest shrine in England and much visited by pilgrims.

3

That I was of hir felawshipe anon,
And made forward° erly for to ryse,   *agreement*
To take oure wey, ther as I yow devyse.°   *(will) tell*
35   But natheles,° whyl I have tyme and space,   *nevertheless*
Er that I ferther in this tale pace,°   *pass on*
Me thinketh it acordaunt to resoun[5]
To telle yow al the condicioun[6]
Of ech of hem, so as it semed me,°   *seemed to me*
40 And whiche° they weren, and of what degree,°   *what / status*
And eek in what array° that they were inne;   *clothing*
And at a knight than wol° I first beginne.   *will*
    A KNIGHT ther was, and that a worthy man,
That fro° the tyme that he first bigan   *from*
45 To ryden out,° he loved chivalrye,   *ride (on expeditions)*
Trouthe and honour, fredom and curteisye.[7]
Ful worthy was he in his lordes werre,°   *war(s)*
And therto° hadde he riden, no man ferre,°   *in such / further*
As wel in Cristendom as in hethenesse,°   *in pagan lands*
50 And evere honoured for his worthinesse.
    At Alisaundre° he was whan it was wonne;   *Alexandria*
Ful ofte tyme he hadde the bord bigonne°   *headed the table*
Aboven alle naciouns in Pruce.°   **not France**   *Prussia*
In Lettow hadde he reysed and in Ruce,[8]
55 No Cristen man so ofte of his degree.°   *rank*
In Gernade° at the sege° eek hadde he be°   *Granada / siege / been*
Of Algezir,° and riden in Belmarye.°   *Algeciras / Benmarin (in Morocco)*
At Lyeys° was he and at Satalye,°   *Ayas / Adalia (both in Asia Minor)*
Whan they were wonne; and in the Grete See°   *Mediterranean*
60 At many a noble armee° hadde he be.   *armed expedition*
At mortal batailles[9] hadde he been fiftene,
And foughten for oure feith at Tramissene°   *Tlemcen (in Algeria)*
In listes° thryes,° and ay slayn his foo.°   *tournaments / thrice / foe*
This ilke° worthy knight hadde been also   *same*
65 Somtyme with the lord of Palatye,°   *Palatia*
Ageyn° another hethen in Turkye;   *Against*
And everemore he hadde a sovereyn prys.°   *reputation*
And though that he were worthy,° he was wys,°   *i.e., valiant / prudent*
And of his port° as meke as is a mayde.   *deportment*
70 He nevere yet no vileinye° ne sayde   *rudeness*
In al his lyf, unto no maner wight.°   *any sort of person*
He was a verray,° parfit,° gentil° knight.   *true / perfect / noble*
But for to tellen yow of his array,
His hors° were gode, but he was nat gay.°   *horses / brightly dressed*
75 Of fustian° he wered° a gipoun°   *rough cloth / wore / tunic*

5. It seems to me reasonable (proper).
6. Character, estate, condition.
7. Fidelity, honor, generosity of spirit, and courtesy (the central chivalric virtues).
8. He had been on campaigns in Lithuania and in Russia.
9. Tournaments fought to the death.

Al bismotered with° his habergeoun,°   *stained by / coat of mail*
For he was late y-come° from his viage,°   *recently come / expedition*
And wente for to doon° his pilgrimage.   *make*
    With him ther was his sone, a young SQUYER,
80 A lovyere, and a lusty bacheler,[1]
With lokkes crulle, as they were leyd in presse.[2]
Of twenty yeer of age he was, I gesse.
Of° his stature he was of evene lengthe,°   *In / average height*
And wonderly delivere,° and of greet strengthe.   *agile*
85 And he hadde been somtyme in chivachye°   *on expeditions*
In Flaundres,° in Artoys,° and Picardye,°   *Flanders / Artois / Picardy* France
And born him wel, as of so litel space,[3]
In hope to stonden° in his lady° grace.   *stand / lady's*
Embrouded° was he, as it were a mede°   *Embroidered / meadow*
90 Al ful of fresshe floures, whyte and rede.°   Red Cross Knights
Singinge he was, or floytinge,° al the day;   *fluting (whistling?)*
He was as fresh as is the month of May.
Short was his gowne, with sleves longe and wyde.
Wel coude° he sitte on hors, and faire ryde.   *knew how to*
95 He coude songes make and wel endyte,°   *compose verse*
Juste° and eek daunce, and wel purtreye° and wryte.   *Joust / draw*
So hote° he lovede that by nightertale°   *hotly / at night*
He sleep° namore° than dooth a nightingale.   *slept / no more*
Curteys he was, lowly, and servisable,[4]
100 And carf° biforn his fader at the table.   *carved (meat)*
    A YEMAN hadde he, and servaunts namo[5]
At that tyme, for him, liste° ryde so;   *it pleased him to*
And he was clad in cote and hood of grene.
A sheef of pecok arwes° brighte and kene   *arrows*
105 Under his belt he bar° ful thriftily.°   *bore / carefully*
Wel coude he dresse° his takel° yemanly: *keep in order / equipment*
His arwes drouped noght with fetheres lowe,
And in his hand he bar a mighty bowe.
A not-heed° hadde he, with a broun visage.°   *closely cropped head / face*
110 Of wodecraft wel coude° he al the usage.   *knew*
Upon his arm he bar a gay bracer,°   *fine wrist guard*
And by his syde a swerd and a bokeler,°   *shield*
And on that other syde a gay daggere,
Harneised° wel, and sharp as point of spere;   *mounted*
115 A Cristofre° on his brest of silver shene.°   *St. Christopher medal / bright*
An horn he bar, the bawdrik° was of grene;   *shoulder strap*
A forster° was he, soothly, as I gesse.   *forester*
    Ther was also a Nonne, a PRIORESSE,
That of hir smyling was ful simple and coy°—   *modest*

1. A lover, and a vigorous young man, one preparing to become a knight.
2. With locks as curly as if they'd been pressed (by a curling iron).
3. And conducted himself well, considering his inexperience.
4. He was courteous, humble, and willing to be of service.
5. He [the Knight] had a Yeoman [a servant one step above a groom in rank; this one seems to
  be a forester] with him, and no other servants.

120 Hir gretteste ooth was but by Seynte Loy°—   *Eligius (Fr. Eloi)*
And she was cleped° madame Eglentyne.   *called*
Ful wel she song° the service divyne,   *sang*
Entuned° in hir nose ful semely;°   *Intoned / becomingly*
And Frensh she spak ful faire and fetisly,°   *elegantly*
125 After the scole of Stratford atte Bowe,⁶
For Frensh of Paris was to hire unknowe.
At mete° wel y-taught was she with alle: *I.e., at table*
She leet° no morsel from hir lippes falle,   *let*
Ne wette hir fingres in hir sauce depe.°   *(too) deeply*
130 Wel coude she carie a morsel, and wel kepe⁷
That no drope ne fille° upon hire brest.   *fell*
In curteisye° was set ful muchel° hir lest.°   *etiquette / much / delight*
Hir over°-lippe wyped she so clene,   *upper*
That in hir coppe was no ferthing° sene°   *small drop / seen*
135 Of grece,° whan she dronken hadde hir draughte.   *grease*
Ful semely after hir mete she raughte,°   *reached*
And sikerly° she was of greet disport,°   *certainly / cheerfulness*
And ful plesaunt, and amiable of port,°   *deportment*
And peyned hire° to countrefete chere°   *took pains / imitate behavior*
140 Of court, and to been estatlich° of manere,   *stately*
And to ben holden digne° of reverence.   *considered worthy*
But, for to speken of hire conscience,°   *sensibility*
She was so charitable and so pitous,°   *compassionate*
She wolde wepe, if that she sawe a mous°   *mouse*
145 Caught in a trappe, if it were deed or bledde.
Of° smale houndes hadde she, that she fedde   *I.e., some*
With rosted flesh, or milk and wastel-breed.°   *fine white bread*
But sore° wepte she if oon of hem were deed,   *sorely*
Or if men° smoot it with a yerde° smerte;° *(some)one / stick / sharply*
150 And al was conscience and tendre herte.
Ful semely hir wimpel° pinched° was,   *headdress / pleated*
Hir nose tretys,° hir eyen° greye as glas,   *graceful / eyes*
Hir mouth ful smal, and therto softe and reed.
But sikerly° she hadde a fair forheed—   *certainly*
155 It was almost a spanne° brood, I trowe°—   *span / believe*
For hardily° she was nat undergrowe.°   *certainly / undersized*
Ful fetis° was hir cloke, as I was war.°   *elegant / aware*
Of smal coral° aboute hire arm she bar   *i.e., small coral beads*
A peire of bedes, gauded al with grene;⁸
160 And theron heng a broche° of gold ful shene,°   *ornament / bright*
On which ther was first write° a crowned A,⁹   *written*
And after, *Amor vincit omnia*.°   *Love conquers all*
Another NONNE with hire hadde she,

6. I.e., in the English fashion, as it was spoken at Stratford at the Bow—a suburb some two
miles east of London and home of the Benedictine nunnery of St. Leonard's.
7. She knew well how to raise a portion (to her lips) and take care.
8. A string of beads (a rosary), its groups marked off by special stones, called "gauds," of green.
9. The letter A with a symbolic crown fashioned above it.

That was hir chapeleyne,° and PREESTES three.   *chaplain, assistant*
165   A MONK ther was, a fair for the maistrye,°   *a very fine one*
An outrydere° that lovede venerye:°   *estate supervisor / hunting*
A manly man, to been an abbot able.
Ful many a deyntee° hors hadde he in stable,   *valuable*
And whan he rood, men mighte his brydel here°   *hear*
170 Ginglen° in a whistling wind als° clere   *Jingling / as*
And eek° as loude as dooth the chapel belle,   *also*
Ther as° this lord was kepere of the celle.[1]   *Where*
The reule of Seint Maure° or of Seint Beneit,°   *Maurus / Benedict*
By cause that it was old and somdel streit,°   *somewhat strict*
175 This ilke° monk leet olde thinges pace,°   *same / pass away*
And held after the newe world the space.°   *course (i.e., customs)*
He yaf° nat of° that text a pulled° hen,   *gave / for / plucked*
That seith that hunters ben° nat holy men,   *are*
Ne that a monk, whan he is reccheless,°   *negligent of his vows*
180 Is lykned til° a fish that is waterlees°   *likened to / out of water*
(This is to seyn,° a monk out of his cloistre);   *say*
But thilke° text held he nat worth an oistre.°   *that same / oyster*
And I seyde his opinioun was good:
What° sholde he studie, and make himselven wood,°   *Why / mad*
185 Upon a book in cloistre alwey to poure,°   *pore over*
Or swinken° with his handes and laboure   *work*
As Austin bit?° How shal the world be served?   *Augustine bids*
Lat Austin have his swink° to him reserved!   *work*
Therfore he was a pricasour° aright:°   *hard rider / truly*
190 Grehoundes he hadde, as swifte as fowel° in flight;   *bird*
Of priking° and of hunting for the hare   *riding*
Was al his lust,° for no cost wolde he spare.   *pleasure*
I seigh° his sleves purfiled° at the hond   *saw / trimmed*
With grys,° and that the fyneste of a lond;°   *gray fur / land*
195 And, for to festne° his hood under his chin,   *fasten*
He hadde of gold y-wroght° a ful curious pin: *made*
A love-knotte[2] in the gretter° ende ther was.   *larger*
His heed was balled,° that shoon as any glas,   *bald*
And eek his face, as° he had been anoint.°   *as if / anointed*
200 He was a lord ful fat and in good point:°   *condition*
His eyen° stepe,° and rollinge in his heed,   *eyes / prominent*
That stemed as a forneys of a leed;[3]
His bootes souple,° his hors in greet estat°—   *supple / condition*
Now certeinly he was a fair prelat.
205 He was nat pale as a forpyned goost;°   *tormented spirit*
A fat swan loved he best of any roost.
His palfrey° was as broun as is a berye.°   *horse / berry*
    A FRERE° ther was, a wantowne° and a merye,   *Friar / gay (one)*

---

1. A priory or dependent house.
2. An elaborate knot symbolizing true love.
3. That gleamed like a furnace (a fire) under a cauldron.

A limitour,[4] a ful solempne° man.   *distinguished*
210 In alle the ordres foure[5] is noon that can°   *knows*
So muchel of daliaunce and fair langage.
He hadde maad° ful many a mariage   *arranged*
Of yonge wommen, at his owne cost.[6]
Unto his ordre he was a noble post.°   *pillar*
215 Ful wel biloved and famulier was he
With frankeleyns over al in his contree,[7]
And eek with worthy wommen of the toun;
For he hadde power of confessioun,
As seyde himself, more than a curat,°   *parish priest*
220 For of his ordre he was licentiat.°   *licensed to hear confessions*
Ful swetely herde he confessioun,
And plesaunt was his absolucioun;
He was an esy man to yeve° penaunce   *give*
Ther as he wiste to have a good pitaunce.[8]
225 For unto a povre° ordre for to yive°   *poor / give*
Is signe that a man is wel y-shrive°—   *shriven*
For if he yaf,° he dorste make avaunt,°   *gave / (the Friar) dared assert*
He wiste° that a man was repentaunt.   *knew*
For many a man so hard is of his herte,
230 He may nat wepe althogh hym sore smerte:°   *it sorely pain him*
Therfore, in stede of wepinge and preyeres,
Men moot° yeve silver to the povre° freres.   *may / poor*
His tipet° was ay farsed° ful of knyves   *scarf / always stuffed*
And pinnes, for to yeven° faire wyves.   *give to*
235 And certeinly he hadde a murye note;°   *pleasant voice*
Wel coude he singe and pleyen on a rote;°   *stringed instrument*
Of yeddinges he bar outrely the prys.[9]
His nekke whyt was as the flour-de-lys;°   *lily*
Therto° he strong was as a champioun.   *Moreover*
240 He knew the tavernes wel in every toun,
And everich hostiler° and tappestere°   *innkeeper / barmaid*
Bet than a lazar or a beggestere,[1]
For unto swich° a worthy man as he   *such*
Acorded nat, as by his facultee,[2]
245 To have with seke lazars° aqueyntaunce: *sick lepers*
It is nat honest,° it may nat avaunce°   *respectable / be profitable*
For to delen with no swich poraille,°   *such poor people*
But al with riche and selleres of vitaille.°   *victuals*
And over al,° ther as° profit sholde aryse,   *everywhere / wherever*

---

4. One licensed to beg within a certain region or limit.
5. The four orders of friars (Franciscan, Dominican, Carmelite, and Augustinian).
6. I.e., he gave them dowries out of his own funds, perhaps after having first seduced them himself.
7. With rich landholders everywhere in his region.
8. Wherever he knew (that he could expect) to have a good gift in return.
9. At narrative songs, he absolutely took the prize.
1. Better than a leper or beggar woman.
2. It was not fitting, considering his position.

250 Curteys he was, and lowely of° servyse.	*humble in*
Ther nas° no man nowher so vertuous.°	*was not / capable*
He was the beste beggere in his hous,	
252a [And yaf° a certeyn ferme° for the graunt:	*gave / payment*
252b Noon of his bretheren cam ther in his haunt.]°	*area of begging*
For thogh a widwe° hadde noght a sho,°	*widow / shoe*
So plesaunt was his *In principio,°*	*"In the beginning"*
255 Yet wolde he have a ferthing,° er he wente.	*farthing*
His purchas was wel bettre than his rente.[3]	
And rage he coude, as it were right a whelpe;[4]	
In love-dayes° ther coude he muchel° helpe,	*legal arbitrations / much*
For there he was nat lyk a cloisterer,[5]	
260 With a thredbare cope,° as is a povre scoler.	*cape*
But he was lyk a maister° or a pope:	*Master of Arts*
Of double worsted was his semi-cope,°	*half cape*
That rounded as a belle out of the presse.°	*mould*
Somwhat he lipsed, for his wantownesse,[6]	
265 To make his English swete upon his tonge;	
And in his harping, whan that he hadde songe,	
His eyen° twinkled in his heed aright	*eyes*
As doon° the sterres° in the frosty night.	*do / stars*
This worthy limitour was cleped° Huberd.	*called*
270 A MARCHANT was ther with a forked berd,°	*beard*
In mottelee,° and hye[7] on horse he sat;	*figured cloth*
Upon his heed a Flaundrish° bever° hat,	*Flemish / beaver fur*
His bootes clasped° faire and fetisly.°	*tied / neatly*
His resons° he spak ful solempnely,°	*opinions / impressively*
275 Souninge° alway th'encrees° of his winning.°	*Proclaiming / increase / profit*
He wolde the see were kept for any thing[8]	
Bitwixe Middleburgh° and Orewelle.°	*(in Holland) / (in England)*
Wel coude he in eschaunge° sheeldes° selle.	*foreign exchange / French coins*
This worthy man ful wel his wit bisette:°	*used*
280 Ther wiste no wight° that he was in dette,	*no person knew*
So estatly° was he of his governaunce,°	*dignified / conduct*
With his bargaynes and with his chevisaunce.°	*(possibly illegal) lending*
For sothe he was a worthy man with alle,	
But sooth to seyn, I noot° how men him calle.	*know not*
285 A CLERK° ther was of Oxenford° also,	*student / Oxford*
That unto logik hadde longe y-go.[9]	
As leene° was his hors as is a rake,	*lean*
And he nas° nat right fat, I undertake,°	*was not / declare*
But loked holwe,° and therto° soberly.	*hollow / also*

3. His profit from begging was much greater than "his regular income," or "the fee he paid for his exclusive begging rights." (Meaning uncertain.)
4. And he knew how to play and flirt, as if he were a puppy.
5. A religious who knows only the enclosed life of the cloister.
6. He lisped a little, out of affectation.
7. On a high saddle.
8. He wanted the sea to be guarded (against pirates) at any cost. (His profits depended on it.)
9. Who had long since proceeded to (the study of) logic in the university curriculum.

290 Ful thredbar was his overest courtepy,°   *outer short cloak*
    For he hadde geten him° yet no benefyce,   *obtained for himself*
    Ne was so worldly for to have offyce;°   *secular employment*
    For him was levere° have at his beddes heed   *he would rather*
    Twenty bokes, clad° in blak or reed,   *bound*
295 Of Aristotle and his philosophye,
    Than robes riche, or fithele,° or gay sautrye.°   *fiddle / psaltery, harp*
    But al be that° he was a philosophre,[1]   *although*
    Yet hadde he but litel gold in cofre;°   *coffer*
    But al that he mighte of his freendes hente,°   *get*
300 On bokes and on lerninge he it spente,
    And bisily gan for the soules preye[2]
    Of hem that yaf him wherwith° to scoleye.°   *i.e., the means / study*
    Of studie took he most cure° and most hede.°   *care / heed*
    Noght o° word spak he more than was nede,   *Not one*
305 And that was seyd in forme° and reverence,°   *properly / respectfully*
    And short and quik, and ful of hy sentence.°   *serious meaning*
    Souninge° in moral vertu was his speche,   *Resounding*
    And gladly wolde he lerne, and gladly teche.
        A SERGEANT OF THE LAWE,° war° and wys,   *eminent lawyer / alert*
310 That often hadde been at the Parvys,[3]
    Ther was also, ful riche of excellence.
    Discreet he was and of greet reverence:°   *worthy of great respect*
    He semed swich,° his wordes weren so wyse.   *such*
    Justyce° he was ful often in assyse,°   *Judge / local courts*
315 By patente° and by pleyn° commissioun;   *letter of appointment / full*
    For his science° and for his heigh renoun,   *knowledge*
    Of fees and robes hadde he many oon.°   *a one*
    So greet a purchasour° was nowher noon:°   *speculator in land / none*
    Al was fee simple to him in effect;[4]
320 His purchasing mighte nat been infect.°   *invalidated*
    Nowher so bisy a man as he ther nas;
    And yet he semed bisier than he was.
    In termes hadde he caas and domes alle,[5]
    That from the tyme of King William[6] were falle.°   *had taken place*
325 Therto he coude endyte,° and make a thing;°   *write / draw up papers*
    Ther coude no wight pinche at° his wryting,   *no one find fault with*
    And every statut coude° he pleyn by rote.°   *knew / completely by heart*
    He rood but hoomly° in a medlee° cote,   *informally / figured*
    Girt with a ceint° of silk, with barres° smale;   *girdle / metal bars*
330 Of his array telle I no lenger tale.
        A FRANKELEYN° was in his companye.   *wealthy landowner*
    Whyt was his berd as is the dayesye;°   *daisy*
    Of his complexioun° he was sangwyn.°   *temperament / sanguine*

1. With a pun on alchemist, another meaning of the word.
2. And busily did pray for the souls.
3. The porch of St. Paul's Cathedral, a favorite gathering place for lawyers.
4. I.e., he always got unrestricted possession ("fee simple") of the property.
5. He knew the exact terms (details) of all the cases and decisions.
6. I.e., since the Norman Conquest (1066).

Wel loved he by the morwe a sop in wyn.⁷

335 To liven in delyt was evere his wone,°   *custom*

For he was Epicurus⁸ owene sone,

That heeld opinioun that pleyn° delyt   *complete*

Was verray° felicitee parfyt.°   *true / perfect*

An housholdere, and that a greet,° was he;   *a great one*

340 Seint Julian⁹ he was in his contree.°   *region*

His breed, his ale, was alweys after oon;°   *of uniform good quality*

A bettre envyned° man was nowher noon.   *stocked with wine*

Withoute bake mete° was nevere his hous,   *meat pies*

Of fish and flesh,° and that so plentevous°   *meat / plentiful*

345 It snewed° in his hous of mete° and drinke.   *snowed / food*

Of alle deyntees° that men coude thinke,   *delicacies*

After° the sondry sesons of the yeer,   *According to*

So chaunged° he his mete° and his soper.   *varied / dinner*

Ful many a fat partrich° hadde he in mewe,°   *partridge / coop*

350 And many a breem° and many a luce° in stewe.°   *carp / pike / fishpond*

Wo° was his cook, but if° his sauce were   *(Made) sorry / unless*

Poynaunt° and sharp, and redy al his gere.°   *Pungent / utensils*

His table dormant¹ in his halle° alway   *main room*

Stood redy covered° al the longe day.   *set*

355 At sessiouns ther was he lord and sire;²

Ful ofte tyme he was knight of the shire.³

An anlas° and a gipser° al of silk   *dagger / purse*

Heng° at his girdel, whyt as morne° milk.   *Hung / morning*

A shirreve° hadde he been, and a countour;°   *sheriff / auditor*

360 Was nowher such a worthy vavasour.°   *landholder*

An HABERDASSHER and a CARPENTER,

A WEBBE,° a DYERE, and a TAPICER,°   *weaver / tapestry maker*

Were with us eek, clothed in o liveree°   *one livery (uniform)*

Of a solempne° and greet fraternitee.°   *distinguished / (parish) guild*

365 Ful fresh and newe hir gere° apyked° was;   *equipment / adorned*

Hir knyves were chaped° noght with bras,   *mounted*

But al with silver; wroght ful clene and weel

Hire girdles° and hire pouches° everydeel.°   *belts / purses / altogether*

Wel semed ech of hem a fair burgeys°   *citizen, burgher*

370 To sitten in a yeldhalle° on a deys.⁴   *guildhall*

Everich,° for the wisdom that he can,°   *Each one / knows*

Was shaply° for to been an alderman.   *fit*

For catel° hadde they ynogh and rente,°   *property / income*

And eek° hir wyves wolde it wel assente;°   *also / assent to*

---

7. In the morning he dearly loved a sop (a piece of bread or cake) in wine.

8. A Greek philosopher who held that pleasure was the highest good.

9. The patron saint of hospitality.

1. Most tables were made of boards laid on trestles and were taken down after each meal; this one seems to have been permanent.

2. I.e., he presided over meetings of local justices of the peace when they gathered to hear cases.

3. Member of Parliament for his county.

4. The dais (a raised platform) on which the mayor or alderman of a city sat.

375 And elles° certein were they to blame.°   otherwise / deserving of blame
It is ful fair to been y-clept° "*Madame*,"°   called / "my lady"
And goon to vigilyës al bifore,[5]
And have a mantel royalliche y-bore.°   royally carried
    A Cook they hadde with hem for the nones,°   occasion
380 To boille the chiknes° with the mary-bones°   chickens / marrowbones
And poudre-marchant tart and galingale.[6]
Wel coude he knowe° a draughte of London ale.   recognize
He coude° roste, and sethe,° and broille, and frye,   knew how to / boil
Maken mortreux,° and wel bake a pye.   stews
385 But greet harm° was it, as it thoughte° me,   misfortune / seemed to
That on his shine° a mormal° hadde he.   shin / ulcerous sore
For blankmanger,[7] that made he with the beste.
    A Shipman was ther, woninge fer by weste:[8]
For aught I woot,° he was of Dertemouthe.°   know / Dartmouth (in Devon)
390 He rood upon a rouncy, as he couthe,[9]
In a gowne of falding° to the knee.   heavy wool
A daggere hanginge on a laas° hadde he   cord
Aboute his nekke, under his arm adoun.
The hote somer° hadde maad his hewe al broun;   summer
395 And certeinly he was a good felawe.°   cheerful companion
Ful many a draughte of wyn had he y-drawe°   drawn off
Fro Burdeux-ward, whyl that the chapman sleep.[1]
Of nyce° conscience took he no keep:°   scrupulous / heed
If that he faught, and hadde the hyer hond,°   upper hand
400 By water he sente hem hoom° to every lond.   i.e., drowned them
But of his craft, to rekene wel his tydes,[2]
His stremes° and his daungers him bisydes,°   currents / close to him
His herberwe° and his mone,° his lodemenage,°   harbor / moon / pilotage
Ther nas noon swich° from Hulle to Cartage.[3]   such
405 Hardy he was, and wys to undertake;[4]
With many a tempest hadde his berd been shake.
He knew wel alle the havenes,° as they were,   harbors
From Gootlond to the cape of Finistere,[5]
And every cryke° in Britayne° and in Spayne;   creek / Brittany
410 His barge y-cleped° was the Maudelayne.°   called / Magdalen
    With us ther was a Doctour of Phisyk;°   a physician
In al this world ne was ther noon him lyk
To speke of phisik° and of surgerye,   In regard to medicine
For he was grounded in astronomye.°   astrology

5. And go to church vigils at the head of the procession.
6. Both are spices, one tart and one sweet.
7. An elaborate dish of chicken in a sweet milk-and-rice sauce.
8. There was a shipmaster, dwelling far off to the west.
9. He rode on a small sturdy horse, as (well as) he knew how. (A man more used to ships than
   horses.)
1. On the way from Bordeaux, while the (wine-) merchant slept.
2. But at his craft, in calculating well the tides.
3. From Hull (in England) to Carthage (in northern Africa) or possibly Cartagena (in Spain).
4. Prudent in the risks he undertook.
5. From Gotland (an island in the Baltic Sea) to Cape Finisterre (in Spain).

415 He kepte° his pacient a ful greet deel   *watched*
    In houres, by his magik naturel.[6]
    Wel coude he fortunen the ascendent
    Of his images for his pacient.[7]
    He knew the cause of everich maladye,
420 Were it of hoot or cold, or moiste, or drye,[8]
    And where engendred,° and of what humour;   *originated*
    He was a verrey° parfit practisour.°   *true / practitioner*
    The cause y-knowe,° and of his harm° the roote,°   *known / malady / cause*
    Anon° he yaf° the seke man his boote.°   *Quickly / gave / remedy*
425 Ful redy hadde he his apothecaries[9]
    To sende him drogges and his letuaries,°   *medicinal syrups*
    For ech of hem made other for to winne;°   *profit*
    Hir° frendschipe nas nat newe to biginne.°   *Their / recently begun*
    Wel knew he the olde Esculapius,
430 And Deiscorides, and eek Rufus,
    Old Ypocras, Haly, and Galien,
    Serapion, Razis, and Avicen,
    Averrois, Damascien, and Constantyn,
    Bernard, and Gatesden, and Gilbertyn.[1]
435 Of his diete mesurable° was he,   *moderate*
    For it was of no superfluitee
    But of greet norissing° and digestible.   *nourishment*
    His studie was but litel on the Bible.[2]
    In sangwin° and in pers° he clad was al,   *bloodred / blue*
440 Lyned with taffata and with sendal;[3]
    And yet he was but esy of dispence.°   *slow to spend*
    He kepte that he wan in pestilence,
    For gold in phisik is a cordial;[4]
    Therefore he lovede gold in special.°   *particularly*
445   A good WYF was ther of bisyde BATHE,°   *from near Bath*
    But she was somdel° deef, and that was scathe.°   *somewhat / a pity*
    Of clooth-making she hadde swiche an haunt,°   *such practiced skill*
    She passed° hem of Ypres and of Gaunt.[5]   *surpassed*
    In al the parisshe wyf ne was ther noon
450 That to the offringe° bifore hir sholde goon;° *offering in church / go*

6. During those hours (best for treatment), through his knowledge of natural magic (i.e., astrology).
7. He knew well how to determine the most favorable position of the stars for (making astrological) images for his patient.
8. The four fundamental qualities, which were thought to combine in pairs to form the four elements and the four humors (melancholia, cholera, phlegm, and blood); bodily health depended upon the existence of a proper equilibrium among them.
9. I.e., pharmacists.
1. A list of the best medical authorities, ancient and modern (e.g., John of Gaddesden, an Englishman, died ca. 1349).
2. Doctors were often held to be skeptical in religious matters.
3. With linings of taffeta and fine silk.
4. He kept what he had earned during time of plague, for gold in medicine is good for the heart. (An ironic reference to *aurum potabile*, a liquid medicine compounded of gold and held to be a sovereign remedy for disease.)
5. Cloth-making in the Low Countries (here represented by Ypres and Ghent) was of high repute.

And if ther dide, certeyn so wrooth° was she,   *angry*
That she was out of alle charitee.
Hir coverchiefs° ful fyne were of ground;°   *kerchiefs / texture*
I dorste° swere they weyeden° ten pound   *would dare / weighed*
455 That on a Sonday weren upon hir heed.
Hir hosen° weren of fyn scarlet reed,   *hose*
Ful streite y-teyd,° and shoos ful moiste° and newe.   *tightly tied / soft*
Bold was hir face, and fair, and reed of hewe.°   *hue*
She was a worthy womman al hir lyve:
460 Housbondes at chirche dore⁶ she hadde fyve,
Withouten° other companye in youthe—   *Not to mention*
But therof nedeth nat to speke as nouthe°—   *at present*
And thryes° hadde she been at Jerusalem.   *thrice*
She hadde passed many a straunge streem:⁷
465 At Rome she hadde been, and at Boloigne,°   *Boulogne (France)*
In Galice at Seint Jame, and at Coloigne;⁸
She coude° muchel of wandringe by the weye.°   *knew / along the road(s)*
Gat-tothed° was she, soothly for to seye.   *Gap-toothed*
Upon an amblere° esily° she sat,   *saddle horse / comfortably*
470 Y-wimpled° wel, and on hir heed an hat   *Covered with a wimple*
As brood as is a bokeler° or a targe;°   *shields*
A foot-mantel° aboute hir hipes large,   *outer skirt*
And on hir feet a paire of spores° sharpe.   *spurs*
In felawschipe wel coude she laughe and carpe.°   *talk*
475 Of remedyes of love she knew per chaunce,°   *as it happened*
For she coude° of that art the olde daunce.°   *knew / (steps of the) dance*
    A good man was ther of religioun,
And was a povre PERSOUN° of a toun,   *poor parson*
But riche he was of holy thoght and werk.
480 He was also a lerned man, a clerk,°   *scholar*
That Cristes gospel trewely wolde preche;
His parisshens° devoutly wolde he teche.   *parishioners*
Benigne° he was, and wonder° diligent,   *Kindly / very*
And in adversitee ful pacient,
485 And swich he was y-preved ofte sythes.⁹
Ful looth° were him to cursen° for his tithes,   *loath / excommunicate*
But rather wolde he yeven,° out of doute,°   *give / there is no doubt*
Unto his povre parisshens aboute
Of° his offring, and eek of his substaunce.°   *From / income*
490 He coude in litel thing han suffisaunce.¹
Wyd was his parisshe, and houses fer asonder,
But he ne lafte° nat, for reyn ne° thonder,   *ceased / nor*
In siknes nor in meschief,° to visyte   *misfortune*

---

6. The medieval marriage ceremony was customarily performed by the priest on the church
   porch. Afterward the company entered the church to hear the nuptial mass.
7. She had crossed many a foreign river.
8. In Galicia (in Spain) at (the shrine of) St. James of Compostella, and at Cologne.
9. And he was proved (to be) such many times.
1. He knew how to have enough in very little.

The ferreste in his parisshe, muche and lyte,[2]
495 Upon his feet, and in his hand a staf.
This noble ensample° to his sheep he yaf,°   *example / gave*
That first he wroghte,° and afterward he taughte.   *did (what was right)*
Out of the gospel he tho° wordes caughte,°   *those / took*
And this figure° he added eek therto,   *metaphor, image*
500 That if gold ruste, what shal iren° do?   *iron*
For if a preest be foul,° on whom we truste,   *corrupted*
No wonder is a lewed man to ruste;[3]
And shame it is, if a preest take keep,°   *heed (it)*
A shiten° shepherde and a clene sheep.   *i.e., covered with excrement*
505 Wel oghte a preest ensample for to yive,°   *give*
By his clennesse, how that his sheep sholde live.
He sette nat his benefice to hyre,[4]
And leet° his sheep encombred in the myre,   *left*
And ran to London unto Seynte Poules°   *St. Paul's cathedral*
510 To seken him a chaunterie for soules,
Or with a bretherhed to been withholde,[5]
But dwelte at hoom, and kepte° wel his folde,   *took care of*
So that the wolf ne made it nat miscarie;°   *come to harm*
He was a shepherde and noght a mercenarie.
515 And though he holy were, and vertuous,
He was to sinful men nat despitous,°   *scornful*
Ne of his speche daungerous ne digne,°   *haughty nor disdainful*
But in his teching discreet and benigne.
To drawen folk to heven by fairnesse,
520 By good ensample, this was his bisinesse;°   *endeavor*
But it were° any persone obstinat,   *were there*
What so° he were, of heigh or lough estat,°   *Whatever / condition, class*
Him wolde he snibben° sharply for the nones.° *rebuke / on such an occasion*
A bettre preest I trowe° that nowher noon is.   *believe*
525 He wayted after° no pompe and reverence,   *looked for*
Ne maked him a spyced conscience,[6]
But Cristes lore,° and his apostles twelve,   *teaching*
He taughte, and first he folwed it himselve.
     With him ther was a PLOWMAN, was his brother,
530 That hadde y-lad° of dong° ful many a fother.° *hauled / dung / cartload*
A trewe swinkere° and a good was he,   *worker*
Livinge in pees° and parfit charitee.   *peace*
God loved he best with al his hole° herte   *whole*
At alle tymes, thogh him gamed or smerte,[7]
535 And thanne his neighebour right as himselve.

2. The furthest (members) of his parish, great and humble.
3. It is no wonder that an unlearned man (should go) to rust.
4. He did not hire out (i.e., engage a substitute for) his benefice (church appointment).
5. To seek for himself an appointment as a chantry-priest singing masses for the souls of the
   dead or to be retained (as a chaplain) by a guild. (Both sorts of positions were relatively un-
   demanding and paid enough for such a priest to retain a curate at home and have money to
   spare.)
6. Nor affected an overly scrupulous nature.
7. At all times, whether he was glad or in distress.

He wolde thresshe, and therto dyke° and delve,° *make ditches / dig*
For Cristes sake, for every povre wight,° *poor man*
Withouten hyre,° if it lay in his might.° *wages / power*
His tythes° payed he ful faire and wel, *tithes*
540 Bothe of his propre swink° and his catel.° *own work / possessions*
In a tabard° he rood upon a mere.° *smock / mare*
    Ther was also a Reve° and a Millere, *Reeve*
A Somnour° and a Pardoner also, *Summoner*
A Maunciple,° and myself—ther were namo.° *Manciple / no more*
545   The MILLERE was a stout carl° for the nones;[8] *exceedingly strong man*
Ful big he was of brawn, and eek of bones—
That proved wel, for over al ther he cam,
At wrastling he wolde have alwey the ram.[9]
He was short-sholdred, brood, a thikke knarre:° *knotty fellow*
550 Ther nas no dore that he nolde heve of harre,[1]
Or breke it at a renning° with his heed. *(by butting it)*
His berd as any sowe or fox was reed,
And therto brood, as though it were a spade.
Upon the cop right° of his nose he hade *very top*
555 A werte,° and theron stood a tuft of herys, *wart*
Reed as the bristles of a sowes erys;° *ears*
His nosethirles° blake were and wyde. *nostrils*
A swerd and a bokeler° bar he by his syde. *small shield*
His mouth as greet° was as a greet forneys;° *large / furnace*
560 He was a janglere° and a goliardeys,° *chatterer / teller of jests*
And that was most of sinne and harlotryes.° *vulgarities*
Wel coude he stelen corn, and tollen thryes,[2]
And yet he hadde a thombe of gold, pardee.[3]
A whyt cote and a blew hood wered° he. *wore*
565 A baggepype wel coude he blowe and sowne,° *play*
And therwithal° he broghte us out of towne. *with it*
    A gentil° MAUNCIPLE was ther of a temple,[4] *worthy, proper*
Of which° achatours° mighte take exemple *From whom / buyers*
For to be wyse in bying of vitaille,° *provisions*
570 For whether that he payde, or took by taille,° *on account*
Algate he wayted so in his achat[5]
That he was ay biforn° and in good stat. *always ahead*
Now is nat that of God a ful fair grace,
That swich a lewed° mannes wit shal pace° *unlearned / surpass*

---

8. A tag-ending, useful to fill out the line metrically but almost wholly devoid of meaning (cf. l. 523).
9. That (was) well proved, for everywhere he went, at wrestling contests he would always win the ram (a usual prize).
1. There was no door he wasn't willing to heave off (its) hinges.
2. He knew well how to steal corn (grain) and take his toll (his percentage for grinding it) three times over.
3. The proverb "An honest miller hath a golden thumb" implies there are no honest millers; "pardee" is a weak form of "by God" (Fr. *par Dieu*), perhaps best translated simply as "I swear."
4. A manciple was in charge of purchasing provisions for a college or (as here) for an inn of court, where law was studied.
5. He was always so watchful in his purchasing.

575 The wisdom of an heep of lerned men?
 Of maistres hadde he mo° than thryes ten   *more*
 That weren of° lawe expert and curious,°   *in / skillful*
 Of which° ther were a doseyn° in that hous   *Among whom / dozen*
 Worthy to been stiwardes of rente° and lond   *income*
580 Of any lord that is in Engelond,
 To make him live by his propre good°   *within his own income*
 In honour, dettelees,° but° he were wood,°   *debtless / unless / mad*
 Or live as scarsly as him list desire,⁶
 And⁷ able for to helpen al a shire°   *an entire county*
585 In any cas° that mighte falle° or happe;   *eventuality / befall*
 And yit this maunciple sette hir aller cappe.°   *made fools of them all*
      The REVE was a sclendre colerik man.⁸
 His berd was shave as ny° as ever he can;   *close*
 His heer was by his eres° ful round y-shorn,°   *ears / cut off*
590 His top was dokked° lyk a preest biforn.°   *cut short / in front*
 Ful longe were his legges, and ful lene,
 Ylyk° a staf; ther was no calf y-sene.°   *Like / to be seen*
 Wel coude he kepe a gerner° and a binne—   *granary*
 Ther was noon auditour coude on him winne.°   *catch him short*
595 Wel wiste° he by the droghte and by the reyn   *knew*
 The yeldinge of his seed and of his greyn.
 His lordes sheep, his neet,° his dayerye,°   *cattle / dairy cows*
 His swyn, his hors, his stoor,° and his pultrye,°   *livestock / poultry*
 Was hoolly° in this reves governinge,   *wholly*
600 And by his covenaunt° yaf° the rekeninge,   *contract / (he) gave*
 Sin that° his lord was twenty yeer of age.   *Since*
 Ther coude no man bringe him in arrerage.°   *arrears*
 Ther nas baillif, ne herde, ne other hyne,⁹
 That he ne knew his sleighte° and his covyne;°   *cunning / deceit*
605 They were adrad° of him as of the deeth.¹   *afraid*
 His woning° was ful fair upon an heeth;   *dwelling*
 With grene trees shadwed was his place.
 He coude bettre than his lord purchace.²
 Ful riche he was astored prively;°   *privately stocked*
610 His lord wel coude he plesen subtilly,
 To yeve and lene him of his owne good,
 And have a thank, and yet a cote and hood.³
 In youthe he hadde lerned a good mister:°   *trade*
 He was a wel good wrighte,° a carpenter.   *craftsman*
615 This reve sat upon a ful good stot°   *farm horse*

---

6. Or live as frugally as it pleases him to wish.
7. The subject is again the "doseyn" men of l. 578 worthy to be stewards.
8. A reeve was manager and accountant of an estate or manor and was chosen from among the serfs. This one is choleric, i.e., dominated by the humor called choler (or yellow bile), and thus hot-tempered by nature.
9. There was no overseer, nor herdsman, nor (any) other servant.
1. Death in general, or perhaps the Black Death (plague).
2. He knew, better than his lord, how to increase one's possessions.
3. He knew well how to please his lord in sly ways, giving and lending to him from his (the lord's) own resources, and earn thanks (for it) and a coat and hood besides.

That was al pomely° grey and highte° Scot.   *dappled / named*
A long surcote° of pers° upon he hade,   *outer coat / blue cloth*
And by his syde he bar° a rusty blade.   *bore*
Of Northfolk° was this reve of which I tell,   *Norfolk*
620 Bisyde° a toun men clepen° Baldeswelle.   *(From) near / call*
Tukked° he was as is a frere° aboute;   *Belted / friar*
And evere he rood the hindreste° of oure route.°   *hindmost / company*
    A SOMONOUR[4] was ther with us in that place,
That hadde a fyr-reed cherubinnes face,[5]
625 For sawcefleem° he was, with eyen° narwe.   *pimpled / eyes*
As hoot° he was and lecherous as a sparwe,°   *passionate / sparrow*
With scalled° browes blake, and piled berd;°   *scabby / scraggy beard*
Of his visage° children were aferd.°   *face / afraid*
Ther nas quiksilver, litarge,° ne brimstoon,   *lead oxide*
630 Boras,° ceruce,° ne oille° of tartre noon,   *Borax / white lead / cream*
Ne oynement that wolde clense and byte,°   *sting*
That him mighte helpen of° his whelkes° whyte,   *cure / pimples*
Nor of the knobbes° sittinge on his chekes.   *lumps*
Wel loved he garleek, oynons, and eek lekes,°   *leeks*
635 And for to drinken strong wyn, reed as blood.
Thanne wolde he speke, and crye° as° he were wood;° *shout / as if / mad*
And whan that he wel dronken hadde the wyn,
Thanne wolde he speke no word but Latyn.°   *(in) Latin*
A fewe termes° hadde he, two or three,   *technical phrases*
640 That he had lerned out of som decree—
No wonder is,° he herde it al the day;   *it is*
And eek ye knowen wel how that a jay°   *a chattering bird*
Can clepen "Watte" as well as can the Pope.[6]
But whoso coude in other thing him grope,°   *question*
645 Thanne hadde he spent° al his philosophye;   *exhausted*
Ay *"Questio quid iuris"* wolde he crye.[7]
He was a gentil° harlot° and a kinde;°   *worthy / rascal / natural one*
A bettre felawe° sholde men noght finde: *companion*
He wolde suffre,° for a quart of wyn,   *allow*
650 A good felawe to have his concubyn
A° twelf-month, and excuse him atte fulle;°   *(For) a / fully*
Ful prively a finch eek coude he pulle.[8]
And if he fond° owher° a good felawe,   *found / anywhere*
He wolde techen him to have non awe°   *fear*
655 In swich cas of the erchedeknes curs,[9]

---

4. A summoner was an officer who cited ("summoned") malefactors to appear before an ecclesiastical court: in this case, an archdeacon's, having jurisdiction over matrimonial cases,
adultery, and fornication.
5. Cherubim, the second order of angels, were sometimes painted brilliant red ("fire-red") in
medieval art. The summoner resembles them, not through beatitude but through a skin disease.
6. Knows how to say "Walter" as well as does the Pope.
7. He would always cry, "The question is, what point of law applies?"
8. He was skilled in secretly seducing girls. ("To pull a finch," i.e., to pluck a bird, was an ob-
scene expression.)
9. Curse, the power of excommunication.

But-if° a mannes soule were in his purs,   *Unless*
For in his purs he sholde y-punisshed be.
"Purs is the erchedeknes helle," seyde he.
But wel I woot° he lyed right in dede: *know*
660 Of cursing oghte ech gilty man him drede—
For curs wol slee, right as assoilling saveth—
And also war him of a *significavit.*[1]
In daunger° hadde he at° his owene gyse°   *his power / in / way*
The yonge girles° of the diocyse,   *wenches*
665 And knew hir counseil,° and was al hir reed.°   *their secrets / adviser to them all*
A gerland° hadde he set upon his heed,   *garland*
As greet as it were for an ale-stake;°   *tavern sign*
A bokeler° hadde he maad him of a cake.°   *shield / round bread*
    With him ther rood a gentil PARDONER[2]
670 Of Rouncival,[3] his freend and his compeer,°   *companion*
That streight was comen fro the court of Rome.
Ful loude he song,° "Com hider,° love, to me."   *sang / hither*
This somnour bar to° him a stif burdoun,°   *accompanied / sturdy bass*
Was nevere trompe° of half so greet a soun.°   *trumpet / sound*
675 This pardoner hadde heer° as yelow as wex,°   *hair / wax*
But smothe it heng,° as dooth a strike of flex;°   *hung / bunch of flax*
By ounces° henge his lokkes that he hadde,   *In thin strands*
And therwith° he his shuldres overspradde;°   *with it / covered*
But thinne it lay, by colpons° oon and oon;   *in small bunches*
680 But hood, for jolitee,° wered° he noon,   *sportiveness / wore*
For it was trussed° up in his walet.°   *packed / pouch*
Him thoughte he rood al of the newe jet;
Dischevele, save his cappe, he rood al bare.[4]
Swiche glaringe eyen° hadde he as an hare.   *staring eyes*
685 A vernicle[5] hadde he sowed on his cappe.
His walet lay biforn° him in his lappe,   *in front of*
Bretful of pardoun comen from Rome al hoot.[6]
A voys he hadde as smal as hath a goot.°   *goat*
No berd hadde he, ne nevere sholde have,
690 As smothe it was as it were late shave:°   *recently shaved*
I trowe° he were a gelding or a mare.   *believe*
But of his craft, fro Berwik into Ware,°   *i.e., from north to south*
Ne was ther swich another pardoner.
For in his male° he hadde a pilwe-beer,°   *bag / pillowcase*

---

1. Every guilty man ought to be fearful of excommunication, for it will slay (the soul eternally), just as absolution (the forgiveness granted through the sacrament of penance) saves—and (he ought) also beware a *significavit* (a writ of arrest).
2. A pardoner was a seller of papal indulgences (remissions of punishment for sin), whose proceeds were often intended to build or support a religious house. Many pardoners were fraudulent, and their abuses were much criticized.
3. Near Charing Cross in London.
4. It seemed to him he rode in the very latest fashion; (his hair) loose, he rode bareheaded except for his cap.
5. A copy of the veil St. Veronica gave to Christ when He was carrying the cross, that He might wipe His brow; it received the imprint of Christ's face.
6. Brimful of pardons, come all hot (fresh) from Rome.

695 Which that he seyde was Oure Lady veyl.°   *Our Lady's veil*
    He seyde he hadde a gobet° of the seyl°   *piece / sail*
    That seynt Peter hadde, whan that he wente°   *walked*
    Upon the see, til Jesu Christ him hente.°   *took hold of*
    He hadde a croys° of latoun,° ful of stones,°   *cross / metal / gems*
700 And in a glas° he hadde pigges bones.   *glass container*
    But with thise relikes,° whan that he fond   *relics*
    A povre person dwellinge upon lond,[7]
    Upon a° day he gat him more moneye   *In one*
    Than that the person gat in monthes tweye.°   *two*
705 And thus, with feyned flaterye and japes,°   *tricks*
    He made the person and the peple his apes.°   *fools*
    But trewely to tellen, atte laste,°   *after all*
    He was in chirche a noble ecclesiaste.°   *preacher*
    Wel coude he rede a lessoun or a storie,°   *religious tale*
710 But alderbest° he song° an offertorie;   *best of all / sang*
    For wel he wiste,° whan that song was songe,   *knew*
    He moste preche, and wel affyle° his tonge   *make smooth*
    To winne silver, as he ful wel coude—
    Therefore he song the murierly° and loude.   *more merrily*
715   Now have I told you soothly, in a clause,°   *briefly*
    Th'estaat, th'array, the nombre, and eek the cause
    Why that assembled was this compaignye
    In Southwerk, at this gentil° hostelrye,   *worthy*
    That highte° the Tabard, faste° by the Belle.°   *was called / close / Bell Inn*
720 But now is tyme to yow for to telle
    How that we baren us° that ilke° night,   *conducted ourselves / same*
    Whan we were in that hostelrye alight;°   *alighted*
    And after wol I telle of our viage,°   *journey*
    And al the remenaunt° of oure pilgrimage.   *remainder*
725 But first I pray yow, of youre curteisye,
    That ye n'arette it nat my vileinye,[8]
    Thogh that° I pleynly speke in this matere,   *Even though*
    To tell yow hir° wordes and hir chere,°   *their / behavior*
    Ne thogh I speke hir wordes properly.°   *exactly*
730 For this ye knowen al so wel as I:
    Whoso shal telle a tale after a man,[9]
    He moot reherce° as ny° as evere he can   *must repeat / closely*
    Everich a word, if it be in his charge,
    Al speke he never so rudeliche and large;[1]
735 Or elles° he moot° telle his tale untrewe,   *else / may*
    Or feyne thing,° or finde wordes newe.   *invent something*
    He may nat spare,° althogh he[2] were his brother;   *hold back*
    He moot° as wel seye o° word as another.   *must / one*

7. A poor parson living in the country.
8. That you do not attribute it to my churlishness.
9. I.e., repeats another man's story.
1. Every word, if that be the responsibility he's charged with, however roughly and broadly he
   (may) speak.
2. I.e., the original teller.

Crist spak himself ful brode° in Holy Writ,   *broadly*
740 And wel ye woot,° no vileinye° is it.   *know / churlishness*
Eek Plato seith, whoso can him rede,
The wordes mote be cosin° to the dede.   *cousin*
Also I prey yow to foryeve° it me,   *forgive*
Al have I nat set folk in hir degree³
745 Here in this tale, as that they sholde stonde;
My wit is short, ye may wel understonde.
      Greet chere made oure Hoste us everichon,⁴
And to the soper sette he us anon;°   *immediately*
He served us with vitaille° at the beste.   *victuals*
750 Strong was the wyn, and wel to drinke us leste.°   *it pleased us*
A semely° man oure hoste was withalle   *suitable*
For to been a marshal in an halle;⁵
A large man he was with eyen stepe°—   *protruding eyes*
A fairer burgeys° was ther noon in Chepe.°   *citizen / Cheapside (in London)*
755 Bold of his speche, and wys, and wel y-taught,
And of manhod him lakkede° right naught.   *he lacked*
Eek therto he was right° a mery man,   *truly*
And after soper pleyen° he bigan,   *to jest*
And spak of mirthe amonges othere thinges—
760 Whan that we hadde maad oure rekeninges°—   *paid our bills*
And seyde thus: "Now, lordinges, trewely,
Ye been° to me right welcome hertely.°   *are / heartily*
For by my trouthe, if that I shal nat lye,
I saugh nat this yeer so mery a compaignye
765 Atones° in this herberwe° as is now.   *At one time / inn*
Fayn wolde I doon yow mirthe, wiste I how,
And of a mirthe I am right now bithoght,⁶
To doon yow ese,° and it shal coste noght.   *give you pleasure*
      Ye goon° to Caunterbury—God yow spede;   *are going*
770 The blisful martir quyte° yow your mede.°   *pay / reward*
And wel I woot, as ye goon by the weye,
Ye shapen yow to talen and to pleye;⁷
For trewely, confort° ne mirthe is noon°   *pleasure / (there) is none*
To ryde by the weye doumb as a stoon;
775 And therfore wol I maken yow disport,°   *amusement*
As I seyde erst,° and doon yow som confort.   *before*
And if yow lyketh° alle, by oon° assent,   *it pleases you / one*
Now for to stonden at° my jugement,   *abide by*
And for to werken° as I shal yow seye,   *do*
780 To-morwe, whan ye ryden by the weye—
Now by my fader° soule that is deed—   *father's*
But° ye be merye, I wol yeve° yow myn heed.°   *Unless / give / head*

3. Although I haven't described (these) people in (the order of) their social rank.
4. Our host made great welcome to every one of us.
5. I.e., the officer in charge of the serving of meals and banquets in a great hall.
6. I would gladly make you (some) amusement if I knew how, and I have just now thought of
   some fun.
7. You plan to tell tales and to play.

Hold up youre hondes, withouten more speche."
Oure counseil° was nat longe for to seche;°   *decision / seek*
785 Us thoughte it was noght worth to make it wys,[8]
And graunted him withouten more avys,°   *further consideration*
And bad him seye his voirdit° as him leste.°   *verdict / it pleased him*
"Lordinges," quod° he, "now herkneth° for the beste,   *said / listen*
But tak it nought, I prey yow, in desdeyn.°   *disdain*
790 This is the poynt, to speken short and pleyn:
That ech of yow, to shorte with° oure weye,   *with which to shorten*
In this viage° shal telle tales tweye,°   *journey / two*
To Caunterbury-ward,° I mene° it so,   *toward Canterbury / intend*
And homward he shal tellen othere two,
795 Of aventures that whylom° han bifalle.   *once upon a time*
And which° of yow that bereth° him best of alle,   *whichever / conducts*
That is to seyn, that telleth in this cas°   *on this occasion*
Tales of best sentence° and most solas,°   *wisdom, instruction / delight*
Shal have a soper at oure aller cost°   *the expense of us all*
800 Here in this place, sittinge by this post,°   *column*
Whan that we come agayn fro Caunterbury.
And for to make yow the more mery,°   *merry*
I wol myselven goodly° with yow ryde,   *gladly*
Right at myn owne cost, and be youre gyde.
805 And whoso wole my jugement withseye°   *oppose*
Shal paye al that we spenden by the weye.
And if ye vouchesauf° that it be so,   *grant*
Tel me anon,° withouten wordes mo,°   *immediately / more*
And I wol erly shape me° therfore."   *prepare myself*
810 This thing was graunted, and oure othes° swore°   *oaths / sworn*
With ful glad herte, and preyden° him also   *we begged*
That he wolde vouchesauf for° to do so,   *grant*
And that he wolde been oure governour
And of oure tales juge and reportour,°   *referee(?)*
815 And sette a soper at a certeyn prys;°   *price*
And we wol reuled been at his devys°   *desire, will*
In heigh and lowe;° and thus, by oon assent,   *In all respects*
We been acorded to his jugement.
And therupon the wyn was fet° anon;°   *fetched / at once*
820 We dronken, and to reste wente echon,°   *each one*
Withouten any lenger taryinge.
Amorwe,° whan that day bigan to springe,   *In the morning*
Up roos oure Host and was oure aller cok,[9]
And gadrede° us togidre,° alle in a flok;   *gathered / together*
825 And forth we riden,° a° litel more than pas,°   *rode / at a / walking speed*
Unto the watering of Seint Thomas,[1]
And there oure Host bigan his hors areste,°   *stopped his horse*
And seyde, "Lordinges, herkneth, if yow leste.°   *it may please*

8. It seemed to us (that) it was not worth pondering over.
9. The rooster who wakened us all.
1. St. Thomas a Watering was a brook two miles from London on the Canterbury road.

Ye woot° youre forward,° and I it yow recorde.°   *know / agreement / recall*
830 If even-song and morwe-song° acorde,   *morning song*
Lat se° now who shal telle the firste tale.   *Let us see*
As evere mote° I drinke wyn or ale,   *may*
Whoso be rebel to my jugement
Shal paye for al that by the weye is spent.
835 Now draweth cut,° er that we ferrer twinne;°   *lots, cut straws / go farther*
He which that hath the shortest shal biginne.
Sire Knight," quod he, "my maister and my lord,
Now draweth cut for that is myn acord.°   *decision*
Cometh neer,"° quod he, "my lady Prioresse;   *nearer*
840 And ye, sire Clerk, lat be° youre shamfastnesse,°   *leave off / shyness*
Ne studieth° noght. Ley hond to, every man!"   *deliberate*
Anon° to drawen every wight° bigan,   *At once / person*
And shortly for to tellen as it was,
Were it by aventure,° or sort,° or cas,°   *chance / fate / fortune*
845 The sothe° is this, the cut fil° to the Knight,   *truth / fell*
Of which ful blythe and glad was every wight;
And telle he moste° his tale, as was resoun,°   *must / right*
By forward° and by composicioun,°   *agreement / arrangement*
As ye han herd. What nedeth wordes mo?°   *more*
850 And whan this gode man saugh it was so,
As he that wys was and obedient
To kepe his forward by his free assent,
He seyde: "Sin° I shal biginne the game,   *Since*
What,° welcome be the cut, a Goddes° name!   *Why / in God's*
855 Now lat us ryde, and herkneth what I seye."
And with that word we riden° forth oure weye;   *rode*
And he bigan with right a mery chere°   *in a very merry mood*
His tale anon, and seyde as ye may heere.

The Knight's Tale

PART ONE

Whylom,° as olde stories tellen us,   *Once, formerly*
860 Ther was a duk that highte° Theseus;   *was called*
Of Athenes he was lord and governour,
And in his tyme swich° a conquerour,   *such*
That gretter was ther noon under the sonne.
Ful many a riche contree hadde he wonne;
865 What with his wisdom and his chivalrye,°   *knightly prowess*
He conquered al the regne° of Femenye,[1]   *kingdom, realm*
That whylom was y-cleped° Scithia,   *called*
And weddede the quene Ipolita,°   *Hippolyta*
And broghte hire hoom with him in his contree

---

1. The country of the Amazons.

870 With muchel glorie and greet solempnitee,°   *pomp, ceremony*
    And eek hire yonge suster Emelye.
    And thus with victorie and with melodye
    Lete I this noble duk to Athenes ryde,
    And al his hoost, in armes, him bisyde.
875   And certes,° if it nere° to long to here,   *certainly / were not*
    I wolde have told yow fully the manere
    How wonnen was the regne of Femenye
    By Theseus, and by his chivalrye;°   *host of knights*
    And of the grete bataille for the nones°   *occasion, purpose*
880 Bitwixen Athenës and Amazones;
    And how asseged° was Ipolita,   *besieged*
    The faire hardy quene of Scithia;
    And of the feste that was at hir° weddinge,   *their*
    And of the tempest at hir hoomcominge;
885 But al that thing I moot° as now° forbere.   *must / at this time*
    I have, God woot,° a large feeld to ere,°   *knows / harrow, plough*
    And wayke° been the oxen in my plough.   *weak*
    The remenant of the tale is long ynough.
    I wol nat letten° eek noon of this route;°   *hinder / company*
890 Lat every felawe telle his tale aboute,°   *in turn*
    And lat see now who shall the soper winne;
    And ther° I lefte, I wol ageyn biginne.   *where*
        This duk, of whom I make mencioun,
    When he was come almost unto the toun,
895 In al his wele° and in his moste pryde,   *success, happiness*
    He was war,° as he caste his eye asyde,   *aware*
    Where that ther kneled in the hye weye
    A companye of ladies, tweye and tweye,°   *two by two*
    Ech after other clad in clothes blake;
900 But swich a cry and swich a wo they make,
    That in this world nis° creature livinge,   *(there) is not*
    That herde swich another weymentinge;°   *lamenting*
    And of this cry they nolde° nevere stenten,°   *would not / cease*
    Til they the reynes of his brydel henten.°   *seized*
905   "What folk ben ye, that at myn hoomcominge
    Perturben so my feste with cryinge?"
    Quod Theseus. "Have ye so greet envye
    Of myn honour, that° thus compleyne and crye?   *that ye*
    Or who hath yow misboden° or offended?   *insulted, harmed*
910 And telleth me if it may been amended,
    And why that ye ben clothed thus in blak."
        The eldeste lady of hem alle spak,
    When she hadde swowned° with a deedly chere° *fainted / deathly appearance*
    That it was routhe° for to seen and here.   *a pity*
915 She seyde: "Lord, to whom Fortune hath yiven°   *given*
    Victorie, and as a conquerour to liven,
    Noght greveth us° youre glorie and youre honour;   *We do not resent*
    But we biseken° mercy and socour.°   *beseech / aid, comfort*

Have mercy on oure wo and oure distresse.
920 Som drope of pitee, thurgh thy gentillesse,
Upon us wrecched wommen lat thou falle.
For certes, lord, ther nis noon of us alle,
That she ne hath been a duchesse or a quene;
Now be we caitifs,° as it is wel sene,   *wretches*
925 Thanked be Fortune and hire false wheel,
That noon estat assureth to be weel.[2]
And certes, lord, to abyden° your presence,   *await*
Here in this temple of the goddesse Clemence°   *Mercy*
We han ben waytinge al this fourtenight;°   *fourteen nights*
930 Now help us, lord, sith° it is in thy might.   *since*
      I, wrecche, which that wepe and waille thus,
Was whylom° wyf to king Capaneus,   *once*
That starf° at Thebes—cursed be that day!   *died*
And alle we that been in this array°   *condition*
935 And maken al this lamentacioun,
We losten alle oure housbondes at that toun,
Whyl that the sege° theraboute lay.   *siege*
And yet now the olde Creon, weylaway,°   *alas*
That lord is now of Thebes the citee,
940 Fulfild° of ire and of iniquitee,   *Filled full*
He, for despyt° and for his tirannye,   *malice, spite*
To do the dede bodyes vileinye,°   *outrage*
Of alle oure lordes whiche that ben y-slawe,°   *slain*
Hath alle the bodyes on an heep y-drawe,°   *dragged*
945 And wol nat suffren° hem, by noon assent,°   *allow / on any terms*
Neither to been y-buried nor y-brent,°   *burned*
But maketh houndes ete hem in despyt."
And with that word, withouten more respyt,°   *further delay*
They fillen gruf° and cryden pitously,   *fell face downward*
950 "Have on us wrecched wommen som mercy,
And lat oure sorwe sinken in thyn herte."
      This gentil duk doun from his courser sterte°   *leaped*
With herte pitous,° whan he herde hem speke.   *pitying, merciful*
Him thoughte° that his herte wolde breke,   *It seemed to him*
955 Whan he saugh hem so pitous° and so mat,°   *pitiable / dejected*
That whylom° weren of so greet estat.   *formerly*
And in his armes he hem alle up hente,°   *took*
And hem conforteth in ful good entente;
And swoor his ooth, as he was trewe knight,
960 He wolde doon so ferforthly° his might   *exert to such an extent*
Upon the tyraunt Creon hem to wreke,°   *avenge*
That al the peple of Grece sholde speke
How Creon was of° Theseus y-served,°   *by / treated*
As he that hadde his deeth ful wel deserved.
965 And right anoon, withouten more abood,°   *delay*

2. Who ensures that no estate will be (permanently) in prosperity.

His baner he desplayeth, and forth rood
To Thebes-ward,° and al his host bisyde.°   *Toward Thebes / with him*
No neer° Athenës wolde he go° ne ryde,   *nearer / walk*
Ne take his ese fully half a day,
970 But onward on his wey that night he lay,°   *lodged*
And sente anoon° Ipolita the quene   *at once*
And Emelye, hir yonge suster shene,°   *bright, fair*
Unto the toun of Athenës to dwelle;
And forth he rit;° ther is namore to telle.   *rides*
975   The rede statue° of Mars, with spere and targe,°   *red image / shield*
So shyneth in his whyte baner large,
That alle the feeldes gliteren up and doun;
And by his baner born is his penoun°   *pennant*
Of gold ful riche, in which ther was y-bete°   *embroidered*
980 The Minotaur, which that he slough° in Crete.   *slew*
Thus rit this duk, thus rit this conquerour,
And in his host of chivalrye the flour,°   *the flower of knighthood*
Til that he cam to Thebes, and alighte°   *alighted*
Faire in a feeld, ther as° he thoghte to fighte.   *where*
985 But shortly for to speken of this thing,
With Creon, which that was of Thebes king,
He faught, and slough him manly° as a knight   *in a manly fashion, boldly*
In pleyn° bataille, and putte the folk to flight;   *open*
And by assaut° he wan° the citee after,   *assault / conquered*
990 And rente° adoun bothe wal and sparre° and rafter;   *tore / beam*
And to the ladyes he restored agayn
The bones of hir housbondes that were slayn,
To doon obsequies, as was tho° the gyse.°   *then / custom*
But it were al to longe for to devyse°   *tell, describe*
995 The grete clamour and the waymentinge°   *lamentation*
That the ladyes made at the brenninge°   *burning*
Of the bodyes, and the grete honour
That Theseus, the noble conquerour,
Doth to the ladyes, whan they from him wente;
1000 But shortly for to telle is myn entente.
Whan that this worthy duk, this Theseus,
Hath Creon slayn and wonne Thebes thus,
Stille in that feeld he took al night his reste,
And dide with al the contree as him leste.°   *as it pleased him*
1005   To ransake in the tas° of bodyes dede,   *pile, heap*
Hem for to strepe° of harneys° and of wede,°   *strip / armor / clothing*
The pilours° diden bisinesse and cure°   *pillagers / worked busily and carefully*
After the bataille and disconfiture.°   *defeat*
And so bifel,° that in the tas they founde,   *it happened*
1010 Thurgh-girt° with many a grevous blody wounde,   *Pierced through*
Two yonge knightes ligginge° by and by,°   *lying / side by side*
Bothe in oon armes,³ wroght° ful richely,   *made*

---

3. Having the same coat of arms.

Of whiche two, Arcita highte that oon,
And that other knight highte Palamon.
1015 Nat fully quike° ne fully dede they were, — alive
But by hir cote-armures[4] and by hir gere° — accoutrements
The heraudes° knew hem best in special° — heralds / especially well
As they that weren of the blood royal
Of Thebes, and of sustren° two y-born. — sisters
1020 Out of the tas the pilours han hem torn,
And han hem caried softe° unto the tente — gently
Of Theseus, and he ful sone hem sente
To Athenës, to dwellen in prisoun
Perpetuelly: he nolde no raunsoun.° — would not (accept) ransom
1025 And whan this worthy duk hath thus y-don,
He took his host, and hoom he rit anon
With laurer° crowned as a conquerour; — laurel
And there he liveth in joye and in honour
Terme° of his lyf; what nedeth wordes mo?° — The remainder / more
1030 And in a tour,° in angwish and in wo, — tower
Dwellen this Palamoun and eek Arcite
For everemore; ther may no gold hem quyte.° — ransom
This passeth yeer by yeer and day by day,
Til it fil° ones, in a morwe° of May, — befell, happened / morning
1035 That Emelye, that fairer was to sene° — see
Than is the lilie upon his° stalke grene, — its
And fressher than the May with floures newe—
For with the rose colour stroof° hire hewe,° — strove / hue, complexion
I noot° which was the fairer of hem two— — know not
1040 Er° it were day, as was hir wone° to do, — Before / wont, custom
She was arisen and al redy dight;° — promptly dressed
For May wole have no slogardye° a-night.° — laziness / at night
The sesoun priketh° every gentil herte, — incites, rouses
And maketh him out of his sleep to sterte,° — start, wake up
1045 And seith "Arys, and do thyn observaunce."
This maked Emelye have remembraunce
To doon honour to May, and for to ryse.
Y-clothed was she fresh, for to devyse:° — as I may tell
Hir yelow heer was broyded° in a tresse — braided
1050 Bihinde hir bak, a yerde long, I gesse.
And in the gardin, at the sonne upriste,° — sun's uprising
She walketh up and doun, and as hire liste° — it pleased her
She gadereth floures, party° whyte and rede, — particolored
To make a sotil° gerland for hire hede, — skillfully woven
1055 And as an aungel hevenysshly she song.
The grete tour, that was so thikke and strong,
Which of the castel was the chief dongeoun
(Theras the knightes weren in prisoun,
Of whiche I tolde yow and tellen shal),

---

4. Coat-armor: a vest displaying a knight's heraldic emblems that is worn over armor.

1060 Was evene joynant to° the gardin wal   *directly adjoining*
    Ther as this Emelye hadde hir pleyinge.°   *amusement*
    Bright was the sonne and cleer that morweninge,
    And Palamon, this woful prisoner,
    As was his wone, by leve° of his gayler,°   *permission, leave / jailer*
1065 Was risen and romed in a chambre on heigh,
    In which he al the noble citee seigh,°   *saw*
    And eek the gardin, ful of braunches grene,
    Theras this fresshe Emelye the shene°   *bright, beautiful*
    Was in hire walk, and romed up and doun.
1070 This sorweful prisoner, this Palamoun,
    Goth in the chambre rominge to and fro,
    And to himself compleyninge of his wo.
    That he was born, ful ofte he seyde, "Alas!"
    And so bifel, by aventure° or cas,°   *chance / accident*
1075 That thurgh a window, thikke of° many a barre   *thickset with*
    Of yren greet and square° as any sparre,°   *sturdy / beam*
    He caste his eye upon Emelya,
    And therwithal he bleynte° and cryde "A!"   *flinched*
    As though he stongen were unto the herte.
1080 And with that cry Arcite anon up sterte
    And seyde, "Cosin myn, what eyleth° thee,   *ails*
    That art so pale and deedly° on to see?°   *deathly / to look at*
    Why crydestow?° Who hath thee doon offence?   *didst thou cry*
    For Goddes love, tak al in pacience
1085 Oure prisoun, for it may non other be;°   *may not be otherwise*
    Fortune hath yeven° us this adversitee.   *given*
    Som wikke aspect or disposicioun
    Of Saturne, by sum constellacioun,
    Hath yeven us this, although we hadde it sworn:[5]
1090 So stood the hevene whan that we were born.
    We moste endure it; this is the short and pleyn."
       This Palamon answerde and seyde ageyn,°   *in reply*
    "Cosyn, for sothe,° of this opinioun   *in truth*
    Thou hast a veyn imaginacioun.°   *foolish, mistaken idea*
1095 This prison caused me nat for to crye,
    But I was hurt right now thurghout myn yë°   *eye*
    Into myn herte, that wol my bane° be.   *destruction*
    The fairnesse of that lady that I see
    Yond° in the gardin romen to and fro   *Yonder*
1100 Is cause of al my crying and my wo.
    I noot wher° she be womman or goddesse,   *do not know whether*
    But Venus is it soothly, as I gesse."
    And therwithal on knees doun he fil,°   *fell*
    And seyde: "Venus, if it be thy wil
1105 Yow° in this gardin thus to transfigure   *Yourself*

---

5. Some ill-omened aspect or disposition of Saturn, in relation to the other stars, has given us this (adversity), no matter what we might have done.

Bifore me, sorweful wrecched creature,
Out of this prisoun help that we may scapen.°   escape
And if so be my destinee be shapen°   shaped, determined
By eterne° word to dyen in prisoun,   eternal
1110 Of oure linage have som compassioun,
That is so lowe y-broght by tirannye."
And with that word Arcite gan° espye   did
Wher as this lady romed to and fro;
And with that sighte hir beautee hurte him so,
1115 That, if that Palamon was wounded sore,
Arcite is hurt as muche as he, or more.
And with a sigh he seyde pitously:
"The fresshe beautee sleeth° me sodeynly   slays
Of hire that rometh in the yonder place;
1120 And, but° I have hir mercy and hir grace,   unless
That I may seen hire atte leeste weye,°   at least
I nam but deed;° ther nis namore to seye."   I am (not) but dead
This Palamon, whan he tho° wordes herde,   those
Dispitously° he loked and answerde: Angrily
1125 "Whether seistow° this in ernest or in pley?"   sayest thou
"Nay," quod Arcite, "in ernest, by my fey!°   faith
God help me so, me list ful yvele pleye."°   I have no desire to jest
This Palamon gan knitte his browes tweye:
"It nere,"° quod he, "to thee no greet honour   were not
1130 For to be fals, ne for to be traytour
To me, that am thy cosin and thy brother
Y-sworn ful depe,[6] and ech of us til° other,   to
That nevere, for to dyen in the peyne,[7]
Til that the deeth departe° shal us tweyne,°   part / two
1135 Neither of us in love to hindre other,
Ne in non other cas, my leve° brother;   dear
But that thou sholdest trewely forthren° me   assist
In every cas, as I shal forthren thee.
This was thyn ooth, and myn also, certeyn;
1140 I wot right wel, thou darst° it nat withseyn.°   darest / deny
Thus artow of my counseil,° out of doute,°   in on my secrets / beyond doubt
And now thou woldest falsly been aboute°   set about
To love my lady, whom I love and serve,
And evere shal til that myn herte sterve.°   die
1145 Now certes,° false Arcite, thou shalt nat so.   surely
I loved hire first, and tolde thee my wo
As to my counseil° and my brother sworn   confidant
To forthre me, as I have told biforn.
For which thou art y-bounden as a knight
1150 To helpen me, if it lay in thy might,
Or elles artow fals, I dar wel seyn."

6. I.e., deeply sworn to you in blood brotherhood.
7. Even should it mean death by torture.

This Arcite ful proudly spak ageyn:°   *in reply*
"Thou shalt," quod he, "be rather° fals than I;   *sooner*
But thou art fals, I telle thee outrely;°   *plainly*
1155 For paramour° I loved hire first er thow.   *With passionate love*
What wiltow seyn? Thou woost° nat yet now   *knowest*
Whether she be a womman or goddesse!
Thyn is affeccioun of° holinesse,   *pertaining to*
And myn is love, as to a creature;
1160 For which I tolde thee myn aventure
As to my cosin and my brother sworn.
I pose° that thou lovedest hire biforn:°   *I put the case (hypothetically) / first*
Wostow° nat wel the olde clerkes sawe,°   *Knowest thou / saying*
That 'who shal yeve° a lovere any lawe?'   *give*
1165 Love is a gretter lawe, by my pan,°   *brainpan, skull*
Than may be yeve to any erthly man.
And therefore positif lawe[8] and swich decree
Is broken al day° for love in ech degree.°   *every day / every social rank*
A man moot nedes love, maugree his heed.[9]
1170 He may nat fleen° it, thogh he sholde be deed,   *flee, escape*
Al be she° mayde or widwe or elles wyf.   *Whether she be*
And eek it is nat lykly al° thy lyf   *during*
To stonden in hir grace; namore shal I;
For wel thou woost° thyselven verraily,   *knowest*
1175 That thou and I be dampned° to prisoun   *condemned*
Perpetuelly; us gayneth° no raunsoun.   *we shall gain*
We stryve as dide the houndes for the boon:°   *bone*
They foughte al day, and yet hir part° was noon;   *their share*
Ther cam a kyte,° whyl that they were so wrothe,   *kite (bird)*
1180 And bar awey the boon bitwixe hem bothe.
And therfore, at the kinges court, my brother,
Ech man for himself: ther is non other.°   *no other way*
Love if thee list;° for I love and ay° shal;   *if it pleases thee / always*
And soothly, leve° brother, this is al.   *dear*
1185 Here in this prisoun mote° we endure,°   *must / remain*
And everich° of us take his aventure."°   *each / what befalls him*
   Greet was the stryf and long bitwixe hem tweye,
If that I hadde leyser° for to seye,   *leisure, opportunity*
But to th'effect.° It happed on a day,   *outcome*
1190 To telle it yow as shortly as I may,
A worthy duk that highte Perotheus,
That felawe° was unto duk Theseus   *fellow, friend*
Sin° thilke day that they were children lyte,°   *Since / little*
Was come to Athenes his felawe to visyte,
1195 And for to pleye as he was wont to do;
For in this world he loved no man so,
And he loved him as tendrely ageyn.

8. Laws made by man rather than natural law.
9. A man must necessarily love despite his intention (not to).

So wel they lovede, as olde bokes seyn,
That whan that oon was deed, sothly to telle,
1200 His felawe wente and soghte him doun in helle;
But of that story list me nat to wryte.
Duk Perotheus loved wel Arcite,
And hadde him knowe° at Thebes yeer by° yere;   *known / after*
And fynally, at requeste and preyere
1205 Of Perotheus, withouten any raunsoun,
Duk Theseus him leet out of prisoun
Freely to goon wher that him liste over al,°   *anywhere it pleased him*
In swich a gyse° as I you tellen shal.   *manner*
     This was the forward,° pleynly for t'endyte,° *agreement / write*
1210 Bitwixen Theseus and him Arcite:
That if so were, that Arcite were y-founde
Evere in his lyf, by day or night, o stounde°   *one moment*
In any contree of this Theseus,
And he were caught, it was acorded° thus,   *agreed*
1215 That with a swerd he sholde lese° his heed;   *lose*
Ther nas non other remedye ne reed;°   *option*
But taketh his leve, and homward he him spedde;
Let him be war, his nekke lyth to wedde.°   *lies as a pledge*
     How greet a sorwe suffreth now Arcite!
1220 The deeth he feleth thurgh his herte smyte;°   *smite, strike*
He wepeth, wayleth, cryeth pitously;
To sleen himself he wayteth prively.[1]
He seyde, "Allas that day that I was born!
Now is my prison worse than biforn;
1225 Now is me shape° eternally to dwelle   *it is destined for me*
Noght in purgatorie but in helle.
Allas, that evere knew I Perotheus!
For elles hadde I dwelled with Theseus
Y-fetered° in his prisoun everemo.   *Fettered, confined*
1230 Than hadde I been in blisse, and nat in wo.
Only the sighte of hire whom that I serve,
Though that I nevere hir grace may deserve,
Wolde han suffised right ynough for me.
O dere cosin Palamon," quod he,
1235 "Thyn is the victorie of this aventure:
Ful blisfully in prison maistow dure.°   *endure, remain*
In prison? certes nay, but in paradys!
Wel hath Fortune y-turned thee the dys,°   *dice*
That hast the sighte of hire, and I th'absence.
1240 For possible is, sin° thou hast hire presence,   *since*
And art a knight, a worthy and an able,
That by som cas,° sin Fortune is chaungeable,   *case, chance*
Thou mayst to thy desyr somtyme atteyne.°   *attain*
But I, that am exyled and bareyne°   *barren*

1. He secretly looks for a chance to slay himself.

1245 Of alle grace, and in so greet despeir
    That ther nis erthe, water, fyr, ne eir,°   *air*
    Ne creature that of hem maked is
    That may me helpe or doon confort in this,
    Wel oughte I sterve° in wanhope° and distresse.   *die / despair*
1250 Farwel my lyf, my lust,° and my gladnesse!   *joy*
       Allas, why pleynen° folk so in commune°   *complain / commonly*
    On purveyaunce° of God, or of Fortune,   *About the providence*
    That yeveth° hem ful ofte in many a gyse   *gives*
    Wel bettre than they can hemself devyse?
1255 Som man desyreth for to han° richesse,   *have*
    That cause is of his mordre° or greet siknesse.   *murder*
    And som man wolde° out of his prison fayn,°   *would be / gladly*
    That in his hous is of his meynee° slayn.   *household, retinue*
    Infinite harmes been in this matere;
1260 We witen° nat what thing we preyen° here.   *know / pray for*
    We faren° as he that dronke° is as a mous: *fare, behave / drunk*
    A dronke man wot° wel he hath an hous,   *knows*
    But he noot° which the righte wey is thider;   *does not know*
    And to a dronke man the wey is slider.°   *slippery*
1265 And certes, in this world so faren we;
    We seken faste° after felicitee,   *seek steadily*
    But we goon wrong ful often, trewely.
    Thus may we seyen alle, and namely° I,   *especially*
    That wende° and hadde a greet opinioun   *thought*
1270 That if I mighte escapen from prisoun,
    Than hadde I been in joye and perfit hele,°   *perfect well-being*
    Ther° now I am exyled fro my wele.°   *Whereas / happiness*
    Sin that I may nat seen yow, Emelye,
    I nam but deed; ther nis no remedye."
1275   Upon that other syde Palamon,
    Whan that he wiste° Arcite was agon,°   *knew / gone*
    Swich sorwe he maketh that the grete tour
    Resouneth° of his youling° and clamour.   *Resounds / howling*
    The pure° fettres on his shines grete°   *very / swollen shins*
1280 Weren of his bittre salte teres wete.
    "Allas!" quod he, "Arcita, cosin myn,
    Of al our stryf, God woot, the fruyt is thyn.
    Thow walkest now in Thebes at thy large,°   *freely, at large*
    And of my wo thou yevest litel charge.°   *care, consideration*
1285 Thou mayst, sin thou hast wisdom and manhede,°   *manliness*
    Assemblen alle the folk of our kinrede,°   *kindred*
    And make a werre° so sharp on this citee,   *war*
    That by som aventure, or some tretee,°   *treaty, agreement*
    Thou mayst have hir to lady and to wyf,
1290 For whom that I moste nedes lese° my lyf.   *lose*
    For, as by wey of possibilitee,
    Sith° thou art at thy large,° of prison free,   *Since / at large*
    And art a lord, greet is thyn avauntage

More than is myn, that sterve° here in a cage.°   *die / prison*
1295 For I mot wepe and wayle, whyl I live,
With al the wo that prison may me yive,
And eek with peyne that love me yiveth also,
That doubleth al my torment and my wo."
Therwith the fyr of jalousye up sterte
1300 Withinne his brest, and hente° him by the herte   *seized*
So woodly,° that he lyk was to biholde   *madly*
The boxtree or the asshen° dede and colde.   *ashes*
Thanne seyde he: "O cruel goddes, that governe
This world with binding of youre word eterne,
1305 And wryten in the table of athamaunt°   *adamant, hardest stone*
Your parlement° and youre eterne graunt,°   *decision / grant, decree*
What is mankinde more unto yow holde
Than is the sheep that rouketh in the folde?²
For slayn is man right as another beste,
1310 And dwelleth eek in prison and areste,°   *arrest, detention*
And hath siknesse and greet adversitee,
And ofte tymes giltelees, pardee!°   *certainly*
    What governaunce is in this prescience³
That giltelees tormenteth innocence?
1315 And yet encreseth° this al my penaunce,°   *increases / suffering*
That man is bounden to his observaunce,°   *bound to the obligation*
For Goddes sake, to letten of° his wille,   *restrain*
Ther as° a beest may al his lust° fulfille.   *Whereas / desire*
And whan a beest is deed, he hath no peyne;
1320 But man after his deeth moot wepe and pleyne,°   *lament, complain*
Though in this world he have care and wo.
Withouten doute it may stonden so.
The answere of this I lete° to divynis,°   *leave / theologians*
But wel I woot, that in this world gret pyne° is.   *suffering*
1325 Allas! I see a serpent or a theef,
That many a trewe man hath doon mescheef,°   *harm*
Goon at his large, and where him list may turne.
But I mot° been in prison thurgh Saturne,   *must*
And eek thurgh Juno,⁴ jalous and eek wood,°   *mad, angry*
1330 That hath destroyed wel ny° al the blood   *near*
Of Thebes, with his waste° walles wyde.   *its wasted, destroyed*
And Venus sleeth° me on that other syde   *slays*
For jalousye, and fere of him Arcite."
    Now wol I stinte° of Palamon a lyte,°   *cease (to tell) / little*
1335 And lete him to his prison stille dwelle,
And of Arcita forth I wol yow telle.
    The somer passeth, and the nightes longe

---

2. In what way is mankind more highly valued by you than is the sheep that cowers in the fold?
3. What sort of governing purpose is there in such foreknowledge.
4. Through the influence of the planet Saturn, whose characteristic workings are enumerated
   in ll. 2453–69, and through the hostility toward Thebes of the goddess Juno, occasioned by
   Jove's several infidelities with Theban women.

Encresen double wyse° the peynes stronge   *twofold*
Bothe of the lovere and the prisoner.
1340 I noot° which hath the wofullere mester.°   *do not know / sadder situation*
For, shortly for to seyn, this Palamoun
Perpetuelly is dampned° to prisoun,   *condemned*
In cheynes and in fettres to ben deed;
And Arcite is exyled upon his heed°   *on pain of losing his head*
1345 For evermo as out of that contree,
Ne neveremo ne shal his lady see.
         Yow loveres axe° I now this questioun: *ask*
Who hath the worse, Arcite or Palamoun?
That oon may seen his lady day by day,
1350 But in prison he moot dwelle alway.
That other wher him list may ryde or go,°   *walk*
But seen his lady shal he neveremo.
Now demeth° as yow liste, ye that can,°   *judge, decide / know how*
For I wol telle forth as I bigan.

PART TWO

1355   Whan that Arcite to Thebes comen was,
Ful ofte a day he swelte° and seyde "allas,"   *fainted*
For seen his lady shal he neveremo.
And shortly to concluden° al his wo,   *briefly to sum up*
So muche sorwe hadde nevere creature
1360 That is, or shal,° whyl that the world may dure.°   *shall (be) / endure*
His sleep, his mete,° his drink is him biraft,°   *(appetite for) food / bereft*
That lene he wex and drye as is a shaft.⁵
His eyen holwe,° and grisly° to biholde;   *hollow / horrible*
His hewe falow° and pale as asshen colde;   *faded*
1365 And solitarie he was and evere allone,
And waillinge al the night, makinge his mone.°   *moan, lament*
And if he herde song or instrument,
Thanne wolde he wepe, he mighte nat be stent.°   *stopped*
So feble eek were his spirits, and so lowe,
1370 And chaunged so, that no man coude knowe
His speche nor his vois, though men it herde.
And in his gere° for al the world he ferde°   *erratic behavior / fared*
Nat oonly lyk° the loveres maladye   *like (one afflicted with)*
Of Hereos,⁶ but rather lyk manye°   *mania*
1375 Engendred of humour malencolyk°   *Born of the melancholic humor*
Biforen,° in his celle fantastyk.⁷   *In the front (of the brain)*
And shortly, turned was al up so doun°   *upside down*
Bothe habit° and eek disposicioun   *outward form*

---

5. So that he became as thin and dry as the shaft of an arrow.
6. An illness caused by passionate love. Its symptoms, according to medieval medical authorities, are those attributed to Arcite in ll. 1356–71.
7. Medieval medicine divided the brain into three cells, the front one containing the imagination (fantasy), the middle cell judgment, the back cell memory. Mania was a disease of the
   imagination.

Of him, this woful lovere daun° Arcite.   *sir, lord*
1380 What sholde I al day of his wo endyte?°   *write*
Whan he endured hadde a yeer or two
This cruel torment and this peyne and wo,
At Thebes, in his contree, as I seyde,
Upon a night, in sleep as he him leyde,°   *laid*
1385 Him thoughte how that the winged god Mercurie
Biforn him stood and bad° him to be murye.°   *bade, requested / merry*
His slepy yerde° in hond he bar uprighte;   *sleep-bringing wand*
An hat he werede° upon his heres° brighte.   *wore / hair*
Arrayed was this god, as he took keep,°   *as (Arcite) took note*
1390 As he was whan that Argus⁸ took his sleep;
And seyde him thus: "To Athenes shaltou° wende: *shalt thou*
Ther is thee shapen° of thy wo an ende."   *destined, determined*
And with that word Arcite wook° and sterte.°   *woke / gave a start*
"Now trewely, how° sore that me smerte,"°   *however / it may hurt me*
1395 Quod he, "to Athenes right now wol I fare;
Ne for the drede of deeth shal I nat spare°   *refrain*
To see my lady, that I love and serve.
In hire presence I recche° nat to sterve."°   *care / if I die*
      And with that word he caughte° a greet mirour,   *seized*
1400 And saugh° that chaunged was al his colour,   *saw*
And saugh his visage al in another kinde.°   *totally altered*
And right anoon it ran him in his minde,
That, sith his face was so disfigured
Of maladye,° the which he hadde endured,   *By illness*
1405 He mighte wel, if that he bar him lowe,°   *behaved humbly*
Live in Athenes everemore unknowe,°   *unknown*
And seen his lady wel ny° day by day.   *nearly*
And right anon he chaunged his array,
And cladde him as a povre° laborer,   *poor*
1410 And al allone, save° oonly a squyer   *except for*
That knew his privetee° and al his cas,°   *private affairs / condition*
Which° was disgysed povrely as he was,   *Who*
To Athenes is he goon the nexte° way.   *nearest*
And to the court he wente upon a day,
1415 And at the gate he profreth his servyse
To drugge° and drawe,° what so men wol devyse.° *drudge / carry / require*
And shortly of this matere for to seyn,
He fil in office° with a chamberleyn,   *got a job*
The which that dwellinge was with Emelye;
1420 For he was wys, and coude soone aspye°   *discover*
Of every servaunt, which that serveth here.°   *her*
Wel coude he hewen° wode and water bere,   *cut*
For he was yong and mighty for the nones,°   *occasion, purpose*
And therto he was strong and big of bones
1425 To doon that° any wight can him devyse.   *what*

---

8. Argus, the monster with a hundred eyes, had likewise been put to sleep by Mercury.

A yeer or two he was in this servyse,
Page of the chambre of Emelye the brighte;
And Philostrate he seide that he highte.°   *was named*
But half so wel biloved a man as he
1430 Ne was ther nevere in court of his degree;°   *social position*
He was so gentil of condicioun°   *disposition*
That thurghout al the court was his renoun.
They seyden that it were° a charitee   *would be*
That Theseus wolde enhauncen his degree°   *improve his rank*
1435 And putten him in worshipful° servyse,   *honorable*
Ther as he mighte his vertu° excercyse.   *natural ability*
And thus withinne a whyle his name is
     spronge,°   *sprung up, become well known*
Bothe of his dedes and his goode tonge,
That Theseus hath taken him so neer°   *so near (to himself)*
1440 That of his chambre he made him a squyer,
And gaf him gold to mayntene his degree;
And eek men broghte him out of his contree
From yeer to yeer, ful prively, his rente;°   *income*
But honestly° and slyly° he it spente,   *fittingly / discreetly*
1445 That no man wondred how that he it hadde.
And three yeer in this wyse° his lyf he ladde,°   *manner / led*
And bar him so in pees and eek in werre,
Ther was no man that Theseus hath derre.°   *holds more dear*
And in this blisse lete° I now Arcite,   *leave*
1450 And speke I wol of Palamon a lyte.
     In derknesse and horrible and strong prisoun
Thise seven yeer hath seten° Palamoun,   *dwelt*
Forpyned,° what for wo and for distresse;   *Wasted away*
Who feleth double soor° and hevinesse   *sorrow*
1455 But Palamon, that love destreyneth° so   *distresses*
That wood° out of his wit he gooth for wo?   *mad*
And eek therto he is a prisoner
Perpetuelly, noght oonly for a yeer.
Who coude ryme in English proprely
1460 His martirdom? For sothe, it am nat I;
Therefore I passe as lightly° as I may.   *quickly*
     It fel° that in the seventhe yeer, of May   *befell*
The thridde night, as olde bokes seyn,
That al this storie tellen more pleyn,°   *fully*
1465 Were it by aventure° or destinee—   *chance*
As, whan a thing is shapen,° it shal be—   *determined (in advance)*
That sone after the midnight Palamoun,
By helping of a freend, brak° his prisoun   *escaped from*
And fleeth the citee faste as he may go;
1470 For he hadde yive his gayler° drinke so   *jailor*
Of a clarree° maad of a certeyn wyn,   *spiced wine*
With nercotikes and opie of Thebes fyn,[9]

---

9. Fine opium from Thebes (in Egypt).

That al that night, thogh that men° wolde him shake,   *one*

The gayler sleep,° he mighte nat awake;   *slept*

1475 And thus he fleeth as faste as evere he may.

The night was short and faste by the day,°   *near daybreak*

That nedes cost° he moot° himselven hyde,   *of necessity / must*

And til° a grove, faste ther bisyde,   *to*

With dredful° foot thanne stalketh Palamoun.   *fearful*

1480 For, shortly, this was his opinioun:

That in that grove he wolde him hyde al day,

And in the night thanne wolde he take his way

To Thebes-ward,° his freendes for to preye   *Toward Thebes*

On Theseus to helpe him to werreye;°   *make war*

1485 And shortly, outher° he wolde lese° his lyf   *either / lose*

Or winnen Emelye unto his wyf.

This is th'effect° and his entente pleyn.°   *substance / complete intent*

    Now wol I turne to Arcite ageyn,

That litel wiste° how ny° that was his care,   *knew / near*

1490 Til that Fortune had broght him in the snare.

    The bisy larke, messager of day,

Saluëth° in hir song the morwe° gray;   *Salutes, greets / morning*

And fyry Phebus ryseth up so brighte

That al the orient° laugheth of the lighte,   *eastern sky*

1495 And with his stremes° dryeth in the greves°   *beams / bushes*

The silver dropes hanginge on the leves.

And Arcite, that in the court royal

With Theseus is squyer principal,

Is risen and loketh on the myrie day.

1500 And for to doon his observaunce to May,

Remembringe on° the poynt° of his desyr,   *Holding in mind / object*

He on a courser, startlinge° as the fyr,°   *leaping / fire*

Is riden into the feeldes him to pleye,

Out of the court, were it a myle or tweye;

1505 And to the grove of which that I yow tolde,

By aventure his wey he gan to holde,

To maken him a gerland of the greves,°   *branches*

Were it of wodebinde or hawethorn leves,

And loude he song ageyn° the sonne shene:°   *in response to / bright*

1510 "May, with alle thy floures and thy grene,

Welcome be thou, faire fresshe May,

In hope that I som grene° gete may."   *something green*

And from his courser, with a lusty herte,

Into the grove ful hastily he sterte,°   *leaped*

1515 And in a path he rometh up and doun,

Theras,° by aventure, this Palamoun   *Where*

Was in a bush, that no man mighte him see,

For sore afered° of his deeth was he.   *afraid*

Nothing° ne knew he that it was Arcite;   *Not at all*

1520 God wot he wolde have trowed° it ful lyte.   *believed*

But sooth is seyd, go sithen many yeres,°   *since many years ago*

That "feeld hath eyen° and the wode hath eres."   *the field has eyes*
It is ful fair° a man to bere him evene,°   *desirable (for)* / *with restraint*
For al day° meeteth men at unset stevene.[1]   *every day*
1525 Ful litel woot Arcite of his felawe,
That was so ny° to herknen al his sawe,°   *near* / *speech*
For in the bush he sitteth now ful stille.
    Whan that Arcite hadde romed al his fille,
And songen al the roundel° lustily,   *song*
1530 Into a studie° he fil sodeynly,   *i.e., deep thought*
As doon thise loveres in hir queynte geres,°   *strange behaviors*
Now in the croppe,° now doun in the breres,°   *treetop* / *briars*
Now up, now doun, as boket in a welle.
Right as° the Friday, soothly for to telle,   *Just as*
1535 Now it shyneth, now it reyneth faste,
Right so can gery° Venus overcaste°   *changeable* / *cloud over, darken*
The hertes of hir folk; right as hir day
Is gereful, right so chaungeth she array.°   *the order, disposition of things*
Selde is the Friday al the wyke ylyke.[2]
1540   Whan that Arcite had songe, he gan to syke,°   *sigh*
And sette him doun withouten any more.°   *without further delay*
"Alas!" quod he, "that day that I was bore!
How longe, Juno, thurgh thy crueltee,
Woltow° werreyen° Thebes the citee?   *Wilt thou* / *make war on*
1545 Allas! y-broght is to confusioun
The blood royal of Cadme° and Amphioun—   *Cadmus*
Of Cadmus, which that was the firste man
That Thebes bulte,° or first the toun bigan,   *built*
And of the citee first was crouned king.
1550 Of his lynage° am I, and his ofspring   *lineage*
By verray ligne,° as of the stok royal;   *true descent*
And now I am so caitif° and so thral°   *wretched* / *enslaved*
That he that is my mortal enemy,
I serve him as his squyer povrely.°   *in a lowly manner*
1555 And yet doth Juno me wel more shame,
For I dar noght biknowe° myn owne name;   *acknowledge*
But ther as I was wont to highte° Arcite,   *be called*
Now highte I Philostrate, noght worth a myte.
Allas, thou felle° Mars! allas, Juno!   *cruel, deadly*
1560 Thus hath youre ire our lynage al fordo,°   *destroyed*
Save only me and wrecched Palamoun,
That Theseus martyreth in prisoun.
And over al this, to sleen me outrely,°   *utterly*
Love hath his fyry dart so brenningly°   *burningly*
1565 Y-stiked° thurgh my trewe careful° herte,   *stabbed* / *woeful*
That shapen was my deeth erst than° my sherte.°   *before* / *shirt*
Ye sleen° me with youre eyen, Emelye!   *slay*

---

1. For people are always meeting at unexpected moments.
2. Seldom is Friday like the other days of the week.

Ye been the cause wherfore that I dye.

Of all the remenant of myn other care°   woe
1570 Ne sette I nat the mountaunce° of a tare,°   amount / weed
So° that I coude don aught to your plesaunce!"   If
And with that word he fil down in a traunce
A longe tyme; and after he up sterte.

     This Palamoun, that thoughte that thurgh his herte
1575 He felte a cold swerd sodeynliche° glyde,   suddenly
For ire he quook,° no lenger wolde he byde.   quaked
And whan that he had herd Arcites tale,
As he were wood,° with face deed° and pale,   mad / deathly
He sterte him up out of the buskes° thikke,   bushes
1580 And seyde: "Arcite, false traitour wikke,°   wicked
Now artow hent,° that lovest my lady so,   art thou caught
For whom that I have al this peyne and wo,
And art my blood, and to my counseil° sworn,   secret counsel
As I ful ofte have told thee heerbiforn,
1585 And hast byjaped° here duk Theseus,   tricked
And falsly chaunged hast thy name thus!
I wol be deed, or elles° thou shalt dye.   else
Thou shalt nat love my lady Emelye,
But I wol love hire only, and namo;°   no one else
1590 For I am Palamoun, thy mortal fo.
And though that I no wepne° have in this place,   weapon
But out of prison am astert° by grace,   escaped
I drede noght° that outher° thou shalt dye   doubt not / either
Or thou ne shalt nat loven Emelye.
1595 Chees° which thou wolt,° for thou shalt nat asterte."   Choose / wish
     This Arcitë, with ful despitous° herte,   scornful
Whan he him knew, and hadde his tale herd,
As fiers as leoun pulled out his swerd
And seyde thus: "By God that sit° above,   sits
1600 Nere it° that thou art sik and wood for love,   Were it not
And eek that thou no wepne hast in this place,
Thou sholdest nevere out of this grove pace,°   pass, leave
That thou ne sholdest dyen of myn hond.
For I defye° the seuretee° and the bond   scorn, disclaim / pledge
1605 Which that thou seyst that I have maad to thee.
What, verray° fool, I think wel that love is free,   true
And I wol love hire maugre° al thy might!   in spite of
But, for as muche thou art a worthy knight,
And wilnest° to darreyne hire° by batayle,   wish / decide the claim to her
1610 Have heer my trouthe:° tomorwe I wol nat fayle,   troth, promise
Withoute witing° of any other wight,°   knowledge / person
That here I wol be founden as° a knight,   (on my honor) as
And bringen harneys° right ynough for thee;   armor
And chees° the beste, and leve the worste for me.   (you may) choose
1615 And mete and drinke this night wol I bringe
Ynough for thee, and clothes for thy beddinge.

And if so be that thou my lady winne,
And slee° me in this wode ther° I am inne,   slay / where
Thou mayst wel have thy lady, as for me."°   as far as I am concerned
1620 This Palamon answerde: "I graunte it thee."
And thus they been departed° til amorwe,°   parted / the next morning
Whan ech of hem had leyd his feith to borwe.°   as a pledge
    O Cupide, out of° alle charitee!°   devoid of / unselfish love
O regne,° that wolt no felawe° have with thee!   sovereign rule / associate
1625 Ful sooth is seyd that love ne lordshipe
Wol noght, his thankes,° have no felaweshipe;   willingly
Wel finden that Arcite and Palamoun.
Arcite is riden anon unto the toun,
And on the morwe, er it were dayes light,
1630 Ful prively two harneys hath he dight,°   prepared
Bothe suffisaunt° and mete° to darreyne°   sufficient / suitable / decide
The bataille in the feeld bitwix hem tweyne.°   two
And on his hors, allone as he was born,
He carieth al this harneys him biforn;
1635 And in the grove, at tyme and place y-set,
This Arcite and this Palamon ben met.
    To chaungen gan the colour in hir face,
Right as the hunters° in the regne° of Trace,°   hunter's / kingdom / Thrace
That stondeth at the gappe° with a spere,   gap (in the forest)
1640 Whan hunted is the leoun or the bere,°   bear
And hereth him come russhing in the greves,°   bushes
And breketh bothe bowes° and the leves,   boughs
And thinketh, "Heere cometh my mortel enemy!
Withoute faile, he moot° be deed or I;   must
1645 For outher° I mot sleen him at the gappe,   either
Or he mot sleen me, if that me mishappe,"°—   if it should go ill for me
So ferden° they in chaunging of hir hewe.   acted
    As fer as° everich° of hem other knewe,   Although / each
Ther nas no "good day," ne no saluing;°   saluting, greeting
1650 But streight, withouten word or rehersing,°   restating (their pact)
Everich of hem heelp° for to armen other   helped
As freendly as he were his owne brother;
And after that, with sharpe speres stronge
They foynen° ech at other wonder longe.   thrust
1655 Thou mightest wene° that this Palamoun   suppose
In his fighting were a wood leoun,
And as a cruel tygre was Arcite;
As wilde bores gonne they to° smyte,   they did
That frothen whyte as foom for ire wood.°   mad anger
1660 Up to the ancle° foghte they in hir blood.   ankle
And in this wyse I lete° hem fighting dwelle,°   leave / continuing to fight
And forth I wole of Theseus yow telle.
    The destinee, ministre° general,   agent
That executeth in the world over al°   everywhere
1665 The purveyaunce° that God hath seyn biforn,°   providential plan / foreseen

So strong it is that, though the world had sworn
The contrarie of a thing by ye or nay,
Yet somtyme it shal fallen° on a day   *befall, happen*
That falleth nat eft° withinne a thousand yere.   *again*
1670 For certeinly, oure appetytes° here,   *desires*
Be it of werre, or pees, or hate, or love,
Al is this reuled by the sighte° above.   *foresight*
This mene I now by° mighty Theseus,   *in relation to*
That for to hunten is so desirous,
1675 And namely° at the grete hert° in May,   *especially / hart*
That in his bed ther daweth him° no day   *dawns for him*
That he nis clad and redy for to ryde
With hunte° and horn and houndes him bisyde.   *huntsman*
For in his hunting hath he swich delyt
1680 That it is al his joye and appetyt
To been himself the grete hertes bane;°   *slayer*
For after Mars° he serveth now Diane.°   *god of war / goddess of the hunt*
    Cleer was the day, as I have told er this,
And Theseus, with alle joye and blis,
1685 With his Ipolita, the fayre quene,
And Emelye, clothed al in grene,
On hunting be they riden royally.
And to the grove that stood ful faste by,
In which ther was an hert, as men him tolde,
1690 Duk Theseus the streighte wey hath holde.°   *has taken*
And to the launde he rydeth him ful right,[3]
For thider was the hert wont have his flight,
And over a brook, and so forth on his weye.
This duk wol han a cours° at him or tweye,   *chase*
1695 With houndes swiche as that him list° comaunde.   *it pleases him*
    And whan this duk was come unto the launde,
Under the sonne he loketh, and anon
He was war of Arcite and Palamon,
That foughten breme° as it were bores two.   *furiously*
1700 The brighte swerdes wenten to and fro
So hidously that with the leeste strook
It seemed as it wolde felle an ook;
But what° they were, no thing he ne woot.   *who*
This duk his courser with his spores° smoot,°   *spurs / struck*
1705 And at a stert° he was bitwix hem two,   *in an instant*
And pulled out a swerd and cryed, "Ho!
Namore, up° peyne of lesinge° of youre heed!   *upon / losing*
By mighty Mars, he shal anon be deed
That smyteth° any strook that I may seen.   *strikes*
1710 But telleth me what mister men° ye been,   *what kind of men*
That been so hardy° for to fighten here   *audacious*
Withouten juge or other officere,

3. And he rides directly to the clearing in the forest.

As it were in a listes° royally?"   *lists (of a tournament)*
   This Palamon answerde hastily,
1715 And seyde: "Sire, what nedeth wordes mo?
We have the deeth deserved bothe two.
Two woful wrecches been we, two caytyves,°   *captives*
That been encombred° of our owne lyves;   *weary*
And as thou art a rightful lord and juge,
1720 Ne yeve° us neither mercy ne refuge,°   *give / protection*
But slee° me first, for seynte° charitee.   *slay / holy*
But slee my felawe eek as wel as me,
Or slee him first: for though thou knowest it lyte,°   *little*
This is thy mortal fo, this is Arcite,
1725 That fro thy lond is banished on his heed,°   *on pain of losing his head*
For which he hath deserved to be deed.
For this is he that cam unto thy gate
And seyde that he highte Philostrate.
Thus hath he japed° thee ful many a yeer,   *tricked*
1730 And thou hast maked him thy chief squyer;
And this is he that loveth Emelye.
For sith° the day is come that I shal dye,   *since*
I make pleynly° my confessioun   *frankly, fully*
That I am thilke° woful Palamoun   *that*
1735 That hath thy prison broken wikkedly.
I am thy mortal fo, and it am I
That loveth so hote° Emelye the brighte   *fervently*
That I wol dye present° in hir sighte.   *at once*
Wherfore I axe° deeth and my juwyse;°   *ask (for) / just sentence*
1740 But slee my felawe in the same wyse,°   *way*
For bothe han we deserved to be slayn."
   This worthy duk answerde anon agayn,
And seyde, "This is a short conclusioun.°   *quick decision*
Youre owne mouth, by your confessioun,
1745 Hath dampned you, and I wol it recorde;°   *declare it as my verdict*
It nedeth noght to pyne° yow with the corde.°   *torture / rope*
Ye shul be deed, by mighty Mars the rede!"
   The quene anon, for verray° wommanhede,   *true*
Gan for to wepe, and so dide Emelye,
1750 And alle the ladies in the companye.
Gret pitee was it, as it thoughte hem° alle,   *it seemed to them*
That ever swich a chaunce sholde falle;°   *befall, occur*
For gentil° men they were of greet estat,   *well-born, courteous*
And no thing but for love was this debat;°   *conflict*
1755 And sawe hir blody woundes wyde and sore,
And alle cryden, bothe lasse and more,°   *the lesser and the greater*
"Have mercy, lord, upon us wommen alle!"
And on hir bare knees adoun they falle,
And wolde have kist his feet ther as he stood,
1760 Til at the laste aslaked° was his mood;°   *diminished / anger*
For pitee renneth° sone in gentil herte.   *runs*

And though he first for ire quook° and sterte,°   *quaked / started*
He hath considered shortly, in a clause,°   *a brief while*
The trespas of hem bothe, and eek the cause,
1765 And although that his ire hir gilt accused,°   *blamed their offense*
Yet in his resoun he hem bothe excused,
As thus: he thoghte wel that every man
Wol helpe himself in love, if that he can,
And eek delivere himself out of prisoun.
1770 And eek his herte had compassioun
Of wommen, for they wepen evere in oon.°   *i.e., continued to weep*
And in his gentil herte he thoghte anoon,
And softe unto himself he seyde: "Fy
Upon a lord that wol have no mercy,
1775 But been a leoun, bothe in word and dede,
To hem that been in repentaunce and drede
As well as to a proud despitous° man   *scornful*
That wol maynteyne that° he first bigan!   *what*
That lord hath litel of discrecioun°   *discernment*
1780 That in swich cas can° no divisioun,°   *knows (how to make) / distinction*
But weyeth° pryde and humblesse after oon."°   *weighs, judges / alike*
And shortly, whan his ire is thus agoon,°   *passed away*
He gan to loken up with eyen lighte,°   *cheerful*
And spak thise same wordes al on highte:°   *aloud*
1785 "The god of love, a, *benedicite*,°   *bless us*
How mighty and how greet a lord is he!
Ayeins° his might ther gayneth° none obstacles.   *Against / prevails*
He may be cleped° a god for his miracles,   *called*
For he can maken at his owne gyse°   *as he chooses*
1790 Of everich herte as that him list devyse.°   *whatever it pleases him to contrive*
Lo heere, this Arcite and this Palamoun,
That quitly° weren out of my prisoun,   *freely, entirely*
And mighte han lived in Thebes royally,
And witen° I am hir mortal enemy   *know*
1795 And that hir deeth lyth in my might also;
And yet hath love, maugree hir eyen two,⁴
Broght hem hider bothe for to dye!
Now loketh, is nat that an heigh° folye?   *great*
Who may been a fool but if° he love?   *unless*
1800 Bihold, for Goddes sake that sit° above,   *sits*
Se how they blede! be they noght wel arrayed?
Thus hath hir lord, the god of love, y-payed
Hir wages and hir fees for hir servyse!
And yet they wenen° for to been ful wyse   *think (themselves)*
1805 That serven love, for aught that may bifalle.
But this is yet the beste game° of alle: *joke*
That she, for whom they han this jolitee,°   *frolic, diversion*

---

4. Despite their two eyes (i.e., despite anything they can do).

Can hem therfore as muche thank as me;[5]
She woot° namore of al this hote fare,°   *knows / frantic business*
1810 By God, than woot a cokkow° or an hare!   *cuckoo*
But al mot been assayed,° hoot and cold;   *tried, experienced*
A man mot been a fool, or yong or old;
I woot it by myself ful yore agoon,°   *long ago*
For in my tyme a servant° was I oon.   *i.e., of love*
1815 And therefore, sin° I knowe of loves peyne,   *since*
And woot how sore it can a man distreyne,°   *distress, torment*
As he that° hath ben caught ofte in his las,°   *one who / net*
I yow foryeve al hoolly° this trespas,   *wholly*
At requeste of the quene that kneleth here,
1820 And eek of Emelye, my suster dere.
And ye shul bothe anon unto me swere
That neveremo ye shul my contree dere,°   *harm*
Ne make werre upon me night ne day,
But been my freendes in al that ye may.
1825 I yow foryeve this trespas every del."°   *in every respect*
And they him swore his axing° fayre and wel,   *request*
And him of lordshipe° and of mercy preyde,   *his protection as their overlord*
And he hem graunteth grace, and thus he seyde:
"To speke of royal linage and richesse,
1830 Though that she were a quene or a princesse,
Ech of yow bothe is worthy, doutelees,
To wedden whan tyme is, but nathelees°—   *nevertheless*
I speke as for my suster Emelye,
For whom ye have this stryf and jalousye—
1835 Ye woot yourself she may not wedden two
Atones,° though ye fighten everemo: *At one time*
That oon of yow, al be him looth or leef,°   *whether he like it or not*
He moot go pypen° in an ivy leef;   *go whistle*
This is to seyn, she may nat now han bothe,
1840 Al be ye never so jalous ne so wrothe.
And forthy° I yow putte in this degree,°   *therefore / condition, position*
That ech of yow shal have his destinee
As him is shape,° and herkneth in what wyse;   *determined*
Lo heer your ende° of that I shal devyse.   *fate*
1845   My wil is this, for plat° conclusioun,   *blunt, plain*
Withouten any replicacioun°—   *reply*
If that yow lyketh, tak it for the beste:
That everich of yow shal gon wher him leste
Frely, withouten raunson° or daunger;°   *ransom / control*
1850 And this day fifty wykes, fer ne ner,°   *neither later nor sooner*
Everich of yow shal bringe an hundred knightes
Armed for listes° up at alle rightes,°   *tournament / points*
Al redy to darreyne hire° by bataille.   *to settle claim to her*
And this bihote° I yow withouten faille,   *promise*

---

5. I.e., has no more to thank them for than I do.

1855 Upon my trouthe, and as I am a knight,
That whether° of yow bothe that hath might—   *whichever*
This is to seyn, that whether he or thou
May with his hundred, as I spak of now,
Sleen° his contrarie° or out of listes dryve—   *Slay / opponent*
1860 Thanne shal I yeve Emelya to wyve°   *as wife*
To whom that Fortune yeveth so fair a grace.
The listes° shal I maken in this place,   *tournament arena*
And God so wisly° on my soule rewe,°   *surely / have pity*
As I shal even° juge been and trewe.   *impartial*
1865 Ye shul non other ende° with me maken,   *agreement*
That oon of yow ne shal be deed or taken.
And if yow thinketh this is wel y-sayd,
Seyeth your avys,° and holdeth yow apayd.°   *opinion / content*
This is your ende and youre conclusioun."
1870   Who loketh lightly now but Palamoun?
Who springeth up for joye but Arcite?
Who couthe telle, or who couthe it endyte,°   *write*
The joye that is maked in the place
Whan Theseus hath doon so fair a grace?
1875 But doun on knees wente every maner wight,
And thanked him with al hir herte and might,
And namely° the Thebans often sythe.°   *especially / many times*
And thus with good hope and with herte blythe°   *glad*
They take hir leve, and homward gonne° they ryde   *did*
1880 To Thebes, with his° olde walles wyde.   *its*

PART THREE

        I trowe° men wolde deme it necligence   *believe*
If I foryete° to tellen the dispence°   *forget / spending*
Of Theseus, that goth so bisily
To maken up the listes royally,
1885 That swich a noble theatre° as it was,   *amphitheater*
I dar wel seyn that in this world ther nas.
The circuit a myle was aboute,
Walled of stoon, and diched° al withoute.   *ditched*
Round was the shap, in manere of compas,°   *circle*
1890 Ful of degrees,° the heighte of sixty pas,°   *steps / paces*
That whan a man was set on o° degree,   *one*
He letted° nat his felawe for to see.   *hindered*
        Estward ther stood a gate of marbel whyt,
Westward right swich another in the opposit.
1895 And shortly to concluden, swich a place
Was noon in erthe, as in so litel space;°   *(built) in such a short time*
For in the lond ther was no crafty° man   *skilled*
That geometrie or ars-metrike° can,°   *arithmetic / knows*
Ne purtreyour,° ne kervere° of images,   *painter / carver*
1900 That Theseus ne yaf° him mete and wages   *gave*

The theatre for to maken and devyse.
And for to doon his ryte and sacrifyse,
He estward hath, upon the gate above,
In worshipe of Venus, goddesse of love,
1905 Don make° an auter° and an oratorie;   *Had made / altar*
And on the gate westward, in memorie
Of Mars, he maked hath right swich another,
That coste largely of gold a fother.°   *load, large quantity*
And northward, in a touret° on the wal,   *turret*
1910 Of alabastre whyt and reed° coral,   *red*
An oratorie riche for to see,
In worshipe of Dyane° of chastitee,   *Diana*
Hath Theseus don wroght° in noble wyse.   *had constructed*
     But yet hadde I foryeten to devyse
1915 The noble kerving and the portreitures,°   *representations*
The shap, the countenaunce, and the figures,
That weren in thise oratories three.
     First in the temple of Venus maystow° see   *mayest thou*
Wroght on the wal, ful pitous to biholde,
1920 The broken slepes and the sykes° colde,°   *sighs / chilling, fatal*
The sacred teres and the waymentinge,°   *lamenting*
The fyry strokes of the desiringe
That loves servaunts in this lyf enduren;
The othes that hir covenants assuren;°   *bind their vows*
1925 Plesaunce and Hope, Desyr, Foolhardinesse,
Beautee and Youthe, Bauderie,° Richesse,   *Pandering*
Charmes and Force, Lesinges,° Flaterye,   *Deceits*
Dispense,° Bisynesse, and Jalousye,   *Expense*
That wered of yelwe goldes° a gerland,   *marigolds*
1930 And a cokkow sitting on hir hand;
Festes,° instruments, caroles,° daunces,   *Feasts / songs sung dancing*
Lust° and array, and alle the circumstaunces   *Pleasure*
Of love, whiche that I rekned° and rekne shal,   *reckoned, considered*
By ordre weren peynted on the wal,
1935 And mo than I can make of mencioun.°   *i.e., make mention of*
For soothly, al the mount of Citheroun,°   *Cithaeron*
Ther° Venus hath hir principal dwellinge,   *Where*
Was shewed on the wal in portreyinge,
With al the gardin and the lustinesse.
1940 Nat was foryeten the porter, Ydelnesse,
Ne Narcisus the faire of yore agon,°   *long ago*
Ne yet the folye of king Salamon,
Ne yet the grete strengthe of Hercules,
Th'enchauntements of Medea and Circes,
1945 Ne of Turnus, with the hardy fiers corage,°   *proud heart*
The riche Cresus, caytif in servage.°   *wretched in bondage*
Thus may ye seen that wisdom ne richesse,
Beautee ne sleighte,° strengthe ne hardinesse,   *cleverness / boldness*
Ne may with Venus holde champartye,°   *equal power*

1950 For as hir list the world than may she gye.°   *guide, govern*
Lo, alle thise folk so caught were in hir las,°   *net*
Til they for wo ful ofte seyde "Allas!"
Suffyceth heer ensamples oon or two,
And though° I coude rekne a thousand mo.   *Although*
1955   The statue of Venus, glorious for to see,
Was naked fletinge° in the large see,   *floating*
And fro the navele doun all covered was
With wawes° grene, and brighte as any glas.   *waves*
A citole° in hir right hand hadde she,   *cithara (a stringed instrument)*
1960 And on hir heed, ful semely° for to see,   *seemly, comely*
A rose gerland, fresh and wel smellinge;
Above hir heed hir dowves flikeringe.°   *doves fluttering*
Biforn hir stood hir sone Cupido,
Upon his shuldres winges hadde he two,
1965 And blind he was, as it is ofte sene.
A bowe he bar° and arwes brighte and kene.   *carried*
    Why sholde I noght as wel eek telle yow al
The portreiture that was upon the wal
Withinne the temple of mighty Mars the rede?
1970 Al peynted was the wal, in lengthe and brede,°   *breadth*
Lyk to the estres° of the grisly place   *like the interior*
That highte° the grete temple of Mars in Trace,°   *is called / Thrace*
In thilke° colde frosty regioun   *that*
Ther as° Mars hath his sovereyn mansioun.   *Where*
1975   First on the wal was peynted a foreste,
In which ther dwelleth neither man ne beste,
With knotty knarry° bareyne° treës olde,   *gnarled / barren*
Of stubbes° sharpe and hidouse to biholde,   *With stublike branches*
In° which ther ran a rumbel in a swough,°   *Through / sough, noise (of wind)*
1980 As though a storm sholde bresten° every bough.   *break*
And downward from an hille, under a bente,°   *below a grassy slope*
Ther stood the temple of Mars armipotente,°   *powerful in arms*
Wroght al of burned° steel, of which the entree°   *burnished / entrance*
Was long and streit,° and gastly for to see.   *narrow*
1985 And therout cam a rage° and such a vese°   *roar (of wind) / blast*
That it made al the gate for to rese.°   *shake*
The northren light in at the dores shoon,°   *shone*
For windowe on the wal ne was ther noon,
Thurgh which men mighten any light discerne.
1990 The dore was al of adamant eterne,
Y-clenched° overthwart° and endelong°   *Braced / crosswise / lengthwise*
With iren tough; and for to make it strong,
Every piler,° the temple to sustene,   *pillar*
Was tonne-greet,° of iren bright and shene.°   *big as a cask / shiny*
1995   Ther saugh I first the derke imagining
Of Felonye,° and al the compassing;°   *Crime, Treachery / plotting*
The cruel Ire, reed as any glede;°   *live coal*
The pykepurs,° and eek the pale Drede;   *pick-purse*

The smylere with the knyf under the cloke;
2000 The shepne° brenning° with the blake smoke; *stable, shed / burning*
The treson of the mordring° in the bedde; *murdering*
The open werre, with woundes al bibledde;° *bloodstained*
Contek,° with blody knyf and sharp manace.° *Strife / menace, threat*
Al ful of chirking° was that sory place. *harsh noises*
2005 The sleere of himself° yet saugh I ther: *i.e., the suicide (self-slayer)*
His herte-blood hath bathed al his heer;° *hair*
The nayl y-driven in the shode⁶ a-night;
The colde deeth, with mouth gaping upright.
Amiddes of° the temple sat Meschaunce,° *In the middle of / Misfortune*
2010 With disconfort° and sory contenaunce. *discouragement*
Yet saugh I Woodnesse° laughing in his rage, *Madness*
Armed Compleint, Outhees,° and fiers Outrage; *Outcry*
The careyne° in the bush, with throte y-corve;° *corpse / cut*
A thousand slayn, and nat of qualm y-storve;° *dead by plague*
2015 The tiraunt, with the prey° by force y-raft;° *plunder / seized*
The toun destroyed, ther was nothing laft.
Yet saugh I brent the shippes hoppesteres;° *dancing, bobbing*
The hunte° strangled with° the wilde beres; *hunter / killed by*
The sowe freten° the child right in the cradel; *devour*
2020 The cook y-scalded, for al his longe ladel—
Noght was foryeten by the infortune of Marte⁷—
The carter overriden with° his carte, *run over by*
Under the wheel ful lowe he lay adoun.
Ther were also, of Martes divisioun,° *company, category*
2025 The barbour and the bocher° and the smith, *butcher*
That forgeth sharpe swerdes on his stith.° *anvil*
And al above, depeynted° in a tour, *depicted*
Saw I Conquest, sitting in greet honour,
With the sharpe swerde over his heed
2030 Hanginge by a sotil twynes threed.° *thin thread of twine*
Depeynted was the slaughtre of Julius,° *Julius Caesar*
Of grete Nero, and of Antonius;° *Mark Antony*
Al be that thilke tyme they were unborn,
Yet was hir deeth depeynted ther-biforn
2035 By manasinge of Mars, right by figure.⁸
So was it shewed in that portreiture,
As is depeynted in the sterres° above *stars*
Who shal be slayn or elles deed for love.
Sufficeth oon ensample in° stories olde: *from*
2040 I may not rekene hem alle, thogh I wolde.
　　The statue of Mars upon a carte stood
Armed, and loked grim as he were wood;
And over his heed ther shynen° two figures *shine*

---

6. The top of the head, where the hair parts.
7. Nothing was forgotten concerning the evil influence of Mars.
8. Yet their death through the menacing influence of Mars was depicted beforehand, in an image.

Of sterres, that been cleped° in scriptures°   *called / writings*
2045 That oon Puella, that other Rubeus:[9]
This god of armes was arrayed thus.
A wolf ther stood biforn him at his feet
With eyen rede, and of a man he eet.°   *ate*
With sotil° pencel was depeynted this storie   *subtle*
2050 In redoutinge° of Mars and of his glorie.   *fearful reverence*
   Now to the temple of Diane the chaste,
As shortly as I can, I wol me haste
To telle yow al the descripcioun.
Depeynted been the walles up and doun
2055 Of hunting and of shamfast° chastitee.   *modest*
Ther saugh° I how woful Calistopee,°   *saw / Callisto*
Whan that Diane agreved° was with here,°   *aggrieved, angry / her*
Was turned from a womman til° a bere,°   *into / bear*
And after was she maad the lode-sterre;°   *lodestar (North Star)*
2060 Thus was it peynted, I can say yow no ferre;°   *further*
Hir sone is eek a sterre, as men may see.
Ther saugh I Dane,° y-turned til a tree—   *Daphne*
I mene nat the goddesse Diane,
But Penneus doughter, which that highte Dane.
2065 Ther saugh I Attheon° an hert° y-maked,   *Actaeon / hart*
For vengeaunce that he saugh Diane al naked;
I saugh how that his houndes have him caught
And freten° him, for that they knewe him naught.   *devoured*
Yet° peynted was a litel forther moor,°   *In addition / along*
2070 How Atthalante° hunted the wilde boor,   *Atalanta*
And Meleagre,° and many another mo,   *Meleager*
For which Diane wroghte him care and wo.
Ther saugh I many another wonder storie,
The whiche me list nat drawen to memorie.°   *remember*
2075   This goddesse on an hert ful hye° seet,°   *high / sat*
With smale houndes al aboute hir feet;
And undernethe hir feet she hadde a mone,°   *moon*
Wexinge it was, and sholde wanie° sone.   *wane*
In gaude° grene hir statue clothed was,   *yellowish*
2080 With bowe in honde, and arwes in a cas.°   *quiver*
Hir eyen caste she ful lowe adoun,
Ther Pluto hath his derke regioun.
A womman travailinge° was hir biforn,   *in labor*
But for° hir child so longe was unborn,   *because*
2085 Ful pitously Lucyna[1] gan she calle,
And seyde, "Help, for thou mayst best of alle."
Wel koude he peynten lyfly° that it wroghte;   *in a lifelike way*
With many a florin he the hewes° boghte.   *colors, pigments*
   Now been thise listes maad, and Theseus,

9. Puella and Rubeus are the names of two patterns of dots (not stars) used in geomancy—a
   form of divination—to determine astrological influences.
1. Lucina, goddess of childbirth, a role attributed to Diana.

2090 That at his grete cost arrayed° thus   *adorned*
      The temples and the theatre every del,°   *in every part*
      Whan it was doon, him lyked° wonder wel.   *it pleased him*
      But stinte° I wole of Theseus a lyte,   *stop (talking)*
      And speke of Palamon and of Arcite.
2095   The day approcheth of hir retourninge,
      That everich° sholde an hundred knightes bringe   *each*
      The bataille to darreyne,° as I yow tolde;   *decide*
      And til Athenes, hir covenant for to holde,
      Hath everich of hem broght an hundred knightes
2100 Wel armed for the werre at alle rightes.°   *points*
      And sikerly,° ther trowed° many a man   *surely / believed, thought*
      That never, sithen that the world bigan,
      As for to speke of knighthod of hir hond,[2]
      As fer as God hath maked see or lond,
2105 Nas of so fewe so noble a companye.
      For every wight that lovede chivalrye,
      And wolde, his thankes,° han a passant° name,   *gladly / outstanding*
      Hath preyed that he mighte ben of that game;
      And wel was him that therto chosen was.
2110 For if ther fille° tomorwe swich a cas,°   *befell / case, situation*
      Ye knowen wel that every lusty knight
      That loveth paramours° and hath his might,°   *passionately / the power*
      Were it in Engelond or elleswhere
      They wolde, hir thankes, wilnen° to be there.   *wish*
2115 To fighte for a lady, *benedicite!*°   *bless us*
      It were° a lusty° sighte for to see.   *would be / joyful*
       And right so ferden° they with Palamon.   *fared, did*
      With him ther wenten knightes many oon;°   *a one*
      Som° wol ben armed in an habergeoun,°   *One / hauberk, coat of mail*
2120 And in a brest plate and a light gipoun;°   *tunic (worn under hauberk)*
      And som wol have a peyre° plates large;   *pair, suit of*
      And som wol have a Pruce° sheeld or a targe;°   *Prussian / light shield*
      Som wol ben armed on his legges weel,°   *well*
      And have an ax, and som a mace of steel.
2125 Ther nis no newe gyse that it nas old.[3]
      Armed were they, as I have you told,
      Everich after his opinioun.
       Ther maistow° seen, coming with Palamoun,   *mayest thou*
      Ligurge° himself, the grete king of Trace.°   *Lycurgus / Thrace*
2130 Blak was his berd, and manly was his face.
      The cercles° of his eyen in his heed,   *irises*
      They gloweden bitwixen yelow and reed;
      And lyk a griffon loked he aboute,
      With kempe° heres on his browes stoute;°   *shaggy / large*
2135 His limes° grete, his braunes° harde and stronge,   *limbs / muscles*

---

2. I.e., the deeds of knighthood.
3. There is no new fashion (in arms) that did not exist long ago.

His shuldres brode, his armes rounde and longe;
And as the gyse was in his contree,
Ful hye upon a char° of gold stood he,   chariot
With foure whyte boles° in the trays.°   bulls / traces
2140 In stede of cote-armure[4] over his harnays,°   armor
With nayles° yelewe and brighte as any gold   claws
He hadde a beres skin, col-blak for old.°   because of age
His longe heer was kembd° bihinde his bak—   combed
As any ravenes fethere it shoon° for° blak;   shone / very
2145 A wrethe of gold arm-greet,° of huge wighte,°   thick as an arm / weight
Upon his heed, set ful of stones brighte,
Of fyne rubies and of dyamaunts.°   diamonds
Aboute his char ther wenten whyte alaunts,°   wolfhounds
Twenty and mo, as grete as any steer,
2150 To hunten at the leoun or the deer,
And folwed him with mosel° faste y-bounde,   muzzle
Colered° of gold, and tourettes[5] fyled° rounde.   Wearing collars / filed
An hundred lordes hadde he in his route,°   retinue
Armed ful wel, with hertes sterne and stoute.
2155   With Arcita, in stories as men finde,
The grete Emetreus, the king of Inde,°   India
Upon a steede bay° trapped in steel,°   bay-colored / with steel trappings
Covered in cloth of gold diapred weel,°   finely patterned
Cam ryding lyk the god of armes, Mars.
2160 His cote-armure was of cloth of Tars,°   Tarsia, in Turkestan
Couched° with perles whyte and rounde and grete.   Set, overlaid
His sadel was of brend° gold newe y-bete;°   burnished / hammered, crafted
A mantelet° upon his shuldre hanginge   short cloak
Bret-ful° of rubies rede as fyr sparklinge.   Brimful
2165 His crispe° heer lyk ringes was y-ronne,°   curly / i.e., hung down
And that was yelow, and glitered as the sonne.
His nose was heigh, his eyen bright citryn,°   lemon-colored
His lippes rounde, his colour was sangwyn;°   bloodred
A fewe frakenes° in his face y-spreynd,°   freckles / scattered
2170 Betwixen yelow and somdel blak y-meynd;°   mingled
And as a leoun he his loking caste.
Of fyve and twenty yeer his age I caste:°   estimate
His berd was wel bigonne for to springe.
His voys was as a trompe° thunderinge.   trumpet
2175 Upon his heed he wered of laurer° grene   laurel
A gerland fresh and lusty for to sene.
Upon his hand he bar for his deduyt°   delight
An egle tame, as any lilie whyt.
An hundred lordes hadde he with him there,
2180 Al armed, sauf° hir heddes, in al hir gere,°   except / gear, armor
Ful richely in alle maner thinges.
For trusteth wel that dukes, erles, kinges

4. See n. 4, p. 27.
5. Rings on the collar for attaching a leash.

Were gadered° in this noble companye — *gathered*
For love and for encrees° of chivalrye. — *increase*
2185 Aboute this king ther ran on every part° — *side*
Ful many a tame leoun and leopart.
And in this wyse° thise lordes, alle and some,° — *way / one and all*
Ben on the Sonday to the citee come
Aboute pryme,° and in the toun alight. — *between 6 and 9 A.M.*
2190   This Theseus, this duk, this worthy knight,
Whan he had broght hem into his citee,
And inned° hem, everich in his degree,° — *housed / each according to his rank*
He festeth hem, and dooth so greet labour
To esen° hem and doon hem al honour, — *set at ease*
2195 That yet men wenen° that no mannes wit — *think*
Of noon estat ne coude amenden° it. — *improve on*
The minstralcye, the service at the feste,
The grete yiftes° to the moste and leste,° — *gifts / highest and lowest (in rank)*
The riche array of Theseus paleys,
2200 Ne who sat first ne last upon the deys,° — *dais, platform*
What ladies fairest been or best daunsinge,
Or which of hem can dauncen best and singe,
Ne who most felingly° speketh of love; — *sensitively*
What haukes sitten on the perche above,
2205 What houndes liggen° on the floor adoun— — *lie*
Of al this make I now no mencioun;
But al° th'effect, that thinketh me° the beste. — *only / seems to me*
Now comth the poynt, and herkneth if yow leste.° — *it please you*
   The Sonday night, er day bigan to springe,
2210 When Palamon the larke herde singe
(Although it nere° nat day by houres two, — *were*
Yet song the larke) and Palamon right tho
With holy herte and with an heigh corage,° — *spirit*
He roos° to wenden on his pilgrimage — *arose*
2215 Unto the blisful Citherea benigne—
I mene Venus, honurable and digne.° — *worthy*
And in hir houre[6] he walketh forth a pas° — *slowly, at a footpace*
Unto the listes ther° hir temple was, — *where*
And doun he kneleth, and with humble chere
2220 And herte soor,° he seyde as ye shul here: — *sore (with love)*
   "Faireste of faire, O lady myn, Venus,
Doughter to Jove and spouse of Vulcanus,
Thou gladere° of the mount of Citheroun. — *gladdener*
For thilke love thou haddest to Adoun,° — *Adonis*
2225 Have pitee of my bittre teres smerte,
And tak myn humble preyere at thyn herte.
Allas! I ne have no langage to telle

6. An hour of the day assigned astrologically to Venus. The hours were assigned to the planets
in rotation, beginning at sunrise with the planet specially associated with that day. All three
characters pray to their deities at the appropriate hours: Palamon to Venus two hours before
Monday's sunrise; Emily to Diana during the first hour of Monday, the moon's day
(ll. 2271–74); and Arcite to Mars during the fourth hour (ll. 2367–69).

Th'effectes ne the torments of myn helle;
Myn herte may myne harmes nat biwreye;°   *reveal*
2230 I am so confus° that I can noght seye   *bewildered*
But mercy, lady bright, that knowest weele
My thought, and seest what harmes that I feele.
Considere al this, and rewe° upon my sore,°   *have pity / pain*
As wisly° as I shal for everemore,   *surely*
2235 Emforth° my might, thy trewe servant be,   *To the extent of*
And holden werre° alwey with chastitee.   *war*
That make I myn avow,° so ye me helpe.   *vow*
I kepe° noght of armes for to yelpe,°   *dare / boast*
Ne I ne axe nat tomorwe to have victorie,
2240 Ne renoun in this cas,° ne veyne glorie   *event*
Of pris° of armes blowen up and doun,   *reputation, praise*
But I wolde have fully possessioun
Of Emelye, and dye in thy servyse.
Find thou the manere how, and in what wyse:
2245 I recche° nat but° it may bettre be   *care / whether*
To have victorie of hem, or they of me,
So that I have my lady in myne armes.
For though so be that Mars is god of armes,
Youre vertu is so greet in hevene above,
2250 That if yow list, I shal wel have my love.
Thy temple wol I worshipe everemo,
And on thyn auter,° where° I ryde or go,°   *altar / whether / walk*
I wol don sacrifice and fyres bete.°   *kindle*
And if ye wol nat so, my lady swete,
2255 Than preye I thee, tomorwe with a spere
That Arcita me thurgh the herte bere.°   *pierce*
Thanne rekke I noght, whan I have lost my lyf,
Though that Arcita winne hire to his wyf.
This is th'effect° and ende of my preyere: *essence*
2260 Yif° me my love, thou blisful lady dere."   *Give*
    Whan the orison° was doon of Palamon,   *prayer*
His sacrifice he dide, and that anon,°   *promptly*
Ful pitously, with alle circumstaunces,°   *attendant details*
Al° telle I noght as now his observaunces.   *Although*
2265 But atte laste the statue of Venus shook,
And made a signe, wherby that he took
That his preyere accepted was that day.
For thogh the signe shewed a delay,
Yet wiste° he wel that graunted was his bone;°   *knew / boon, request*
2270 And with glad herte he wente him hoom ful sone.
    The thridde houre inequal[7] that° Palamon   *after*
Bigan to Venus temple for to goon,
Up roos the sonne, and up roos Emelye,

---

7. The hours assigned to the planets (see n. 6 above) were based on a system that divided them into twelve each of daylight and darkness. Hence they would almost always be unequal in duration, since day and night are the same length only at the equinoxes.

And to the temple of Diane gan hye.°   *hastened*
2275 Hir maydens, that she thider with hir ladde,°   *led*
Ful redily with hem the fyr they hadde,
Th'encens,° the clothes,° and the remenant al   *incense / cloths, hangings*
That to the sacrifyce longen shal;°   *should belong*
The hornes fulle of meth,° as was the gyse,°   *mead / fashion*
2280 Ther lakked noght to doon hir sacrifyse.
Smokinge the temple, full of clothes faire,[8]
This Emelye, with herte debonaire,°   *gracious, humble*
Hir body wessh° with water of a welle,°   *washed / spring*
But how she dide hir ryte I dar nat telle,
2285 But° it be any thing in general;   *Unless*
And yet it were a game° to heren al;   *pleasure*
To him that meneth wel it were no charge,°   *it wouldn't matter*
But it is good a man ben at his large.°   *at liberty (to speak or not)*
Hir brighte heer was kembd,° untressed° al;   *combed / loose*
2290 A coroune° of a grene ook cerial°   *garland / a species of oak*
Upon hir heed was set ful fair and mete.°   *fitting*
Two fyres on the auter gan she bete,
And dide hir thinges, as men may biholde
In Stace° of Thebes and thise bokes olde.   *Statius*
2295 Whan kindled was the fyr, with pitous chere°   *countenance*
Unto Diane she spak as ye may here:
  "O chaste goddesse of the wodes grene,
To whom bothe hevene and erthe and see is sene,°   *visible*
Quene of the regne° of Pluto derk and lowe,   *realm*
2300 Goddesse of maydens, that myn herte hast knowe
Ful many a yeer, and woost° what I desire,   *knowest*
As keepe me fro thy vengeaunce and thyn ire,
That Attheon° aboughte° cruelly.   *Actaeon / suffered for*
Chaste goddesse, wel wostow° that I   *knowest thou*
2305 Desire to been a mayden al my lyf,
Ne never wol I be° no love° ne wyf.   *do I wish to be / lover*
I am, thou woost, yet of thy companye,
A mayde, and love hunting and venerye,°   *hunting, the chase*
And for to walken in the wodes wilde,
2310 And noght to been a wyf and be with childe.
Noght wol I knowe companye of man.
Now help me, lady, sith ye may and can,
For tho° thre formes[9] that thou hast in thee.   *those*
And Palamon, that hath swich love to me,
2315 And eek Arcite, that loveth me so sore,
This grace I preye thee withoute more:
As sende love and pees° bitwixe hem two,   *peace*
And fro me turne awey hir hertes so
That al hir hote love and hir desyr,

8. Censing the temple, full of beautiful cloth hangings.
9. The goddess appears as Diana on earth, Luna in heaven, and Proserpina in the underworld (the "regne of Pluto" referred to in l. 2299).

2320 And al hir bisy° torment and hir fyr,   *intense*
     Be queynt° or turned in another place.°   *quenched / direction*
     And if so be thou wolt° not do me grace,   *will*
     Or if my destinee be shapen° so,   *shaped, determined*
     That I shal nedes° have oon of hem two,   *must necessarily*
2325 As sende me him that most desireth me.
     Bihold, goddesse of clene chastitee,
     The bittre teres that on my chekes falle.
     Sin° thou art mayde° and kepere° of us alle,   *Since / a virgin / guardian*
     My maydenhede thou kepe and wel conserve,
2330 And whyl I live a mayde, I wol thee serve."
         The fyres brenne° upon the auter° clere,°   *burn / altar / brightly*
     Whyl Emelye was thus in hir preyere.
     But sodeinly she saugh a sighte queynte,°   *strange*
     For right anon oon of the fyres queynte,°   *died out*
2335 And quiked° agayn, and after that anon   *became alive, flamed up*
     That other fyr was queynt, and al agon;°   *gone*
     And as it queynte, it made a whistelinge,
     As doon thise wete brondes° in hir brenninge,   *pieces of burning wood*
     And at the brondes ende out ran anoon
2340 As it were° blody dropes many oon;   *What seemed like*
     For which so sore agast was Emelye
     That she was wel ny° mad, and gan to crye,   *near*
     For she ne wiste what it signifyed;
     But only for the fere° thus hath she cryed,   *fear*
2345 And weep,° that it was pitee for to here.   *wept*
     And therwithal Diane gan appere,
     With bowe in hond, right as an hunteresse,
     And seyde: "Doghter, stint° thyn hevinesse.°   *stop / sorrow*
     Among the goddes hye° it is affermed,   *high*
2350 And by eterne word writen and confermed,
     Thou shalt ben wedded unto oon of tho°   *those*
     That han° for thee so muchel care and wo;   *have*
     But unto which of hem I may nat telle.
     Farwel, for I ne may no lenger dwelle.
2355 The fyres which that on myn auter brenne
     Shulle thee declaren, er that thou go henne,°   *hence*
     Thyn aventure° of love, as in this cas."   *What will befall thee*
     And with that word, the arwes in the cas°   *quiver*
     Of the goddesse clateren faste and ringe,
2360 And forth she wente, and made a vanisshinge;
     For which this Emelye astoned° was,   *stunned, astonished*
     And seyde, "What amounteth° this, allas!   *means*
     I putte me in thy proteccioun,
     Diane, and in° thy disposicioun."°   *at / disposing*
2365 And hoom she gooth anon the nexte° weye.   *nearest*
     This is th'effect, ther is namore to seye.
         The nexte houre of Mars folwinge this,
     Arcite unto the temple walked is°   *has walked*

Of fierse Mars, to doon his sacrifyse,
2370 With alle the rytes of his payen wyse.°   *pagan customs*
With pitous herte and heigh devocioun,
Right thus to Mars he seyde his orisoun:°   *prayer*
  "O stronge god, that in the regnes° colde   *realms*
Of Trace° honoured art and lord y-holde,°   *Thrace / considered*
2375 And hast in every regne and every lond
Of armes al the brydel° in thyn hond,   *i.e., control*
And hem fortunest as thee list devyse,[1]
Accepte of me my pitous sacrifyse.
If so be that my youthe may deserve,
2380 And that my might be worthy for to serve
Thy godhede, that I may be oon of thyne,
Thanne preye I thee to rewe° upon my pyne.°   *take pity / suffering*
For thilke° peyne and thilke hote fyr   *that same*
In which thou whylom° brendest° for desyr,   *once / burned*
2385 Whan that thou usedest° the beautee   *enjoyed*
Of fayre yonge fresshe Venus free,°   *noble, generous*
And haddest hir in armes at thy wille—
Although thee ones° on a tyme misfille°   *once / it went wrong with*
Whan Vulcanus hadde caught thee in his las,°   *net*
2390 And fond° thee ligginge° by his wyf, allas!—   *found / lying*
For thilke sorwe that was in thyn herte,
Have routhe° as wel upon my peynes smerte.°   *pity / sharp*
I am yong and unkonning,° as thou wost,°   *ignorant / knowest*
And, as I trowe,° with love offended° most   *believe / assailed*
2395 That evere was any lyves° creature;   *living*
For she that dooth° me al this wo endure,   *makes*
Ne reccheth° nevere wher° I sinke or flete.°   *cares / whether / float*
And wel I woot, er she me mercy hete,°   *promise*
I moot with strengthe winne hire in the place;°   *i.e., the tournament lists*
2400 And wel I woot, withouten help or grace
Of thee, ne may my strengthe noght availle.
Than help me, lord, tomorwe in my bataille,
For thilke fyr that whylom brente° thee,   *burned*
As wel as thilke fyr now brenneth me;
2405 And do° that I tomorwe have victorie.   *bring it about*
Myn be the travaille,° and thyn be the glorie!   *labor*
Thy soverein temple wol I most honouren
Of any place, and alwey most labouren
In° thy plesaunce° and in thy craftes° stronge,   *For / pleasure / activities*
2410 And in thy temple I wol my baner honge,°   *hang*
And alle the armes of my companye;
And everemo, unto that day I dye,
Eterne fyr I wol biforn thee finde.°   *provide*
And eek° to this avow I wol me binde: *also*
2415 My berd, myn heer, that hongeth long adoun,

1. And give them (whatever) fortune it pleases you to devise.

That never yet ne felte offensioun°   damage
Of rasour nor of shere,° I wol thee yive,   shears
And ben thy trewe servant whyl I live.
Now lord, have routhe upon my sorwes sore:
2420 Yif° me the victorie, I aske thee namore."   Give
     The preyere stinte° of Arcita the stronge,   being ended
The ringes on the temple dore that honge,
And eek the dores, clatereden ful faste,
Of which Arcita somwhat him agaste.°   took fright
2425 The fyres brenden up on the auter brighte,
That it gan al the temple for to lighte;
And swete smel the ground anon up yaf,°   gave
And Arcita anon his hand up haf,°   lifted
And more encens° into the fyr he caste,   incense
2430 With othere rytes mo; and atte laste
The statue of Mars bigan his hauberk° ringe.   coat of mail
And with that soun he herde a murmuringe
Ful lowe and dim, that sayde thus, "Victorie,"
For which he yaf to Mars honour and glorie.
2435 And thus with joye and hope wel to fare,
Arcite anon unto his in° is fare,°   dwelling / gone
As fayn° as fowel° is of the brighte sonne.   glad / fowl, bird
     And right anon swich stryf ther is bigonne,
For thilke graunting, in the hevene above,
2440 Bitwixe Venus, the goddesse of love,
And Mars, the sterne god armipotente,°   strong in arms
That Jupiter was bisy it to stente;°   stop
Til that the pale Saturnus the colde,²
That knew so manye of aventures olde,
2445 Fond° in his olde experience an art   Found
That he ful sone hath plesed every part.°   side
As sooth is sayd, elde° hath greet avantage;   old age
In elde is bothe wisdom and usage;°   experience
Men may the olde atrenne° and noght atrede.°   outrun / outwit
2450 Saturne anon, to stinten stryf and drede,
Al be it that it is agayn° his kynde,°   against / nature
Of al this stryf he gan remedie fynde.
     "My dere doghter Venus," quod Saturne,
"My cours,° that hath so wyde for to turne,   orbit
2455 Hath more power than wot° any man: knows
Myn is the drenching° in the see so wan;°   drowning / pale, colorless
Myn is the prison° in the derke cote;°   imprisonment / hut, cell
Myn is the strangling and hanging by the throte;
The murmure and the cherles° rebelling,   churls', peasants'
2460 The groyninge° and the pryvee° empoysoning.   grumbling / secret
I do vengeance and pleyn° correccioun°   full / punishment

---

2. In describing Saturn, the word not only indicates his imbalance of humors but also means
ominous, baleful.

Whyl I dwelle in the signe of the leoun.³
Myn is the ruine of the hye halles,
The falling of the toures and of the walles
2465 Upon the mynour° or the carpenter.   *miner*
I slow° Sampsoun, shakinge the piler;   *slew*
And myne be the maladyes colde,
The derke tresons, and the castes° olde;   *plots, deceits*
My loking° is the fader of pestilence.   *aspect*
2470 Now weep namore, I shal doon diligence
That Palamon, that is thyn owne knight,
Shal have his lady, as thou hast him hight.°   *promised*
Though Mars shal helpe his knight, yet nathelees
Bitwixe yow ther moot be som tyme pees,°   *peace*
2475 Al be ye noght of o complexioun,°   *the same temperament*
That causeth al day swich divisioun.
I am thin ayel,° redy at thy wille;   *grandfather*
Weep now namore, I wol thy lust° fulfille."   *desire*
     Now wol I stinten° of the goddes above,   *cease (to tell)*
2480 Of Mars and of Venus, goddesse of love,
And telle yow as pleynly as I can
The grete effect° for which that I bigan.   *outcome*

PART FOUR

     Greet was the feste in Athenes that day,
And eek the lusty seson of that May
2485 Made every wight to been in swich plesaunce,°   *pleasure*
That al that Monday justen° they and daunce,   *joust*
And spenden it in Venus heigh servyse.
But by the cause that° they sholde ryse   *i.e., because*
Erly, for to seen the grete fight,
2490 Unto hir reste wenten they at night.
And on the morwe, whan that day gan springe,
Of hors and harneys° noyse and clateringe   *equipment*
Ther was in hostelryes al aboute;
And to the paleys rood ther many a route°   *company*
2495 Of lordes upon stedes and palfreys.
Ther maystow seen devysing° of harneys   *fashioning, preparation*
So uncouth° and so riche, and wroght so weel°   *curious, unusual / well*
Of goldsmithrie, of browdinge,° and of steel;   *embroidery*
The sheeldes brighte, testeres,° and trappures;° *headpieces / trappings*
2500 Gold-hewen helmes, hauberkes, cote-armures;
Lordes in paraments° on hir courseres,°   *decorated robes / coursers, chargers*
Knightes of retenue,° and eek squyeres   *in service*
Nailinge the speres,⁴ and helmes bokelinge;
Gigginge of° sheeldes with layneres° lacinge—   *Putting straps on / thongs*

---

3. Saturn is most malign while in the astrological house of Leo.
4. I.e., nailing the head to the shaft.

2505 Ther as° need is, they weren no thing ydel; — *Wherever*
The fomy steedes on the golden brydel
Gnawinge, and faste the armurers also
With fyle and hamer prikinge° to and fro; — *riding*
Yemen° on foote and communes° many oon — *Yeomen / common people*
2510 With shorte staves, thikke as they may goon;
Pypes, trompes,° nakers,° clariounes — *trumpets / kettledrums*
That in the bataille blowen blody sounes,° — *warlike sounds*
The paleys ful of peple up and doun,
Heer three, ther ten, holding hir questioun,
2515 Divyninge of° thise Thebane knightes two. — *Speculating about*
Somme seyden thus, somme seyde it shal be so;
Somme helden with° him with the blake berd, — *sided with*
Somme with the balled,° somme with the thikke herd;° — *bald / haired*
Somme sayde he° loked grim, and he wolde fighte— — *that one*
2520 "He hath a sparth° of twenty pound of wighte."° — *battle-ax / weight*
Thus was the halle ful of divyninge,
Longe after that the sonne gan to springe.
        The grete Theseus, that of° his sleep awaked — *out of*
With minstralcye and noyse that was maked,
2525 Held yet the chambre of his paleys riche,
Til that the Thebane knightes, bothe yliche° — *equally*
Honoured, were into the paleys fet.° — *summoned*
Duk Theseus was at a window set,
Arrayed right as he were a god in trone.° — *throne*
2530 The peple preesseth thiderward ful sone
Him for to seen, and doon heigh reverence,
And eek to herkne° his heste° and his sentence.° — *hear / command / decision*
        An heraud on a scaffold made an "Oo!"
Til al the noyse of peple was ydo;° — *done, finished*
2535 And whan he saugh the peple of noyse al stille,
Thus showed he the mighty dukes wille:
        "The lord hath of his heigh discrecioun° — *acumen*
Considered that it were destruccioun
To gentil blood to fighten in the gyse° — *manner*
2540 Of mortal bataille now in this empryse.° — *undertaking*
Wherfore, to shapen° that they shal not dye, — *arrange things so*
He wol his firste purpos modifye.
No man therfore, up° peyne of los of lyf, — *upon*
No maner shot,° ne polax,° ne short knyf — *arrow, missile / battle-ax*
2545 Into the listes sende,° or thider bringe; — *may send*
Ne short swerd, for to stoke° with poynt bytinge,° — *stab / piercing*
No man ne drawe ne bere it by his syde.
Ne no man shal unto his felawe° ryde — *against his opponent*
But o cours° with a sharp y-grounde spere; — *one charge*
2550 Foyne,° if him list, on fote, himself to were.° — *He may parry / defend*
And he that is at meschief° shal be take,° — *in trouble / taken, captured*
And noght slayn, but be broght unto the stake

That shal ben ordeyned° on either syde;   *set up*
But thider he shal by force, and ther abyde.[5]
2555 And if so falle° the chieftayn be take   *befall, happen*
On either syde, or elles° sleen° his make,[6]   *else / slay*
No lenger shal the turneyinge laste.
God spede yow! goth forth, and ley on faste.
With long swerd and with mace fighteth youre fille.
2560 Goth now youre wey—this is the lordes wille."
    The voys of peple touchede the hevene,
So loude cryde they with mery stevene:°   *voice*
"God save swich a lord, that is so good,
He wilneth° no destruccioun of blood!"   *desires*
2565 Up goon the trompes° and the melodye,   *trumpets*
And to the listes rit° the companye,   *rides*
By ordinaunce,° thurghout the citee large,   *In order*
Hanged with cloth of gold and nat with sarge.°   *serge*
Ful lyk a lord this noble duk gan ryde,
2570 Thise two Thebans upon either syde;
And after rood the quene and Emelye,
And after that another companye
Of oon and other, after hir degree.°   *according to their rank*
And thus they passen thurghout the citee,
2575 And to the listes come they bytyme.°   *promptly*
It nas° not of the day yet fully pryme°   *was / 9 A.M.*
Whan set was Theseus ful riche and hye,
Ipolita the quene and Emelye,
And othere ladies in degrees° aboute.   *tiers*
2580 Unto the seetes preesseth al the route.°   *crowd*
    And westward, thurgh the gates under Marte,°   *Mars*
Arcite, and eek the hundred of his parte,°   *on his side*
With baner° reed is entred right anon;   *banner*
And in that selve° moment Palamon   *same*
2585 Is under Venus, estward in the place,
With baner whyt, and hardy chere° and face.   *countenance*
In al the world, to seken up and doun,
So evene° withouten variacioun,   *equal*
Ther nere° swiche companyes tweye.   *were not*
2590 For ther was noon so wys that coude seye
That any hadde of other avauntage
Of° worthinesse, ne of estaat ne age,   *In*
So evene were they chosen, for to gesse.°   *one would guess*
And in two renges° faire they hem dresse.°   *rows / place themselves*
2595 Whan that hir names rad° were everichoon,°   *read / every one*
That° in hir nombre gyle° were ther noon,   *So that / deception*
Tho° were the gates shet,° and cryed was loude: *Then / shut*
"Do now your devoir,° yonge knightes proude!"   *duty*
    The heraudes lefte hir priking° up and doun;   *their riding*

5. But there he must be brought by force, and there remain.
6. I.e., the opposing leader.

2600 Now ringen trompes loude and clarioun.
      Ther is namore to seyn, but west and est
      In goon the speres ful sadly° in th'arest;°   *firmly / into the spear rests*
      In goth the sharpe spore° into the syde.   *spur*
      Ther seen men who can juste° and who can ryde;   *joust*
2605 Ther shiveren shaftes upon sheeldes thikke;
      He° feleth thurgh the herte-spoon° the prikke.   *One / breastbone*
      Up springen speres twenty foot on highte;°   *on high*
      Out goon the swerdes as the silver brighte.
      The helmes they tohewen and toshrede;°   *hew and shred to pieces*
2610 Out brest° the blood, with sterne° stremes rede.   *bursts / powerful, violent*
      With mighty maces the bones they tobreste.°   *smash to bits*
      He thurgh the thikkeste of the throng gan threste;°   *thrust*
      Ther stomblen stedes stronge, and doun goth al;
      He rolleth under foot as dooth a bal.
2615 He foyneth° on his feet with his   *parries*
              tronchoun,°   *truncheon, shattered spear*
      And he him hurtleth° with his hors adoun.   *strikes*
      He thurgh the body is hurt and sithen° y-take,   *then*
      Maugree his heed,° and broght unto the stake.   *In spite of all he could do*
      As forward° was, right ther he moste abyde;   *agreement*
2620 Another lad° is on that other syde.   *led, carried off*
      And som tyme dooth° hem Theseus to reste,   *causes*
      Hem to refresshe and drinken, if hem leste.°   *if it please them*
      Ful ofte a day° han thise Thebanes two   *during this day*
      Togidre y-met, and wroght his felawe wo;°   *done harm to each other*
2625 Unhorsed hath ech other of hem tweye.°   *twice*
      Ther nas no tygre° in the vale of Galgopheye,[7]   *tigress*
      Whan that hir whelp is stole whan it is lyte,°   *little*
      So cruel on the hunte° as is Arcite   *toward the hunter*
      For jelous herte upon° this Palamoun.   *toward*
2630 Ne in Belmarye ther nis so fel° leoun   *fierce*
      That hunted is, or for° his hunger wood,°   *because of / enraged*
      Ne of his praye desireth so the blood,
      As Palamon to sleen° his foo Arcite.   *slay*
      The jelous strokes on hir helmes byte;
2635 Out renneth° blood on bothe hir sydes rede.   *runs*
              Som tyme an ende ther is of every dede.
      For er the sonne unto the reste wente,
      The stronge king Emetreus gan hente°   *seize*
      This Palamon, as he faught with Arcite,
2640 And made his swerd depe in his flesh to byte;
      And by the force of twenty is he take
      Unyolden° and y-drawe° unto the stake.   *Not having yielded / drawn, dragged*
      And in the rescus° of this Palamoun   *(attempted) rescue*
      The stronge king Ligurge is born adoun;

7. Probably the valley of Gargaphie, where according to Ovid's *Metamorphoses* Actaeon was
   killed by his hounds. Chaucer describes the event in ll. 2065–68. For Belmarye (l. 2630),
   see *General Prologue*, l. 57.

2645 And king Emetreus, for al his strengthe,
    Is born° out of his sadel a swerdes lengthe,   *carried, knocked*
    So hitte him Palamon er he were take.
    But al for noght: he was broght to the stake.
    His hardy herte mighte him helpe naught;
2650 He moste abyde, whan that he was caught,
    By force° and eek by composicioun.°   *necessity / agreement*
    Who sorweth now but woful Palamoun,
    That moot° namore goon agayn to fighte?   *may*
       And whan that Theseus had seyn this sighte,
2655 Unto the folk that foghten thus echoon
    He cryde, "Ho! namore, for it is doon!
    I wol be trewe juge, and nat partye.°   *partisan*
    Arcite of Thebes shal have Emelye,
    That by his fortune hath hir faire° y-wonne."   *fairly*
2660 Anon ther is a noyse of peple bigonne
    For joye of this, so loude and heighe° withalle,   *great*
    It semed that the listes sholde falle.
       What can now faire Venus doon above?
    What seith she now? what dooth this quene of love
2665 But wepeth so, for wanting° of hir wille,   *lacking*
    Til that hir teres in the listes fille?°   *fell*
    She seyde, "I am ashamed,° doutelees."   *shamed, disgraced*
       Saturnus seyde, "Doghter, hold thy pees.°   *peace*
    Mars hath his wille: his knight hath al his bone;°   *request*
2670 And, by myn heed,° thou shalt ben esed° sone."   *head / eased, satisfied*
       The trompours° with the loude minstralcye,°   *trumpeters / music*
    The heraudes that ful loude yelle and crye,
    Been in hir wele° for joye of daun° Arcite.   *happiness / sir, master*
    But herkneth me, and stinteth° noyse a lyte,°   *cease / little*
2675 Which° a miracle ther bifel anon.   *What*
       This fierse° Arcite hath of° his helm y-don,°   *bold / off / taken*
    And on a courser, for to shewe his face,
    He priketh endelong° the large place,   *the length of*
    Loking upward upon this Emelye;
2680 And she agayn° him caste a freendlich yë   *toward*
    (For wommen, as to speken in comune,°   *generally*
    They folwen alle the favour of fortune)
    And she was al his chere,° as in his herte.   *happiness*
       Out of the ground a furie infernal sterte,°   *started, leaped*
2685 From Pluto sent at requeste of Saturne,
    For which his hors for fere° gan to turne   *fear*
    And leep° asyde, and foundred° as he leep;   *leaped / foundered, stumbled*
    And er that Arcite may taken keep,°   *heed*
    He pighte° him on the pomel° of his heed,   *pitched / crown, top*
2690 That in the place he lay as he were deed,
    His brest tobrosten° with° his sadel-bowe.[8]   *broken, shattered / by*

8. The high arched front of a saddle. Arcite's horse, after rearing and pitching him off, falls backward on top of him.

As blak he lay as any cole° or crowe, coal
So was the blood y-ronnen in° his face. into
Anon he was y-born out of the place,
2695 With herte soor, to Theseus paleys.
Tho° was he corven° out of his harneys,° Then / cut / armor
And in a bed y-brought ful faire and blyve,° quickly
For he was yet in memorie° and alyve, conscious
And alway crying after Emelye.
2700   Duk Theseus, with al his companye,
Is comen hoom to Athenes his citee,
With alle blisse and greet solempnitee.
Al be it that this aventure° was falle,° accident / had occurred
He nolde noght disconforten° hem alle. dishearten
2705 Men seyde eek that Arcite shal nat dye;
He shal ben heled of his maladye.
And of another thing they were as fayn:° glad
That of hem alle was ther noon y-slayn,
Al° were they sore y-hurt, and namely° oon, Although / especially
2710 That with a spere was thirled° his brest-boon. pierced
To° othere woundes and to broken armes For
Some hadden salves, and some hadden charmes;
Fermacies° of herbes, and eek save° Medicines / a drink made of herbs
They dronken, for they wolde hir limes° have.° limbs / keep, preserve
2715 For which this noble duk, as he wel can,° knows how
Conforteth and honoureth every man,
And made revel al the longe night
Unto the straunge° lordes, as was right. foreign
Ne ther was holden no disconfitinge
2720 But as a justes or a tourneyinge;
For soothly ther was no disconfiture,
For falling nis nat but an aventure.⁹
Ne to be lad° with fors unto the stake led, carried
Unyolden,° and with twenty knightes take, Not having yielded
2725 O° persone allone, withouten mo, One
And haried° forth by arme, foot, and to,° dragged / toe
And eek his steede driven forth with staves
With° footmen, bothe yemen and eek knaves°— By / servants
It nas aretted° him no vileinye,° attributed to / disgrace
2730 Ther may no man clepen° it cowardye.° call / cowardice
    For which anon duk Theseus leet crye,° caused to be proclaimed
To stinten° alle rancour and envye,° stop / bad will
The gree° as wel of o syde as of other, worthiness
And either syde ylyk° as otheres brother; alike
2735 And yaf hem yiftes after hir degree,
And fully heeld a feste dayes three;
And conveyed the kinges worthily
Out of his toun a journee° largely.° a day's journey / fully

---

9. Nor was anything accounted a defeat except as is proper to a jousting or a tournament; for
truly there was no dishonor, since falling (in a joust) is nothing but an accident.

And hoom wente every man the righte way.
2740 Ther was namore but "Farewel, have good day!"
Of this bataille I wol namore endyte,°   tell, make verses
But speke of Palamon and of Arcite.
    Swelleth the brest of Arcite, and the sore
Encreesseth at his herte more and more.
2745 The clothered° blood, for° any lechecraft,°   clotted / despite / medical care
Corrupteth and is in his bouk° y-laft,°   body / left
That neither veyne-blood,° ne ventusinge,°   bloodletting / cupping
Ne drinke of herbes may ben his helpinge.
The vertu expulsif, or animal,
2750 Fro thilke vertu cleped natural¹
Ne may the venim voyden° ne expelle.   void, remove
The pypes° of his longes° gonne to swelle,   tubes / lungs
And every lacerte° in his brest adoun   muscle
Is shent° with venim and corrupcioun.°   damaged / decay
2755 Him gayneth° neither, for to gete° his lyf,   It helps him / save
Vomyt upward ne dounward laxatif;
Al is tobrosten° thilke regioun.   shattered
Nature hath now no dominacioun;°   dominion, power
And certeinly, ther nature wol nat wirche,°   work
2760 Farewel, phisyk;° go ber the man to chirche.   medicine
This al and som,° that Arcita mot° dye;   This is the entire matter / must
For which he sendeth after Emelye
And Palamon, that was his cosin dere.
Than seyde he thus, as ye shul after here:
2765   "Naught may the woful spirit in myn herte
Declare o poynt° of alle my sorwes smerte°   one part / painful
To yow, my lady, that I love most;
But I biquethe° the service of my gost°   bequeath / spirit, soul
To yow aboven every creature,
2770 Sin° that my lyf may no lenger dure.°   Since / last
Allas, the wo! allas, the peynes stronge,
That I for yow have suffred, and so longe!
Allas, the deeth! allas, myn Emelye!
Allas, departinge° of oure companye!   separation
2775 Allas, myn hertes quene! allas, my wyf!
Myn hertes lady, endere of my lyf!
What is this world? what asketh men° to have?   does one ask
Now with his love, now in his colde grave
Allone, withouten any companye.
2780 Farewel, my swete fo, myn Emelye!
And softe tak me in your armes tweye,
For love of God, and herkneth what I seye:
    I have heer with my cosin Palamon

---

1. Medieval medicine thought three powers ("virtues") controlled the functions of the body. Here the animal virtue, located in the brain, is unable to force the muscles to expel the corrupted blood from the natural virtue, located in the liver. Hence the natural virtue is powerless to perform one of its normal tasks, cleansing the lungs of corrupt substances.

Had stryf and rancour many a day agon,°   *past*
2785 For love of yow and for my jalousye.
And Jupiter so wis° my soule gye,°   *wise / guide*
To speken of° a servant° proprely,   *about / servant (of love)*
With alle circumstaunces° trewely—   *necessary qualities*
That is to seyn, trouthe,° honour, knighthede,   *fidelity*
2790 Wisdom, humblesse,° estaat,° and heigh kinrede,°   *humility / position / kindred*
Fredom,° and al that longeth° to that art—   *Generosity / belongs*
So Jupiter have of my soule part,°   *i.e., receive after death*
As in this world right now ne knowe I non
So worthy to ben loved as Palamon,
2795 That serveth yow and wol don al his lyf.
And if that evere ye shul been a wyf,
Foryet nat Palamon, the gentil° man."   *noble, virtuous*
And with that word his speche faille gan,°   *began to*
For from his feet up to his brest was come
2800 The cold of deeth, that hadde him overcome,
And yet moreover, in his armes two
The vital strengthe is lost and al ago.
Only° the intellect, withouten more,°   *Only then / without delay*
That dwelled in his herte syk and sore,
2805 Gan faillen when the herte felte deeth.
Dusked° his eyen two, and failled breeth,   *Became dim*
But on his lady yet caste he his yë;
His laste word was, "Mercy, Emelye!"
His spirit chaunged hous and wente ther
2810 As° I cam never, I can nat tellen wher.   *Where*
Therfor I stinte,° I nam no divinistre;°   *stop / diviner, theologian*
Of soules finde I nat in this registre,°   *register, list*
Ne me ne list° thilke° opiniouns to telle   *It does not please me / those*
Of hem, though that they wryten wher they dwelle.
2815 Arcite is cold, ther° Mars his soule gye.°   *wherefore may / guide*
Now wol I speken forth of Emelye.
      Shrighte° Emelye and howleth Palamon,   *Shrieked*
And Theseus his suster took anon
Swowninge, and bar° hire fro the corps away.   *bore, carried*
2820 What helpeth it to tarien forth the day²
To tellen how she weep° bothe eve and morwe?   *wept*
For in swich cas wommen have swich sorwe,
Whan that hir housbondes been from hem ago,°   *gone*
That for the more part they sorwen so,°   *thus, in that manner*
2825 Or elles fallen in swich a maladye
That at the laste certeinly they dye.
      Infinite been the sorwes and the teres
Of olde folk and folk of tendre yeres
In al the toun, for deeth of this Theban;
2830 For him ther wepeth bothe child and man.

2. What does it serve to while away the day.

So greet weping was ther noon, certayn,
Whan Ector° was y-broght, al fresh y-slayn,   *Hector*
To Troye. Allas, the pitee that was ther:
Cracchinge° of chekes, renting° eek of heer.   *Scratching / rending, tearing*
2835 "Why woldestow° be deed," thise wommen crye,   *didst thou wish to*
"And haddest gold ynough, and Emelye?"
      No man mighte gladen Theseus
Savinge° his olde fader Egeus,   *Except*
That knew this worldes transmutacioun,°   *mutability*
2840 As he had seyn it chaunge bothe up and doun—
Joye after wo, and wo after gladnesse—
And shewed hem ensamples and lyknesse.°   *i.e., analogies*
      "Right as ther deyed° nevere man," quod he,   *died*
"That he ne livede in erthe in some degree,
2845 Right so ther livede never man," he seyde,
"In al this world, that som tyme he ne deyde.
This world nis but a thurghfare° ful of wo,   *thoroughfare, roadway*
And we ben pilgrimes, passinge to and fro:
Deeth is an ende of every worldly sore."°   *pain, sorrow*
2850 And over° al this yet seyde he muchel more   *beyond*
To this effect, ful wysely to enhorte°   *exhort*
The peple that they sholde hem reconforte.°   *be comforted*
      Duk Theseus, with al his bisy cure,°   *diligent concern*
Caste° now wher that the sepulture°   *Considered / burial*
2855 Of goode Arcite may best y-maked be,
And eek most honurable in° his degree.°   *according to / rank*
And at the laste he took conclusioun,
That ther as° first Arcite and Palamoun   *where*
Hadden for love the bataille hem bitwene,
2860 That in that selve° grove, swote° and grene,   *same / sweet*
Ther as he hadde his amorouse desires,
His compleynte,° and for love his hote fires,   *lament*
He wolde make a fyr, in which the office°   *duties, rites*
Funeral he mighte al accomplice;
2865 And leet comaunde° anon to hakke and hewe   *had commands given*
The okes olde, and leye hem on a rewe°   *row*
In colpons° wel arrayed° for to brenne.°   *pieces / arranged / burn*
His officers with swifte feet they renne°   *run*
And ryde anon at his comaundement.
2870 And after this, Theseus hath y-sent
After a bere,° and it al overspradde°   *bier / covered*
With cloth of gold, the richeste that he hadde;
And of the same suyte° he cladde Arcite.   *material*
Upon his hondes hadde he gloves whyte,
2875 Eek on his heed a croune of laurer° grene,   *laurel*
And in his hond a swerd ful bright and kene.
He leyde him, bare the visage,° on the bere;   *with face uncovered*
Therwith he weep° that pitee was to here.   *wept*
And for° the people sholde seen him alle,   *so that*

2880 Whan it was day he broghte him to the halle,
That roreth of the crying and the soun.
  Tho cam this woful Theban Palamoun,
With flotery° berd and ruggy,° asshy° heres,   *fluttering / unkempt / ash-covered*
In clothes blake, y-dropped° al with teres;   *wet*
2885 And, passinge othere of° weping, Emelye,   *surpassing others in*
The rewfulleste° of al the companye.   *most rueful, sorrowful*
In as muche as the service sholde be
The more noble and riche in° his degree,   *according to*
Duk Theseus leet° forth three stedes bringe,°   *caused / to be brought*
2890 That trapped° were in steel al gliteringe   *outfitted*
And covered with the armes° of daun Arcite.   *coat of arms*
Upon thise stedes, that weren grete and whyte,
Ther seten° folk, of which oon bar° his sheeld,   *sat / bore*
Another his spere up in his hondes heeld,
2895 The thridde bar with him his bowe Turkeys°—   *Turkish*
Of brend° gold was the cas° and eek the harneys;°   *refined / quiver / fittings*
And riden° forth a pas° with sorweful   *(they) rode / at a walk*
  chere°   *countenance*
Toward the grove, as ye shul after here.
  The nobleste of the Grekes that ther were
2900 Upon hir shuldres carieden the bere,
With slakke pas° and eyen rede and wete,   *slow pace*
Thurghout the citee by the maister° strete,   *principal*
That sprad° was al with blak; and wonder hye°   *spread / wondrously high*
Right of the same is the strete y-wrye.[3]
2905 Upon the right hond wente old Egeus,
And on that other syde duk Theseus,
With vessels in hir hand of gold ful fyn,
Al ful of hony, milk, and blood, and wyn;
Eek Palamon, with ful greet companye;
2910 And after that cam woful Emelye,
With fyr in honde, as was that tyme the gyse,°   *custom*
To do the office of funeral servyse.
  Heigh° labour and ful greet apparaillinge°   *Great / preparation*
Was at the service and the fyr-makinge,
2915 That with his° grene top the hevene raughte,°   *its / reached*
And twenty fadme of brede the armes straughte[4]—
This is to seyn, the bowes° were so brode.   *boughs*
Of stree° first ther was leyd ful many a lode;   *straw*
But how the fyr was maked upon highte,°   *in height*
2920 Ne eek the names how the treës highte°—   *were called*
As ook, firre, birch, aspe,° alder, holm,° popler,   *aspen / holm oak (holly)*
Wilow, elm, plane, ash, box, chasteyn,° lind,° laurer,   *chestnut / linden*
Mapul, thorn, beech, hasel, ew,° whippeltree°—   *yew / dogwood*
How they weren feld shal nat be told for me;
2925 Ne how the goddes° ronnen° up and doun,   *i.e., tree spirits / ran*

3. With the same material the street fronts were draped.
4. And twenty fathoms in breadth the sides stretched.

Disherited° of hire habitacioun, *Disinherited*
In which they woneden° in reste and pees— *dwelled*
Nymphes, faunes, and amadrides,° *hamadryads*
Ne how the bestes and the briddes alle
2930 Fledden for fere whan the wode was falle,° *felled*
Ne how the ground agast was of the light,
That was nat wont° to seen the sonne bright; *accustomed*
Ne how the fyr was couched° first with stree,° *laid / straw*
And thanne with drye stikkes cloven a° three, *in*
2935 And thanne with grene wode and spycerye,° *spices*
And thanne with cloth of gold and with perrye,° *jewels*
And gerlandes hanginge with ful many a flour,
The mirre,° th'encens,° with al so greet odour; *myrrh / incense*
Ne how Arcite lay among al this,
2940 Ne what richesse aboute his body is;
Ne how that Emelye, as was the gyse,° *custom*
Putte in° the fyr of funeral servyse; *I.e., lit*
Ne how she swowned whan men made the fyr,
Ne what she spak, ne what was hir desyr;
2945 Ne what jeweles men in the fyr caste,
Whan that the fyr was greet and brente° faste; *burned*
Ne how som caste hir sheeld, and som hir spere,
And of hire° vestiments whiche that they were,° *part of their / were wearing*
And cuppes ful of milk and wyn and blood,
2950 Into the fyr that brente as it were wood;° *mad*
Ne how the Grekes with an huge route° *company*
Thryës° riden al the fyr aboute *Thrice*
Upon the left hand, with a loud shoutinge,
And thryës with hir speres clateringe;
2955 And thryës how the ladies gonne crye;° *cried out*
Ne how that lad° was homward Emelye; *led*
Ne how Arcite is brent to asshen colde;
Ne how that liche-wake° was y-holde° *funeral wake / held*
Al thilke night; ne how the Grekes pleye
2960 The wake-pleyes,° ne kepe° I nat to seye— *funeral games / care*
Who wrastleth best naked with oille enoynt,° *anointed*
Ne who that bar him best in no disjoynt.° *in any difficulty*
I wol nat tellen eek how that they goon
Hoom til° Athenes whan the pley is doon; *to*
2965 But shortly to the poynt than wol I wende,° *proceed*
And maken of my longe tale an ende.
   By processe° and by lengthe of certeyn° *In course / a certain number of*
     yeres
Al stinted° is the moorninge and the teres *ceased*
Of Grekes, by oon general assent.
2970 Thanne semed me ther was a parlement
At Athenes, upon certeyn poynts and cas;° *matters*
Among the whiche poynts y-spoken was
To have with certeyn contrees alliaunce,

And have fully of Thebans obeisaunce.°   *submission*
2975 For which this noble Theseus anon
Leet° senden after gentil Palamon,   *Caused*
Unwist of° him what was the cause and why;   *Unknown to*
But in his blake clothes sorwefully
He cam at his comaundement in hye.°   *haste*
2980 Tho sente Theseus for Emelye.
Whan they were set, and hust° was al the place,   *hushed*
And Theseus abiden hadde a space°   *space of time*
Er any word cam from his wyse brest,
His eyen sette he ther as was his lest,°   *pleasure*
2985 And with a sad visage he syked stille,°   *sighed quietly*
And after that right thus he seyde his wille:
"The Firste Moevere of the cause above,
Whan he first made the faire cheyne of love,
Greet was th'effect, and heigh° was his entente.   *noble*
2990 Wel wiste he why, and what thereof he mente,°   *intended*
For with that faire cheyne of love he bond°   *bound*
The fyr, the eyr, the water, and the lond
In certeyn boundes, that they may nat flee.
That same Prince and that Moevere," quod he,
2995 "Hath stablissed° in this wrecched world adoun°   *established / below*
Certeyne⁵ dayes and duracioun
To al that is engendred in this place,
Over° the whiche day they may nat pace,°   *Beyond / pass*
Al mowe they° yet tho dayes wel abregge.°   *Although they may / abridge, shorten*
3000 Ther needeth non auctoritee to allegge,°   *cite*
For it is preved° by experience,   *proved*
But that me list° declaren my sentence.°   *it pleases me / thought*
Than may men by this ordre wel discerne
That thilke Moevere stable is and eterne.°   *eternal*
3005 Wel may men knowe, but it be a fool,
That every part deryveth° from his hool.°   *derives, descends / its own whole*
For nature hath nat taken his beginning
Of no partye° or cantel° of a thing,   *part / portion*
But of° a thing that parfit is and stable,   *from*
3010 Descendinge so° til it be corrumpable.°   *i.e., from heaven / corruptible*
And therfore, of his wyse purveyaunce,°   *providence, foresight*
He hath so wel biset° his ordinaunce°   *arranged / plan*
That speces° of thinges and progressiouns°   *species / natural changes*
Shullen enduren by successiouns°   *succession of generations*
3015 And nat eterne,° withouten any lye.   *by being eternal*
This maistow° understonde and seen at eye:°   *mayest thou / by looking*
Lo, the ook, that hath so long a norisshinge°   *growth*
From tyme that it first biginneth springe,
And hath so long a lyf, as we may see,
3020 Yet at the laste wasted is the tree.

5. I.e., a certain number of.

Considereth eek, how that the harde stoon
Under oure feet, on which we trede and goon,
Yet wasteth it, as it lyth by the weye.
The brode river somtyme wexeth dreye;°   *becomes dry*
3025 The grete tounes see we wane and wende.°   *pass away*
Than may ye see that al this thing hath ende.
    Of man and womman seen we wel also
That nedes,° in oon of thise termes° two,   *by necessity / times*
This is to seyn, in youthe or elles age,
3030 He moot be deed, the king as shal a page;
Som° in his bed, som in the depe see,   *One*
Som in the large feeld, as men may see.
Ther helpeth noght: al goth that ilke° weye.   *same*
Thanne may I seyn that al this thing moot deye.°   *must die*
3035 What° maketh this but Jupiter the king,   *Who*
That is prince and cause of alle thing,
Convertinge al unto his° propre welle°   *its / source*
From which it is deryved, sooth to telle?
And here-agayns° no creature on lyve,°   *against this / alive*
3040 Of no degree, availleth° for to stryve.   *it avails*
    Thanne is it wisdom, as it thinketh° me,   *seems to*
To maken vertu of necessitee,
And take it wel that° we may nat eschue,°   *what / eschew, avoid*
And namely° that to us alle is due.   *especially*
3045 And whoso gruccheth° ought,° he dooth   *grouches, complains / in any way*
    folye,
And rebel is to him that al may gye.°   *govern*
And certeinly a man hath most honour
To dyen in his excellence and flour,
Whan he is siker° of his gode name;   *sure*
3050 Than hath he doon his freend ne him° no shame.   *himself*
And gladder oghte his freend ben of his deeth
Whan with honour up yolden° is his breeth,   *yielded*
Than whan his name apalled° is for age,   *faded, dimmed*
For al forgeten is his vasselage.°   *prowess*
3055 Than is it best, as for a worthy fame,
To dyen whan that he is best of name.
    The contrarie of al this is wilfulnesse.
Why grucchen we, why have we hevinesse,°   *sorrow*
That goode Arcite, of chivalrye flour,°   *the flower*
3060 Departed is with duetee° and honour   *due respect*
Out of this foule prison of this lyf?
Why grucchen heer his cosin and his wyf
Of his welfare, that loveth hem so weel?
Can he hem thank? Nay, God wot, never a deel,°   *not a bit*
3065 That° bothe his soule and eek hemself° offende,°   *Who / themselves / hurt*
And yet they mowe° hir lustes° nat amende.°   *can / happiness / advance*
    What may I conclude of this longe serie,°   *sequence of arguments*
But after wo I rede° us to be merie,   *advise*

And thanken Jupiter of al his grace;
3070 And er that we departen from this place,
I rede° that we make of sorwes two   *advise*
O° parfyt joye, lastinge everemo;   *One*
And loketh now, wher most sorwe is herinne,
Ther wol we first amenden and biginne.
3075   Suster," quod he, "this is my fulle assent,°   *desire*
With al th'avys° heer of my parlement: *advice*
That gentil Palamon, your owne knight,
That serveth yow with wille, herte, and might,
And ever hath doon sin° ye first him knewe,   *since*
3080 That ye shul of your grace upon him rewe,°   *take pity*
And taken him for housbonde and for lord.
Leene° me your hond, for this is our acord.°   *Give / agreement*
Lat see now of youre wommanly pitee.
He is a kinges brother° sone, pardee;°   *brother's / indeed (Fr. par Dieu)*
3085 And though he were a povre bacheler,°   *young knight*
Sin he hath served yow so many a yeer,
And had for yow so greet adversitee,
It moste been considered, leveth° me;   *believe*
For gentil mercy oghte to passen° right."°   *surpass, prevail over / justice*
3090   Than seyde he thus to Palamon the knyght:
"I trowe° ther nedeth litel sermoning°   *believe / preaching, persuading*
To make yow assente to this thing.
Com neer, and tak your lady by the hond."
Bitwixen hem was maad anon° the bond   *at once*
3095 That highte matrimoigne° or marriage,   *matrimony*
By al the counseil° and the baronage.   *council*
And thus with alle blisse and melodye
Hath Palamon y-wedded Emelye.
And God, that al this wyde world hath wroght,
3100 Sende him his love that hath it dere aboght.°   *who has paid dearly for it*
For now is Palamon in alle wele,°   *happiness*
Livinge in blisse, in richesse, and in hele,°   *health, well-being*
And Emelye him loveth so tendrely,
And he hir serveth so gentilly
3105 That nevere was ther no word hem bitwene
Of jalousye or any other tene.°   *trouble, vexation*
Thus endeth Palamon and Emelye;
And God save al this faire companye! Amen.

The Miller's Prologue and Tale

The Prologue

Whan that the Knight had thus his tale y-told,
3110 In al the route° nas° ther yong ne old   *company / was not*
That he ne seyde it was a noble storie,
And worthy for to drawen to° memorie,   *hold in*

And namely the gentils everichoon.[1]
Oure Hoste lough° and swoor, "So moot I goon,[2]   *laughed*
3115 This gooth aright;° unbokeled° is the male.°   *well / opened / bag*
Lat see now who shal telle another tale,
For trewely, the game is wel bigonne.
Now telleth ye, sir Monk, if that ye conne,°   *know how*
Sumwhat° to quyte with° the Knightes tale."   *Something / match (repay)*
3120 The Miller, that fordronken° was al pale,   *totally drunk*
So that unnethe° upon his hors he sat,   *with difficulty*
He nolde avalen° neither hood ne hat,   *take off*
Ne abyde° no man for his° curteisye,   *wait for / out of*
But in Pilates vois he gan to crye,[3]
3125 And swoor, "By armes° and by blood and bones,   *(Christ's) arms*
I can° a noble tale for the nones,°   *know / occasion*
With which I wol now quyte° the Knightes tale."   *repay*
    Oure Hoste saugh that he was dronke of° ale,   *drunken from*
And seyde, "Abyd,° Robin, my leve° brother,   *Wait / dear*
3130 Som bettre man shal telle us first another:
Abyd, and lat us werken thriftily."°   *proceed properly*
    "By Goddes soul," quod° he, "that wol nat I;   *said*
For I wol speke or elles° go my wey."   *else*
Oure Hoste answerde, "Tel on, a devel wey!°   *what the devil*
3135 Thou art a fool, thy wit is overcome."
    "Now herkneth,"° quod the Miller, "alle and some!°   *listen / one and all*
But first I make a protestacioun
That I am dronke, I knowe it by my soun.°   *the sound of my voice*
And therfore, if that I misspeke or seye,°   *speak or talk amiss*
3140 Wyte it° the ale of Southwerk, I yow preye;°   *Blame it on / beseech*
For I wol telle a legende and a lyf
Bothe of a carpenter and of his wyf,
How that a clerk hath set the wrightes cappe."[4]
    The Reve[5] answerde and seyde, "Stint thy clappe!°   *Stop your chatter*
3145 Lat be thy lewed° dronken harlotrye.°   *coarse / ribaldry*
It is a sinne and eek° a greet folye°   *also / folly*
To apeiren° any man, or him diffame,   *injure*
And eek to bringen wyves in swich fame.°   *into such (bad) repute*
Thou mayst ynogh of othere thinges seyn."°   *speak*
3150   This dronken Miller spak ful sone ageyn,°   *in response*
And seyde, "Leve brother Osewold,
Who hath no wyf, he is no cokewold.°   *cuckold*
But I sey nat therfore that thou art oon;
Ther been ful gode wyves many oon,°   *a one*
3155 And ever a thousand gode ayeyns° oon badde.   *(to set) against*
That knowestow wel thyself, but if thou madde.[6]

1. And particularly the well-born (pilgrims), every one.
2. Roughly, "As I may hope to live."
3. He cried aloud in a voice like Pilate's (familiar from the mystery plays: a ranting voice conventionally high and hoarse).
4. How a student made a fool of the carpenter.
5. The Reeve is the general manager of an estate; see the *General Prologue*, ll. 587–622.
6. Thou knowest that well thyself, unless thou art mad.

Why artow° angry with my tale now?   *art thou*
I have a wyf, pardee,° as well as thou,   *by God*
Yet nolde° I, for the oxen in my plogh,°   *would not / plow*
3160 Take upon me more° than ynogh,°   *more (cares) / necessary*
As demen of myself that I were oon;[7]
I wol beleve wel that I am noon.
An housbond shal nat been inquisitif
Of Goddes privetee,° nor of his wyf.   *secrets*
3165 So he may finde Goddes foyson° there,   *plenty*
Of the remenant nedeth nat enquere."[8]
    What sholde I more seyn, but this Millere
He nolde° his wordes for no man forbere,°   *would not / spare*
But tolde his cherles° tale in his manere.   *churl's*
3170 M'athynketh° that I shal° reherce it here.   *I regret / must*
And therfore every gentil wight° I preye,°   *person / beg*
For Goddes love, demeth° nat that I seye°   *judge / speak*
Of° evel entente, but that I moot° reherce   *From / must*
Hir° tales alle, be they bettre or werse,   *Their*
3175 Or elles falsen° som of my matere.   *falsify*
And therfore, whoso list° it nat y-here,°   *desires / to hear*
Turne over the leef,° and chese° another tale;   *page / choose*
For he shal finde ynowe,° grete and smale,   *enough*
Of storial° thing that toucheth° gentillesse,   *historical / treats of*
3180 And eek° moralitee and holinesse.   *also*
Blameth nat me if that ye chese amis.
The Millere is a cherl,° ye knowe wel this;   *churl, rude fellow*
So was the Reve eek and othere mo,°   *more*
And harlotrye° they tolden bothe two.   *ribaldry*
3185 Avyseth yow° and putte me out of blame;   *Think (before you choose)*
And eek men shal nat maken ernest of game.[9]

The Tale

    Whylom° ther was dwellinge at Oxenford°   *Once / Oxford*
A riche gnof,° that gestes heeld to bord,°   *churl / took in lodgers*
And of his craft° he was a carpenter.   *by trade*
3190 With him ther was dwellinge a povre scoler,°   *poor student*
Hadde lerned art, but al his fantasye[1]
Was turned for to lerne astrologye,
And coude a certeyn of conclusiouns
To demen by interrogaciouns,[2]
3195 If that men asked him in certein houres
Whan that men sholde have droghte or elles shoures,°   *else showers*
Or if men asked him what sholde bifalle

---

7. As to think that I am one (i.e., a cuckold).
8. There is no need to inquire about the rest.
9. And furthermore one should not treat game as something serious.
1. Who had studied the liberal arts, but all his fancy.
2. And he knew a certain (number) of propositions by which to arrive at an opinion on questions.

Of every thing, I may nat rekene hem° alle.   *count them*
This clerk was cleped hende Nicholas.[3]
3200 Of derne° love he coude° and of solas;°   *secret / knew / pleasure*
And therto he was sleigh° and ful privee,°   *sly / secretive*
And lyk a mayden meke for to see.°   *meek to look at*
A chambre hadde he in that hostelrye°   *lodging house*
Allone, withouten any companye,
3205 Ful fetisly y-dight° with herbes swote;°   *neatly arrayed / sweet*
And he himself as swete as is the rote°   *root*
Of licorys, or any cetewale.[4]
His Almageste[5] and bokes grete and smale,
His astrelabie,° longinge for° his art,   *astrolabe / belonging to*
3210 His augrim-stones[6] layen faire apart
On shelves couched° at his beddes heed;   *placed*
His presse y-covered with a falding reed.[7]
And al above ther lay a gay sautrye,[8]
On which he made a-nightes° melodye   *by night*
3215 So swetely, that al the chambre rong,°   *rang*
And *Angelus ad virginem*° he song,   *(an Annunciation hymn)*
And after that he song the kinges note;°   *(an unidentified song)*
Ful often blessed was his mery throte.
And thus this swete clerk his tyme spente
3220 After his freendes finding and his rente.[9]
     This carpenter hadde wedded newe° a wyf   *recently*
Which that he lovede more than his lyf;
Of eightetene yeer she was of age.
Jalous he was, and heeld hire narwe in cage,°   *confined, as in a cage*
3225 For she was wilde and yong, and he was old
And demed himself ben lyk° a cokewold.°   *likely to be / cuckold*
He knew nat Catoun, for his wit was rude,[1]
That bad° man sholde wedde his similitude.°   *bade / his like*
Men sholde wedden after hire estaat,°   *according to their condition*
3230 For youthe and elde° is often at debaat.°   *old age / strife*
But sith that° he was fallen in the snare,   *since*
He moste° endure, as other folk, his care.   *must*
Fair was this yonge wyf, and therwithal
As any wesele° hir body gent° and smal.   *weasel / graceful*
3235 A ceynt° she werede° barred° al of silk;   *belt / wore / striped*
A barmclooth eek as whyt as morne milk[2]
Upon hir lendes,° ful of many a gore.°   *loins / very fully cut*
Whyt was hir smok,° and broyden° al bifore   *dress / embroidered*

3. This scholar was called gentle (pleasant) Nicholas.
4. A spice of the ginger family.
5. An astronomical treatise by Ptolemy.
6. Counters for doing arithmetic.
7. His clothes chest covered with red wool cloth.
8. Psaltery, a flat, stringed instrument.
9. In accordance with the money provided (for him) by his relatives, and his income.
1. He didn't know Cato (the *Distichs*, a Latin reader used in the schools), for his intelligence
   was untutored.
2. An apron also, as white as morning milk.

And eek bihinde, on hir coler° aboute,   *collar*
3240 Of col-blak silk, withinne and eek withoute.
The tapes° of hir whyte voluper°   *strings / bonnet*
Were of the same suyte of° hir coler;°   *kind as / collar*
Hir filet° brood of silk and set ful hye.°   *headband / high*
And sikerly° she hadde a likerous yë.°   *certainly / lecherous eye*
3245 Ful smale y-pulled° were hire browes° two,   *plucked / eyebrows*
And tho° were bent, and blake as any sloo.³   *they*
She was ful more blisful on to see°   *to look on*
Than is the newe pere-jonette° tree;   *newly (blossomed) pear*
And softer than the wolle° is of a wether.°   *wool / sheep*
3250 And by hir girdel heeng° a purs of lether   *hung*
Tasseled with silk, and perled with latoun.°   *studded with metal*
In al this world, to seken up and doun,
There nis° no man so wys° that coude thenche°   *is not / wise / imagine*
So gay a popelote,° or swich° a wenche.   *plaything (puppet-doll) / such*
3255 Ful brighter was the shyning of hir hewe°   *complexion*
Than in the Tour° the noble° y-forged°   *Tower of London / gold coin / minted*
    newe.
But of° hir song, it was as loude and yerne°   *in regard to / lively*
As any swalwe° sittinge on a berne.°   *swallow / barn*
Therto she coude skippe and make game,°   *play*
3260 As any kide or calf folwinge his dame.°   *mother*
Hir mouth was swete as bragot or the meeth,⁴
Or hord of apples leyd in hey or heeth.°   *heather*
Winsinge° she was, as is a joly colt,   *Skittish*
Long as a mast, and upright° as a bolt.°   *straight / crossbow bolt*
3265 A brooch she baar° upon hir lowe coler,°   *wore / collar*
As brood as is the bos of a bocler;⁵
Hir shoes were laced on hir legges hye.°   *high*
She was a prymerole,° a piggesnye,°   *primrose / cuckooflower*
For any lord to leggen° in his bedde,   *lay*
3270 Or yet for any good yeman° to wedde.   *yeoman*
    Now sire, and eft° sire, so bifel the cas,°   *again / affair*
That on a day this hende° Nicholas   *gracious, gentle, clever*
Fil with this yonge wyf to rage° and pleye,   *dally*
Whyl that hir housbond was at Oseneye,°   *Osney (a town near Oxford)*
3275 As clerkes ben ful subtile and ful queynte.°   *sly*
And prively he caughte hire by the queynte,⁶
And seyde, "Ywis, but if ich° have my wille,   *Surely, unless I*
For derne° love of thee, lemman,° I spille,"°   *hidden / sweetheart / perish*
And heeld hire harde° by the haunche-bones,°   *firmly / hips*
3280 And seyde, "Lemman, love me al atones,°   *immediately*
Or I wol dyen, also° God me save!"   *as*
And she sprong as a colt doth in the trave,⁷

3. Sloeberry, a purple-black fruit.
4. "Bragot" and "meeth" (mead) are drinks made of ale and honey.
5. And broad as is the boss (the central fitting) of a shield.
6. And when they were alone he grabbed her between her legs. ("Queynte" puns on ME "cunte.")
7. A stall for shoeing unruly horses.

And with hir heed she wryed° faste awey,   *twisted*
And seyde, "I wol nat kisse thee, by my fey.°   *faith*
3285 Why, lat be,"° quod° she, "lat be, Nicholas,   *leave off / said*
Or I wol crye 'out, harrow'° and 'allas.'   *help*
Do wey your handes° for your curteisye!"   *Take your hands away*
   This Nicholas gan° mercy for to crye,   *began*
And spak so faire, and profred him° so faste,° *offered himself / eagerly*
3290 That she hir love him graunted atte laste,°   *at (the) last*
And swoor hir ooth, by Seint Thomas of Kent,° *Thomas Becket*
That she wol been at his comandement,
Whan that she may hir leyser° wel espye.° *chance, opportunity / perceive*
"Myn housbond is so ful of jalousye,
3295 That but ye wayte° wel and been privee,°   *watch out / secretive*
I woot° right wel I nam but° deed," quod she. *know / I'm as good as*
"Ye moste been ful derne,° as in this cas."   *secret*
   "Nay, therof care thee noght," quod Nicholas.
"A clerk had litherly biset his whyle,°   *poorly used his time*
3300 But if° he coude a carpenter bigyle."°   *Unless / trick*
And thus they been acorded and y-sworn
To wayte a tyme, as I have told biforn.
Whan Nicholas had doon thus everydeel,°   *all this so*
And thakked° hire aboute the lendes° weel,   *stroked / loins*
3305 He kiste° hire swete, and taketh his sautrye,° *kissed / psaltery*
And pleyeth faste, and maketh melodye.
   Thanne fil° it thus, that to the parish chirche,   *befell*
Cristes owene werkes for to wirche,°   *perform*
This gode wyf wente on an haliday;°   *holy day*
3310 Hir forheed shoon as bright as any day,
So was it wasshen whan she leet° hir werk.   *left*
   Now was ther of that chirche a parish clerk,[8]
The which that was y-cleped° Absolon.   *called*
Crul° was his heer, and as the gold it shoon,   *Curly*
3315 And strouted° as a fanne large and brode;   *spread out*
Ful streight and evene lay his joly shode.° *the part in his hair*
His rode° was reed, his eyen greye as goos;° *complexion / a goose*
With Powles window corven on his shoos,[9]
In hoses rede° he wente fetisly.°   *red stockings / neatly*
3320 Y-clad he was ful smal° and properly,   *tightly*
Al in a kirtel° of a light waget°—   *coat / blue*
Ful faire and thikke° been the poyntes° set— *close together / laces*
And therupon he hadde a gay surplys°   *loose robe*
As whyt as is the blosme upon the rys.°   *twig*
3325 A mery child° he was, so God me save.   *young man*
Wel coude he laten° blood and clippe° and shave, *let / cut hair*
And make a chartre° of lond or acquitaunce.° *charter / deed of release*
In twenty manere° coude he trippe and daunce   *ways*
After the scole° of Oxenforde° tho,° *fashion / Oxford / then*

8. Assistant to the parish priest.
9. With (a design like) the window of St. Paul's (Cathedral) cut into the leather of his shoes.

3330 And with his legges casten to and fro,
     And pleyen songes on a small rubible,°   *fiddle*
     Therto he song som tyme a loud quinible;°   *high treble*
     And as wel coude he pleye on a giterne.°   *guitar*
     In al the toun nas° brewhous ne taverne   *there was no*
3335 That he ne visited with his solas,°   *entertainment*
     Ther° any gaylard tappestere° was.   *Where / gay barmaid*
     But sooth to seyn, he was somdel squaymous°   *somewhat squeamish*
     Of farting, and of speche daungerous.°   *fastidious*
         This Absolon, that jolif° was and gay,   *jolly, amorous*
3340 Gooth with a sencer° on the haliday,°   *(incense) censer / holy day*
     Sensinge the wyves of the parish faste,°   *diligently*
     And many a lovely look on hem° he caste,   *them*
     And namely° on this carpenteres wyf: *especially*
     To loke on hire him thoughte a mery lyf.
3345 She was so propre° and swete and likerous,°   *comely / flirtatious*
     I dar wel seyn, if she had been a mous,
     And he a cat, he wolde hire hente anon.°   *seize immediately*
     This parish clerk, this joly Absolon,
     Hath in his herte swich° a love-longinge,   *such*
3350 That of° no wyf ne took he noon offringe;   *from*
     For curteisye, he seyde, he wolde noon.°   *wanted none*
         The mone, whan it was night, ful brighte shoon,
     And Absolon his giterne hath y-take;
     For paramours he thoghte for to wake.[1]
3355 And forth he gooth, jolif and amorous,
     Til he cam to the carpenteres hous
     A litel after cokkes° hadde y-crowe,°   *cocks / crowed*
     And dressed him up by a shot-windowe[2]
     That was upon the carpenteres wal.°   *wall*
3360 He singeth in his vois gentil and smal,°   *high, thin*
     "Now, dere lady, if thy wille be,
     I preye yow that ye wol rewe° on me,"   *have pity*
     Ful wel acordaunt to his giterninge.[3]
     This carpenter awook and herde him singe,
3365 And spak unto his wyf, and seyde anon,
     "What, Alison, herestow° nat Absolon   *hearest thou*
     That chaunteth° thus under oure boures° wal?"   *sings / bedroom's*
     And she answerde hir housbond therwithal,
     "Yis, God wot,° John, I here it every deel."°   *knows / every bit*
3370   This passeth forth; what wol ye bet than wel?°   *what more do you want?*
     Fro day to day this joly Absolon
     So woweth hire, that him is wo bigon.[4]
     He waketh° al the night and al the day;   *remains awake*
     He kembeth° hise lokkes brode, and made him gay;   *combs*

1. For love's sake, he intended to stay awake.
2. And took a place up near a casement window, one that opens and closes.
3. In fine harmony with his guitar-playing.
4. Woos her so that he is utterly wretched (woebegone).

3375 He woweth hire by menes and brocage,[5]
And swoor he wolde been hir owene page;
He singeth, brokkinge° as a nightingale;   *quavering*
He sente hire piment,° meeth,° and spyced ale,   *spiced wine / mead*
And wafres,° pyping hote out of the glede;°   *wafer cakes / embers*
3380 And for° she was of toune, he profred mede.°   *because / money, bribes*
For som folk wol ben wonnen for° richesse,   *by*
And som for strokes,° and som for gentillesse.   *blows*
    Somtyme, to shewe his lightness° and maistrye,°   *agility / skill*
He pleyeth Herodes on a scaffold hye.[6]
3385 But what availleth him as in this cas?
She loveth so this hende Nicholas,
That Absolon may blowe the bukkes horn;[7]
He ne hadde for his labour but a scorn.
And thus she maketh Absolon hire ape,°   *monkey*
3390 And al his ernest turneth til° a jape.°   *into / joke*
Ful sooth is this proverbe, it is no lye,°   *lie*
Men seyn right thus, "Alwey the nye slye°   *nearby sly (one)*
Maketh the ferre leve to be looth."[8]
For though that Absolon be wood° or wrooth,°   *mad / angry*
3395 By cause that he fer° was from hir sighte,   *far*
This nye° Nicholas stood in his lighte.   *nearby*
    Now bere thee wel, thou hende Nicholas!
For Absolon may waille and singe "allas."
And so bifel it on a Saterday,
3400 This carpenter was goon til° Osenay,°   *gone to / Osney*
And hende Nicholas and Alisoun
Acorded been to° this conclusioun,   *Were agreed on*
That Nicholas shal shapen him a wyle°   *prepare a stratagem*
This sely° jalous housbond to bigyle;°   *foolish, simple / trick*
3405 And if so be the game wente aright,
She sholde slepen in his arm al night,
For this was his desyr and hire° also.   *hers*
And right anon,° withouten wordes mo,°   *at once / more*
This Nicholas no lenger wolde tarie,
3410 But doth ful softe° unto his chambre carie°   *quietly / carry*
Bothe mete and drinke for a day or tweye,°   *two*
And to hire housbonde bad° hire for to seye,   *bade*
If that he axed after° Nicholas,   *asked about*
She sholde seye she niste° where he was,   *did not know*
3415 Of° al that day she saugh him nat with yë;   *During*
She trowed° that he was in maladye,°   *believed / sickness*
For for no cry hir mayde coude him calle
He nolde° answere, for thing° that mighte falle.°   *wouldn't / anything / befall*
    This passeth forth° al thilke° Saterday,   *goes on / that same*

5. Through (the use of) go-betweens and agents, intermediaries.
6. He plays Herod (in a mystery play), high on a scaffold (stage).
7. I.e., doesn't have a chance.
8. Makes the far-off dear (one) to be hated.

3420 That Nicholas stille in his chambre lay,
     And eet° and sleep, or dide what him leste,°   ate / pleased
     Til Sonday, that° the sonne gooth to reste.   when
     This sely carpenter hath greet merveyle°   marveled greatly
     Of Nicholas, or what thing mighte him eyle,°   ail
3425 And seyde, "I am adrad,° by Seint Thomas,   afraid
     It stondeth nat aright with Nicholas.
     God shilde° that he deyde° sodeynly!   forbid / should die
     This world is now ful tikel,° sikerly:°   unstable / surely
     I saugh to-day a cors° y-born° to chirche   corpse / carried
3430 That now, on Monday last, I saugh him wirche.°   work
     Go up," quod he unto his knave° anoon,°   servant / at once
     "Clepe° at his dore, or knokke with a stoon,   Call
     Loke how it is, and tel me boldely."°   straightway
        This knave gooth him up ful sturdily,
3435 And at the chambre dore, whyl that he stood,
     He cryde and knokked as that° he were wood:°   as if / insane
     "What! how! what do ye, maister Nicholay?
     How may° ye slepen al the longe day?"   can
     But al for noght, he herde nat a word.
3440   An hole he fond, ful lowe upon a bord,
     Ther as the cat was wont in for to crepe;⁹
     And at that hole he looked in ful depe,
     And at the laste he hadde of him a sighte.
     This Nicholas sat evere caping uprighte,°   staring upward
3445 As he had kyked on the newe mone.¹
     Adoun° he gooth, and tolde his maister sone°   Down / at once
     In what array° he saugh this ilke° man.   state / same
        This carpenter to blessen him° bigan,   cross himself
     And seyde, "Help us, Seinte Frideswyde!°   patron saint of Oxford
3450 A man woot° litel what him shal bityde.°   knows / happen to
     This man is falle, with his astromye,²
     In som woodnesse° or in som agonye;°   madness / fit
     I thoghte ay° wel how that it sholde be!°   ever / might happen
     Men sholde nat knowe of Goddes privetee.°   secrets
3455 Ye, blessed be alwey a lewed° man   unlearned
     That noght but oonly his bileve° can!°   creed / knows
     So ferde° another clerk° with astromye: fared / scholar
     He walked in the feeldes for to prye°   spy
     Upon the sterres, what ther sholde bifalle,
3460 Til he was in a marle-pit³ y-falle—
     He saugh nat that. But yet, by Seint Thomas,
     Me reweth sore of° hende Nicholas.   I pity greatly
     He shal be rated of° his studying,   berated for
     If that I may, by Jesus, hevene° king!   heaven's

9. There where the cat was accustomed to creep in.
1. As if he were gazing (half-crazed) at the new moon.
2. This man has fallen, because of his astronomy (John mispronounces "astronomye").
3. A pit from which clay is dug.

3465 Get me a staf, that I may underspore,°   pry up
      Whyl that thou, Robin, hevest up° the dore.   push on
      He shal° out of his studying, as I gesse."   shall (come)
      And to the chambre dore he gan him dresse.°   directed his attentions
      His knave was a strong carl° for the nones,°   fellow / for this purpose
3470 And by the haspe he haf it up atones;°   heaved it off at once
      Into° the floor the dore fil anon.°   On to / straightway
      This Nicholas sat ay° as stille as stoon,   ever
      And ever caped° upward into the eir.°   stared / air
      This carpenter wende° he were in despeir,   thought
3475 And hente° him by the sholdres mightily,   seized
      And shook him harde, and cryde spitously,°   violently
      "What, Nicholay! what, how! what, loke adoun!
      Awake, and thenk on Cristes passioun!
      I crouche thee from elves and fro wightes!"[4]
3480 Therwith the night-spel[5] seyde he anon-rightes°   at once
      On foure halves° of the hous aboute,   sides
      And on the threshfold° of the dore withoute:°   threshold / outside
      "Jesu Crist, and Seynte Benedight,°   Benedict
      Blesse this hous from every wikked wight,°   creature
3485 For nightes verye, the white *pater-noster!*[6]
      Where wentestow, seynt Petres soster?"[7]
          And atte laste° this hende Nicholas   finally
      Gan for to syke° sore,° and seyde, "Allas!   began to sigh / deeply
      Shal al the world be lost eftsones° now?"   so soon again
3490   This carpenter answerde, "What seystow?°   sayest thou
      What! thenk on God, as we don, men that swinke!"°   labor
          This Nicholas answerde, "Fecche me drinke;
      And after wol I speke in privitee°   secretly
      Of certeyn thing that toucheth me and thee;
3495 I wol telle it non other man, certeyn."
          This carpenter goth doun and comth ageyn,
      And broghte of mighty ale a large quart;
      And whan that ech of hem° had dronke his part,   them
      This Nicholas his dore faste shette,°   shut
3500 And doun the carpenter by him he sette.
      He seyde, "John, myn hoste lief° and dere,   beloved
      Thou shalt upon thy trouthe° swere me here,   honor
      That to no wight° thou shalt this conseil° wreye;° person / secret / betray
      For it is Cristes conseil that I seye,
3505 And if thou telle it man,° thou art forlore;°   to anyone / lost
      For this vengeaunce thou shalt han therfore,
      That if thou wreye° me, thou shalt be wood!"°   betray / go mad
      "Nay, Crist forbede it, for° his holy blood!"   by

---

4. I make the sign of the cross over thee (to protect thee) from elves and from (other such) creatures.
5. A charm against evil spirits, said at night.
6. A bedtime blessing, "white" because black magic plays no part in it.
7. The sense of these lines is confused and comically intended: they represent a carpenter's version of "white" magic. Line 3486 means literally "Where didst thou go, St. Peter's sister?"

Quod tho this sely man, "I nam no labbe,
3510 Ne, though I seye, I nam nat lief to gabbe.[8]
Sey what thou wolt, I shal it nevere telle
To child ne wyf, by him° that harwed° helle!"   *i.e., Christ / harrowed*
     "Now John," quod Nicholas, "I wol nat lye.
I have y-founde in myn astrologye,
3515 As I have loked in the mone bright,
That now, a Monday next, at quarter night,°   *about 9 P.M.*
Shal falle a reyn° and that so wilde and wood,°   *rain / furious*
That half so greet was nevere Noës° flood.   *Noah's*
This world," he seyde, "in lasse° than in an hour   *less*
3520 Shal al be dreynt,° so hidous is the shour;°   *drowned / shower, storm*
Thus shal mankynde drenche° and lese° hir lyf."   *drown / lose*
     This carpenter answerde, "Allas, my wyf!
And shal she drenche?° allas, myn Alisoun!"   *drown*
For sorwe of this he fil almost adoun,
3525 And seyde, "Is ther no remedie in this cas?"
     "Why, yis, for° Gode," quod hende Nicholas,   *before*
"If thou wolt werken after lore and reed;[9]
Thou mayst nat werken after thyn owene heed;°   *head, wits*
For thus seith Salomon, that was ful trewe,°   *trustworthy*
3530 'Werk al by conseil,° and thou shalt nat rewe.'°   *advice / be sorry*
And if thou werken wolt by good conseil,
I undertake,° withouten mast and seyl,°   *promise / sail*
Yet shal I saven hire and thee and me.
Hastow° nat herd° how saved was Noë,°   *Hast thou / heard / Noah*
3535 Whan that Oure Lord hadde warned him biforn
That al the world with water sholde be lorn?"°   *lost*
     "Yis," quod this carpenter, "ful yore° ago."   *long*
     "Hastow nat herd," quod Nicholas, "also
The sorwe of Noë with his felawshipe?[1]
3540 Er that° he mighte gete his wyf to shipe,   *Before*
Him hadde be levere, I dar wel undertake,[2]
At thilke° tyme than alle hise wetheres° blake   *that same / sheep*
That she hadde had a ship hirself allone.
And therfore, wostou° what is best to done?°   *knowest thou / do*
3545 This asketh° haste, and of an hastif° thing   *requires / urgent*
Men may nat preche or maken tarying.
     Anon° go gete us faste into this in°   *At once / dwelling*
A kneding trogh° or elles a kymelyn°   *(dough-)kneading trough / shallow tub*
For ech of us, but loke that they be large,
3550 In whiche we mowe swimme° as in a barge,   *may float*
And han therinne vitaille suffisant°   *provisions sufficient*
But for a day; fy on the remenant!
The water shal aslake° and goon away   *diminish*

8. This foolish man said then, "I am no blabbermouth, nor, though I say (it myself), am I fond
of chattering."
9. If thou wilt work according to learning and good counsel.
1. The trouble(s) of Noah and his companions (as portrayed in the mystery plays).
2. He would have rather, I dare declare.

Aboute pryme° upon the nexte day.   near sunrise
3555 But Robin may nat wite° of this, thy knave,°   know / servant
Ne eek° thy mayde° Gille I may nat save.   Nor / maid
Axe° nat why, for though thou aske me,   Ask
I wol nat tellen Goddes privetee.°   secret things
Suffiseth thee, but if° thy wittes madde,°   unless / are gone (insane)
3560 To han as greet a grace as Noë hadde.
Thy wyf shal I wel saven, out of° doute.   without
Go now thy wey, and speed thee heer-aboute.
     But whan thou hast, for hire and thee and me,
Y-geten us thise kneding tubbes three,
3565 Than shaltow° hange hem in the roof ful hye,°   must thou / high
That no man of oure purveyaunce° espye.°   provision / catch sight
And whan thou thus hast doon, as I have seyd,
And hast oure vitaille faire in hem y-leyd,°   laid
And eek an ax, to smyte the corde atwo°   in two
3570 When that the water comth, that we may go,
And breke an hole an heigh° upon the gable   on high
Unto the gardin-ward,° over the stable,   Toward the garden
That we may frely passen forth our way
Whan that the grete shour° is goon away—   shower, storm
3575 Than shaltow swimme as myrie, I undertake,[3]
As doth the whyte doke° after hire° drake.   duck / its
Thanne wol I clepe,° 'How, Alison! how, John!   call
Be myrie, for the flood wol passe anon!'°   at once
And thou wolt seyn, 'Hayl, maister Nicholay!
3580 Good morwe, I se thee wel, for it is day.'
And thanne shul we be lordes al oure lyf
Of al the world, as° Noë and his wyf.   as (were)
     But of o thyng I warne thee ful right:
Be wel avysed° on that ilke° night   forewarned / same
3585 That we ben entred into shippes bord°   on board the ship
That noon of us ne speke nat a word,
Ne clepe, ne crye, but been in his preyere;[4]
For it is Goddes owene heste° dere.   commandment
     Thy wyf and thou mote° hange fer atwinne,°   must / far apart
3590 For that° bitwixe yow shal be no sinne   So that
No more in looking than ther shal° in dede;   shall (be)
This ordinance is seyd, go, God thee spede!°   give thee success
Tomorwe at night, whan men ben alle aslepe,
Into oure kneding tubbes wol we crepe,
3595 And sitten ther, abyding° Goddes grace.   awaiting
Go now thy wey, I have no lenger space°   no more time
To make of this no lenger sermoning.
Men seyn thus, 'Send the wyse, and sey no thing.'
Thou art so wys, it nedeth thee nat teche;[5]

3. Then shalt thou swim as merrily, I declare.
4. Nor call, nor cry out, but be at his prayer(s).
5. It's not necessary to teach thee.

₃₆₀₀ Go, save oure lyf, and that I thee biseche."
　　This sely carpenter goth forth his wey.
　Ful ofte he seith "allas" and "weylawey,"
　And to his wyf he tolde his privetee;°   *secret*
　And she was war,° and knew it bet° than he,   *aware / better*
₃₆₀₅ What al this queynte cast was for to seye.[6]
　But nathelees she ferde as° she wolde deye,°   *acted as if / die*
　And seyde, "Allas! go forth thy wey anon,°   *immediately*
　Help us to scape,° or we ben dede echon.°   *escape / each one*
　I am thy trewe verray° wedded wyf;   *real*
₃₆₁₀ Go, dere spouse, and help to save oure lyf."
　　Lo, which° a greet thyng is affeccioun!°   *what / emotion*
　Men may dyen° of imaginacioun,   *die*
　So depe may impressioun be take.°   *taken*
　This sely° carpenter biginneth quake;   *foolish, simple*
₃₆₁₅ Him thinketh verraily° that he may see   *truly*
　Noës flood come walwing° as the see°   *rolling / sea*
　To drenchen° Alisoun, his hony dere.   *drown*
　He wepeth, weyleth, maketh sory chere,°   *a long face*
　He syketh° with ful many a sory swogh.°   *sighs / groan*
₃₆₂₀ He gooth and geteth him a kneding trogh,°   *kneading trough*
　And after that a tubbe and a kymelyn,°   *a shallow tub*
　And prively° he sente hem to his in,°   *secretly / house*
　And heng° hem in the roof in privetee.°   *hung / secret*
　His owene° hand he made laddres three,   *(With) his own*
₃₆₂₅ To climben by the ronges° and the stalkes°   *rungs / shafts*
　Unto the tubbes hanginge in the balkes,°   *beams*
　And hem vitailled,° bothe trogh and tubbe,   *provisioned*
　With breed and chese, and good ale in a jubbe,°   *jug*
　Suffysinge right ynogh as for a day.
₃₆₃₀ But er that° he had maad al this array,°   *before / preparation*
　He sente his knave° and eek his wench° also   *servant / maid*
　Upon his nede° to London for to go.   *business*
　And on the Monday, whan it drow° to night,   *drew near*
　He shette° his dore withoute candel-light,   *shut*
₃₆₃₅ And dressed° al thing as it sholde be.   *arranged*
　And shortly, up they clomben° alle three;   *climbed*
　They sitten stille wel a furlong-way.°   *short time*
　　"Now, *Pater-noster*, clom!" seyde Nicholay,[7]
　And "clom," quod John, and "clom," seyde Alisoun.
₃₆₄₀ This carpenter seyde his devocioun,
　And stille he sit,° and biddeth° his preyere,   *sits / offers*
　Awaytinge on° the reyn,° if he it here.   *Waiting for / rain*
　　The dede sleep, for wery bisinesse,[8]
　Fil° on this carpenter right as I gesse   *Fell*
₃₆₄₅ Aboute corfew°-tyme, or litel more;   *curfew (8 P.M.)*

6. What all this elaborate stratagem meant.
7. "Now, (an) 'Our Father' (and then) 'mum!' " said Nicholas.
8. A dead sleep, because of (his) tiring labor.

For travail of his goost° he groneth sore,   *spirit*
And eft he routeth, for his heed mislay.⁹
Doun of° the laddre stalketh° Nicholay,   *from / creeps*
And Alisoun, ful softe adoun she spedde;°   *hastened*
3650 Withouten wordes mo,° they goon to bedde   *more*
Theras° the carpenter is wont to lye.   *Where*
Ther was the revel and the melodye;
And thus lyth° Alison and Nicholas   *lie*
In bisinesse of mirthe and of solas,°   *pleasure*
3655 Til that the belle of Laudes gan to ringe,¹
And freres° in the chauncel° gonne° singe.   *friars / chancel / began to*
    This parish clerk, this amorous Absolon,
That is for love alwey so wo bigon,
Upon the Monday was at Oseneye
3660 With compaignye him to disporte° and pleye,   *to amuse himself*
And axed upon cas a cloisterer²
Ful prively after John the carpenter;
And he drough° him apart° out of the chirche,   *drew / aside*
And seyde, "I noot,° I saugh him here nat wirche°   *don't know / work*
3665 Sin° Saterday. I trow° that he be went   *Since / believe*
For timber, ther° oure abbot hath him sent,   *where*
For he is wont for timber for to go,
And dwellen at the grange° a day or two;   *monastery's farmhouse*
Or elles° he is at his hous, certeyn.°   *else / for sure*
3670 Wher that he be, I can nat sothly° seyn."   *truly*
    This Absolon ful joly was and light,°   *joyous*
And thoghte, "Now is tyme to wake° al night;   *to stay awake*
For sikirly° I saugh him nat stiringe   *surely*
Aboute his dore sin° day bigan to springe.   *since*
3675 So moot I thryve,° I shal, at cokkes° crowe,   *So may I thrive / cock's*
Ful prively° knokken at his windowe   *secretly*
That stant° ful lowe upon his boures° wal.   *stands / bedroom's*
To Alison now wol I tellen al
My love-longing, for yet I shal nat misse
3680 That at the leste wey° I shal hire kisse.   *at least*
Som maner° confort shal I have, parfay.°   *kind of / by my faith*
My mouth hath icched al this longe day;
That is a signe of kissing atte leste.°   *at the least*
Al night me mette eek, I was at a feste.³
3685 Therfore I wol gon slepe an houre or tweye,°   *two*
And al the night than wol I wake and pleye."
    Whan that the firste cok hath crowe, anon°   *immediately*
Up rist° this joly lovere Absolon,   *rises*
And him arrayeth gay, at point-devys.°   *to perfection*
3690 But first he cheweth greyn° and lycorys   *an aromatic spice*

9. And also he snores, for his head lay uncomfortably.
1. Till the chapel bell began to ring Lauds (a canonical hour, about 4 A.M.).
2. And asked by chance a resident of the cloister.
3. Also I dreamt all night (that) I was at a feast.

To smellen swete, er° he had kembd° his heer.   *before / combed*
Under his tonge a trewe-love he beer,[4]
For therby wende° he to ben gracious.   *thought*
He rometh to the carpenteres hous,
3695 And stille he stant° under the shot-windowe—   *stood*
Unto his brest it raughte,° it was so lowe—   *reached*
And softe he cougheth with a semi-soun:°   *small sound*
"What do ye, hony-comb, swete Alisoun,
My faire brid,° my swete cinamome?°   *bird / cinnamon*
3700 Awaketh, lemman° myn, and speketh to me!   *sweetheart*
Wel litel thenken ye upon my wo,
That for youre love I swete° ther° I go.   *sweat / wherever*
No wonder is thogh that I swelte° and swete;   *swelter*
I moorne° as doth a lamb after the tete.°   *yearn / teat*
3705 Ywis,° lemman, I have swich° love-longinge,   *Truly / such*
That lyk a turtel° trewe is my moorninge;°   *turtledove / mourning*
I may nat ete na more than a mayde."
    "Go fro the window, Jakke fool,"° she sayde,   *you Jack-fool*
"As help me God, it wol nat be 'com pa me.'°   *come kiss me*
3710 I love another, and elles° I were to blame,   *otherwise*
Wel bet° than thee, by Jesu, Absolon!   *Much better*
Go forth thy wey or I wol caste a ston,
And lat me slepe, a twenty devel wey!"°   *in the devil's name*
    "Allas," quod Absolon, "and weylawey,
3715 That trewe love was evere so yvel biset!°   *ill-bestowed*
Thanne kisse me, sin° it may be no bet,°   *since / better*
For Jesus love and for the love of me."
    "Wiltow thanne go thy wey therwith?" quod she.
    "Ye, certes,° lemman,"° quod this Absolon.   *truly / lover*
3720   "Thanne make thee redy," quod she, "I come anon;"°   *at once*
And unto Nicholas she seyde stille,°   *quietly*
"Now hust,° and thou shalt laughen al thy fille."   *hush*
    This Absolon doun sette him on his knees,
And seyde, "I am a lord at alle degrees;[5]
3725 For after this I hope ther cometh more.
Lemman, thy grace, and swete brid, thyn ore!"°   *mercy*
    The window she undoth,° and that in haste,   *opens*
"Have do,"° quod she, "com of,° and speed thee faste,   *done / on*
Lest that oure neighebores thee espye."
3730   This Absolon gan° wype his mouth ful drye: *did*
Derk was the night as pich,° or as the cole,°   *pitch / coal*
And at the window out she putte hir hole,
And Absolon, him fil no bet ne wers,[6]
But with his mouth he kiste hir naked ers°   *arse*
3735 Ful savourly, er° he was war° of this.   *before / aware*

---

4. He bore a true-love (the leaf of a plant evidently thought to bring good fortune in love)
   under his tongue.
5. I am (equal to) a lord, in every way.
6. And Absolom, it befell him neither better nor worse.

Abak he stirte,° and thoghte it was amis,   leaped
For wel he wiste a womman hath no berd;°   beard
He felte a thing al rough and long y-herd,°   haired
And seyde, "Fy! allas, what have I do?"°   done
3740   "Tehee!" quod she, and clapte the window to;°   shut
And Absolon goth forth a sory pas.°   with a sad step
"A berd,° a berd!" quod hende Nicholas,   trick, joke
"By Goddes *corpus*,° this goth faire and weel!"   body
This sely° Absolon herde every deel,°   poor / bit
3745 And on his lippe he gan° for anger byte;   began
And to himself he seyde, "I shal thee quyte."°   repay
Who rubbeth now, who froteth° now his lippes   chafes
With dust,° with sond,° with straw, with clooth, with   dirt / sand
    chippes,°   bark
But Absolon, that seith ful ofte, "Allas!
3750 My soule bitake° I unto Sathanas,°   commit / Satan
But me wer levere° than al this toun," quod he,   If I would not rather
"Of this despyt° awroken° for to be.   insult / avenged
Allas!" quod he, "allas, I ne hadde y-bleynt!"°   that I did not abstain
His hote love was cold and al y-queynt;°   quenched
3755 For fro that tyme that he had kiste hir ers,
Of paramours he sette nat a kers,[7]
For he was heeled° of his maladye.   cured
Ful ofte paramours he gan deffye,°   denounce
And weep° as dooth a child that is y-bete.°   wept / beaten
3760 A softe paas° he wente over the strete   (With) a soft step
Until° a smith men cleped daun° Gerveys,   To / sir, mister
That in his forge smithed plough harneys:°   parts
He sharpeth shaar and culter[8] bisily.
This Absolon knokketh al esily,°   quietly
3765 And seyde, "Undo,° Gerveys, and that anon."   Open up
"What, who artow?"° "It am I, Absolon."   art thou
"What, Absolon! for Cristes swete tree,°   cross
Why ryse ye so rathe,° ey, *benedicite!*°   early / bless us all
What eyleth° yow? som gay gerl, God it woot,°   ails / knows
3770 Hath broght yow thus upon the viritoot;°   astir(?)
By Seynt Note,° ye woot wel what I mene."   St. Neot
This Absolon ne roghte° nat a bene°   cared / bean
Of° al his pley. No word agayn° he yaf;°   For / in response / gave
He hadde more tow on his distaf[9]
3775 Than Gerveys knew, and seyde, "Freend so dere,
That hote culter in the chimenee° here,   forge
As lene° it me: I have therwith to done,   Do lend
And I wol bringe it thee agayn ful sone."
Gerveys answerde, "Certes,° were it gold,   Truly
3780 Or in a poke° nobles alle untold,°   sack / coins uncounted

7. For stylish love affairs he didn't care a cress (a common waterweed).
8. A plowshare and colter (the front part of a plow).
9. I.e., more business in hand.

Thou sholdest have,° as I am trewe smith.   *have (it)*
Ey, Cristes foo!° what wol ye do therwith?"   *i.e., the devil*
   "Therof," quod Absolon, "be as be may:
I shal wel telle it thee tomorwe day,"
3785 And caughte the culter by the colde stele.°   *handle*
Ful softe out at the dore he gan to stele,°   *stole away*
And wente unto the carpenteres wal.
He cogheth first, and knokketh therwithal
Upon the windowe, right as° he dide er.°   *just as / before*
3790   This Alison answerde, "Who is ther
That knokketh so? I warante it° a theef."   *believe it (is)*
   "Why, nay," quod he, "God woot, my swete leef,°   *dear one*
I am thyn Absolon, my dereling.°   *darling*
Of gold," quod he, "I have thee brought a ring—
3795 My moder yaf° it me, so God me save—   *gave*
Ful fyn it is, and therto wel y-grave.°   *engraved*
This wol I yeve° thee, if thou me kisse!"   *give*
   This Nicholas was risen for to pisse,
And thoghte he wolde amenden° al the jape;°   *improve / joke*
3800 He sholde kisse his ers° er that° he scape.°   *arse / before / escape*
And up the windowe dide° he hastily,   *put*
And out his ers he putteth prively
Over the buttok, to the haunche-bon;
And therwith spak this clerk, this Absolon,
3805 "Spek, swete brid,° I noot° nat wher thou art."   *bird / know not*
   This Nicholas anon° leet fle° a fart,   *at once / fly*
As greet as it had been a thonder-dent,°   *thunderclap*
That with the strook he was almost y-blent;°   *blinded*
And he was redy with his iren hoot,
3810 And Nicholas amidde the ers he smoot.°   *struck*
   Of gooth the skin an hande-brede aboute,[1]
The hote culter brende° so his toute,°   *burned / rump*
And for the smert he wende° for to dye.   *expected*
As° he were wood,° for wo he gan to crye°—   *As if / mad / cried out*
3815 "Help! water! water! help, for Goddes herte!"
   This carpenter out of his slomber sterte,
And herde oon° cryen "water" as° he were wood,°   *someone / as if / mad*
And thoghte, "Allas! now comth Nowelis flood!"[2]
He sit° him up withouten wordes mo,°   *sits / more*
3820 And with his ax he smoot the corde atwo,°   *in two*
And doun goth al; he fond° neither to selle   *found time*
Ne breed ne ale, til he cam to the celle°   *floorboards*
Upon the floor; and ther aswowne° he lay.   *in a faint*
   Up sterte hire° Alison and Nicholay,   *leaped*
3825 And cryden "out" and "harrow"° in the strete.   *help*
The neighebores, bothe smale and grete,
In ronnen° for to gauren° on this man,   *ran / stare*

1. Off goes the skin (from an area) a hand's-breadth around.
2. John confuses "Noah" with "Nowell" (Noel, or Christmas).

That yet° aswowne lay, bothe pale and wan;   *still*
For with the fal he brosten° hadde his arm.   *broken*
3830 But stonde he moste unto his owene harm.³
For whan he spak, he was anon° bore doun°   *at once / shouted down*
With° hende Nicholas and Alisoun.   *By*
They tolden every man that he was wood,°   *crazy*
He was agast so of "Nowelis flood"
3835 Thurgh fantasye,° that of his vanitee°   *delusion / foolish pride*
He hadde y-boght him kneding tubbes three,
And hadde hem hanged in the roof above;
And that he preyed hem, for Goddes love,
To sitten in the roof, *par*° *compaignye*.   *for the sake of*
3840   The folk gan laughen° at his fantasye;   *laughed heartily*
Into the roof they kyken° and they cape,°   *gaze / gape*
And turned al his harm° unto a jape.°   *misfortune / joke*
For what so that this carpenter answerde,
It was for noght; no man his reson° herde.   *explanation*
3845 With othes° grete he was so sworn adoun,   *oaths*
That he was holden° wood° in al the toun.   *considered / mad*
For every clerk° anonright° heeld° with other: *scholar / at once / agreed*
They seyde, "The man is wood, my leve° brother;"   *dear*
And every wight° gan laughen at this stryf.   *person*
3850   Thus swyved° was this carpenteres wyf   *made love to*
For al his keping° and his jalousye;   *watchfulness*
And Absolon hath kist hir nether yë;°   *lower eye*
And Nicholas is scalded in the toute.°   *rump*
This tale is doon, and God save al the route!°   *company*

The Reeve's Prologue and Tale

The Prologue

3855   Whan folk had laughen at this nyce cas°   *foolish matter*
Of Absolon and hende° Nicholas,   *courteous, gentle*
Diverse folk diversely they seyde,
But, for the more° part, they loughe° and pleyde;°   *greater / laughed / jested*
Ne at this tale I saugh no man him greve,°   *become vexed*
3860 But° it were only Osewold the Reve.   *Except*
By cause he was of carpenteres craft,
A litel ire° is in his herte y-laft.°   *anger / left*
He gan° to grucche° and blamed it a lyte.°   *began / grumble / little*
    "So theek," quod he, "ful wel coude I thee quyte
3865 With blering of a proud milleres yë,¹
If that me liste° speke of ribaudye.°   *it pleased me / ribaldry*

---

3. But he must accept responsibility for his own misfortune.
1. "So may I thrive," said he, "I could very well pay you back with (a story of) the deceiving of a proud miller" (*lit.*, "the blearing of his eye").

But ik° am old; me list not pley for° age; — *I / because of*
Gras-tyme is doon, my fodder° is now forage,[2] — *food*
This whyte top wryteth° myne olde yeres. — *declares*
3870 Myn herte is also mowled° as myne heres,° — *as moldy / hair(s)*
But if° I fare as dooth an open-ers;[3] — *Unless*
That ilke° fruit is ever lenger the wers,° — *same / the older the worse*
Til it be roten in mullok° or in stree.° — *muck / straw*
We olde men, I drede,° so fare we: — *fear*
3875 Til we be roten, can we nat be rype;
We hoppen alwey whyl that the world wol pype.
For in oure wil ther stiketh evere a nayl,[4]
To have an hoor° heed and a grene tayl — *hoary*
As hath a leek,[5] for thogh our might° be goon,° — *power, force / gone*
3880 Oure wil desireth folie evere in oon.° — *always the same*
For whan we may nat doon,° than wol we speke; — *act*
Yet in oure asshen° olde is fyr y-reke.° — *ashes / raked up*
  Foure gledes° han we, whiche I shal devyse:° — *burning coals / mention*
Avaunting,° lying, anger, coveityse.° — *Boasting / avarice*
3885 Thise foure sparkles° longen° unto elde.° — *sparks / belong / old age*
Our olde lemes° mowe° wel been unwelde,° — *limbs / may / weak*
But wil ne shal nat faillen, that is sooth.
And yet ik have alwey a coltes tooth,[6]
As many a yeer as it is passed henne° — *hence*
3890 Sin that my tappe of lyf bigan to renne.[7]
For sikerly,° whan I was bore,° anon° — *truly / born / at once*
Deeth drogh the tappe° of lyf and leet it gon;° — *drew the tap / run*
And ever sithe° hath so the tappe y-ronne, — *afterward*
Til that almost al empty is the tonne.° — *tun, cask*
3895 The streem of lyf now droppeth on the chimbe.° — *rim of the cask*
The sely° tonge° may wel ringe and chimbe° — *foolish / tongue / chime*
Of wrecchednesse that passed is ful yore;° — *long ago*
With olde folk, save° dotage, is° namore." — *except for / there is*
  Whan that oure Host hadde herd this sermoning,° — *preaching*
3900 He gan to speke as lordly as a king.
He seide, "What amounteth al this wit?[8]
What shul° we speke alday of Holy Writ? — *Why must*
The devel made a reve for to preche,
Or of a soutere° a shipman or a leche.° — *shoemaker / doctor*
3905 Sey forth thy tale, and tarie° nat the tyme; — *delay*
Lo, Depeford, and it is half-way pryme!
Lo, Grenewich, ther many a shrewe is inne![9]

2. Hay laid up for winter.
3. The medlar fruit, inedible until it is mushy and decayed.
4. We dance on always, as long as the world will pipe. For in our will (desire), there is always an obstruction (*lit.*, a nail sticking up).
5. A kind of onion.
6. And even now I have in every way the desire of youth (*lit.*, a colt's tooth).
7. Since my tap of life began to run. (The figure is that of a wine cask.)
8. He said, "What does all this wisdom amount to?"
9. Lo, Deptford, and it's half past seven in the morning! Lo, Greenwich, wherein there is many a rascal! (Both are suburbs of London; Chaucer lived in Greenwich for a time.)

It were al tyme thy tale to biginne."
    "Now, sires," quod this Osewold the Reve,
3910 "I pray yow alle that ye nat yow greve,°   take (it) amiss
Thogh I answere and somdel sette his howve;¹
For leveful is with force force of-showve.²
    This dronke millere hath y-told us heer
How that bigyled° was a carpenteer,   deceived
3915 Peraventure° in scorn for I am oon.   Perhaps
And, by youre leve,° I shal him quyte° anoon;   permission / pay back
Right in his cherles° termes wol I speke.   churl's
I pray to God his nekke mote tobreke°—   may break
He can wel in myn yë seen a stalke,°   straw
3920 But in his owne he can nat seen a balke."°   beam

The Tale

    At Trumpyngtoun,° nat fer° fro Cantebrigge,° Trumpington / far / Cambridge
Ther goth a brook and over that a brigge;°   bridge
Upon the whiche brook ther stant a melle;°   mill
And this is verray soth° that I yow telle.   the real truth
3925 A millere was ther dwelling many a day;
As eny pecok° he was proud and gay.   peacock
Pypen he coude and fisshe, and nettes bete,
And turne coppes, and wel wrastle and shete;³
Ay by his belt he baar a long panade,°   cutlass
3930 And of a swerd ful trenchant° was the blade.   sharp
A joly popper° baar he in his pouche—   dagger
Ther was no man for peril dorste° him touche—   dared
A Sheffeld thwitel° baar he in his hose.   knife
Round was his face, and camus° was his nose;   flat, pug
3935 As piled° as an ape was his skulle.   bald
He was a market-betere atte fulle.⁴
Ther dorste no wight hand upon him legge,°   lay
That he ne swoor he sholde anon abegge.°   pay for it
A theef he was for sothe° of corn° and mele,°   truly / grain / meal
3940 And that a sly,° and usaunt for° to stele.   sly one / accustomed
His name was hote° deynous° Simkin.   called / scornful, proud
A wyf he hadde, y-comen of noble kin:
The person of the toun hir fader was.⁵
With hire he yaf° ful many a panne° of bras,   gave / pan (as dowry)
3945 For that Simkin sholde in his blood allye.⁶
She was y-fostred° in a nonnerye   raised
For Simkin wolde° no wyf, as he sayde,   desired
But° she were wel y-norissed° and a mayde,° Unless / brought up / virgin

1. Somewhat adjust his hood (i.e., make a fool of him).
2. For it is lawful to repel force with force.
3. He knew how to play bagpipes and fish and mend (fishing) nets and turn (wooden) cups on a lathe and wrestle well and shoot.
4. He was a great swaggerer at markets.
5. The parson of the town was her father. (She was therefore born out of wedlock.)
6. I.e., marry her (with a pun on "alloy").

To saven his estaat of yomanrye.[7]
3950 And she was proud, and pert as is a pye.°   *magpie*
A ful fair sighte was it upon hem two;[8]
On halydayes° biforn hire wolde he go   *holy days*
With his tipet° wounde about his heed,   *scarf*
And she cam after in a gyte of reed;°   *red gown*
3955 And Simkin hadde hosen° of the same.   *stockings*
Ther dorste no wight clepen° hire but "Dame."°   *call / Lady*
Was noon so hardy that wente by the weye
That with hir dorste rage° or ones° pleye,   *dally / once*
But if° he wolde° be slayn of Simkin   *Unless / wished (to)*
3960 With panade,° or with knyf, or boydekin,°   *cutlass / dagger*
For jalous folk ben perilous° everemo—   *dangerous*
Algate they wolde hire wyves wenden so.[9]
And eek, for she was somdel smoterlich,[1]
She was as digne° as water in a dich,   *dignified, worthy*
3965 And ful of hoker° and of bisemare.°   *scorn / disdain*
Hir thoughte that a lady sholde hire spare,[2]
What for hire kinrede° and hir nortelrye°   *family / education*
That she had lerned in the nonnerye.
    A doghter hadde they bitwixe hem two
3970 Of twenty yeer, withouten any mo,°   *more*
Savinge° a child that was of half-yeer age;   *Except for*
In cradel it lay and was a propre page.°   *fine boy*
This wenche thikke° and wel y-growen was,   *stout*
With camuse° nose and eyen greye as glas,   *pug*
3975 With buttokes brode and brestes rounde and hye;
But right fair was hire heer,° I wol nat lye.   *hair*
    The person° of the toun, for° she was feir,   *parson / because*
In purpos was to maken hire his heir
Bothe of his catel° and his messuage,°   *property / house*
3980 And straunge he made it of hir mariage.[3]
His purpos was for to bistowe hire hye°   *in a high place*
Into som worthy blood of auncetrye;°   *old lineage*
For holy chirches good° moot° been despended°   *goods / must / spent*
On holy chirches blood, that is descended.
3985 Therfore he wolde his holy blood honoure,
Though that he holy chirche sholde devoure.
    Gret soken° hath this miller, out of doute,°   *monopoly / doubtless*
With° whete and malt of al the land aboute;   *On*
And nameliche ther was a greet collegge
3990 Men clepen° the Soler Halle° at Cantebregge;°   *call / Solar Hall / Cambridge*
Ther was hir whete and eek° hir malt y-grounde.   *also*
And on a day it happed, in a stounde,°   *at one time*

7. To preserve his rank as a freeman.
8. It was a handsome sight (to look) upon the two of them.
9. At any rate, they would like their wives to believe so.
1. And also, because she was somewhat besmirched (i.e., by her illegitimate birth).
2. It seemed to her that a lady ought to treat her with respect.
3. And he made (the question of) her marriage difficult.

Sik lay the maunciple on a maladye:[4]

Men wenden wisly° that he sholde dye,   expected for certain

3995 For which this millere stal° bothe mele and corn   stole

An hundred tyme more than biforn;

For ther-biforn he stal but curteisly,[5]

But now he was a theef outrageously.

For which the wardeyn chidde and made fare,[6]

4000 But therof sette° the millere nat a tare;°   cared / whit

He craketh boost,° and swoor it was nat so.   talks loudly

      Than were ther yonge povre scolers° two   poor scholars

That dwelten in this halle of which I seye.°   speak

Testif° they were, and lusty for to pleye,   Headstrong

4005 And, only for hire mirthe and revelrye,

Upon the wardeyn bisily they crye

To yeve° hem leve° but a litel stounde°   give / permission / while

To goon to mille and seen hir corn° y-grounde;   grain

And hardily° they dorste leye° hir nekke,   boldly / wager

4010 The millere shold nat stele hem° half a pekke°   from them / peck

Of corn by sleighte, ne by force hem reve;°   rob

And at the laste the wardeyn yaf hem leve.°   gave them permission

John highte° that oon, and Aleyn highte that other;   was named

Of o° toun were they born, that highte Strother,   one

4015 Fer in the north—I can nat telle where.[7]

      This Aleyn maketh redy al his gere,°   gear, equipment

And on an hors the sak° he caste anon.°   sack (of grain) / at once

Forth goth Aleyn the clerk,° and also John,   scholar

With good swerd and with bokeler° by hir syde.   buckler, shield

4020 John knew the wey, hem nedede° no gyde,   they needed

And at the mille the sak adoun he layth.

Aleyn spak first, "Al hayl, Symond, y-fayth!°   in faith

How fares thy faire doghter and thy wyf?"

      "Aleyn, welcome," quod° Simkin, "by my lyf!   said

4025 And John also, how now, what do ye heer?"°   here

      "Symond," quod John, "by God, nede has na peer.°   need has no equal

Him boes serve himselve that has na swayn,[8]

Or elles he is a fool, as clerkes sayn.

Oure manciple, I hope° he wil be deed,   expect

4030 Swa werkes ay the wanges in his heed.[9]

And forthy° is I come, and eek° Alayn,   therefore / also

To grinde our corn and carie it ham° agayn;   home

I pray yow spede us hethen° that° ye may."   hence / as much as

---

4. The college steward lay sick with an illness.
5. For previously he stole only in a polite fashion.
6. On account of which the warden (the college head) chided (him) and made a fuss.
7. The town has not been identified, though there was a Strother castle in Northumberland. The speech of the students firmly characterizes them as Northerners: words such as "boes," "lathe," "fonne," "hethyng," "taa"; the substitution of long *a* for normal long *o* (as in "gas," "swa," "ham"); present indicative verbs in -*es* or -*s*, and so on, are used to create a distinct and slightly comic dialect.
8. It behooves him who has no servant to serve himself.
9. The molars in his head keep aching so.

"It shal be doon," quod Simkin, "by my fay.°   *faith*

4035 What wol ye doon whyl that it is in hande?"°   *being processed*

     "By God, right by the hopur° will I stande,"   *hopper*

Quod John, "and se how that the corn gas° in.   *goes*

Yet saugh I never, by my fader° kin,   *father's*

How that the hopur° wagges til and fra."°   *hopper / to and fro*

4040   Aleyn answerde, "John, and wiltow swa?°   *wilt thou (do) so*

Than wil I be bynethe, by my croun,°   *head*

And se how that the mele° falles doun   *meal*

Into the trough; that sal° be my disport.   *shall*

For John, in faith, I may° been of youre sort: *must*

4045 I is as ille° a millere as are ye."   *bad*

     This miller smyled of° hir nycetee,°   *at / foolishness*

And thoghte, "Al this nis doon but for a wyle.°   *only as a trick*

They wene° that no man may hem bigyle,°   *think / beguile, trick*

But, by my thrift, yet shal I blere hire yë°   *blur their eye(s)*

4050 For al the sleighte° in hir philosophye.   *craftiness*

The more queynte crekes° that they make,   *sly tricks*

The more wol I stele whan I take.

In stide of flour, yet wol I yeve° hem bren.°   *give / bran*

'The gretteste clerkes been noght wysest men,'

4055 As whylom° to the wolf thus spak the mare;[1]   *once*

Of al hir° art counte I noght a tare."°   *their / whit*

     Out at the dore he gooth ful prively,°   *secretly*

Whan that he saugh his tyme, softely;

He loketh up and doun til he hath founde

4060 The clerkes hors, ther as° it stood y-bounde   *where*

Bihinde the mille, under a levesel.°   *leafy arbor*

And to the hors he gooth him faire and wel;

He strepeth of° the brydel right anon.   *strips off*

And whan the hors was laus,° he ginneth gon°   *loose / dashes off*

4065 Toward the fen,° ther° wilde mares renne,°   *marsh / where / run*

Forth with "wehee,"° thurgh thikke and thurgh thenne.°   *a whinny / thin*

     This miller gooth agayn, no word he seyde,

But dooth his note,° and with the clerkes pleyde,°   *job / jested*

Til that hir corn° was faire and wel y-grounde.   *grain*

4070 And whan the mele° is sakked° and y-bounde,°   *flour / sacked / tied*

This John goth out and fynt° his hors away,   *finds*

And gan to crye "harrow" and "weylaway!"[2]

Oure hors is lorn!° Alayn, for goddes banes°   *lost / bones*

Step on thy feet! com of, man, al atanes!°   *right now*

4075 Allas, our wardeyn has his palfrey° lorn!"°   *riding horse / lost*

This Aleyn al forgat bothe mele and corn;

Al was out of his mynde his housbondrye.°   *shrewd management*

"What, whilk° way is he geen?"° he gan to crye.°   *which / gone / cried out*

     The wyf cam lepinge inward with a ren;°   *run*

---

1. Refers to a fable in which the wolf, very hungry, is kicked by a mare while trying to read on her hind foot the price of her foal.
2. And cried out "help" and "alas-alack."

4080 She seyde, "Allas! youre hors goth to the fen
With wilde mares, as faste as he may go.
Unthank° come on his hand that boond him so,   *Bad luck*
And he that bettre sholde han knit the reyne."°   *tied the reins*
"Allas," quod John, "Aleyn, for Cristes peyne,°   *pain*
4085 Lay doun thy swerd, and I will myn alswa.°   *also*
I is ful wight,° God waat,° as is a raa;°   *swift / knows / roe*
By Goddes herte he sal° nat scape° us bathe!°   *shall / escape / both*
Why ne had thou pit° the capul° in the lathe?°   *put / horse / barn*
Il-hayl,° by God, Aleyn, thou is a fonne!"°   *Bad luck / fool*
4090   This sely clerkes° han ful faste y-ronne   *These poor scholars*
Toward the fen, bothe Aleyn and eek John.
And whan the millere saugh° that they were gon,   *saw*
He half a busshel of hir flour hath take,
And bad his wyf go knede it in a cake.³
4095 He seyde, "I trowe° the clerkes were aferd,°   *believe / afraid, suspicious*
Yet can a millere make a clerkes berd°   *outwit a scholar*
For al his art; now lat hem goon hir weye.
Lo, wher he gooth! ye, lat the children pleye.
They gete him nat so lightly, by my croun!"⁴
4100   Thise sely clerkes rennen up and doun
With "Keep! keep! stand! stand! jossa! warderere!⁵
Ga° whistle thou, and I shal kepe him here!"   *Go*
But shortly,° til that it was verray° night,   *in short / real*
They coude nat, though they dide al hir might,°   *their best*
4105 Hir capul cacche,° he ran alwey so faste,   *Catch their horse*
Til in a dich they caughte him atte laste.
Wery and weet,° as beest° is in the reyn,°   *wet / animal / rain*
Comth sely John, and with him comth Aleyn.
"Allas," quod John, "the day that I was born!
4110 Now are we drive til hething° and til scorn.   *driven into derision*
Oure corn° is stole, men wil us foles° calle,   *grain / fools*
Bathe° the wardeyn and our felawes° alle,   *Both / companions*
And namely° the millere, weylaway!"°   *especially / alas*
Thus pleyneth° John as he goth by° the way   *complains / on*
4115 Toward the mille, and Bayard° in his hond.   *the horse's name*
The millere sitting by the fyr he fond,
For it was night, and forther° mighte they noght. *go farther*
But for the love of God they him bisoght
Of herberwe° and of ese,° as for hir peny.°   *lodging / rest / money*
4120   The millere seyde agayn,° "If ther be eny,   *in response*
Swich° as it is, yet shal ye have youre part.   *Such*
Myn hous is streit,° but ye han lerned art: *narrow, small*
Ye conne° by argumentes make a place   *know how to*
A myle brood of° twenty foot of space.   *out of*
4125 Lat see now if this place may suffyse—

3. And told his wife to go knead it into a loaf.
4. They won't catch him so easily, by my head!
5. Down here! look out behind!

Or make it roum° with speche, as is youre gyse."°   *roomy / way*
   "Now, Symond," seyde John, "by Seint Cutberd,°   *Cuthbert*
Ay° is thou mery, and this is faire answerd.   *Ever*
I have herd seyd, 'man sal taa of twa thinges:
4130 Slyk as he fyndes, or taa slyk as he bringes.'⁶
But specially, I pray thee, hoste dere,
Get us som mete and drinke and make us chere,°   *good cheer*
And we will payen trewely atte fulle;
With empty hand men may na haukes tulle.°   *lure no hawks*
4135 Lo, here oure silver, redy for to spende."
   This millere into toun his doghter sende°   *sent*
For ale and breed, and rosted hem° a goos,   *roasted for them*
And bond hir hors, it sholde namoore go loos;
And in his owene chambre hem made a bed
4140 With shetes and with chalons° faire y-spred,   *bedspreads*
Noght from his owene bed ten foot or twelve.
His doghter hadde a bed, al by hirselve,
Right in the same chambre, by and by.°   *side by side*
It mighte be no bet, and cause why,⁷
4145 Ther was no roumer° herberwe° in the place.   *larger / lodgings*
They soupen° and they speke, hem to solace,°   *sup / for amusement*
And drinken evere strong ale atte beste.°   *of the best*
Aboute midnight wente they to rest.
   Wel hath this millere vernisshed his heed:⁸
4150 Ful pale he was fordronken,° and nat reed;   *very drunk*
He yexeth,° and he speketh thurgh the nose   *hiccups*
As he were on the quakke,° or on the pose.°   *hoarse / had a cold*
To bedde he gooth, and with him gooth his wyf—
As any jay she light° was and jolyf,°   *cheerful / jolly*
4155 So was hir joly whistle wel y-wet.
The cradel at hir beddes feet is set,
To rokken,° and to yeve° the child to souke.°   *rock / give / suck*
And whan that dronken al was in the crouke,°   *jug*
To bedde went the doghter right anon;
4160 To bedde gooth Aleyn and also John;
Ther nas na more, hem nedede no dwale.°   *sleeping potion*
This millere hath so wisly° bibbed° ale,   *deeply / imbibed*
That as° an hors he fnorteth° in his sleep,   *like / snores*
Ne of his tayl bihinde he took no keep.°   *heed*
4165 His wyf bar him a burdon,° a ful strong: *bass accompaniment*
Men mighte hir routing° here two furlong;   *snoring*
The wenche routeth eek *par compaignye*.°   *to keep (them) company*
   Aleyn the clerk, that herd this melodye,
He poked John, and seyde, "Slepestow?°   *Art thou asleep?*
4170 Herdestow evere slyk° a sang° er° now?   *such / song / before*

6. I have heard said, "a man must take one of two things: such as he finds, or take such as he brings."
7. No better could be (arranged), and (this is the) reason why.
8. *Lit.*, varnished his head (with ale).

Lo, swilk° a compline° is y-mel° hem alle!   *such / evening song / among*
A wilde fyr⁹ upon thair bodyes falle!
Wha herkned° ever slyk° a ferly° thing?   *Who heard / such / weird*
Ye, they sal have the flour of il ending.¹
4175 This lange° night ther tydes° me na° reste;   *long / comes to / no*
But yet, na fors,° al sal° be for the beste.   *no matter / shall*
For John," seyde he, "als evere moot I thryve,°   *may I thrive*
If that I may, yon wenche wil I swyve.°   *lie with*
Som esement° has lawe y-shapen° us.   *redress / provided*
4180 For John, ther is a lawe that says thus,
That gif° a man in a° point be agreved,°   *if / one / aggrieved*
That in another he sal be releved.°   *relieved*
Oure corn is stoln, sothly, it is na nay,°   *there is no denial*
And we han had an il fit° al this day.   *sorry time of it*
4185 And sin° I sal have neen amendement°   *since / no amends*
Agayn my los,° I wil have esement.°   *loss / redress*
By Goddes saule, it sal neen other be!"²
   This John answerde, "Alayn, avyse thee,°   *consider*
The miller is a perilous° man," he seyde,   *dangerous*
4190 "And gif° that he out of his sleep abreyde,°   *if / awake*
He mighte doon us bathe° a vileinye."°   *both / harm*
   Aleyn answerde, "I count him nat a flye."
And up he rist,° and by the wenche he crepte.   *rises*
This wenche lay upright,° and faste° slepte   *face up / soundly*
4195 Til he so ny° was, er° she mighte espye,°   *near / before / see (him)*
That it had been to° late for to crye,   *too*
And shortly for to seyn, they were aton;°   *at one, united*
Now pley, Aleyn! for I wol speke of John.
   This John lyth stille a furlong-wey or two,³
4200 And to himself he maketh routhe° and wo: *lamentation*
"Allas!" quod he, "this is a wikked jape.°   *joke*
Now may I seyn° that I is but an ape.   *say*
Yet has my felawe° somwhat° for his harm: *companion / something*
He has the milleris° doghter in his arm.   *miller's*
4205 He auntred him,° and has his nedes sped,°   *took a chance / satisfied*
And I lye as a draf-sak° in my bed.   *bag of straw or refuse*
And when this jape is tald° another day,   *told*
I sal been halde° a daf,° a cokenay!°   *held / fool / milksop*
I wil aryse and auntre° it, by my fayth!   *chance*
4210 Unhardy is unsely,⁴ thus men sayth."
And up he roos° and softely he wente   *arose*
Unto the cradel, and in his hand it hente,°   *took*
And baar° it softe unto his beddes feet.   *bore*
   Sone after this the wyf hir routing leet,°   *ceased snoring*

9. A painful skin disease.
1. The best of bad ending(s).
2. By God's soul, it shall not be otherwise!
3. This John lies still for a moment or two (*lit.*, the length of time it takes to walk a furlong or two. A furlong is an eighth of a mile).
4. (He who is) not bold is unlucky.

4215 And gan awake,° and wente hir out to pisse,   *woke up*
     And cam agayn, and gan hir cradel misse,
     And groped heer and ther, but she fond noon.
     "Allas!" quod she, "I hadde almost misgoon;°   *gone amiss*
     I hadde almost gon to the clerkes bed—
4220 Ey, *benedicite*, thanne hadde I foule y-sped!"⁵
     And forth she gooth til she the cradel fond;
     She gropeth alwey° forther with hir hond,   *ever*
     And fond the bed, and thoghte noght but good,°   *everything was well*
     By cause that the cradel by it stood,
4225 And niste° wher she was, for it was derk;   *knew not*
     But faire and wel she creep° in to the clerk,°   *crept / scholar*
     And lyth° ful stille, and wolde han caught a sleep.°   *lies / fallen asleep*
     Withinne a whyl this John the clerk up leep,°   *leapt*
     And on this gode wyf he leyth on sore.°   *sets to it vigorously*
4230 So mery a fit ne hadde she nat ful yore;⁶
     He priketh harde and depe as he were mad.
     This joly lyf han thise two clerkes lad°   *led*
     Til that the thridde cok⁷ bigan to singe.
        Aleyn wex° wery in the daweninge,°   *grew / at dawn*
4235 For he had swonken° al the longe night,   *labored*
     And seyde, "Fare weel, Malyne, swete wight!
     The day is come; I may no lenger byde;°   *remain*
     But everemo, wher so° I go° or ryde,   *wherever / walk*
     I is thyn awen clerk, swa have I seel!"⁸
4240   "Now, dere lemman,"° quod she, "go, far weel!   *sweetheart*
     But er° thou go, o° thing I wol thee telle: *before / one*
     Whan that thou wendest homward by the melle,°   *mill*
     Right at the entree of the dore bihinde,
     Thou shalt a cake° of half a busshel finde   *loaf*
4245 That was y-maked of thyn owene mele,°   *meal*
     Which that I heelp° my sire for to stele.   *helped*
     And, gode lemman, God thee save and kepe!"
     And with that word almost she gan to wepe.°   *fell to weeping*
        Aleyn up rist,° and thoughte, "Er° that it dawe,°   *rises / Before / dawns*
4250 I wol go crepen in by my felawe,"
     And fond the cradel with his hand anon.°   *at once*
     "By God," thoghte he, "al wrang° I have misgon.°   *wrong / gone amiss*
     Myn heed is toty° of° my swink° tonight: *dizzy / from / labor*
     That maketh me that I go nat aright.
4255 I woot° wel by the cradel I have misgo—   *know*
     Heere lyth the miller and his wyf also."
     And forth he goth, a twenty devel way,°   *straight to the devil*
     Unto the bed ther as° the miller lay—   *there where*
     He wende have cropen by his felawe John⁹—

5. Aye, bless me! then I would have fared badly.
6. She hadn't had so merry a bout for a long time.
7. The third crow of the cock that heralds dawn.
8. I'm your very own scholar, as I hope to have bliss.
9. He thought to have crept in alongside his friend John.

4260 And by the millere in he creep° anon,   *crept*
     And caughte hym by the nekke, and softe he spak.
     He seyde, "Thou, John, thou swynes-heed,° awak   *swine's-head*
     For Cristes saule, and heer a noble game.°   *great joke*
     For by that lord that called is Seint Jame,°   *James*
4265 As° I have thryes° in this shorte night   *So / thrice*
     Swyved the milleres doghter bolt upright,[1]
     Whyl thow hast as a coward been agast.°   *afraid*
         "Ye, false harlot,"° quod the millere, "hast?   *rascal*
     A! false traitour! false clerk!" quod he,
4270 "Thou shalt be deed, by Goddes dignitee!
     Who dorste° be so bold to disparage°   *would dare / dishonor*
     My doghter, that is come of swich linage?"°   *such (high) birth*
     And by the throte-bolle° he caughte Alayn;   *Adam's apple*
     And he hente hym despitously agayn,[2]
4275 And on the nose he smoot him with his fest°—   *fist*
     Doun ran the blody streem upon his brest.
     And in° the floor, with nose and mouth tobroke,°   *on / smashed*
     They walwe° as doon two pigges in a poke.   *wallow*
     And up they goon, and doun agayn anon,°   *immediately*
4280 Til that the miller sporned at a stoon,[3]
     And doun he fil bakward upon his wyf,
     That wiste° no thing of this nyce° stryf,   *Who knew / foolish*
     For she was falle aslepe a lyte wight°   *little bit*
     With John the clerk, that waked hadde al night;
4285 And with the fal, out of hir sleep she breyde.°   *started*
     "Help, holy croys of Bromeholm," she seyde,[4]
     "*In manus tuas!*° Lord, to thee I calle!   *Into thy hands*
     Awak, Symond! the feend° is on me falle,°   *fiend / fallen*
     Myn herte is broken, help, I nam but° deed: *am just about*
4290 There lyth oon upon my wombe° and on myn heed.   *belly*
     Help, Simkin, for the false clerkes fighte."
         This John sterte° up as faste as ever he mighte,   *leaped*
     And graspeth by° the walles to and fro,   *gropes along*
     To finde a staf; and she sterte° up also,   *leaped*
4295 And knew the estres° bet° than dide this John,   *interior / better*
     And by the wal a staf she fond anon,
     And saugh° a litel shimering of a light—   *saw*
     For at an hole in shoon the mone bright—
     And by that light she saugh hem bothe two,
4300 But sikerly° she niste° who was who,   *truly / knew not*
     But as° she saugh a whyt° thing in hir yë   *Except that / white*
     And whan she gan° this whyte thing espye,   *did*
     She wende the clerk hadde wered a volupeer,[5]

1. Made love to the miller's daughter (as she lay) flat on her back.
2. And he (Alan) grabbed him fiercely in return.
3. Until the miller tripped on a stone.
4. "Help, holy cross of Bromholm," she said (a famous relic, supposed to be a piece of the true cross of Christ, brought to Bromholm in Norfolk in 1223).
5. She thought the scholar had worn a nightcap.

And with the staf she drough° ay neer° and neer,   *drew / ever nearer*
4305 And wende han hit this Aleyn at the fulle,[6]
And smoot the millere on the pyled° skulle   *bald*
That° doun he gooth and cryde, "Harrow!° I dye!"   *So that / Help!*
Thise clerkes bete° him weel and lete him lye,   *beat*
And greythen hem,° and toke hir hors anon,   *get themselves ready*
4310 And eek hire mele,° and on hir wey they gon.   *meal*
And at the mille yet they toke hir cake
Of half a busshel flour, ful wel y-bake.°   *baked*
　　Thus is the proude millere wel y-bete,°   *beaten*
And hath y-lost the grinding of the whete,
4315 And payed for the soper everideel°   *completely*
Of Aleyn and of John, that bette° him weel;   *beat*
His wyf is swyved, and his doghter als.[7]
Lo, swich it is° a millere to be fals!   *thus it is for*
And therefore this proverbe is seyd ful sooth,
4320 "Him thar nat wene wel that yvel dooth;[8]
A gylour° shal himself bigyled° be."   *beguiler, deceiver / deceived*
And God, that sitteth heighe in magestee,
Save al this compaignye grete and smale!
Thus have I quit° the Millere in my tale.   *repaid*

The Cook's Prologue and Tale

The Prologue

4325 　　The Cook of London, whyl the Reve spak,
For joye him thoughte he clawed him on the bak.[1]
"Ha ha!" quod he, "for Cristes passioun,
This millere hadde a sharp conclusioun
Upon° his argument of herbergage!"°   *To / discussion about lodging(s)*
4330 Wel seyde Salomon° in his langage,   *Solomon*
'Ne bringe nat every man into thyn house.'°   *(cf. Ecclesiasticus 11:31)*
For herberwinge° by nighte is perilous.   *lodging*
Wel oghte a man avysed° for to be   *cautious*
Whom that he broughte into his privetee.°   *privacy*
4335 I pray to God, so yeve° me sorwe and care   *give*
If ever, sith I highte Hogge of Ware,[2]
Herde I a millere bettre y-set a-werk.°   *set to work, tricked*
He hadde a jape° of malice in the derk.   *joke*
But God forbede that we stinten° here,   *leave off*
4340 And therfore, if ye vouchesauf to here°   *agree to hear*
A tale of me, that am a povre man,
I wol you telle as wel as evere I can

6. And thought to have hit this Alan square-on.
7. His wife's been made love to, and his daughter as well.
8. He need not expect good who does evil.
1. For the joy (he felt), it seemed to him the Reeve was scratching him on the back.
2. If ever, since I first was called Hodge (Roger) of Ware (in Hertfordshire).

A little jape that fil° in our citee."   *befell, occurred*
    Our Host answerde and seide, "I graunte it thee;°   *i.e., I agree*
4345 Now telle on, Roger, loke that° it be good;   *see to it that*
For many a pastee° hastow laten blood,[3]   *meat pie*
And many a Jakke of Dover[4] hastow sold
That hath been twyes° hoot and twyes cold.   *twice*
Of many a pilgrim hastow Cristes curs,°   *curse, i.e., been damned*
4350 For of thy persly° yet they fare the wors,°   *parsley / worse*
That they han eten° with thy stubbel-goos,[5]   *have eaten*
For in thy shoppe is many a flye loos.
Now telle on, gentil° Roger, by thy name.   *noble*
But yet I pray thee, be nat wrooth for game.[6]
4355 A man may seye ful sooth° in game and pley."   *say the whole truth*
    "Thou seist ful sooth," quod Roger, "by my fey,°   *faith*
But 'sooth pley, quaad pley,' as the Fleming seith.[7]
And therfore, Herry° Bailly, by thy feith,   *i.e., Harry*
Be thou nat wrooth, er we departen° heer,   *before we part company*
4360 Though that my tale be of an hostileer.°   *innkeeper*
But nathelees° I wol nat telle it yit,°   *nevertheless / yet*
But er we parte, ywis,° thou shalt be quit."°   *certainly / paid back*
And therwithal he lough° and made chere,°   *laughed / acted cheerfully*
And seyde his tale, as ye shul after here.

The Tale

4365   A prentis whylom° dwelled in our citee,   *apprentice once*
And of a craft of vitaillers° was he.   *victualers, foodsellers*
Gaillard° he was as goldfinch in the shawe,°   *Lively / wood, thicket*
Broun° as a berie, a propre° short felawe,   *Dark-complexioned / handsome*
With lokkes blake, y-kempt° ful fetisly.°   *combed / elegantly*
4370 Dauncen he coude so wel and jolily
That he was cleped° Perkin Revelour.°   *called / Reveller*
He was as ful of love and paramour°   *sexual desire*
As is the hyve° ful of hony° swete;   *beehive / honey*
Wel was the wenche with him mighte mete.°   *i.e., who might encounter him*
4375 At every brydale° wolde he singe and hoppe.°   *wedding party / dance*
He loved bet° the taverne than the shoppe.   *better*
For whan ther any ryding° was in Chepe,[8]   *procession, parade*
Out of the shoppe thider° wolde he lepe.°   *thither, to that place / leap*
Til that he hadde al the sighte y-seyn°   *seen*
4380 And daunced wel, he wolde nat come ageyn.°   *i.e., come back to work*
And gadered him a meinee of his sort[9]

---

3. Thou hast let blood, i.e., drawn off the gravy from unsold pies (to keep them from getting soggy).
4. Probably a name for some kind of reheated pie.
5. Goose fed only on stubble, stalks, and stumps of harvested grain.
6. Do not be wroth, angry, (at what is said) in sport.
7. "A true jest is a bad jest," as the Flemish say.
8. Cheapside, a busy market area of London with many shops.
9. And (he) gathered around him a group of (people of) his type.

To hoppe and singe and maken swich disport.°   *have such entertainment*
And ther they setten steven for to mete°   *set a time to meet*
To pleyen at the dys° in swich a strete,°   *dice / a certain street*
4385 For in the toune nas ther no° prentys   *there was no*
That fairer° coude caste a paire of dys   *more skillfully*
Than Perkin coude, and therto° he was   *in that (activity)*
    free°   *unrestrained*
Of his dispense,° in place of privetee.°   *spending / in private place(s)*
That fond° his maister wel in his chaffare,°   *i.e., discovered that fact / business*
4390 For often tyme he fond his box° ful bare.   *money box*
For sikerly° a prentis revelour   *certainly*
That haunteth dys, riot, or paramour,[1]
His maister shal it in his shoppe abye,°   *pay for*
Al° have he no part of the minstralcye.°   *Even though / i.e., entertainment*
4395 For thefte and riot, they ben convertible,°   *interchangeable*
Al conne he pleye on giterne or ribible.[2]
Revel and trouthe, as in a low degree,
They been ful wrothe al day, as men may see.[3]
    This joly prentis with his maister bood,°   *stayed*
4400 Til he were ny° out of his prentishood,°   *nearly / apprenticeship*
Al were he snibbed° bothe erly and late,   *Even though he was rebuked*
And somtyme lad with revel to Newgate.[4]
But atte laste his maister him bithoghte,°   *thought to himself*
Upon a day whan he his paper soghte,[5]
4405 Of a proverbe that seith this same word:
"Wel bet° is roten appel out of hord°   *better / hoard, barrel*
Than that it rotie al the remenaunt."°   *cause all the rest to rot*
So fareth it by° a riotous servaunt—   *So it is in regard to*
It is ful lasse° harm to lete him pace,°   *much less / go, leave*
4410 Than he shende° alle the servants in the place.   *ruin*
Therefore his maister yaf° him acquitance,°   *gave / discharge*
And bad him go, with sorwe and with meschance.°   *bad luck (to him)*
And thus this joly prentis hadde his leve.°   *permission to go*
Now lat him riote al the night or leve.°   *leave off*
4415   And for° ther is no theef withoute a louke,°   *since / accomplice*
That helpeth him to wasten° and to souke°   *spend lavishly / suck, extract*
Of that° he brybe° can or borwe may,   *Whatever (money) / steal*
Anon° he sente his bed and his array°   *Quickly / clothing*
Unto a compeer° of his owne sort,   *comrade*
4420 That lovede dys and revel and disport,

1. Who haunts (pursues) dicing, riotous living, or womanizing.
2. However well he (the apprentice) can play a cittern (guitar) or a rebec (fiddle); i.e., whatever his charms and skills. Some critics think "he" in this line refers to the master, whose musical accomplishments contrast with the "minstrelsy" of Perkin and his friends.
3. Revelry and honesty in a person of low social standing are always at odds, as people can see.
4. And sometimes led away to Newgate Prison with revelry. (Minstrels often accompanied people led off to prison in order to shame them publicly.)
5. One day when he (Perkin) sought his certificate (that would indicate release from his contract as an apprentice).

And hadde a wyf that heeld for countenance°   *for the sake of appearances*
A shoppe, and swyved° for hir sustenance.°⁶   *had sex / livelihood*

The Wife of Bath's Prologue and Tale

The Prologue

"Experience, though noon auctoritee¹
Were in this world, is right ynough° for me   *certainly enough*
To speke of wo that is in mariage:
For, lordinges, sith° I twelf yeer was of age,   *since*
5 Thonked be God that is eterne on lyve,°   *alive eternally*
Housbondes at chirche dore I have had fyve²
(If I so ofte myghte have y-wedded be)
And alle were worthy men in hir degree.°   *within their station*
But me was told, certeyn,° nat longe agon is,°   *truly / not long ago*
10 That sith that Crist ne wente nevere but onis°   *once*
To wedding in the Cane° of Galilee,   *Cana*
That by the same ensample° taughte he me   *example*
That I ne sholde wedded be but ones.°   *once*
Herkne eek, lo, which a sharp word for the nones³
15 Besyde a welle, Jesus, God and man,
Spak in repreve° of the Samaritan: *reproof*
'Thou hast y-had fyve housbondes,' quod he,
'And that ilke° man that now hath thee   *that same*
Is noght thyn housbond'—thus seyde he certeyn.
20 What that he mente therby, I can nat seyn,°   *say*
But that° I axe,° why that the fifthe man   *Except / ask*
Was noon housbond to the Samaritan?
How manye mighte she have in mariage?
Yet herde I nevere tellen in myn age°   *in all my days*
25 Upon° this nombre diffinicioun.°   *Of / definition, explanation*
Men may devyne° and glosen° up and doun,   *guess / interpret, comment upon*
But wel I woot expres,° withoute lye,°   *know particularly / lie*
God bad us for to wexe° and multiplye: *wax, increase*
That gentil° text can I wel understonde.   *noble*
30 Eek° wel I woot° he seyde, myn housbonde   *Also / know*
Sholde lete° fader and moder, and take to me;   *leave*
But of no nombre mencioun made he,

6. Most scholars believe that for one reason or another Chaucer never finished the Cook's Tale. Scribes of the *Canterbury Tales* seem to have expected something more—one wrote in the margin of an early manuscript, "Of this Cokes tale maked Chaucer na moore." In some cases scribes added short endings to the tale or substituted the non-Chaucerian outlaw romance, the *Tale of Gamelyn*.

1. The authoritative truths of learned tradition, preserved in writings from the past.

2. Medieval marriages were performed at the church door. Only the nuptial mass was within the church.

3. (And) lo, hear also what a sharp word on the matter ("for the nones" is a tag-ending: "for the occasion," "to the purpose," but often nearly meaningless). The incident referred to can be found in John 4:5–42, printed on pp. 379–80.

Of bigamye or of octogamye.[4]
Why sholde men thanne speke of it vileinye?°   *rude things, reproach*
35   Lo, here the wyse king, daun Salomon;[5]
I trowe° he hadde wyves mo than oon.   *believe*
As wolde° God it leveful° were unto me   *Would to / lawful*
To be refresshed° half so ofte as he!   *i.e., sexually*
Which yifte° of God hadde he for alle his wyvis!   *What a gift*
40   No man hath swich° that in this world alyve is.   *such*
God woot° this noble king, as to my wit,°   *knows / understanding*
The firste night had many a mery fit°   *bout, turn*
With ech of hem, so wel was him on lyve![6]
Blessed be God that I have wedded fyve,
44a   Of whiche I have pyked out° the beste,[7]   *extracted*
Bothe of here nether purs and of here cheste.[8]
Diverse scoles° maken parfyt clerkes,°   *schools / perfect scholars*
And diverse practyk° in many sondry° werkes   *practice / sundry, varied*
Maketh the werkman parfyt sekirly:°   *assuredly*
44f   Of fyve husbondes scoleiyng° am I.   *schooling*
45   Welcome the sixte, whan that evere he shall!°   *shall (come along)*
For sothe I wol nat kepe me chast in al.°   *entirely chaste*
Whan myn housbond is fro the world y-gon,
Som Cristen man shal wedde me anon;°   *at once*
For thanne th'Apostle° seith that I am free   *St. Paul*
50   To wedde, a Goddes half,° where it lyketh° me.   *on God's behalf / pleases*
He seith that to be wedded is no sinne:
Bet° is to be wedded than to brinne.°   *Better / burn*
What rekketh me° thogh folk seye vileinye°   *do I care / speak ill*
Of shrewed Lameth° and his bigamye?   *accursed Lamech*
55   I woot° wel Abraham was an holy man,   *know*
And Jacob eek, as ferforth° as I can;°   *far / know*
And ech of hem° hadde wyves mo° than two,   *each of them / more*
And many another holy man also.
Wher can ye seye,° in any manere age,°   *say / any age whatever*
60   That hye° God defended° mariage   *high / forbade*
By expres word? I pray you, telleth me.
Or where comanded he virginitee?
I woot as wel as ye, it is no drede,°   *no doubt about it*
Th'Apostel,° whan he speketh of maydenhede,   *St. Paul*
65   He seyde that precept° therof hadde he noon.   *i.e., commandment*
Men may conseille° a womman to been oon,   *advise*
But conseilling is no comandement:
He putte it in oure owene° jugement.   *own*
For hadde God comanded maydenhede,
70   Thanne hadde he dampned° wedding with the° dede.   *damned / in that*

4. Here, marriages in succession.
5. Consider the wise king, lord Solomon. (According to 1 Kings 11:3, he had seven hundred wives and three hundred concubines.)
6. With each of them, so fortunate was his life.
7. Lines 44a–44f are probably a late addition; the best manuscripts exclude them.
8. Both from their lower purse (i.e., testicles) and from their (money-)chest.

And certes, if ther were no seed y-sowe,°   *sown*
Virginitee, thanne wherof sholde it growe?
Poul dorste nat comanden, atte leste,[9]
A thing of which his maister yaf noon heste.°   *gave no order*
75 The dart° is set up for virginitee;   *dart (given as prize)*
Cacche who so may: who renneth best lat see.[1]
   But this word is nat take of every wight,
But ther as God list give it of his might.[2]
I woot° wel that th'Apostel was a mayde,°   *know / virgin*
80 But natheless,° thogh that he wroot° and sayde   *nevertheless / wrote*
He wolde° that every wight° were swich° as he,   *wished / person / such*
Al nis° but conseil to virginitee,   *All (this) is nothing*
And for to been a wyf, he yaf° me leve°   *gave / leave, permission*
Of° indulgence. So nis it no repreve°   *By / reproach*
85 To wedde me, if that my make dye,
Withoute excepcioun of bigamye,[3]
Al° were it good no womman for to touche—   *Although*
He mente as in his bed or in his couche—
For peril is bothe fyr and tow t'assemble;[4]
90 Ye knowe what this ensample° may resemble.   *example*
This al and som: he heeld virginitee
More parfit than wedding in freletee.
Freletee clepe I, but if that he and she[5]
Wolde leden° al hir lyf in chastitee.   *Should wish to lead*
95   I graunte it wel, I have noon envye
Thogh maydenhede preferre° bigamye.   *be preferred over*
Hem lyketh° to be clene, body and goost.°   *They wish / soul, spirit*
Of myn estaat° I nil nat° make no boost: *condition / will not*
For wel ye knowe, a lord in his houshold
100 He hath nat every vessel al of gold;
Somme been of tree,° and doon hir lord servyse.   *wood*
God clepeth° folk to him in sondry wyse,°   *calls / various ways*
And everich hath of God a propre yifte,°   *his own special gift*
Som this, som that, as Him lyketh shifte.°   *it pleases Him to ordain*
105   Virginitee is greet perfeccioun,
And continence eek with devocioun.[6]
But Crist, that of perfeccioun is welle,°   *the well, the source*
Bad° nat every wight° he sholde go selle   *Commanded / person*
All that he hadde and give it to the pore,°   *poor*
110 And in swich wyse° folwe him and his fore.°   *such a way / footsteps*
He spak to hem that wolde live parfitly,
And lordinges, by youre leve,° that am nat I.   *leave*
I wol bistowe the flour° of al myn age   *the flower, the best part*

9. (St.) Paul did not dare in the least command.
1. Catch (win) it whoever may: let's see who runs the best.
2. But this counsel (i.e., the preference for virginity) is not required of every person but (only)
   there where God is pleased to impose it by His might.
3. To wed (again) if my mate die, without being criticized for bigamy.
4. For it is perilous to bring together both fire and flax.
5. "Frailty" I call it, unless he and she.
6. And continence also (when) accompanied by devotion.

In the actes and in fruit of mariage.
115   Telle me also, to what conclusioun°   *end, purpose*
Were membres maad of generacioun
And of so parfit wys a wright y-wroght?[7]
Trusteth right wel, they were nat maad for noght.
Glose° whoso wole,° and seye bothe up and doun   *Interpret / will*
120 That they were maked for purgacioun
Of urine, and oure bothe° thinges smale   *both our*
Were eek to knowe° a female from a male,   *to distinguish*
And for noon other cause: sey ye no?
The experience° woot° wel it is noght so.   *experience (in general) / knows*
125 So that the clerkes be nat with me wrothe,°   *wroth, angry*
I sey this, that they maked been for bothe—
This is to seye, for office,° and for ese°   *natural duty / pleasure*
Of engendrure,° ther° we nat God displese.   *In procreation / there where*
Why sholde men elles° in hir bokes sette   *otherwise*
130 That man shal yelde° to his wyf hire dette?°   *pay / what is owing her*
Now wherwith° sholde he make his payement   *by what means*
If he ne used his sely° instrument?   *simple, blessed*
Thanne° were they maad upon a creature   *Therefore*
To purge uryne, and eek for engendrure.
135   But I seye noght that every wight is holde,°   *beholden, bound*
That hath swich harneys° as I to yow tolde,   *such equipment*
To goon and usen hem in engendrure:
Thanne sholde men take of chastitee no cure.[8]
Crist was a mayde° and shapen as° a man,   *virgin / formed like*
140 And many a seint, sith that° the world bigan,   *since*
Yet lived they evere in parfit chastitee.
I nil° envye no virginitee: *will not*
Lat hem be breed° of pured whete-seed,°   *bread / finest wheat*
And lat us wyves hoten° barly-breed.°   *be called / barley bread*
145 And yet with barly-breed, Mark° telle can,   *St. Mark*
Oure Lord Jesu refresshed° many a man.   *i.e., fed*
In swich estaat° as God hath cleped° us   *condition / called*
I wol persevere, I nam nat precious.[9]
In wyfhode I wol use myn instrument
150 As frely° as my Makere hath it sent.   *generously*
If I be daungerous,° God yeve° me sorwe!   *standoffish / give*
Myn housbond shal it have bothe eve and morwe,°   *morning*
Whan that him list° com forth and paye his dette.   *it pleases him to*
An housbonde I wol have, I wol nat lette,°   *will not leave off*
155 Which shal be bothe my dettour and my thral,°   *thrall, slave*
And have his tribulacioun withal°   *besides*
Upon his flessh, whyl that I am his wyf.
I have the power duringe al my lyf
Upon° his propre° body, and noght he: *Over / own*

---

7. And by so perfect and wise a workman? (i.e., God).
8. Then people wouldn't be concerned about chastity.
9. I will continue; I'm not overly fastidious.

160 Right thus th'Apostel° tolde it unto me, *St. Paul*
And bad oure housbondes for to love us weel.
Al this sentence me lyketh every deel."[1]
     Up sterte the Pardoner, and that anon.[2]
"Now dame," quod he, "by God and by Seint John,
165 Ye been a noble prechour° in this cas!° *preacher / matter*
I was aboute to wedde a wyf. Allas,
What° sholde I bye° it on my flesh so dere? *Why / pay for*
Yet hadde I levere° wedde no wyf to-yere!"° *rather / this year*
     "Abyde!"° quod° she, "my tale is nat bigonne. *Wait / said*
170 Nay, thou shalt drinken of another tonne° *tun, cask*
Er that I go, shal savoure wors than ale.[3]
And whan that I have told thee forth my tale
Of tribulacioun in mariage,
Of which I am expert in al myn age—[4]
175 This° to seyn, myself° have been the whippe— *This is / (I) myself*
Than maystow chese° whether thou wolt sippe° *mayst thou choose / sip*
Of thilke° tonne that I shal abroche.° *that same / open*
Be war° of it, er thou to ny° approche, *wary / too near*
For I shall telle ensamples° mo° than ten. *examples / more*
180 'Whoso that nil be war° by othere men, *Whoever will not be warned*
By him shul othere men corrected be.'
The same wordes wryteth Ptholomee:° *Ptolemy*
Rede in his Almageste,° and take it there." *an astronomical treatise*
     "Dame, I wolde praye yow, if youre wil it were,"
185 Seyde this Pardoner, "as ye bigan,
Telle forth youre tale, spareth° for no man, *hold back*
And teche us yonge men of youre praktike."° *practice*
     "Gladly," quod she, "sith it may yow lyke.° *please*
But yet I praye to al this companye,
190 If that I speke after my fantasye,° *according to my fancy*
As taketh not agrief of that I seye;[5]
For myn entente° nis° but for to pleye. *intention / is not*
     Now sires, now wol I telle forth my tale.
As evere mote° I drinken wyn or ale, *might*
195 I shal seye sooth,° tho° housbondes that I *tell the truth / (of) those*
     hadde,
As three of hem were gode and two were badde.
The three men were gode, and riche, and olde;
Unnethe mighte they the statut holde[6]
In° which that they were bounden unto me. *By*
200 Ye woot° wel what I mene of this, pardee!° *know / by God*
As help me God, I laughe whan I thinke
How pitously° a-night° I made hem swinke,° *pitiably / at night / labor*

1. All this lesson pleases me, every bit (of it).
2. The Pardoner broke in (*lit.*, started up) at once.
3. Before I go, (which) shall taste worse than ale.
4. About which I have been expert all my life.
5. Not to take amiss that (which) I say.
6. They could scarcely observe the statute (law).

And by my fey, I tolde of it no stoor.[7]
They had me yeven° hir lond and hir tresoor;°   *given / wealth*
205 Me neded nat do lenger diligence[8]
To winne hir love, or doon hem reverence.°   *to honor them*
They loved me so wel, by God above,
That I ne tolde no deyntee of° hir love!   *took no pleasure in*
A wys womman wol bisye hire evere in oon[9]
210 To gete hire love, ye, ther as° she hath noon.   *there where*
But sith I hadde hem hoolly° in myn hond,   *wholly*
And sith they hadde me yeven° all hir lond,   *given*
What° sholde I taken keep° hem for to plese,   *Why / heed*
But° it were for my profit and myn ese?°   *Unless / comfort*
215 I sette hem so a-werke,° by my fey,°   *working / faith*
That many a night they songen° 'weilawey!'°   *sang / woe is me*
The bacoun was nat fet for hem, I trowe,[1]
That som men han in Essex at Dunmowe.
I governed hem so wel after° my lawe   *according to*
220 That ech° of hem ful blisful° was and fawe°   *each / happy / fain, eager*
To bringe me gaye thinges fro the fayre.°   *fair*
They were ful glad whan I spak to hem fayre,°   *nicely*
For God it woot, I chidde° hem spitously.°   *chided, scolded / spitefully*
     Now herkneth° how I bar me° proprely: *listen / conducted myself*
225 Ye wyse° wyves, that can understonde,   *prudent*
Thus shul ye speke and bere hem wrong on honde,°   *put them in the wrong*
For half so boldely can ther no man
Swere and lyen as a womman can.
I sey nat this by° wyves that ben wyse,   *concerning*
230 But if° it be whan they hem misavyse.°   *Unless / act ill-advisedly*
A wys wyf, if that she can hir good,
Shal beren him on hond the cow is wood,[2]
And take witnesse of° hir owene mayde   *take as witness*
Of° hir assent.° But herkneth° how I sayde: *With / consent / listen*
235 'Sire olde kaynard, is this thyn array?[3]
Why is my neighebores wyf so gay?°   *gaily dressed*
She is honoured over al ther° she goth:°   *everywhere / goes*
I sitte at hoom, I have no thrifty cloth.°   *suitable clothing*
What dostow° at my neighebores hous?   *dost thou*
240 Is she so fair?° artow° so amorous?   *beautiful / art thou*
What rowne° ye with oure mayde? *benedicite!*°   *whisper / God bless us*
Sire olde lechour, lat thy japes be!°   *leave off thy pranks*
And if I have a gossib° or a freend,   *gossip, confidante*

---

7. And by my faith, I set no store by it.
8. It wasn't necessary that I be diligent any longer.
9. A prudent woman will exert herself constantly.
1. The bacon wasn't fetched for them I'm sure. (A side of bacon was awarded annually at Dun-
   mow in Essex to couples who could claim they had not quarreled or been unhappy in their
   marriage that year.)
2. A prudent (skillful) wife, if she knows her (own) good, shall trick him into believing the
   chough is mad (refers to common stories—Chaucer's own *Manciple's Tale* is an example—in
   which a speaking bird tells tales to the husband of a wife's infidelity).
3. Old dotard, sir, is this how you dress me?

Withouten gilt, thou chydest as a feend,[4]
245 If that I walke or pleye unto his hous!
    Thou comest hoom as dronken as a mous,°   *mouse*
    And prechest on thy bench, with yvel preef![5]
    Thou seist° to me, it is a greet meschief°   *sayst / misfortune*
    To wedde a povre womman, for costage.°   *because of expense*
250 And if that she be riche, of heigh parage,°   *parentage, blood*
    Thanne seistow° that it is a tormentrye°   *sayst thou / torment*
    To suffre° hire pryde and hire malencolye.°   *endure / melancholy, moodiness*
    And if that she be fair,° thou verray knave,°   *pretty / true rascal*
    Thou seyst that every holour° wol hire have: *lecher*
255 She may no whyle in chastitee abyde°   *abide, remain*
    That° is assailled upon ech a syde.°   *Who / on every side*
       Thou seyst som folk desyren us for richesse,°   *(our) money*
    Somme for oure shap,° and somme for oure fairnesse,° *figure / beauty*
    And som for° she can outher° singe or daunce,   *because / either*
260 And som for gentillesse° and daliaunce,°   *good breeding / flirtatiousness*
    Som for hir handes and hir armes smale;°   *slender*
    Thus goth al to the devel, by thy tale.°   *according to thy account*
    Thou seyst men may nat kepe° a castel wal,   *hold*
    It may so longe assailled been over al.°   *everywhere*
265   And if that she be foul,° thou seist that she   *ugly*
    Coveiteth° every man that she may se;   *Desires*
    For as a spaynel° she wol on him lepe,   *spaniel*
    Til that she finde som man hire to chepe.°   *to buy her wares*
    Ne noon so grey goos goth ther in the lake[6]
270 As, seistow,° that wol been withoute make.°   *sayst thou / a mate*
    And seyst, it is an hard thing for to welde°   *control*
    A thing that no man wol, his thankes,° helde.°   *willingly / hold*
    Thus seistow, lorel,° whan thow goost to bedde,   *you wretch*
    And that no wys man nedeth for to wedde,
275 Ne no man that entendeth unto° hevene.   *aims to get to*
    With wilde thonder-dint° and firy levene° *thunderclap / fiery lightning*
    Mote° thy welked° nekke be to-broke!°   *May / withered / broken*
       Thow seyst that dropping° houses and eek smoke   *leaking*
    And chyding wyves maken men to flee
280 Out of hir owene hous; a, *benedicite!*°   *God bless us*
    What eyleth° swich an old man for to chyde?   *ails*
    Thow seyst we wyves wol oure vyces° hyde   *vices*
    Til we be fast,° and thanne we wol hem shewe°— *secure (married) / show*
    Wel may that be a proverbe of a shrewe!°   *(fit) for a villain*
285   Thou seist that oxen, asses, hors,° and houndes,   *horses*
    They been assayed° at diverse stoundes;°   *tested / various times*
    Bacins,° lavours,° er° that men hem bye,° *Basins / washbowls / before / buy*
    Spones° and stoles,° and al swich   *Spoons / stools*
       housbondrye,°   *all such housewares*

4. Without guilt (on our part), thou scoldest like a devil.
5. And preachest (sermons, sitting) on thy bench—bad luck to you!
6. There swims in the lake no goose so gray.

And so been pottes, clothes, and array;°   *ornament(s)*
290 But folk of wyves maken noon assay°   *test*
Til they be wedded. Olde dotard shrewe!°   *wretched rascal*
And thanne, seistow,° we wol oure vices shewe.   *sayst thou*
        Thou seist also that it displeseth me
But if that° thou wolt preyse° my beautee,   *Unless / praise*
295 And but° thou poure° alwey upon my face,   *unless / gaze intently*
And clepe° me "faire dame" in every place;   *call*
And but thou make a feste° on thilke° day   *feast / that same*
That I was born, and make me fresh and gay,
And but thou do to my norice° honour,   *nurse*
300 And to my chamberere° withinne my bour,°   *chambermaid / bower, bedroom*
And to my fadres folk° and his allyes°—   *relatives / connections*
Thus seistow, olde barel ful of lyes!°   *lies (pun on lees)*
        And yet of oure apprentice Janekyn,
For his crispe heer,° shyninge as gold so fyn,   *curly hair*
305 And for° he squiereth° me bothe up and doun,   *because / escorts*
Yet hastow caught a fals suspecioun.[7]
I wol hym noght,° thogh thou were deed tomorwe.   *I don't want him*
        But tel me this, why hydestow, with sorwe,[8]
The keyes of thy cheste° awey fro me?   *for storing valuables*
310 It is my good° as wel as thyn, pardee.°   *property / by God*
What, wenestow make an idiot of oure dame?[9]
Now by that lord that called is Seint Jame,°   *St. James*
Thou shalt nat bothe, thogh that thou were wood,°   *mad (with rage)*
Be maister of my body and of my good;°   *goods, possessions*
315 That oon thou shalt forgo, maugree thyne yën;[1]
What helpith thee of me to enquere° or spyën?   *inquire*
I trowe,° thou woldest loke° me in thy chiste!°   *believe / lock / chest*
Thou sholdest seye, "Wyf, go wher thee liste;°   *it pleases thee*
Tak your disport,° I wol nat leve no talis.°   *pleasure / believe any tales*
320 I knowe yow for a trewe wyf, dame Alis."°   *Alice*
We love no man that taketh kepe or charge°   *takes heed or cares*
Wher that we goon; we wol ben at oure large.°   *liberty*
        Of alle men y-blessed moot° he be,   *may*
The wyse astrologien° Daun Ptholome,°   *astrologer / Lord Ptolemy*
325 That seith this proverbe in his Almageste:
"Of alle men his wisdom is the hyeste,°   *greatest*
That rekketh° nevere who hath the world in honde."°   *cares / in (his) control*
By this proverbe thou shalt understonde,
Have thou ynogh, what thar thee recche or care[2]
330 How merily that othere folkes fare?°   *get along*
For certeyn, olde dotard, by youre leve,°   *leave*
Ye shul have queynte° right ynough at eve.   *i.e., sex (punning on ME "cunte")*

7. I.e., become wrongly suspicious.
8. But tell me this, why dost thou hide (may you have sorrow).
9. What, do you think to make an idiot of our mistress? (She here uses a kind of royal plural:
she means herself.)
1. Thou shalt give up one (of them), despite thy eyes (i.e., despite anything you can do).
2. As long as thou hast enough, what need for thee to take heed or care.

He is to° greet a nigard that wol werne°   *too / refuse*
A man to lighte a candle at his lanterne;
335 He shal have never the lasse° light, pardee.   *less*
Have thou ynough, thee thar nat pleyne thee.°   *thou needst not complain*
     Thou seyst also that if we make us gay
With clothing and with precious array,°   *ornaments*
That it is peril of° oure chastitee;   *a danger to*
340 And yet, with sorwe, thou most enforce thee,[3]
And seye thise wordes in th'Apostles° name: *St. Paul*
"In habit° maad with chastitee and shame,   *garment(s)*
Ye wommen shul apparaille yow,"° quod he,   *dress yourselves*
"And noght in tressed heer° and gay perree,°   *braided hair / precious stones*
345 As° perles, ne with gold, ne clothes riche."   *Such as*
After thy text, ne after thy rubriche
I wol nat wirche as muchel as a gnat.[4]
     Thou seydest this, that I was lyk a cat:
For whoso wolde senge° a cattes skin,°   *singe / i.e., fur*
350 Thanne wolde the cat wel dwellen in his in;°   *lodgings*
And if the cattes skin be slyk° and gay,   *sleek*
She wol nat dwelle in house half a day,
But forth she wole, er° any day be dawed,°   *before / has dawned*
To shewe hir skin and goon a-caterwawed.°   *caterwauling*
355 This is to seye, if I be gay, sire shrewe,°   *wretch*
I wol renne out,° my borel° for to shewe.   *run about / clothing*
     Sire olde fool, what helpeth thee to spyën?
Thogh thou preye° Argus, with his hundred yën,°   *beg / eyes*
To be my warde-cors,° as he can° best,   *bodyguard / knows how*
360 In feith, he shal nat kepe me but me lest;°   *unless I wish*
Yet coude I make his berd, so moot I thee.[5]
     Thou seydest eek that ther ben thinges three,
The whiche thinges troublen al this erthe,
And that no wight ne may endure the ferthe.°   *fourth*
365 O leve° sire shrewe, Jesu shorte° thy lyf!   *dear / may Jesus shorten*
Yet prechestow° and seyst an hateful wyf   *Still thou preachest*
Y-rekened° is for° oon of thise meschances.°   *Counted / as / misfortunes*
Been ther none othere maner° resemblances   *kind of*
That ye may lykne° youre parables to,   *liken*
370 But if° a sely° wyf be oon of tho?°   *Unless / innocent / those*
     Thou lykenest eek wommanes love to helle,
To bareyne° lond, ther° water may not dwelle;   *barren / where*
Thou lyknest it also to wilde fyr.[6]
The more it brenneth,° the more it hath desyr   *burns*
375 To consume every thing that brent wol be.°   *can be burned*
Thou seyst that right° as wormes shende° a tree,   *just / damage*
Right so a wyf destroyeth hire housbonde;

3. And further—sorrow beset thee!—thou must strengthen thyself (in the argument).
4. I will not behave according to thy text or thy rubric (i.e., interpretation) as much as (would)
   a gnat.
5. I could still trick him, as I hope to thrive.
6. "Greek fire," a highly inflammable compound used in sea warfare.

This knowe they that been to wyves bonde.'°   *bound*
     Lordinges, right thus, as ye have understonde,
380 Bar I stifly myne olde housbondes on honde⁷
    That thus they seyden in hir dronkenesse;
    And al was fals, but that° I took witnesse   *and yet*
    On° Janekin and on my nece° also.   *From / niece*
    O Lord, the peyne I dide° hem and the wo,   *suffering I caused*
385 Ful giltelees, by Goddes swete pyne!°   *suffering*
    For as° an hors I coude byte° and whyne.°   *like / bite / whinny*
    I coude pleyne,° thogh I were in the gilt,°   *complain / wrong*
    Or elles° often tyme hadde I ben spilt.°   *otherwise / ruined*
    Whoso that first to mille comth, first grint.°   *grinds (his grain)*
390 I pleyned first: so was oure werre° y-stint.°   *strife / concluded*
    They were ful glad to excusen hem° ful blyve°   *themselves / quickly*
    Of thing of which they nevere agilte° hir lyve.   *were guilty (in)*
    Of wenches wolde I beren hem on honde,°   *accuse them (falsely)*
    Whan that for syk° unnethes° mighte they stonde.   *illness / scarcely*
395   Yet tikled° I his herte, for that he   *tickled, pleased*
    Wende° that I hadde of him so greet chiertee.°   *Thought / affection*
    I swoor that al my walkinge out by nighte
    Was for t'espye° wenches that he dighte.°   *to spy out / lay with*
    Under that colour° hadde I many a mirthe,°   *pretense / merry time*
400 For al swich wit° is yeven° us in oure birthe.   *such cleverness / given*
    Deceite, weping, spinning God hath yive°   *given*
    To wommen kindely° whyl they may live.   *by nature*
    And thus of o° thing I avaunte° me: *one / boast*
    Atte° ende I hadde the bettre in ech degree,°   *At the / in every way*
405 By sleighte,° or force, or by som maner° thing,   *trick / kind of*
    As by continuel murmur or grucching.°   *grumbling*
    Namely abedde° hadden they meschaunce:°   *Especially in bed / misfortune*
    Ther wolde I chyde° and do° hem no plesaunce;°   *scold / give / pleasure*
    I wolde no lenger in the bed abyde,
410 If that I felte his arm over my syde,
    Til he had maad his raunson° unto me;   *paid his ransom*
    Thanne wolde I suffre° him do his nycetee.°   *endure, allow / foolishness, lust*
    And therfore every man this tale I telle,
    Winne whoso may, for al is for to selle.⁸
415 With empty hand men may none haukes° lure.   *hawks*
    For winning° wolde I al his lust endure,   *profit*
    And make me a feyned° appetyt—   *feigned*
    And yet in bacon° hadde I nevere delyt.   *old meat (aged men)*
    That made me that evere I wolde hem chyde.
420 For thogh the Pope had seten hem biside,°   *sat next to them*
    I wolde nat spare hem at hir owene bord.°   *table*
    For by my trouthe,° I quitte° hem word for word. *troth / requited, paid back*
    As° help me verray° God omnipotent,   *So / true*
    Thogh I right now sholde make my testament,°   *will*

7. I firmly deceived my old husbands into thinking.
8. Profit whoever may, for all is for sale.

425 I ne owe hem nat a word that it nis quit.° —— *is not paid back*
I broghte it so aboute, by my wit,° —— *cleverness*
That they moste yeve it up,° as for the beste, —— *give up*
Or elles° hadde we nevere been in reste. —— *else*
For thogh he loked as a wood leoun,° —— *like a mad lion*
430 Yet sholde he faille of his conclusioun.° —— *fail in the end*
　　　Thanne wolde I seye, 'Godelief,° tak keep° —— *Sweetheart / heed*
How mekely loketh Wilkin oure sheep!
Com neer, my spouse, lat me ba° thy cheke! —— *kiss*
Ye sholde been al pacient and meke,
435 And han a swete spyced conscience,° —— *sweetly seasoned disposition*
Sith° ye so preche of Jobes° pacience. —— *Since / Job's*
Suffreth° alwey, sin° ye so wel can preche; —— *Endure / since*
And but° ye do, certein we shal yow teche —— *unless*
That it is fair° to have a wyf in pees.° —— *good / peace*
440 Oon of us two moste bowen,° doutelees, —— *bow (to the other's will)*
And sith° a man is more resonable —— *since*
Than womman is, ye moste been suffrable.° —— *patient*
What eyleth° yow to grucche° thus and grone?° —— *ails / grumble / groan*
Is it for ye wolde have my queynte° allone? —— *(cf. ME "cunte")*
445 Why taak it al! lo, have it every-deel!° —— *every bit of it*
Peter!° I shrewe° yow but ye love it weel! —— *(By St.) Peter / curse*
For if I wolde° selle my *bele chose*,° —— *wished to / pretty thing*
I coude walke as fresh as is a rose;
But I wol kepe it for your owene tooth.⁹
450 Ye be to blame. By God, I sey yow sooth.'° —— *tell you the truth*
Swiche manere° wordes hadde we on honde. —— *kind of*
Now wol I speken of my fourthe housbonde.
　　　My fourthe housebonde was a revelour°— —— *reveler, rioter*
This is to seyn, he hadde a paramour°— —— *mistress*
455 And I was yong and ful of ragerye,° —— *wantonness, passion*
Stiborn° and strong, and joly as a pye.° —— *Stubborn / magpie*
Wel coude I daunce to an harpe smale,
And singe, ywis,° as any nightingale, —— *truly*
Whan I had dronke a draughte of swete wyn.
460 Metellius, the foule cherl, the swyn,° —— *swine*
That with a staf birafte° his wyf hir lyf —— *bereft*
For she drank wyn, thogh° I hadde been his wyf, —— *if*
He sholde nat han daunted° me fro drinke! —— *frightened*
And after wyn on Venus moste° I thinke, —— *must*
465 For al so siker° as cold engendreth° hayl,° —— *surely / engenders / hail*
A likerous mouth moste han a likerous tayl.¹
In wommen vinolent° is no defence°— —— *full of wine / resistance*
This knowen lechours by experience.
　　　But, Lord Crist! whan that it remembreth me° —— *I think*
470 Upon my yowthe, and on my jolitee,° —— *gaiety*
It tikleth° me aboute myn herte rote.° —— *tickles / heart's root*

9. I.e., your own sexual appetite.
1. A gluttonous mouth must have (i.e., necessarily implies) a lecherous tail.

Unto this day it dooth myn herte bote°   good
That I have had my world as in my tyme.
But age, allas! that al wol envenyme,°   poison
475 Hath me biraft° my beautee and my pith.°   bereft of / vigor
Lat go,° farewel! the devel go therwith!   Let it go
The flour is goon, ther is namore to telle:
The bren,° as I best can, now moste I selle;   bran, husks
But yet to be right mery wol I fonde.°   try
480 Now wol I tellen of my fourthe housbonde.
        I seye, I hadde in herte greet despyt°   malice
That he of any other° had delyt.   other woman
But he was quit,° by God and by Seint Joce!°   repaid / a Breton saint
I made him of the same wode° a croce°—   wood / cross
485 Nat of my body in no foul° manere,   unclean
But certeinly, I made folk swich chere°   such good cheer
That in his owene grece° I made him frye   grease
For angre and for verray° jalousye.   pure
By God, in erthe° I was his purgatorie,   on earth
490 For which I hope his soule be in glorie.
For God it woot,° he sat ful ofte and song°   knows / sang
Whan that his shoo° ful bitterly him wrong.°   shoe / hurt
Ther was no wight,° save° God and he, that wiste°   person / except / knew
In many wyse° how sore° I him twiste.°   ways / sorely / tormented
495 He deyde whan I cam fro° Jerusalem,   from (a pilgrimage to)
And lyth y-grave under the rode-beem,²
Al° is his tombe noght so curious°   Although / elaborate
As was the sepulcre° of him Darius,   a very famous tomb
Which that Appelles wroghte subtilly;°   made skillfully
500 It nis but wast to burie him preciously.³
Lat him° farewel, God yeve his soule reste!   May he
He is now in the grave and in his cheste.°   coffin
        Now of my fifthe housbond wol I telle—
God lete his soule nevere come in helle!
505 And yet was he to me the moste shrewe.°   worst rascal
That fele° I on my ribbes al by rewe,°   feel / in a row
And evere shal unto myn ending day.°   i.e., dying day
But in oure bed he was so fresh and gay,
And therwithal so wel coude he me glose°   cajole, flatter
510 Whan that he wolde han my *bele chose*,°   pretty thing
That thogh he hadde me bet° on every boon,°   beaten / bone
He coude winne agayn my love anoon.°   at once
I trowe° I loved him beste for that he   believe
Was of his love daungerous° to me.   standoffish, grudging
515 We wommen han, if that I shal nat lye,
In this matere a queynte fantasye:°   an odd fancy
Wayte what° thing we may nat lightly have,   Whatever

2. And lies buried under the rood-beam (a timber separating the nave from the chancel in a church).
3. It is (i.e., would have been) nothing but a waste to bury him expensively.

Thereafter wol we crye al day and crave.
Forbede us thing,° and that desyren we;   *something*
520 Prees on° us faste,° and thanne wol we flee.   *Crowd, pursue / hard*
With daunger° oute° we al oure chaffare:°   *haughtiness / set out / wares*
Greet prees° at market maketh dere° ware,   *press, crowd / expensive*
And to° greet cheep° is holde at litel prys.°   *too / a bargain / worth*
This knoweth every womman that is wys.
525   My fifthe housbonde, God his soule blesse!
Which that I took for love and no richesse,
He som tyme° was a clerk° of Oxenford,°   *once / scholar / Oxford*
And had left scole, and wente at hoom to bord°   *to board at home*
With my gossib,° dwellinge in oure toun—   *gossip, intimate friend*
530 God have hir soule! hir name was Alisoun.
She knew myn herte and eek° my privetee°   *also / secrets*
Bet° than oure parisshe preest, so moot I thee!°   *Better / as I may thrive*
To hire biwreyed° I my conseil° al,   *disclosed / thoughts*
For had myn housebonde pissed on a wal,
535 Or doon a thing that sholde han cost his lyf,
To hire and to another worthy wyf,
And to my nece,° which that I loved weel,   *niece*
I wolde han told his conseil° every deel.°   *secrets / (in) every detail*
And so I dide ful often, God it woot,°   *knows*
540 That made his face ful often reed and hoot
For verray° shame, and blamed himself for° he   *pure / because*
Had told to me so greet a privetee.°   *secret*
        And so bifel° that ones° in a Lente°—   *it happened / once / at Lent*
So often tymes I to my gossib wente,
545 For evere yet I lovede to be gay,
And for to walke in March, Averille,° and May,   *April*
Fro hous to hous, to here° sondry talis°—   *hear / various tales*
That Jankin clerk° and my gossib dame Alis   *Jankin (the) clerk*
And I myself into the feldes° wente.   *fields*
550 Myn housbond was at London al that Lente:
I hadde the bettre leyser° for to pleye,   *leisure, opportunity*
And for to see, and eek° for to be seye°   *also / seen*
Of lusty folk. What wiste I wher my grace
Was shapen for to be, or in what place?[4]
555 Therefore I made my visitaciouns,°   *visits*
To vigilies and to processiouns,[5]
To preching eek and to thise pilgrimages,
To pleyes° of miracles, and mariages,   *(stage) plays*
And wered upon° my gaye scarlet gytes.°   *wore / gowns*
560 Thise wormes, ne thise motthes,° ne thise mytes,°   *moths / mites*
Upon my peril, frete hem never a deel;[6]

4. By pleasure-loving folk. How could I know where grace was destined to befall me, or in what place?
5. "Vigilies": vigils (services on the eve of a feast day); "processiouns": ceremonial processions within a church service.
6. On peril (of my soul), ate into them not at all.

And wostow° why? for° they were used weel.   knowest thou / because
   Now wol I tellen forth what happed° me.   befell
I seye that in the feeldes walked we,
565 Til trewely we hadde swich daliance,[7]
This clerk and I, that of my purveyance°   by my foresight
I spak to him and seyde him how that he,
If I were widwe,° sholde wedde me.   a widow
For certeinly, I sey for no bobance,°   not as a boast
570 Yet was I nevere withouten purveyance°   (future) provision
Of° mariage, n'of° othere thinges eek.   Concerning / nor concerning
I holde a mouses herte nat worth a leek°   leek, onion
That hath but oon hole for to sterte° to,   run
And if that faille,° thanne is al y-do.°   fails / done for
575   I bar him on honde° he hadde enchanted me—   made him believe
My dame° taughte me that soutiltee°—   mother / subtlety, trick
And eek I seyde I mette° of him al night: dreamed
He wolde han slayn° me as I lay upright,°   wanted to slay / face-up
And al my bed was ful of verray° blood;   real
580 But yet I hope that he shal do me good,
For blood bitokeneth gold, as me was taught.
And al was fals—I dremed of it right naught,
But as° I folwed ay° my dames lore°   But / ever / teaching
As wel of° this as of othere thinges more.   concerning
585   But now sire, lat me see, what I shal seyn?
Aha! by God, I have my tale ageyn.
   Whan that my fourthe housbond was on bere,°   (his) bier
I weep algate, and made sory chere[8]
As wyves moten,° for it is usage,°   must / the custom
590 And with my coverchief° covered my visage;°   kerchief / face
But for that° I was purveyed of° a make,°   because / provided with / mate
I wepte but smal,° and that I undertake.°   little / declare
   To chirche was myn housbond born° a-morwe°   borne / in the morning
With° neighebores, that for him maden sorwe;   By
595 And Jankin oure clerk was oon of tho.°   them
As° help me God! whan that I saugh° him go°   So / saw / walk
After the bere, me thoughte he hadde a paire
Of legges and of feet so clene° and faire,   neat
That al myn herte I yaf° unto his hold.°   gave / possession
600 He was, I trowe,° twenty winter old,   believe
And I was fourty, if I shal seye sooth;°   tell the truth
But yet I hadde alwey a coltes tooth.°   i.e., youthful appetites
Gat-tothed I was, and that bicam me weel;[9]
I hadde the prente of Seynte Venus seel.[1]
605 As help me God, I was a lusty° oon,   vigorous

7. I.e., were getting along so well.
8. I wept, of course, and put on a sad look.
9. I was gap-toothed, and that suited me well. (In medieval handbooks of physiognomy, gap teeth are said to indicate a bold and lascivious nature.)
1. I had the print of St. Venus's seal—i.e., Venus had given me a birthmark (again indicative of amorousness).

And faire, and riche, and yong, and wel bigoon;°   *well-off*
And trewely, as myne housbondes tolde me,
I had the beste *quoniam*° mighte be.   *i.e., pudendum*
For certes, I am al Venerien
610   In felinge, and myn herte is Marcien:[2]
Venus me yaf° my lust, my likerousnesse,°   *gave / lecherousness*
And Mars yaf me my sturdy hardinesse;°   *boldness*
Myn ascendent was Taur, and Mars therinne.[3]
Allas! allas! that evere love was sinne!
615   I folwed ay° myn inclinacioun   *ever*
By vertu of my constellacioun;[4]
That made me I coude noght withdrawe°   *withhold*
My chambre of Venus from a good felawe.°   *companion*
Yet have I Martes° mark upon my face,   *Mars's*
620   And also in another privee° place.   *secret*
For, God so wis be my savacioun,°   *salvation*
I ne loved nevere by no discrecioun,°   *with any wisdom*
But evere folwede myn appetyt:
Al° were he short or long,° or blak or whyt,   *Whether / tall*
625   I took no kepe, so that he lyked me,[5]
How pore he was, ne eek° of what degree.°   *nor / social rank*
    What sholde I seye but, at the monthes ende,
This joly clerk Jankin, that was so hende,°   *pleasant*
Hath wedded me with greet solempnitee;°   *ceremony*
630   And to him yaf° I al the lond° and fee°   *gave / land / property*
That evere was me yeven° therbifore.   *given (by earlier husbands)*
But afterward repented me° ful sore;°   *I regretted it / deeply*
He nolde suffre nothing of my list.[6]
By God, he smoot° me ones° on the list°   *hit / once / ear*
635   For that° I rente° out of his book a leef,°   *Because / tore / leaf, page*
That of the strook myn ere wex al deef.[7]
Stiborn° I was as is a leonesse,°   *Stubborn / lionness*
And of my tonge a verray jangleresse,°   *real ranter*
And walke I wolde, as I had doon biforn,
640   From hous to hous, although he had it sworn.[8]
For which he often tymes wolde preche,
And me of° olde Romayn gestes° teche,   *from / Roman stories*
How he Simplicius Gallus lefte his wyf,
And hire forsook for terme° of al his lyf,   *the duration*
645   Noght but for open-heveded he hir say[9]
Lokinge out at his dore upon a day.
    Another Romayn tolde he me by name,

2. "Venerien": under the influence of the planet Venus; "Marcien": under the influence of the
    planet Mars. Together they determine her appetites for love and marital strife.
3. (When I was born) the sign of Taurus was ascendant, and Mars was in it.
4. Through the influence of my horoscope (the planets reigning over my birth).
5. I took no heed, as long as he was pleasing to me.
6. He wouldn't allow (me) anything I wanted.
7. So that from the blow my ear grew wholly deaf.
8. I.e., he had sworn I shouldn't.
9. Only because he saw her bareheaded.

That, for° his wyf was at a someres game°   *because / summer's revel*
Withoute his witing,° he forsook hire eke.°   *knowledge / also*
650 And thanne wolde he upon° his Bible seke   *in*
That ilke° proverbe of Ecclesiaste°   *same / Ecclesiasticus*
Wher he comandeth and forbedeth faste°   *firmly*
Man shal nat suffre° his wyf go roule° aboute;   *allow / to go roaming*
Thanne wolde he seye right thus, withouten doute:
655   'Whoso that° buildeth his hous al of salwes,° *Whoever / willow twigs*
And priketh° his blinde hors over the falwes,°   *spurs / fallow (plowed) land*
And suffreth° his wyf to go seken halwes,°   *allows / shrines*
Is worthy to been hanged on the galwes!'°   *gallows*
But al for noght; I sette noght an hawe°   *haw (hawthorn berry)*
660 Of his proverbes n'of his olde sawe,°   *saw, proverb*
Ne I wolde nat of° him corrected be.   *by*
I hate him that° my vices telleth me,   *the one who*
And so do mo,° God woot,° of us than I.   *more / knows*
This made him with me wood° al outrely:°   *mad / completely*
665 I nolde noght forbere him in no cas.[1]
    Now wol I seye yow sooth,° by Seint Thomas,   *tell you the truth*
Why that I rente° out of his book a leef,°   *tore / leaf*
For which he smoot° me so that I was deef.   *struck*
    He hadde a book that gladly, night and day,
670 For his desport° he wolde rede alway.   *amusement*
He cleped it Valerie and Theofraste,[2]
At which book he lough° alwey ful faste.°   *laughed / strongly*
And eek ther was somtyme° a clerk° at Rome,   *once / scholar*
A cardinal, that highte° Seint Jerome,   *was called*
675 That made a book agayn Jovinian;
In which book eek ther was Tertulan,
Crisippus, Trotula, and Helowys,[3]
That was abbesse nat fer fro Parys;°   *Paris*
And eek the Parables° of Salomon,   *Proverbs*
680 Ovydes Art,° and bokes many on,°   *Ovid's Art (of Love) / a one*
And alle thise were bounden in o° volume.   *one*
And every night and day was his custume,
Whan he hadde leyser° and vacacioun°   *leisure / free time*
From other worldly occupacioun,
685 To reden on this book of wikked° wyves.   *wicked*
He knew of hem mo° legendes and lyves   *more*
Than been° of gode wyves in the Bible.   *there are*
For trusteth wel, it is an impossible°   *impossibility*
That any clerk wol speke good of wyves,

---

1. I wouldn't give way to him on any occasion.
2. Jankyn's "book of wikked wyves" includes several antifeminist works: Walter Map's *Letter of Valerius*, Theophrastus's *On Marriage*, and St. Jerome's *Against Jovinian*; they quote other authorities in turn (Tertullian, Chrysippus, etc.). For these texts, see the Sources and Backgrounds section on *The Wife of Bath's Prologue and Tale*.
3. "Trotula": the supposed woman author of a well-known medieval treatise on the diseases of women; "Helowys": Eloise, who loved the great scholar Abelard but argued in her letters against marrying him; she later became a nun and abbess.

690 But if° it be of holy seintes lyves,   *Unless*
     Ne of noon other womman never the mo.°   *in any way*
     Who peyntede the leoun, tel me, who?[4]
     By God, if wommen hadde writen stories,
     As clerkes han withinne hir oratories,°   *chapels, studies*
695 They wolde han writen of men more wikkednesse
     Than all the mark° of Adam may redresse.   *sex*
     The children[5] of Mercurie and of Venus
     Been in hir wirking° ful contrarious:°   *actions / contrary*
     Mercurie loveth wisdom and science,°   *knowledge*
700 And Venus loveth ryot° and dispence;°   *revelry / spending*
     And, for° hire diverse disposicioun,   *because of*
     Ech° falleth in otheres exaltacioun,°   *Each / moment of highest ascent*
     And thus, God woot, Mercurie is desolat°   *without influence*
     In Pisces wher Venus is exaltat,°   *in her greatest influence*
705 And Venus falleth ther° Mercurie is reysed;°   *there where / has risen*
     Therfore no womman of° no clerk is preysed.   *by*
     The clerk, whan he is old and may noght do
     Of Venus werkes worth° his olde sho°—   *to the value of / shoe*
     Thanne sit he doun and writ in his dotage
710 That wommen can nat kepe° hir mariage!   *i.e., be faithful in*
     But now to purpos why I tolde thee
     That I was beten° for a book, pardee.°   *beaten / by God*
     Upon a night Jankin, that was our syre,°   *lord, husband*
     Redde on his book as he sat by the fyre
715 Of Eva° first, that for hir wikkednesse   *Eve*
     Was al mankinde broght to wrecchednesse,
     For which that Jesu Crist himself was slayn,
     That boghte us with his herteblood agayn.
     Lo, here expres° of womman may ye finde   *specifically*
720 That womman was the los° of all mankinde.   *destruction*
     Tho° redde he me how Sampson loste his heres:°   *Then / hair(s)*
     Slepinge, his lemman° kitte° hem° with hir sheres,   *lover / cut / it (them)*
     Thurgh whiche tresoun loste he bothe his yën.°   *eyes*
     Tho° redde he me, if that I shal nat lyen,   *Then*
725 Of Hercules and of his Dianyre,°   *Deianira*
     That caused him to sette himself afyre.°   *on fire*
     Nothing forgat he the sorwe and the wo
     That Socrates had with hise wyves two—
     How Xantippa caste pisse upon his heed:
730 This sely° man sat stille, as° he were deed;   *poor / as if*
     He wyped his heed; namore dorste° he seyn   *dared*
     But 'Er° that thonder stinte,° comth a reyn.'°   *Before / ceases / rain, shower*
     Of Phasipha[6] that was the quene of Crete—
     For shrewednesse° him thoughte the tale swete—   *Out of cursedness*

---

4. In the *Fables* of Marie de France (#37), a peasant shows a lion a painting of a lion being
   killed by a peasant; the lion asks pointedly who painted that picture, a man or a lion.
5. Those born under the sign.
6. Pasiphaë, who loved a bull and gave birth to the Minotaur.

735 Fy! spek namore, it is a grisly thing,
Of hire horrible lust and hir lyking.°   *desire*
    Of Clitermistra,[7] for hire lecherye,
That falsly made hire housbond for to dye,
He redde it with ful good devocioun.
740   He tolde me eek for what occasioun
Amphiorax[8] at Thebes loste his lyf.
Myn housbond hadde a legende of his wyf,
Eriphilem, that° for an ouche° of gold   *Eryphile, who / brooch*
Hath prively° unto the Grekes told   *secretly*
745 Wher that hir housbonde hidde him in a place,
For which he hadde at Thebes sory grace.°   *ill fortune*
    Of Lyvia tolde he me, and of Lucye.[9]
They bothe made hir housbondes for to dye,
That oon for love, that other was for hate.
750 Lyvia hir housbond, on an even° late,   *evening*
Empoysoned° hath, for that she was his fo.°   *Poisoned / foe*
Lucya, likerous,° loved hire housbond so,   *lecherous*
That, for° he sholde alwey upon hire thinke, *so that*
She yaf° him swich a manere° love-drinke, *gave / such a kind of*
755 That he was deed er° it were by the morwe;° *before / morning*
And thus algates° housbondes han sorwe.   *in every way*
    Thanne tolde he me how oon Latumius
Compleyned unto his felawe° Arrius,   *companion*
That in his gardin growed swich a° tree   *a certain*
760 On which he seyde how that his wyves three
Hanged hemself° for herte despitous.°   *themselves / spiteful*
'O leve° brother,' quod this Arrius,   *dear*
'Yif° me a plante° of thilke° blissed tree, *Give / slip / that same*
And in my gardin planted shal it be!'
765   Of latter date, of wyves hath he red
That somme han slayn hir housbondes in hir bed,
And lete hir lechour° dighte° hire al the night *lecher, lover / lie with*
Whyl that the corps lay in° the floor upright.° *on / faceup*
And somme han drive° nayles° in hir brayn° *driven / nails / brain*
770 Whyl that they slepte, and thus they han hem slayn.
Somme han hem yeve° poysoun in hire drinke. *given*
He spak more harm than herte may bithinke,° *imagine*
And therwithal° he knew of mo° proverbes *in addition / more*
Than in this world ther growen gras or herbes.° *plants*
775 'Bet is,'° quod he, 'thyn habitacioun   *Better it is (that)*
Be with a leoun or a foul dragoun,
Than with a womman usinge for° to chyde.   *accustomed*

7. Clytemnestra, who murdered her husband, Agamemnon, to keep Aegisthus, her lover.
8. Amphiaraus, a soothsayer who prophesied his own death if he fought at Thebes; he was persuaded into battle by his wife.
9. Livia poisoned her husband, Drusus, at Sejanus's instigation; Lucilia, wife to the poet Lucretius, poisoned him with a love potion meant to increase his amorousness.

Bet is,' quod he, 'hye in° the roof abyde°   *high on / to stay*
Than with an angry wyf doun in the hous;
780 They been so wikked and contrarious°   *contradictory*
They haten that° hir housbondes loveth ay.'° *what / ever*
He seyde, 'A womman cast° hir shame away *casts*
Whan she cast of° hir smok;'° and   *off / smock, underdress*
 forthermo,°   *furthermore*
'A fair° womman, but° she be chaast also, *beautiful / unless*
785 Is lyk a gold ring in a sowes° nose.'   *sow's*
Who wolde wene,° or who wolde suppose° *think / imagine*
The wo that in myn herte was, and pyne?° *suffering*
 And whan I saugh° he wolde nevere fyne° *saw / finish*
To reden on this cursed book al night,
790 Al sodeynly° three leves° have I plight° *suddenly / pages / plucked*
Out of his book, right° as he radde,° and eke° *just / read / also*
I with my fist so took° him on the cheke *hit*
That in oure fyr he fil° bakward adoun. *fell*
And he upstirte° as dooth a wood leoun,° *jumped up / mad lion*
795 And with his fist he smoot° me on the heed *struck*
That in° the floor I lay as° I were deed. *(So) that on / as if*
And when he saugh° how stille that I lay, *saw*
He was agast,° and wolde han fled his way, *frightened*
Til atte laste out of my swogh° I breyde.° *swoon, faint / started up*
800 'O! hastow° slayn me, false theef?'° I seyde, *hast thou / criminal*
'And for my land thus hastow mordred° me? *murdered*
Er° I be deed, yet wol I kisse thee.'   *Before*
 And neer he cam, and kneled faire° adoun, *courteously*
And seyde, 'Dere suster Alisoun,
805 As° help me God, I shall thee nevere smyte;° *So / strike*
That I have doon, it is thyself to wyte.[1]
Foryeve° it me, and that I thee biseke'°— *Forgive / beseech*
And yet eftsones° I hitte him on the cheke *again*
And seyde, 'Theef! thus muchel° am I wreke.° *much / avenged*
810 Now wol I dye: I may no lenger speke.'
But atte laste, with muchel care and wo,
We fille acorded° by us selven two.   *came to an agreement*
He yaf me al° the brydel° in myn hond, *completely / bridle*
To han the governance° of hous and lond, *direction*
815 And of his tonge and of his hond also;
And made him brenne his book anon right tho.[2]
And whan that I hadde geten unto me,° *gotten for myself*
By maistrie,° al the soveraynetee,°   *mastery / supremacy, sovereignty*
And that he seyde, 'Myn owene trewe wyf,
820 Do as thee lust° the terme° of al thy lyf; *please / (to the) end*
Keep° thyn honour, and keep eek myn estaat'°— *Preserve / public position*
After that day we hadden never debaat.° *contention*
God help me so, I was to him as kinde

---

1. For what I've done, it's thyself (who is) to blame.
2. And (I) made him burn his book then at once.

As any wyf from Denmark unto Inde,°   *India*
825 And also° trewe, and so was he to me.   *equally as*
I prey to God that sit° in magestee,°   *who sits / majesty*
So blesse his soule for his° mercy dere!   *by his*
Now wol I seye my tale, if ye wol here."

  Biholde the wordes bitween the Somonour and the Frere.

The Frere° lough° whan he hadde herd al this.   *Friar / laughed*
830 "Now, dame," quod° he, "so have I° joye or blis,   *said / as I may have*
This is a long preamble of° a tale!"   *i.e., introduction to*
And whan the Somnour herde the Frere gale,°   *exclaim aloud*
"Lo,"° quod the Somnour, "Goddes armes two,°   *Behold / by God's two arms*
A frere wol entremette him° everemo!   *intrude himself*
835 Lo, gode men, a flye and eek a frere
Wol falle in every dish and eek matere.°   *subject*
What spekestow° of preambulacioun?°   *Why speakest thou / preambling*
What!° amble, or trotte, or [pace,]° or go sit doun!   *Lo / walk*
Thou lettest° oure disport° in this manere."   *hinderest / pleasure*
840   "Ye, woltow so,° sire Somnour?" quod the Frere; *wouldst thou (have it) so*
"Now by my feith, I shal, er that I go,
Telle of a somnour swich° a tale or two   *such*
That alle the folk shal laughen in this place."
  "Now elles,° Frere, I wol bishrewe° thy face,"   *otherwise / curse*
845 Quod this Somnour, "and I bishrewe me
But if° I telle tales two or thre   *Unless*
Of freres, er I come to Sidingborne,³
That° I shal make thyn herte for to morne°—   *So that / mourn*
For wel I woot° thy pacience is goon."   *know*
850   Oure Hoste cryde "Pees!° and that anoon!"°   *Peace / at once*
And seyde, "Lat the womman telle hire tale.
Ye fare° as folk that dronken been of ale.   *act*
Do, dame, tel forth youre tale, and that is best."
  "Al redy, sire," quod she, "right as yow lest,⁴
855 If I have licence° of this worthy Frere."   *the permission*
  "Yis, dame," quod he, "tel forth, and I wol here."°   *listen*

The Tale

In th'olde dayes of the King Arthour,
Of which that Britons speken greet honour,
All was this land fulfild of fayerye.°   *filled with fairy people*
860 The elf-queen with hir joly companye
Daunced ful ofte in many a grene mede.°   *meadow*
This was the olde opinion, as I rede—
I speke of manye hundred yeres ago—
But now can no man see none elves mo.°   *more*
865 For now the grete charitee and prayeres

3. Sittingbourne, a town roughly two-thirds of the way to Canterbury.
4. "(I am) all ready, sir," she said, "just as you wish."

Of limitours⁵ and othere holy freres,
That serchen° every lond and every streem,   *visit*
As thikke° as motes in the sonne-beem,°   *thick / sunbeam*
Blessinge halles, chambres, kichenes, boures,°   *bowers, sleeping rooms*
870 Citees, burghes,° castels, hye toures,°   *towns / high towers*
Thropes, bernes, shipnes, dayeryes⁶—
This maketh° that ther been no fayeryes.   *is the cause*
For ther as wont to walken was an elf,⁷
Ther walketh now the limitour himself
875 In undermeles° and in morweninges,°   *afternoons / mornings*
And seyth his Matins° and his holy thinges   *morning service*
As he goth in his limitacioun.°   *licensed begging area*
Wommen may go now saufly° up and doun: *safely*
In every bush or under every tree⁸
880 Ther is noon other incubus⁹ but he,
And he ne wol doon hem but dishonour.¹
     And so bifel° that this King Arthour   *it happened*
Hadde in his hous a lusty bacheler,°   *young knight*
That on a day cam rydinge fro river;²
885 And happed that, allone as he was born,
He saugh° a mayde walkinge him biforn,   *saw*
Of whiche mayde anon, maugree hir heed,³
By verray force° he rafte° hire maydenheed.   *force itself / took*
For which oppressioun° was swich° clamour   *wrong / such*
890 And swich pursute° unto the King Arthour,   *suing (for justice)*
That dampned° was this knight for to be deed   *condemned*
By cours of lawe, and sholde han° lost his heed—   *was to have*
Paraventure° swich was the statut° tho°—   *By chance / statute, law / then*
But that° the quene and othere ladies mo°   *Except / besides*
895 So longe preyeden° the king of° grace   *begged / for*
Til he his lyf him graunted in the place,
And yaf° him to the quene al at hir wille,   *gave*
To chese whether she wolde him save or spille.°   *destroy*
     The quene thanketh the king with al hir might,
900 And after this thus spak she to the knight
Whan that she saugh hir tyme, upon a day:
"Thou standest yet," quod she, "in swich array°   *such a condition*
That of thy lyf yet hastow° no suretee.°   *hast thou / security, guarantee*
I grante thee lyf, if thou canst tellen me
905 What thing is it that wommen most desyren.
Be war, and keep thy nekke-boon from yren.⁴
And if thou canst nat tellen it anon,°   *right away*

5. Friars given exclusive rights by license to beg within a certain area, or "limits."
6. Villages, barns, sheds, dairies.
7. For there where an elf was accustomed to walk.
8. Places popularly thought to be haunted by fairies.
9. An evil spirit supposed to lie upon women in their sleep and have intercourse with them.
1. Shame, dishonor; as opposed to the begetting of devils upon them.
2. From hawking; riverbanks were favorite places for the sport.
3. (And) from this maid at once, in spite of anything she could do.
4. Be wary, and keep thy neck from the ax (*lit.*, iron).

Yet wol I yeve° thee leve° for to gon   *give / leave*
A twelf-month and a day, to seche° and lere°   *seek out / learn*
910 An answere suffisant° in this matere.°   *sufficient / subject*
And suretee° wol I han, er that thou pace,°   *a pledge, security / walk off*
Thy body for to yelden° in this place."   *yield up, return*
    Wo° was this knight and sorwefully he syketh.°   *Woeful / sighs*
But what! he may nat do al as him lyketh,⁵
915 And at the laste he chees him for to wende,°   *decided to go off*
And come agayn, right° at the yeres ende,   *exactly*
With swich answere as God wolde him purveye;°   *provide for him*
And taketh his leve and wendeth forth his weye.
    He seketh every hous and every place
920 Wheras° he hopeth for to finde grace,°   *Where / good fortune*
To lerne what thing wommen loven most;
But he ne coude arryven in no cost°   *coast, country*
Wheras he mighte finde in this matere°   *subject*
Two creatures accordinge in-fere.°   *agreeing together*
925   Somme seyde wommen loven best richesse,
Somme seyde honour, somme seyde jolynesse;
Somme riche array,° somme seyden lust abedde,°   *adornment / pleasure in bed*
And ofte tyme to be widwe° and wedde.°   *widowed / (re)married*
    Somme seyde that oure hertes been most esed
930 Whan that we been y-flatered and y-plesed.
He gooth ful ny the sothe,° I wol nat lye: *very near the truth*
A man shal winne us best with flaterye;
And with attendance° and with bisinesse°   *attention / diligence*
Been we y-lymed, bothe more and lesse.⁶
935   And somme seyn how that we loven best
For to be free and do right as us lest,°   *just as we please*
And that no man repreve us of° oure vyce,   *reproach us for*
But seye that we be wyse, and no thing nyce.°   *not at all foolish*
For trewely, ther is noon of us alle,
940 If any wight wol clawe° us on the galle,°   *scratch / sore spot*
That we nil kike for he seith us sooth:⁷
Assay,° and he shal finde it that so dooth.   *Try*
For be we never so vicious withinne,
We wol been holden° wyse, and clene of sinne.   *wish to be considered*
945   And somme seyn that greet delyt han we
For to ben holden stable° and eek secree,°   *steadfast / discreet*
And in o° purpos stedefastly to dwelle,   *one*
And nat biwreye° thing that men us telle—   *reveal*
But that tale is nat worth a rake-stele.°   *rake handle*
950 Pardee, we wommen conne nothing hele:⁸
Witnesse on Myda°—wol ye here the tale?   *Midas*
    Ovyde,° amonges othere thinges smale,   *Ovid*

---

5. But lo! he cannot do everything just as he pleases.
6. We are ensnared (caught, as with birdlime), both great and small.
7. Who will not kick back, because he tells us the truth. (The metaphor is of horses.)
8. By heaven, we women don't know how to conceal anything.

Seyde Myda hadde under his longe heres,°   *hair*
Growinge upon his heed two asses eres,°   *ears*
955 The whiche vyce° he hidde as he best mighte°   *deformity / could*
Ful subtilly° from every mannes sighte,   *cleverly*
That, save his wyf, ther wiste of it namo.[9]
He loved hire most, and trusted hire also;
He preyede° hire that to no creature   *begged*
960 She sholde tellen of his disfigure.°   *disfigurement*
    She swoor him nay, for al this world to winne,
She nolde° do that vileinye° or sinne,   *would not / bad deed*
To make hir housbond han so foul a name.
She nolde nat telle it for° hir owene shame.   *i.e., to spare*
965 But nathelees, hir thoughte that she dyde[1]
That° she so longe sholde a conseil° hyde.   *If / secret*
Hir thoughte it swal° so sore° aboute hir herte   *swelled / painfully*
That nedely som word hire moste asterte,[2]
And sith° she dorste° telle it to no man,   *since / dared*
970 Doun to a mareys° faste by° she ran.   *marsh / close by*
Til she came there hir herte was afyre,°   *on fire*
And as a bitore bombleth in the myre,[3]
She leyde° hir mouth unto the water doun: *laid*
"Biwreye° me nat, thou water, with thy soun,"°   *Betray / sound*
975 Quod she, "to thee I telle it, and namo;°   *no one else*
Myn housbond hath longe asses eres° two!   *ears*
Now is myn herte all hool,° now is it oute.   *whole (again)*
I mighte no lenger kepe it, out of doute."
Heer° may ye se, thogh we a tyme abyde,°   *Here / wait for a time*
980 Yet out it moot,° we can no conseil° hyde.   *must / secret*
The remenant of the tale[4] if ye wol here,
Redeth Ovyde,° and ther ye may it lere.°   *Read Ovid / learn*
    This knight of which my tale is specially,
Whan that he saugh he mighte nat come therby,°   *i.e., learn the answer*
985 This is to seye, what wommen loven moost,
Withinne his brest ful sorweful was the goost,°   *spirit*
But hoom he gooth, he mighte nat sojourne.°   *linger*
The day was come that hoomward moste° he tourne,   *must*
And in his wey it happed him to ryde
990 In al this care under a forest-syde,°   *on the edge of a forest*
Wheras he saugh° upon a daunce go°   *saw / moving in a dance*
Of ladies foure and twenty and yet mo;
Toward the whiche daunce he drow° ful yerne,°   *drew / eagerly*
In hope that som wisdom sholde he lerne.
995 But certeinly, er° he came fully there,   *before*
Vanisshed was this daunce, he niste° where.   *knew not*

9. So that no one else knew about it except his wife.
1. But nonetheless, it seemed to her that she would die.
2. That of necessity some word must burst out of her.
3. And as a bittern (a marsh bird) booms in the mire.
4. In Ovid's conclusion—his version differs in several ways from the Wife of Bath's—the marsh
   reeds whisper the secret aloud whenever the wind blows.

No creature saugh he that bar° lyf,   *bore*
Save on the grene° he saugh sittinge a wyf°—   *grass / woman*
A fouler wight° ther may no man devyse.°   *An uglier being / imagine*
1000 Agayn° the knight this olde wyf gan ryse,°   *i.e., to meet / rose up*
And seyde, "Sire knight, heerforth° ne lyth no wey.   *through here*
Tel me what that ye seken,° by youre fey!°   *seek / faith*
Paraventure° it may the bettre be: *By chance*
Thise olde folk can muchel thing," quod she.[5]
1005   "My leve° mooder," quod this knight, "certeyn°   *dear / certainly*
I nam but deed, but if that I can seyn[6]
What thing it is that wommen most desyre.
Coude ye me wisse,° I wolde wel quyte your   *inform*
      hyre."°   *repay your trouble*
      "Plighte° me thy trouthe,° heer in myn hand,"   *Pledge / promise*
      quod she,
1010 "The nexte thing that I requere° thee,   *request of*
Thou shalt it do, if it lye in thy might,°   *power*
And I wol telle it yow er it be night."
      "Have heer my trouthe,"° quod the knight, "I grante."°   *pledge / grant (it)*
      "Thanne," quod she, "I dar me wel avante°   *dare well boast*
1015 Thy lyf is sauf,° for I wol stonde therby.°   *safe / i.e., I guarantee it*
Upon my lyf, the queen wol seye as I.
Lat see which is the proudeste of hem alle,
That wereth° on a coverchief° or a calle,°   *wears / kerchief / hairnet*
That dar° seye nay of that° I shal thee teche.   *dares to / to that which*
1020 Lat us go forth withouten lenger speche."
Tho rouned° she a pistel° in his ere,°   *Then whispered / message / ear*
And bad him to be glad and have no fere.
      Whan they be comen to the court, this knight
Seyde he had holde° his day, as he hadde hight,°   *kept to / promised*
1025 And redy was his answere, as he sayde.
Ful many a noble wyf, and many a mayde,
And many a widwe°—for that° they ben wyse—   *widow / because*
The quene hirself sittinge as a justyse,°   *judge*
Assembled been, his answere for to here;
1030 And afterward this knight was bode appere.°   *bidden to appear*
      To every wight° comanded was silence,   *person*
And that the knight sholde telle in audience°   *in open hearing*
What thing that worldly wommen loven best.
This knight ne stood nat stille as doth a best,°   *beast*
1035 But to his questioun anon° answerde   *at once*
With manly voys,° that° al the court it herde: *voice / so that*
      "My lige° lady, generally," quod he,   *liege*
"Wommen desyren to have sovereyntee°   *sovereignty, domination*
As wel over hir housbond as hir love,[7]
1040 And for to been in maistrie° him above.   *mastery, control*

5. "These old folk (i.e., *we* old folk) know many things," said she.
6. I'm as good as dead unless I can say.
7. Over their husband(s) as well as over their lover(s).

This is youre moste° desyr, thogh ye me kille.   greatest
Doth as yow list°—I am heer at your wille."   it please you
In al the court ne was ther wyf, ne mayde,
Ne widwe that contraried° that° he sayde,   opposed / what
1045 But seyden he was worthy han° his lyf.   to have
And with that word up stirte° the olde wyf,   started up
Which that the knight saugh° sittinge in the grene: saw (had seen)
"Mercy," quod she, "my sovereyn lady quene!
Er that youre court departe, do me right.°   give me justice
1050 I taughte this answere unto the knight;
For which he plighte me his trouthe there,
The firste thing I wolde of him requere°   request
He wolde it do, if it lay in his might.°   power
Bifore the court thanne preye I thee, sir knight,"
1055 Quod she, "that thou me take unto thy wyf,
For wel thou wost° that I have kept° thy lyf.   knowest / preserved
If I sey fals, sey nay, upon thy fey!"°   faith
        This knight answerde, "Allas and weylawey!°   woe is me
I woot° right wel that swich° was my biheste.°   know / such / promise
1060 For Goddes love, as chees° a newe requeste: choose
Tak al my good,° and lat my body go."   goods, property
        "Nay thanne," quod she, ' "I shrewe° us bothe two!   curse
For thogh that I be foul° and old and pore,   ugly
I nolde° for al the metal ne for ore   would not
1065 That under erthe is grave° or lyth° above   buried / lies
But if° thy wyf I were, and eek thy love."   (Have anything) except
        "My love?" quod he, "Nay, my dampnacioun!°   damnation
Allas! that any of my nacioun°   birth, lineage
Sholde evere so foule disparaged° be!"   disgracefully degraded
1070 But al for noght, the ende° is this, that he   outcome
Constreyned was: he nedes moste° hire wedde,   needs must
And taketh his olde wyf and gooth to bedde.
        Now wolden som men seye, paraventure,°   perchance
That for° my necligence I do no cure°   out of / omit
1075 To tellen yow the joye and al th'array°   the pomp
That at the feste° was that ilke° day.   feast / same
To whiche thing shortly° answere I shal: in brief
I seye ther nas° no joye ne feste at al;   was not
Ther nas but° hevinesse and muche sorwe,   was only
1080 For prively° he wedded hire on morwe,°   privately / in the morning
And al day after hidde him as an oule,°   like an owl
So wo was him, his wyf looked so foule.[8]
        Greet was the wo the knight hadde in his thoght,
Whan he was with his wyf abedde° y-broght;   to bed
1085 He walweth,° and he turneth to and fro.   tosses about
His olde wyf lay smylinge everemo,°   all the while
And seyde, "O dere housbond, *benedicite!*°   bless us

---

8. So woeful was he, (because) his wife looked so ugly.

Fareth° every knight thus with his wyf as ye?   *Acts, behaves*
Is this the lawe of King Arthures hous?
1090 Is every knight of his so dangerous?°   *haughty, reluctant*
I am youre owene love and eek youre wyf;
I am she which that saved hath youre lyf;
And certes yet dide I yow nevere unright.°   *wrong*
Why fare° ye thus with me this firste night?   *act*
1095 Ye faren lyk a man had° lost his wit!   *(who) had*
What is my gilt?° for Goddes love, tel me it,   *error*
And it shal been amended, if I may."°   *can*
    "Amended?" quod this knight, "allas! nay, nay!
It wol nat been amended nevere mo!°   *more*
1100 Thou art so loothly,° and so old also,   *loathsome, ugly*
And therto comen of so lowe a kinde,°   *such low birth*
That litel wonder is° thogh I walwe and winde.°   *it is / toss and turn*
So wolde God myn herte wolde breste!"°   *burst*
    "Is this," quod she, "the cause of youre unreste?"
1105   "Ye, certainly," quod he, "no wonder is."°   *it is*
    "Now, sire," quod she, "I coude amende al this,
If that me liste, er it were dayes three,
So wel ye mighte bere yow unto me.⁹
    But for ye speken of swich gentillesse¹
1110 As is descended out of old richesse°—   *wealth*
That therfore sholden ye be gentil men²—
Swich° arrogance is nat worth an hen.   *Such*
Loke who that° is most vertuous alway,   *See who*
Privee and apert, and most entendeth ay³
1115 To do the gentil dedes that he can,
And tak him for the grettest gentil man.
Crist wol° we clayme of° him oure gentillesse,   *desires (that) / from*
Nat of oure eldres° for hire old richesse.   *elders, ancestors*
For thogh they yeve° us al hir heritage—   *give*
1120 For which we clayme to been of heigh parage°—   *parentage, birth*
Yet may they nat biquethe,° for no thing,°   *bestow / by any means*
To noon of us hir vertuous living
That made hem gentil men y-called be,
And bad us folwen hem in swich degree.°   *in a similar condition*
1125   Wel can the wyse poete of Florence,
That highte Dant, speken in this sentence;⁴
Lo, in swich maner rym° is Dantes tale: *this sort of rhyme*
'Ful selde° up ryseth by his branches⁵ smale   *seldom*
Prowesse° of man, for God of° his goodnesse   *The excellence / out of*

9. If it pleased me, before three days were past, if you could behave well toward me.
1. "Gentillesse" implies the kind of behavior and sensibility proper to good ("gentil") birth—
   openness, generosity, compassion, courtesy—but as the Wife points out (with learned authority to support her), a high ancestry is no guarantee of these things, nor does low birth
   necessarily preclude them.
2. That because of this, you must necessarily be "gentle"-men.
3. In private and in public, and always seeks most diligently.
4. Who is called Dante, speak on this theme.
5. I.e., of the family tree.

1130 Wol° that of° him we clayme oure gentillesse;'   *Desires / from*
For of oure eldres may we no thing clayme
But temporel thing, that man may hurte and mayme.⁶
    Eek° every wight° wot° this as wel as I,   *Also / being / knows*
If gentillesse were planted naturelly°   *by nature*
1135 Unto a certeyn linage doun the lyne,
Privee and apert, than wolde they nevere fyne°   *cease*
To doon of gentillesse the faire offyce°—   *function(s)*
They mighte° do no vileinye or vyce.°   *could / vicious act*
    Tak fyr, and ber it in° the derkeste hous   *bear it into*
1140 Bitwix this° and the Mount of Caucasus,   *here*
And lat men shette° the dores and go thenne,°   *shut / away*
Yet wol the fyr as faire lye and brenne,°   *burn*
As° twenty thousand men mighte it biholde: *As when*
His office° naturel ay° wol it holde,°   *Its function / ever / perform*
1145 Up° peril of my lyf, til that it dye.°   *Upon / die out*
    Heer may ye see wel how that genterye°   *nobility*
Is nat annexed° to possessioun,   *attached*
Sith° folk ne doon hir operacioun°   *Since / perform their function*
Alwey, as dooth the fyr, lo, in his kinde.°   *according to its nature*
1150 For, God it woot, men may wel often finde
A lordes sone° do° shame and vileinye;   *son / doing*
And he that wol han prys of° his gentrye   *have praise (esteem) for*
For° he was boren° of a gentil hous,   *Because / born*
And hadde his eldres noble and vertuous,
1155 And nil° himselven do no gentil dedis,   *will not*
Ne folwe his gentil auncestre° that deed is,°   *ancestry / which is dead*
He nis nat° gentil, be he duk or erl;   *is not*
For vileyns° sinful dedes make a cherl.°   *villainous / churl*
For gentillesse nis° but renomee°   *is nothing / the renown*
1160 Of thyne auncestres, for hire heigh bountee,°   *their great goodness*
Which is a straunge thing° to thy persone.   *a thing foreign*
Thy gentillesse cometh fro God allone.
Thanne comth oure verray gentillesse of grace:
It was nothing biquethe us with oure place.⁷
1165   Thenketh how noble, as seith Valerius,°   *Valerius Maximus*
Was thilke Tullius Hostilius,⁸
That out of povert° roos° to heigh noblesse.   *poverty / rose*
Redeth Senek,° and redeth eek° Boëce:°   *Seneca / also / Boethius*
Ther shul ye seen expres° that it no drede° is   *explicitly / doubt*
1170 That he is gentil that doth gentil dedis.°   *deeds*
And therfore, leve° housbond, I thus conclude: *dear*
Al were it that° myne auncestres were rude,°   *Even though / humble*
Yet may the hye° God, and so hope I,   *high*
Grante me grace to liven vertuously.

6. But temporal (worldly) things, which can harm and maim man.
7. Then our real *gentillesse* comes from (God's) grace; it was in no way bestowed upon us with our social position.
8. Third legendary king of Rome.

1175 Thanne am I gentil, whan that I biginne
    To liven vertuously and weyve° sinne.   *put aside*
      And ther as ye of povert° me repreve,°   *poverty / reproach*
    The hye God, on° whom that we bileve,   *in*
    In wilful° povert chees° to live his lyf.   *voluntary / chose*
1180 And certes every man, mayden, or wyf,
    May understonde that Jesus, hevene king,
    Ne wolde nat chese a vicious living.°   *way of living*
    Glad° povert is an honest thing, certeyn;°   *Contented / certainly*
    This wol Senek and othere clerkes seyn.
1185 Whoso that halt him payd of his poverte,[9]
    I holde him riche, al° hadde he nat a sherte.°   *although / shirt*
    He that coveyteth° is a povre wight,°   *covets / poor creature*
    For he wolde han that° is nat in his might.°   *what / power*
    But he that noght hath, ne coveyteth have,°   *desires (to) have*
1190 Is riche, although ye holde him but a knave.°   *one of low estate*
    Verray° povert, it singeth proprely.°   *True / by its nature*
    Juvenal seith of povert merily:
    'The povre man, whan he goth by the weye,
    Bifore the theves he may singe and pleye.'
1195 Poverte is hateful good,° and as I gesse,   *a hated good*
    A ful greet bringere out of bisinesse;°   *anxiety, care*
    A greet amendere eek of sapience°   *wisdom*
    To him that taketh it in° pacience.   *accepts it with*
    Poverte is this, although it seme elenge,°   *miserable*
1200 Possessioun that no wight wol chalenge;°   *claim (as his own)*
    Poverte ful ofte, whan a man is lowe,
    Maketh° his God and eek himself to knowe;   *Makes (him)*
    Poverte a spectacle° is, as thinketh me,   *eyeglass*
    Thurgh which he may his verray frendes see.
1205 And therfore, sire, sin that I noght yow greve,[1]
    Of° my povert namore ye me repreve.°   *For / reproach*
      Now, sire, of elde° ye repreve me: *old age*
    And certes, sire, thogh° noon auctoritee   *even if*
    Were in no book, ye gentils of honour°   *who are honorable*
1210 Seyn that men sholde an old wight° doon favour   *(to) an old person*
    And clepe° him fader, for° youre gentillesse;   *call / out of*
    And auctours° shal I finden, as I gesse.   *authorities (for this opinion)*
      Now ther ye seye that I am foul° and old,   *ugly*
    Than drede° you noght to been a cokewold,°   *fear / cuckold*
1215 For filthe and elde, also moot I thee,°   *as I may prosper*
    Been grete wardeyns upon° chastitee.   *guardians of*
    But nathelees, sin° I knowe youre delyt,°   *since / pleasure, wish*
    I shal fulfille youre worldly appetyt.°   *appetite, lust*
      Chese° now," quod she, "oon of thise thinges tweye:°   *Choose / two*
1220 To han me foul and old til that I deye°   *die*
    And be to yow a trewe° humble wyf,   *faithful*

9. Whosoever considers himself satisfied with his poverty.
1. And therefore, sir, since I don't trouble you (with it).

And nevere yow displese in al my lyf,

Or elles° ye wol han me yong and fair,   *else*

And take youre aventure of° the repair°   *chance with / i.e., the crowd*

1225 That shal be to youre hous, by cause of me,

Or in som other place, may wel be.°   *(it) may well be*

Now chese yourselven whether that yow lyketh."°   *whichever pleases you*

    This knight avyseth him and sore syketh,[2]

But atte laste he seyde in this manere:

1230 "My lady and my love, and wyf so dere,

I put me in youre wyse governance:°   *under your wise control*

Cheseth° youreself which may be most   *Choose*

    plesance°   *the greatest pleasure*

And most honour to yow and me also.

I do no fors the whether of the two,

1235 For as yow lyketh, it suffiseth me."[3]

    "Thanne have I gete of° yow maistrye,"° quod she, *gotten from / mastery*

"Sin° I may chese and governe as me lest?"°   *Since / I please*

    "Ye, certes,° wyf," quod he, "I holde° it best."   *certainly / consider*

    "Kis me," quod she. "We be no lenger wrothe,° *longer wroth (angry)*

1240 For by my trouthe,° I wol be to yow bothe,   *i.e., I swear*

This is to seyn, ye,° bothe fair and good.   *yes*

I prey to God that I mot sterven wood,°   *may die mad*

But° I to yow be also° good and trewe   *Unless / just as*

As evere was wyf, sin° that the world was newe.   *since*

1245 And but I be to-morn as fair to sene[4]

As any lady, emperyce,° or quene,   *empress*

That is bitwixe the est and eke the west,

Doth with my lyf and deeth right as yow lest.°   *just as you please*

Cast° up the curtin:° loke how that it is."   *Lift / (bed-)curtain*

1250   And whan the knight saugh° verraily° al this,   *saw / in truth*

That she so fair was and so yong therto,

For joye he hente° hire in his armes two;   *clasped*

His herte bathed in a bath of blisse.

A thousand tyme a-rewe° he gan hire kisse,°   *in a row / did kiss her*

1255 And she obeyed him in every thing

That mighte doon° him plesance° or lyking.°   *give / pleasure / delight*

    And thus they live unto hir lyves ende

In parfit° joye. And Jesu Crist us sende   *perfect*

Housbondes meke,° yonge, and fresshe abedde,° *meek / in bed*

1260 And grace t'overbyde hem that we wedde.[5]

And eek I preye Jesu shorte hir lyves°   *to shorten their lives*

That° noght wol be governed by hir wyves;   *Who*

And olde and angry nigardes of dispence,° *niggards with their money*

God sende hem sone° verray° pestilence.   *soon / a real*

---

2. This knight thinks it over and sorrowfully sighs.
3. I don't care which of the two (it be), for as it is pleasing to you, (so) it suffices me.
4. And unless I am in the morning as fair to look upon.
5. And the grace to outlive them that we wed.

The Friar's Prologue and Tale

The Prologue

1265 This worthy limitour,° this noble Frere,   *(see GP l. 209 and note)*
He made alwey a maner louring chere°   *a sort of glowering expression*
Upon° the Somnour, but for honestee°   *Toward / for (the sake of) propriety*
No vileyns° word as yet to him spak he.   *churlish, indecent*
But atte laste he seyde unto the Wyf,
1270 "Dame," quod he, "God yeve° yow right good lyf!   *give*
Ye han° heer touched, also moot I thee,°   *have / as I may thrive*
In scole-matere greet difficultee.°   *Upon scholastic questions of great difficulty*
Ye han seyd muchel thing° right wel, I seye.   *many things*
But dame, here as we ryden by the weye
1275 Us nedeth nat to speken but of game,°   *entertaining subjects*
And lete auctoritees,° on° Goddes name,   *leave (citing) authorities / in*
To preching and to scoles of clergye.°   *to the learned schools*
But if it lyke to° this companye,   *please*
I wol yow of a somnour telle a game.°   *jest, funny story*
1280 Pardee,° ye may wel knowe by the name°   *By God / the term itself*
That of a somnour may no good be sayd.
I praye that noon of you be yvel apayd.°   *be offended*
A somnour is a renner° up and doun   *runner*
With mandements° for fornicacioun,   *summonses*
1285 And is y-bet° at every tounes ende."   *beaten, assailed*
     Our Host tho° spak, "A, sire, ye sholde be hende°   *then / polite*
And curteys, as° a man of your estaat;°   *as (befits) / position*
In companye we wol have no debaat.°   *quarreling, strife*
Telleth your tale, and lat the Somnour be."
1290 "Nay," quod° the Somnour, "lat him seye to me   *said*
What so him list.° Whan it comth to my lot,°   *Whatever pleases him / turn*
By God, I shal him quyten° every grot.°   *repay / groat (a coin)*
I shal him tellen which° a greet honour   *what*
It is to be a flateringe limitour,
1295 And of many another manere crime
Which nedeth nat rehercen for° this tyme.   *mention at*
And his offyce I shal him telle, ywis."[1]
     Our Host answerde, "Pees,° namore of this."   *Peace*
And after this he seyde unto the Frere,
1300 "Tel forth your tale, leve° maister deere."   *dear*

The Tale

     Whilom° ther was dwellinge in my contree°   *Once / district*
An erchedeken,[2] a man of heigh degree,°   *rank*
That boldely dide execucioun°   *carried out (church) law*

---

1. And I will reveal to him, indeed, (the true nature) of his office (his official duties).
2. The archdeacon was a church official in charge of local ecclesiastical courts in a diocese. The list of offenses that follows indicates what sorts of behavior were typically tried in church courts rather than secular ones.

In punisshinge of fornicacioun,
1305 Of wicchecraft and eek° of bauderye,°   *also / pandering*
Of diffamacioun° and avoutrye,°   *slander / adultery*
Of chirche-reves and of testaments,
Of contractes and of lakke of sacraments,[3]
Of usure° and of symonye[4] also.   *usury*
1310 But certes,° lechours° dide he grettest wo—   *certainly / lechers*
They sholde singen° if that they were hent.°   *sing, i.e., lament / caught*
And smale tytheres weren foule y-shent:
If any persone wolde upon hem pleyne,
Ther mighte asterte him no pecunial peyne.[5]
1315 For smale tythes and for smal offringe,
He made the peple pitously to singe.
For er° the bisshop caughte hem with his hook,°   *before / staff, crozier*
They weren in the erchedeknes book.
Thanne hadde he, thurgh his jurisdiccioun,
1320 Power to doon on hem correccioun.°   *inflict punishment on them*
He hadde a somnour redy to his hond.°   *ready to do his bidding*
A slyer boy° nas noon in Engelond,   *knave*
For subtilly° he hadde his espiaille°   *subtly, cunningly / spies*
That taughte him wher that him mighte availle.°   *he would profit*
1325 He coude spare of lechours oon or two,
To techen° him to foure and twenty mo.   *direct, lead*
For thogh this Somnour wood° were as an hare,   *crazy*
To telle his harlotrye° I wol nat spare,   *evil doings, immorality*
For we been out of his correccioun.[6]
1330 They han of us no jurisdiccioun,
Ne never shullen,° terme of alle hir lyves.°   *shall / for as long as they live*
    "Peter!° so been the wommen of the styves,"°   *By St. Peter / brothels*
Quod the Somnour, "y-put out of my cure!"°   *beyond my authority*
    "Pees, with mischance and with misaventure,"°   *bad luck (to you)*
1335 Thus seyde our Host, "and lat him telle his tale.
Now telleth forth, thogh that the Somnour gale.°   *protest*
Ne spareth nat, myn owene maister dere."
    This false theef, this somnour, quod the Frere,
Hadde alwey baudes redy to his hond,°   *pimps ready at hand (cf. l. 1321)*
1340 As any hauk to lure in Engelond,[7]
That° tolde him al the secree° that they knewe,   *Who / secrets*
For hir acqueyntance was nat come of newe.°   *had not come about recently*
They weren hise approwours° prively.°   *agents / privately, secretly*

---

3. Of churchwardens' misbehavior, and of (violations in regard to) wills and marriage contracts,
   and of failing to perform the sacraments (most likely confession and communion).
4. Simony is the buying and selling of church offices, the corruption of spiritual benefits and
   responsibilities by financial motives.
5. And those who did not pay all the tithes they owed (ten percent of one's income) were dealt
   with severely: if any parish priest complained about them, they could not escape financial
   pain (punishment).
6. For we are outside of his authority. (Charges against friars were handled within their orders,
   not by the ecclesiastical courts.)
7. Just as in England any hawk (returns) to the lure (a feathered device a falconer uses to call
   back a hawk).

He took himself a greet profit therby.

1345 His maister knew nat alwey what he wan.° *won, gained*
Withouten mandement,° a lewed° man *a summons / ignorant*
He coude somne,° on peyne of Cristes curs,° *summon / excommunication*
And they were gladde for to fille his purs,
And make him grete festes atte nale.° *entertain him at the ale(house)*

1350 And right° as Judas hadde purses smale *just*
And was a theef,[8] right swich a theef was he.
His maister hadde but half his duetee.° *amount due him*
He was, if I shal yeven him his laude,° *give him the praise (he deserves)*
A theef, and eek° a somnour, and a baude. *also*

1355 He hadde eek wenches at his retenue,° *at his command*
That—whether that sir Robert or sir Huwe,
Or Jakke or Rauf or whoso° that it were *whoever*
That lay by hem—they tolde it in his ere.
Thus was the wenche and he of oon assent,° *in collusion*

1360 And he wolde fecche a feyned mandement° *bring a fake summons*
And somne hem to the chapitre° bothe two, *i.e., the ecclesiastical court*
And pile° the man, and lete the wenche go. *rob, plunder*
Thanne wolde he seye, "Frend, I shal for thy sake
Do stryken hire out of° our lettres blake. *have her (name) erased from*

1365 Thee thar° namore as in this cas travaille.° *need / labor, go to any trouble*
I am thy freend, ther° I thee may availle."° *where / help*
Certeyn° he knew of bryberyes mo° *Certainly / more ways to extort money*
Than possible is to telle in yeres two.
For in this world nis dogge for the bowe,° *hunting dog*

1370 That can an hurt deer from an hool° knowe, *healthy (one)*
Bet° than this somnour knew a sly lechour *Better*
Or an avouter° or a paramour.° *adulterer / lover*
And, for° that was the fruit° of al his rente,° *since / major part / income*
Therfore on it he sette al his entente.° *intentions*

1375 And so bifel° that ones on a day° *it befell, happened / one day*
This somnour, ever waiting on° his pray,° *always on watch for / prey*
Rood for to somne an old widwe,° a ribybe,[9] *widow*
Feynynge a cause,° for he wolde brybe.° *charge / extort money*
And happed° that he saugh bifore him ryde *it happened*

1380 A gay yeman, under a forest syde.[1]
A bowe he bar,° and arwes° brighte and kene.° *bore / arrows / keen, sharp*
He hadde upon a courtepy of grene,° *wore a short green jacket*
An hat upon his heed with frenges° blake. *fringes*
"Sir," quod this somnour, "hayl and wel atake!"° *well met*

1385 "Welcome," quod he, "and every good felawe!
Wher rydestow° under this grene-wode shawe?"° *dost thou ride / grove*
Seyde this yeman. "Wiltow fer° to day?" *Wilt thou (ride) far*
This somnour him answerde and seyde, "Nay.

---

8. Judas, as the purse-keeper for the poor apostles, would have had only a small amount of money; John 12:6 says he was a thief.
9. Rebec, fiddle, a derogatory term for an old woman; see l. 1573.
1. A merry yeoman (see *GP* ll. 101–17), by the edge of a forest.

Heer faste by,"° quod he, "is myn entente   *Close to here*

1390 To ryden, for to reysen up a rent°   *collect some revenue*

That longeth° to my lordes duetee."°   *belongs / what is due my lord*

  "Artow thanne a bailly?"[2] "Ye,"° quod he.   *Yes*

He dorste° nat, for verray° filthe and shame,   *dared / true, sheer*

Seye that he was a somnour, for the name.°   *due to the word (being hateful)*

1395   "*Depardieux*,"° quod this yeman, "dere brother,   *By God*

Thou art a bailly and I am another.

I am unknowen as in° this contree.°   *in / region*

Of thyn aqueyntance I wolde praye thee,

And eek of brotherhede,° if that yow leste.°   *sworn brotherhood / it please you*

1400 I have gold and silver in my cheste;

If that thee happe° to comen in our shyre,°   *happen / shire*

Al shal be thyn, right as thou wolt desyre."°   *whatever thou wilt desire*

  "Grant mercy,"° quod this somnour, "by my feith."   *Thank you*

Everich in otheres hand his trouthe leith,[3]

1405 For to be sworne bretheren til they deye.

In daliance° they ryden forth and pleye.   *friendly conversation*

  This somnour, which that was as ful of jangles,°   *idle, inappropriate speech*

As ful of venim° been thise wariangles,°   *venom / shrikes, butcherbirds*

And ever enquering upon° every thing,   *always inquiring about*

1410   "Brother," quod he, "where is now your dwelling,

Another day if that I sholde yow seche?"°   *seek*

This yeman him answerde in softe° speche,   *quiet, easygoing*

  "Brother," quod he, "fer in the north contree,[4]

Wher as I hope° som tyme I shal thee see.   *Where I hope (or expect)*

1415 Er we departe,° I shal thee so wel wisse°   *part company / inform*

That of myn hous ne shaltow never misse."°   *thou shalt not fail to find*

  "Now, brother," quod this somnour, "I yow preye,

Teche me, whyl that we ryden by the weye,

Sin° that ye been a baillif as am I,   *Since*

1420 Som subtiltee,° and tel me feithfully   *clever stratagem*

In myn offyce how I may most winne.°   *gain*

And spareth nat° for conscience ne sinne,   *do not hold back*

But as my brother tel me—how do ye?"°   *how do you (operate)?*

  "Now, by my trouthe,° brother dere," seyde he,   *troth*

1425 "As I shal tellen thee a feithful tale,°   *accurate account*

My wages been ful streite° and ful smale.   *very limited*

My lord is hard to me and daungerous,°   *haughty, ungenerous*

And myn offyce° is ful laborous,°   *position / laborious*

And therfore by extorcions I live.

1430 For sothe,° I take al that men wol me yive.°   *Truly / give*

Algate,° by sleyghte° or by violence,   *Always / sleight, trickery*

Fro yeer to yeer I winne° al my dispence.°   *earn / living expenses*

---

2. A bailiff. The term was used for local magistrates and for sheriffs' officers but here probably refers to an agent who collects rents for the lord of a manor.

3. Each lays his hand in the other's to pledge his troth.

4. Hell was often thought to be in the north. These lines, plus the earlier detail of his green coat, hint at the yeoman's soon-to-be-revealed identity.

I can no bettre telle, feithfully."
"Now, certes,"° quod this somnour, "so fare I.   *certainly*
1435 I spare nat to taken, God it woot,°   *knows*
But if° it be to hevy° or to hoot.°   *Unless / too heavy / too hot*
What° I may gete in conseil prively,°   *Whatever / in secret*
No maner conscience of that have I.
Nere° myn extorcioun, I mighte nat liven,   *If it were not for*
1440 Ne of swiche japes wol I nat be shriven.[5]
Stomak° ne conscience ne knowe I noon.   *Stomach, i.e., feeling*
I shrewe thise shrifte-fadres everichoon.[6]
Wel be we met, by God and by Seint Jame!°   *St. James*
But, leve° brother, tel me than thy name,"   *dear*
1445 Quod this somnour. In this mene whyle°   *Meanwhile*
This yeman gan° a litel for to smyle.   *began*
"Brother," quod he, "wiltow° that I thee telle?   *wilt thou*
I am a feend.° My dwelling is in helle,   *fiend, devil*
And here I ryde about my purchasing,°   *for my acquisitions*
1450 To wite wher° men wolde yeve me any thing.   *know whether*
My purchas° is th'effect° of al my rente.°   *What I take / sum / income*
Loke how thou rydest for the same entente,
To winne good,° thou rekkest° never how;   *goods, profit / carest*
Right so fare I, for ryde wolde I now
1455 Unto the worldes ende for a preye."°   *prey, victim*
"A," quod this somnour, "*benedicite!*° What sey ye?   *bless us*
I wende° ye were a yeman trewely.   *thought*
Ye han a mannes shap° as wel as I.   *shape, appearance*
Han ye a figure than determinat
1460 In helle, ther ye been in your estat?"[7]
"Nay, certeinly," quod he, "ther have we noon;°   *none*
But whan us lyketh, we can take us oon,°   *assume one (shape)*
Or elles make yow seme° we ben shape   *make it seem to you*
Somtyme lyk a man, or lyk an ape,
1465 Or lyk an angel can I ryde or go.°   *ride or walk, i.e., move*
It is no wonder thing thogh it be so.
A lousy jogelour° can deceyve thee,   *lice-ridden conjurer*
And pardee,° yet can I more craft° than he."   *by God / I know more tricks*
"Why," quod the somnour, "ryde ye thanne or goon
1470 In sondry shap,° and nat alwey in oon?"   *various shapes*
"For° we," quod he, "wol us swich formes   *Because*
make°   *take such shapes*
As most able° is our preyes° for to take."°   *effective / victims / seize*
"What maketh° yow to han al this labour?"   *causes*
"Ful many a cause, leve sir somnour,"
1475 Seyde this feend, "but alle thing hath tyme.°   *(see Ecclesiastes 3:1)*
The day is short, and it is passed pryme,°   *prime, 9:00 A.M.*

5. Nor do I want to be absolved of such tricks through confession.
6. I curse every one of these confessors. (A proper confession would include the summoner's
making restitution for his extortions.)
7. Do you then have a fixed shape in hell, where you are in your normal state?

And yet° ne wan° I nothing in this day.   *as yet / won, gained*
I wol entende° to winnen, if I may,   *concentrate, focus upon*
And nat entende our wittes to declare.°   *discussing our talents*
1480 For, brother myn, thy wit° is al to bare°   *intelligence / all too bare, inadequate*
To understonde, althogh I tolde hem thee.°   *them (to) thee*
But for thou axest° why labouren we: *since thou askest*
For somtyme we ben Goddes instruments
And menes to don° his comandements,   *(the) means of enacting*
1485 Whan that him list,° upon his creatures,   *it pleases him*
In divers art° and in diverse figures.°   *methods / shapes*
Withouten him we have no might,° certayn,   *power*
If that him list to stonden ther-agayn.°   *oppose (our actions)*
And somtyme, at our prayere,° han we leve°   *prayer, request / leave, permission*
1490 Only the body and nat the soule greve;°   *grieve, torment*
Witnesse on° Job, whom that we diden wo.   *Take as evidence*
And somtyme han we might of° bothe two,   *power over*
This is to seyn, of soule and body eke.°   *also*
And somtyme be we suffred° for to seke   *permitted*
1495 Upon° a man and doon his soule unreste°   *i.e., harass / disturb his soul*
And nat his body, and al is for the beste.
Whan he withstandeth our temptacioun,
It is a cause of his savacioun,°   *salvation*
Al be it° that it was nat our entente   *Albeit, although*
1500 He sholde be sauf° but that we wolde him hente.°   *saved / seize, take*
And somtyme be we servant unto man,
As to the erchebisshop Seint Dunstan,
And to the apostles servant eek was I."[8]
"Yet tel me," quod the somnour, "feithfully,
1505 Make ye yow° newe bodies thus alway   *for yourselves*
Of elements?"° The feend answerde,   *Out of the elements (earth, air, fire, water)*
"Nay.
Somtyme we feyne,° and somtyme we aryse   *i.e., produce an illusion*
With° dede bodies in ful sondry wyse,°   *enter into / many ways*
And speke as renably° and faire and wel   *reasonably*
1510 As to the Phitonissa dide Samuel.[9]
(And yet wol som men seye it was nat he;
I do no fors of° your divinitee.)°   *do not care about / theology*
But o° thing warne I thee, I wol nat jape:°   *one / jest*
Thou wolt algates° wite° how we ben shape.   *in any case / know*
1515 Thou shalt herafterward, my brother dere,
Com ther° thee nedeth nat of me to lere.°   *where / learn from me*
For thou shalt by thyn owene experience
Conne in a chayer rede of this sentence[1]
Bet° than Virgyle,° whyl he was on lyve,°   *Better / Virgil / alive*

---

8. Medieval stories tell of the power over demons or devils possessed by Saint Dunstan, a tenth-century Archbishop of Canterbury, and by various apostles.
9. As Samuel did to the Witch of Endor. (See 1 Sam. 28:7–19; the Witch of Endor is referred to elsewhere in the Vulgate Bible as "pythonissam" [1 Par. 10:13].)
1. Be able to lecture on this subject from a professorial chair.

1520 Or Dant also.² Now lat us ryde blyve,°   *ride on quickly*
     For I wol holde companye with thee
     Til it be so that thou forsake me."
         "Nay," quod this somnour, "that shal nat bityde.°   *happen*
     I am a yeman, knowen is ful wyde.
1525 My trouthe° wol I holde as in this cas.   *troth, promise (see ll. 1404–05)*
     For though thou were the devel Sathanas,°   *Satan (himself)*
     My trouthe wol I holde to my brother,
     As I am sworn—and ech of us til other—
     For to be trewe brother in this cas.
1530 And bothe we goon abouten our purchas.°   *acquisitions*
     Tak thou thy part, what that° men wol thee yive,   *whatever*
     And I shal myn. Thus may we bothe live.
     And if that any of us have more than other,
     Lat him be trewe and parte° it with his brother."   *share*
1535   "I graunte,"° quod the devel, "by my fey."°   *agree (to that) / faith*
     And with that word they ryden forth hir wey.
     And right at the entring of the tounes ende°   *town limits*
     To which this somnour shoop him for to wende,°   *intended to go*
     They saugh° a cart, that charged° was with hey,°   *saw / loaded / hay*
1540 Which that a carter droof° forth in his wey.   *drove*
     Deep° was the wey, for which the carte   *Deep (in mud)*
         stood.°   *stuck, stood still*
     The carter smoot° and cryde as he were wood,°   *smote, struck / mad*
     "Hayt, Brok! Hayt, Scot! What, spare ye° for   *do you hold back*
         the stones?³
     The feend," quod he, "yow fecche,° body and bones, *May the devil take you*
1545 As ferforthly° as ever were ye foled,°   *surely / foaled (born)*
     So muche wo as I have with yow tholed!°   *suffered*
     The devel have al, bothe hors and cart and hey!"
         This somnour seyde, "Heer shal we have a pley,"°   *some amusement*
     And neer the feend he drough, as noght ne were,⁴
1550 Ful prively,° and rouned° in his ere: *privately / whispered*
     "Herkne,° my brother, herkne, by thy feith.   *Harken, listen*
     Herestow nat° how that the carter seith?°   *Dost thou not hear / speaks*
     Hent it anon,° for he hath yeve° it thee,   *Seize it immediately / given*
     Bothe hey and cart, and eek hise caples° three."   *also his horses*
1555   "Nay," quod the devel, "God wot,° never a deel.°   *knows / not at all*
     It is nat his entente,° trust me weel.   *intention*
     Axe° him thyself, if thou nat trowest° me,   *Ask / dost not believe*
     Or elles stint° a while and thou shalt see."   *stop, hold off*
     This carter thakketh° his hors upon the croupe,°   *slaps / rump*
1560 And they bigonne drawen° and to stoupe.°   *to draw, pull / stoop, strain*
         "Heyt, now!" quod he, "ther° Jesu Crist yow blesse,   *i.e., may*

2. These lines allude to the famous descriptions of the underworld in the *Aeneid* and the *Divine Comedy*.
3. "Hayt" is a word used to drive horses, like our modern "Giddyap!" "Brok" and "Scot" are the horses' names. The carter accuses them of not pulling hard enough because of the stones in the road.
4. And he drew nearer to the fiend as if it were nothing (i.e., very nonchalantly).

And al his handwerk,° bothe more and lesse!   *handiwork, creation*
That was wel twight,° myn owene lyard° boy.   *pulled / dappled gray*
I pray God save thee and Seynte Loy.[5]
1565 Now is my cart out of the slow,° pardee."°   *slough, mud / by God*
    "Lo, brother," quod the feend, "what tolde I thee?
Heer may ye see, myn owene dere brother,
The carl° spak oo° thing, but he thoghte another.   *churl, fellow / one*
Lat us go forth abouten our viage.°   *on our journey*
1570 Heer winne I nothing upon cariage."°   *by my (feudal) rights*
    Whan that they comen somwhat out of toune,
This somnour to his brother gan to roune.°   *whisper*
"Brother," quod he, "heer woneth° an old   *dwells*
    rebekke°   *fiddle (i.e., woman)*
That hadde almost as lief to lese° hir nekke   *would be almost as willing to lose*
1575 As for to yeve° a peny of hir good.°   *give, surrender / goods*
I wol han twelf pens, though that she be wood,°   *mad*
Or I wol sompne° hir unto our offyce.°   *summon / court*
And yet, God woot,° of hir knowe I no vyce.°   *knows / nothing wrong*
But for° thou canst nat, as in this contree,   *since*
1580 Winne thy cost,° tak heer ensample of me."   *Cover thy expenses*
    This somnour clappeth° at the widwes gate.   *raps*
"Com out," quod he, "thou olde viritrate!°   *hag, witch*
I trowe° thou hast som frere or preest with thee."   *believe*
    "Who clappeth?" seyde this widwe. "*Benedicite!*°   *Bless us*
1585 God save you, sire, what is your swete wille?"
    "I have," quod he, "of somonce here a bille.°   *a writ of summons*
Up peyne of cursing,° loke that thou be   *On pain of excommunication*
Tomorn° bifore the erchedeknes knee   *In the morning*
T'answere to the court of° certeyn thinges."   *in regard to*
1590   "Now, Lord," quod she, "Crist Jesu, king of kinges,
So wisly° helpe me, as I ne may.°   *Surely / I cannot (go to court)*
I have been syk, and that ful many a day.
I may nat go° so fer," quod she, "ne ryde,   *walk*
But I be deed,° so priketh it° in my syde.   *Without dying / it is so painful*
1595 May I nat axe a libel,° sir somnour,   *request a written copy of the charge*
And answere there by my procutour°   *agent, proxy*
To swich thing as men wol opposen me?"°   *charge me with*
    "Yis," quod this somnour, "pay anon°—lat se—°   *now / let us see*
Twelf pens to me, and I wol thee acquyte.
1600 I shall no profit han therby but lyte;°   *except a little*
My maister hath the profit and nat I.
Com of,° and lat me ryden hastily.   *Come on, i.e., hurry*
Yif me twelf pens. I may no lenger tarie."°   *tarry, delay*
    "Twelf pens!" quod she, "Now lady Seinte Marie
1605 So wisly help me out of care and sinne,
This wyde world thogh that I sholde winne,°   *win, gain*
Ne have I nat twelf pens withinne myn hold.°   *possession*
Ye knowen wel that I am povre° and old.   *poor*

5. St. Eligius, the patron saint of carters. See also *GP* 1. 120.

Kythe your almesse on° me, povre wrecche."   *Show your charity to*
1610   "Nay than," quod he, "the foule feend me fecche°   *fetch, take*
If I th'excuse, though thou shul be spilt!"°   *ruined*
"Alas," quod she, "God woot,° I have no gilt!"   *knows*
"Pay me," quod he, "or by the swete Seinte Anne,°   *(Mary's mother)*
As I wol° bere awey thy newe panne   *I.e., I will*
1615 For dette which that thou owest me of old.
Whan that thou madest thyn housbond cokewold,°   *cuckold*
I payde at hoom for thy correccioun."°   *punishment, fine*
"Thou lixt!"° quod she. "By my savacioun,°   *liest / salvation*
Ne was I nevere er° now, widwe ne wyf,   *before*
1620 Somoned unto your court in al my lyf,
Ne nevere I nas° but of my body trewe.   *Nor was I ever*
Unto the devel blak and rough of hewe°   *in appearance*
Yeve° I thy body and my panne also!"   *Give*
And whan the devel herde hir cursen so
1625 Upon hir knees, he seyde in this manere,
"Now, Mabely, myn owene moder dere,
Is this your wil° in ernest that ye seye?"   *will, wish*
"The devel," quod she, "so fecche him er he deye,⁶
And panne and al, but° he wol him repente!"   *unless*
1630 "Nay, olde stot,° that is nat myn entente,"   *(you) old horse*
Quod this somnour, "for to repente me
For any thing that I have had of° thee.   *gotten from*
I wolde I hadde thy smok and every clooth!"⁷
"Now, brother," quod the devel, "be nat wrooth.°   *wroth, angry*
1635 Thy body and this panne ben myne by right.
Thou shalt with me to helle yet tonight,
Where thou shalt knowen of oure privetee°   *secrets*
More than a maister of divinitee."°   *theology*
And with that word this foule feend him hente.°   *seized*
1640 Body and soule, he with the devel wente
Wher as° that somnours han hir heritage.°   *There where / inheritance*
And God, that maked after his image
Mankinde, save and gyde us, alle and some,
And leve° thise somnours good men to bicome.   *let*
1645   Lordinges, I coude han told yow, quod this Frere,
Hadde I had leyser for° this Somnour here,   *Were I given (enough) time by*
After the text° of Crist, Poul,° and John,   *teaching / (St.) Paul*
And of oure othere doctours° many oon,   *authorities on theology*
Swiche peynes° that your hertes mighte   *Such pains, torments*
agryse,°   *shudder*
1650 Al be it so° no tonge may devyse—°   *Even though / describe*
Thogh that I mighte a thousand winter° telle—   *winters, i.e., years*
The peynes of thilke cursed hous of helle.
But for to kepe us fro that cursed place,
Waketh,° and preyeth Jesu for his grace   *Be awake, watchful*
1655 So kepe us fro the temptour Sathanas.°   *Satan*

---

6. She said, "May the devil carry him off before he dies."
7. I wish I had thy shift (undergarment) and every (bit of thy) clothing.

Herketh this word, beth war° as in this cas:　　　　　　　*be aware, wary*
"The leoun sit in his await° alway　　　　　　　*lies in ambush*
To slee the innocent, if that he may."[8]
Disposeth ay° your hertes to withstonde°　　　　　　*always / resist*
1660　The feend, that yow wolde make thral° and bonde.°　　*captive / enslaved*
He may nat tempte yow over youre might,°　　　　*beyond your power*
For Crist wol be your champion[9] and knight.
And prayeth that thise somnours hem repente°　　*repent (themselves)*
Of hir misdedes, er that the feend hem hente.°　*before the devil seizes them*

The Summoner's Prologue and Tale

The Prologue

1665　This Somnour in his stiropes° hye° stood.　　　　　*stirrups / high up*
Upon this Frere° his herte was so wood°　　　　　　*Friar / angry*
That lyk an aspen leef he quook° for yre.°　　　　*trembled / ire*
　　　"Lordinges," quod° he, "but o° thing I desyre.　　*said / just one*
I yow biseke° that, of your curteisye,　　　　　　*beseech*
1670　Sin° ye han° herd this false Frere lye,°　　　　　*Since / have / lie*
As suffereth° me I may my tale telle.　　　　　　*Permit*
This Frere bosteth° that he knoweth helle,　　　　*boasts*
And God it woot° that it is litel wonder:　　　　*God knows*
Freres and feendes° been but lyte asonder.°　*fiends, devils / not far apart*
1675　For, pardee,° ye han ofte tyme herd telle　　　　*by God*
How that a frere ravisshed° was to helle　　　　*carried off*
In spirit ones° by a visioun.°　　　　　　　　*once / in a dream*
And as an angel ladde° him up and doun　　　　　*led*
To shewen him the peynes° that ther were,　　　*pains*
1680　In al the place saugh° he nat a frere.　　　　　*saw*
Of other folk he saugh ynowe° in wo.°　　*enough / woe, torment*
Unto this angel spak the frere tho:°　　　　　　*then*
　　　'Now, sire,' quod he, 'han° freres swich° a grace　*have / such*
That noon° of hem° shal come to this place?'　　*none / them*
1685　'Yis,'° quod this angel, 'many a millioun!'　　*Yes (indeed)*
And unto Sathanas° he ladde° him doun.　　　　　*Satan / led*
'And now hath Sathanas,' seith he, 'a tayl
Brodder° than of a carrik° is the sayl.　*Broader / large sailing ship*
Hold up thy tayl, thou Sathanas,' quod he.
1690　'Shewe forth thyn ers,° and lat the frere see　　*arse*
Wher is the nest of freres in this place.'
And er that half a furlong wey of space,[1]
Right so as bees out swarmen from an hyve,
Out of the develes ers ther gonne dryve°　　　　*did rush*
1695　Twenty thousand freres in a route,°　　　　　　*crowd*

8. See Psalm 10:8–9.
9. One who fights on behalf of someone else in a judicial duel.
1. And in a few moments (literally, the time it takes to walk half a furlong, or about 100 yards).

And thurghout helle swarmeden aboute,
And comen° agayn as faste as they may gon,   *came, returned*
And in° his ers they crepten everichon.°   *into / every one*
He clapte° his tayl agayn, and lay ful stille.   *clapped shut*
1700 This frere, whan he loked hadde his fille
Upon the torments of this sory° place,   *sorrowful*
His spirit God restored of° His grace   *by*
Unto his body agayn, and he awook.°   *awoke*
But natheles° for fere yet° he quook,°   *nevertheless / still / trembled*
1705 So was the develes ers ay° in his minde,   *always*
That is his heritage° of verray kinde.°   *inheritance / by true nature*
God save° yow alle, save° this   *protect / except (with pun on prior meaning)*
       cursed Frere!
My prologe wol I ende in this manere."

The Tale

Lordinges, ther is in Yorkshire, as I gesse,
1710 A mersshy contree° called Holdernesse,°   *marshy region / (in SE Yorkshire)*
In which ther wente a limitour° aboute   *begging friar (see GP l. 209)*
To preche and eek° to begge, it is no doute.   *also*
And so bifel° that on a day this frere   *it happened*
Had preched at a chirche in his manere,
1715 And specially, aboven every thing,
Excited° he the peple in his preching   *Exhorted*
To trentals,[2] and to yeve,° for Goddes sake,   *give (money)*
Wherwith° men mighten holy houses make°   *With which / build*
Ther as° divyne service is honoured,   *Where*
1720 Nat ther as° it is wasted and devoured,   *where*
Ne ther° it nedeth nat for to be yive,°   *Nor where / given*
As to possessioners,[3] that mowen° live—   *who are able to*
Thanked be God—in wele° and habundaunce.   *prosperity*
Trentals, seyde he, deliveren fro penaunce
1725 Hir° freendes soules, as wel olde as yonge,   *Their*
Ye,° whan that they been hastily° y-songe,   *Yes / without delay*
Nat for to holde° a preest joly° and gay: *keep, support / jolly, merry*
He singeth nat but o° masse in a day.   *only one*
"Delivereth out,"° quod he, "anon° the   *Release (from Purgatory) / at once*
       soules!
1730 Ful hard it is with fleshhook° or with oules°   *meathooks / awls*
To been y-clawed,° or to brenne° or bake.   *torn, lacerated / burn*
Now spede yow° hastily, for Cristes sake!"   *help yourselves*
And whan this frere had seyd al his entente,
With *qui cum patre*[4] forth his wey he wente.
1735 Whan folk in chirche had yeve° him what hem leste,°   *given / they wished*
He wente his wey, no lenger wolde he reste.

2. The purchase of thirty requiem masses ("trentals") sung for a soul in Purgatory.
3. Monks and beneficed clergy living on endowments and regular income, unlike the mendicant friars, who are supposed to have no property and so must beg for alms.
4. "Who with the Father" (a liturgical formula for concluding prayers and sermons).

With scrippe and tipped staf, y-tukked hye,[5]
In every hous he gan to poure° and prye,   *look about*
And beggeth mele° and chese or elles corn.°   *meal, flour / grain*
His felawe° hadde a staf tipped with horn,   *companion friar*   1740
A peyre of tables al of yvory,[6]
And a poyntel° polisshed fetisly,°   *stylus / elegantly*
And wroot the names alwey, as he stood,
Of alle folk that yaf hem° any good,°   *gave them / goods*
Ascaunces° that he wolde for hem preye.   *As if*   1745
"Yeve us a busshel whete, malt, or reye,°   *rye*
A Goddes kechil° or a trip° of chese,   *small alms cake / bit, morsel*
Or elles what yow list—we may nat chese°—   *choose*
A Goddes halfpeny or a masse-peny,[7]
Or yeve us of your brawn,° if ye have eny,   *meat*   1750
A dagon° of your blanket,° leve dame,°   *piece / woolen cloth / dear lady*
Our suster dere—lo, here I write your name—
Bacon or beef, or swich thing as ye finde."
    A sturdy harlot° wente ay° hem bihinde,   *fellow / always*
That was hir hostes man,[8] and bar° a sak,   *bore, carried*   1755
And what men yaf hem,° leyde it on his bak.   *whatever people gave them*
And whan that he was out at dore, anon°   *at once*
He planed° awey the names everichon   *smoothed*
That he biforn had writen in his tables.
He served hem with nyfles° and with fables.°   *trifles / lies*   1760
    "Nay, ther thou lixt,° thou Somnour!" quod the Frere.   *liest*
    "Pees!"° quod our Host, "for Cristes moder° dere!   *Peace / mother*
Tel forth thy tale and spare it nat at al."
    "So thryve I,"° quod this Somnour, "so I shal."   *As I may thrive*
So longe he wente, hous by hous, til he   1765
Cam til an hous ther° he was wont° to be   *where / accustomed*
Refresshed° more than in an hundred placis.   *I.e., with food and drink*
Sik lay the gode man° whos that the place is.   *goodman, head of household*
Bedrede° upon a couche lowe he lay.   *Bedridden*
    "Deus hic,"° quod he, "O Thomas, freend, good day,"   *God be here*   1770
Seyde this frere curteisly° and softe.°   *courteously / quietly*
"Thomas," quod he, "God yelde° yow! Ful ofte   *reward*
Have I upon this bench faren ful weel.°   *fared very well, prospered*
Here have I eten many a mery meel."
And fro the bench he droof° awey the cat,   *drove*   1775
And leyde adoun his potente° and his hat,   *staff*
And eek° his scrippe,° and sette him softe adoun.   *also / satchel*
His felawe was go walked° into toun   *had gone walking*
Forth with his knave,° into that hostelrye°   *servant / inn*
Whereas° he shoop him° thilke° night to lye.   *Where / intended / that*   1780
    "O dere maister," quod this syke° man,   *sick*

5. With satchel and a staff tipped with metal and with his robe tucked up high (for easier walking).
6. A folding pair of writing tablets made of ivory. The tablets were wax-coated, written on with a stylus ("poyntel"), and could be easily erased by scraping (see ll. 1757–59).
7. A half-penny as alms or a penny for saying mass.
8. Possibly the servant of the host at the inn where the two friars were staying (see ll. 1778–80).

"How han ye fare sith° that March bigan?   *since*
I saugh° yow noght this fourtenight° or more."   *saw / fortnight (two weeks)*
"God woot,"° quod he, "laboured have I ful sore,°   *knows / exceedingly*
1785 And specially for thy savacioun°   *salvation*
Have I seyd many a precious orisoun,°   *prayer*
And for our othere frendes, God hem° blesse.   *them*
I have today been at your chirche at messe°   *mass*
And seyd a sermon after my simple wit,
1790 Nat al after° the text of holy writ,   *according to*
For it is hard to yow,° as I suppose,   *for you (to understand)*
And therfore wol I teche° yow al the glose.⁹   *teach*
Glosinge° is a glorious thing, certeyn,   *Interpretation*
For lettre sleeth,° so as we clerkes° seyn.   *slays, kills / scholars*
1795 Ther° have I taught hem to be charitable   *I.e., in church*
And spende hir good ther° it is resonable,   *their money where*
And ther I saugh our dame°—a! wher is she?"   *i.e., your wife*
"Yond in the yerd° I trowe° that she be,"   *yard, garden / believe*
Seyde this man, "and she wol come anon."°   *at once*
1800   "Ey, maister! Welcome be ye, by Seint John,"
Seyde this wyf. "How fare ye, hertely?"°   *(I ask it) sincerely*
The frere aryseth up ful curteisly,
And hir embraceth in his armes narwe,°   *closely*
And kiste° hir swete,° and chirketh° as a   *kissed / sweetly / chirps*
     sparwe°   *sparrow*
1805 With his lippes. "Dame," quod he, "right weel,
As he that is your servant every deel,°   *every bit, completely*
Thanked be God, that yow yaf° soule and lyf.   *gave*
Yet saugh° I nat this day so fair° a wyf   *saw / lovely*
In al the chirche, God so save me!"
1810   "Ye, God amende defautes,° sir," quod she.   *repair (my) faults*
"Algates,° welcome be ye, by my fey."°   *In any case / faith*
"Graunt mercy,° dame, this have I founde alwey.   *Many thanks*
But of your grete goodnesse, by your leve,°   *with your permission*
I wolde prey yow that ye nat yow greve—°   *get angry*
1815 I wol with Thomas speke a litel throwe.°   *while*
Thise curats° been ful necligent and slowe°   *parish priests / slothful*
To grope tendrely° a conscience   *search sensitively*
In shrift.° In preching is my diligence,   *confession*
And studie in Petres° wordes and in Poules.°   *St. Peter's / St. Paul's*
1820 I walke and fisshe° Cristen° mennes soules   *fish for / Christian*
To yelden° Jesu Crist his propre rente.°   *give to / due tribute*
To sprede his word is set al myn entente."
"Now, by your leve, o dere sir," quod she,
"Chydeth° him weel, for seinte Trinitee.°   *Admonish / Holy Trinity*
1825 He is as angry as a pissemyre,°   *pismire, ant*
Though that he have al that he can desyre.

9. The "glose" (gloss) offers a spiritual interpretation of a sacred text rather than a literal reading. "The letter killeth, but the spirit giveth life" (2 Cor. 3:6, paraphrased below, l. 1794).
   But "glossing" came also to mean wilfully misinterpreting a text for ulterior purposes; see
   ll. 1918–28 for an example.

Though I him wrye° a-night and make him warm — cover
And on hym leye my leg outher° myn arm, — or
He groneth lyk our boor,° lyth° in our sty. — pig / that lies
1830 Other desport° right noon of him have I. — pleasure
I may nat plese him in no maner cas."° — in any way
　　"O Thomas! *Je vous dy,*° Thomas, Thomas, — I tell you
This maketh the feend.° This moste ben — This is the work of the devil
　　amended.
Ire° is a thing that hye God defended,° — Anger (a deadly sin) / forbade
1835 And therof wol I speke a word or two." — before
　　"Now maister," quod the wyf, "er° that I go, — before
What wol ye dyne?° I wol go theraboute."° — eat for dinner / see about it
　　"Now dame," quod he, "*Je vous dy sanz doute,*° — I say to you indeed
Have I° nat of a capon but the livere,° — If I were to have / just the liver
1840 And of your softe breed nat but° a shivere,° — nothing but / sliver
And after that a rosted pigges heed
(But that I nolde no beest for me were deed),[1]
Thanne hadde I with yow hoomly suffisaunce.° — plain food enough
I am a man of litel sustenaunce.° — who eats little
1845 My spirit hath his fostring° in the Bible. — its nourishment
The body is ay so redy and penyble
To wake that my stomak is destroyed.[2]
I prey yow, dame, ye be nat anoyed,
Though I so freendly yow my conseil° shewe. — secrets
1850 By God, I wolde nat telle it° but a fewe." — tell it (to)
　　"Now sir," quod she, "but o word er I go.
My child is deed° withinne thise wykes° two, — died / weeks
Sone° after that ye wente out of this toun." — Soon
　　"His deeth saugh° I by revelacioun," — saw
1855 Seith this frere, "at hoom in our dortour.° — dormitory (in the convent)
I dar wel seyn that er° that half an hour — before
After his deeth, I saugh him born to blisse° — carried to heaven
In myn avisioun,° so God me wisse.° — vision / guide
So dide our sexteyn° and our fermerer,° — sacristan / infirmary keeper
1860 That han° been trewe freres fifty yeer. — Who have
(They may now—God be thanked of his lone—
Maken hir jubilee and walke allone.)[3]
And up I roos° and al our covent eke,° — rose / also
With many a tere° trikling on my cheke, — tear
1865 Withouten noyse or clateringe of belles.
Te deum[4] was our song and nothing elles,
Save° that to Crist I seyde an orisoun° — Except / prayer
Thankinge him of his revelacioun.
For, sir and dame,° trusteth me right weel, — dear sir and madam
1870 Our orisons been more effectueel,° — valid, effective

1. But I would not want any animal killed (just) for me.
2. [My] body is always so ready and inured to staying awake (at prayers and vigils) that my appetite has been destroyed.
3. They may now—thank God for his gift—celebrate their jubilee (fiftieth year in the convent) and go about alone (instead of in pairs).
4. A hymn of praise, usually sung at Matins.

And more we seen of Cristes secree° thinges	*secret, hidden*
Than burel° folk, although they weren kinges.	*secular*
We live in poverte and in abstinence,	
And burel folk in richesse and despence°	*(wasteful) expenditure*
1875 Of mete and drinke, and in hir foul delyt.°	*their foul pleasure(s)*
We han° this worldes lust° al in despyt.°	*hold / pleasure / contempt*
Lazar and Dives liveden° diversly,⁵	*lived*
And diverse guerdon° hadden they therby.°	*different rewards / as a result*
Whoso wol preye, he moot° faste and be clene,°	*must / chaste*
1880 And fatte° his soule and make his body lene.°	*fatten / lean*
We fare as seith th'apostle:⁶ cloth° and fode°	*clothing / food*
Suffysen° us, though they be nat ful gode.	*Suffice for*
The clennesse° and the fastinge of us freres	*chaste living*
Maketh that° Crist accepteth our preyeres.	*Is the reason why*
1885 Lo, Moyses° fourty dayes and fourty night	*Moses*
Fasted, er° that the heighe God of might	*before*
Spak with him in the mountain of Sinay.°	*Sinai (cf. Exodus 34:28)*
With empty wombe,° fastinge many a day,	*stomach*
Receyved he the lawe that was writen	
1890 With Goddes finger; and Elie,° wel ye witen,°	*Elijah / know*
In mount Oreb,° er he hadde any speche	*Horeb*
With hye° God, that is our lyves leche,°	*high / healer, physician*
He fasted longe and was in contemplaunce.°	*contemplation (cf. 1 Kings 19:8)*
Aaron, that hadde the temple in governaunce,	
1895 And eek° the othere preestes everichon,°	*also / every one*
Into the temple whan they sholde gon	
To preye for the peple and do servyse,	
They nolden° drinken in no maner wyse°	*would not / in any way*
No drinke which that mighte hem dronke make,	
1900 But there in abstinence preye and wake,	
Lest that they deyden.° Tak heed what I seye.	*died (cf. Leviticus 10:8–11)*
But° they be sobre that for the peple preye,	*Unless*
War° that—I seye namore, for it suffyseth.	*Beware*
Our lord Jesu, as holy writ devyseth,°	*relates*
1905 Yaf° us ensample of fastinge and preyeres.	*Gave*
Therfor we mendinants,° we sely° freres,	*mendicants / good, simple*
Been° wedded to poverte and continence,	*Are*
To charitee, humblesse, and abstinence,	
To persecucion for rightwisnesse,°	*for the sake of righteousness*
1910 To wepinge, misericorde,° and clennesse.°	*mercy / chastity*
And therfor may ye see that our preyeres—	
I speke of us, we mendinants, we freres—	
Ben to the hye God more acceptable	
Than youres, with your festes° at the table.	*feasts*
1915 Fro Paradys first, if I shal nat lye,	
Was man out chaced° for his glotonye;	*chased*

5. In Jesus' parable (Luke 16:19–31), Lazarus, a beggar denied even the crumbs from the rich man's (Dives's) table, is carried by angels after his death to Abraham's bosom, while the rich man suffers horribly in hell.
6. St. Paul (in 1 Timothy 6:8).

And chaast° was man in Paradys, certeyn.   *chaste*
   But herkne now, Thomas, what I shal seyn.°   *say*
I ne have no text° of it, as I suppose,   *i.e., biblical source*
1920 But I shall finde it in a maner glose,°   *a kind of gloss (see ll. 1792–94)*
That specially our swete lord Jesus
Spak this by° freres, whan he seyde thus: *concerning*
'Blessed be they that povre° in spirit been.'   *poor (cf. Matthew 5:3)*
And so forth al the gospel may ye seen,
1925 Wher it be lyker our professioun,
Or hirs that swimmen in possessioun.[7]
Fy on hir° pompe and on hir glotonye!   *their*
And for hir lewednesse° I hem diffye.°   *ignorance / scorn them*
   Me thinketh they ben lyk Jovinian,[8]
1930 Fat as a whale and walkinge as° a swan,   *waddling like*
Al vinolent° as botel° in the spence.°   *full of wine / bottle / pantry*
Hir° preyer is of ful gret reverence,   *Their*
Whan they for soules seye the psalm of Davit:°   *David*
Lo, 'Buf!'° they seye, 'cor meum eructavit.'[9]   *(sound of a belch)*
1935 Who folweth Cristes gospel and his fore°   *footsteps (i.e., example)*
But we that humble been and chast° and pore,   *chaste*
Werkers° of Goddes word, not auditours?°   *Doers / (merely) listeners*
Therfore, right° as an hauk up at a sours°   *just / in rising flight*
Up springeth into th'eir,° right so prayeres   *air*
1940 Of charitable and chaste bisy freres
Maken hir sours° to Goddes eres° two.   *upward flight / ears*
Thomas, Thomas, so mote° I ryde or go,°   *may / walk*
And by that lord that clepid is Seint Yve,
Nere thou our brother, sholdestou nat thryve.[1]
1945 In our chapitre° praye we day and night   *In devotions at our friary*
To Crist, that he thee sende hele° and might,°   *health / strength*
Thy body for to welden hastily."°   *quickly (re)gain the use of*
   "God woot,"° quod he, "nothing therof° fele° I.   *knows / from that / feel*
As help me Crist, as° I in fewe yeres   *i.e., although*
1950 Have spended upon dyvers maner° freres   *many sorts of*
Ful many a pound, yet fare I never the bet.°   *better*
Certeyn, my good° have I almost biset.°   *goods, wealth / used up*
Farwel my gold, for it is al ago!"
   The frere answerde, "O Thomas, dostow° so?   *dost thou*
1955 What nedeth yow diverse° freres seche?°   *different / seek out*
What nedeth him that hath a parfit leche°   *perfect doctor*

---

7. And so you can see throughout the gospel whether it (as a statement of Christian principles) is more like our (fraternal) orders or theirs (the beneficed clergy) that swim in endowments.
8. Jovinian was a fourth-century monk whose heretical views on marriage and the good life prompted St. Jerome's *Adversus Jovinianum*, to which the Wife of Bath responds in her Prologue; see esp. ll. 673–75 and the excerpts from Jerome reprinted in the "Sources and Backgrounds" section of this Norton Critical Edition.
9. "My heart hath uttered [a good word]." This is the opening of Psalm 45, but *eructare* can also mean to belch.
1. And by that great man called St. Ivo, wert thou not our brother, thou shouldst not prosper. Thomas is a "brother" by having been admitted to lay-brotherhood in the friar's order. Scholars disagree about the identity of St. Ivo.

To sechen othere leches in the toun?
Your inconstance° is your confusioun.°   *inconstancy / ruin*
Holde ye than° me or elles our covent°   *Do you then consider / convent, friary*
1960 To praye for yow ben insufficient?
Thomas, that jape° nis nat worth a myte.°   *foolish notion / coin of small value*
Your maladye is for° we han to lyte.°   *because / too little (from you)*
'A! yif° that covent half a quarter otes.°   *give / quarter-load of oats*
A! yif that covent four and twenty grotes.°   *groats (coin worth four pence)*
1965 A! yif that frere a peny, and lat him go.'
Nay, nay, Thomas! It may no thing° be so!   *not at all*
What is a ferthing° worth parted in twelve?   *farthing*
Lo, ech thing that is oned° in himselve°   *united / itself*
Is more strong than whan it is toscatered.°   *scattered, dispersed*
1970 Thomas, of° me thou shalt nat been y-flatered:°   *by / flattered*
Thou woldest han° our labour al for noght.°   *have / nothing*
The hye God, that al this world hath wroght,°   *made*
Seith that the werkman worthy is his hyre.°   *is worthy of his wages (Luke 10:7)*
Thomas, noght of your tresor I desyre
1975 As for myself, but that al our covent
To preye for yow is ay° so diligent,   *always*
And for to builden Cristes owene chirche.
Thomas, if ye wol lernen for to wirche,°   *to do good works*
Of° buildinge up of chirches may ye finde   *Concerning*
1980 If it be good in Thomas lyf of Inde.²
Ye lye heer° ful of anger and of yre,°   *lie here / ire, wrath*
With which the devel set° your herte afyre,   *sets*
And chyden° heer this sely° innocent,   *scold / poor, simple*
Your wyf, that° is so meke and pacient.   *who*
1985 And therfor, Thomas, trowe° me if thee leste,°   *believe / will*
Ne stryve° nat with thy wyf, as for thy beste;°   *argue, fight / for thy own good*
And ber° this word awey now, by thy feith.   *bear*
Touchinge° swich thing, lo, what the wyse man seith: *Concerning*
'Within thyn hous ne be thou no leoun.°   *lion (cf. Ecclesiasticus 34:5)*
1990 To thy subgits° do noon oppressioun,   *subjects*
Ne make thyne aqueyntances nat to flee.'
And Thomas, yet eftsones° I charge° thee,   *again / command*
Be war from° ire that in thy bosom slepeth,   *Beware of*
War fro the serpent that so slyly crepeth°   *creeps*
1995 Under the gras and stingeth subtilly.°   *secretly*
Be war, my sone, and herkne° paciently   *harken, hear*
That twenty thousand men han lost hir lyves
For stryving with hir lemmans° and hir wyves.   *their lovers*
Now sith° ye han so holy° meke a wyf,   *since / wholly, entirely*
2000 What nedeth yow, Thomas, to maken stryf?°   *create strife*
Ther nis,° ywis,° no serpent so cruel   *is not / indeed*
Whan man tret° on his° tayl, ne half so fel°   *treads / its / dangerous*
As womman is whan she hath caught an ire.°   *become angry*

2. The saint's life of the apostle Thomas, some versions of which tell of his building churches
in India.

Vengeance is thanne al that they desyre.
2005 Ire is a sinne, oon of the grete of sevene,°   *chief of the seven (deadly sins)*
Abhominable unto the God of hevene,
And to himself° it is destruccion.   *a man himself*
This every lewed viker° or person°   *ignorant vicar / parson*
Can seye—how Ire engendreth homicyde.
2010 Ire is, in sooth,° executour° of pryde.   *truth / i.e., agent*
I coude of ire seye so muche sorwe,
My tale sholde laste til tomorwe.
And therfor preye I God bothe day and night:
An irous° man, God sende° him litel might!°   *angry / may God send / power*
2015 It is greet harm and certes° gret pitee   *certainly*
To sette an irous man in heigh degree.°   *social rank*
    Whilom° ther was an irous potestat,°   *Once / potentate*
As seith Senek,° that, duringe his estaat,°   *Seneca / term of office*
Upon a day out riden° knightes two,   *rode*
2020 And as fortune wolde° that it were so,   *willed, desired*
That oon of hem° cam hoom, that other noght.°   *one of them / did not*
Anon° the knight bifore the juge° is broght,   *Promptly / judge*
That seyde thus: 'Thou hast thy felawe° slayn,   *fellow, companion*
For which I deme° thee to the deeth, certayn.'   *condemn*
2025 And to another knight comanded he,
'Go lede° him to the deeth, I charge thee.'   *lead, bring*
And happed,° as they wente by the weye   *it happened*
Toward the place ther° he sholde deye,°   *where / die*
The knight cam which men wenden° had be deed.   *thought*
2030 Thanne thoughte they it was the beste reed°   *plan*
To lede hem bothe to the juge agayn.
They seiden, 'Lord, the knight ne hath nat slayn
His felawe; here he standeth hool° alyve.'   *whole, unharmed*
'Ye shul° be deed,' quod he, 'so moot° I thryve,   *shall / may*
2035 That is to seyn bothe oon and two and three!'
And to the firste knight right thus spak he,
'I dampned° thee. Thou most algate° be deed.   *condemned / therefore*
And thou also most nedes° lese° thyn heed,   *necessarily / lose*
For thou art cause why thy felawe deyth.'
2040 And to the thridde knight right thus he seyth,
'Thou hast nat doon that° I comanded thee.'   *what*
And thus he dide don sleen hem alle three.° *caused all three of them to be slain*
    Irous Cambyses was eek dronkelewe,[3]
And ay delyted him° to been a shrewe.°   *always took pleasure / evil person*
2045 And so bifel, a lord of his meynee,°   *household*
That lovede vertuous moralitee,
Seyde on a day bitwix hem two° right thus: *i.e., confidentially*
'A lord is lost if he be vicious,°   *given to vice*
And dronkenesse is eek a foul record°   *shameful reputation*
2050 Of° any man, and namely° in a lord.   *For / especially*

---

3. Angry Cambises (a king of Persia) was also addicted to drink.

Ther is ful many an eye and many an ere° *ear*
Awaiting on° a lord—he noot nat° where. *Watching / does not know*
For Goddes love, drink more attemprely!° *temperately, moderately*
Wyn maketh man to lesen° wrecchedly *lose*
2055 His minde and eek his limes° everichon.' *(control of) his limbs*
'The revers° shaltou° se,' quod he anon, *reverse / shalt thou*
'And preve° it by thyn owene experience *prove*
That wyn ne dooth to folk no swich offence.° *harm*
Ther is no wyn bireveth me my might° *(that) deprives me of my control*
2060 Of hand ne foot ne of myn eyen sight.'
And for despyt° he drank ful muchel more— *out of spite*
An hondred part°—than he had doon bifore; *a hundred times (more)*
And right anon this irous° cursed wrecche *angry*
Leet° this knightes sone° bifore him fecche,° *Caused / son / to be brought*
2065 Comandinge him he sholde bifore him stonde.
And sodeynly he took his bowe in honde,
And up the streng° he pulled to his ere,° *bowstring / ear*
And with an arwe he slow° the child° right there. *slew, killed / young man*
'Now whether have I a siker hand or noon?'[4]
2070 Quod he. 'Is al my might and minde agoon?
Hath wyn bireved me myn eyen sight?'° *bereft me of my eyesight*
What sholde I telle th'answere of the knight?
His sone was slayn, ther is namore to seye.
Beth war° therfor with lordes how ye pleye. *Beware*
2075 Singeth *Placebo*° and 'I shal if I can,' *I shall please (Psalm 114:9)*
But if° it be unto a povre° man. *Unless / poor*
To a povre man men sholde hise vyces telle,
But nat to a lord, thogh he sholde go to helle.
  Lo irous Cirus, thilke Percien,° *angry Cyrus the Great, the Persian*
2080 How he destroyed the river of Gysen° *river Gyndes*
For that an hors of his was dreynt° therinne, *drowned*
Whan that he wente Babiloigne to winne.° *to conquer Babylon*
He made that the river was so smal[5]
That wommen mighte wade it over al.
2085 Lo, what seyde he° that so wel teche° can? *i.e., Solomon / teach*
'Ne be no felawe to an irous man,
Ne with no wood° man walke by the weye, *mad, crazy*
Lest thee repente.'° I wol no ferther seye. *regret it (cf. Proverbs 22:24–25)*
  Now, Thomas, leve° brother, lef° thyn ire. *dear / leave*
2090 Thou shalt me finde as just° as is a squire.° *exact, true / carpenter's square*
Hold nat the develes knyf ay° at thyn herte— *always*
Thyn angre dooth thee al to sore smerte°— *makes thee suffer all too painfully*
But shewe to me al thy confessioun."° *all you need to confess*
  "Nay," quod the syke° man, "by Seint Simoun!° *sick / Simon (the apostle)*
2095 I have be shriven° this day at° my curat.° *confessed / by / local priest*
I have him told hoolly° al myn estat.° *wholly / spiritual condition*
Nedeth namore to speke of it, seith he,

4. Now (tell me) whether I have a steady hand or not.
5. I.e., he diverted the river into so many small channels.

But if me list° of myn humilitee."   *Unless I choose*

   "Yif° me thanne of thy gold to make our cloistre,"   *Give*

2100 Quod he, "for many a muscle and many an oistre,[6]

Whan other men han ben ful wel at eyse,°   *ease*

Hath been our fode, our cloistre for to reyse.°   *build*

And yet, God woot, unnethe the fundement

Parfourned is, ne of our pavement

2105 Nis nat a tyle yet withinne our wones.[7]

By God, we owen° fourty pound for stones.   *owe*

Now help, Thomas, for Him° that harwed° helle,   *i.e., Christ / harrowed*

For elles° moste° we our bokes selle.   *otherwise / must*

And if ye lakke our predicacioun,°   *preaching*

2110 Than gooth the world al to destruccioun.

For whoso wolde us fro this world bireve°—   *remove*

So God me save, Thomas, by your leve°—   *leave*

He wolde bireve out of this world the sonne.°   *sun*

For who can teche and werchen° as we conne?   *work, do good deeds*

2115 And that is nat of litel tyme,"° quod he,   *i.e., not just recently*

"But sith° Elie° was, or Elisee,°   *since / Elijah / Elisha*

Han freres been—that finde I of record°—   *recorded, written down*

In charitee, y-thanked be our Lord.[8]

Now Thomas, help, for seinte charitee!"

2120 And doun anon° he sette him on his knee.°   *at once / i.e., he kneeled*

   This syke man wex wel ny wood for ire.°   *went nearly insane out of anger*

He wolde° that the frere had been on fire   *wished*

With his false dissimulacioun.°   *dissimulation, hypocrisy*

"Swich thing as is in my possessioun,"°   *i.e., owned by me*

2125 Quod he, "that may I yeven,° and non other.°   *give / nothing else*

Ye sey me thus, how that I am your brother?"° *lay brother of your order*

   "Ye, certes," quod the frere, "trusteth weel.

I took our dame our lettre with our seel."[9]

   "Now wel," quod he, "and somwhat° shal I yive° *something / give*

2130 Unto your holy covent whyl I live,

And in thyn hand thou shalt it have anoon,°   *at once*

On this condicioun and other noon:°   *no other*

That thou departe it so,° my dere brother,   *divide it in such a way*

That every frere have as muche as other.

2135 This shaltou° swere on thy professioun,°   *shalt thou / religious vows*

Withouten fraude or cavillacioun."°   *quibbling*

   "I swere it," quod this frere, "upon my feith."

And therwithal his hand in his he leith.°   *lays*

"Lo, heer my feith!° In me shal be no lak."° *here is my pledge / lack, fault*

---

6. In the Middle Ages, mussels and oysters were held in some disdain as part of a meatless diet associated with Lenten abstinence, poverty, and penance.

7. And still, God knows, the foundation has scarcely been completed, nor has a tile yet been laid on the floor where we live.

8. The Carmelites, a thirteenth-century order of friars, claimed they were founded by the prophet Elijah and his successor, Elisha.

9. I carried a letter of confraternity (i.e., brotherhood) to our lady (your wife) with our official seal.

2140   "Now thanne, put thyn hand doun by my bak,"
       Seyde this man, "and grope wel bihinde.
       Bynethe my buttok° ther shaltow finde   *buttocks*
       A thing that I have hid in privetee."°   *secrecy*
       "A!" thoghte this frere, "that shal go with me!"
2145   And doun his hand he launcheth° to the clifte°   *thrusts / cleft*
       In hope for to finde ther a yifte.°   *gift*
       And whan this syke man felte this frere
       Aboute his tuwel° grope there and here,   *rectum*
       Amidde his hand he leet° the frere a fart.   *let, released*
2150   Ther nis no capul° drawinge in a cart,   *horse*
       That mighte have lete a fart of swich a soun.°   *such a sound*
          The frere up stirte° as doth a wood leoun.°   *started, leaped / maddened lion*
       "A! false cherl,"° quod he, "for Goddes bones!   *churl, fellow*
       This hastow for despyt doon,° for the nones.°   *done for spite / on purpose*
2155   Thou shalt abye° this fart, if that I may!"   *pay for*
          His meynee,° whiche that herden this affray,°   *servants / disturbance*
       Cam lepinge in and chaced out the frere,
       And forth he gooth with a ful angry chere,°   *appearance*
       And fette his felawe theras lay his stoor.¹
2160   He looked as° he were a wilde boor;   *as though*
       He grinte with° his teeth, so was he wrooth.   *ground, gnashed*
       A sturdy pas° doun to the court° he gooth,   *(At) a furious pace / manor house*
       Wheras° ther woned° a man of greet honour,   *Where / dwelt*
       To whom that he was alwey confessour.
2165   This worthy man was lord° of that village.   *i.e., feudal lord*
       This frere cam, as he were in a rage,
       Wheras this lord sat eting at his bord.°   *table*
       Unnethes° mighte the frere speke a word,   *Scarcely*
       Til atte laste he seyde, "God yow see."°   *May God watch over you*
2170   This lord gan loke and seide, "*Benedicite!*°   *Bless us*
       What, frere John, what maner world is this?°   *i.e., what's wrong*
       I see wel that som thing ther is amis.°   *amiss*
       Ye loken as the wode° were ful of thevis.°   *woods / thieves*
       Sit doun anon and tel me what your greef° is,   *grievance*
2175   And it shal been amended, if I may."
          "I have," quod he, "had a despyt° this day—   *insult (spite)*
       God yelde yow°—adoun in your village,   *May God reward you*
       That in this world is noon so povre a page°   *so lowly a serving boy*
       That he nolde° have abhominacioun°   *would not / loathing, disgust*
2180   Of that° I have receyved in your toun.   *For what*
       And yet ne greveth me nothing so sore°   *sorely, deeply*
       As that this olde cherl with lokkes hore°   *white hair*
       Blasphemed hath our holy covent eke."°   *also*
          "Now maister,"° quod this lord, "I yow biseke°—"   *master / beseech*
2185   "No maister, sire," quod he, "but servitour,°   *servant*
       Thogh I have had in scole that honour.°   *i.e., a master of arts degree*

       1. And fetched his companion friar (at the lodging) where there was all his store (what he had
          collected from begging).

God lyketh nat that 'Raby'° men us calle,   *rabbi (cf. Matthew 23:8)*
Neither in market ne in your large halle."
    "No fors,"° quod he, "but tel me al your grief."   *No matter*
2190   "Sire," quod this frere, "an odious meschief°   *wrong*
This day bitid is° to myn ordre and me,   *has happened*
And so *per consequens*° to ech degree   *consequently*
Of holy chirche. God amende it sone!"
    "Sir," quod the lord, "ye woot° what is to done.   *know*
2195 Distempre yow noght.° Ye be my confessour;   *Do not lose your temper*
Ye been the salt of the erthe and the savour.°   *savor, taste (cf. Matthew 5:13)*
For Goddes love, your pacience ye holde.°   *i.e., calm yourself*
Tel me your grief." And he anon him tolde
As ye han herd biforn—ye woot wel what.
2200   The lady of the hous ay° stille sat,   *all the time*
Til she had herd what the frere sayde.
"Ey, Goddes moder,"° quod she, "blisful mayde!   *mother*
Is ther oght elles?° Telle me feithfully."   *anything else*
    "Madame," quod he, "how thinketh yow herby?"°   *about this*
2205   "How that me thinketh?" quod she. "So God me speede,
I seye a cherl° hath doon a cherles dede.   *churl, common fellow*
What shold I seye? God lat him never thee!°   *thrive, prosper*
His syke heed is ful of vanitee.°   *foolishness*
I hold him° in a maner frenesye."°   *believe him (to be) / kind of madness*
2210   "Madame," quod he, "by God, I shal nat lye,
But I on other wise° may be wreke:°   *in another way / avenged*
I shal diffame° him overal ther° I speke,   *defame / everywhere*
This false blasphemour, that charged me
To parte that° wol nat departed be   *divide that which*
2215 To every man yliche,° with meschaunce!"°   *alike (equally) / curse him*
    The lord sat stille as he were in a traunce,°   *trance*
And in his herte he rolled up and doun,°   *turned over (the question)*
"How hadde this cherl imaginacioun°   *the ingenuity*
To shewe° swich a probleme° to the frere?   *present / logical problem*
2220 Never erst er° now herde I of swich matere.°   *before / such an affair*
I trowe° the devel putte it in his minde.   *believe*
In ars-metryke° shal ther no man finde,   *arithmetic (with pun on "arse")*
Biforn this day, of swich a questioun.°   *problem*
Who sholde make a demonstracioun°   *provide a logical proof*
2225 That every man sholde have yliche his part
As of the soun° or savour° of a fart?   *sound / odor*
O nyce,° proude cherl, I shrewe° his face!   *foolish / curse*
Lo, sires," quod the lord, "with harde grace!°   *bad luck to him*
Who ever herde of swich a thing er° now?   *before*
2230 To every man ylyke?° Tel me how.   *alike (equally)*
It is an inpossible°—it may nat be!   *logical impossibility*
Ey, nyce cherl, God lete him never thee!°   *thrive, prosper*
The rumblinge of a fart and every soun
Nis but of eir reverberacioun,°   *Is only reverberation of air*
2235 And ever° it wasteth lyte and lyte° awey.   *always / diminishes little by little*

Ther is no man can demen,° by my fey,°   *judge / faith*
If that it were departed° equally.   *divided*
What, lo, my cherl, lo yet how shrewedly°   *wickedly*
Unto my confessour today he spak.
2240 I holde him certeyn a demoniak!°   *madman (demon-possessed)*
Now ete your mete and lat the cherl go pleye.
Lat him go hange himself a devel weye!"°   *in the devil's name*
    Now stood the lordes squyer° at the bord,°   *squire / table*
That carf° his mete, and herde word by word   *Who carved*
2245 Of alle thinges of which I have yow sayd.
"My lord," quod he, "be ye nat yvel apayd,°   *if you were not displeased*
I coude telle, for a goune-clooth,°   *cloth for a gown*
To yow, sir frere, so ye be nat wrooth,°   *wroth, angry*
How that this fart sholde even deled° be   *evenly distributed*
2250 Among your covent, if it lyked me."
    "Tel," quod the lord, "and thou shalt have anon
A goune-cloth, by God and by Seint John."
    "My lord," quod he, "whan that the weder° is fair,   *weather*
Withouten wind or perturbinge° of air,   *disturbance*
2255 Lat bringe° a cartwheel here into this halle.   *Let there be brought*
But loke° that it have his° spokes alle.   *see to it / its*
Twelf spokes hath a cartwheel comunly.°   *commonly, usually*
And bring me than twelf freres. Woot ye° why?   *Do you know*
For thrittene° is a covent, as I gesse.   *thirteen (twelve and a superior)*
2260 Youre confessour heer, for his worthinesse,
Shal parfourne up° the nombre of his covent.   *complete*
Than shal they knele doun, by oon assent,°   *by one accord, in concord*
And to every spokes ende, in this manere,
Ful sadly° leye° his nose shal a frere.   *firmly, steadily / lay, place*
2265 Your noble confessour—ther God him save—°   *may God preserve him*
Shal holde his nose upright° under the nave.°   *upwards / hub*
Than shal this cherl, with bely stif and toght°   *taut*
As any tabour,° hider° been y-broght;   *drum / hither*
And sette him on the wheel right of this cart,
2270 Upon the nave,° and make him lete a fart.   *hub*
And ye shul seen, up peril of my lyf,°   *i.e., I stake my life on it*
By preve° which that is demonstratif,°   *proof / demonstrable*
That equally the soun° of it wol wende,°   *sound / travel*
And eek° the stink, unto the spokes ende—   *also*
2275 Save° that this worthy man, your confessour,   *Except*
By cause° he is a man of greet honour,   *Because*
Shal have the firste fruit, as reson is.°   *as is right*
The noble usage° of freres yet° is this: *custom / still*
The worthy men of hem° shul first be served;   *among them*
2280 And certeinly he hath it weel deserved.
He hath today taught us so muchel° good   *much*
With° preching in the pulpit ther° he stood,   *Through / where*
That I may vouchesauf, I sey for me,°   *would grant, speaking for myself*
He hadde the firste smel of fartes three.

2285	And so wolde al his covent hardily,°	*assuredly*
	He bereth him° so faire and holily."°	*bears himself, behaves / devoutly*
	The lord, the lady, and ech man save° the frere	*except*
	Seyede that Jankin spak in this matere°	*on this problem*
	As wel as Euclide or Ptholomee.[2]	
2290	Touchinge° this cherl, they seyde subtiltee°	*As for / cleverness*
	And heigh wit° made him speken as he spak;	*intelligence, ingenuity*
	He nis no fool ne no demoniak.°	*madman (see l. 2240)*
	And Jankin hath y-wonne a newe goune.	
	My tale is doon; we been almost at toune.	

The Clerk's Prologue and Tale

The Prologue

	"Sir Clerk of Oxenford,"° our Hoste sayde,	*scholar from Oxford*
	"Ye ryde as coy° and stille as dooth a mayde	*shy*
	Were newe spoused, sittinge at the bord.[1]	
	This day ne herde I of° your tonge a word.	*from*
5	I trowe ye studie aboute som sophyme,[2]	
	But Salomon seith, 'every thing hath tyme.'	
	For Goddes sake, as beth° of bettre chere.	*be*
	It is no tyme for to studien here.	
	Telle us som mery tale, by youre fey!°	*faith*
10	For what man that is entred in a pley,[3]	
	He nedes moot° unto the pley assente.	*needs must*
	But precheth nat,° as freres° doon in Lente,	*don't preach / friars*
	To make us for our olde sinnes wepe,	
	Ne that thy tale make us nat to slepe.	
15	Telle us som mery thing of aventures.	
	Youre termes, youre colours, and youre figures,[4]	
	Kepe hem in stoor til so be ye endyte[5]	
	Heigh° style, as whan that men to kinges wryte.	*High*
	Speketh so pleyn° at this time, we yow preye,°	*plain / beseech*
20	That we may understonde what ye seye."	
	This worthy Clerk benignely° answerde:	*graciously*
	"Hoste," quod he, "I am under your yerde;°	*rod, rule*
	Ye han° of us as now the governaunce,°	*have / the governing*
	And therfor wol I do yow obeisaunce°	*obey you*
25	As fer° as reson axeth,° hardily.°	*far / demands / certainly*
	I wol yow telle a tale which that I	
	Lerned at Padowe° of a worthy clerk,	*Padua*
	As preved° by his wordes and his werk.	*(was) proved*

2. As well as Euclid (the Greek geometrician) or Ptolemy (the astronomer and mathematician).
1. (Who) is newly wed, sitting at the (wedding) table.
2. I believe you're pondering over some sophism (i.e., clever, specious argument).
3. For whoever has entered into a game.
4. Various learned devices of rhetoric.
5. Keep them in store until you (have occasion to) compose in.

He is now deed° and nayled° in his cheste;°	*dead / nailed / coffin*
30 I prey to God so yeve° his soule reste!	*give*
Fraunceys Petrark,° the laureat poete,	*Francis Petrarch*
Highte° this clerk, whos rethoryke° sweete	*Was called / rhetoric*
Enlumined° al Itaille° of° poetrye,	*Illumined / Italy / with*
As Linian° dide of philosophye	*(Giovanni da) Legnano*
35 Or lawe, or other art° particuler;	*field of knowledge*
But deeth, that wol nat suffre° us dwellen heer°	*allow / here*
But as it were a twinkling of an yë,°	*eye*
Hem° bothe hath slayn, and alle shul we dye.°	*Them / shall die*
But forth to tellen of this worthy man	
40 That taughte me this tale, as I bigan,	
I seye that first with heigh style he endyteth,°	*composes*
Er° he the body° of his tale wryteth,	*Before / main part*
A proheme, in the which discryveth he⁶	
Pemond,° and of Saluces° the contree,	*Piedmont / Saluzzo*
45 And speketh of Apennyn,° the hilles hye,°	*the Apennines / high*
That been the boundes° of West Lumbardye,°	*boundaries / Lombardy*
And of Mount Vesulus° in special,	*Viso*
Where as the Poo,° out of a welle° smal,	*Po River / spring*
Taketh his firste springing and his sours,°	*source*
50 That estward ay encresseth in his cours	
To Emelward, to Ferrare, and Venyse:⁷	
The which a long thing were to devyse,°	*relate*
And trewely, as to my jugement,	
Me thinketh it a thing impertinent,°	*irrelevant*
55 Save that he wol conveyen his matere.⁸	
But this° his tale, which that ye may here."°	*this is / hear*

The Tale

PART ONE

Ther is, at the west syde of Itaille,	
Doun at the rote° of Vesulus° the colde,	*base / Mount Viso*
A lusty playne, habundant of vitaille,⁹	
60 Wher many a tour° and toun thou mayst biholde	*tower*
That founded were in tyme of fadres olde,°	*forefathers*
And many another delitable° sighte,	*delightful*
And Saluces° this noble contree highte.°	*Saluzzo / was called*
A markis° whylom° lord was of that londe,	*marquis / at one time*
65 As were his worthy eldres° him bifore;	*elders*
And obeisant,° ay° redy to his honde	*obedient / ever*
Were alle his liges, bothe lasse and more.¹	

6. A proem (introduction) in which he describes.
7. That eastward ever grows larger in its course, toward Emilia, Ferrara, and Venice.
8. Except that he wishes to introduce his (main) subject.
9. A pleasant plain, abounding in food.
1. Were all his vassals, both small and great.

Thus in delyt he liveth, and hath don yore,°   *for a long time*
Biloved and drad,° thurgh° favour of Fortune,   *feared / through*
70 Bothe of° his lordes and of his commune.°   *by / common people*

Therwith° he was, to speke as of linage,°   *In addition / lineage*
The gentilleste° y-born of Lumbardye,   *i.e., the highest*
A fair° persone, and strong, and yong of age,   *handsome*
And ful of honour and of curteisye;°   *courtesy*
75 Discreet ynogh his contree for to gye²—
Save in somme thinges that° he was to blame°—   *wherein / at fault*
And Walter was this yonge lordes name.

I blame him thus, that he considered noght
In tyme cominge° what mighte him bityde,   *In future time*
80 But on his lust present° was al his thoght,   *immediate pleasure*
As for to hauke° and hunte on every syde;   *hawk*
Wel ny alle othere cures leet he slyde,³
And eek° he nolde°—and that was worst of alle—   *also / would not*
Wedde no wyf, for noght° that may bifalle.   *whatever*

85 Only that point his peple bar so sore°   *took so hard*
That flokmele° on a day they to him wente,   *in flocks, droves*
And oon of hem, that wysest was of lore,°   *in learning*
Or elles that° the lord best wolde assente   *Or because*
That he sholde telle him what his peple mente,
90 Or elles coude he shewe wel swich matere,⁴
He to the markis seyde as ye shul here.

"O noble markis, your humanitee
Assureth us and yeveth° us hardinesse,°   *giveth / the boldness*
As ofte as tyme is of necessitee,°   *it is necessary*
95 That we to yow mowe° telle our hevinesse.   *may*
Accepteth, lord, now of youre gentillesse,
That we with pitous° herte unto yow pleyne,°   *sorrowful / make complaint*
And lete youre eres nat my voys disdeyne.⁵

Al° have I noght to done in this matere   *Although*
100 More than another man hath in this place,
Yet for as muche as ye, my lord so dere,
Han alwey shewed me favour and grace,
I dar the better aske of yow a space°   *opportunity*
Of audience, to shewen° our requeste,   *put forward*
105 And ye, my lord, to doon right as yow leste.⁶

---

2. Wise enough to guide (govern) his country.
3. He let slide almost all other responsibilities.
4. Or else (because) he knew well how to put forward such a subject.
5. And let your ears not disdain (to hear) my voice.
6. And you, my lord, to do just as you please.

For certes, lord, so wel us lyketh yow[7]
And al your werk, and ever han doon, that we
Ne coude nat us self° devysen° how   *ourselves / imagine*
We mighte liven in more felicitee,°   *happiness*
110 Save o° thing, lord, if it youre wille be,   *one*
That for to been a wedded man yow leste:[8]
Than° were your peple in sovereyn hertes reste.°   *Then / supreme happiness*

Boweth youre nekke under that blisful yok
Of soveraynetee, noght of servyse,
115 Which that men clepeth spousaille° or wedlok;   *call marriage*
And thenketh, lord, among your thoghtes wyse,
How that oure dayes passe in sondry wyse;°   *various ways*
For though we slepe or wake, or rome,° or ryde,   *wander about*
Ay fleeth the tyme, it nil no man abyde.[9]

120 And though youre grene youthe floure° as yit,°   *flower / yet*
In crepeth age alwey, as stille as stoon,[1]
And deeth manaceth° every age, and smit°   *threatens / smites*
In each estaat,° for ther escapeth noon.°   *every rank / no one*
And al so° certein as we knowe echoon°   *even as / each one*
125 That we shul deye,° as uncerteyn we alle   *die*
Been of that day whan deeth shal on us falle.

Accepteth than of us the trewe entente,°   *loyal intention*
That never yet refuseden youre heste,°   *command*
And we wol, lord, if that ye wol assente,
130 Chese yow a wyf in short tyme, atte leste,°   *at (the) least*
Born of the gentilleste and of the meste°   *greatest*
Of al this lond, so that it oghte seme
Honour to God and yow, as we can deme.°   *judge*

Delivere us out of al this bisy drede°   *anxious fear*
135 And tak a wyf, for hye° Goddes sake;   *high*
For if it so bifelle, as God forbede,°   *i.e., may God forbid*
That thurgh your deeth your lyne sholde slake,°   *cease*
And that a straunge° successour sholde take   *unknown*
Youre heritage, O, wo were us alyve!
140 Wherfor we pray you hastily to wyve."°   *take a wife*

Hir° meke preyere and hir pitous chere°   *Their / appearance*
Made the markis herte° han pitee.   *marquis's heart*
"Ye wol,"° quod he, "myn owene peple dere,   *wish*
To that° I never erst° thoghte streyne° me.   *what / before / constrain*
145 I me rejoysed of my libertee

7. For truly, lord, you please us so well.
8. That it may please you to become a married man.
9. Time always flees, it will not wait for any man.
1. Age creeps in steadily, as quietly as (a) stone.

That selde tyme° is founde in mariage;   *seldom*
Ther I was free, I moot been in servage.²

But nathelees° I see your trewe entente,   *nevertheless*
And truste upon youre wit,° and have don ay;   *judgment*
150 Wherfore of my free wil I wole assente
To wedde me, as sone as evere I may.
But theras° ye han profred° me today   *where / offered*
To chese° me a wyf, I yow relesse°   *choose / release*
That choys, and prey yow of that profre cesse.³

155 For God it woot,° that children ofte been   *knows*
Unlyk hir worthy eldres° hem bifore;°   *ancestors / before them*
Bountee° comth al of God, nat of the streen°   *Goodness / strain, lineage*
Of which they been engendred and y-bore.°   *born*
I truste in Goddes bountee and therfore
160 My mariage and myn estaat° and reste°   *noble station / quiet peace*
I him bitake; he may don as him leste.⁴

Lat me alone in chesinge° of my wyf—   *the choosing*
That charge° upon my bak I wol endure;   *load*
But I yow preye, and charge upon youre lyf,
165 That what° wyf that I take, ye me assure   *whatever*
To worshipe hire° whyl that hir lyf may dure,°   *revere her / last*
In word and werk,° bothe here and everywhere,   *deed*
As° she an emperoures doghter were.   *As if*

And forthermore this shal ye swere,° that ye   *swear*
170 Agayn my choys shul neither grucche° ne stryve;°   *grumble / oppose*
For sith° I shal forgoon° my libertee   *since / forgo*
At your requeste, as ever moot I thryve,°   *I may prosper*
Ther as° myn herte is set, ther wol I wyve.°   *There where / marry*
And but° ye wole assente in swich manere,   *unless*
175 I prey yow, speketh namore of this matere."

With hertely° wil they sworen and assenten   *sincere, good*
To al this thing—ther seyde no wight° nay—   *person*
Bisekinge him of grace, er that they wenten,⁵
That he wolde graunten hem° a certein day   *grant (to name) them*
180 Of° his spousaille, as sone as evere he may;   *For*
For yet alwey° the peple somwhat dredde°   *still / feared*
Lest that this markis no wyf wolde wedde.

2. Where I (once) was free, I must be in servitude.
3. (From) that choice and ask you to withdraw that offer.
4. I entrust to Him; He may do as it pleases Him.
5. Beseeching him of (his) grace, before they departed.

He graunted hem a day, swich as him leste,⁶
On which he wolde be wedded sikerly,°   *certainly*
185 And seyde he dide al this at hir° requeste.   *their*
And they, with humble entente, buxomly,°   *submissively*
Knelinge upon hir knees ful reverently,
Him thanken alle; and thus they han an ende
Of hire entente,° and hoom agayn they wende.   *purpose*

190 And heerupon he to his officeres°   *household officials*
Comaundeth for the feste° to purveye,°   *feast / provide*
And to his privee° knightes and squyeres   *personal*
Swich charge yaf as him liste on hem leye;⁷
And they to his comandement obeye,
195 And ech of them doth al his diligence
To doon unto the feste reverence.°   *honor*

PART TWO

Noght fer fro thilke paleys honurable
Wheras this markis shoop his mariage,⁸
Ther stood a throp,° of site delitable,°   *village / pleasant*
200 In which that povre° folk of that village   *poor*
Hadden hir bestes° and hir herbergage,°   *animals / lodgings*
And of° hire labour took hir sustenance   *by*
After that the erthe yaf hem habundance.⁹

Amonges thise povre folk ther dwelte a man
205 Which that was holden° povrest of hem alle;   *Who was held to be*
But hye° God somtyme senden can   *high*
His grace into a litel oxes stalle.
Janicula men of that throp him calle;
A doghter hadde he, fair ynogh to sighte,°   *to the eye*
210 And Grisildis this yonge mayden highte.°   *was named*

But for to speke of vertuous beautee,
Than was she oon the faireste° under sonne;   *one of the loveliest*
For povreliche y-fostred up was she,
No likerous lust was thurgh hire herte y-ronne.¹
215 Wel ofter of the welle° than of the tonne°   *spring / (wine) cask*
She drank; and for she wolde vertu plese,
She knew wel labour, but non ydel ese.°   *no idle ease*

But thogh this mayde tendre were of age,°   *i.e., young in years*
Yet in the brest of hir virginitee
220 Ther was enclosed rype and sad corage;°   *a mature and firm heart*

6. Such as it pleased him.
7. (He) gave such responsibility as it pleased him to lay on them.
8. Not far from that same worthy palace where this marquis prepared for his marriage.
9. In whatever abundance the earth yielded them.
1. Because she was raised in poverty, no wanton desire had run through her heart.

And in greet reverence and charitee
Hir° olde povre fader fostred° she.   *Her / cared for*
A fewe sheep, spinninge, on feeld she kepte;[2]
She wolde noght been ydel til she slepte.

225 And whan she hoomward cam, she wolde bringe
Wortes° or othere herbes tymes ofte,   *Plants*
The whiche she shredde and seeth° for hir° livinge,   *boiled / their*
And made hir° bed ful harde and nothing softe;   *her*
And ay she kepte hir fadres lyf on lofte°   *sustained her father's life*
230 With everich° obeisaunce and diligence   *every*
That child may doon to fadres reverence.

Upon Grisilde, this povre creature,
Ful ofte sythe° this markis sette his yë   *oftentimes*
As he on hunting rood paraventure;°   *rode by chance*
235 And whan it fil° that he mighte hire espye,°   *befell / see*
He noght with wantoun loking of folye[3]
His eyen° caste on hire, but in sad° wyse   *eyes / serious*
Upon hir chere° he wolde him ofte avyse,°   *countenance / often ponder*

Commendinge in his herte hir wommanhede,
240 And eek hir vertu, passinge° any wight°   *surpassing / person*
Of so yong age, as wel in chere° as dede.   *appearance*
For thogh the peple have no greet insight
In vertu, he considered ful right
Hir bountee,° and disposed° that he wolde   *goodness / decided*
245 Wedde hire only, if ever he wedde sholde.

The day of wedding cam, but no wight° can   *nobody*
Telle what womman that it sholde be;
For which merveille wondred many a man,
And seyden, whan they were in privetee,°   *private*
250 "Wol nat our lord yet leve his vanitee?°   *foolishness*
Wol he nat wedde? allas, allas the whyle!
Why wol he thus himself and us bigyle?"°   *deceive*

But natheles this markis hath don make°   *has had made*
Of gemmes, set in gold and in asure,°   *azure, blue*
255 Broches and ringes, for Grisildis sake,
And of hir clothing took he the mesure
By a mayde, lyk to hire stature,
And eek of othere ornamentes° alle   *adornments*
That unto switch° a wedding sholde falle.   *such*

2. (While) spinning, she watched over a few sheep in the field.
3. He did not with wanton, foolish looks.

260 The tyme of undern° of the same day   *midmorning*
     Approcheth, that this wedding sholde be;
     And al the paleys° put was in array,°   *palace / order*
     Bothe halle and chambres, ech in his° degree;   *its*
     Houses of office⁴ stuffed with plentee
265 Ther maystow° seen, of deyntevous vitaille°   *mayest thou / dainty foods*
     That may be founde as fer as last Itaille.°   *Italy extends*

     This royal markis, richely arrayed,
     Lordes and ladyes in his companye,
     The whiche unto the feste were y-prayed,°   *asked*
270 And of his retenue the bachelrye,°   *young knights*
     With many a soun° of sondry° melodye,   *sound / various*
     Unto the village of the which I tolde,
     In this array the righte wey° han holde.°   *direct way / taken*

     Grisilde of this, God woot,° ful innocent°   *knows / entirely unaware*
275 That for hire shapen° was al this array,   *prepared*
     To fecchen water at a welle is went,°   *has gone*
     And cometh hoom as sone as ever she may.
     For wel she hadde herd seyd that thilke° day   *that same*
     The markis sholde wedde, and, if she mighte,
280 She wolde fayn° han seyn some of that sighte.   *gladly*

     She thoghte, "I wol with othere maydens stonde,
     That been my felawes,° in our dore and see   *companions*
     The markisesse,° and therfor wol I fonde°   *marchioness / try*
     To doon° at hoom as sone as it may be   *I.e., to finish*
285 The labour which that longeth° unto me;   *belongs*
     And than I may at leyser° hire biholde,   *leisure*
     If she this wey unto the castel holde."°   *takes*

     And as she wolde over hir threshfold° goon,   *threshold*
     The markis cam and gan hire for to calle,°   *did call her*
290 And she sette doun hir water pot anoon°   *at once*
     Bisyde the threshfold, in an oxes stalle,
     And doun upon hir knees she gan to falle,°   *fell*
     And with sad° contenance kneleth stille   *earnest*
     Til she had herd what was the lordes wille.

295 This thoghtful° markis spak unto this mayde   *pensive*
     Ful sobrely,° and seyde in this manere: *gravely*
     "Wher is your fader, Grisildis?" he sayde,
     And she with reverence, in humble chere,°   *manner*
     Answerde, "Lord, he is al redy° here."   *right at hand*
300 And in she gooth withouten lenger lette,°   *delay*
     And to the markis she hir fader fette.°   *fetched*

----

4. Service buildings (storerooms, kitchens, etc.).

He by the hond than took this olde man,
And seyde thus whan he him hadde asyde,°   *off to the side*
"Janicula, I neither may ne can
305 Lenger the plesance° of myn herte hyde.   *pleasure, desire*
If that thou vouche sauf, what so bityde,[5]
Thy doghter wol I take er that° I wende°   *before / depart*
As for my wyf, unto hir lyves ende.

Thou lovest me, I woot it wel, certeyn,
310 And art my feithful lige man y-bore;[6]
And al that lyketh° me, I dar wel seyn   *all that which pleases*
It lyketh thee; and specially therfore
Tel me that poynt that I have seyd bifore:[7]
If that thou wolt unto that purpos drawe°   *incline*
315 To take me as for thy sone-in-lawe."

This sodeyn cas this man astoned so
That reed he wex; abayst and al quaking
He stood.[8] Unnethes° seyde he wordes mo,°   *Scarcely / more*
But only thus: "Lord," quod he, "my willinge
320 Is as ye wole, ne ayeines° your lykinge   *contrary to*
I wol° no thing, ye be my lord so dere.   *wish*
Right as yow lust° governeth this matere."   *Just as you please*

"Yet wol I," quod this markis softely,
"That in thy chambre I and thou and she
325 Have a collacion,° and wostow° why?   *conference / knowest thou*
For I wol axe° if it hire wille be   *ask*
To be my wyf, and reule hire after me.[9]
And al this shal be doon in thy presence—
I wol noght speke out of thyn audience."°   *hearing*

330 And in the chambre whyl they were aboute
Hir tretis,° which as ye shal after here,   *Their contract*
The peple cam unto the hous withoute,°   *outside*
And wondred hem in how honest manere
And tentifly she kepte hir fader dere.[1]
335 But outerly° Grisildis wondre mighte,   *truly*
For never erst° ne saugh° she swich° a sighte.   *before / saw / such*

No wonder is thogh that she were astoned°   *bewildered*
To seen so greet a gest° come in that place;   *guest*
She never was to swiche gestes woned,°   *accustomed*
340 For° which she loked with ful pale face.   *On account of*

5. If thou will permit (it), whatever may happen.
6. And were born my faithful vassal.
7. Answer me in that particular that I have named before.
8. This sudden event astonished this man so much that he grew red; he stood abashed and trembling all over.
9. To be my wife and govern herself according to my will.
1. And they marveled at how decently and attentively she cared for her dear father.

But shortly forth this matere for to chace,°   *pursue*
Thise arn° the wordes that the markis sayde   *are*
To this benigne,° verray,° feithful mayde.   *gracious / true*

"Grisilde," he seyde, "ye shul wel understonde
345 It lyketh to° your fader and to me   *It pleases*
That I yow wedde, and eek° it may so stonde,°   *also / be the case*
As I suppose, ye wol that it so be.
But thise demandes axe I first," quod he,
"That sith° it shal be doon in hastif wyse,°   *since / hastily*
350 Wol ye assente, or elles yow avyse?°   *deliberate*

I seye this, be ye redy with good herte
To al my lust,[2] and that I frely may,
As me best thinketh, do yow laughe or smerte,[3]
And never ye to grucche° it, night ne day?   *grumble about*
355 And eek° whan I sey 'ye,'° ne sey nat 'nay,'   *also / yes*
Neither by word ne frowning contenance?
Swere this, and here I swere our alliance."

Wondringe upon this word,° quakinge for drede,   *speech*
She seyde, "Lord, undigne° and unworthy   *undeserving*
360 Am I to thilke° honour that ye me bede;°   *that same / offer*
But as ye wol yourself, right so wol I.
And heer I swere that nevere willingly
In werk° ne thoght I nil° yow disobeye,   *deed / will not*
For to be deed, though me were looth to deye."[4]

365 "This is ynogh, Grisilde myn!" quod he.
And forth he gooth with a ful sobre chere
Out at the dore, and after that cam she,
And to the peple he seyde in this manere:
"This is my wyf," quod he, "that standeth here.
370 Honoureth hire and loveth hire I preye
Whoso° me loveth; ther is namore to seye."   *Whosoever*

And for that° nothing of hir olde gere°   *in order that / apparel*
She sholde bringe into his hous, he bad
That wommen sholde dispoilen° hire right there;   *strip*
375 Of which thise ladyes were nat right glad
To handle hir clothes wherinne she was clad.
But natheles,° this mayde bright of hewe°   *nevertheless / hue*
Fro foot to heed they clothed han al newe.

Hir heres° han they kembd,° that lay untressed°   *hair / combed / all loose*
380 Ful rudely,° and with hir° fingres smale   *Artlessly / their*

2. To (honor) my every wish.
3. As it seems best to me, make you laugh or suffer.
4. Even to die, though I would be loath to die.

A corone° on hire heed they han y-dressed,°   *crown / set*
And sette° hire ful of nowches° grete and smale.   *adorned / jewels*
Of hire array what sholde I make a tale?
Unnethe° the peple hir knew for hire fairnesse,   *Scarcely*
385 Whan she translated° was in swich richesse.   *transformed, elevated*

This markis hath hire spoused° with a ring   *married*
Broght for the same cause, and thanne hire sette
Upon an hors, snow-whyt and wel ambling,°   *paced*
And to his paleys,° er° he lenger lette,°   *palace / before / delayed*
390 With joyful peple that hire ladde° and mette,   *led*
Conveyed hire; and thus the day they spende
In revel, til the sonne gan descende.°   *did set*

And shortly forth this tale for to chace,°   *pursue*
I seye that to this newe markisesse°   *marchioness*
395 God hath swich° favour sent hire of his grace,   *such*
That it ne semed nat by lyklinesse°   *likely*
That she was born and fed in rudenesse,°   *lowliness*
As in a cote° or in an oxe-stalle,   *cottage*
But norished in an emperoures halle.

400 To every wight° she woxen is° so dere   *person / has grown*
And worshipful, that folk ther she was bore[5]
And from hire birthe knewe hire yeer by yere,
Unnethe trowed they—but dorste han swore—[6]
That to Janicle, of which I spak bifore,
405 She doghter were, for, as by conjecture,
Hem thoughte° she was another creature.   *It seemed to them*

For thogh that evere vertuous was she,
She was encressed in swich excellence
Of thewes° gode, y-set in heigh bountee,°   *qualities / goodness*
410 And so discreet° and fair of eloquence,°   *wise / speech*
So benigne° and so digne° of reverence,°   *gracious / worthy / honor*
And coude so the peples herte embrace,[7]
That ech hire lovede that loked on hir face.

Noght only of Saluces° in the toun   *Saluzzo*
415 Publiced° was the bountee° of hir name,   *Made known / goodness*
But eek° bisyde in many a regioun: *also*
If oon° seyde wel, another seyde the same.   *one*
So spradde° of hire heighe bountee the fame   *spread*
That men and wommen, as wel yonge as olde,
420 Gon to Saluce upon hire to biholde.

5. And worthy of honor, that people where she was born.
6. They could scarcely believe—though they'd have dared to swear it.
7. And so (well) knew how to hold fast the hearts of the people.

Thus Walter lowly—nay but royally—
Wedded with fortunat honestetee,°   *honor*
In Goddes pees° liveth ful esily   *God's peace*
At hoom, and outward grace ynogh had he;
425 And for° he saugh° that under low degree   *because / saw*
Was ofte vertu hid, the peple him helde
A prudent man, and that is seyn° ful selde.°   *seen / seldom*

Nat only this Grisildis thurgh hir wit
Coude al the feet of wyfly hoomlinesse,⁸
430 But eek,° whan that the cas requyred it,   *also*
The commune profit° coude she redresse.°   *general welfare / amend*
Ther nas° discord, rancour, ne hevinesse°   *was not / i.e., of heart*
In al that lond that she ne coude apese,°   *appease*
And wysly bringe hem alle in reste and ese.

435 Though that hire housbonde absent were, anoon°   *at once*
If gentil men or othere of hire contree
Were wrothe,° she wolde bringen hem atoon;°   *angered / into accord*
So wyse and rype° wordes hadde she,   *mature*
And jugements of so greet equitee,°   *fairness*
440 That she from heven sent was, as men wende,°   *they supposed*
Peple to save and every wrong t'amende.°   *to amend*

Nat longe tyme after that this Grisild
Was wedded, she a doughter hath y-bore.°   *borne*
Al had hire levere have born a knave child,⁹
445 Glad was this markis and the folk therfore;
For though a mayde child come al bifore,
She may unto a knave child atteyne
By lyklihed, sin she nis nat bareyne.¹

PART THREE

Ther fil, as it bifalleth tymes mo,²
450 Whan that this child had souked° but a throwe,°   *nursed / short time*
This markis° in his herte longeth so   *marquis*
To tempte his wyf, hir sadnesse° for to knowe,   *steadfastness*
That he ne mighte out of his herte throwe
This merveillous° desyr, his wyf t'assaye;°   *strange / to test*
455 Needless,° God woot,° he thoughte hire   *Needlessly / knows*
        for t'affraye.°   *to frighten*

He hadde assayed hire ynogh bifore
And fond hire evere good. What needed it
Hire for to tempte and alwey° more and more,   *continually*

8. Knew all the feats (skills) of a wife's household duties.
9. Although she had rather have borne a male child.
1. Quite probably, since she is not barren.
2. It happened, as it often happens.

Though som men preise it for a subtil wit?
460 But as for me, I seye that yvel it sit[3]
T'assaye a wyf whan that it is no nede,
And putten hire in anguish and in drede.

For which this markis wroghte in this manere:
He cam alone a-night,° ther as° she lay,   *by night / there where*
465 With sterne face and with ful trouble chere,°   *troubled countenance*
And seyde thus: "Grisilde," quod he, "that day
That I yow took out of your povre array°   *condition of poverty*
And putte yow in estaat of heigh noblesse,
Ye have nat that forgeten, as I gesse.

470 I seye, Grisild, this present dignitee,
In which that I have put yow, as I trowe,°   *believe*
Maketh yow nat foryetful° for to be   *forgetful*
That I yow took in povre estaat ful lowe.
For any wele° ye moot° yourselven knowe,   *happiness / may*
475 Take hede of every word that I yow seye:
Ther is no wight° that hereth it but we tweye.°   *no one / two*

Ye woot° yourself wel how that ye cam here   *know*
Into this hous, it is nat longe ago,
And though to me that ye be lief° and dere,   *beloved*
480 Unto my gentils° ye be no thing° so;   *gentlefolk / not at all*
They seyn, to hem it is greet shame and wo
For to be subgets° and ben in servage°   *subjects / waiting, servitude*
To thee, that born art of a smal village.

And namely sith thy doghter was y-bore°   *born*
485 Thise wordes han they spoken, doutelees;
But I desyre, as I have doon bifore,
To live my lyf with hem in reste and pees;°   *peace*
I may nat in this caas° be recchelees.°   *matter / heedless*
I moot° don with thy doghter for the beste,   *must*
490 Nat as I wolde, but as my peple leste.[4]

And yet, God wot,° this is ful looth° to me.   *knows / hateful*
But nathelees° withoute your witing°   *nevertheless / knowledge*
I wol nat doon;° but this wol I," quod he,   *act*
"That ye to me assente as in this thing.
495 Shewe now youre pacience in youre werking°   *deeds*
That ye me highte° and swore in your village   *promised*
That day that maked was oure mariage."

Whan she had herd al this, she noght ameved°   *made no motion*
Neither in word or chere° or countenaunce;   *manner*

3. It ill becomes (a man), i.e., is evil.
4. Not as I would wish, but as my people desire.

500 For as it semed, she was nat agreved.
     She seyde, "Lord, al lyth° in youre plesaunce;   *lies*
     My child and I with hertely° obeisaunce   *sincere*
     Ben youres al,° and ye mowe° save or spille°   *wholly / may / destroy*
     Youre owene thing: werketh after° youre wille.   *according to*

505 Ther may no thing, God so my soule save,
     Lyken to yow° that may displese me;   *Please you*
     Ne I desyre no thing for to have,
     Ne drede for to lese, save only ye;
     This wil is in myn herte and ay° shal be.   *ever*
510 No lengthe of tyme or deeth may this deface,
     Ne chaunge my corage° to another place."   *heart*

     Glad was this markis of° hire answering,   *for*
     But yet he feyned° as he were nat so;   *feigned*
     Al drery° was his chere° and his loking   *sad / face*
515 Whan that he sholde out of the chambre go.
     Sone after this, a furlong wey or two,⁵
     He prively° hath told al his entente°   *secretly / plan, intention*
     Unto a man, and to his wyf him sente.

     A maner sergeant was this privee man,⁶
520 The which that feithful ofte he founden hadde
     In thinges grete, and eek° swich° folk wel can   *also / such*
     Don execucioun in° thinges badde.   *Perform*
     The lord knew wel that he him loved and dradde;°   *feared*
     And whan this sergeant wiste° his lordes wille,   *knew*
525 Into the chambre he stalked him ful stille.°   *crept very quietly*

     "Madame," he seyde, "ye mote foryeve° it me,   *must forgive*
     Thogh I do thing to which I am constreyned.
     Ye ben so wys that ful wel knowe ye
     That lordes hestes° mowe° nat been y-feyned;°   *commands / may / avoided*
530 They mowe wel been biwailled or compleyned,°   *lamented*
     But men mot nede° unto hire lust° obeye,   *needs must / their will*
     And so wol I; ther is na more to seye.

     This child I am comanded for to take"—
     And spak na more, but out the child he hente°   *seized*
535 Despitously,° and gan a chere make°   *Cruelly / i.e., acted*
     As though he wolde han slayn it er° he wente.°   *before / left*
     Grisildis mot° al suffren and al consente;   *must*
     And as a lamb she sitteth meke and stille,
     And leet this cruel sergeant doon his wille.

---

5. I.e., within a little while (the length of time it takes to walk a furlong—one-eighth of a
   mile—or two).
6. This trusted man was a kind of sergeant-at-law.

540 Suspecious was the diffame° of this man,   *bad reputation*
     Suspect[7] his face, suspect his word also;
     Suspect the tyme in which he this bigan.
     Allas! hir doghter that she lovede so,
     She wende° he wolde han slawen° it right tho.°   *thought / slain / then*
545 But natheles she neither weep ne syked,°   *wept nor sighed*
     Conforminge hire to that the markis lyked.[8]

     But atte laste° speken she bigan,   *finally*
     And mekely she to the sergeant preyde,°   *begged*
     So as he was a worthy gentil man,
550 That she moste° kisse hire child er° that it deyde;°   *might / before / died*
     And in hir barm° this litel child she leyde°   *lap / laid*
     With ful sad face, and gan the child to blisse[9]
     And lulled it, and after gan it kisse.

     And thus she seyde in hire benigne voys,°   *gracious voice*
555 "Far weel, my child; I shal thee nevere see.
     But, sith° I thee have marked with the croys°   *since / cross*
     Of thilke° Fader, blessed mote he be,   *that same*
     That for us deyde upon a croys of tree,°   *wood*
     Thy soule, litel child, I him bitake,°   *entrust to Him*
560 For this night shaltow° dyen for my sake."   *shalt thou*

     I trowe° that to a norice° in this cas   *believe / nurse*
     It had ben hard this rewthe° for to se;   *pitiful sight*
     Wel° mighte a mooder than han cryed "allas!"   *I.e., well more*
     But nathelees so sad° stedfast was she   *firmly*
565 That she endured all adversitee,
     And to the sergeant mekely she sayde,
     "Have heer agayn your litel yonge mayde.

     Goth now," quod she, "and dooth my lordes heste.°   *command*
     But o° thing wol I preye yow of youre grace,   *one*
570 That, but° my lord forbad yow, atte leste°   *unless / at (the) least*
     Burieth this litel body in som place
     That bestes ne no briddes it torace."[1]
     But he no word wol to that purpos seye,
     But took the child and wente upon his weye.

575 This sergeant cam unto his lord ageyn,
     And of Grisildis wordes and hire chere°   *behavior*
     He tolde him point for point, in short and playn,°   *briefly and clearly*
     And him presenteth with his doghter dere.
     Somwhat this lord hath rewthe in his manere,[2]

7. I.e., ominous, foreboding (causing suspicion).
8. Conforming her (conduct) to what was pleasing to the marquis.
9. With a most somber face, and blessed the child.
1. (So) that no beasts or birds tear it to pieces.
2. This lord showed something of pity in his behavior.

580 But nathelees his purpos heeld he stille,
   As lordes doon whan they wol han hir wille.

   And bad this sergeant that he prively°   *in secret*
   Sholde this child softe winde and wrappe°   *i.e., cover with clothing*
   With alle circumstances° tendrely,   *In every detail*
585 And carie it in a cofre° or in a lappe;°   *box / cloth*
   But, upon peyne his heed of for to swappe,³
   That no man sholde knowe of his entente,°   *purpose*
   Ne whenne° he cam, ne whider° that he wente;   *whence / whither*

   But at Boloigne° to his suster° dere,   *Bologna / sister*
590 That thilke° tyme of Panik⁴ was countesse,   *(at) that same*
   He sholde it take, and shewe hire° this matere,   *explain*
   Bisekinge hire to don hire bisinesse
   This child to fostre in alle gentilesse;⁵
   And whos child that it was he bad hire hyde
595 From every wight, for oght that may bityde.⁶

   The sergeant gooth, and hath fulfild this thing;
   But to this markis now retourne we.
   For now goth he ful faste imagining°   *intently wondering*
   If by his wyves chere° he mighte see,   *countenance*
600 Or by hire word aperceyve,° that she   *perceive*
   Were chaunged; but he never hire coude finde
   But ever in oon ylyke sad° and kinde.   *consistently steadfast*

   As glad, as humble, as bisy in servyse,
   And eek° in love as she was wont° to be,   *also / accustomed*
605 Was she to him in every manner wyse;°   *sort of way*
   Ne of hir doghter noght a word spak she.
   Non accident° for noon adversitee   *outward sign*
   Was seyn in hire, ne never hir doghter° name   *daughter's*
   Ne nempned° she, in ernest nor in game.°   *named / play*

PART FOUR

610 In this estaat° ther passed been foure yeer   *condition*
   Er° she with childe was; but, as God wolde,   *Before*
   A knave° child she bar° by this Walter,   *male / bore*
   Ful gracious and fair° for to biholde.   *handsome*
   And whan that folk it to his fader tolde,
615 Nat only he, but al his contree, merie
   Was for this child, and God they thanke and herie.°   *praise*

---

3. But on pain of having his head struck off.
4. Panico, near Bologna.
5. Beseeching her to give her careful attention to the raising of this child, in all things proper to gentle birth.
6. From every man, no matter what might happen.

When it was two yeer old and fro the brest
Departed of his norice,° on a day   *nurse*
This markis caughte° yet another lest°   *conceived / desire*
620 To tempte his wyf yet ofter,° if he may.   *more often*
O needles was she tempted in assay!°   *trial*
But wedded men ne knowe no mesure°   *moderation*
Whan that they finde a pacient creature.

"Wyf," quod this markis, "ye han herd er° this,   *before*
625 My peple sikly berth° oure mariage,   *bear ill, dislike*
And namely, sith° my sone y-boren° is,   *since / born*
Now is it worse than ever in al our age.°   *time*
The murmur sleeth° myn herte and my corage,°   *slays / spirit*
For to myne eres° comth the voys so smerte°   *ears / sharply*
630 That it wel ny° destroyed hath myn herte.   *well nigh, almost*

Now sey they thus, 'Whan Walter is agoon,°   *gone, dead*
Thanne shal the blood of Janicle succede
And been our Lord, for other have we noon;'
Swiche wordes seith my peple, out of drede.°   *there is no doubt*
635 Wel oughte I of swich° murmur taken hede,   *such*
For certeinly, I drede swich sentence,°   *opinion*
Though they nat pleyn° speke in myn audience.°   *plainly / hearing*

I wolde live in pees° if that I mighte;   *peace*
Wherfor I am disposed outerly,°   *entirely*
640 As I his suster servede° by nighte,   *dealt with*
Right so thenke I to serve him prively.°   *in secret*
This warne I yow, that ye nat sodeynly
Out of youreself for no wo sholde outraye:[7]
Beth pacient, and therof I yow preye."

645 "I have," quod she, "seyd thus, and ever shal,
I wol no thing ne nil° no thing, certayn,   *desire not*
But as yow list; noght greveth me at al,[8]
Thogh that my doghter and my sone be slayn—
At your comandement, this is to sayn.
650 I have noght had no part of children tweyne°   *the two children*
But first siknesse,° and after wo and peyne.   *i.e., in childbearing*

Ye been oure lord, doth with youre owene thing
Right as yow list; axeth no reed at me.[9]
For as I lefte at hoom° al my clothing   *home*
655 Whan I first cam to yow, right so," quod she,
"Left I my wil and al my libertee,

7. Should lose control of yourself for any sorrow.
8. But as it pleases you; it doesn't grieve me at all.
9. Just as you please; ask no advice from me.

And took your clothing. Wherfore I yow preye,
Doth your plesaunce; I wol youre lust° obeye.   *desire*

And certes,° if I hadde prescience°   *certainly / foreknowledge*
660 Your will to knowe er° ye youre lust° me tolde,   *before / pleasure, will*
I wolde it doon withouten necligence.
But now I woot° youre lust and what ye wolde,   *know*
Al youre plesaunce ferme° and stable° I holde;   *firmly / steadfastly*
For wiste I° that my deeth wolde do yow ese,°   *if I knew / give you pleasure*
665 Right gladly wolde I dyen, yow to plese.

Deth may noght make no comparisoun
Unto youre love." And whan this markis sey°   *saw*
The constance° of his wyf, he caste adoun   *constancy*
His eyen two,° and wondreth that she may   *two eyes*
670 In pacience suffre al this array.°   *all these things*
And forth he gooth with drery° contenaunce,   *doleful*
But to his herte it was ful greet plesaunce.

This ugly° sergeant, in the same wyse°   *fearsome / way*
That he hire doghter caughte,° right so he—   *took away*
675 Or worse, if men worse can devyse—
Hath hent° hire sone that ful was of beautee.   *seized*
And evere in oon° so pacient was she   *always*
That she no chere° made of hevinesse,[1]   *appearance*
But kiste° hir sone, and after gan it blesse.°   *kissed / blessed him*

680 Save this:° she preyede him that if he mighte   *Except for this*
Hir litel sone he wolde in erthe grave,°   *bury*
His tendre limes,° delicat to sighte,   *limbs*
Fro foules° and fro bestes for to save.   *birds*
But she non answer of him mighte have.
685 He wente his wey, as him nothing ne roghte,[2]
But to Boloigne he tendrely it broghte.

This markis wondreth evere lenger the more°   *i.e., increasingly*
Upon hir pacience, and if that he
Ne hadde soothly° knowen ther-bifore   *truly*
690 That parfitly hir children loved she,
He wolde have wend° that of° som subtiltee,°   *thought / out of / trick*
And of malice or for cruel corage,°   *heart*
That she had suffred this with sad visage.°   *unchanged countenance*

But wel he knew that next himself, certayn,°   *certainly*
695 She loved hir children best in every wyse.
But now of wommen wolde I axen fayn,[3]

1. I.e., of a heavy heart.
2. He went on his way as though he didn't care at all.
3. But now I would like to ask of (you) women.

If thise assayes° mighte nat suffyse?   trials
What coude a sturdy° housbond more devyse   cruel
To preve° hir wyfhod and hir stedfastnesse,   prove, test
700 And he continuinge evere in sturdinesse?°   cruelty

But ther ben folk of swich condicioun°   such disposition
That, whan they have a certein purpos take,°   decided on
They can nat stinte° of hire entencioun;°   stop short / intention
But right as° they were bounden to a stake,   just as if
705 They wol nat of that firste purpos slake.°   leave off
Right so this markis fulliche° hath purposed°   fully / intended
To tempte his wyf as he was first disposed.

He waiteth° if by word or contenance   watched
That she to him was changed of corage,°   in her heart
710 But never coude he finde variance:
She was ay° oon in herte and in visage.   ever
And ay the forther° that she was in age,   i.e., older
The more trewe, if that it were possible,
She was to him in love, and more penible.°   painstaking

715 For which it semed thus, that of hem two°   for them both
Ther nas° but o° wil; for, as Walter leste,°   was not / one / wished
The same lust° was hire plesance also;   desire
And, God be thanked, al fil° for the beste.   turned out
She shewed wel for no worldly unreste[4]
720 A wyf, as of hirself,° no thing ne sholde   for her own sake
Wille in effect° but as hir housbond wolde.   Wish in fact

The sclaundre° of Walter ofte and wyde spradde°   scandalous report / spread
That of a cruel herte he wikkedly,
For° he a povre womman wedded hadde,   Because
725 Hath mordred° bothe his children prively.°   murdered / secretly
Swich° murmur was among hem comunly.°   Such / them generally
No wonder is, for to the peples ere°   ear
Ther cam no word but that they mordred were.

For which, wher as his peple therbifore
730 Had loved him wel, the sclaundre of his diffame°   ill repute
Made hem that they him hatede therfore:°   for it
To been a mordrer is an hateful name.
But natheles, for ernest ne for game,
He of his cruel purpos nolde stente.°   would not desist
735 To tempte his wyf was set al his entente.

Whan that his doghter twelf yeer was of age,
He to the court of Rome, in subtil wyse°   secretly

4. (That) for no earthly distress.

Enformed of his wil, sente his message,°   *messenger(s)*
Comaundinge hem swiche bulles to devyse⁵
740 As to his cruel purpos may suffyse:
How that the Pope, as for his peples reste,
Bad° him to wedde another if him leste.°   *Bid / if he wished*

I seye, he bad they sholde countrefete°   *counterfeit*
The Popes bulles, makinge mencioun
745 That he hath leve° his firste wyf to lete,°   *permission / to leave*
As by the Popes dispensacioun,
To stinte° rancour and dissencioun   *stop*
Bitwixe his peple and him—thus seyde the bulle,
The which they han publiced atte fulle.°   *published widely*

750 The rude° peple, as it no wonder is,   *ignorant*
Wenden° ful wel that it had been right so;   *Thought*
But whan thise tydinges cam to Grisildis,
I deme° that hire herte was ful wo.   *i.e., am certain*
But she, ylyke sad° for evermo,   *uniformly steadfast*
755 Disposed was, this humble creature,
Th'adversitee of Fortune al t'endure,°   *wholly to endure*

Abydinge evere° his lust and his plesaunce,   *Waiting ever upon*
To whom that she was yeven° herte and al,   *given*
As to hire verray worldly suffisaunce.⁶
760 But shortly if this storie I tellen shal,
This markis writen hath in special
A lettre in which he sheweth° his entente,   *reveals*
And secrely he to Boloigne it sente.

To the Erl° of Panik,° which that hadde tho°   *Earl / Panico / then*
765 Wedded his suster, preyde° he specially   *requested*
To bringen hoom agayn his children two
In honurable estaat° al openly.   *state*
But o° thing he him preyede outerly,°   *one / above all*
That he to no wight,° though men wolde enquere,°   *nobody / inquire*
770 Sholde nat telle whos° children that they were,   *whose*

But seye the mayden sholde y-wedded be°   *was to be wed*
Unto the Markis of Saluce° anon.°   *Saluzzo / immediately*
And as this erl was preyed, so dide he,
For at day set° he on his wey is goon   *on the day appointed*
775 Toward Saluce, and lordes many oon°   *many a lord*
In riche array, this mayden for to gyde,°   *conduct*
Hir yonge brother rydinge hire bisyde.

5. Commanding them (i.e., those at the court of Rome) to contrive such (papal) bulls.
6. As (being) her true, earthly contentment (refers back to "his lust and his plesaunce" in
l. 757).

Arrayed was toward° hir mariage *for*
This fresshe mayde, ful of gemmes clere;° *shining jewels*
780 Hir brother, which that seven yeer was of age,
Arrayed eek° ful fresh in his manere. *also*
And thus in greet noblesse° and with glad chere,° *magnificence / aspect*
Toward Saluces shapinge° hir journey, *making*
Fro day to day they ryden in hir° wey. *on their*

PART FIVE

785 Among al this, after his wikke usage,° *wicked custom*
This markis yet his wyf to tempte more
To the uttereste preve° of hir corage,° *utmost proof / heart, spirit*
Fully to han experience and lore° *knowledge*
If that she were as stedfast as bifore,
790 He on a day in open audience° *assembly*
Ful boistously° hath seyd hire this sentence:° *roughly / decision*

"Certes,° Grisilde, I hadde ynough plesaunce *Truly*
To han yow to my wyf for youre goodnesse—
As for youre trouthe and for youre obeisaunce—
795 Nought for youre linage ne for your richesse.
But now knowe I in verray soothfastnesse° *certain truth*
That in gret lordshipe, if I wel avyse,° *discern*
Ther is gret servitute in sondry wyse.° *in sundry ways*

I may nat don as every° plowman may. *any*
800 My peple me constreyneth° for to take *constrain*
Another wyf, and cryen° day by day; *call (for it)*
And eek the Pope, rancour for to slake,° *appease*
Consenteth it,° that dar I undertake,° *Consents to it / declare*
And treweliche thus muche I wol yow seye,
805 My newe wyf is coming by° the weye. *along*

Be strong of herte, and voyde anon° hir place; *vacate at once*
And thilke° dowere that ye broghten me *that same*
Tak it agayn, I graunte it of my grace.
Retourneth to your fadres hous," quod he.
810 "No man may alwey han prosperitee;
With evene° herte I rede° yow t'endure *steady / advise*
The strook° of Fortune or of aventure."° *stroke / chance*

And she agayn answerde in pacience,
"My lord," quod she, "I woot,° and wiste° alway, *know / knew*
815 How that bitwixen° youre magnificence *between*
And my poverte no wight° can ne may *no one*
Maken comparison; it is no nay.° *it cannot be denied*
I ne heeld me nevere digne° in no manere *worthy*
To be youre wyf, no, ne youre chamberere.° *chambermaid*

820 And in this hous ther° ye me lady made—   *where*
    The heighe God take I for my witnesse,
    And also wisly° he my soule glade°—   *as surely / may gladden*
    I nevere heeld me° lady ne maistresse,   *considered myself*
    But humble servant to youre worthinesse,
825 And ever shal, whyl that my lyf may dure,°   *last*
    Aboven every worldly creature.

    That ye so longe of youre benignitee°   *graciousness*
    Han holden me in honour and nobleye,°   *nobleness*
    Wher as I was noght worthy for to be,
830 That thonke I God and yow, to whom I preye
    Foryelde° it yow. There is namore to seye.   *Repay*
    Unto my fader gladly wol I wende,°   *go*
    And with him dwelle unto my lyves ende.

    Ther I was fostred of° a child ful smal,   *raised from*
835 Til I be deed, my lyf ther wol I lede:
    A widwe clene,° in body, herte, and al.   *widow pure*
    For sith I yaf° to yow my maydenhede,   *gave*
    And am youre trewe wyf, it is no drede,°   *without doubt*
    God shilde° swich a lordes wyf to take   *forbid*
840 Another man to housbonde or to make.°   *as mate*

    And of youre newe wyf, God of his grace
    So graunte yow wele° and prosperitee!   *happiness*
    For I wol gladly yelden hire° my place,   *yield to her*
    In which that I was blisful wont° to be.   *accustomed*
845 For sith it lyketh yow,° my lord," quod she,   *since it pleases you*
    "That° whylom° weren al myn hertes reste,   *Who / formerly*
    That I shal goon,° I wol gon whan yow leste.   *must go*

    But ther as ye me profre swich dowaire°   *such a dowry*
    As I first broghte, it is wel in my minde
850 It were my wrecched clothes, nothing° faire,   *in no way*
    The which to me were hard now for to finde.
    O gode God! how gentil and how kynde
    Ye semed by youre speche and youre visage°   *face, appearance*
    The day that maked was oure mariage!

855 But sooth is seyd—algate I finde it trewe,[7]
    For in effect it preved is on° me—   *is proven in*
    Love is noght° old as whan that it is newe.   *not (the same)*
    But certes, lord, for noon adversitee,
    To dyen in the cas, it shal nat be[8]
860 That evere in word or werk° I shal repente   *deed*
    That I yow yaf° myn herte in hool entente.°   *gave / wholeheartedly*

7. But it is truly said—in any case, I find it true.
8. (Even) if I should die in this affair, it shall not be.

My lord, ye woot° that in my fadres place   know
Ye dide me strepe out of my povre wede,[9]
And richely me cladden, of° youre grace.   by
865 To yow broghte I noght elles, out of drede,°   there is no doubt
But feyth° and nakednesse and maydenhede.   loyalty
And here agayn your clothing I restore,
And eek° your wedding ring, for everemore.   also

The remenant of your jewels redy be°   is prepared
870 Inwith° your chambre, dar I saufly° sayn.   Within / safely
Naked out of my fadres hous," quod she,
"I cam, and naked moot° I turne° agayn.   must / return
Al youre plesaunce wol I folwen fayn.°   follow willingly
But yet I hope it be nat youre entente
875 That I smoklees[1] out of youre paleys wente.°   should go

Ye coude nat doon so dishoneste a thing
That thilke wombe in which youre children leye°   lay
Sholde biforn the peple, in my walking,
Be seyn al bare;° wherfore I yow preye,   naked
880 Lat me nat lyk a worm go by° the weye.   along
Remembre yow, myn owene lord so dere,
I was youre wyf, thogh I unworthy were.

Wherfore in guerdon° of my maydenhede,   recompense
Which that I broghte, and noght agayn I bere,°   bear
885 As voucheth sauf to yeve me to my mede[2]
But swich° a smok as I was wont° to were,   Only such / used
That I therwith may wrye° the wombe of here°   hide / her
That was youre wyf. And heer take I my leve°   leave
Of yow, myn owene lord, lest I yow greve."°   vex

890 "The smok," quod he, "that thou hast on thy bak,
Lat it be° stille, and bere° it forth with thee."   remain / bear
But wel unnethes° thilke° word he spak   hardly / that same
But wente his wey for rewthe° and for pitee.   compassion
Biforn the folk hirselven strepeth° she,   strips
895 And in hir smok, with heed and foot al bare,
Toward hir fader hous forth is she fare.[3]

The folk hire folwe wepinge in hir weye,°   on their way
And Fortune ay they cursen as they goon.
But she fro weping kepte hire eyen dreye,°   eyes dry
900 Ne in this tyme word ne spak she noon.
Hir fader, that this tydinge° herde anoon,   news

9. You had me stripped out of my poor clothing.
1. Smockless, without even an undergarment.
2. Just allow me to be given as my reward (my pay).
3. She has journeyed forth toward her father's house.

Curseth the day and tyme that nature
Shoop° him to been a lyves° creature.   *Created / living*

For out of doute° this olde povre man   *certainly*
905 Was evere in suspect° of hir mariage;   *doubtful*
For evere he demed,° sith° that it bigan,   *thought / since*
That whan the lord fulfild hadde his corage,°   *desire*
Him wolde thinke it were a disparage[4]
To his estaat° so lowe for t'alighte,°   *rank / to settle*
910 And voyden° hire as sone as ever he mighte.   *(would) get rid of*

Agayns° his doghter hastilich° goth he,   *Toward / hastily*
For he by noyse of folk knew hire cominge,
And with hire old cote, as it mighte be,[5]
He covered hire ful sorwefully wepinge.
915 But on° hire body mighte he it nat bringe,   *around*
For rude was the cloth and she more of age
By dayes fele° than at hire mariage.   *many*

Thus with hire fader for a certeyn space°   *space of time*
Dwelleth this flour° of wyfly pacience,   *flower*
920 That neither by hire wordes ne hire face
Biforn° the folk, ne eek in hire° absence,   *In front of / their*
Ne shewed she that hire° was doon offence;   *to her*
Ne of hire heighe estaat no remembraunce
Ne hadde she, as by° hire countenaunce.   *to judge by*

925 No wonder is, for in hire grete° estaat   *high*
Hire goost° was evere in pleyn° humylitee: *spirit / perfect*
No tendre mouth, noon herte delicaat,
No pompe, no semblant° of royaltee,   *semblance*
But ful of pacient benignitee,°   *graciousness*
930 Discreet and prydeles,° ay° honurable,   *without pride / ever*
And to hire housbonde evere meke and stable.°   *constant*

Men speke of Job and most° for his humblesse,°   *above all / humbleness*
As clerkes, whan hem list, can wel endyte,°   *write*
Namely of men; but as in soothfastnesse,°   *with regard to truth*
935 Thogh clerkes preyse wommen but a lyte,°   *very little*
Ther can no man in humblesse him acquyte°   *acquit himself*
As womman can, ne can ben half so trewe
As wommen been, but it be falle of newe.[6]

---

4. It would seem to him that it was a disgrace.
5. And with her old cloak, as well as he could.
6. Unless it has happened just recently.

PART SIX

Fro Boloigne is this Erl of Panik come,
940 Of which the fame up sprang° to more and lesse,°   *arose / great and small*
And in the peples eres° alle and some°   *ears / i.e., one and all*
Was couth eek° that a newe markisesse   *It was known also*
He with him broghte, in swich pompe and richesse,
That never was ther seyn with mannes yë°   *eye*
945 So noble array in al West Lumbardye.

The markis, which that shoop° and knew al this,   *planned*
Er that° this erl was° come sente his message°   *Before / had / messenger*
For thilke° sely° povre Grisildis;   *that same / good*
And she with humble herte and glad visage,
950 Nat with no swollen° thoght in hire corage,°   *i.e., prideful / heart*
Cam at his heste,° and on hire knees hire sette,   *command*
And reverently and wysly° she him grette.°   *discreetly / greeted*

"Grisild," quod he, "my wille is outrely°   *completely*
This mayden, that shal wedded been to me,
955 Receyved be tomorwe as royally
As it possible is in myn hous to be,
And eek that every wight° in his degree   *person*
Have his estaat in sitting° and servyse   *proper place at table*
And heigh plesaunce, as I can best devyse.

960 I have no wommen suffisaunt,° certayn,   *not women enough*
The chambres for t'arraye in ordinaunce°   *to put in order*
After my lust, and therfor wolde I fayn⁷
That thyn° were al swich maner governaunce;   *thine*
Thou knowest eek of old al my plesaunce.
965 Though thyn array° be badde and yvel biseye,°   *apparel / poor to see*
Do thou thy devoir° at the leeste weye."°   *duty / all the same*

"Nat only, lord, that I am glad," quod she,
"To doon youre lust, but I desyre also
Yow for to serve and plese in my degree°   *according to my station*
970 Withouten feynting,° and shal everemo.   *weariness*
Ne nevere, for no wele ne no wo,
Ne shal the gost° withinne myn herte stente°   *spirit / cease*
To love yow best with al my trewe entente."

And with that word she gan° the hous to dighte,°   *began / to make ready*
975 And tables for to sette and beddes make;
And peyned hir° to doon al that she mighte,   *she took pains*
Preying the chambereres,° for Goddes sake,   *Urging the chambermaids*
To hasten hem,° and faste swepe and shake.   *To hurry*

---

7. According to my desire, and therefore I would be pleased.

And she, the most servisable° of alle,   *diligent*
980 Hath every chambre arrayed and his halle.

Abouten undern gan this erl alighte,[8]
That with him broghte thise noble children tweye,
For which the peple ran to seen the sighte
Of hire° array, so richely biseye;°   *their / rich to see*
985 And thanne at erst amonges hem they seye[9]
That Walter was no fool thogh that him leste°   *it pleased him*
To chaunge his wyf, for it was for the beste.

For she is fairer, as they demen° alle,   *judge*
Than is Grisild, and more tendre° of age,   *young*
990 And fairer fruit° bitwene hem sholde falle,   *offspring*
And more plesant, for hire heigh linage;[1]
Hir brother eek so fair was of visage
That hem° to seen the peple hath caught° plesaunce,   *them / taken*
Commendinge now the markis governaunce.°   *conduct*

995 "O stormy peple! unsad and evere untrewe!
Ay undiscreet and chaunging as a vane![2]
Delytinge evere in rumbel° that is newe,   *rumor*
For lyk the mone ay wexe° ye and wane!   *wax, grow larger*
Ay ful of clapping, dere ynogh a jane![3]
1000 Youre doom is fals, youre constance yvel preveth,[4]
A ful greet fool is he that on yow leveth!"°   *believes in you*

Thus seyden sadde° folk in that citee,   *steadfast*
Whan that the peple gazed up and doun,
For they were glad, right° for the noveltee,   *just*
1005 To han a newe lady of hir toun.
Namore of this make I now mencioun,
But to Grisilde agayn wol I me dresse,°   *address myself*
And telle hir constance and hir bisinesse.

Ful bisy was Grisilde in every thing
1010 That to the feste was apertinent;°   *appertained*
Right noght was she abayst° of hire clothing,   *ashamed*
Though it were rude and somdel eek torent.°   *also somewhat torn*
But with glad chere to the yate° is went°   *gate / has gone*
With other folk, to grete the markisesse,
1015 And after that doth forth° hire bisinesse.   *continues*

---

8. About midmorning this earl arrived (*lit.*, dismounted).
9. And then for the first time they say amongst themselves.
1. Because of her noble birth (lineage).
2. Ever unwise, and changeable as a weather vane.
3. Ever full of chatter, not worth a penny (a "jane").
4. Your judgment is false, your constancy proves poor.

With so glad chere his gestes she receyveth,
And so conningly, everich in his degree,
That no defaute no man aperceyveth;[5]
But ay they wondren what she mighte be
1020 That in so povre array was for to see,
And coude° swich honour and reverence;   understood
And worthily they preisen° hire prudence.   praise

In al this mene whyle she ne stente°   did not cease
This mayde and eek hir brother to commende
1025 With al hir herte, in ful benigne entente,
So wel that no man coude hir prys° amende.°   praise / improve
But atte laste,° whan that thise lordes wende°   at (the) last / thought
To sitten doun to mete,° he gan to calle   to the meal
Grisilde, as she was bisy in his halle.

1030 "Grisilde," quod he, as° it were in his pley,   as if
"How lyketh thee my wyf and hire beautee?"
"Right wel," quod she, "my lord, for in good fey,°   faith
A fairer say° I nevere noon than she.   saw
I prey to God yeve° hire prosperitee,   give
1035 And so hope I that he wol to yow sende
Plesance ynogh unto youre lyves ende.

O° thing biseke° I yow, and warne also,   One / beseech
That ye ne prikke° with no tormentinge   goad
This tendre mayden, as ye han don mo.°   others
1040 For she is fostred° in hire norishinge°   raised / upbringing
More tendrely, and to my supposinge,
She coude nat adversitee endure
As coude a povre fostred° creature."   raised in poverty

And whan this Walter saugh° hire pacience,   saw
1045 Hir glade chere and no malice at al—
And he so ofte had doon to hire offence,
And she ay sad° and constant as a wal,   ever firm
Continuinge evere hire innocence overal°—   in every respect
This sturdy markis gan his herte dresse[6]
1050 To rewen° upon hire wyfly stedfastnesse.   take pity

"This is ynogh,° Grisilde myn," quod he,   enough
"Be now namore agast° ne yvel apayed;°   afraid / ill-pleased
I have thy feith° and thy benignitee,   faithfulness
As wel as ever womman was, assayed.°   tested
1055 In greet° estaat, and povreliche° arrayed,   high / poorly
Now knowe I, dere wyf, thy stedfastnesse,"
And hire in armes took and gan hire kesse.°   kissed her

5. She receives his guests in so happy a mood and (so) skillfully—every one according to his
   rank—that no one (could) discover anything lacking.
6. This cruel (stern) marquis did turn his heart.

And she for wonder took of it no keep;°   heed
She herde nat what thing he to hire seyde;
1060 She ferde as° she had stert° out of a sleep,   acted as if / started
Til she out of hir masednesse° abreyde.°   bewilderment / awoke
"Grisilde," quod he, "by God that for us deyde,
Thou art my wyf, ne noon other I have,
Ne never hadde, as God my soule save!

1065 This is thy doghter which thou hast supposed
To be my wyf; that other feithfully
Shal be myn heir, as I have ay disposed;°   ever intended
Thou bare° him in thy body trewely.   bore
At Boloigne have I kept hem prively;°   secretly
1070 Tak hem agayn, for now maystow° nat seye   mayest thou
That thou hast lorn° non of thy children tweye.   lost

And folk that otherweyes° han seyd of me,   otherwise
I warne hem wel that I have doon this dede
For no malice ne for no crueltee,
1075 But for t'assaye in thee thy wommanhede,
And nat to sleen° my children, God forbede!   slay
But for to kepe hem prively and stille,°   quietly
Til I thy purpos knewe and al thy wille."

Whan she this herde, aswowne° doun she falleth   in a faint
1080 For pitous joye, and after hire swowninge
She bothe hire yonge children to hire calleth,
And in hire armes, pitously wepinge,
Embraceth hem, and tendrely kissinge,
Ful lyk a mooder, with hire salte teres
1085 She batheth bothe hire visage° and hire heres.°   their faces / hair

O, which a° pitous thing it was to see   what a
Hir swowning, and hire humble voys° to here!   voice
"Grauntmercy,° lord, God thanke° it yow," quod she,   Great thanks / reward
"That ye han saved me my children dere!
1090 Now rekke I never to ben deed right here;[7]
Sith° I stonde in youre love and in youre grace,   Since
No fors of deeth, ne whan my spirit pace![8]

O tendre, o dere, o yonge children myne,
Your woful mooder wende° stedfastly   thought
1095 That cruel houndes or som foul vermyne°   low animal
Hadde eten yow; but God of his mercy,
And youre benigne° fader, tendrely   gracious
Hath doon yow kept;" and in that same stounde[9]
Al sodeynly she swapte° adoun to grounde.   fell

7. Now I do not care if I should die right here.
8. Death is of no consequence, nor (the time) when my spirit (shall) go hence.
9. Have had you cared for;" and in that same moment.

1100 And in her swough° so sadly° holdeth she   *faint / firmly*
Hire children two, whan she gan hem t'embrace,°   *embraced them*
That with greet sleighte° and greet difficultee   *skill*
The children from hire arm they gonne arace.°   *tore away*
O many a teer on many a pitous face
1105 Doun ran of hem that stoden hire bisyde;
Unnethe° abouten hire mighte they abyde.°   *Scarcely / remain*

Walter hire gladeth° and hire sorwe slaketh;°   *cheers her / eases*
She ryseth up, abaysed,° from hire traunce,   *embarrassed*
And every wight hire joye and feste maketh[1]
1110 Til she hath caught° agayn hire contenaunce.°   *got / composure*
Walter hire dooth so feithfully plesaunce
That it was deyntee° for to seen the chere°   *delight / happiness*
Bitwixe hem two, now they ben met yfere.°   *together*

Thise ladyes, whan that they hir° tyme say,°   *their / saw*
1115 Han taken hire and into chambre goon,
And strepen° hire out of hire rude array,   *undress*
And in a cloth of gold that brighte shoon,
With a coroune° of many a riche stoon°   *crown / stone, jewel*
Upon hire heed, they into halle hire broghte,
1120 And ther she was honoured as hire oghte.°   *was due her*

Thus hath this pitous day a blisful ende,
For every man and womman dooth his might
This day in murthe and revel to dispende°   *spend*
Til on the welkne° shoon the sterres light.   *in the sky*
1125 For more solempne° in every mannes sight   *splendid*
This feste was, and gretter of costage,°   *cost*
Than was the revel of hire mariage.

Ful many a yeer in heigh prosperitee
Liven thise two in concord and in reste,
1130 And richely his doghter maried he
Unto a lord, oon of the worthieste
Of al Itaille; and than in pees° and reste   *peace*
His wyves fader in his court he kepeth,
Til that the soule out of his body crepeth.

1135 His sone succedeth in his heritage,
In reste and pees, after his fader° day,   *father's*
And fortunat was eek in mariage,
Al° putte he nat his wyf in greet assay.   *Although*
This world is nat so strong, it is no nay,°   *it cannot be denied*
1140 As it hath been in olde tymes yore.°   *long ago*
And herkneth° what this auctour° seith therfore: *listen to / Petrarch*

---

1. And every person makes joy for her and good cheer.

This storie is seyd, nat for that wyves sholde
Folwen Grisilde as in humilitee,
For it were importable, though they wolde;[2]
1145 But for that every wight° in his degree   person
Sholde be constant in adversitee
As was Grisilde. Therfore Petrark wryteth
This storie, which with heigh style he endyteth.°   composes

For sith° a womman was so pacient   since
1150 Unto a mortal man, wel more us oghte
Receyven al in gree° that God us sent.   good will
For greet skile is he preve that he wroghte,[3]
But he ne tempteth° no man that he boghte°—   tempts / redeemed
As seith Seint Jame,° if ye his pistel° rede.   James / epistle
1155 He preveth folk al day, it is no drede,°   doubtless

And suffreth° us, as for our excercyse,°   allows / discipline
With sharpe scourges of adversitee
Ful ofte to be bete° in sondry wyse,°   beaten / ways
Nat for to knowe oure wil; for certes he,
1160 Er we were born, knew al oure freletee.°   frailty
And for our beste is al his governaunce:
Lat us than live in vertuous suffraunce.°   patience

But o word, lordinges, herkneth° er I go: listen
It were ful hard to finde now-a-dayes
1165 In al a° toun Grisildes three or two;   In an entire
For if that they were put to swiche assayes,
The gold of hem hath now so° badde alayes°   such / alloys
With bras, that thogh the coyne be fair at yë,°   to the eye
It wolde rather breste a-two° than plye.°   break in two / bend

1170 For which heer, for the Wyves love of Bathe[4]—
Whos lyf and al hire secte° God mayntene   sect
In heigh maistrye,° and elles were it scathe°—   mastery / a pity
I wol with lusty° herte fresshe and grene   vigorous
Seyn yow a song to glade° yow, I wene,°   gladden / think
1175 And lat us stinte of ernestful matere.[5]
Herkneth my song, that seith in this manere:

2. For it would be intolerable (*lit.*, unbearable), even if they should wish to.
3. For there is good reason why He (should) test what He created.
4. For which right now, for love of the Wife of Bath.
5. And let's stop (talking) of serious matters.

THE ENVOY

Grisilde is deed, and eek° hire pacience,   *also*
And bothe atones° buried in Itaille.   *together*
For which I crye in open audience:°   *hearing*
1180 No wedded man so hardy° be t'assaille   *bold*
His wyves pacience, in hope to finde
Grisildes, for in certein he shall faille!

O noble wyves, ful of heigh prudence,
Lat noon humilitee your tonge naille,°   *nail down*
1185 Ne lat no clerk have cause or diligence
To wryte of yow a storie of swich mervaille
As of Grisildis, pacient and kinde,
Lest Chichevache yow swelwe in hire entraille!⁶

Folweth Ekko,° that holdeth no silence,   *Echo*
1190 But evere answereth at the countretaille;°   *in counterreply*
Beth nat bidaffed for your innocence,⁷
But sharply tak on yow the governaille.°   *control*
Emprinteth wel this lesson in youre minde
For commune profit, sith it may availle.

1195 Ye archewyves, stondeth at defence⁸—
Sin° ye be stronge as is a greet camaille°—   *Since / camel*
Ne suffreth° nat that men yow doon offence.   *allow*
And sclendre° wyves, feble as in bataille,   *slender*
Beth egre° as is a tygre yond° in Inde;°   *fierce / yonder / India*
1200 Ay clappeth as a mille, I yow consaille.⁹

Ne dreed° hem nat, doth hem no reverence;°   *fear / honor*
For though thyn housbonde armed be in maille,°   *mail*
The arwes° of thy crabbed eloquence   *arrows*
Shal perce his brest, and eek his aventaille.°   *helmet's faceplate*
1205 In jalousye I rede eek° thou him binde,   *advise also*
And thou shalt make him couche° as dooth a quaille.   *cower*

If thou be fair, ther° folk ben in presence°   *where / present*
Shew thou thy visage and thyn apparaille;°   *clothing*
If thou be foul, be free of thy dispence;°   *spending*
1210 To gete thee freendes ay do thy travaille.°   *take thy pains*
Be ay of chere as light as leef on linde,¹
And lat him care,° and wepe, and wringe, and waille!   *worry*

---

6. Lest Chichevache swallow you into her entrails. (Chichevache was a fabled cow who fed
   only on patient wives and hence was very lean.)
7. Don't be made a fool of because of (your) simplemindedness.
8. You archwives (dominating women), stand up in self-defense.
9. Always be noisy (clatter, chatter), I advise you, like a mill.
1. In behavior, always be as light as a leaf of the linden tree.

[THE WORDS OF THE HOST

1212a This worthy Clerk, whan ended was his tale,
       Our Hoste seyde and swoor, "By Goddes bones,
       Me were lever than a barel ale[2]
       My wyf at hoom had herd this legende ones.°   *once*
       This is a gentil tale for the nones,°   *occasion*
       As to my purpos, wiste ye° my wille;   *if you know*
1212g But thing that wol nat be, lat it be stille."][3]

The Merchant's Prologue and Tale

The Prologue

       "Weping and wayling, care and other sorwe
       I know ynogh, on even and a-morwe,"°   *i.e., by night and day*
1215   Quod the Marchant, "and so doon othere mo°   *many others*
       That wedded been. I trowe° that it be so,   *believe*
       For wel I woot° it fareth so° with me.   *know / that's how it goes*
       I have a wyf, the worste that may be;
       For thogh the feend° to hir y-coupled were,   *devil*
1220   She wolde him overmacche,° I dare wel swere.   *overmatch, master*
       What° sholde I yow reherce in special°   *Why / rehearse in detail*
       Hir hye° malice? She is a shrewe at al.° *proud / in every respect*
       There is a long and large difference
       Bitwix° Grisildis grete pacience   *Between*
1225   And of my wyf the passing° crueltee.   *surpassing*
       Were I unbounden, also moot I thee,[1]
       I wolde nevere eft° comen in the snare.   *again*
       We wedded men live in sorwe and care.
       Assaye° whoso wol, and he shal finde   *Test (it)*
1230   That I seye sooth, by Seint Thomas of Inde,[2]
       As for the more part°—I sey nat alle.   *i.e., the majority*
       God shilde° that it sholde so bifalle!   *forbid*
          A! Goode sire Host, I have y-wedded be
       Thise monthes two—and more nat, pardee°—   *no more, by God*
1235   And yet, I trowe, he that all his lyve
       Wyflees° hath been, though that men wolde him ryve° *I.e., a bachelor / stab*
       Unto the herte, ne coude in no manere
       Tellen so muchel sorwe as I now heere
       Coude tellen of my wyves cursednesse."°   *shrewishness*
1240   "Now," quod our Hoost, "Marchaunt, so God yow blesse,
       Sin° ye so muchel knowen of that art,   *Since*
       Ful hertely° I pray yow telle us part."   *heartily*

2. I'd sooner than a barrel of ale (that).
3. This stanza appears in some manuscripts and seems to have been an earlier draft canceled
   when Chaucer chose to have the Merchant respond directly to the Clerk's tale.
1. Were I freed of the marriage bond, so may I thrive.
2. St. Thomas of India ("Doubting Thomas," who tested Christ's wounds).

"Gladly," quod he, "but of myn owene sore,°   *misery*
For sory° herte, I telle may namore."   *(a) vexed*

The Tale

1245   Whylom° ther was dwellinge in Lumbardye°   *Once / Lombardy*
       A worthy knight that born was of Pavye,°   *Pavia (near Milan)*
       In which he lived in greet prosperitee.
       And sixty yeer a wyflees° man was he,   *wifeless*
       And folwed ay° his bodily delyt°   *always pursued / pleasure, desire*
1250   On° wommen, ther as° was his appetyt,   *In / where*
       As doon thise foles° that ben seculeer.°   *As these fools do / secular, i.e., laymen*
       And whan that he was passed sixty yeer—
       Were it for° holinesse or for dotage°   *Whether it was due to / senility*
       I can nat seye—but swich a greet corage°   *spirit, desire*
1255   Hadde this knight to been a wedded man
       That day and night he dooth al that he can
       T'espyen° where he mighte wedded be,   *To spy out, discover*
       Preyinge our Lord to graunten him that he
       Mighte ones knowe of thilke° blisful lyf   *Might once experience that*
1260   That is bitwixe an housbond and his wyf,
       And for to live under that holy bond
       With which that first° God man and womman bond.°   *originally / bound*
       "Non other lyf," seyde he, "is worth a bene,°   *bean*
       For wedlok is so esy° and so clene°   *easy, comfortable / pure*
1265   That in this world it is a paradys."
       Thus seyde this olde knight, that was so wys.
           And certeinly, as sooth° as God is king,   *truly*
       To take a wyf it is a glorious thing,
       And namely° whan a man is old and hoor;°   *especially / white-haired*
1270   Thanne is a wyf the fruit° of his tresor.°   *best part / treasure, wealth*
       Thanne sholde he take a yong wyf and a feir,°   *fair one*
       On which he mighte engendren him an heir,
       And lede his lyf in joye and in solas,°   *solace, pleasure*
       Wheras thise bacheleres singe "Allas!"
1275   Whan that they finden any adversitee
       In love, which nis but° childish vanitee.   *is only*
       And trewely it sit wel° to be so,   *it is fitting*
       That bacheleres have often peyne and wo:
       On brotel° ground they builde, and brotelnesse   *brittle, fragile*
1280   They finde whan they wene sikernesse.°   *expect security*
       They live but° as a brid° or as a beest,°   *merely / bird / beast*
       In libertee and under non arreest,°   *restraint*
       Ther as° a wedded man in his estaat°   *Whereas / state, condition*
       Liveth a lyf blisful and ordinaat,°   *well-ordered*
1285   Under the yok° of mariage y-bounde.   *yoke*
       Wel may his herte in joye and blisse habounde.°   *abound*
       For who can be so buxom° as a wyf?   *obedient*
       Who is so trewe and eek° so ententyf°   *also / eager, attentive*

To kepe° him, syk and hool,° as is his make?°   *look after / healthy / mate*
1290 For wele or wo° she wol him nat forsake.   *In joy or sorrow*
She nis nat wery° him to love and serve,   *i.e., never gets tired*
Thogh that he lye bedrede° til he sterve.°   *bedridden / die*
And yet somme clerkes seyn° it nis nat so,   *scholars (authorities) say*
Of whiche he, Theofraste,³ is oon of tho.°   *those*
1295 What force though° Theofraste liste° lye?   *What does it matter that / liked to*
"Ne take no wyf," quod he, "for housbondrye,°   *frugality, i.e., economy's sake*
As for to spare° in houshold thy dispence.°   *to be sparing / expenditure*
A trewe servant dooth more diligence
Thy good° to kepe than thyn owene wyf,   *goods, wealth*
1300 For she wol clayme half part al hir lyf.
And if that thou be syk, so God me save,
Thy verray° frendes or a trewe knave°   *true / male servant*
Wol kepe thee bet° than she that waiteth ay°   *take better care of thee / always*
After° thy good and hath don many a day.   *I.e., to inherit*
1305 And if thou take a wyf unto thyn hold,°   *into thy keeping*
Ful lightly° maystow been a cokewold."°   *Very easily / cuckold*
This sentence° and an hundred thinges worse   *opinion*
Wryteth this man—ther° God his bones corse!°   *may / curse*
But take no kepe° of al swich vanitee.°   *heed / nonsense, foolishness*
1310 Deffye° Theofraste and herke° me.   *Defy, reject / listen to*
    A wyf is Goddes yifte, verraily.°   *truly*
Alle other maner yiftes, hardily,°   *All other sorts of gifts, certainly*
As° londes, rentes,° pasture, or commune,⁴   *Such as / income*
Or moebles,° alle ben yiftes of Fortune,   *moveable goods*
1315 That passen as a shadwe° upon a wal.   *shadow*
But dredelees,° if pleynly speke I shal,   *doubtless*
A wyf wol laste and in thyn hous endure,
Wel lenger than thee list,° paraventure.°   *it please thee / perhaps*
    Marriage is a ful gret sacrement.
1320 He which that hath no wyf, I holde him shent:°   *ruined, lost*
He liveth helplees and al desolat°   *lonely*
(I speke of folk in seculer estaat).°   *layfolk (as opposed to clergy)*
And herke why—I sey nat this for noght—
That womman is for mannes help y-wroght:°   *made*
1325 The hye God, whan he hadde Adam maked
And saugh° him al allone, bely-naked,°   *saw / stark naked*
God of his grete goodnesse seyde than,
"Lat us now make an helpe° unto this man   *helpmate*
Lyk to himself," and thanne he made him Eve.
1330 Heer may ye se, and heerby may ye preve,°   *prove*
That wyf is mannes help and his confort,
His paradys terrestre° and his disport.°   *earthly paradise / delight*
So buxom° and so vertuous is she,   *submissive, obedient*

---

3. Theophrastus, author of *The Golden Book on Marriage*, a tract (now lost) satirically attack-
   ing marriage, excerpted by St. Jerome in his *Against Jovinian*, an important source for
   Chaucer's *Wife of Bath's Tale*. We print it in A. G. Rigg's translation, pp. 357–59.
4. Rights to use land held in common, for grazing, woodcutting, etc.

They moste nedes° live in unitee. — *must necessarily*
1335 O° flesh they been, and o flesh as I gesse° — *One / suppose*
Hath but on° herte, in wele° and in distresse. — *one / happy times*
 A wyf—a,° Seinte Marie, *benedicite!*° — *ah, oh / bless us all*
How mighte a man han° any adversitee — *have*
That hath a wyf? Certes,° I can nat seye. — *Certainly*
1340 The blisse which that is bitwixe hem tweye° — *the two of them*
Ther may no tonge telle or herte thinke.
If he be povre,° she helpeth him to swinke.° — *poor / work*
She kepeth° his good° and wasteth never a — *looks after / goods*
     deel.° — *not a bit*
Al that hir housbonde lust° hir lyketh weel.° — *desires / pleases her greatly*
1345 She seith not ones° "nay" whan he seith "ye."° — *once / yes*
"Do this," seith he; "Al redy, sir," seith she.
O blisful ordre of wedlok precious,
Thou art so mery and eek° so vertuous, — *also*
And so commended and approved eek,
1350 That every man that halt him° worth a leek° — *considers himself / i.e., anything*
Upon his bare knees oghte al his lyf
Thanken his God that him hath sent a wyf,
Or elles preye to God him for to sende
A wyf to laste unto his lyves ende,
1355 For thanne his lyf is set in sikernesse.° — *security*
He may nat be deceyved, as I gesse,
So that° he werke after° his wyves reed.° — *Provided / act according to / advice*
Than may he boldly beren up° his heed. — *hold up*
They been so trewe and therwithal so wyse,
1360 For which, if thou wolt werken as the wyse,° — *act as wise men (do)*
Do alwey so as° wommen wol thee rede.° — *just as / advise*
 Lo, how that Jacob, as thise clerkes rede,° — *tell, lecture on*
By good conseil° of his moder Rebekke,° — *counsel / Rebecca*
Bond° the kides° skin aboute his nekke, — *Bound, fastened / goat kid's*
1365 Thurgh which his fadres benisoun° he wan. — *blessing*
 Lo Judith, as the storie eek° telle can, — *also*
By wys conseil she Goddes peple kepte,° — *protected*
And slow° him Olofernus° whyl he slepte. — *slew / Holofernes*
 Lo Abigayl, by good conseil how she
1370 Saved hir housbonde Nabal whan that he
Sholde han be slayn; and loke, Ester also
By good conseil delivered out of wo
The peple of God, and made him Mardochee
Of Assuere enhaunced for to be.[5]
1375 Ther nis no thing in gree superlatyf,° — *superior in degree*
As seith Senek,° above an humble wyf. — *Seneca*
 Suffre° thy wyves tonge, as Caton bit;° — *Endure / Cato bids*

5. And look, Esther also, by good counsel, delivered from their woe the people of God and caused
Mordecai (her uncle) to be advanced by Ahasuerus (her husband). For these biblical examples
of feminine deception, violence, and skillful pleading see Genesis 27:1–29 (Rebecca, Jacob,
and Esau); Judith, chaps. 10–13 (Judith and Holofernes, whom she beheads); 1 Samuel
25:1–35 (Abigail, Nabal, and King David); and Esther, chaps. 7–8 (Esther and Ahasuerus).

She shal comande and thou shalt suffren it,
And yet she wol obeye of° curteisye.   *out of*
1380 A wyf is keper of thyn housbondrye.°   *domestic affairs*
Wel may the syke man biwaille and wepe,
Ther as° ther nis no wyf the hous to kepe.   *Wherever*
I warne thee, if wisely thou wolt wirche,°   *work, act*
Love wel thy wyf, as Crist loveth his chirche.
1385 If thou lovest thyself, thou lovest thy wyf.
No man hateth his flesh, but in his lyf
He fostreth° it, and therfore bidde I thee   *nourishes*
Cherisse thy wyf, or thou shalt never thee.°   *prosper*
Housbond and wyf, what so° men jape° or pleye,   *however much / joke*
1390 Of worldly° folk holden the siker° weye.   *Among secular / surer*
They been so knit° ther may noon harm bityde,°   *united / happen*
And namely° upon the wyves syde.   *especially*
For which this Januarie, of whom I tolde,
Considered hath, inwith his dayes olde,°   *in his old age*
1395 The lusty° lyf, the vertuous quiete,   *pleasurable*
That is in mariage hony-swete;
And for his freendes on a day° he sente,   *one day*
To tellen hem th'effect° of his entente.   *the substance*
    With face sad° his tale he hath hem told.   *sober, solemn*
1400 He seyde, "Freendes, I am hoor° and old   *white-haired*
And almost, God wot,° on my pittes brinke.°   *knows / the edge of my grave*
Upon my soule somwhat moste I thinke.
I have my body folily despended°—   *foolishly wasted*
Blessed be God that it shal been amended!
1405 For I wol be, certeyn, a wedded man,
And that anoon° in al the haste I can,   *promptly*
Unto som mayde fair and tendre of age.
I prey yow, shapeth° for my mariage   *prepare*
Al sodeynly,° for I wol nat abyde,°   *At once / wait*
1410 And I wol fonde t'espyen,° on my syde,°   *try to discover / for my part*
To whom I may be wedded hastily.
But forasmuche as ye ben mo° than I,   *more (in number)*
Ye shullen rather° swich a thing espyen   *sooner*
Than I, and wher me best were to allyen.°   *ally myself, marry*
1415   But o° thing warne I yow, my freendes dere,   *one*
I wol non old wyf han in no manere.°   *i.e., in any way*
She shal nat passe twenty yeer, certayn.
Old° fish and yong flesh° wolde I have fayn.°   *Fully grown / meat / eagerly*
Bet is," quod he, "a pyk° than a pikerel,°   *pike / young pike*
1420 And bet than old boef° is the tendre veel.°   *beef / veal*
I wol no womman thritty yeer of age;
It is but bene-straw° and greet forage.°   *dry beanstalks / coarse animal food*
And eek° thise olde widwes,° God it woot,°   *also / widows / knows*
They conne so muchel craft,° on Wades boot,[6]   *have so much cunning*

6. By Wade's boat. Wade was a legendary hero, but the meaning of this oath or allusion is unclear.

1425 So muchel broken harm,° whan that — petty wickedness
        hem leste,° — it pleases them
That with hem sholde I never live in reste.
For sondry scoles maken sotil clerkis;
Womman of manye scoles half a clerk is.[7]
But certeynly, a yong thing may men gye,° — guide
1430 Right as men may warm wex° with handes plye.° — wax / ply, shape
Wherfore I sey yow pleynly, in a clause,° — in a few words
I wol non old wyf han right for this cause.
For if so were I hadde swich mischaunce° — bad luck
That I in hir ne coude han no plesaunce,° — sexual pleasure
1435 Thanne sholde I lede my lyf in avoutrye° — adultery
And go streight to the devel whan I dye,
Ne children sholde I none upon hir geten.° — beget
Yet were me levere° houndes had me eten° — I would rather / eaten
Than that myn heritage° sholde falle — inheritance
1440 In straunge hand,° and this I tell yow alle. — To anyone not my kin
I dote nat.° I woot° the cause why — do not dote / know
Men sholde wedde, and forthermore woot I
Ther speketh many a man of mariage
That woot namore of it than woot my page° — serving boy
1445 For whiche causes man sholde take a wyf:
If he ne may nat liven chast° his lyf, — chastely
Take him° a wyf with greet devocioun — Let him take
By cause° of leveful° procreacioun — For the purpose / lawful
Of children to th'onour° of God above, — the honor
1450 And nat only for paramour° or love; — amorous feeling
And for° they sholde lecherye eschue° — so that / eschew, avoid
And yelde hir dettes whan that they ben due;[8]
Or for that ech of hem sholde helpen other
In meschief,° as a suster shal the brother, — misfortune
1455 And live in chastitee ful holily.
But sires, by your leve,° that am nat I. — by your leave, with your allowance
For God be thanked, I dar make avaunt,° — boast
I fele my limes° stark° and suffisaunt — limbs / strong
To do al that a man bilongeth to.° — is proper for a man to (do)
1460 I woot myselven best what I may do.
Though I be hoor,° I fare as dooth a tree — hoar, white-haired
That blosmeth er that fruyt y-woxen be,° — blossoms before the fruit has grown
And blosmy° tree nis neither drye ne deed. — (a) blossoming
I fele me nowher hoor but on myn heed.
1465 Myn herte and alle my limes been as grene
As laurer° thurgh the yeer is for to sene.° — laurel (an evergreen) / see
And sin° that ye han herd al myn entente,° — since / intentions, desires
I prey yow to my wil ye wole assente."

---

7. For different schools make students (scholars) clever; a woman who's been to many schools (i.e., been married often) is half a scholar.
8. And pay their debts when they are due. "Dettes" here echoes the biblical language for sexual intercourse as a marital obligation (1 Corinthians 7:3).

Diverse men diversely him tolde
1470 Of mariage manye ensamples olde.
Somme blamed it, somme preysed it, certeyn.
But atte laste, shortly for to seyn,
As al day falleth° altercacioun   *All the time happens*
Bitwixen freendes in disputisoun,°   *debate, discussion*
1475 Ther fil a stryf° bitwixe his bretheren two,   *An argument took place*
Of whiche that oon was cleped° Placebo;   *named*
Justinus soothly° called was that other.⁹   *truly*
      Placebo seyde, "O Januarie, brother,
Ful litel nede had ye, my lord so dere,
1480 Conseil to axe° of any that is here,   *To ask the counsel*
But° that ye been so ful of sapience°   *Except / wisdom*
That yow ne lyketh, for your heighe prudence,
To weyven fro° the word of Salomon.   *depart from*
This word seyde he unto us everichon:°   *every one of us*
1485 'Wirk alle thing by conseil,' thus seyde he,
'And thanne shaltow° nat repente thee.'   *shalt thou*
But though that Salomon spak swich a word,
Myn owene dere brother and my lord,
So wisly God° my soule bringe at reste,   *As surely as God (may)*
1490 I hold° your owene conseil is the beste.   *believe, affirm*
For, brother myn, of me tak this motyf:°   *idea, thought*
I have now been a court-man° al my lyf,   *courtier*
And God it woot,° though I unworthy be,   *knows*
I have stonden in ful greet degree°   *very high rank*
1495 Abouten lordes of ful heigh estaat,
Yet hadde I never with noon of hem° debaat.°   *them / disagreement*
I never hem contraried,° trewely.   *contradicted*
I woot wel that my lord can° more than I.   *knows*
What that he seith, I holde it ferme° and stable.   *firm, true*
1500 I seye the same or elles thing semblable.°   *something like it*
A ful gret fool is any conseillour
That serveth any lord of heigh honour
That dar presume or elles thenken it°   *even imagine*
That his conseil sholde passe° his lordes wit.°   *surpass / reason, intelligence*
1505 Nay, lordes been no fooles, by my fay.°   *faith*
Ye han yourselven shewed heer today
So heigh sentence,° so holily° and weel,   *Such good judgment / virtuously*
That I consente and conferme everydeel°   *completely*
Your wordes alle and your opinioun.
1510 By God, ther nis no man in al this toun
Ne in Itaille that coude bet han sayd.°   *could have spoken better*
Crist halt him° of this conseil wel apayd.°   *considers himself (i.e., is) / pleased*
And trewely, it is an heigh corage°   *a high-spirited deed*
Of any man that stapen° is in age   *advanced (lit., stepped)*
1515 To take a yong wyf. By my fader° kin,   *father's*

9. "Placebo": "I shall please," "I shall be found pleasing" (Latin); "Justinus" evokes Latin *justus:* "just," "rightful," "the just one."

Your herte hangeth on a joly pin!°   *i.e., is jolly, lively*
Doth now in this matere right as yow leste,°   *exactly as it pleases you*
For finally I holde it for the beste."
    Justinus, that ay° stille sat and herde,   *all this time*
1520 Right in this wyse° he to Placebo answerde: *manner*
"Now, brother myn, be pacient, I preye,
Sin ye han seyd,° and herkneth what I seye.   *Since you have spoken*
Senek,° among his othere wordes wyse,   *Seneca*
Seith that a man oghte him right wel avyse°   *to consider very carefully*
1525 To whom he yeveth° his lond or his catel.°   *gives / chattels, property*
And sin I oghte avyse me right wel
To whom I yeve my good awey fro me,
Wel muchel more I oghte avysed be
To whom I yeve my body for alwey.
1530 I warne yow wel, it is no childes pley
To take a wyf withoute avysement.°   *deliberation*
Men moste enquere—this is myn assent°—   *opinion*
Wher° she be wys or sobre or dronkelewe,°   *Whether / given to drunkenness*
Or proud or elles otherweys a shrewe,°   *wicked person*
1535 A chydester° or wastour° of thy good,   *scold / waster*
Or riche or poore, or elles mannish wood.°   *man-crazy, a virago (?)*
Al be it so that° no man finden shal   *Even though*
Noon° in this world that trotteth hool in al°— *No one / trots (i.e., acts) perfectly*
Ne° man ne° beest, swich as men coude devyse°—   *Neither / nor / imagine*
1540 But nathelees° it oghte ynough suffise   *nevertheless*
With any wyf if so were that she hadde
Mo° goode thewes° than hir vyces badde;   *More / qualities*
And al this axeth leyser for t'enquere.°   *requires leisure (time) to look into*
For God it woot,° I have wept many a tere   *knows*
1545 Ful prively° sin° I have had a wyf.   *secretly / since*
Preyse° whoso wole a wedded mannes lyf,   *Praise*
Certein° I finde in it but cost° and care   *Certainly / only expense*
And observances° of alle blisses bare.°   *duties / i.e., joyless*
And yet, God woot,° my neighebores aboute,°   *knows / round about*
1550 And namely of wommen many a route,°   *throng*
Seyn° that I have the moste stedefast wyf   *Say*
And eek° the mekeste° oon that bereth lyf.   *also / meekest*
But I wot best wher wringeth me my sho.°   *my shoe pinches me*
Ye mowe,° for me,° right as yow lyketh do.   *may / as far as I'm concerned*
1555 Avyseth yow°—ye been a man of age—   *Think carefully*
How that ye entren into mariage,
And namely with a yong wyf and a fair.
By Him that made water, erthe, and air,
The yongest man that is in al this route°   *company*
1560 Is bisy ynogh to bringen it aboute
To han his wyf allone.° Trusteth me,   *have his wife solely to himself*
Ye shul nat plese hir fully yeres three
(This is to seyn, to doon hir ful plesaunce).°   *sexual pleasure*
A wyf axeth° ful many an observaunce.°   *asks, requires / much attention*

1565 I prey yow that ye be nat yvel apayd."°   *displeased*
     "Wel," quod this Januarie, "and hastow sayd?°   *i.e., have you finished?*
     Straw for thy Senek and for thy proverbes!
     I counte nat a panier ful of herbes
     Of scole-termes.¹ Wyser men than thow,
1570 As thou hast herd, assenteden right now
     To my purpos. Placebo, what sey ye?"
          "I seye it is a cursed man," quod he,
     "That letteth° matrimoine, sikerly."°   *hinders / surely*
     And with that word they rysen sodeynly,
1575 And been assented fully that he sholde
     Be wedded whanne him list° and wher he wolde.   *it pleased him*
          Heigh fantasye and curious bisinesse°   *obsessive preoccupation*
     Fro day to day gan° in the soule impresse°   *did / make a mark*
     Of Januarie aboute° his mariage.   *concerning*
1580 Many fair shape and many a fair visage
     Ther passeth thurgh his herte, night by night.
     As whoso toke° a mirour polished bright   *If someone took*
     And sette it in a commune market-place,
     Than sholde he see many a figure pace
1585 By his mirour; and in the same wyse°   *manner*
     Gan Januarie inwith° his thoght devyse°   *within / fantasize*
     Of° maydens whiche that dwelten him bisyde.°   *About / nearby*
     He wiste° nat wher that he mighte abyde,°   *knew / (best) settle*
     For if that oon° have beaute in hir face,   *if one*
1590 Another stant° so in the peples grace   *stands*
     For hir sadnesse° and hir benignitee°   *seriousness / graciousness*
     That of the peple grettest voys° hath she.   *praise*
     And somme were riche and hadden badde name.°   *i.e., reputation*
     But nathelees, bitwixe ernest and game,°   *jest*
1595 He atte laste apoynted him° on oon,   *decided*
     And leet alle othere° from his herte goon,   *others*
     And chees° hir of° his owene auctoritee;°   *chose / on / authority, judgment*
     For love is blind al day° and may nat see.   *always*
     And whan that he was in his bed y-broght,
1600 He purtreyed° in his herte and in his thoght   *pictured*
     Hir fresshe beautee and hir age tendre,
     Hir myddel° smal, hir armes longe and sclendre,°   *waist / slender*
     Hir wyse governaunce,° hir gentillesse,°   *behavior / gentility*
     Hir wommanly beringe and hir sadnesse.°   *seriousness*
1605 And whan that he on hir was condescended,°   *settled*
     Him thoughte his chois mighte nat ben amended.°   *bettered*
     For whan that he himself concluded hadde,
     Him thoughte ech other mannes wit so badde
     That inpossible it were to replye°   *speak*
1610 Agayn° his chois—this was his fantasye.   *Against*
     His freendes sente he to at his instaunce°   *request*

---

1. I value this scholar-talk no more than a basket full of greens.

And preyed hem° to doon him that plesaunce,   *asked them*
That hastily they wolden to him come.
He wolde abregge° hir° labour, alle and some: *abridge, shorten / their*
1615 Nedeth namore for him to go ne ryde;°   *i.e., to search about on his behalf*
He was apoynted° ther° he wolde   *had decided / where (i.e., on whom)*
            abyde.°   *settle*
Placebo cam and eek his freendes sone,°   *soon*
And alderfirst° he bad hem alle a bone,°   *first of all / asked them all a favor*
That noon of hem° none argumentes make   *none of them*
1620 Agayn the purpos which that he hath take,°   *has decided on*
Which purpos was plesant° to God, seyde he,   *pleasing*
And verray ground° of his prosperitee.   *true foundation*
        He seyde ther was a mayden in the toun,
Which that of beautee hadde greet renoun.
1625 Al were it so° she were of smal degree,°   *Although / low rank*
Suffyseth him hir youthe and hir beautee.
Which mayde, he seyde, he wolde han to° his wyf,   *have as*
To lede in ese° and holinesse his lyf,   *ease, comfort*
And thanked God that he mighte han hire al,°   *entirely*
1630 That no wight° his blisse parten° shal,   *person / share*
And preyed hem to laboure in this nede°   *business*
And shapen° that he faille nat to spede.°   *arrange matters / succeed*
For thanne, he seyde, his spirit was at ese.
"Thanne is," quod he, "no thing may me displese,
1635 Save o° thing priketh in my conscience,   *But one*
The which I wol reherce in your presence.
        I have," quod he, "herd seyd ful yore ago°   *a long time ago*
Ther may no man han parfite° blisses two,   *perfect*
This is to seye, in erthe and eek° in hevene.   *also*
1640 For though he kepe him fro the sinnes sevene,°   *seven deadly sins*
And eek from every branche of thilke tree,°   *that tree (of sins)*
Yet is ther so parfit felicitee°   *such perfect happiness*
And so greet ese and lust° in mariage   *pleasure*
That ever° I am agast° now in myn age   *constantly / terrified*
1645 That I shal lede now so mery a lyf,
So delicat,° withouten wo and stryf,   *delightful*
That I shal have myn hevene in erthe here.
For sith that° verray° hevene is boght so   *since / the real*
            deere°   *at such expense*
With tribulacioun and greet penaunce,
1650 How sholde I thanne, that live in swich plesaunce
As alle wedded men don° with hir wyvis,   *do*
Come to the blisse ther° Crist eterne on lyve° is?   *where / eternally alive*
This is my drede,° and ye, my bretheren tweye,   *fear*
Assoilleth me this questioun,° I preye."   *Resolve this problem for me*
1655   Justinus, which that hated his folye,°   *folly*
Answerde anon,° right° in his japerye,°   *at once / directly / mockery*
And for° he wolde his longe tale° abregge,°   *because / speech / abridge*
He wolde noon auctoritee allegge°   *cite, appeal to*
But seyde, "Sire, so° ther be noon obstacle   *as long as*

1660 Other than this, God of his hye miracle°   *miraculous power*
And of his mercy may so for yow wirche°   *work*
That, er° ye have your right° of holy chirche,   *before / last rites*
Ye may repente of wedded mannes lyf,
In which ye seyn ther is no wo ne stryf.
1665 And elles,° God forbede but° he sente   *further / but (that)*
A wedded man him grace° to repente   *i.e., reasons*
Wel ofte rather° than a sengle man!   *more often*
And therfore, sire, the beste reed I can:°   *advice I know*
Dispeire yow noght, but have° in your memorie,   *hold*
1670 Paraunter° she may be your purgatorie!   *By chance, perhaps*
She may be Goddes mene° and Goddes whippe.   *means, instrument*
Than shal your soule up to hevene skippe
Swifter than dooth an arwe° out of the bowe.   *arrow*
I hope to God herafter shul ye knowe
1675 That ther nis no so greet felicitee
In mariage, ne never mo shal be,
That yow shal lette of° your savacioun,   *shall keep you from*
So that° ye use, as skile is and resoun,°   *Provided / as is proper and reasonable*
The lustes° of your wyf attemprely,°   *pleasures / moderately*
1680 And that ye plese hir nat to° amorously,   *too*
And that ye kepe yow eek° from other sinne.   *also*
My tale is doon, for my wit is thinne.°   *weak*
Beth nat agast herof,° my brother dere.   *Do not be afraid of this*
But lat us waden° out of this matere.   *wade, go*
1685 The Wyf of Bathe, if ye han understonde,
Of mariage, which we have on honde,°   *i.e., is our present subject*
Declared hath ful wel in litel space.
Fareth now wel; God have yow in his grace."
      And with this word this Justin and his brother
1690 Han take hir leve, and ech of hem of other.
For whan they sawe it moste nedes be,
They wroghten° so by sly° and wys tretee°   *arranged it / skillful / negotiation*
That she, this mayden which that Mayus highte,°   *who was called May*
As hastily as ever that she mighte
1695 Shal wedded be unto this Januarie.
I trowe it were to° longe yow to tarie°   *too / delay*
If I yow tolde of every scrit° and bond   *writ, legal document*
By which that she was feffed° in his lond,   *enfeoffed, put in possession of*
Or for to herknen° of hir riche array.°   *hear / clothing*
1700 But finally y-comen is the day
That to the chirche bothe be they went
For to receyve the holy sacrement.°   *i.e., of marriage*
Forth comth the preest, with stole° aboute his nekke, *(a liturgical vestment)*
And bad hir be lyk Sarra and Rebekke
1705 In wisdom and in trouthe° of mariage,[2]   *troth, fidelity*
And seyde his orisons° as is usage,°   *prayers / customary*

---

2. These lines refer to a prayer in the medieval marriage ceremony: the priest asks that the wife
   be as wise as Rebecca and as faithful as Sarah.

And croucheth hem,[3] and bad° God sholde hem blesse,   *prayed*
And made al siker° ynogh with holinesse.   *secure*
   Thus been they wedded with solempnitee,
1710 And at the feste° sitteth he and she   *feast*
With other worthy folk upon the deys.°   *dais*
Al ful of joye and blisse is the paleys,
And ful of instruments and of vitaille,°   *food*
The moste deyntevous° of al Itaille.   *choice, delicious*
1715 Biforn hem stoode instruments of swich soun°   *of such sound*
That Orpheus ne of Thebes Amphioun
Ne maden never swich a melodye.[4]
At every cours° than cam loud minstralcye   *course of the meal*
That never tromped° Joab for to here,°   *trumpeted / hear*
1720 Nor he Theodomas yet half so clere
At Thebes whan the citee was in doute.°   *danger*
Bacus° the wyn hem skinketh° al aboute,   *Bacchus, god of wine / pours*
And Venus° laugheth upon every wight°—   *goddess of love / person*
For Januarie was bicome hir knight
1725 And wolde bothe assayen his corage°   *test his spirit (and sexual potency)*
In libertee° and eek in mariage—   *i.e., bachelorhood*
And with hir fyrbrond° in hir hand aboute   *her (Venus's) torch*
Daunceth biforn the bryde and al the route.°   *company*
And certeinly, I dar right wel seyn this,
1730 Ymeneus,° that god of wedding is,   *Hymen*
Saugh never his lyf° so mery a wedded man.   *in his life*
Hold thou thy pees,° thou poete Marcian,[5]   *Hold thy peace (keep silent)*
That wrytest us that ilke° wedding murie°   *very same / merry*
Of hir, Philologye, and him, Mercurie,
1735 And of the songes that the Muses songe.
To smal° is bothe thy penne and eek thy tonge   *Too small, inadequate*
For to descryven of this mariage.
Whan tendre youthe hath wedded stouping° age,   *stooping, bent*
Ther is swich mirthe that it may nat be writen.
1740 Assayeth° it yourself; than may ye witen°   *Try / know*
If that I lye or noon° in this matere.   *or not*
   Mayus,[6] that sit with so benigne a chere,°   *so gracious an expression*
Hir to biholde it semed fayerye.°   *something enchanting, like a fairy tale*
Quene Ester° loked never with swich an yë°   *Esther / eye*
1745 On Assuer,° so meke a look hath she.   *Ahasuerus (see ll. 1371–74 and note)*
I may yow nat devyse° al hir beautee,   *describe*
But thus muche of hir beautee telle I may,
That she was lyk the brighte morwe° of May,   *morning*
Fulfild of alle beautee and plesaunce.

3. And makes the sign of the cross over them.
4. Orpheus won Euridyce back from the underworld (for a time) by the power of his music.
   Amphion raised the walls of Thebes by the same means. Joab (1. 1719) was the chief general of King David and blew the trumpet for his army. The auguries of Thiodamas (1. 1720)
   at the siege of Thebes were answered by the sound of trumpets.
5. Martianus Capella, author of *The Marriage of Philology and Mercury*, an allegory of the
   seven liberal arts.
6. Chaucer here calls her by the Latin name for the month of May; cf. 1. 2157.

1750   This Januarie is ravisshed in a traunce
       At every time he loked on hir face;
       But in his herte he gan hir to manace°   menace, threaten
       That he that night in armes wolde hir streyne°   clasp
       Harder than ever Paris dide Eleyne.[7]
1755   But nathelees yet hadde he greet pitee
       That thilke night offenden° hir moste he,   hurt physically
       And thoughte, "Allas! O tendre creature,
       Now wolde God ye mighte wel endure
       Al my corage,° it is so sharp and kene.°   desire / keen
1760   I am agast° ye shul it nat sustene.°   afraid / endure
       (But God forbede that I dide al my might!)
       Now wolde God that it were woxen night°   had become night
       And that the night wolde lasten evermo.
       I wolde that al this peple were ago."°   had gone, departed
1765   And finally he doth al his labour°   i.e., all he can
       As he best mighte, savinge his honour,°   without injuring his reputation
       To haste° hem fro the mete° in subtil wyse.   hasten / (wedding) feast
          The tyme cam that reson was° to ryse,   it was appropriate
       And after that men° daunce and drinken faste,   i.e., folk (impersonal pronoun)
1770   And spyces al aboute the hous they caste,°   scattered
       And ful of joye and blisse is every man—
       All but a squyer highte° Damian,   named
       Which carf° biforn the knight ful many a day.   Who carved (cf. GP l. 100)
       He was so ravisshed on° his lady May   by
1775   That for the verray peyne° he was ny wood.°   sheer agony / almost crazy
       Almost he swelte° and swowned ther he stood,   fainted
       So sore hath Venus hurt him with hir brond,
       As that she bar it° daunsinge in hir hond;   When she bore it
       And to his bed he wente him hastily.
1780   Namore of him at this tyme speke I,
       But ther I lete him wepe ynough and pleyne,°   make complaints
       Til fresshe May wol rewen° on his peyne.   have pity
          O perilous fyr° that in the bedstraw bredeth!°   fire / breeds, begins
       O famulier[8] foo that° his servyce bedeth!°   foe who / offers
1785   O servant traitour, false hoomly hewe,°   faithless domestic servant
       Lyk to the naddre° in bosom sly° untrewe,   adder, serpent / deceitful
       God shilde us alle from your aqueyntaunce!
       O Januarie, dronken in plesaunce°   pleasure
       Of mariage, see how thy Damian,
1790   Thyn owene squyer and thy borne man,°   i.e., servant from birth
       Entendeth for to do thee vileinye.°   wrong
       God graunte thee thyn hoomly fo t'espye,°   to see (spy out)
       For in this world nis worse pestilence
       Than hoomly foo al day in thy presence.
1795   Parfourned° hath the sonne° his ark diurne.°   Completed / sun / daily arc
       No lenger may the body of him° sojurne°   (i.e., the sun) / remain

7. Paris, a Trojan prince, ravished Helen of Troy, originally Greek, initiating the Trojan war.
8. Intimate, belonging to one's household.

On th'orisonte° as in that latitude. — *the horizon*
Night with his mantel° that is derk and rude° — *mantle, cloak / rough*
Gan oversprede the hemisperie° aboute, — *hemisphere*
1800 For which departed is this lusty route° — *joyful company*
Fro Januarie, with thank on every syde.
Hom to hir houses lustily they ryde,
Wher as they doon hir thinges as hem leste,° — *whatever pleased them*
And whan they sye hir° tyme, goon to reste. — *saw their*
1805 Sone after that this hastif° Januarie — *eager, impatient*
Wolde go to bedde—he wolde no lenger tarie.
He drinketh ipocras, clarree, and vernage[9]
Of spyces hote, t'encresen his corage,° — *desire*
And many a letuarie° hadde he, ful fyn,° — *medicine / quite choice*
1810 Swiche as the cursed monk dan Constantyn
Hath writen in his book, *De Coitu.*[1]
To eten hem° alle he nas no thing eschu.° — *consume them / was in no way averse*
And to his privee° freendes thus seyde he: — *closest*
"For Goddes love, as sone as it may be,
1815 Lat voyden° al this hous in curteys° wyse." — *Clear out / courteous*
And they had doon right° as he wol devyse. — *exactly*
Men drinken, and the travers[2] drawe anon.
The bryde was broght abedde as stille as stoon,
And whan the bed was with° the preest y-blessed, — *by*
1820 Out of the chambre hath every wight him dressed,° — *removed himself*
And Januarie hath faste° in armes take — *quickly, firmly*
His fresshe May, his paradys, his make.° — *mate*
He lulleth° hir, he kisseth hir ful ofte. — *soothes*
With thikke bristles of his berd unsofte—
1825 Lyk to the skin of houndfish,° sharp as brere,° — *dogfish / briar*
For he was shave al newe° in his manere— — *had recently shaved*
He rubbeth hir aboute hir tendre face
And seyde thus: "Allas! I moot trespace° — *commit offense*
To yow, my spouse, and yow gretly offende,° — *displease, hurt*
1830 Er tyme come that I wil doun descende.° — *get down (or off)*
But nathelees, considereth this," quod he,
"Ther nis no werkman, whatsoever he be,
That may bothe werke wel and hastily.
This wol° be doon at leyser° parfitly.° — *must / leisure / perfectly*
1835 It is no fors° how longe that we pleye. — *It does not matter*
In trewe wedlok coupled be we tweye,° — *two*
And blessed be the yok° that we been inne, — *yoke*
For in our actes we mowe° do no sinne. — *may*
A man may do no sinne with his wyf,
1840 Ne hurte himselven with his owene knyf,

9. Hippocras, clary, and vernaccia are all strongly spiced sweet wines, thought to increase sexual desire.
1. "Dan" or "don": *dominus,* a familiar title for a monk. Constantinus Africanus's treatise on sexual intercourse, *De Coitu,* written ca. 1080, contained recipes for aphrodisiacs.
2. A curtain drawn to divide the room, creating a private bedchamber.

For we han leve to pleye us by the lawe."³

Thus laboureth he til that the day gan dawe,°   *began to dawn*

And than he taketh a sop in fyn clarree,°   *piece of bread dipped in wine*

And upright in his bed than sitteth he,

1845 And after that he sang ful loude and clere,

And kiste his wyf and made wantoun chere.°   *behaved amorously*

He was al coltish,° ful of ragerye,°   *frisky as a colt / wantonness*

And ful of jargon° as a flekked pye.°   *chatter / spotted magpie*

The slakke° skin aboute his nekke shaketh   *loose*

1850 Whyl that he sang, so chaunteth° he and craketh.°   *sings / croaks*

But God wot° what that May thoughte in hir herte,   *knows*

Whan she him saugh up sittinge in his sherte,°   *nightshirt*

In his night-cappe, and with his nekke lene.°   *lean, skinny*

She preyseth° nat his pleying° worth a bene.   *values / i.e., love-making*

1855 Than seide he thus, "My reste wol I take.

Now day is come, I may no lenger wake."

And doun he leyde his heed and sleep° til pryme.°   *slept / 9 A.M.*

And afterward, whan that he saugh his tyme,

Up ryseth Januarie; but fresshe May

1860 Held hir chambre° unto the fourthe day,   *Remained in her bedroom*

As usage° is of wyves for the beste.   *the custom*

For every labour somtyme moot han° reste,   *must have*

Or elles longe may he nat endure—

This is to seyn,° no lyves° creature,   *say / living*

1865 Be it of fish or brid° or beest or man.   *bird*

    Now wol I speke of woful Damian,

That languissheth for love, as ye shul here.

Therfore I speke to him in this manere:

I seye, "O sely° Damian, allas!   *hapless, unfortunate*

1870 Answere to my demaunde,° as in this cas.   *question*

How shaltow to thy lady, fresshe May,

Telle thy wo? She wole alwey seye 'nay.'

Eek° if thou speke, she wol thy wo biwreye.°   *And / reveal, betray*

God be thyn help—I can no bettre seye."

1875   This syke° Damian in Venus fyr   *sick, sorrowful*

So brenneth° that he dyeth for desyr,   *burns*

For which he putte his lyf in aventure.°   *at risk*

No lenger mighte he in this wyse endure,

But prively° a penner° gan he borwe,   *secretly / pen case*

1880 And in a lettre wroot he al his sorwe,

In manere of a compleynt° or a lay,°   *a poetic lament / song*

Unto his faire, fresshe lady May.

And in a purs of silk, heng° on his sherte,   *which hung*

He hath it put and leyde it at his herte.

1885 The mone that at noon was thilke day

That Januarie hath wedded fresshe May

3. For we have permission to enjoy ourselves (sexually) by law.

In two of Taur, was into Cancre gliden.[4]
So longe hath Maius in hir chambre biden,°   *stayed*
As custume is unto thise nobles alle.
1890   A bryde shal nat eten° in the halle   *eat, dine*
Til dayes foure, or three dayes atte leste,
Y-passed been; than lat hir go to feste.
The fourthe day compleet° fro noon to noon,   *being completed*
Whan that the heighe masse° was y-doon,   *High Mass*
1895   In halle sit this Januarie and May,
As fresh as is the brighte someres day.
And so bifel how that this gode man
Remembred him upon this Damian
And seyde, "Seinte Marie! How may this be
1900   That Damian entendeth nat° to me?   *does not attend (wait on)*
Is he ay syk,° or how may this bityde?"°   *Has he been sick all this time / happen*
His squyeres whiche that stoden ther bisyde
Excused him bycause of his siknesse,
Which letted° him to doon his bisinesse.°   *prevented / duties*
1905   Noon other cause mighte make him tarie.
    "That me forthinketh,"° quod this Januarie,   *worries me*
"He is a gentil° squyer, by my trouthe!   *noble*
If that he deyde,° it were harm° and routhe.°   *died / grief / pity*
He is as wys, discreet, and as secree°   *able to keep secrets*
1910   As any man I woot° of his degree,°   *know / rank*
And therto manly and eek servisable,°   *also willing to serve*
And for to been a thrifty° man right able.   *successful*
But after mete,° as sone as ever I may,   *dinner*
I wol myself visyte him, and eek May,
1915   To doon him al the confort that I can."
And for that word him blessed every man,
That of° his bountee° and his gentillesse°   *out of / goodness / nobility*
He wolde so conforten in siknesse
His squyer, for it was a gentil dede.
1920   "Dame," quod this Januarie, "tak good hede,°   *heed*
At after-mete° ye with your wommen alle,   *After dinner*
Whan ye han been in chambre° out of this halle,   *i.e., go to your chamber*
That alle ye go see this Damian.
Doth him disport°—he is a gentil man—   *Provide him (some) amusement*
1925   And telleth him that I wol him visyte,
Have I no thing but° rested me a lyte;°   *When I have merely / little*
And spede yow faste,° for I wole abyde°   *go quickly / wait*
Til that ye slepe faste by° my syde."   *close to*
And with that word be gan to him to calle
1930   A squyer that was marchal° of his halle,   *i.e., in charge of arrangements*
And tolde him certeyn thinges what he wolde.
    This fresshe May hath streight hir wey y-holde,°   *taken*
With alle hir wommen, unto Damian.

4. The moon, which at noon on the day of the wedding was in the second degree of Taurus,
had (four days later) slid (through Gemini) into Cancer.

Doun by his beddes syde sit° she than,   *sits*
1935 Confortinge him as goodly° as she may.   *pleasantly*
This Damian, whan that his tyme he say,°   *saw*
In secree wise his purs and eek his bille,°   *letter*
In which that he y-writen hadde his wille,°   *desire*
Hath put into hir hand, withouten more,°   *without more ado*
1940 Save° that he syketh° wonder° depe and sore,   *Except / sighs / wondrously*
And softely to hir right thus seyde he:
"Mercy—and that ye nat discovere° me!   *reveal*
For I am deed° if that this thing be kid."°   *dead / known*
This purs hath she inwith hir bosom hid,
1945 And wente hir wey; ye gete namore of me.
But unto Januarie y-comen is she,
That on his beddes syde sit ful softe.
He taketh hir and kisseth hir ful ofte
And leyde him doun to slepe, and that anon.°   *soon*
1950 She feyned hir° as that she moste gon°   *pretended / must go*
There as ye woot that every wight mot nede.[5]
And whan she of this bille hath taken hede,°   *has taken heed, attended to*
She rente° it al to cloutes° atte laste,   *tore / bits*
And in the privee° softely° it caste.   *privy / quietly*
1955   Who studieth° now but faire fresshe May?   *ponders*
Adoun by olde Januarie she lay,
That sleep° til that the coughe hath him awaked.   *Who slept*
Anon° he preyde° hir strepen hir al naked.   *At once / beseeched*
He wolde of hir, he seyde, han som plesaunce,
1960 And seyde hir clothes dide him encombraunce,°   *got in his way*
And she obeyeth, be hir lief or looth.°   *whether she likes it or not*
But lest that precious° folk be with me wrooth,°   *fussy, prudish / angry*
How that he wroghte° I dar nat to yow telle,   *How he did what he did*
Or whether hir thoughte it° paradys or helle;   *it seemed to her*
1965 But here I lete hem werken in hir wyse°   *in their fashion*
Til evensong° rong and that they moste aryse.   *the bell for vespers*
          Were it by destinee or aventure,°   *chance*
Were it by influence° or by nature   *(of the stars)*
Or constellacion,° that in swich estat°   *astrological disposition / such condition*
1970 The hevene stood that tyme fortunat
Was for to putte a bille of° Venus werkes   *present a petition for*
(For alle thing hath tyme,° as seyn thise clerkes)   *its time*
To any womman, for to gete hir love,
I can nat seye—but grete God above,
1975 That knoweth that non act is causelees,
He deme° of al, for I wol holde my pees.   *May he judge*
But sooth° is this: how that this fresshe May   *the truth*
Hath take swich impression° that day   *i.e., has been so moved*
For pitee of this syke Damian
1980 That from hir herte she ne dryve can

5. There where you know every person must needs go (i.e., to the privy).

The remembraunce for to doon him ese.°   *make him comfortable*
"Certeyn," thoghte she, "whom that this thing displese
I rekke° noght, for here I him assure°   *care / promise*
To love him best of any creature,
1985 Though he namore hadde than his sherte."°   *undershirt*
Lo, pitee renneth sone in° gentil herte.   *flows quickly in*
　　Heer may ye se° how excellent franchyse°   *see / generosity*
In wommen is whan they hem narwe avyse.°   *think things through closely*
Som tyrant is, as ther be many oon[6]
1990 That hath an herte as hard as any stoon,°   *stone*
Which wolde han lete him sterven° in the place   *Who would have let him die*
Wel rather than han graunted him hir grace;
And hem reioysen° in hir cruel pryde,   *And (such women) rejoice*
And rekke nat to been° an homicyde.   *do not care if they are*
1995 　　This gentil May, fulfilled of pitee,
Right of hir hande a lettre made she,
In which she graunteth him hir verray grace.
Ther lakketh noght but only day and place
Wher that she mighte unto his lust suffyse,°   *satisfy his desire*
2000 For it shal be right° as he wol devyse.°   *exactly / arrange*
And whan she saugh hir time upon a day,
To visite this Damian goth May,
And sotilly° this lettre doun she threste°   *craftily / thrust*
Under his pilwe°—rede it if him leste.°   *pillow / it pleased him*
2005 She taketh him by the hand and harde him twiste°   *squeezed*
So secrely that no wight° of it wiste,°   *person / knew*
And bad° him been al hool,° and forth she wente   *told / well, healthy*
To Januarie, whan that he for hir sente.
　　Up ryseth Damian the nexte morwe.°   *morning*
2010 Al passed was his siknesse and his sorwe.
He kembeth° him, he proyneth° him and pyketh,°   *combs / preens / prinks*
He dooth al that his lady lust° and lyketh,   *desires*
And eek° to Januarie he gooth as lowe°   *also / humbly, obediently*
As ever dide a dogge for the bowe.[7]
2015 He is so plesant unto every man
(For craft° is al, whoso that do it can°)   *skill, trickery / knows how to use it*
That every wight is fayn° to speke him° good,   *eager / of him*
And fully in his lady grace he stood.
Thus lete° I Damian aboute his nede,   *let go*
2020 And in my tale forth I wol procede.
　　Somme clerkes holden that felicitee°   *supreme happiness*
Stant in delyt,° and therefor certeyn he,   *Consists of pleasure*
This noble Januarie, with al his might,
In honest wyse,° as longeth to° a knight,   *honorable manner / befits*
2025 Shoop him° to live ful deliciously.°   *Arranged / very sumptuously*
His housinge, his array,° as honestly°   *clothing / worthily*
To his degree° was maked as a kinges.   *For his rank*
Amonges othere of his honest° thinges   *worthy, suitable*

6. Some (women) are tyrants; indeed, there is many a one.
7. A dog trained to track game wounded by arrows from archers' bows.

He made a gardin, walled al with stoon.
2030 So fair a gardin woot° I nowher noon.°   know / none
     For out of doute, I verraily° suppose   truly
     That he° that wroot the Romance of the Rose   i.e., Guillaume de Lorris
     Ne coude of it the beautee wel devyse;°   describe
     Ne Priapus⁸ ne mighte nat suffyse,
2035 Though he be god of gardins, for to telle
     The beautee of the gardin and the welle°   spring
     That stood under a laurer° alwey grene.   laurel
     Ful ofte tyme he Pluto° and his quene   god of the underworld
     Proserpina and al hir fayerye°   their band of fairies
2040 Disporten hem and maken melodye
     Aboute that welle, and daunced, as men tolde.
         This noble knight, this Januarie the olde,
     Swich deintee hath° in it to walke and pleye   Takes such pleasure
     That he wol no wight suffren bere° the keye   allow no person to bear, carry
2045 Save he himself—for of the smale wiket°   gate
     He bar alwey of silver a smal cliket,°   small latchkey
     With which, whan that him leste,° he it unshette.°   it pleased him / unlocked
     And whan he wolde paye his wyf hir dette°   marital debt (see l. 1452 and note)
     In somer seson, thider° wolde he go,   thither, to that place
2050 And May his wyf, and no wight but they two.
     And thinges whiche that were nat doon abedde
     He in the gardin parfourned° hem and   performed
          spedde.°   i.e., successfully so
     And in this wyse° many a mery day   manner
     Lived this Januarie and fresshe May.
2055 But worldly joye may nat alwey dure°   last
     To Januarie, ne to no creature.
         O sodeyn hap!° O thou Fortune unstable,   sudden chance
     Lyk to the scorpion so deceivable,
     That flaterest with thyn heed when thou wolt stinge;
2060 Thy tayl is deeth thurgh thyn envenyminge.°   through thy poisoning
     O brotil° joye! O swete venim queynte!⁹   brittle, fragile
     O monstre, that so subtilly canst peynte°   disguise
     Thy yiftes° under hewe° of stedfastnesse,   gifts / color
     That° thou deceyvest bothe more and lesse!°   So that / great and small
2065 Why hastow Januarie thus deceyved,
     That haddest him for thy ful frend receyved?
     And now thou hast biraft him° bothe hise yën,°   deprived him of / eyes
     For sorwe of which desyreth he to dyen.
         Allas! this noble Januarie free,°   gracious
2070 Amidde his lust° and his prosperitee   pleasure
     Is woxen° blind, and that al sodeynly.   Has become
     He wepeth and he wayleth pitously,
     And therwithal° the fyr of jalousye—°   following upon that / fire of jealousy
     Lest that his wyf sholde falle in som folye°—   into some folly

8. Priapus: a phallic god of gardens, fruitfulness, fecundity.
9. "Queynte": "strange," "curious"; also a slang word for female genitalia.

2075 So brente° his herte that he wolde fayn°	*burned / very much wanted*
That som man bothe him and hir had slayn.	
For neither after his deeth nor in his lyf	
Ne wolde he that she were love° ne wyf,	*(anyone else's) sweetheart*
But ever live as widwe° in clothes blake,	*widow*
2080 Soul° as the turtle° that lost hath hir make.°	*Solitary / turtledove / mate*
But atte laste, after a monthe or tweye	
His sorwe gan aswage,° sooth to seye;	*began to lessen*
For whan he wiste it may noon other° be,	*not otherwise*
He paciently took his adversitee,	
2085 Save,° out of doute, he may nat forgoon°	*Except that / refrain*
That he nas° jalous evermore in oon.°	*From being / continually*
Which jalousye it was so outrageous°	*excessive*
That neither in halle n'in° noon other hous,	*nor in*
Ne in noon other place, neverthemo°	*no longer*
2090 He nolde suffre° hir for to ryde or go	*would not allow*
But if° that he had hand on hir alway.	*Unless*
For which ful ofte wepeth fresshe May,	
That loveth Damian so benignely°	*graciously*
That she mot outher° dyen sodeynly	*must either*
2095 Or elles she mot han him as hir leste.°	*have him as she desired*
She wayteth° whan hir herte wolde breste.°	*waits for (the time) / burst*
Upon that other syde Damian	
Bicomen is the sorwefulleste man	
That ever was, for neither night ne day	
2100 Ne mighte he speke a word to fresshe May	
As to his purpos, of no swich matere,°	*on no subject of that sort*
But if that Januarie moste it here,°	*Without January hearing it*
That° hadde an hand upon hir evermo.	*Who*
But nathelees, by wryting to and fro	
2105 And privee° signes, wiste° he what she mente,	*hidden, secret / knew*
And she knew eek° the fyn° of his entente.	*also / end, aim*
O Januarie, what mighte it thee availle°	*avail, benefit*
Thou mightest° see as fer as shippes saille?	*(Even) if thou couldst*
For as good is blind deceyved be	
2110 As to be deceyved whan a man may se.	
Lo Argus,[1] which that hadde an hondred yën,°	*eyes*
For al that ever he coude poure or pryen,°	*pore over or pry into (= see)*
Yet was he blent,° and God wot° so ben mo°	*deceived / knows / others*
That wenen wisly° that it be nat so.	*confidently believe*
2115 Passe over° is an ese;° I sey namore.	*To ignore (such deceptions) / relief*
This fresshe May, that I spak of so yore,°	*earlier*
In warme wex° hath emprented the cliket°	*wax / made an imprint of the key*
That Januarie bar of the smale wiket°	*gate*
By which into his gardin ofte he wente.	
2120 And Damian, that knew al hir entente,	

---

1. Juno, jealous of Jupiter's love for Io, charged Argus, a monster with a hundred eyes, to keep watch over her. Argus did not succeed.

The cliket countrefeted prively.°   copied secretly
Ther nis namore to seye, but hastily
Som wonder by° this cliket shal bityde,°   because of / happen
Which ye shul heren if ye wole abyde.°   wait, be patient
2125   O noble Ovyde,° ful sooth seystou,° God woot!   Ovid / truly thou speakest
What sleighte is it,° thogh it be long and hoot,°   What trick is there / difficult
That he° nil finde it out° in som manere?   i.e., Love / will not discover it
By Piramus and Tesbee° may men lere:°   Thisbe / people learn (this)
Thogh they were kept ful longe streite overal,°   guarded strictly in every way
2130 They been accorded, rouninge thurgh a wal,²
Ther no wight° coude han founde out swich a sleighte.   Where no one
        But now to purpos:° er that° dayes eighte   I.e., back to the story / before
Were passed er the monthe of Juil,° bifil°   July / it happened
That Januarie hath caught so greet a wil°—   will, desire
2135 Thurgh egging° of his wyf—him for to pleye   incitement
In his gardin, and no wight but they tweye,
That in a morwe° unto this May seith he: So that one morning
"Rys up, my wyf, my love, my lady free!°   gracious
The turtles° vois is herd, my douve° swete.   turtledove's / dove
2140 The winter is goon, with alle his reynes wete.°   its wet rains
Com forth now, with thyn eyen columbyn.°   eyes like a dove's
How fairer been thy brestes than is wyn.°   wine
The gardin is enclosed al aboute;
Com forth, my whyte° spouse. Out of doute   chaste; clothed in white?
2145 Thou hast me wounded in myn herte, o wyf.
No spot° of thee ne knew I al my lyf.   blemish, flaw
Com forth, and lat us taken our disport.
I chees° thee for my wyf and my confort."   choose
        Swiche olde lewed³ wordes used he.
2150 On° Damian a signe made she   To
That he sholde go biforen with his cliket.°   key
This Damian thanne hath opened the wiket°   gate
And in he stirte,° and that in swich manere   went quickly
That no wight mighte it see neither y-here,°   nor hear
2155 And stille he sit° under a bush anoon.   sits
        This Januarie, as blind as is a stoon,
With Maius in his hand and no wight mo,
Into his fresshe gardin is ago°   has gone
And clapte to° the wiket sodeynly.   closed shut
2160 "Now, wyf," quod he, "heer nis but thou and I,
That art the creature that I best love.
For, by that Lord that sit in heven above,
Lever ich hadde° dyen on a knyf   I would rather
Than thee offende, trewe dere wyf!
2165 For Goddes sake, thenk how I thee chees:°   chose

---

2. They communicated (reached an understanding) by whispering through (a chink in) a wall.
3. "Lewed": "stupid," "ignorant," "unlearned," and here perhaps "lascivious" as well, meanings
all ironically inappropriate to January's speech of invitation, which resounds with echoes
from the biblical *Song of Songs*.

Noght for no coveityse,° doutelees,   greed (for any dowry)
But only for the love I had to thee.
And though that I be old and may nat see,
Beth to me trewe, and I shal telle yow why.
2170 Three thinges, certes,° shul ye winne therby: certainly
First, love of Crist, and to yourself honour,
And al myn heritage,° toun and tour,°   inheritance / tower
I yeve it yow, maketh chartres° as yow leste.°   charters, deeds / it pleases you
This shal be doon tomorwe er sonne reste,°   before sunset
2175 So wisly God° my soule bringe in blisse.   As surely as God may
I prey yow first in covenant° ye me kisse,   i.e., to seal our union
And thogh that I be jalous, wyte° me noght.   blame
Ye been so depe enprented° in my thoght   deeply imprinted
That whan that I considere your beautee
2180 And therwithal the unlykly elde° of me,   unsuitable age
I may nat, certes, thogh I sholde dye,
Forbere to been out of your companye
For verray° love—this is withouten doute.   true
Now kis me, wyf, and lat us rome° aboute."   roam, stroll
2185   This fresshe May, whan she thise wordes herde,
Benignely° to Januarie answerde,   Graciously
But first and forward° she bigan to wepe.°   first of all / weep
"I have," quod she, "a soule for to kepe
As wel as ye, and also myn honour,
2190 And of my wyfhod thilke° tendre flour°   that / flower
Which that I have assured in° your hond   entrusted to
Whan that the preest to yow my body bond.°   bound
Wherfore I wole answere in this manere
By the leve of yow,° my lord so dere: With your permission
2195 I prey to God that never dawe the day°   the day may never dawn
That I ne sterve° as foule° as womman may,   die / shamefully
If ever I do unto my kin that shame,
Or elles° I empeyre° so my name°   otherwise / injure / reputation
That I be° fals. And if I do that lakke,°   I.e., by being / misdeed
2200 Do strepe° me and put me in a sakke   strip
And in the nexte° river do me drenche.°   nearest / have me drowned
I am a gentil° womman and no wenche.   well born, decent
Why speke ye thus? But men ben ever untrewe,
And wommen have repreve of yow ay newe.°   reproof from you always
2205 Ye han non other contenance,° I leve,°   way of behaving / believe
But° speke to us of untrust° and repreve."°   Except (to) / distrust / reproof
    And with that word she saugh wher Damian
Sat in the bush, and coughen° she bigan,   to cough
And with hir finger signes made she
2210 That Damian sholde climbe upon a tree
That charged° was with fruit; and up he wente,   loaded
For verraily° he knew al hir entente   truly
And every signe that she coude mak
Wel bet° than Januarie, hir owene make.   Much better

2215 For in a lettre she had told him al
 Of this matere, how he werchen shal.°   *i.e., what he must do*
 And thus I lete him sitte upon the pyrie,°   *up in the pear tree*
 And Januarie and May rominge myrie.°   *roaming merrily*
  Bright was the day, and blew° the firmament.   *blue*
2220 Phebus° hath of gold his stremes° doun y-sent   *God of the sun / beams, rays*
 To gladen every flour with his warmnesse.
 He was that tyme *in Geminis*, as I gesse,
 But litel fro his declinacioun
 Of Cancer, Jovis exaltacioun.[4]
2225 And so bifel that brighte morwe-tyde°   *morning-time*
 That in that gardin, in the ferther syde,
 Pluto, that is the king of Fayerye,°   *the fairy world (also of Hades)*
 And many a lady in his companye
 Folwinge his wyf, the quene Proserpyna,°   *Proserpina*
2230 Which that he ravysshed out of Ethna°   *Whom he abducted from Mt. Etna*
 Whil that she gadered floures in the mede.°   *meadow*
 (In Claudian ye may the story rede,
 How in his grisly carte he hir fette.)[5]
 This king of Fairye thanne adoun him sette
2235 Upon a bench of turves° fresh and grene,   *pieces of turf*
 And right anon thus seyde he to his quene:
  "My wyf," quod he, "ther may no wight° sey nay.   *person*
 Th'experience so preveth° every day   *indeed proves*
 The tresons° whiche that wommen doon to man.   *treasons, betrayals*
2240 Ten hondred thousand stories telle I can
 Notable of your untrouthe and brotilnesse.°   *frailty, fickleness*
 O Salomon,° wys, richest of richesse,°   *Solomon / in wealth*
 Fulfild of sapience° and of worldly glorie,   *Filled with wisdom*
 Ful worthy been thy wordes to memorie°   *to (hold in) memory*
2245 To every wight that wit and reson can.°   *has intelligence and reason*
 Thus preiseth° he yet the bountee° of man: *appraises / goodness*
 'Amonges a thousand men yet fond I oon,°   *I found but one (good one)*
 But of wommen alle fond I noon.'°   *(see Ecclesiastes 7:29)*
  Thus seith the king that knoweth your wikkednesse.
2250 And Jesus *filius Syrak*, as I gesse,
 Ne speketh of yow but selde reverence.[6]
 A wilde fyr° and corrupt pestilence°   *burning skin disease / infectious plague*
 So falle upon your bodies yet tonight!
 Ne see ye nat this honurable knight?
2255 Bycause, allas, that he is blind and old,
 His owene man° shal make him cokewold.°   *manservant / cuckold*
 Lo, heer he sit,° the lechour,° in the tree.   *sits / lecher (with a pun on "healer")*
 Now wol I graunten, of my magestee,°   *through my majesty*

4. The sun was in the sign of Gemini (the Twins), just short of entering Cancer on June 12, the
 sign over which Jupiter exerted his maximum influence ("Jove's exaltacioun").
5. You may read the story in Claudian, how Pluto carried her off in his frightening chariot.
 Claudius Claudianus wrote an unfinished poem, *The Rape of Proserpina*, ca. 400.
6. And I think Jesus the son of Syrach (the supposed author of *Ecclesiasticus*) spoke of you
 (women) only seldom with respect.

Unto this olde, blinde, worthy knight
2260 That he shal have ayeyn° his eyen sight,   *again*
Whan that his wyf wold doon him vileinye.°   *bring him dishonor*
Than shal he knowen al his harlotrye°   *wickedness*
Both in repreve° of hir and othere mo."   *reproof / other (women) more*
     "Ye shal?" quod Proserpyne. "Wol ye so?
2265 Now, by my modres sires soule,[7] I swere
That I shal yeven° hir suffisant answere—   *give*
And alle wommen after, for hir sake—
That though they be in any gilt y-take,°   *caught in any offense*
With face bold° they shulle hemself° excuse,   *assured, brazen / themselves*
2270 And bere hem doun° that wolden hem accuse.   *beat down those*
For lakke of answer noon of hem shal dyen.
Al hadde man seyn° a thing with bothe his yën,°   *Even if one had seen / eyes*
Yit shul we wommen visage it hardily°   *put a bold face on it*
And wepe and swere and chyde subtilly,°   *complain cleverly*
2275 So that ye men shul been as lewed as gees.°   *ignorant as geese*
     What rekketh me of° your auctoritees?   *What do I care about*
I woot° wel that this Jew, this Salomon,   *know*
Fond of° us wommen foles many oon.°   *Found among / many a fool*
But though that he ne fond no good womman,
2280 Yet hath ther founde many another man
Wommen ful trewe, ful gode and vertuous.
Witnesse on hem° that dwelle in Cristes hous: *them*
With martirdom they preved hir constance.°   *proved their constancy*
The Romayn gestes eek maken remembrance°   *Roman histories also remind us*
2285 Of many a verray,° trewe wyf also.   *faithful*
But sire—ne be nat wrooth°—al be it so   *angry*
Though that he seyde he fond no good womman,
I prey yow take the sentence° of the man.   *meaning*
He mente thus: that in sovereyn bontee°   *supreme goodness*
2290 Nis noon but God, but neither he ne she.°   *man nor woman*
     Ey! For verray° God that nis but oon,°   *true / i.e., the one and only*
What° make ye so muche of Salomon?   *Why*
What though° he made a temple, Goddes hous?   *So what if*
What though he were riche and glorious?
2295 So made he eek a temple of° false goddis.   *to*
How mighte he do a thing that more forbode° is?   *forbidden*
Pardee,° as faire° as ye his name emplastre,°   *Certainly / favorably / whitewash*
He was a lechour and an ydolastre,°   *idolater*
And in his elde° he verray God forsook.   *old age*
2300 And if that God ne hadde, as seith the book,[8]
Y-spared him for his fadres° sake, he sholde   *father's*
Have lost his regne° rather than he wolde.°   *kingdom / sooner than he wanted*
I sette right noght, of al the vileinye
That ye of wommen wryte, a boterflye.[9]

7. By the soul of my mother's father. The father of Ceres, Proserpina's mother, was Saturn.
8. I.e., the Bible. See 3 Kings 11:1–13 (Vulgate) or 1 Kings 11:1–13 (Authorized Version).
9. I don't care a bit (*lit.*, a butterfly) for all the villainous things you men write about women.

2305 I am a womman—nedes moot° I speke   *necessarily must*
Or elles swelle til myn herte breke.
For sithen° he seyde that we ben jangleresses,°   *since / chattering women*
As ever hool I mote brouke my tresses,¹
I shal nat spare, for no curteisye,
2310 To speke him harm° that wolde us vileinye."°   *speak ill of him / do us shame*
    "Dame," quod this Pluto, "be no lenger° wrooth.   *longer*
I yeve it up.° But sith° I swoor myn ooth   *give up, yield / since*
That I wolde graunten him his sighte ageyn,
My word shal stonde, I warne yow, certeyn.
2315 I am a king; it sit° me noght to lye."°   *suits, befits / lie, i.e., break my word*
    "And I," quod she, "a queene of Fayerye.°   *the fairy world*
Hir answere shal she have, I undertake.°   *declare*
Lat us namore wordes heerof make,°   *Let's have no more debate about this*
For sothe° I wol° no lenger yow contrarie."°   *truly / wish, want / argue with*
2320   Now lat us turne agayn to Januarie,
That in the gardin with his faire May
Singeth ful merier° than the papejay,°   *more merrily / parrot*
"Yow love I best, and shal, and other noon."°   *no one else*
So longe aboute the aleyes° is he goon°   *garden paths (alleys) / has he walked*
2325 Til he was come agaynes thilke pyrie°   *in front of that very pear tree*
Wher as° this Damian sitteth ful myrie   *Where*
An heigh° among the fresshe leves grene.   *On high*
    This fresshe May, that is so bright and shene,°   *fair, beautiful*
Gan for to syke° and seyde, "Allas, my syde!   *Began to sigh*
2330 Now sir," quod she, "for aught that may bityde,°   *whatever may happen*
I moste han of the peres° that I see   *must have (some) of the pears*
Or I mot° dye, so sore longeth me°   *must / intensely I long*
To eten° of the smale peres grene.   *eat*
Help, for hir love that is of hevene quene!°   *i.e., the Virgin Mary*
2335 I telle yow wel, a womman in my plyt°   *condition (implying pregnancy)*
May han to fruit so greet an appetyt
That she may dyen but° she of it have."   *unless*
    "Allas," quod he, "that I ne had heer a knave°   *servant*
That coude climbe! Allas, allas," quod he,
2340 "That I am blind!" "Ye, sir, no fors,"° quod she,   *no matter*
"But wolde ye vouchesauf,° for Goddes sake,   *But if you would agree*
The pyrie inwith° your armes for to take   *within*
(For wel I woot° that ye mistruste me),   *know*
Thanne sholde I climbe wel ynogh," quod she,
2345 "So° I my foot mighte sette upon your bak."   *Provided that*
    "Certes," quod he, "theron shal be no lak,°   *i.e., I will not fail to do that*
Mighte° I yow helpen with myn herte blood."   *I.e., even if it meant that*
He stoupeth doun, and on his bak she stood,
And caughte hir by a twiste,° and up she gooth—   *grabbed hold of a branch*
2350 Ladies, I prey yow that ye be nat wrooth;°   *angry*
I can nat glose;° I am a rude° man—   *gloss over with fine words / rough, plain*

1. Literally, "as surely as I mean to keep all my hair," i.e., stay alive.

And sodeynly anon this Damian
Gan pullen° up the smok, and in he throng.°   *Began to pull / thrust*
   And whan that Pluto saugh this grete wrong,
2355 To Januarie he gaf° agayn his sighte   *gave*
And made him see as wel as ever he mighte.
And whan that he hadde caught his sighte agayn,
Ne was ther never man of thing so fayn.°   *happy*
But on his wyf his thoght was evermo;
2360 Up to the tree he caste his eyen two
And saugh that Damian his wyf had dressed°   *dealt with*
In swich° manere it may nat ben expressed   *such*
But if° I wolde speke uncurteisly.°   *Unless / crudely*
   And up he yaf a roring and a cry
2365 As doth the moder° whan the child shal dye.   *mother*
"Out! Help! Allas! Harrow!"° he gan to crye.   *Help*
"O stronge lady store,° what dostow?"°   *bold, brazen woman / doest thou*
   And she answerde, "Sir, what eyleth° yow?   *ails*
Have pacience and reson in your minde.
2370 I have yow holpe° on bothe your eyen blinde.   *helped*
Up° peril of my soule I shal nat lyen: *Upon*
As me was taught, to hele with° your yën   *heal*
Was nothing bet° to make yow to see   *better, more effective*
Than strugle° with a man upon a tree.   *wrestle*
2375 God woot° I dide it in ful good entente."   *knows*
   "Strugle?" quod he. "Ye, algate° in it wente!   *nevertheless*
God yeve° yow bothe on shames deeth° to dyen!   *give / a shameful death*
He swyved° thee! I saugh it with myne yën,°   *had sex with / eyes*
And elles° be I hanged by the hals!"°   *Or else / neck*
2380 "Thanne is," quod she, "my medicyne al fals.°   *wrong, useless*
For certeinly, if that ye mighte° see,   *were able to*
Ye wolde nat seyn thise wordes unto me.
Ye han° som glimsing° and no parfit°   *have / glimpse, fleeting look / perfect*
   sighte."
   "I see," quod he, "as wel as ever I mighte,
2385 Thonked be God, with bothe myne eyen two,
And by my trouthe, me thoughte° he dide thee so."   *it seemed to me*
   "Ye maze,° maze, gode sire," quod she.   *are confused, dazed*
"This thank have I for I have maad° yow see.   *made*
Allas," quod she, "that ever I was so kinde!"°   *(with pun on "natural")*
2390 "Now, dame," quod he, "lat al passe out of minde.
Com doun, my lief,° and if I have missayd,°   *love / misspoken*
God help me so, as I am yvel apayd.°   *sorry*
But by my fader soule, I wende han seyn°   *thought I saw*
How that this Damian had by thee leyn,°   *i.e., pressed against*
2395 And that thy smok had leyn upon his brest."
   "Ye, sire," quod she, "ye may wene° as yow lest;°   *believe / wish*
But, sire, a man that waketh out of his sleep,
He may nat sodeynly wel taken keep°   *take good notice*
Upon a thing, ne seen it parfitly°   *perfectly*

2400 Til that he be adawed verraily.°   *truly awakened*
Right so a man that longe hath blind y-be
Ne may nat sodeynly so wel y-see
First,° whan his sighte is newe come ageyn,   *At first*
As he that hath a day or two y-seyn.
2405 Til that your sighte y-satled° be a whyle,   *settled*
Ther may ful many a sighte yow bigyle.°   *deceive*
Beth war,° I prey yow, for by hevene° king,   *Be aware / heaven's*
Ful many a man weneth to seen° a thing,   *thinks to have seen*
And it is al another° than it semeth.   *completely other*
2410 He that misconceyveth,° he misdemeth."°   *misapprehends / misjudges*
And with that word she leep° doun fro the tree.   *leaped*
    This Januarie, who is glad but he?
He kisseth hir and clippeth° hir ful ofte,   *embraces*
And on hir wombe° he stroketh hir ful softe,   *stomach*
2415 And to his palays° hoom he hath hir lad.°   *palace / led*
Now, gode men, I pray yow to be glad.
Thus endeth heer my tale of Januarie.
God bless us, and his moder Seinte Marie!

The Epilogue

    "Ey! Goddes mercy!" seyde our Hoste tho.°   *then*
2420 "Now swich° a wyf I pray God kepe me fro!   *such*
Lo, whiche sleightes° and subtilitees   *what tricks*
In wommen been, for ay° as bisy as bees   *always*
Ben they, us sely° men for to deceyve,   *simple, innocent*
And from a sothe° ever wol they weyve.°   *truth / turn away, avoid*
2425 By this Marchauntes tale it preveth weel.°   *surely proves true*
But doutelees,° as trewe as any steel   *without doubt*
I have a wyf, though that she povre° be;   *poor*
But of hir tonge a labbing° shrewe is she,   *blabbing*
And yet° she hath an heep° of vyces mo.°   *also / heap, great number / more*
2430 Therof no fors°—lat alle swiche thinges go.   *no matter*
But wite ye what?° In conseil° be it seyd,   *do you know what / confidence*
Me reweth sore° I am unto hir teyd.°   *It grieves me painfully / tied*
For and° I sholde rekenen° every vyce   *if / reckon, count up*
Which that she hath, ywis I were to nyce.°   *truly I would be too foolish*
2435 And cause why? It sholde reported be
And told to hir of° somme of this meynee,°   *by / company*
Of° whom it nedeth nat for to declare,   *By*
Sin° wommen connen outen°   *Since / know how to spread*
    swich chaffare.°   *wares, matters*
And eek° my wit suffyseth nat therto   *also*
2440 To tellen al, wherfor my tale is do."°   *done*

The Franklin's Prologue and Tale

The Introduction

"In feith, Squier, thou hast thee wel y-quit°   *acquitted*
And gentilly.° I preise wel thy wit,"   *i.e., like a gentleman*
675 Quod the Frankeleyn. "Consideringe thy youthe,
So feelingly thou spekest, sire, I allow the:°   *commend thee*
As to my doom,° there is non that is here   *judgment*
Of eloquence that shal be thy pere,°   *peer, equal*
If that thou live. God yeve° thee good chaunce,°   *give / fortune*
680 And in vertu sende thee continuaunce,
For of thy speche I have greet deyntee.°   *pleasure*
I have a sone, and by the Trinitee,
I hadde levere than twenty pound worth lond—[1]
Though it right now were fallen in myn hond—
685 He were a man of swich discrecioun
As that ye been. Fy on possessioun,°   *property, wealth*
But if° a man be vertuous withal!   *Unless*
I have my sone snibbed,° and yet shal,   *rebuked*
For he to vertu listeth nat entende;[2]
690 But for to pleye at dees,° and to despende,°   *dice / spend freely*
And lese° al that he hath, is his usage.°   *lose / custom*
And he hath levere° talken with a page°   *rather / young servant*
Than to comune° with any gentil wight°   *talk / gentlemanly person*
Where he mighte lerne gentilesse° aright."   *gentility*
695   "Straw for your gentillesse!" quod our Host.
"What, Frankeleyn! pardee,° sire, wel thou wost°   *by God / knowest*
That eche of yow mot° tellen atte leste°   *must / at (the) least*
A tale or two, or breken his biheste."°   *promise*
   "That knowe I wel, sire," quod the Frankeleyn;
700 "I prey yow, haveth me nat in desdeyn°   *don't disdain me*
Though to this man I speke a word or two."
   "Telle on thy tale withouten wordes mo."°   *more*
   "Gladly, sire Host," quod he, "I wol obeye
Unto your wil; now herkneth° what I seye.   *listen to*
705 I wol yow nat contrarien° in no wyse   *oppose*
As fer as that my wittes wol suffyse.
I prey to God that it may plesen yow:
Thanne woot I wel that it is good ynow."°   *enough*

The Prologue

Thise olde gentil Britons° in hir° dayes   *Bretons / their*
710 Of diverse aventures maden layes,°   *lays, poems*
Rymeyed° in hir firste° Briton tonge;   *Rhymed / original*

---

1. I would rather than land worth twenty pounds a year.
2. Because he does not care to concern himself with (the development of his) capacities. ("Vertu" involves notions of power, strength, and efficacy as well as moral goodness.)

Which layes with hir instruments they songe,
Or elles redden hem° for hir plesaunce;°   *else read them / pleasure*
And oon of hem have I in remembraunce,
715   Which I shal seyn with good wil as I can.
      But, sires, by cause° I am a burel° man,   *because / plain, untutored*
At my biginning first I yow biseche
Have me excused of my rude° speche.   *crude, inartistic*
I lerned nevere rethoryk,° certeyn:°   *rhetoric / in truth*
720   Thing that I speke, it moot° be bare and pleyn.°   *must / plain*
I sleep° nevere on the Mount of Pernaso,°   *slept / Parnassus*
Ne lerned Marcus Tullius Cithero.°   *Cicero*
Colours ne knowe I none, withouten drede,³
But swiche° colours as growen in the mede,°   *Only such / meadow*
725   Or elles swiche as men dye or peynte.°   *paint*
Colours of rethoryk ben to me queynte:°   *too abstruse for me*
My spirit feleth noght of° swich matere.   *has no feeling for*
But if yow list,° my tale shul ye here.   *it pleases you*

The Tale

      In Armorik,° that called is Britayne,°   *Armorica / Brittany*
730   Ther was a knight that loved and dide his payne°   *took pains*
To serve a lady in his beste wyse;
And many a labour, many a greet empryse°   *undertaking, exploit*
He for his lady wroghte,° er° she were wonne.   *performed / before*
For she was oon the faireste° under sonne,   *one of the loveliest*
735   And eek° therto come of so heigh kinrede,°   *also / high lineage*
That wel unnethes dorste° this knight, for drede,°   *scarcely dared / fear*
Telle hire his wo, his peyne, and his distresse.
But atte laste° she, for his worthinesse,   *at (the) last*
And namely° for his meke obeysaunce,°   *especially / obedience*
740   Hath swich° a pitee caught of° his penaunce°   *such / felt for / suffering*
That prively° she fil of his accord°   *secretly / i.e., consented*
To take him for hir housbonde and hir lord,
Of swich lordshipe as men han over hir wyves.
And for to lede° the more in blisse hir° lyves,   *lead / their*
745   Of his free wil he swoor hire° as a knight   *swore to her*
That nevere in al his lyf he, day ne night,
Ne sholde upon him take no maistrye°   *mastery, domination*
Agayn hir wil, ne kythe hire° jalousye,   *display to her*
But hire obeye and folwe hir wil in al
750   As any lovere to his lady shal°—   *must*
Save that the name° of soveraynetee,   *title, appearance*
That wolde he have for shame of his degree.⁴
      She thanked him, and with ful greet humblesse
She seyde, "Sire, sith° of youre gentillesse   *since*

---

3. I don't know any rhetorical "colors" (devices)—no fear of that. (The Franklin's modest apology is of a traditional kind, recommended by the very art he claims not to know.)
4. That would he retain, lest it reflect on his rank.

755 Ye profre me to have so large° a reyne,°   *free / rein*
     Ne wolde nevere God bitwixe us tweyne,
     As in my gilt, were outher werre or stryf.⁵
     Sire, I wol be youre humble trewe wyf:
     Have heer my trouthe,° til that myn herte breste."°   *loyal pledge / burst*
760 Thus been they bothe in quiete and in° reste.   *at*
         For o° thing, sires, saufly° dar I seye,   *one / safely*
     That frendes everich other° moot° obeye,   *each other / must*
     If they wol longe holden companye.
     Love wol nat ben constreyned by maistrye.⁶
765 When maistrie comth, the God of Love anon°   *at once*
     Beteth° hise winges, and farewel, he is gon!   *Beats*
     Love is a thing as° any spirit free.   *like*
     Wommen of kinde° desiren libertee,   *by nature*
     And nat to ben constreyned as a thral;°   *thrall, slave*
770 And so don men, if I soth° seyen shal.   *truth*
     Loke who that° is most pacient in love: *Consider the man who*
     He is at his avantage al above.°   *above all others*
     Pacience is an heigh vertu, certeyn,
     For it venquisseth,° as thise clerkes° seyn,   *vanquishes / scholars*
775 Thinges that rigour° sholde° never atteyne.   *harshness, strictness / could*
     For every word men may nat chyde or pleyne.°   *complain*
     Lerneth to suffre, or elles, so moot I goon,°   *as I may live*
     Ye shul it lerne, wher so ye wole or noon.°   *whether you wish to or not*
     For in this world, certein, ther no wight° is   *person*
780 That he ne dooth or seith somtyme amis.°   *wrongly*
     Ire,° siknesse, or constellacioun,°   *Anger / fate, his stars*
     Wyn, wo, or chaunginge of complexioun⁷
     Causeth ful ofte to doon amis or speken.
     On every wrong a man may nat be wreken:°   *avenged*
785 After° the tyme moste be temperaunce°   *According to / moderation*
     To every wight that can on governaunce.°   *understands self-control*
     And therfore hath this wyse worthy knight,
     To live in ese, suffrance hire bihight,°   *promised her (his) forbearance*
     And she to him ful wisly gan to swere°   *truly did swear*
790 That nevere sholde ther be defaute in here.°   *a lacking in her*
         Heere may men seen an humble wys accord:°   *agreeing*
     Thus hath she take hir servant and hir lord,
     Servant in love, and lord in mariage;
     Thanne was he bothe in lordship and servage.°   *servitude*
795 Servage? Nay, but in lordshipe above,
     Sith he hath bothe his lady and his love;
     His lady, certes,° and his wyf also,   *certainly*
     The which that lawe of love acordeth to.

5. God would not wish that there should ever be either war or strife between us two for any
   fault (guilt) of mine.
6. Love will not be constrained by mastery (i.e., by one partner exercising absolute power over
   the other).
7. Wine, woe, or a change in the balance of humors ("complexioun") that determine a man's
   temperament.

And whan he was in this prosperitee,

800 Hoom with his wyf he gooth to his contree,°   *region*
    Nat fer fro Pedmark, ther his dwelling was,[8]
    Where as he liveth in blisse and in solas.°   *solace, joy*
       Who coude telle, but he hadde wedded be,°   *unless he'd been married*
    The joye, the ese, and the prosperitee

805 That is bitwixe an housbonde and his wyf?
    A yeer and more lasted this blisful lyf,
    Til that the knight of which I speke of thus,
    That of Kayrrud° was cleped° Arveragus,   *from Kerru / called*
    Shoop him° to goon and dwelle a yeer or tweyne°   *Prepared himself / two*

810 In Engelond, that cleped was eek° Briteyne,°   *also / Britain*
    To seke in armes worshipe and honour—
    For al his lust° he sette° in swich° labour—   *pleasure / took / such*
    And dwelled ther two yeer; the book seith thus.
       Now wol I stinten of° this Arveragus,   *cease concerning*

815 And speken I wole of Dorigene his wyf,
    That loveth hire housbonde as hire hertes lyf.
    For his absence wepeth she and syketh,°   *sighs*
    As doon thise noble wyves whan hem lyketh.°   *it pleases them*
    She moorneth, waketh,° wayleth, fasteth, pleyneth;°   *stays awake / laments*

820 Desyr of his presence hire so distreyneth°   *afflicts*
    That al this wyde world she sette at noght.°   *holds to be nothing*
    Hire frendes, whiche that knewe hir hevy thoght,
    Conforten hire in al that ever they may:
    They prechen° hire, they telle hire night and day,   *preach to*

825 That causelees she sleeth° hirself, allas!   *is killing*
    And every confort possible in this cas
    They doon to hire with al hire bisinesse,°   *their diligence*
    Al for to make hire leve hire hevinesse.
       By proces,° as ye knowen everichoon,°   *In course of time / every one*

830 Men may so longe graven in° a stoon   *engrave*
    Til som figure therinne emprented be.
    So longe han° they conforted hire til she   *have*
    Receyved hath, by hope and by resoun,
    The emprenting° of hire° consolacioun,   *imprint / their*

835 Thurgh which hir grete sorwe gan aswage:°   *was assuaged*
    She may nat alwey duren° in swich rage.°   *continue / passion*
       And eek° Arveragus, in al this care,   *also*
    Hath sent hire lettres hoom of his welfare,°   *well-being*
    And that he wol come hastily agayn;

840 Or elles hadde this sorwe hir herte slayn.
       Hire freendes sawe hir sorwe gan to slake,°   *was abating*
    And preyde hire on knees, for Goddes sake,
    To come and romen hire° in companye,   *walk about*
    Awey to dryve hire derke fantasye.°   *dark imagining(s)*

845 And finally, she graunted that requeste,

---

8. Not far from Penmarch (on the coast of Finistère, in Brittany), where his dwelling was.

For wel she saugh° that it was for the beste.   saw
   Now stood hire castel faste° by the see,   close
And often with hire freendes walketh she
Hire to disporte° upon the bank an heigh,°   amuse / on high
850 Where as she many a ship and barge seigh°   saw
Seilinge hir° cours, where as hem liste go.   their
But thanne was that a parcel° of hire wo,   portion
For to hirself ful ofte "Allas!" seith she,
"Is ther no ship, of so manye as I see,
855 Wol bringen hom my lord? Thanne were myn herte
Al warisshed° of his bittre peynes smerte."°   cured / smart, sharp
   Another tyme ther wolde she sitte and thinke,
And caste hir eyen dounward fro the brinke.°   edge
But whan she saugh the grisly rokkes blake,°   black rocks
860 For verray fere° so wolde hir herte quake   Out of real fear
That on hire feet she mighte hire noght sustene.
Than wolde she sitte adoun upon the grene,°   grass
And pitously into the see biholde,
And seyn right thus, with sorweful sykes° colde: sighs
865   "Eterne God, that thurgh thy purveyaunce°   foresight, providence
Ledest° the world by certein governaunce,°   Guidest / rule
In ydel,° as men seyn, ye no thing make.   vain
But Lord, thise grisly feendly° rokkes blake,   hostile, devilish
That semen° rather a foul confusioun   seem (to be)
870 Of werk, than any fair creacioun
Of swich a parfit wys° God and a stable,°   wise / steadfast
Why han ye wroght this werk unresonable?°   i.e., that confounds reason
For by this werk, south, north, ne west, ne eest,
Ther nis y-fostred° man, ne brid, ne beest.   is not served, supported
875 It dooth no good, to my wit,° but anoyeth.°   understanding / injures
See ye nat, Lord, how mankinde it destroyeth?
An hundred thousand bodies of mankinde
Han rokkes slayn, al be they nat in minde:° although they be unremembered
Which mankinde is so fair part of thy werk
880 That thou it madest lyk to thyn owene merk.°   image
Thanne semed it ye hadde a greet chiertee°   affection
Toward mankinde; but how thanne may it be
That ye swiche meenes° make it to destroyen,   such means
Which meenes do no good, but evere anoyen?
885 I woot wel clerkes° wol seyn as hem leste,°   scholars / they please
By arguments,° that al is for the beste,   i.e., of philosophy
Though I ne can the causes nat y-knowe.
But thilke° God that made wind to blowe,   that same
As kepe° my lord! This° my conclusioun.   May He protect / This is
890 To clerkes lete° I al disputisoun,°   leave / debate
But wolde° God that alle thise rokkes blake   would (to)
Were sonken° into helle for his sake!   sunken
Thise rokkes sleen° myn herte for the fere."°   slay / fear
Thus wolde she seyn, with many a pitous tere.

895 Hire freendes sawe that it was no disport°   *pleasure (for her)*
     To romen by the see, but disconfort,
     And shopen° for to pleyen somewher elles.°   *arranged / else*
     They leden hire by riveres and by welles,°   *springs*
     And eek in othere places delitables;°   *pleasant*
900 They dauncen, and they pleyen at ches° and tables.° *chess / backgammon*
        So on a day, right in the morwe-tyde,°   *morning*
     Unto a gardin that was ther bisyde,
     In which that they hadde maad hir ordinaunce°   *their arrangements*
     Of vitaille° and of other purveyaunce,°   *For food / provisions*
905 They goon and pleye hem al the longe day.
     And this was on the sixte morwe° of May,   *morning*
     Which May had peynted° with his softe shoures°   *painted / showers*
     This gardin ful of leves and of floures;
     And craft of mannes hand so curiously°   *skillfully*
910 Arrayed° hadde this gardin, trewely,   *Adorned*
     That nevere was ther gardin of swich prys,°   *so priceless*
     But if° it were the verray Paradys.°   *Unless / Paradise itself*
     The odour of floures and the fresshe sighte
     Wolde han maked any herte lighte
915 That evere was born, but if to gret° siknesse   *too great*
     Or to gret sorwe helde it in distresse,
     So ful it was of beautee with plesaunce.°   *delight*
     At after-diner gonne they to daunce,⁹
     And singe also, save° Dorigen allone,   *except*
920 Which made alwey hir compleint° and hir mone,°   *lament / moan*
     For she ne saugh° him on the daunce go,   *saw*
     That was hir housbonde and hir love also.
     But nathelees° she moste° a tyme abyde,   *nevertheless / must*
     And with good hope lete hir sorwe slyde.°   *pass*
925   Upon° this daunce, amonges othere men,   *In*
     Daunced a squyer biforen Dorigen,
     That fressher was and jolyer of array,°   *dress*
     As to my doom,° than is the monthe of May.   *judgment*
     He singeth, daunceth, passinge° any man   *surpassing*
930 That is, or was, sith° that the world bigan.   *since*
     Therwith he was, if men sholde him discryve,°   *describe*
     Oon of the beste faringe° man on lyve:°   *handsomest / alive*
     Yong, strong, right vertuous, and riche and wys,
     And wel biloved, and holden in gret prys.°   *held in great esteem*
935 And shortly, if the sothe° I tellen shal,   *truth*
     Unwiting of° this Dorigen at al,   *Unknown to*
     This lusty° squyer, servant to Venus,   *vigorous, joyful*
     Which that y-cleped° was Aurelius,   *called*
     Hadde loved hire best of any creature
940 Two yeer and more, as was his aventure,°   *lot*
     But never dorste° he telle hire his grevaunce:°   *dared / sorrow*

9. After dinner (the first big meal of the day, between 9 A.M. and noon), they began to dance.

Withouten coppe he drank al his penaunce.[1]
He was despeyred;° no thing dorste° he seye,   *in despair / dared*
Save in his songes somwhat wolde he wreye°   *disclose*
945 His wo, as in a general compleyning;°   *lamentation*
He seyde he lovede, and was biloved no thing.°   *not at all*
Of swich matere° made he manye layes,   *such substance*
Songes, compleintes, roundels, virelayes,[2]
How that he dorste nat his sorwe telle,
950 But languissheth as a furie dooth in helle;
And dye he moste, he seyde, as dide Ekko
For Narcisus, that dorste nat telle hir wo.[3]
In other manere than ye here me seye,
Ne dorste he nat to hire his wo biwreye,°   *reveal*
955 Save that, paraventure,° somtyme at daunces,   *by chance*
Ther° yonge folk kepen hir observaunces,° *Where / perform their devotions*
It may wel be he loked on hir face
In swich a wyse as man that asketh grace,
But nothing wiste° she of his entente.°   *knew / purpose(s)*
960 Nathelees, it happed, er they thennes wente,° *before they departed thence*
By cause that he was hire neighebour,
And was a man of worshipe and honour,
And hadde y-knowen him of tyme yore,[4]
They fille in speche;° and forth more and more   *fell into conversation*
965 Unto his purpos drough° Aurelius,   *drew*
And when he saugh° his tyme, he seyde thus: *saw*
  "Madame," quod he, "by God that this world made,
So that° I wiste° it mighte youre herte glade,° *If only / knew / gladden*
I wolde that day that youre Arveragus
970 Wente over the see, that I, Aurelius,
Had went ther° nevere I sholde have come agayn.   *there where*
For wel I woot° my service is in vayn: *know*
My guerdon° is but bresting° of myn herte.   *reward / breaking*
Madame, reweth° upon my peynes smerte,°   *take pity / sharp*
975 For with a word ye may me sleen° or save.   *slay*
Heere at your feet God wolde that I were grave!°   *buried*
I ne have as now no leyser° more to seye: *leisure, opportunity*
Have mercy, swete, or ye wol do me deye!"°   *make me die*
  She gan to loke upon° Aurelius: *stared at*
980 "Is this youre wil," quod she, "and sey ye thus?
Nevere erst,"° quod she, "ne wiste° I what ye mente. *before / knew*
But now, Aurelie, I knowe youre entente,
By thilke° God that yaf° me soule and lyf,   *that same / gave*
Ne shal I nevere been untrewe° wyf,   *unfaithful*

---

1. Literally, "He drank all his penance without cup," but the exact meaning is unclear: perhaps "He had to swallow his pain," being unable to speak of it to her.
2. Various forms of lyric.
3. Echo, unable to speak in her own right, could not tell Narcissus of her love for him; she died in despair, ever faithful to that love.
4. The subject "she" must be supplied; "of tyme yore": for a long time past.

985 In word ne werk,° as fer as I have wit.   *deed*
    I wol ben his to whom that I am knit:°   *i.e., in matrimony*
    Tak this for fynal answere as of me."
    But after that in pley thus seyde she:
      "Aurelie," quod she, "by heighe God above,
990 Yet wolde I graunte yow to been youre love,
    Sin° I yow see so pitously complayne.   *Since*
    Loke what° day that, endelong° Britayne,   *Whatever / along the edge of*
    Ye remoeve alle the rokkes, stoon by stoon,
    That they ne lette° ship ne boot to goon°—   *prevent / from passing*
995 I seye, whan ye han maad the coost so clene
    Of rokkes, that ther nis° no stoon y-sene—   *is not*
    Thanne wol I love yow best of any man;
    Have heer my trouthe,° in al that evere I can."   *pledge*
      "Is ther non other grace° in yow?" quod he.   *mercy*
1000   "No, by that Lord," quod she, "that maked me!
    For wel I woot° that it shal never bityde.°   *know / happen*
    Lat swiche° folies out of youre herte slyde.°   *such / pass*
    What deyntee° sholde a man han in his lyf   *delight*
    For to go love another mannes wyf,
1005 That hath hir body whan so that him lyketh?"⁵
      Aurelius ful ofte sore syketh;°   *painfully sighs*
    Wo was Aurelie, whan that he this herde,
    And with a sorweful herte he thus answerde:
    "Madame," quod he, "this were an inpossible!°   *impossibility*
1010 Than° moot° I dye of sodein deth horrible."   *Then / must*
    And with that word he turned him anoon.°   *at once*
    Tho° come hir othere freendes many oon,   *Then*
    And in the aleyes° romeden° up and doun,   *garden walks / strolled*
    And nothing wiste° of this conclusioun;°   *knew / outcome*
1015 But sodeinly bigonne revel newe°   *began new revelry*
    Til that the brighte sonne loste his hewe,°   *hue*
    For th'orisonte° hath reft° the sonne his light— *the horizon / taken from*
    This is as muche to seye as it was night—
    And hoom they goon in joye and in solas,
1020 Save only wrecche° Aurelius, allas!   *wretched*
    He to his hous is goon with sorweful herte.
    He seeth° he may nat fro his deeth asterte:°   *sees / escape*
    Him semed that he felte his herte colde.⁶
    Up to the hevene° his handes he gan holde,°   *heavens / did raise*
1025 And on his knowes° bare he sette him doun,   *knees*
    And in his raving seyde his orisoun.°   *prayer*
    For verray wo out of his wit he breyde.⁷
    He niste° what he spak, but thus he seyde;   *knew not*
    With pitous herte his pleynt° hath he bigonne   *complaint*
1030 Unto the goddes, and first unto the sonne:°   *sun*

---

5. Who possesses her body (in the act of love) whensoever it pleases him.
6. It seemed to him that he felt his heart grow cold.
7. For sheer grief he went out of his mind.

He seyde, "Appollo, god and governour
Of every plaunte,° herbe, tree and flour,   plant
That yevest, after thy declinacioun,[8]
To ech of hem° his tyme and his sesoun,   each of them
1035 As thyn herberwe° chaungeth lowe or hye,   lodging, zodiacal position
Lord Phebus, cast thy merciable yë°   merciful eye
On wrecche Aurelie, which that am but lorn.°   lost
Lo, lord! my lady hath my deeth y-sworn
Withoute gilt, but° thy benignitee°   unless / kindness
1040 Upon my dedly° herte have som pitee!   dying
For wel I woot,° lord Phebus, if yow lest,°   know / if it please you
Ye may me helpen, save° my lady, best.   except for
Now voucheth sauf° that I may yow devyse°   grant / describe
How that I may been holpe° and in what wyse.°   helped / way
1045   Youre blisful suster, Lucina the shene,°   bright
That of the see° is chief goddesse and quene[9]—   sea
Though Neptunus have deitee in the see,
Yet emperesse aboven him is she—
Ye knowen wel, lord, that right as hir desyr
1050 Is to be quiked and lighted of youre fyr,[1]
For which she folweth yow ful bisily,
Right° so the see desyreth naturelly   Just
To folwen hire, as she that is goddesse
Bothe in° the see and riveres more and lesse.   i.e., goddess of
1055 Wherfore, lord Phebus, this is my requeste:
Do this miracle—or do° myn herte breste°—   make / burst
That now, next at this opposicioun,°   opposition (of the sun and moon)
Which in the signe° shal be of the Leoun,°   (zodiacal) sign / Lion (Leo)
As preyeth hire so greet a flood to bringe
1060 That fyve fadme° at the leeste it overspringe°   fathoms / tower over
The hyeste rokke in Armorik Briteyne;
And lat this flood endure yeres tweyne.°   two
Thanne certes to my lady may I seye:
'Holdeth youre heste,° the rokkes been aweye.'   promise
1065   Lord Phebus, dooth this miracle for me!
Preye hire she go no faster cours than ye;
I seye, preyeth your suster° that she go   sister
No faster cours than ye thise yeres two.[2]
Than shal she been evene atte fulle° alway,   just at the full
1070 And spring-flood laste bothe night and day.
And but° she vouche sauf° in swiche manere°   unless / grant / such a way
To graunte me my sovereyn lady dere,
Prey hire to sinken every rok adoun

8. That givest, according to thy distance from the equator ("declinacioun").
9. Lucina is the goddess of light, here identified with Diana, the moon.
1. "Quiked": given life; "lighted of": illumined by. The simple fact referred to here is that the
   moon depends on the sun for its light. (Cf. the explanation of tides in ll. 1052–54).
2. The miracle requested would keep the sun and moon in perfect opposition for two years, so
   that the high tide covering the rocks might not wane.

Into hir owene derke regioun[3]
1075 Under the ground, ther° Pluto dwelleth inne,   *where*
Or nevere mo shal I my lady winne.
Thy temple in Delphos wol I barefoot seke.°   *seek (visit)*
Lord Phebus, see the teres on my cheke,
And of my peyne have som compassioun."
1080 And with that word in swowne° he fil adoun,   *a faint*
And longe tyme he lay forth° in a traunce.   *thereafter*
   His brother, which that knew of his penaunce,°   *suffering*
Up caughte him and to bedde he hath him broght.
Dispeyred° in this torment and this thoght   *Filled with despair*
1085 Lete I this woful creature lye:
Chese he, for me, wher he wol live or dye.[4]
   Arveragus, with hele° and greet honour,   *in health*
As he that was of chivalrye the flour,
Is comen hoom, and othere worthy men.
1090 O blisful artow° now, thou Dorigen,   *art thou*
That hast thy lusty° housbonde in thyne armes, *vigorous, merry*
The fresshe° knight, the worthy man of armes,   *lively*
That loveth thee as his owene hertes lyf.
No thing list him to been imaginatyf[5]
1095 If any wight° hadde spoke, whyl he was oute,° *person / away*
To hire of love; he hadde of it no doute.°   *fear*
He noght entendeth° to no swich matere,   *paid no attention*
But daunceth, justeth,° maketh hire good chere; *jousts*
And thus in joye and blisse I lete hem dwelle,
1100 And of the syke° Aurelius wol I telle.   *sick*
   In langour° and in torment furious   *sickness*
Two yeer and more lay wrecche Aurelius,
Er° any foot he mighte on erthe goon.°   *Before / walk*
Ne confort in this tyme hadde he noon,
1105 Save of his brother, which that was a clerk:°   *scholar*
He knew of al this wo and al this werk,°   *affair*
For to non other creature, certeyn,°   *certainly*
Of this matere he dorste° no word seyn.   *dared*
Under° his brest he bar it more secree   *Within*
1110 Than evere dide Pamphilus for Galathee.[6]
His brest was hool° withoute for to sene,° *whole / seen from outside*
But in his herte ay was the arwe° kene;   *arrow*
And wel ye knowe that of a sursanure[7]
In surgerye is perilous the cure,
1115 But° men mighte touche the arwe, or come therby.° *Unless / near to it*
His brother weep° and wayled prively,°   *wept / secretly*
Til atte laste him fil in remembraunce,°   *it occurred to him*

3. Lucina is here also identified with Proserpina, Pluto's queen in the underworld.
4. Let *him* choose, for my part, whether he will live or die.
5. He has no wish at all to be suspicious (full of imaginings).
6. Pamphilus and Galatea were lovers in a widely circulated twelfth-century dialogue, *Pamphilus de Amore*.
7. A wound healed only on the surface.

That whiles he was at Orliens° in Fraunce, *Orléans (university)*
As yonge clerkes that been likerous° *desirous*
1120 To reden artes that been curious° *recondite, subtle*
Seken in every halke° and every herne° *nook / corner*
Particuler° sciences for to lerne— *Little-known*
He him remembred that, upon a day,
At Orliens in studie a book he say° *saw*
1125 Of magik naturel,[8] which his felawe,° *companion*
That was that tyme a bacheler of lawe—
Al° were he ther to lerne another craft— *Although*
Had prively° upon his desk y-laft:° *secretly / left*
Which book spak muchel of the operaciouns
1130 Touchinge the eighte and twenty mansiouns° *positions in the heavens*
That longen° to the mone°—and swich folye *belong / moon (in a month)*
As in oure dayes is nat worth a flye;° *fly*
For holy chirches feith in our bileve
Ne suffreth noon illusion° us to greve.° *deception / vex*
1135 And whan this book was in his remembraunce,
Anon° for joye his herte gan° to daunce, *Immediately / began*
And to himself he seyde prively:° *secretly*
"My brother shal be warisshed° hastily; *cured*
For I am siker° that ther be sciences° *certain / kinds of knowledge*
1140 By whiche men make diverse apparences° *apparitions*
Swiche as thise subtile tregetoures° pleye.° *magicians / perform*
For ofte at festes° have I wel herd seye *feasts*
That tregetours withinne an halle° large *(dining) hall*
Have maad come in a water° and a barge, *some water*
1145 And in the halle rowen° up and doun; *rowed*
Somtyme hath semed come a grim leoun;° *lion*
And somtyme floures springe as in a mede;° *meadow*
Somtyme a vyne, and grapes whyte and rede;
Somtyme a castel,° al of lym° and stoon— *castle / lime*
1150 And whan hem lyked, voyded it anoon.[9]
Thus semed it to every mannes sighte.
　　Now thanne conclude I thus, that if I mighte
At Orliens som old felawe° y-find *companion*
That hadde this° mones mansions in minde, *these*
1155 Or other magik naturel above,° *i.e., even higher*
He sholde wel make my brother han his love.
For with an apparence° a clerk° may make *illusion / scholar*
To mannes sighte, that alle the rokkes blake
Of Britaigne weren y-voyded° everichon,° *removed / every one*
1160 And shippes by the brinke° comen and gon, *coast*
And in swich forme endure a wowke° or two. *week*
Than were my brother warisshed° of his wo; *cured*

8. I.e., employing astronomy.
9. And when it pleased them, caused it at once to disappear. (The "tregetours" are as much artisans as magicians, working the kind of "magic" ordinarily associated with stage sets and properties. A feast given for Charles V in Paris in 1378 included an entertainment much like this.)

Than moste she nedes holden hir biheste,[1]
Or elles he shal shame hire atte leste."
1165   What° sholde I make a lenger tale of this?   *Why*
Unto his brotheres bed he comen is,
And swich confort he yaf° him for to gon   *gave*
To Orliens, that he up stirte anon,°   *jumped up at once*
And on his wey forthward thanne is he fare,°   *has he traveled*
1170 In hope for to ben lissed° of his care.   *eased*
     Whan they were come almost to that citee,
But if it were a two furlong or three,[2]
A yong clerk rominge° by himself they mette,   *strolling*
Which that in Latin thriftily hem grette,°   *suitably greeted them*
1175 And after that he seyde a wonder° thing: *wondrous*
"I knowe," quod he, "the cause of youre coming."
And er° they ferther any fote° wente,   *before / a foot further*
He tolde hem al that was in hire entente.
     This Briton clerk him asked of felawes
1180 The whiche that he had knowe in olde dawes;°   *days*
And he answerde him that they dede were,
For which he weep° ful ofte many a tere.   *wept*
     Doun of his hors Aurelius lighte° anon,   *alighted*
And forth with this magicien is he gon
1185 Hoom to his hous, and maden hem° wel at ese.   *made themselves*
Hem lakked° no vitaille° that mighte hem plese;   *They lacked / food*
So wel arrayed° hous as ther was oon   *furnished (a)*
Aurelius in his lyf saugh nevere noon.
     He shewed him, er° he wente to sopeer,°   *before / supper*
1190 Forestes, parkes ful of wilde deer:
Ther saugh he hertes° with hir hornes hye,°   *harts / tall*
The gretteste° that evere were seyn with yë,°   *largest / eye*
He saugh of hem an hondred slayn with houndes,
And somme with arwes° blede of° bittre woundes.   *arrows / bled from*
1195 He saugh, whan voided° were thise wilde deer,   *departed*
Thise fauconers° upon a fair river,°   *Some falconers / riverbank*
That with hir haukes han the heron slayn.
     Tho saugh° he knightes justing° in a playn;   *Then saw / jousting*
And after this he dide him swich plesaunce
1200 That he him shewed his lady on° a daunce   *in*
On which himself he daunced, as him thoughte.°   *so it seemed to him*
And whan this maister° that this magik wroughte   *Master of Arts*
Saugh it was tyme, he clapte his handes two,
And farewel! al oure revel was ago.°   *gone*
1205 And yet remoeved° they nevere out of the hous   *moved*
Whyl they saugh al this sighte merveillous,
But in his studie, ther as° his bookes be,   *where*
They seten stille, and no wight but they three.
     To him this maister called his squyer,

1. Then she needs must keep her promise.
2. Unless it was two or three furlongs before. (A furlong is one-eighth of a mile.)

1210 And seyde him thus: "Is redy oure soper?
Almost an houre it is, I undertake,°   *declare*
Sith° I yow bad° oure soper for to make,   *Since / ordered*
Whan that thise worthy men wenten with me
Into my studie, ther as my bookes be."
1215   "Sire," quod this squyer, "whan it lyketh yow,°   *it pleases*
It is al redy, though ye wol° right now."   *wish (it)*
"Go we than soupe,"° quod he, "as for the beste: *to eat supper*
This° amorous folk somtyme mote° han reste."   *These / must*
    At after-soper fille° they in tretee°   *fell / negotiations*
1220 What somme° sholde this maistres guerdon° be,   *sum / reward*
To remoeven alle the rokkes of Britayne,
And eek from Gerounde to the mouth of Sayne.³
    He made it straunge,° and swoor,° so God him save,   *difficult / swore*
Lasse° than a thousand pound he wolde nat have,   *Less*
1225 Ne gladly for that somme he wolde nat goon.⁴
    Aurelius with blisful herte anoon°   *at once*
Answerde thus, "Fy on a thousand pound!
This wyde world, which that men seye is round,
I wolde it yeve,° if I were lord of it.   *give*
1230 This bargayn is ful drive,° for we ben knit.°   *driven, concluded / agreed*
Ye shal be payed trewely, by my trouthe!°   *loyalty, fidelity*
But loketh now, for no necligence or slouthe,°   *sloth*
Ye tarie us heer° no lenger than tomorwe."   *delay us here*
"Nay," quod this clerk, "have heer my feith to borwe."°   *i.e., as pledge*
1235   To bedde is goon Aurelius whan him leste,°   *it pleased him*
And wel ny° al that night he hadde his reste: *well nigh, almost*
What for his labour and his hope of blisse,
His woful herte of penaunce° hadde a lisse.°   *suffering / relief*
    Upon the morwe,° whan that it was day,   *morning*
1240 To Britaigne toke they the righte° way,   *direct*
Aurelius and this magicien bisyde,°   *at his side*
And been descended° ther° they wolde abyde;°   *have dismounted / where / stay*
And this was, as thise bokes me remembre,°   *remind me*
The colde frosty seson of Decembre.
1245   Phebus wex old, and hewed lyk latoun,⁵
That in his hote declinacioun⁶
Shoon as the burned° gold with stremes° brighte;   *burnished / beams*
But now in Capricorn adoun he lighte,°   *alighted*
Where as he shoon ful pale, I dar wel seyn.
1250 The bittre frostes, with the sleet and reyn,°   *rain*
Destroyed hath the grene in every yerd.°   *garden, yard*
Janus⁷ sit by the fyr with double berd,

3. And also from the Gironde to the mouth of the Seine.
4. I.e., the price is his absolute minimum, nothing to cause him delight.
5. Phoebus (the sun) grew old, and colored like brass.
6. I.e., in the Tropic of Cancer.
7. The two-headed Roman god (hence double-bearded), who looks both forward and backward, to the future and the past. The month of January is named for him, and medieval calendars (in the Books of Hours) often show him feasting, in the character of a medieval prince or rich landowner.

And drinketh of his bugle-horn° the wyn;   *goblet made of ox horn*
Biforn him stant° brawen° of the tusked swyn,°   *stands / brawn, meat / boar*
1255 And "Nowel"° cryeth every lusty man.   *Noel, Christmas*
    Aurelius, in al that evere he can,
Doth° to this maister chere° and reverence,   *Makes / good cheer*
And preyeth him to doon his diligence
To bringen him out of his peynes smerte,
1260 Or with a swerd that he wolde slitte his herte.
    This subtil° clerk swich routhe° had of this man   *skillful / compassion*
That night and day he spedde him that° he can,   *hurried as much as*
To wayten a tyme of his conclusioun;[8]
This is to seye, to maken illusioun,
1265 By swich an apparence° or jogelrye°—   *apparition / magic, jugglery*
I ne can° no termes of astrologye—   *do not know*
That she and every wight° sholde wene° and seye   *person / suppose*
That of Britaigne the rokkes were aweye,
Or elles they were sonken under grounde.
1270 So atte laste he hath his tyme y-founde
To maken his japes° and his wrecchednesse°   *tricks / miserable actions*
Of swich° a supersticious cursednesse.   *From such*
His tables Toletanes[9] forth he broght,
Ful wel corrected, ne ther lakked noght,
1275 Neither his collect ne his expans yeres,[1]
Ne his rotes° ne his othere geres,°   *statistics / gear*
As been his centres and his arguments,
And his proporcionels convenients
For his equacions in every thing.[2]
1280 And by his eighte spere[3] in his wirking
He knew ful wel how fer Alnath° was shove°   *the star / advanced*
Fro the heed° of thilke fixe° Aries above   *head / that same fixed (constellation)*
That in the ninthe speere considered is:[4]
Ful subtilly he calculed at this.
1285   Whan he had founde his firste mansioun,°   *position (of the moon)*
He knew the remenant° by proporcioun,   *remainder*
And knew the arysing° of his mone° weel,   *rising / moon*
And in whos face, and terme,[5] and everydeel;
And knew ful weel the mones mansioun,
1290 Acordaunt to his operacioun,
And knew also his othere observaunces°   *ceremonies*
For swiche illusiouns and swiche meschaunces°   *mischief*
As hethen° folk used in thilke° days.   *heathen / those same*
For which no lenger maked he delayes,

8. To watch for a time to conclude the matter.
9. Astronomical tables calculated for the city of Toledo, which gives them their name.
1. The "collect" recorded movements of the planets over long periods of years; the "expans yeres" for shorter periods of up to twenty years.
2. Astronomical instruments and formulae used to determine astrological positions.
3. The eighth sphere, of the fixed stars.
4. That is held to be in the ninth sphere (the Primum Mobile).
5. Divisions, even and uneven, of zodiacal signs.

1295 But thurgh his magik, for a wyke or tweye,°   *week or two*
It semed that alle the rokkes were aweye.
    Aurelius, which that yet despeired° is   *despairing*
Wher° he shal han his love or fare amis,   *Whether*
Awaiteth night and day on this miracle;
1300 And whan he knew that ther was noon obstacle—
That voided° were thise rokkes everichon°—   *removed / every one*
Doun to his maistres feet he fil anon°   *fell at once*
And seyde, "I woful wrecche, Aurelius,
Thanke yow, lord, and lady myn Venus,
1305 That me han holpen fro my cares colde."°   *bitter, fatal*
And to the temple his wey forth hath he holde,
Where as he knew he sholde his lady see.
And whan he saugh° his tyme, anonright° he,   *saw / right away*
With dredful° herte and with ful humble chere,°   *fearful / appearance*
1310 Salewed° hath his sovereyn lady dere: *Greeted*
    "My righte° lady," quod this woful man,   *own true*
"Whom I most drede° and love as I best can,   *fear*
And lothest° were of al this world displese,   *most loath*
Nere it° that I for yow have swich disese°   *Were it not / misery*
1315 That I moste° dyen heer at youre foot anon,   *must*
Noght wolde I telle how me is wo bigon.°   *woebegone I am*
But certes outher° moste I dye or pleyne;°   *either / speak my grief*
Ye slee° me, giltelees, for verray° peyne.   *slay / real*
But of my deeth, thogh that ye have no routhe,°   *compassion*
1320 Avyseth yow,° er° that ye breke your trouthe.°   *Take heed / before / pledge*
Repenteth yow, for thilke God above,⁶
Er ye me sleen° by cause that I yow love.   *slay*
For, madame, wel ye woot what ye han hight°—   *promised*
Nat that I chalange° any thing of right°   *claim / by rights*
1325 Of yow, my sovereyn lady, but youre grace°—   *mercy, favor*
But in a gardin yond,° at swich a place,   *yonder*
Ye woot right wel° what ye bihighten° me;   *know full well / promised*
And in myn hand youre trouthe plighten° ye   *pledged*
To love me best. God woot, ye seyde so,
1330 Al be° that I unworthy be therto.   *Although*
Madame, I speke it for the honour of yow
More than to save myn hertes lyf right now.
I have do° so as ye comanded me;   *done*
And if ye vouchesauf,° ye may go see.   *(will) grant (it)*
1335 Doth as yow list, have youre biheste in minde,
For, quik° or deed, right there ye shul me finde.   *living*
In yow lyth al to do° me live or deye: *make*
But wel I woot the rokkes been aweye!"
    He taketh his leve, and she astonied° stood;   *astonished*
1340 In al hir face nas° a drope of blood.   *was not*
She wende° never han come in swich a trappe.   *thought*

6. Repent you, for (the sake of) that same God on high.

"Allas!" quod she, "that evere this sholde happe!°   occur
For wende I nevere, by possibilitee,
That swich a monstre° or merveille mighte be!   strange thing
1345 It is agayns the proces° of nature."   course
And hoom she gooth a sorweful creature.
For verray fere° unnethe° may she go.°   deep fear / scarcely / walk
She wepeth, wailleth, al a day° or two,   a whole day
And swowneth,° that it routhe° was to see;   faints / pity
1350 But why it was, to no wight° tolde she,   person
For out of toune was goon Arveragus.
But to hirself she spak, and seyde thus,
With face pale and with ful sorweful chere,°   countenance
In hire compleynt,° as ye shul after here: lament
1355 "Allas," quod she, "on thee, Fortune, I pleyne,°   make complaint
That unwar° wrapped has me in thy cheyne,°   unawares / chain
Fro which t'escape woot° I no socour°   know / help
Save only deeth or elles° dishonour;   else
Oon of thise two bihoveth me° to chese.   it's necessary for me
1360 But nathelees yet have I lever to lese°   would I rather lose
My lyf, than of my body to have a shame,
Or knowe° myselven fals, or lese my name;   acknowledge
And with my deth I may be quit,° ywis.   freed (from the debt)
Hath ther nat many a noble wyf er this,°   before now
1365 And many a mayde, y-slayn hirself, allas!
Rather than with hir body doon trepas?°   commit a sin
     Yis, certes, lo, thise stories[7] beren witnesse;
Whan thretty° tyraunts, ful of cursednesse,   thirty
Hadde slayn Phidoun in Athenes atte feste,°   at (the) feasting
1370 They commanded his doghtres for t'areste,°   to be seized
And bringen hem biforn hem in despyt°   scorn
Al naked, to fulfille hir foul delyt,°   pleasure
And in hir fadres blood they made hem daunce
Upon the pavement, God yeve hem mischaunce!°   give them misfortune
1375 For which thise woful maydens, ful of drede,°   fear
Rather than they wolde lese hir maydenhede,
They prively° ben stirt° into a welle,   secretly / have leaped
And dreynte° hemselven, as the bokes telle.   drowned
     They of Messene lete enquere and seke[8]
1380 Of Lacedomie° fifty maydens eke,°   From Sparta / also
On whiche they wolden doon° hir lecherye;   perform
But was ther noon of al that compaignye
That she nas° slayn, and with a good entente°   was not / will, purpose
Chees° rather for to dye than assente   Chose
1385 To been oppressed° of hir maydenhede.   ravished
Why sholde I thanne to dye been in drede?
Lo eek the tiraunt Aristoclides°   a tyrant of Arcadia

---

7. The examples of virtuous women she brings to mind, from Phidon's daughters on, are all
found in St. Jerome's treatise against Jovinian.
8. The men of Messene (in the Peloponnesus) had inquiries made and sought.

That loved a mayden, heet° Stimphalides,   *named*
Whan that hir fader slayn was on a night,
1390 Unto Dianes temple goth she right,°   *directly*
And hente° the image° in hir handes two,   *clasped / of the goddess*
Fro which image wolde she nevere go.
No wight° ne mighte hir handes of it arace,°   *person / tear away*
Til she was slayn right in the selve place.
1395   Now sith that° maydens hadden swich despyt°   *since / disdain, scorn*
To been defouled with mannes foul delyt,
Wel oghte a wyf rather hirselven slee
Than be defouled,° as it thinketh me.°   *defiled / it seems to me*
What shal I seyn of Hasdrubales° wyf,   *Hasdrubal's*
1400 That at Cartage° birafte° hirself hir lyf?   *Carthage / took from*
For whan she saugh° that Romayns wan° the toun,   *saw / won*
She took hir children alle, and skipte° adoun   *jumped*
Into the fyr, and chees rather to dye
Than any Romayn dide° hire vileinye.   *should do*
1405 Hath nat Lucresse° y-slayn hirself, allas!   *Lucretia*
At Rome, whanne she oppressed° was   *violated*
Of° Tarquin, for hire thoughte° it was a shame   *By / it seemed to her*
To liven whan she hadde lost hir name?
The sevene maydens of Milesie° also   *Miletus, in Asia Minor*
1410 Han slayn hemself,° for verray° drede and wo,   *themselves / great*
Rather than folk of Gaule° hem sholde oppresse.   *the Galatians*
Mo than a thousand stories, as I gesse,
Coude I now telle as touchinge this matere.
When Habradate° was slayn, his wyf so dere   *Abradates, king of the Susi*
1415 Hirselven slow,° and leet hir blood to glyde   *slew*
In Habradates woundes depe and wyde,
And seyde, 'My body, at the leeste way,°   *at least*
Ther shal no wight defoulen, if I may.'°   *if I can help it*
   What sholde I mo ensamples heerof sayn,
1420 Sith that so manye han hemselven slayn
Wel rather than they wolde defouled be?
I wol conclude that it is bet° for me   *better*
To sleen myself than been defouled thus.
I wol be trewe unto Arveragus,
1425 Or rather sleen myself in som manere—
As dide Demociones° doghter dere,   *Demotion's*
By cause that she wolde nat defouled be.
O Cedasus!° it is ful greet pitee   *Seedasus, of Boeotia*
To reden how thy doghtren° deyde, allas!   *daughters*
1430 That slowe hemself for swich manere cas.°   *such a kind of occurrence*
As greet a pitee was it, or wel more,
The Theban mayden that for Nichanore°   *Nichanor, an Alexandrian*
Hirselven slow° right for swich manere wo.   *slew*
Another Theban mayden dide right so:
1435 For° oon of Macedoine° hadde hire oppressed,° *Because / Macedonia / violated*
She with hire deeth hir maydenhede redressed.°   *made amends for*

What shal I seye of Nicerates° wyf   *Niceratus's, an Athenian*
That for swich cas birafte hirself hir lyf?
How trewe eek was to Alcebiades°   *Alcibiades, friend of Socrates*
1440 His love, that rather for to dyen chees°   *chose*
Than for to suffre his body unburied be!
Lo, which a⁹ wyf was Alceste," quod she.
"What seith Omer° of gode Penalopee?°   *Homer / Penelope, Ulysses' wife*
Al Grece knoweth of hire chastitee.
1445 Pardee, of Laodomya° is writen thus,   *Laodamia*
That whan at Troye was slayn Protheselaus,°   *Protesilaus*
No lenger wolde she live after his day.
The same of noble Porcia° telle I may: *Portia*
Withoute Brutus coude she nat live,
1450 To whom she hadde al hool° hir herte yive.°   *completely / given*
The parfit wyfhod of Arthemesye¹
Honoured is thurgh al the Barbarye.°   *heathendom*
O Teuta,° queen! thy wyfly chastitee   *queen of Illirica*
To alle wyves may a mirour be.
1455 The same thing I seye of Bilia,°   *wife of Gaius Duillius*
Of Rodogone, and eek Valeria."²

    Thus pleyned° Dorigene a day or tweye,   *lamented*
Purposinge evere that she wolde deye.°   *die*
But natheless, upon the thridde night,
1460 Hom cam Arveragus, this worthy knight,
And asked hire why that she weep° so sore;°   *wept / painfully*
And she gan wepen ever lenger the more.°   *ever more and more*
"Allas!" quod she, "that ever was I born!
Thus have I seyd," quod she, "thus have I sworn,"
1465 And told him al as ye han herd bifore;
It nedeth nat reherce it yow namore.°   *repeat it again to you*
This housbonde, with glade chere,° in freendly   *expression, countenance*
    wyse,
Answerde and seyde as I shal yow devyse.°   *relate*
"Is ther oght elles, Dorigen, but this?"
1470   "Nay, nay," quod she, "God help me so as wis;°   *indeed*
This is to° muche, and° it were Goddes wille."   *too / if*
    "Ye, wyf," quod he, "lat slepen that° is stille.°   *what / quiet*
It may be wel, paraventure,° yet today.   *by chance*
Ye shul youre trouthe holden,° by my fay!   *keep your pledge*
1475 For God so wisly° have mercy on me,   *surely*
I hadde wel levere° y-stiked° for to be,   *rather / stabbed*
For verray° love which that I to yow have,   *true*
But if ye sholde youre trouthe kepe and save.°   *guard and preserve*
Trouthe is the hyeste thing that man may kepe."³

9. What a. Alcestis, wife of Admetus, died his death for him.
1. Artemisia, queen of Caria, built a famous tomb for her husband.
2. Rhodogune, wife of Darius; Valeria, daughter of Diocletian.
3. "Trouthe" is a central concept in this poem, for which no single modern equivalent can be
   found. In certain idioms, it can be defined as "pledge" or "promise"; but its larger sense (as
   here) is fidelity, steadfastness, integrity—the capacity to embody a single "entente" without

1480 But with that word he brast anon to wepe,[4]
And seyde, "I yow forbede, up° peyne of deeth,   *on*
That nevere, whyl thee lasteth lyf ne breeth,
To no wight° tel thou of this aventure—   *person*
As I may best, I wol my wo endure—
1485 Ne make no contenance of hevinesse,°   *i.e., look sorrowful*
That folk of yow may demen° harm or gesse."°   *suppose / guess (at it)*
    And forth he cleped° a squyer and a mayde: *called*
"Goth forth anon° with Dorigen," he sayde,   *at once*
"And bringeth hire to swich a° place anon."   *a certain*
1490 They take hir° leve, and on hir wey they gon,   *their*
But they ne wiste° why she thider° wente: *knew / thither*
He nolde° no wight tellen his entente.   *would not*
    Paraventure° an heep° of yow, ywis,°   *Perhaps / many / certainly*
Wol holden him a lewed° man in this,   *thoughtless, foolish*
1495 That he wol putte his wyf in jupartye.°   *jeopardy*
Herkneth the tale, er ye upon hire crye.[5]
She may have bettre fortune than yow semeth,°   *i.e., expect*
And whan that ye han herd the tale, demeth.°   *judge*
    This squyer, which that highte° Aurelius,   *was called*
1500 On Dorigen that was so amorous,
Of aventure° happed hire to mete   *By chance*
Amidde the toun, right in the quikkest° strete,   *busiest*
As she was boun° to goon the wey forth right°   *ready / directly*
Toward the gardin ther as she had hight;°   *promised*
1505 And he was to the gardinward° also,   *(going) toward the garden*
For wel he spyed° whan she wolde go   *he watched closely*
Out of hir hous to any maner° place.   *kind of*
But thus they mette, of aventure or grace;°   *by chance or good fortune*
And he saleweth° hire with glad entente,°   *greets / cheerfully*
1510 And asked of hire whiderward she wente;
And she answerde, half as she were mad,
"Unto the gardin, as myn housbond bad,
My trouthe for to holde, allas! allas!"
    Aurelius gan wondren° on this cas,°   *fell to wondering / event*
1515 And in his herte hadde greet compassioun
Of° hire and of hire lamentacioun,   *For*
And of Arveragus, the worthy knight,
That bad hire holden° al that she had hight,°   *keep / promised*
So looth him was[6] his wyf sholde breke hir trouthe.
1520 And in his herte he caughte of this greet routhe,°   *took great pity on this*
Consideringe the beste on every syde,
That fro his lust yet were him levere abyde[7]

---

variance, whatever the circumstances. The keeping of a promise is only symptomatic of the
presence of this deeper, pervasive moral quality.
4. But with that word, he burst at once into tears.
5. Hear the (whole) tale, before you complain about her.
6. So hateful to him was (the notion that).
7. (So) that he thought it better to abstain from his desire.

Than doon so heigh° a cherlish wrecchednesse°   *great / churlish miserable act*
Agayns franchyse° and alle gentillesse;°   *Against generosity / nobleness*
1525 For which in fewe wordes seyde he thus:
    "Madame, seyth to youre lord Arveragus,
That sith° I see his grete gentillesse   *since*
To yow, and eek° I see wel youre distresse,   *also*
That him were levere han shame (and that
    were routhe)°   *would be a pity*
1530 Than ye to me sholde breke thus youre trouthe,
I have wel levere° evere to suffre wo   *would much rather*
Than I departe° the love bitwix yow two.   *(that) I divide*
I yow relesse,° madame, into youre hond,   *release*
Quit° every serement° and every bond   *Discharged of / oath*
1535 That ye han maad to me as heerbiforn,
Sith thilke tyme which that ye were born.[8]
My trouthe I plighte, I shal yow never repreve°   *reproach*
Of no biheste,° and here I take my leve,   *promise*
As of the treweste and the beste wyf
1540 That evere yet I knew in al my lyf.
But every wyf be war° of hire biheste!   *be careful*
On Dorigene remembreth atte leste.°   *at (the) least*
Thus can a squyer doon a gentil dede
As well as can a knight, withouten drede."°   *doubt*
1545   She thonketh him upon hir knees al bare,
And hoom unto hir housbond is she fare,°   *has she gone*
And tolde him al as ye han herd me sayd;
And be ye siker,° he was so weel apayd°   *sure / pleased*
That it were inpossible me to wryte.
1550 What° sholde I lenger of this cas endyte?°   *Why / relate*
    Arveragus and Dorigene his wyf
In sovereyn° blisse leden forth° hir lyf.   *supreme / lead on*
Never eft° ne was ther angre hem bitwene: *again*
He cherisseth hire as though she were a quene,
1555 And she was to him trewe for everemore.
Of° thise two folk ye gete of° me namore.   *Concerning / i.e., hear from*
    Aurelius, that his cost° hath al forlorn,°   *expense / lost*
Curseth the tyme that evere he was born:
"Allas," quod he, "allas! that I bihighte°   *promised*
1560 Of pured° gold a thousand pound of wighte°   *refined / by weight*
Unto this philosophre!° How shal I do?   *philosopher (alchemist?)*
I see namore but that I am fordo.°   *done in, ruined*
Myn heritage° moot I nedes° selle   *inheritance / I needs must*
And been a beggere; heer may I nat dwelle,
1565 And shamen al my kinrede° in this place,   *kindred, family*
But° I of him may gete bettre grace.°   *Unless / i.e., better terms*
But natheless, I wol of him assaye°   *try (to arrange with) him*
At certeyn dayes, yeer by yeer, to paye,

8. Since that same time (in) which you were born.

And thanke him of his grete curteisye;
1570 My trouthe wol I kepe, I wol nat lye."
     With herte soor° he gooth unto his cofre,°   *painful / money chest*
And broghte gold unto this philosophre
The value of fyve hundred pound, I gesse,°   *guess*
And him bisecheth of° his gentillesse   *(out) of*
1575 To graunte him dayes of the remenaunt,⁹
And seyde, "Maister, I dar wel make avaunt,°   *boast*
I failled nevere of my trouthe as yit;
For sikerly° my dette shal be quit°   *surely / repaid*
Towardes yow, howevere that I fare°   *although I may go off*
1580 To goon a-begged° in my kirtle° bare.   *begging / shirt*
But wolde ye vouche sauf,° upon seuretee,°   *grant / surety, pledge*
Two yeer or three for to respyten me,°   *to give me a delay*
Than were I wel; for elles° moot° I selle   *otherwise / must*
Myn heritage; ther is namore to telle."
1585   This philosophre sobrely° answerde,   *gravely*
And seyde thus, whan he thise wordes herde:
"Have I nat holden° covenant unto thee?"   *kept*
    "Yes, certes,° wel and trewely," quod° he.   *certainly / said*
    "Hastow° nat had thy lady as thee lyketh?"   *Hast thou*
1590   "No, no," quod he, and sorwefully he syketh.°   *sighs*
    "What was the cause? tel me if thou can."
    Aurelius his tale anon bigan,
And tolde him al, as ye han herd bifore:
It nedeth nat to yow reherce it more.°   *recite it again*
1595 He seide, "Arveragus, of gentillesse,
Hadde levere° dye in sorwe and in distresse   *rather*
Than that his wyf were of hir trouthe fals."
The sorwe of Dorigen he tolde him als,°   *also*
How looth° hire was to been a wikked wyf,   *loath*
1600 And that she levere had lost that day hir lyf,
And that hir trouthe° she swoor° thurgh innocence: *pledge / swore*
She nevere erst° herde speke of apparence.°   *before / illusion, magic*
"That made me han of hire so greet pitee;
And right as frely° as he sente hire me,   *generously*
1605 As frely sente I hire to him ageyn.
This al and som,° ther is namore to seyn."   *This is the whole*
    This philosophre answerde, "Leve° brother,   *Dear*
Everich° of yow dide gentilly til other.°   *Everyone / toward the other*
Thou art a squyer, and he is a knight;
1610 But God forbede, for his blisful might,
But if° a clerk° coude doon a gentil dede   *Unless / scholar*
As wel as any of yow, it is no drede!°   *doubt*
    Sire, I relesse thee thy thousand pound,
As° thou right now were cropen° out of the ground,   *As if / had crept*
1615 Ne nevere er° now ne haddest knowen me.   *before*

9. To grant him days (i.e., some time) in which to pay the remainder.

For sire, I wol nat take a peny of thee
For al my craft, ne noght for my travaille.°   *labor*
Thou hast y-payed wel for my vitaille;°   *food, entertainment*
It is ynogh.° And farewel, have good day."   *enough*
1620 And took his hors, and forth he gooth his way.
    Lordinges, this question thanne wolde I aske now:
Which was the moste free,° as thinketh yow?[1]   *generous*
Now telleth me, er that° ye ferther wende.°   *before / travel*
I can namore:° my tale is at an ende.   *know no more*

The Pardoner's Prologue and Tale

The Introduction

* * *

"By corpus bones![1] but° I have triacle,°   *unless / medicine*
315 Or elles a draught of moyste° and corny° ale,   *fresh / malty*
Or but° I here anon° a mery tale,   *unless / at once*
Myn herte is lost for pitee of this mayde.[2]
Thou bel amy,° thou Pardoner," he seyde,   *sweet friend*
"Tel us som mirthe or japes° right anon."   *jokes*
320   "It shall be doon," quod° he, "by Seint Ronyon![3]   *said*
But first," quod he, "heer at this ale-stake°   *tavern sign*
I wol both drinke and eten° of a cake."   *eat*
    But right anon thise gentils gonne to crye,[4]
"Nay! lat him telle us of no ribaudye;°   *ribaldry*
325 Tel us som moral thing, that we may lere°   *learn*
Som wit,° and thanne wol we gladly here."°   *Something instructive / listen*
"I graunte,° ywis,"° quod he, "but I mot° thinke   *agree / certainly / must*
Upon som honest° thing whyl that I drinke."   *decent, decorous*

The Prologue

"Lordinges," quod he, "in chirches whan I preche,
330 I peyne me° to han an hauteyn° speche,   *take pains / elevated*
And ringe it out as round as gooth° a belle,   *sounds*
For I can al by rote° that I telle.   *know all by memory*
My theme° is alwey oon,° and evere was—   *text / always the same*
Radix malorum est Cupiditas.[5]
335   First I pronounce° whennes° that I come,   *proclaim / whence, from where*
And thanne my bulles[6] shewe I, alle and somme.°   *one and all*

---

1. I.e., in your judgment.
1. I.e., Christ's bones.
2. The Host is speaking to the Physician, who has just concluded his sad tale of a young Roman girl who allows her father to kill her rather than submit to the lust of a corrupt judge.
3. St. Ronan or St. Ninian, with a possible pun on "runnion," meaning loins (including the sexual organs).
4. But immediately these gentlefolk raised a cry.
5. Avarice (the love of money) is the root of all evil (1 Timothy 6:10).
6. Bulls—writs of indulgence for sin, purchasable in lieu of other forms of penance.

Oure lige lordes seel° on my patente,°   *i.e., bishop's seal / license*
That shewe I first, my body° to warente,°   *person / authorize*
That no man be so bold, ne preest ne clerk,°   *neither priest nor scholar*
340 Me to destourbe of Cristes holy werk;
And after that thanne telle I forth my tales.
Bulles of popes and of cardinales,
Of patriarkes,° and bishoppes I shewe,   *heads of churches*
And in Latyn I speke a wordes fewe,
345 To saffron with my predicacioun,[7]
And for to stire° hem to devocioun.   *stir*
Thanne shewe I forth my longe cristal stones,°   *glass cases*
Y-crammed ful of cloutes° and of bones—   *rags*
Reliks been they, as wenen they echoon.[8]
350 Thanne have I in latoun[9] a sholder-boon
Which that was of an holy Jewes shepe.
'Goode men,' seye I, 'tak of my wordes kepe:°   *heed*
If that this boon be wasshe° in any welle,   *washed, dunked*
If cow, or calf, or sheep, or oxe swelle,°   *swell (up)*
355 That any worm hath ete, or worm y-stonge,[1]
Tak water of that welle, and wash his tonge,
And it is hool° anon;° and forthermore,   *healed / at once*
Of pokkes° and of scabbe and every sore   *pox*
Shal every sheep be hool,° that of this welle   *healed*
360 Drinketh a draughte. Tak kepe° eek° what I telle: *heed / also*
If that the good man that the bestes° oweth°   *animals / owns*
Wol every wike,° er° that the cok him croweth,   *week / before*
Fastinge,° drinken of this welle a draughte—   *(While) fasting*
As thilke° holy Jewe° oure eldres taughte—   *that same / i.e., Jacob*
365 His bestes and his stoor° shal multiplye.   *stock*
    And, sires, also it heleth° jalousye: *heals*
For though a man be falle in jalous rage,
Let maken with this water his potage,[2]
And nevere shal he more his wyf mistriste,°   *mistrust*
370 Though he the sooth° of hir defaute° wiste°—   *truth / erring / should know*
Al° had she taken° preestes two or three.   *Even if / taken (as lovers)*
    Heer is a miteyn° eek, that ye may see: *mitten*
He that his hond wol putte in this miteyn,
He shal have multiplying of his greyn°   *grain*
375 Whan he hath sowen, be it whete° or otes,°   *wheat / oats*
So that he offre pens, or elles grotes.[3]
    Goode men and wommen, o° thing warne° I yow: *one / tell*
If any wight° be in this chirche now,   *person*
That hath doon sinne horrible, that he

---

7. With which to season my preaching. (Saffron is a yellow spice.)
8. They are (saints') relics, or so they all suppose.
9. Latten, a metal like brass.
1. Who has eaten any (poisonous) worm or whom a snake has stung (bitten).
2. Have his soup made with this water.
3. Provided that he offers (to me) pennies or else groats (coins worth fourpence).

380	Dar° nat for shame of it y-shriven⁴ be,	*Dare*
	Or any womman, be she yong or old,	
	That hath y-maked hir housbonde cokewold,°	*a cuckold*
	Swich° folk shul have no power ne no grace	*Such*
	To offren° to my reliks in this place.	*To offer (money)*
385	And whoso findeth him out of swich blame,°	*not deserving such blame*
	He wol com up and offre a° Goddes name,	*make an offering in*
	And I assoille° him by the auctoritee°	*(will) absolve / authority*
	Which that by bulle y-graunted was to me.'	
	By this gaude° have I wonne,° yeer° by yeer,	*trick / earned / year*
390	An hundred mark sith I was pardoner.⁵	
	I stonde lyk a clerk° in my pulpet,	*scholar*
	And whan the lewed° peple is doun y-set,	*ignorant, unlearned*
	I preche, so as ye han herd bifore,	
	And telle an hundred false japes° more.	*tricks, stories*
395	Thanne peyne I me° to strecche forth the nekke,	*I take pains*
	And est and west upon the peple I bekke°	*nod*
	As doth a dowve,° sittinge on a berne.°	*dove / in a barn*
	Myn hondes and my tonge goon so yerne°	*rapidly*
	That it is joye to see my bisinesse.	
400	Of avaryce and of swich° cursednesse	*such*
	Is al my preching, for° to make hem free°	*in order / generous*
	To yeven hir pens, and namely unto me.⁶	
	For myn entente° is nat but for to winne,°	*intention / profit*
	And nothing° for correccioun of sinne:	*not at all*
405	I rekke° nevere, whan that they ben beried,°	*care / buried*
	Though that hir soules goon a-blakeberied!⁷	
	For certes,° many a predicacioun°	*certainly / sermon*
	Comth ofte tyme of yvel° entencioun:	*evil*
	Som for plesaunce° of folk and flaterye,	*the entertainment*
410	To been avaunced by ypocrisye,⁸	
	And som for veyne glorie,° and som for hate.	*vainglory*
	For whan I dar non other weyes debate,⁹	
	Than wol I stinge him¹ with my tonge smerte°	*sharp*
	In preching, so that he shal nat asterte°	*leap up (to protest)*
415	To been° defamed falsly, if that he	*At being*
	Hath trespased to° my brethren² or to me.	*wronged*
	For, though I telle noght his propre° name,	*own*
	Men shal wel knowe that it is the same	
	By signes and by othere circumstances.	
420	Thus quyte° I folk that doon us displesances;°	*requite / offenses*
	Thus spitte I out my venim under hewe°	*hue, coloring*

---

4. I.e., confessed and absolved.
5. A hundred marks (coins worth thirteen shillings fourpence) since I became a pardoner.
6. In giving their pence, and particularly to me.
7. Blackberrying, i.e., wandering.
8. (Thus) to seek advancement through hypocrisy.
9. For when I dare enter into contest (argument) no other way.
1. I.e., some enemy.
2. I.e., fellow pardoners.

Of holynesse, to semen° holy and trewe.   *seem*
　　But shortly° myn entente I wol devyse:°   *briefly / describe*
I preche of no thing but for coveityse.°   *out of covetousness*
425 Therfore my theme is yet, and evere was,
Radix malorum est cupiditas.
Thus can I preche agayn° that same vyce   *against*
Which that I use,° and that is avaryce.   *practice*
But though myself be gilty in that sinne,
430 Yet can I maken other folk to twinne°   *part*
From avaryce, and sore° to repente.   *ardently*
But that is nat my principal entente:
I preche nothing but for coveityse.
Of this matere° it oughte ynogh suffyse.   *subject*
435 　　Than telle I hem ensamples many oon°   *examples many a one*
Of olde stories longe tyme agoon,°   *past*
For lewed° peple loven tales olde;   *unlearned*
Swich° thinges can they wel reporte° and holde.°   *Such / repeat / remember*
What, trowe ye, the whyles I may preche[3]
440 And winne° gold and silver for° I teche,   *obtain / because*
That I wol live in povert° wilfully?°   *poverty / willingly*
Nay, nay, I thoghte° it nevere, trewely!   *considered*
For I wol preche and begge in sondry° londes;   *various*
I wol nat do no labour with myn hondes,
445 Ne make baskettes,[4] and live therby,
By cause I wol nat beggen ydelly.°   *without profit*
I wol non of the Apostles counterfete:°   *imitate*
I wol have money, wolle,° chese, and whete,   *wool*
Al° were it yeven of° the povereste page,°   *Even if / given by / servant*
450 Or of° the povereste widwe° in a village,   *by / poorest widow*
Al sholde hir children sterve for famyne.[5]
Nay! I wol drinke licour° of the vyne,   *liquor, wine*
And have a joly wenche in every toun.
But herkneth,° lordinges, in conclusioun: *listen*
455 Youre lyking is that I shall telle a tale.
Now have I dronke a draughte of corny° ale,   *malty*
By God, I hope I shal yow telle a thing
That shal by resoun° been at° youre lyking.   *with reason / to*
For though myself be a ful vicious° man,   *evil, vice-ridden*
460 A moral tale yet I yow telle can,
Which I am wont to preche for to winne.[6]
Now holde youre pees,° my tale I wol beginne."   *peace*

The Tale

In Flaundres whylom was° a compaignye   *once (there) was*
Of yonge folk, that haunteden folye—

---

3. What? do you believe (that) as long as I can preach.
4. St. Paul was said to have been a basket maker.
5. Even though her children should die of hunger.
6. Which I am in the habit of preaching to make some money.

465 As ryot, hasard, stewes, and tavernes,[7]
   Where as° with harpes, lutes, and giternes,°   *There where / guitars*
   They daunce and pleyen at dees° bothe day and night,   *dice*
   And eten also and drinken over hir might,°   *beyond their capacity*
   Thurgh which they doon the devel sacrifyse°   *make sacrifice to the devil*
470 Withinne that develes temple,° in cursed wyse,°   *i.e., the tavern / way*
   By superfluitee° abhominable.   *excess*
   Hir othes° been so grete and so dampnable,°   *oaths, curses / condemnable*
   That it is grisly for to here hem swere.
   Our blissed Lordes body they totere°—   *tear apart*
475 Hem thoughte° Jewes rente° him noght ynough—   *It seemed to them / tore*
   And ech° of hem at otheres sinne lough.°   *each / laughed*
   And right anon thanne comen tombesteres°   *female tumblers, dancers*
   Fetys and smale, and yonge fruytesteres,[8]
   Singeres with harpes, baudes,° wafereres,°   *bawds / girls selling cakes*
480 Whiche been the verray° develes officeres   *the very*
   To kindle and blowe the fyr of lecherye
   That is annexed° unto glotonye: *joined (as a sin)*
   The Holy Writ take I to my witnesse
   That luxurie° is in wyn and dronkenesse.   *lechery*
485   Lo, how that dronken Loth° unkindely°   *Lot / unnaturally*
   Lay by his doghtres two, unwitingly;°   *unknowingly*
   So dronke he was, he niste° what he wroghte.°   *knew not / did*
      Herodes,° whoso wel the stories soghte,°   *Herod / should seek out*
   Whan he of wyn was repleet° at his feste,   *replete, full*
490 Right at his owene table he yaf° his heste°   *gave / command*
   To sleen the Baptist John ful giltelees.°   *guiltless (innocent)*
      Senek° seith a good word doutelees: *Seneca*
   He seith, he can no difference finde
   Bitwix a man that is out of his minde
495 And a man which that is dronkelewe,°   *drunken*
   But that woodnesse, y-fallen in a shrewe,[9]
   Persevereth lenger° than doth dronkenesse.   *Continues longer*
   O glotonye,° ful of cursednesse!   *gluttony*
   O cause first° of oure confusioun!°   *first cause / ruin*
500 O original° of oure dampnacioun,   *origin*
   Til Crist had boght us with his blood agayn!
   Lo, how dere,° shortly for to sayn,°   *costly / to speak briefly*
   Aboght was thilke cursed vileinye;[1]
   Corrupt° was al this world for glotonye!   *Corrupted*
505 Adam oure fader and his wyf also
   Fro Paradys to labour and to wo
   Were driven for that vyce, it is no drede.°   *doubt*
   For whyl that Adam fasted, as I rede,°   *read*
   He was in Paradys; and whan that he

7. Of young folk who gave themselves up to folly—(such) as excessive revelry, gambling with
   dice, (visiting) brothels and taverns.
8. Shapely and slender, and young girls selling fruit.
9. Except that madness, having afflicted a miserable man.
1. Bought was that same cursed, evil deed.

510 Eet of the fruyt defended° on the tree,   *forbidden*
    Anon° he was outcast to wo and peyne.°   *Immediately / pain*
    O glotonye, on thee wel oghte us pleyne!²
        O, wiste a man° how manye maladyes   *(if) a man knew*
    Folwen of° excesse and of glotonyes,   *Follow on*
515 He wolde been the more mesurable°   *measured, temperate*
    Of his diete, sittinge at his table.
    Allas! the shorte throte, the tendre mouth,³
    Maketh that,° est and west, and north and south,   *Causes*
    In erthe, in eir,° in water, men to swinke°   *air / labor*
520 To gete a glotoun deyntee° mete and drinke!   *dainty*
    Of this matere,° O Paul, wel canstow trete:°   *subject / canst thou treat*
    "Mete° unto wombe,° and wombe eek unto mete,   *Food / belly*
    Shal God destroyen bothe," as Paulus seith.⁴
    Allas! a foul thing is it, by my feith,
525 To seye this word, and fouler is the dede,
    Whan man so drinketh of the whyte and rede°   *i.e., wines*
    That of his throte he maketh his privee,°   *privy (toilet)*
    Thurgh thilke° cursed superfluitee.°   *that same / excess*
        The apostel,⁵ weping, seith ful pitously,
530 "Ther walken manye of whiche yow told have I"—
    I seye it now weping with pitous voys—
    "They been enemys of Cristes croys,°   *cross*
    Of which the ende is deeth: wombe° is her° god!"   *belly / their*
    O wombe! O bely! O stinking cod,⁶
535 Fulfild of donge and of corrupcioun!⁷
    At either ende of thee foul is the soun.°   *sound*
    How° greet labour and cost is thee to finde!°   *What / to provide for*
    Thise cookes, how they stampe,° and streyne,° and grinde, *pound / strain*
    And turnen substance into accident,⁸
540 To fulfille al thy likerous talent!°   *lecherous (here, gluttonous) appetite*
    Out of the harde bones knokke they
    The mary,° for they caste noght° awey   *marrow / nothing*
    That may go thurgh the golet° softe and swote;°   *gullet / sweet*
    Of spicerye° of leef, and bark, and rote°   *spices / root(s)*
545 Shal been his sauce y-maked by delyt,°   *to give pleasure*
    To make him yet a newer° appetyt.   *renewed*
    But certes, he that haunteth swich delyces⁹
    Is deed, whyl that° he liveth in tho° vyces.   *while / those*
        A lecherous thing is wyn, and dronkenesse
550 Is ful of stryving° and of wrecchednesse.   *quarreling*
    O dronke man, disfigured is thy face,

2. Oh, gluttony, we certainly ought to complain against you.
3. I.e., the brief pleasure of swallowing, the mouth accustomed to delicacies.
4. 1 Corinthians 6:13.
5. St. Paul. See Philippians 3:18–19.
6. Bag, i.e., the stomach.
7. Filled up with dung and with decaying matter.
8. And turn substance into accident (a scholastic joke: "substance" means essence, essential qualities; "accident," external appearances).
9. But truly, he that gives himself up to such pleasures.

Sour is thy breeth, foul artow° to embrace, *art thou*
And thurgh thy dronke nose semeth the soun° *sound*
As though thou seydest ay° "Sampsoun, Sampsoun";[1] *ever*
555 And yet, God wot,° Sampsoun drank nevere no wyn. *knows*
Thou fallest,° as it were a stiked swyn;° *i.e., down / stuck pig*
Thy tonge is lost, and al thyn honest cure,° *care for decency*
For dronkenesse is verray sepulture° *the true tomb*
Of mannes wit° and his discrecioun.° *understanding / discretion*
560 In whom that° drinke hath dominacioun, *In him whom*
He can no conseil° kepe, it is no drede.° *secrets / doubt*
Now kepe yow fro the whyte and fro the rede—
And namely° fro the whyte wyn of Lepe° *especially / near Cádiz*
That is to selle° in Fishstrete° or in Chepe.° *for sale / Fish Street / Cheapside*
565 This wyn of Spaigne crepeth subtilly
In othere wynes growinge faste by,[2]
Of° which ther ryseth swich fumositee,° *From / vapor*
That whan a man hath dronken draughtes three
And weneth° that he be at hoom in Chepe, *thinks*
570 He is in Spaigne, right at the toune of Lepe,
Nat at The Rochel,° ne at Burdeux toun;° *La Rochelle / Bordeaux*
And thanne wol he seye, "Sampsoun, Sampsoun."
      But herkneth,° lordinges, o° word I yow preye, *listen / one*
That alle the sovereyn actes,° dar I seye, *supreme deeds*
575 Of victories in the Olde Testament,
Thurgh verray° God, that is omnipotent, *true*
Were doon in abstinence and in preyere:
Loketh the Bible, and ther ye may it lere.° *learn*
      Loke Attila,° the grete conquerour, *the Hun*
580 Deyde° in his sleep, with shame and dishonour, *Died*
Bledinge ay° at his nose in dronkenesse: *continually*
A capitayn shoulde live in sobrenesse.
And over al this, avyseth yow right wel° *be well advised*
What was comaunded unto Lamuel°— *Lemuel*
585 Nat Samuel, but Lamuel, seye I—
Redeth the Bible, and finde it expresly
Of wyn-yeving to hem that han justyse.[3]
Namore of this, for it may wel suffyse.
      And now that I have spoke of glotonye,
590 Now wol I yow defenden° hasardrye.° *forbid / gambling at dice*
Hasard is verray moder° of lesinges,° *the true mother / lies*
And of deceite and cursed forsweringes,° *perjuries*
Blaspheme of Crist, manslaughtre, and wast° also *waste*
Of catel° and of tyme; and forthermo, *goods*
595 It is repreve° and contrarie of honour *a reproach*
For to ben holde a commune hasardour.° *gambler*

---

1. A witty kind of onomatopoeia: the snoring sound seems to say "Samson," who was betrayed (see *Wife of Bath's Prologue*, ll. 721–23).
2. That is, the wines sold as French are often mixed with the cheaper wines of Spain.
3. Concerning the giving of wine to those responsible for the law (see Proverbs 31:4–5).

And ever the hyer° he is of estaat°   *higher / in social rank*
The more is he y-holden desolaat:°   *considered debased*
If that a prince useth° hasardrye,   *practices*
600 In alle governaunce and policye
He is, as by commune opinioun,
Y-holde the lasse in reputacioun.
      Stilbon, that was a wys° embassadour,   *wise*
Was sent to Corinthe in ful greet honour,
605 Fro Lacidomie° to make hire alliaunce.°   *Lacedaemon (Sparta) / their alliance*
And whan he cam, him happede par chaunce°   *it happened by chance*
That alle the grettest° that were of that lond,   *greatest (men)*
Pleyinge atte° hasard he hem fond.   *at (the)*
For which, as sone as it mighte be,°   *could be*
610 He stal him° hoom agayn to his contree,   *stole away*
And seyde, "Ther wol I nat lese° my name,°   *lose / (good) name*
Ne I wol nat take on me so greet defame,°   *dishonor*
Yow for to allye° unto none hasardours.°   *to ally / gamblers*
Sendeth othere wyse embassadours—
615 For by my trouthe, me were levere dye°   *I would rather die*
Than I yow sholde to hasardours allye.
For ye that been so glorious in honours
Shul nat allyen yow with hasardours
As by my wil, ne as by my tretee."°   *negotiations*
620 This wyse philosophre, thus seyde he.
      Loke eek° that to the king Demetrius   *also*
The king of Parthes,° as the book seith us,[4]   *Parthia*
Sente him a paire of dees° of gold in scorn,   *dice*
For he hadde used hasard ther-biforn;
625 For which he heeld his glorie or his renoun°   *renown*
At no value or reputacioun.
Lordes may finden other maner pley
Honeste° ynough to dryve the day awey.   *Honorable*
      Now wol I speke of othes° false and grete   *oaths, curses*
630 A word or two, as olde bokes trete.
Gret swering° is a thing abhominable,   *cursing*
And false swering° is yet more reprevable.°   *i.e., of oaths / reproachable*
The heighe° God forbad swering at al—   *high*
Witnesse on Mathew—but in special
635 Of swering seith the holy Jeremye,°   *Jeremiah*
"Thou shalt swere sooth° thyn othes° and nat lye,   *truly / oaths*
And swere in dome,° and eek in   *(good) judgment*
        rightwisnesse;"°   *righteousness*
But ydel° swering is a cursednesse.°   *vain / wickedness*
Bihold and see, that in the first table°   *tablet (of Moses)*
640 Of heighe Goddes hestes° honurable,   *commandments*
How that the seconde heste of him is this:
"Tak nat my name in ydel° or amis."°   *in vain / amiss (wrongly)*
Lo, rather° he forbedeth swich° swering   *earlier (in the list) / such*

4. The *Policraticus* of John of Salisbury, which also contains the preceding story.

Than homicyde or many a cursed thing—
645 I seye that, as by ordre,° thus it stondeth—   *in terms of the order*
This knoweth, that his hestes understondeth,[5]
How that the second heste of God is that.
And forther over,° I wol thee telle al plat°   *moreover / flatly*
That vengeance shal nat parten° from his hous   *depart*
650 That° of his othes is to° outrageous.   *Who / too*
"By Goddes precious herte," and "By his nayles,"
And "By the blode of Crist that is in Hayles,[6]
Seven is my chaunce,[7] and thyn is cink° and treye;"°   *five / three*
"By Goddes armes, if thou falsly pleye,
655 This dagger shal thurghout thyn herte go!"
This fruyt cometh of the bicched bones two—[8]
Forswering,° ire,° falsnesse, homicyde.   *Perjury / anger*
Now for the love of Crist that for us dyde,
Lete° youre othes, bothe grete and smale.   *Cease*
660 But, sires, now wol I telle forth my tale.
    Thise ryotoures° three of which I telle,   *rioters, revelers*
Longe erst er° pryme° rong of any belle,   *before / 9 A.M.*
Were set hem° in a taverne for to drinke;   *Had set themselves down*
And as they sat, they herde a belle clinke
665 Biforn a cors° was° caried to his grave.   *corpse / (which) was (being)*
That oon of hem gan callen to his knave,
"Go bet," quod he, "and axe redily,[9]
What cors is this that passeth heer forby;°   *by here*
And looke that thou reporte his name wel."°   *i.e., correctly*
670 "Sire," quod this boy, "it nedeth never-a-del.°   *it isn't at all necessary*
It was me told, er° ye cam heer two houres.   *before*
He was, pardee,[1] an old felawe° of youres;   *companion*
And sodeynly he was y-slayn tonight,
Fordronke,° as he sat on his bench upright.   *Dead drunk*
675 Ther cam a privee° theef men clepeth° Deeth,   *secret / call*
That in this contree° al the peple sleeth,°   *region / kills*
And with his spere he smoot his herte atwo,[2]
And wente his wey withouten wordes mo.°   *more*
He hath a thousand slayn this pestilence.°   *(during) this plague*
680 And maister, er° ye come in his presence,   *before*
Me thinketh° that it were necessarie   *It seems to me*
For to be war° of swich an adversarie: *aware, careful*
Beth redy for to mete him everemore.°   *always*
Thus taughte me my dame,° I sey namore."   *mother*

---

5. (He) knows this, who understands His commandments.
6. An abbey in Gloucestershire supposed to possess (as a high relic) some of Christ's blood.
7. I.e., throw.
8. This fruit, i.e., result, comes from the two cursed dice. (Dice were made of bone; hence "bones" here.)
9. The one of them proceeded to call to his servant-boy, "Go quickly," he said, "and ask straightway."
1. A weak form of the oath "by God," based on the French *par dieu.*
2. And with his spear he struck his heart in two. (Death was often shown in the visual arts as a hideous skeleton menacing men with a spear or arrow.)

685   "By Seinte Marie," seyde this taverner,°   *tavernkeeper*
  "The child seith sooth, for he hath slayn this yeer,
  Henne° over a myle, withinne a greet village,   *Hence, from here*
  Bothe man and womman, child, and hyne,° and page;° *laborer / servant*
  I trowe° his habitacioun be there.   *believe*
690 To been avysed° greet wisdom it were,   *forewarned*
  Er that° he dide a man a dishonour."   *Before*
      "Ye,° Goddes armes," quod° this ryotour,° *Aye, yes / said / reveler*
  "Is it swich peril with him for to mete?
  I shal him seke by wey° and eek° by strete,   *road / also*
695 I make avow to° Goddes digne° bones!   *avow (it) by / worthy*
  Herkneth felawes, we three been al ones:°   *all of one mind*
  Lat ech° of us holde up his hond til other,°   *each / to the other*
  And ech of us bicomen otheres° brother,   *the others'*
  And we wol sleen° this false traytour Deeth.   *slay*
700 He shal be slayn, he that so manye sleeth,
  By Goddes dignitee,° er it be night."   *worthiness*
      Togidres° han thise three hir trouthes plight° *Together / plighted their troth*
  To live and dyen ech of hem for other,°   *one another*
  As though he were his owene y-boren° brother.   *born*
705 And up they sterte,° al dronken in this rage,°   *leaped / passion*
  And forth they goon towardes that village
  Of which the taverner hadde spoke biforn,
  And many a grisly ooth thanne han they sworn,
  And Cristes blessed body they to-rente°—   *tore apart*
710 Deeth shal be deed, if that they may him hente.°   *seize*
     Whan they han goon nat fully half a myle,
  Right° as they wolde han troden° over a style,° *Just / stepped / stile*
  An old man and a povre° with hem mette.   *poor (one)*
  This olde man ful mekely° hem grette,°   *meekly / greeted them*
715 And seyde thus, "Now, lordes, God yow see!"° *may God protect you*
    The proudest of thise ryotoures three
  Answerde agayn, "What, carl,° with sory grace!° *Hey, fellow / confound you*
  Why artow al forwrapped save thy face?³
  Why livestow° so longe in so greet age?"   *livest thou*
720   This olde man gan loke in° his visage,   *scrutinized*
  And seyde thus, "For° I ne can nat finde   *Because*
  A man, though that I walked into Inde,°   *India*
  Neither in citee nor in no village,
  That wolde chaunge his youthe for myn age;
725 And therfore moot° I han myn age stille,   *must*
  As longe time as it is Goddes wille.
  Ne Deeth, allas! ne wol nat han my lyf.
  Thus walke I, lyk° a restelees caityf,°   *like / captive*
  And on the ground, which is my modres° gate,   *mother's*
730 I knokke with my staf bothe erly and late,
  And seye, 'Leve° moder, leet me in!   *Dear*

3. Why art thou all wrapped up except for thy face?

Lo, how I vanish,° flesh, and blood, and skin!   *waste away*
Allas! whan shul my bones been at reste?
Moder, with yow wolde I chaunge° my cheste°   *exchange / chest (of clothes)*
735 That in my chambre longe tyme hath be,°   *been*
Ye, for an heyre clout° to wrappe me!'   *haircloth (for burial)*
But yet to me she wol nat do that grace,
For which ful pale and welked° is my face.   *withered*
    But sires, to yow it is no curteisye⁴
740 To speken to an old man vileinye,°   *rudeness*
But° he trespasse° in worde or elles° in dede.   *Unless / offend / else*
In Holy Writ ye may yourself wel rede,°   *read*
'Agayns° an old man, hoor° upon his heed,   *Before / hoary, white*
Ye sholde aryse.' Wherfor I yeve yow reed:⁵
745 Ne dooth unto an old man noon harm now,
Namore than that ye wolde men did to yow
In age, if that ye so longe abyde.°   *remain (alive)*
And God be with yow, wher ye go° or ryde;   *walk*
I moot° go thider as° I have to go."   *must / thither where*
750   "Nay, olde cherl, by God, thou shalt nat so,"
Seyde this other hasardour° anon;°   *gambler / at once*
"Thou partest° nat so lightly, by Seint John!   *departest*
Thou spak right now of thilke° traitour Deeth   *that same*
That in this contree alle oure frendes sleeth.
755 Have heer my trouthe,° as° thou art his espye,°   *pledge / since / spy*
Telle wher he is, or thou shalt it abye,°   *pay for*
By God, and by the holy sacrament!
For soothly thou art oon of his assent°   *in league with him*
To sleen us yonge folk, thou false theef!"
760   "Now, sires," quod he, "if that yow be so leef°   *desirous*
To finde Deeth, turne up this croked° wey,   *crooked*
For in that grove I lafte° him, by my fey,°   *left / faith*
Under a tree, and there he wol abyde:°   *stay*
Nat for youre boost he wole him nothing hyde.⁶
765 See ye that ook?° right ther ye shul him finde.   *oak*
God save yow, that boghte agayn° mankinde,   *redeemed*
And yow amende!"° Thus seyde this olde man.   *make you better*
    And everich° of thise ryotoures° ran,   *each / revelers*
Til he cam to that tree, and ther they founde
770 Of florins° fyne of golde y-coyned° rounde   *florins, coins / coined*
Wel ny an° eighte busshels, as hem thoughte.°   *nearly / it seemed to them*
No lenger thanne° after Deeth they soughte,   *No longer then*
But ech° of hem so glad was of that sighte—   *each*
For that the florins been so faire and brighte—
775 That doun they sette hem by this precious hord.
The worste of hem he spake the firste word.
    "Brethren," quod he, "take kepe° what that I seye: *heed*

4. But, sirs, it is not courteous of you.
5. "You should stand up (in respect)." Therefore I give you (this) advice.
6. He won't conceal himself at all because of your boasting.

My wit° is greet, though that I bourde° and pleye.   *understanding / jest*

This tresor° hath Fortune unto us yiven°   *treasure / given*

780 In mirthe and jolitee° our lyf to liven,   *merriment*

And lightly as it comth, so wol we spende.

Ey! Goddes precious dignitee!° who wende°   *worthiness / would have supposed*

Today that we sholde han so fair a grace?°   *favor*

But° mighte this gold be caried fro this place   *If only*

785 Hoom to myn hous—or elles unto youres—

For wel ye woot° that al this gold is oures—   *know*

Thanne were we in heigh felicitee.°   *supreme happiness*

But trewely, by daye it may nat be:°   *be (done)*

Men wolde seyn that we were theves stronge,°   *flagrant*

790 And for oure owene tresor doon us honge.°   *have us hanged*

This tresor moste y-caried be by nighte,

As wysly° and as slyly° as it mighte.°   *prudently / craftily / can (be)*

Wherfore I rede° that cut° among us alle   *advise / lots, straws*

Be drawe,° and lat se wher the cut wol falle;   *drawn, pulled*

795 And he that hath the cut with herte blythe

Shal renne° to the toune, and that ful swythe,°   *run / quickly*

And bringe us breed and wyn ful prively.°   *secretly*

And two of us shul kepen° subtilly°   *guard / carefully*

This tresor wel; and if he wol nat tarie,°   *tarry*

800 Whan it is night we wol this tresor carie,

By oon assent, where as us thinketh best."[7]

That oon of hem the cut broughte in his fest,°   *fist*

And bad hem drawe, and loke wher it wol falle;

And it fil on the yongeste of hem alle,

805 And forth toward the toun he wente anon.

And also sone as° that he was agon,   *as soon as*

That oon of hem° spak thus unto that other: *The one of them*

"Thou knowest wel thou art my sworne brother;

Thy profit° wol I telle thee anon.   *Something to thy advantage*

810 Thou woost° wel that oure felawe is agon,°   *knowest / gone*

And heer is gold, and that° ful greet plentee,   *that (in)*

That shal departed° been among us three.   *divided*

But natheles,° if I can shape° it so   *nonetheless / arrange*

That it departed were among us two,

815 Hadde I nat doon a freendes torn° to thee?"   *turn*

That other answerde, "I noot° how that may be: *know not*

He woot how that the gold is with us tweye.

What shal we doon? what shal we to him seye?"

"Shal it be conseil?"° seyde the firste shrewe;°   *a secret / wretch*

820 "And I shal tellen in a wordes fewe

What we shal doon, and bringe it wel aboute."

"I graunte,"° quod that other, "out of doute,[8]   *grant (it)*

That, by my trouthe, I wol thee nat biwreye."°   *betray*

"Now," quod the firste, "thou woost° wel we be tweye,°   *knowest / two*

---

7. By common assent, wherever seems to us best.
8. I.e., you can be sure.

825 And two of us shul strenger° be than oon.   *stronger*
Looke whan that he is set,° that right anoon°   *has sat down / right away*
Arys° as though thou woldest with him pleye;   *Arise (get up)*
And I shal ryve° him thurgh the sydes tweye°   *stab / through his two sides*
Whyl that thou strogelest° with him as in game,°   *strugglest / as if in play*
830 And with thy dagger looke° thou do the same;   *take heed*
And thanne shall al this gold departed° be,   *divided*
My dere freend, bitwixen me and thee.
Thanne may we bothe oure lustes° al fulfille,   *desires*
And pleye at dees° right at oure owene wille."   *dice*
835 And thus acorded° been thise shrewes° tweye   *agreed / cursed fellows*
To sleen the thridde, as ye han herd me seye.
    This yongest, which that wente unto the toun,
Ful ofte in herte he rolleth up and doun°   *i.e., thinks on*
The beautee of thise florins newe and brighte.
840 "O Lord!" quod he, "if so were that I mighte
Have al this tresor to myself allone,
Ther is no man that liveth under the trone°   *throne*
Of God that sholde live so mery as I!"
And atte laste° the feend,° our enemy,   *at (the) last / devil*
845 Putte in his thought that he shold poyson beye,°   *buy poison*
With which he mighte sleen his felawes tweye°—   *two companions*
For-why the feend fond him in swich lyvinge⁹
That he had leve° him to sorwe bringe: *permission (from God)*
For this was outrely° his fulle entente,°   *completely / purpose*
850 To sleen hem bothe, and nevere to repente.
And forth he gooth—no lenger wolde he tarie—
Into the toun, unto a pothecarie,°   *apothecary, pharmacist*
And preyed° him that he him wolde selle   *asked*
Som poyson, that° he mighte his rattes quelle,°   *so that / kill his rats*
855 And eek° ther was a polcat° in his hawe,°   *also / weasel / yard*
That, as he seyde, his capouns° hadde y-slawe,°   *capons / killed*
And fayn° he wolde wreke him,° if he mighte,   *gladly / avenge himself*
On vermin, that destroyed° him by nighte.   *were ruining*
    The pothecarie answerde, "And thou shalt have
860 A thing that, also° God my soule save,   *so (may)*
In al this world ther nis no° creature,   *is not any*
That ete or dronke hath of this confiture°   *mixture*
Noght but the mountance of a corn of whete,¹
That he ne shal his lyf anon° forlete.°   *at once / lose*
865 Ye,° sterve° he shal, and that in lasse whyle°   *Yes / die / shorter time*
Than thou wolt goon a paas° nat but° a myle,   *walk at normal pace / only*
This poyson is so strong and violent."
    This cursed man hath in his hond y-hent°   *grasped*
This poyson in a box, and sith° he ran   *afterward*
870 Into the nexte strete unto a man
And borwed [of] him large botels° three,   *bottles (probably of leather)*

9. Because the fiend (the devil) found him living in such a way.
1. No more than the quantity of a grain of wheat.

And in the two his poyson poured he—
The thridde he kepte clene for his° drinke—   his (own)
For al the night he shoop him° for to swinke°   was preparing himself / work
875 In carying of the gold out of that place.
And whan this ryotour, with sory grace,°   i.e., blessed by evil
Hadde filled with wyn his grete botels three,
To his felawes agayn repaireth° he.   returns
    What nedeth it to sermone° of it more?   speak
880 For right as they hadde cast° his deeth bifore,   planned
Right so they han him slayn, and that anon.°   immediately
And whan that this was doon, thus spak that oon:
"Now lat us sitte and drinke, and make us merie,
And afterward we wol his body berie."°   bury
885 And with that word it happed° him, par cas,°   befell / by chance
To take the botel ther° the poyson was,   where
And drank, and yaf° his felawe drink also,   gave
For which anon they storven° bothe two.   died
    But certes, I suppose that Avicen
890 Wroot nevere in no canon, ne in no fen,
Mo wonder signes of empoisoning[2]
Than hadde thise wrecches two, er° hir° ending.   before / their
Thus ended been thise homicydes two,
And eek° the false empoysoner° also.°   also / poisoner / as well
895   O cursed sinne of alle cursednesse!
O traytours° homicyde, O wikkednesse!   traitorous
O glotonye, luxurie,° and hasardrye!   lechery
Thou blasphemour of Crist with vileinye°   vile speech
And othes grete, of usage° and of pryde!   out of habit
900 Allas! mankinde, how may it bityde°   happen
That to thy Creatour which that thee wroghte,
And with his precious herte-blood thee boghte,°   redeemed
Thou art so fals and so unkinde,° allas!   unnatural
    Now, goode men, God forgeve° yow youre trespas,   may God forgive
905 And ware yow fro° the sinne of avaryce.   make you beware of
Myn holy pardoun may yow alle waryce°—   cure
So that ye offre nobles or sterlinges,[3]
Or elles silver broches, spones,° ringes.   spoons
Boweth youre heed° under this holy bulle!   head
910 Cometh up, ye wyves, offreth of youre wolle!°   wool
Youre names I entre heer in my rolle° anon:°   roll, list / at once
Into the blisse of hevene shul ye gon.
I yow assoile,° by myn heigh power—   absolve
Yow that wol offre°—as clene and eek as cleer°   make an offering / pure
915 As ye were born.—And, lo, sires, thus I preche.
And Jesu Crist, that is our soules leche,°   healer, doctor
So graunte° yow his pardon to receyve,   May He grant

2. But truly, I would guess that Avicenna (an Islamic physician and author) never described, in
   any treatise or chapter, more terrible symptoms of poisoning.
3. As long as you offer nobles (gold coins) or silver pennies.

For that is best; I wol yow nat deceyve.
   But sires, o° word forgat I in my tale: *a, one*
920 I have relikes and pardon in my male°   *pouch*
As faire as any man in Engelond,
Whiche were me yeven° by the Popes hond.   *given*
If any of yow wol of devocioun°   *out of devotion*
Offren and han myn absolucioun,
925 Cometh forth anon, and kneleth heer adoun,
And mekely receyveth my pardoun;
Or elles, taketh pardon as ye wende,°   *travel*
Al newe and fresh, at every myles ende—
So that ye offren alwey newe and newe[4]
930 Nobles or pens,° which that be gode and trewe.   *pence*
It is an honour to everich° that is heer   *every one*
That ye mowe° have a suffisant° pardoneer   *may / capable*
T'assoille° yow, in contree as ye ryde,   *To absolve*
For aventures whiche that may bityde.[5]
935 Peraventure° ther may falle oon or two   *By chance*
Doun of his hors, and breke his nekke atwo.°   *in two*
Look which a seuretee° is it to you alle   *what a security*
That I am in youre felaweship y-falle,
That may assoille yow, bothe more and lasse,°   *great and small*
940 Whan that the soule shal fro the body passe.
I rede° that oure Host heer shal biginne,   *advise*
For he is most envoluped° in sinne.   *enveloped, wrapped up*
Com forth, sire Hoste, and offre first anon,°   *first now*
And thou shalt kisse the reliks everichon,°   *every one*
945 Ye, for a grote:° unbokel° anon thy purs."   *groat (four pence) / unbuckle*
   "Nay, nay," quod° he, "thanne have I Cristes curs!   *said*
Lat be," quod he, "it shal nat be, so theech!°   *as I hope to prosper*
Thou woldest make me kisse thyn olde breech°   *breeches*
And swere it were a relik of a seint,
950 Thogh it were with thy fundement° depeint!°   *fundament (rectum) / stained*
But by the croys° which that Seint Eleyne° fond,   *(true) Cross / St. Helena*
I wolde I hadde thy coillons° in myn hond   *testicles*
In stede of relikes or of seintuarie.°   *i.e., holy things*
Lat cutte hem of! I wol thee helpe hem carie.[6]
955 Thay shul be shryned° in an hogges tord!"°   *enshrined / turd*
   This Pardoner answerde nat a word;
So wrooth° he was, no word ne wolde he seye.   *wroth, angered*
   "Now," quod our Host, "I wol no lenger pleye
With thee, ne with noon other angry man."
960 But right anon the worthy Knight bigan,
Whan that he saugh that al the peple lough,°   *laughed*
"Namore of this, for it is right ynough!°   *quite enough*
Sire Pardoner, be glad and mery of chere;°   *mood*

4. As long as you make offering anew each time (of).
5. In respect to things which may befall.
6. Have them cut off! I'll help thee carry them.

And ye, sire Host, that been to me so dere,
965 I prey yow that ye kisse the Pardoner.
And Pardoner, I prey thee, drawe thee neer,
And, as we diden, lat us laughe and pleye."
Anon° they kiste, and riden forth hir weye.°   *At once / (on) their way*

The Prioress's Prologue and Tale

The Introduction

435   "Well seyd, by *corpus dominus*,"° quod° oure Hoste,   *the Lord's body / said*
"Now longe moot° thou sayle by the coste,°   *may / sail along the coast*
Sire gentil maister, gentil marineer![1]
God yeve this monk a thousand last quad yeer![2]
A ha! felawes!° beth ware of swiche° a jape!°   *companions / such / trick*
440 The monk putte in the mannes hood an ape,[3]
And in his wyves eek,° by Seint Austin!°   *as well / Augustine*
Draweth° no monkes more unto youre in.°   *Take / lodging*
     But now passe over,° and lat us seke aboute,   *on*
Who shal now telle first, of al this route,°   *company*
445 Another tale;" and with that word he sayde,
As curteisly as it had been a mayde,[4]
"My lady Prioresse, by your leve,
So that I wiste° I sholde yow nat greve,°   *knew / vex*
I wolde demen° that ye tellen sholde   *would decide*
450 A tale next, if so were that ye wolde.°   *were willing*
Now wol ye vouche sauf,° my lady dere?"   *agree*
     "Gladly," quod she, and seyde as ye shal here.

The Prologue

Domine, dominus noster.°   *Oh Lord, our lord*

     O Lord, oure Lord, thy name how merveillous°   *marvelously*
Is in this large worlde y-sprad°—quod° she—   *spread / said*
455 For noght only thy laude° precious   *praise*
Parfourned° is by men of dignitee,   *Celebrated, performed*
But by the mouth of children thy bountee°   *goodness*
Parfourned is, for on the brest soukinge°   *sucking*
Somtyme shewen° they thyn heryinge.°   *show forth / praise*

460 Wherfore in laude,° as I best can or may,   *praise*
Of thee, and of the whyte lily flour°   *i.e., the Virgin*
Which that thee bar,° and is a mayde° alway,   *Who bore thee / virgin*
To telle a storie I wol do my labour;

---

1. The Shipman has just told his tale of a merchant, his wife, and a lecherous monk.
2. God give this monk a thousand cartloads of bad years.
3. The monk put an ape in the man's hood, i.e., made a fool of him.
4. As courteously as if it had been a maiden (speaking).

Not that I may encresen° hir honour,   *increase*
465 For she hirself is honour, and the rote°   *root*
Of bountee, next° hir sone, and soules bote.°   *next (to) / help*

O moder mayde! o mayde moder free!°   *gracious, bountiful*
O bush unbrent, brenninge in Moyses sighte,[5]
That ravysedest° doun fro the deitee,   *ravished*
470 Thurgh thyn humblesse, the goost° that in   *(Holy) Spirit*
        th'alighte,°   *alighted in thee*
Of whos vertu, whan he thyn herte lighte,
Conceived was the Fadres sapience,[6]
Help me to telle it in thy reverence!

Lady, thy bountee, thy magnificence,
475 Thy vertu, and thy grete humilitee,
Ther may° no tonge expresse in no science;°   *can / whatever its learning*
For somtyme, lady, er° men praye to thee,   *before*
Thou goost biforn° of thy benignitee,   *proceedest*
And getest us the light, of° thy preyere,   *by means of*
480 To gyden° us unto thy Sone so dere.   *guide*

My conning° is so wayk,° o blisful Quene,   *skill / weak*
For to declare thy grete worthinesse,
That I ne may the weighte nat sustene;
But as a child of twelf monthe old, or lesse,
485 That can unnethes° any word expresse,   *hardly*
Right so fare I, and therfor I yow preye,
Gydeth° my song that I shal of yow seye.   *Guide*

The Tale

Ther was in Asie,° in a greet citee,   *Asia (Minor)*
Amonges Cristen folk, a Jewerye°   *Jews' quarter*
490 Sustened by a lord of that contree
For foule usure° and lucre of vileynye,°   *usury / wicked financial gain*
Hateful to Crist and to his compaignye;°   *i.e., Christians*
And thurgh° the strete men mighte ryde or wende,°   *through / go*
For it was free, and open at either ende.

495 A litel scole° of Cristen° folk ther stood   *school / Christian*
Doun at the ferther ende, in which ther were
Children an heep,° y-comen° of Cristen blood,   *many, a crowd / come*
That lerned in that scole yeer by yere
Swich manere doctrine as men used there—[7]

---

5. Oh, bush unburned, burning in Moses's sight (a common figure for the miracle of Mary's
   virginity, preserved even in her motherhood of Christ; ultimately based on Exodus 3:1–5).
6. Through whose power, when he illumined thy heart, was conceived the Wisdom of the Father, i.e., Christ, the Logos.
7. Such kinds of subjects as were usual there.

500 This is to seyn,° to singen and to rede,°   *say / read*
    As smale children doon in hire childhede.

    Among thise children was a widwes° sone,   *widow's*
    A litel clergeoun,° seven yeer of age,   *schoolboy*
    That day by day to° scole was his wone,°   *i.e., to go to / custom*
505 And eek also, where as° he saugh° th'ymage   *wherever / saw*
    Of Cristes moder, hadde he in usage,°   *he was accustomed*
    As him was taught, to knele adoun and seye
    His *Ave Marie,*° as he goth by the weye.   *Hail, Mary*

    Thus hath this widwe hir litel sone y-taught
510 Our blisful Lady, Cristes moder dere,
    To worshipe ay;° and he forgat it naught,   *always*
    For sely child wol alday sone lere.[8]
    But ay,° whan I remembre° on this matere,   *ever / i.e., think, meditate*
    Seint Nicholas[9] stant° evere in my presence,   *stands*
515 For he so yong to Crist did reverence.°   *honored*

    This litel child, his litel book lerninge,
    As he sat in the scole at his prymer,[1]
    He *Alma redemptoris*[2] herde singe,
    As children lerned hire antiphoner,°   *their anthem-book*
520 And, as he dorste, he drough him ner and ner,[3]
    And herkned ay° the wordes and the note,°   *ever / music*
    Til he the firste vers coude° al by rote.°   *knew / by heart*

    Noght wiste° he what this Latin was to seye,°   *knew / meant*
    For he so yong and tendre was of age;
525 But on a day his felaw gan he preye[4]
    T'expounden him this song in his langage,°   *his own language*
    Or telle him why this song was in usage;°   *used*
    This preyde he him to construe° and declare   *interpret*
    Ful ofte tyme upon his knowes° bare.   *knees*

530 His felawe, which that elder was than he,
    Answerde him thus: "This song, I have herd seye,
    Was maked of° our blisful Lady free,°   *about / generous*
    Hire to salue,° and eek° hire for to preye   *salute, greet / also*
    To been oure help and socour° whan we dye.°   *succor, aid / die*
535 I can no more expounde in this matere:
    I lerne song, I can° but smal° grammere."   *know / little*

---

8. For a good child will always learn quickly.
9. St. Nicholas is said to have fasted even as an infant; he took the breast only once on Wednesdays and Fridays. He is also the patron saint of schoolboys.
1. A prayerbook used as an elementary school text.
2. For text and translation of this anthem, see p. 448.
3. And, as (much as) he dared, he drew nearer and nearer.
4. But one day he begged his companion.

"And is this song maked in reverence
Of Cristes moder?" seyde this innocent.
"Now certes,° I wol do my diligence   *certainly*
540 To conne° it al, er° Cristemasse be went.°   *learn / before / is passed*
Though that I for my prymer⁵ shal be shent,°   *scolded*
And shal be beten thryes° in an houre,   *thrice*
I wol it conne, oure Lady for to honoure."

His felaw taughte him homward prively,⁶
545 Fro day to day, til he coude° it by rote,   *knew*
And thanne he song° it wel and boldely°   *sang / forcefully*
Fro word to word, acording with the note;
Twyes° a day it passed thurgh his throte,   *Twice*
To scoleward° and homward whan he wente.   *Toward school*
550 On Cristes moder set was his entente.°   *(heart's) intent*

As I have seyd, thurghout the Jewerye
This litel child, as he cam to and fro,
Ful merily than wolde he singe and crye°   *cry out*
O *Alma redemptoris* everemo.
555 The swetnesse his herte perced° so   *pierced*
Of Cristes moder, that, to hire to preye,
He can nat stinte of° singing by° the weye.   *cease from / along*

Oure firste fo,° the serpent Sathanas,°   *foe / Satan*
That hath in Jewes herte his waspes nest,
560 Up swal° and seide, "O Hebraik peple, allas!   *swelled*
Is this to yow a thing that is honest,°   *honorable, seemly*
That swich° a boy shal walken as him lest°   *such / it pleases him*
In youre despyt, and singe of swich sentence,⁷
Which is agayn° oure lawes reverence?"⁸   *against*

565 Fro thennes forth° the Jewes han° conspyred   *thenceforth / have*
This innocent out of this world to chace:°   *drive*
An homicyde° therto han they hyred,°   *murderer / hired*
That in an aley° hadde a privee° place;   *alley / secret*
And as the child gan forby for to pace,°   *was walking by*
570 This cursed Jew him hente° and heeld him faste,   *seized*
And kitte° his throte, and in a pit him caste.   *cut*

I seye that in a wardrobe° they him threwe   *privy*
Where as these Jewes purgen hir entraille.⁹
O cursed folk of Herodes° al newe,°   *Herod / always renewed*
575 What may youre yvel entente° yow availle?   *evil plan*
Mordre° wol out, certein, it wol nat faille,   *Murder*

5. I.e., for failing to study my primer.
6. His companion taught him (on the way) homeward, privately.
7. In scorn of you, and sing of such a subject.
8. The best manuscripts read "oure," as here; some read "youre."
9. Where these Jews empty their bowels.

And namely ther° th'onour of God shal sprede,   *there where*
The blood out cryeth on your cursed dede.

O martir souded to° virginitee,   *made fast in*
580 Now maystou° singen, folwinge evere in oon°   *mayest thou / forever*
The Whyte Lamb celestial—quod she—
Of which the grete evangelist Seint John
In Pathmos[1] wroot, which seith that they that goon°   *walk*
Biforn° this Lamb and singe a song al newe,°   *Before / wholly new*
585 That nevere, fleshly,° wommen they ne knewe.   *carnally*

This povre widwe° awaiteth al that night   *poor widow*
After hir litel child, but he cam noght;
For which, as sone as it was dayes light,
With face pale of drede° and bisy thoght,°   *fear / anxiety*
590 She hath at scole and elleswhere him soght,
Til finally she gan so fer espye°   *found out this much*
That he last seyn° was in the Jewerye.   *seen*

With modres pitee in hir brest enclosed,
She gooth, as° she were half out of hir minde,   *as if*
595 To every place wher she hath supposed
By lyklihede hir litel child to finde.
And evere on Cristes moder meke and kinde
She cryde, and atte laste thus she wroghte:[2]
Among the cursed Jewes she him soghte.

600 She frayneth° and she preyeth° pitously   *inquires / begs*
To every Jew that dwelte in thilke° place,   *that same*
To telle hire if hir child wente oght forby.°   *by at all*
They seyde "Nay"; but Jesu, of° his grace,   *by*
Yaf in hir thought, inwith a litel space,[3]
605 That° in that place after hir sone she cryde°   *So that / called*
Where he was casten in a pit bisyde.°   *nearby*

O grete God, that parfournest thy laude[4]
By mouth of innocents, lo heer° thy might!   *behold here*
This gemme of chastitee, this emeraude,°   *emerald*
610 And eek° of martirdom the ruby bright,   *also*
Ther he with throte y-corven lay upright,[5]
He *Alma redemptoris* gan° to singe   *began*
So loude that al the place gan to ringe.°   *resounded*

The Cristen folk, that thurgh the strete wente,
615 In coomen° for to wondre upon this thing,   *came*

1. The isle of Patmos in Greece, where St. John wrote the Book of Revelation.
2. She called, and in the end she did thus.
3. Gave her an idea, within a little while.
4. Oh, great God, that (hast) thy praise performed.
5. There where he lay face-up, with his throat cut.

And hastily they for the provost° sente;   *magistrate*
He cam anon withouten tarying,
And herieth° Crist that is of heven king,   *praises*
And eek° his moder, honour of mankinde,   *also*
620 And after that the Jewes leet he binde.°   *he had bound*

This child with pitous lamentacioun
Up taken was, singing his song alway;
And with honour of greet processioun
They carien him unto the nexte abbay.°   *nearest abbey*
625 His moder swowning° by his bere° lay.   *swooning / bier*
Unnethe° might the peple that was there   *Scarcely*
This newe Rachel⁶ bringe fro his bere.

With torment° and with shamful deth echon°   *torture / each one*
This provost dooth° thise Jewes for to sterve°   *causes / die*
630 That of this mordre wiste,° and that anon;°   *knew / immediately*
He nolde no swich cursednesse observe.⁷
"Yvel shal have that yvel wol deserve:"⁸
Therfore with wilde hors° he dide hem   *horses*
    drawe,°   *had them drawn, dragged*
And after that he heng° hem by the lawe.   *hanged (probably on pikes)*

635 Upon his bere al lyth° this innocent   *still lies*
Biforn the chief auter,° whyl the masse° laste,   *altar / the mass*
And after that, the abbot with his covent°   *monks*
Han sped hem° for to burien him ful faste;   *have hastened*
And whan they holy water on him caste,
640 Yet spak this child, whan spreynd° was holy water,   *sprinkled*
And song° O *Alma redemptoris mater!*   *sang*

This abbot, which that was an holy man
As monkes been°—or elles oghten° be—   *are / else ought to*
This yonge child to conjure° he bigan,   *entreat*
645 And seyde, "O dere child, I halse° thee,   *beg*
In vertu of the Holy Trinitee,
Tel me what is thy cause for to singe,
Sith that° thy throte is cut, to my seminge?"°   *Since / it seems to me*

"My throte is cut unto my nekke-boon,"
650 Seyde this child, "and, as by wey of kinde,°   *nature*
I sholde have deyed, ye,° longe tyme agoon,°   *yea, yes / ago*
But Jesu Crist, as ye in bokes finde,
Wil° that his glorie laste and be in minde;   *Wills*

---

6. This second Rachel (a grieving Jewish mother, in Jeremiah 31:15, who was said to prefigure
   the grieving mothers of the innocents slain by command of Herod, in Matthew 2:18).
7. He would not tolerate such evil doings.
8. "He who will deserve evil shall have evil."

And for the worship of his moder dere
655 Yet° may I singe O *Alma* loude and clere.   *Still*

This welle° of mercy, Cristes moder swete,   *spring*
I lovede alwey as after my conninge;°   *as best I could*
And whan that I my lyf sholde forlete,°   *was to leave*
To me she cam, and bad me for to singe
660 This antem° verraily° in my deyinge,   *hymn / truly*
As ye han herd; and whan that I had songe,
Me thoughte she leyde a greyn° upon my tonge.   *seed*

Wherfore I singe, and singe moot certeyn,°   *indeed must*
In honour of that blisful mayden free,°   *generous*
665 Til fro my tonge of° taken is the greyn;   *off*
And afterward thus seyde she to me,
'My litel child, now wol I fecche° thee   *fetch*
Whan that the greyn is fro thy tongue y-take;
Be nat agast,° I wol thee nat forsake.' "   *afraid*

670 This holy monk, this abbot, him mene I,
His tongue out caughte and took awey the greyn,
And he yaf° up the goost ful softely.   *gave*
And whan this abbot had this wonder seyn,°   *seen*
His salte teres° trikled doun as reyn,°   *tears / like rain*
675 And gruf° he fil al plat° upon the grounde,   *face downward / flat*
And stille° he lay as° he had been y-bounde.   *(as) quietly / as if*

The covent° eek° lay on the pavement,   *monks / also*
Weping and herying° Cristes moder dere,   *praising*
And after that they ryse, and forth ben went,°   *have gone*
680 And toke awey this martir fro his bere,°   *bier*
And in a tombe of marbulstones clere°   *bright, splendid*
Enclosen they his litel body swete.
Ther° he is now, God leve° us for to mete.°   *Where / grant / meet*

O yonge Hugh of Lincoln,[9] slayn also
685 With° cursed Jewes, as it is notable°—   *By / well known*
For it nis° but a litel whyle ago—   *is not*
Preye eek° for us, we sinful folk unstable,°   *also / unsteadfast*
That, of his mercy, God so merciable°   *merciful*
On us his grete mercy multiplye,
690 For reverence of his moder Marye. Amen.

9. Hugh of Lincoln was thought to have been murdered by Jews in a similar fashion in 1255.

The Prologue and Tale of Sir Thopas

The Prologue

Whan seyd was al this miracle,° every man	*i.e., the Prioress's tale of a miracle*
As sobre was° that wonder was to se,	*Was so grave, serious*
Til that our Hoste japen tho bigan,°	*began then to jest, joke*
And than at erst° he loked upon me	*for the first time*
695 And seyde thus: "What man artow?"° quod he.	*art thou*
"Thou lokest as° thou woldest finde an hare,	*as if*
For ever upon the ground I see thee stare.	

Approche neer° and loke up merily.	*nearer*
Now war yow,° sirs, and lat this man have place.	*pay attention*
700 He in the waast° is shape as wel as I.	*waist*
This were a popet° in an arm t'enbrace°	*little doll / to embrace*
For any womman, smal and fair of face.	
He semeth elvish by his contenaunce,[1]	
For unto no wight° dooth he daliaunce.°	*person / is he sociable*

705 Sey now somwhat, sin° other folk han sayd.°	*since / have spoken*
Tel us a tale of mirthe, and that anoon."	
"Hoste," quod I, "ne beth nat yvel apayd,°	*do not be displeased*
For other tale certes° can° I noon,	*certainly / know*
But of° a ryme I lerned longe agoon."	*Except*
710 "Ye, that is good," quod he. "Now shul we here	
Som deyntee° thing, me thinketh by his chere."°	*pleasant / look, expression*

The Tale

[THE FIRST FIT][2]

Listeth,° lordes, in good entent,°	*Listen / with good will*
And I wol telle verrayment°	*truly*
Of mirthe and of solas:	
715 Al of a knyght was fair and gent°	*noble, elegant*
In bataille and in tourneyment;	
His name was sir Thopas.°	*topaz (a yellow semiprecious stone)*

Y-born he was in fer° contree,	*far, distant*
In Flaundres° al biyonde the see,	*Flanders (Belgium)*
720 At Popering,° in the place.	*a Flemish market town*
His fader was a man ful free,°	*noble, generous*

---

1. He seems elfish, from the look of him. "Elvish" is often glossed as "distracted, abstracted" but literally means someone mysterious, from another world of being; cf. the realm of "Fairye" (l. 802).
2. We follow John Burrow's argument that the Tale of Sir Thopas is divided into three parts or "fits" (see l. 888), the second fit half as long as the first, the third half as long as the second.

And lord he was of that contree,
  As it was Goddes grace.

Sir Thopas wex a doghty swayn.°   *grew into a bold young man, squire*
725 Whyt was his face as payndemayn,°   *fine white bread*
  His lippes rede as rose.
  His rode° is lyk scarlet in grayn,°   *complexion / scarlet dye*
  And I yow telle in good certayn,°   *in certainty*
    He hadde a semely° nose.   *seemly, handsome*

730 His heer, his berd was lyk saffroun,°   *saffron (deep yellow)*
  That to his girdel° raughte° adoun;   *belt / reached*
    His shoon° of Cordewane.°   *shoes / cordovan (Spanish) leather*
  Of Brugges° were his hosen broun,°   *Bruges (in Flanders) / brown tights*
  His robe was of ciclatoun,°   *costly embroidered silk*
735   That coste many a jane.°   *a silver coin of Genoa*

He coude° hunte at wilde deer,°   *knew how to / animals*
  And ryde an hauking for riveer°   *go hawking for waterfowl*
    With grey goshauk° on honde.   *a kind of hawk*
  Therto° he was a good archeer;   *In addition*
740 Of wrastling was ther noon his peer,°   *equal*
    Ther° any ram shal stonde.°   *Where / be put up as a prize (see GP l. 548)*

Ful many a mayde, bright in bour,°   *bedchamber*
  They moorne° for him paramour,°   *yearn / with love-longing*
    Whan hem were bet° to slepe.   *it would be better for them*
745 But he was chast° and no lechour,°   *chaste / lecher*
  And sweet as is the bremble-flour°   *bramble flower (dog rose)*
    That bereth the rede hepe.°   *rose hip*

And so bifel° upon a day,   *it happened*
  For sothe,° as I yow telle may,   *In truth*
750   Sir Thopas wolde out ryde.°   *decided to ride out*
  He worth upon° his stede° gray,   *gets up on / steed*
  And in his honde a launcegay,°   *a light lance*
    A long swerd by his syde.

He priketh° thurgh a fair forest,   *pricks, spurs his horse*
755 Therinne is many a wilde best,
    Ye, bothe bukke° and hare;   *buck, male deer*
  And as he priketh north and est,
  I telle it yow, him° hadde almest°   *(to) him / almost*
    Bitid° a sory care.°   *Happened / sad misfortune*

760 Ther springen herbes grete and smale,
  The lycorys° and cetewale,°   *licorice / zedoary (like ginger)*
    And many a clowe-gilofre;°   *clove*
  And notemuge° to putte in ale,   *nutmeg*

Whether it be moyste° or stale,°   *fresh / stale, old*
765   Or for to leye in cofre.°³   *put in a chest*

The briddes singe, it is no nay,°   *it cannot be denied*
The sparhauk° and the papeiay,°   *sparrow hawk / parrot*
     That joye it was to here.°   *hear (them)*
The thrustelcok° made eek his lay,°   *male thrush / also sang (composed) his song*
770 The wodedowve° upon the spray°   *wood pigeon / branch*
     She sang ful loude and clere.

Sir Thopas fil° in love-longinge   *fell*
Al whan he herde the thrustel° singe,   *thrush*
     And priked° as he were wood.°   *rode / mad*
775 His faire stede° in° his prikinge   *steed / because of*
So swatte° that men mighte him wringe;   *sweated*
     His sydes were al blood.°   *covered with blood*

Sir Thopas eek so wery was
For prikinge on the softe gras
780   (So fiers° was his corage°)   *fierce, ferocious / heart, spirit*
That doun he leyde him in that plas°   *place*
To make° his stede som solas,°   *give / respite, comfort*
     And yaf° him good forage.°   *gave / feeding*

"O seinte Marie, *benedicite!*°   *bless me*
785 What eyleth this love at me°   *does love have against me*
     To binde me so sore?
Me dremed al this night, pardee,°   *by God*
An elf-queen° shal my lemman° be,   *fairy queen / lover, sweetheart*
     And slepe under my gore.°   *robe, cloak*

790 An elf-queen wol I love, ywis,°   *indeed*
For in this world no womman is
     Worthy to be my make°   *mate, match*
          In toune.°   *in (any) town*
Alle othere wommen I forsake,
795 And to an elf-queen I me take
     By dale° and eek by doune."°   *valley / hill*

Into his sadel he clamb anoon°   *quickly climbed*
And priketh over style° and stoon   *stile*
     An elf-queen for t'espye,°   *to discover*
800 Til he so longe had riden and goon
That he fond, in a privee woon,°   *secret place*
     The contree of Fairye
          So wilde.

---

3. None of the spice-bearing plants named in this stanza would be found growing in Flanders.
Like many other details in the story, they are part of the exotic landscape of romance that
Chaucer playfully invokes throughout.

For in that contree was ther noon
805 That to° him dorste° ryde or goon—   *against / dared*
    Neither wyf ne childe—

    Til that ther cam a greet geaunt;°   *giant*
    His name was sir Olifaunt,°   *Sir Elephant*
    A perilous man of dede.°   *in (his) actions*
810 He seyde, "Child,° by Termagaunt,°   *Noble youth / (supposedly a Saracen god)*
    But if° thou prike° out of myn haunt,°   *Unless / ride / territory*
    Anon I slee° thy stede   *will slay*
        With mace.°   *a spiked warclub*
    Heer is the queen of Fayerye,°   *the magical otherworld*
815 With harpe and pype and simphonye°   *a stringed instrument*
    Dwelling in this place."

    The child seyde, "Also mote I thee,°   *So may I thrive (I swear)*
    Tomorwe wol I mete thee
      Whan I have myn armoure;
820 And yet I hope, *par ma fay*,°   *by my faith*
    That thou shalt with this launcegay°   *light lance*
    Abyen it ful soure.°   *Pay for it very sourly, bitterly*
        Thy mawe°   *stomach, belly*
    Shal I percen,° if I may,   *pierce*
825 Er it be fully pryme° of day,   *9 A.M.*
    For heer thou shalt be slawe."°   *slain*

    Sir Thopas drow° abak ful faste;   *drew*
    This geaunt at him stones caste
    Out of a fel staf-slinge.°   *terrifying sling-shot*
830 But faire° escapeth child Thopas,   *fairly, safely*
    And al it was thurgh Goddes gras°   *grace*
    And thurgh his fair beringe.°   *behavior, conduct*

[THE SECOND FIT]

    Yet listeth,° lordes, to my tale   *listen*
    Merier than the nightingale,
835   For now I wol yow roune°   *tell (whisper)*
    How sir Thopas, with sydes smale,°   *slender waist*
    Priking over hil and dale,
      Is come agayn to toune.

    His merie men° comanded he   *companions in arms*
840 To make him bothe game and glee,°   *entertainment and music*
    For nedes moste he fight
    With a geaunt with hevedes° three,   *heads*
    For paramour° and jolitee°   *love / pleasure*
    Of oon° that shoon ful brighte.   *i.e., the elf queen*

845 "Do come,"° he seyde, "my minstrales,   *Summon*
And gestours° for to tellen tales—   *storytellers*
   Anon in myn arminge—
Of romances that been royales,
Of popes and of cardinales,
850 And eek° of love-lykinge."°   *also / love delights*

They fette° him first the swete wyn,   *fetched*
And mede° eek in a maselyn,°   *mead / mazer (wooden bowl)*
   And royal spicerye°   *mixtures of spices*
Of gingebreed° that was ful fyn,   *preserved ginger*
855 And lycorys,° and eek comyn,°   *licorice / cumin*
   With sugre that is trye.°   *choice, excellent*

He dide° next° his whyte lere°   *put on / next to / flesh*
Of clooth of lake° fyn and clere°   *fine linen / bright*
   A breech° and eek a sherte;   *pair of trousers*
860 And next his sherte an aketoun,°   *padded jacket*
And over that an habergeoun°   *coat of mail*
   For° percinge of his herte;   *To prevent*

And over that a fyn hauberk°   *armor for chest and back*
Was al y-wroght of° Jewes werk,   *made, crafted by*
865 Ful strong it was of plate;°   *plate armor*
And over that his cote-armour°   *heraldic surcoat*
As whyt as is a lily-flour,
   In which he wol debate.°   *fight*

His sheeld was al of gold so reed,°   *red*
870 And therin was a bores° heed,   *boar's*
   A charbocle° bisyde;   *carbuncle (a red gemstone)*
And there he swoor on ale and breed
How that the geaunt shal be deed,
   Bityde what bityde.°   *Come what may*

875 His jambeux° were of quirboilly,°   *leg armor / hardened leather*
His swerdes shethe of yvory,
   His helm° of laton° bright.   *helmet / latten, brass*
His sadel was of rewel-boon,°   *whalebone, ivory*
His brydel as the sonne shoon,°   *shone*
880 Or as the mone light.

His spere was of fyn ciprees,°   *cypress*
That bodeth werre° and nothing pees,°   *forebodes war / in no way peace*
   The heed ful sharpe y-grounde.
His stede was al dappel gray,
885 It gooth an ambel° in the way   *goes at a slow walk*
   Ful softely and rounde°   *easily*
      In londe.

Lo, lordes myne, heer is a fit!°   *canto or section of a poem*
If ye wol any more of it,
890 To telle it wol I fonde.°   *strive, try*

[THE THIRD FIT]

Now hold your mouth, *par charitee*,°   *for charity's sake*
Bothe knight and lady free,°   *noble, generous*
  And herkneth to my spelle.°   *listen to my story*
Of bataille and of chivalry,
895 And of ladyes love-drury°   *love service, courtship*
  Anon I wol yow telle.

Men speke of romances of prys,°   *worthy, excellent*
Of Horn child and of Ypotys,
  Of Bevis and sir Gy,
900 Of sir Libeux and Pleyn-damour.
But sir Thopas—he bereth the flour°   *bears the prize*
  Of royal chivalry.[4]

His gode stede al he bistrood,°   *bestrode*
And forth upon his wey he glood°   *glided, traveled*
905 As sparkle° out of the bronde.°   *sparks / burning brand, torch*
Upon his crest° he bar a tour,°   *the top of his helmet / bore a tower ornament*
And therin stiked° a lily-flour—   *stuck, was fixed*
  God shilde his cors fro shonde!°   *keep his body from harm*

And for° he was a knight auntrous,°   *because / adventurous*
910 He nolde° slepen in non hous,   *would not*
  But liggen° in his hode.°   *lie / hood (i.e., outdoors)*
His brighte helm° was his wonger,°   *helmet / pillow*
And by him baiteth° his dextrer°   *feeds, grazes / warhorse*
  Of herbes° fyne and gode.   *On grasses*

915 Himself drank water of the wel,°   *spring*
As did the knight sir Percivel,°   *Percival (a chaste romance hero)*
  So worly under wede,°   *worthy in his armor, clothing*
Til on a day—[5]

4. Chaucer claims that his hero surpasses those of the popular romances that he parodies in this tale: King Horn (also known as Child Horn), Ypotis (a pious child, Epictetus, who instructs the emperor Hadrian in the Christian faith), Bevis of Hampton and Guy of Warwick, who furnished Chaucer much to satirize here, along with Lybeaux Desconus ("sir Lybeux"), whose disguise-name means "The Fair Unknown," and the almost wholly unknown "Pleyn-damour," whose name means "full of love."
5. After this line the Hengwrt MS has the following rubric: "Here the hoost stynteth [stops] Chaucer of his tale of Thopas and biddeth hym telle another tale."

From The Prologue and Tale of Melibee

The Prologue

"No more of this, for Goddes dignitee,"
920 Quod oure Hoste, "for thou makest me
So wery of thy verray lewednesse°   *sheer incompetence*
That, also wisly° God my soule blesse,°   *as surely as / may bless*
Myn eres° aken of° thy drasty° speche.   *ears / ache from / foul, vile*
Now swiche a rym° the devel I biteche!°   *rhyme, tale in verse / consign to*
925 This may wel be rym dogerel,"° quod he.   *doggerel verse*
    "Why so?" quod I. "Why wiltow lette° me   *wilt thou prevent*
More of my tale than another man,
Sin° that it is the beste rym I can?"°   *Since / know*
    "By God," quod he, "for pleynly at a word,
930 Thy drasty ryming is nat worth a tord.°   *turd*
Thou doost nought elles but despendest° tyme.   *waste*
Sir, at o word,° thou shalt no lenger ryme.   *in short*
Lat see wher thou canst tellen aught in geste[1]
Or telle in prose somwhat° at the leste,   *something*
935 In which ther be som mirthe or som doctryne."°   *useful teaching*
    "Gladly," quod I, "By Goddes swete pyne,°   *pain, i.e., Passion*
I wol yow telle a litel thing in prose
That oghte lyken° yow, as I suppose,   *please*
Or elles, certes,° ye been to daungerous.° *surely / too disdainful, hard to please*
940 It is a moral tale vertuous,
Al be it° told somtyme in sondry wyse°   *Although / in different ways*
Of° sondry folk, as I shal yow devyse°   *By / explain to you*
As thus:° ye woot° that every evangelist°   *As follows / know / Gospel writer*
That telleth us the peyne° of Jesu Crist   *pain, suffering*
945 Ne saith nat al thing as his felaw° dooth,   *fellow evangelist*
But natheles° hir sentence is al sooth,   *nevertheless*
And alle acorden as in hir sentence,[2]
Al be ther° in hir telling difference;   *Although there is*
For somme of hem seyn more and somme lesse
950 Whan they his pitous° passioun expresse   *piteous, sad*
(I mene of Marke, Mathew, Luk and John),
But doutelees hir sentence is al oon.°   *their meaning is the same*
Therfor, lordinges alle, I yow biseche,°   *beseech, ask*
If that ye thinke I varie as in my speche,
955 As thus,° thogh that I telle somwhat more   *In this way*
Of proverbes than ye han herd bifore
Comprehended° in this litel tretis here,   *Contained*
To enforce with° the'effect of my matere,°   *To strengthen / material*
And thogh I nat the same wordes seye

---

1. "Let (us) see whether thou canst tell something in alliterative verse."
2. But nevertheless their essential meaning is true, and they all agree on that meaning. In
   these and the following lines Chaucer uses the different renderings in the four gospels of a
   single set of events to explain how his proverb-laden tale of Melibee contains the same basic
   meaning as other versions of that story.

960 As ye han herd, yet to yow alle I preye,
Blameth me nat; for as in my sentence°   *for in my meaning*
Shul ye nowher fynden difference
Fro the sentence of this tretis lyte°   *little treatise*
After the which° this mery° tale I wryte.   *Which is the source of / pleasant*
965 And therfor herkneth what that I shal seye,
And lat me tellen al my tale, I preye."

From *The Tale*

A yong man called Melibeus, mighty and
riche, bigat° upon his wyf, that called was   *begot*
Prudence, a doghter which that called was
Sophie.° /   *(evoking "Sophia," wisdom)*
Upon a day bifel° that he for his desport°   *it happened / disport, pleasure*
is went into the feeldes° him to pleye.° / His   *fields / to enjoy himself*
wyf and eek° his doghter hath he left in-   *also*
with° his hous, of which the dores° weren   *inside / doors*
fast y-shette.° / Thre of his olde foos° han it   *firmly shut / foes*
espyed° and setten laddres° to the walles of   *saw it / put up ladders*
970 his hous and by the windowes been entred, /
and betten° his wyf and wounded his   *(they) beat, struck*
doghter with fyve mortal woundes in fyve
sondry° places / (this is to seyn, in hir feet,   *different*
in hir handes, in hir eres,° in hir nose, and   *ears*
in hir mouth) and leften hir for deed,° and   *as though dead*
wenten awey. /
Whan Melibeus retourned was into his
hous and saugh° al this meschief,° he, lyk a   *saw / harm, misfortune*
mad man rendinge his clothes, gan to wepe
and crye. /
Prudence his wyf, as ferforth° as she   *far*
dorste,° bisoghte° him of his weping for to   *dared / begged*
stinte,° / but nat forthy° he gan to crye and   *stop / nevertheless*
975 wepen ever lenger the more.° /   *more and more intensely*
This noble wyf Prudence remembered hir
upon° the sentence° of Ovide, in his book   *i.e., recalled / maxim*
that cleped is° The Remedie of Love,° wher   *is titled / Ovid's* Remedia Amoris
as° he seith, / "He is a fool that des-   *in which*
tourbeth° the moder to wepen in the deeth   *who prevents*
of hir child til she have wept hir fille° as for   *as much as she desires*
a certein tyme, /and thanne shal man doon
his diligence° with amiable wordes hir to re-   *a person make every effort*
conforte,° and preyen° hir of hir weping for   *to comfort her / beg*
to stinte."/ For which resoun this noble wyf
Prudence suffred° hir housbond for to wepe   *allowed*
and crye as for a certein space,° / and whan   *space of time*
she saugh° hir tyme, she seyde him° in this   *saw / spoke to him*
wyse:° "Allas, my lord," quod° she, "why   *way / said*

980 make ye yourself for to be lyk a fool? / For
sothe,° it aperteneth nat to° a wys man to   *truly / is not suitable for*
maken swiche a sorwe. / Your doghter, with
the grace of God, shal warisshe° and es-   *recover*
cape. / And al were it° so that she right now   *even if it were*
were deed, ye ne oghte nat as for hir deeth
yourself to destroye. / Senek° seith, 'The   *Seneca*
wise man shal nat take to° greet disconfort   *too*
for the deeth of his children, / but certes°   *certainly*
he sholde suffren° it in pacience, as wel as   *endure*
he abydeth° the deeth of his owene propre   *waits for*
985 persone.' "° /   *i.e., his own death*
     This Melibeus answerde anon° and   *immediately*
seyde: "What man," quod he, "sholde of his
weping stinte° that hath so greet a cause for   *cease*
to wepe? / Jesu Crist, our Lord, himself
wepte for the deeth of Lazarus his freend." /
Prudence answerde, "Certes, wel I woot°   *know (that)*
attempree° weping is no thing defended° to   *moderate / not at all forbidden*
him that sorweful is amonges folk in sorwe,
but it is rather graunted him to wepe. / The
Apostle Paul unto the Romayns wryteth,
'Man shal rejoyse with hem that° maken   *those who*
joye and wepen with swich folk as wepen.' /
But thogh attempree weping be y-graunted,
990 outrageous° weping certes is defended. /   *excessive*
Mesure of° weping sholde be considered   *Moderation in*
after the lore° that techeth us Senek: /   *according to the wisdom*
'Whan that thy freend is deed,' quod he, 'lat
nat thyne eyen° to° moyste been of teres, ne   *do not let thine eyes / too*
to muche drye. Althogh the teres come to
thyne eyen, lat hem nat falle. / And whan
thou hast forgoon° thy freend, do diligence°   *lost / make every effort*
to gete another freend. And this is more
wysdom° than for to wepe for thy freend   *i.e., wiser*
which that thou hast lorn,° for therinne is   *lost*
no bote.'° / And therfore, if ye governe yow°   *benefit, remedy / yourself*
by sapience,° put awey sorwe out of your   *wisdom*
herte. / Remembre yow that° Jesus Syrak³   *Remember what*
seith: 'A man that is joyous and glad in
herte, it him conserveth florisshing° in his   *keeps him healthy*
age; but soothly sorweful herte maketh his
995 bones drye.' / He seith eek thus that sorwe
in herte sleeth ful many a man. / Salomon

---

3. Jesus, son of Sirach, was the author of Ecclesiasticus (a canonical book in the Catholic but
   not the Protestant Bible). The passage quoted here is actually from Proverbs 17:22. The
   mistake is in Chaucer's source, *Le Livre de Mellibee et Prudence*, by the fourteenth-century
   friar Reynaud de Louens. Chaucer's Tale of Melibee is a rather close translation of Reynaud's work, which itself is a translation/adaptation of a Latin work by the thirteenth-
   century Italian orator, Albertano of Brescia.

seith that right as motthes° in the shepes | *just as moths*
flees° anoyeth° to the clothes, and the | *fleece / do damage*
smale wormes to the tree, right so anoyeth
sorwe to the herte. / Wherfore us oghte,° as | *we ought to*
wel in the deeth of our children as in the
losse of our othere goodes temporels,° have | *temporal, transitory*
pacience. / Remembre yow upon the pa-
cient Job. Whan he hadde lost his children
and his temporel substance,° and in his | *worldly wealth*
body endured and receyved ful many a
grevous tribulacioun, yet seyde he thus: /
'Our Lord hath yeven it me,° our Lord hath | *given it to me*
biraft it me.° Right as our Lord hath wold,° | *taken it from me / willed*
right so it is doon. Blessed be the name of
1000 our Lord.' " /

To thise foreseide thinges answerde Melibeus unto his wyf Prudence: "Alle thy
wordes," quod he, "been sothe and therto° | *on that (subject)*
profitable, but trewely myn herte is troubled
with this sorwe so grevously that I noot
what to done."° / | *know not what to do*

"Lat calle,"° quod Prudence, "thy trewe freen- | *I.e., call, summon*
des alle and thy linage° whiche that been | *kinfolk*
wyse. Telleth your cas° and herkneth° what | *case, situation / listen to*
they seye in conseiling, and yow governe° | *conduct yourself*
after hir sentence.° Salomon seith, 'Werk | *according to their opinion*
alle thy thinges by conseil,° and thou shalt | *Do everything through counsel*
never repente.' " /

Thanne° by the conseil of his wyf Pru- | *Then*
dence, this Melibeus leet callen° a greet | *i.e., summoned*
congregacioun of folk, / as surgiens,° phisi- | *such as surgeons*
ciens, olde folk and yonge, and somme of
hise olde enemys reconciled (as by hir sem-
1005 blaunt°) to his love and into his grace; / and | *as it appeared*
therwithal ther comen somme of hise
neighebores that diden him reverence° more | *showed him respect*
for drede° than for love, as it happeth ofte. / | *out of fear*
Ther comen also ful many subtile flatereres
and wyse advocates° lerned in the lawe. / | *lawyers*

And whan this folk togidre° assembled | *together*
weren, this Melibeus in sorweful wyse
shewed hem his cas,° and by the manere of | *revealed to them what happened*
his speche it semed that in herte he bar° a | *carried*
cruel ire,° redy to doon° vengeaunce upon | *anger / take*
hise foos,° and sodeynly° desired that the | *foes / impetuously*
werre° sholde biginne; / but nathelees yet | *war, conflict*
axed he hir conseil° upon this matere. / | *he asked their advice*

[*Summary of lines 1010–1805*: The majority of these friends and kin
support Melibee's wish to take vengeance. Prudence advises him not

to act hastily and to listen to her counsel. Melibee says he will not listen to her, for reasons chiefly based on her status as a woman and a wife. Prudence refutes each of these arguments, and Melibee then agrees to follow her counsel. Prudence first addresses the issue of taking counsel, discussing how counselors should be chosen and calling into question the advice he received. Melibee, seeing the direction of her argument, gives various reasons why taking vengeance is necessary and appropriate, but Prudence challenges all of them. She counsels Melibee to make peace with his enemies, and when he claims that she does not care about his "honor," she pretends to be angry with him, prompting Melibee to see that his own anger has clouded his judgment. He promises Prudence that he will follow her counsel. She tells him first to make peace between himself and God. Having secured his good will, she talks privately with his three enemies, who acknowledge they have done wrong, and persuades them to submit themselves to Melibee's judgment. Melibee agrees to pardon them if they are repentant but does not want to act without the counsel of others. This time, to Prudence's pleasure, the counselors invited to his court are "trewe and wyse" rather than self-interested friends. They advise him to pursue peace. Following his wife's counsel, Melibee asks his enemies to come to him to discuss a peaceful resolution of their conflict.]

And right anon they token hir wey° to the	*took their way*
court of Melibee / and token with hem	
somme of hir trewe freendes to maken	
feith° for hem and for to been hir borwes.° /	*stand surety / guarantors*
And whan they were comen to the presence	
of Melibee, he seyde hem° thise wordes: /	*spoke to them*
"It standeth thus," quod Melibee, "and	
sooth° it is, that ye / —causeless and with-	*true*
1810 outen skile° and resoun / —han doon grete	*grounds*
injuries and wronges to me and to my wyf	
Prudence and to my doghter also. / For ye	
han entred into myn hous by violence / and	
have doon swich outrage that alle men	
knowen wel that ye have deserved the	
deeth; / and therfore wol I knowe and	
wite° of yow / whether ye wol putte the	*understand*
punissement and the chastysinge and the	
vengeance of this outrage in the wil of	
me° and of my wyf Prudence, or ye wol	*in my will, choice*
1815 nat?" /	
Thanne the wysest of hem thre° answerde	*the three of them*
for hem alle and seyde: / "Sire," quod he,	
"we knowen wel that we been unworthy to	
comen unto the court of so greet a lord and	
so worthy as ye been. / For we han so greetly	
mistaken us° and han offended and agilt in	*acted wrongly*
swich a wyse agayn° your heigh lordshipe /	*done such wrong against*

that trewely we han deserved the deeth.° /   *i.e., to die*
But yet, for the grete goodnesse and
debonairetee° that all the world witnesseth   *kindness*
1820 of your persone,° / we submitten us to the   *i.e., in yourself*
excellence and benignitee° of your gracious   *goodness*
lordshipe / and been° redy to obeie to alle   *are*
your comandements, / bisekinge° yow that   *beseeching*
of° your merciable° pitee ye wol considere   *out of / merciful*
our grete repentaunce and lowe° submis-   *humble*
sioun / and graunten us foryevenesse° of   *forgiveness*
our outrageous trespas and offence. / For
wel we knowe that your liberal grace and
mercy strecchen hem ferther° into good-   *extend further*
nesse than doon° our outrageouse giltes   *do*
1825 and trespas into wikkednesse, / al be it that°   *even though*
cursedly and dampnably we han agilt agayn
your heigh lordshipe." /

Thanne Melibee took hem up fro the
ground ful benignely° / and receyved hir   *very graciously*
obligaciouns and hir bondes by hir othes
upon hir plegges and borwes,[4] / and assigned hem a certeyn day to retourne unto
his court / for to accepte and receyve the
sentence° and jugement that Melibee wolde   *decision*
comande to be doon° on hem by° the   *imposed / for*
1830 causes aforeseyd. / Whiche thinges or-
deyned,° every man retourned to his hous. /   *ordained, arranged*

And whan that dame Prudence saugh°   *saw*
hir tyme, she freyned° and axed hir lord   *inquired*
Melibee / what vengeance he thoughte to
taken of° hise adversaries. /   *against*

To which Melibee answerde and seyde:
"Certes,"° quod he, "I thinke and purpose   *Surely*
me fully / to desherite° hem of al that ever   *dispossess*
they han and for to putte hem in exil° for   *exile*
1835 ever." /

"Certes," quod dame Prudence, "this
were a cruel sentence and muchel° agayn   *much*
resoun. / For ye been riche ynough and han
no nede of other mennes good,° / and ye   *goods, property*
mighte lightly in this wyse gete yow a cov-
eitous name,° / which is a vicious thing and   *a reputation for greed*
oghte been eschewed of° every good man. /   *shunned by*
For after the sawe° of the word of the apos-   *according to the maxim*
1840 tle, 'Coveitise is rote of all harmes.'[5] / And

---

4. And accepted the obligations and commitments they made by oath, supported by their
pledges and sureties.
5. Avarice is the root of all evil (1 Timothy 6:10). This is the text on which the Pardoner says
he always preaches.

therfore it were bettre for yow to lese° so   *lose*
muchel good of your owene than for to
taken of hir good in this manere. / For bet-
tre it is to lesen good with worshipe° than it   *honor*
is to winne good with vileinye° and shame, /   *dishonor*
and every man oghte to doon his diligence
and his bisinesse to geten him° a good   *himself*
name. / And yet shal he nat only bisie him
in kepinge of his good name, / but he shal
also enforcen him° alwey to do somthing by   *strive*
1845 which he may renovelle° his good name, /   *renew*
for it is writen that the olde good loos° or   *reputation*
good name of a man is sone goon° and   *soon lost*
passed whan it is nat newed° ne renovelled.   *renewed*
/ And as touchinge° that ye seyn° ye wole   *considering / say*
exile your adversaries, / that thinketh me
muchel agayn resoun and out of mesure,° /   *excessive*
considered° the power that they han yeve°   *considering / have given*
yow upon° hemself. / And it is writen that   *over*
he is worthy to lesen° his privilege that mis-   *lose*
useth the might and the power that is yeven
1850 him. / And I sette cas° ye mighte enjoyne   *i.e., supposing*
hem that peyne° by right and by lawe /   *impose that punishment on them*
(which I trowe° ye mowe° nat do), / I seye   *believe / may*
ye mighte nat putten it to execucioun° per-   *carry it out / by (some) chance*
aventure,° / and thanne were it lykly° to re-   *the situation would be likely*
tourne to the werre° as it was biforn. / And   *conflict*
therefore if ye wole° that men do yow obei-   *will, wish*
1855 sance,° ye moste demen° more curteisly° /   *obey you / pass judgments / gently*
—this is to seyn, ye moste yeven° more esy°   *must give / lenient*
sentences and jugements. / For it is writen
that he that most curteisly comandeth, to
him men most obeyen. / And therfore I
prey° yow that in this necessitee and in this   *beg*
nede ye caste yow° to overcome your herte.   *make an effort*
/ For Senek[6] seith that he that overcometh
his herte overcometh twyes.° / And Tullius°   *twice / Cicero*
seith ther is no thing so comendable in a
1860 greet lord / as whan he is debonaire° and   *kind*
meke° and appeseth him lightly.° / And I   *meek / is easily appeased*
prey yow that ye wole forbere° now to do   *refrain*
vengeance / in swich a manere that your
goode name may be kept and conserved, /
and that men mowe° have cause and   *may*
matere° to preyse° yow of° pitee and of   *reason / praise / for*
mercy, / and that ye have no cause to re-
1865 pente yow of thing that ye doon. / For

6. Seneca; but the author here and in line 1866 is actually Publilius Syrus.

Senek seith, 'He overcometh in an yvel°
manere that° repenteth him of his victorie.'[7] /
Wherfore I pray yow, lat mercy been in your
minde and in your herte, / to th'effect and
entente° that God Almighty have mercy on
yow in His laste jugement. / For Seint Jame
seith in his epistle, 'Jugement withouten
mercy shal be doon to° him that hath no
mercy of° another wight.'"° /

Whanne Melibee hadde herd the grete
1870 skiles° and resouns of dame Prudence and
hir wise informaciouns° and techinges, / his
herte gan enclyne° to the wil of his wyf,
consideringe hir trewe entente, / and con-
formed him anon° and assented fully to
werken after° hir conseil, / and thonked
God, of° whom procedeth al vertu and alle
goodnesse, that him sente a wyf of so greet
discrecioun.° / And whan the day cam that
hise adversaries sholde apperen° in his
presence, / he spak unto hem ful goodly°
1875 and seyde in this wyse: / "Al be it so that° of°
your pryde and presumpcioun and folie,°
and of your necligence and unconninge,° /
ye have misborn yow° and trespassed unto
me, / yet for as much as I see and biholde
your grete humilitee / and that ye been sory
and repentant of your giltes,° / it con-
1880 streyneth me to doon° yow grace and mercy. /
Therfore I receyve yow to° my grace / and
foryeve yow outrely° alle the offences, injuries, and wronges that ye have doon
agayn° me and myne, / to this effect and to
this ende: that God of his endelees mercy /
wole at the time of our dyinge foryeven us
our giltes that we han trespassed to° him in
this wrecched world. / For doutelees,° if we
be sory and repentant of the sinnes and
giltes whiche we han trespassed in the
1885 sighte of our Lord God, / he is so free° and
so merciable° that he wole foryeven us our
giltes / and bringen us to his blisse that
never hath ende." Amen. /

	evil
	who
	for the purpose
	inflicted on
	on / person
	arguments
	instruction
	incline, bend
	resolved promptly
	act according to
	from
	discernment, understanding
	appear
	kindly, sensibly
	Although / out of
	foolishness, sin
	ignorance
	misbehaved
	sins
	i.e., I am compelled to grant
	accept you (back) into
	forgive you utterly, completely
	against
	sinned against
	without doubt
	generous
	merciful

---

7. He who has cause to repent his victory has won it in an evil [dishonorable] way.

The Nun's Priest's Prologue and Tale

The Prologue

"Ho!"° quod° the Knight, "good sir, namore of this: *Stop / said*
That° ye han seyd is right ynough, ywis,°¹   *What / indeed*
And mochel more; for litel hevinesse²
2770 Is right ynough to mochel° folk, I gesse.   *for many*
I seye for me it is a greet disese,°   *discomfort*
Where as° men han ben in greet welthe and ese,   *There where*
To heeren° of hire sodeyn° fal, allas!   *hear / sudden*
And the contrarie is joie° and greet solas,°   *joy / comfort*
2775 As whan a man hath been in povre estaat,°   *a condition of poverty*
And clymbeth up, and wexeth° fortunat,   *becomes increasingly*
And ther abydeth in prosperitee—
Swich° thing is gladsom, as it thinketh me,   *Such*
And of swich thing were goodly for to telle."
2780 "Ye," quod our Hoste, "by Seinte Poules° belle,   *St. Paul's (cathedral)*
Ye seye right sooth:° this Monk, he clappeth loude.°   *truly / chatters loudly*
He spak 'how Fortune covered with a cloude'—
I noot° never what. And als° of a 'tragedie'   *know not / besides*
Right now ye herde, and pardee!° no remedie   *by God*
2785 It is for to biwaille° ne compleyne   *bewail*
That that° is doon, and als° it is a peyne,   *which / besides*
As ye han seyd, to heere° of hevinesse.   *hear*
    Sire Monk, namore of this, so God yow blesse!
Your tale anoyeth al this compaignye.
2790 Swich talking is nat worth a boterflye,°   *butterfly*
For therinne is ther no desport° ne game.   *pleasure*
Wherfore sir Monk, or daun° Piers by youre name,   *sir*
I preye yow hertely° telle us somwhat elles,°   *heartily / something else*
For sikerly, nere clinking of youre belles³
2795 That on your brydel hange on every syde,
By hevene° king that for us alle dyde,°   *heaven's / died*
I sholde er° this han fallen doun for slepe,   *before*
Althogh the slough° had never been so depe.   *mire*
Than had your tale al be° told in vayn;   *been*
2800 For certainly, as that° thise clerkes seyn,   *just as*
'Whereas° a man may have noon audience,   *There where*
Noght helpeth it to tellen his sentence.'°   *meaning*
    And wel I woot the substance is in me,⁴
If any thing shal wel reported be.
2805 Sir, sey somwhat of hunting, I yow preye."
    "Nay," quod this Monk, "I have no lust° to pleye;   *desire*

1. The Knight here breaks off the Monk's tale, a recital of "tragedies," i.e., stories of the fall of great ones from high fortune into misery.
2. And much more (than enough); for a little seriousness.
3. For certainly, were it not for the clinking of your bells.
4. Sense uncertain: *either* I know well I have the capacity to understand; *or* I know I've got the meaning (if it's been well told).

Now let another telle, as I have told."
Than spak our Host, with rude speche and bold,
And seyde unto the Nonnes Preest° anon,   *Nun's Priest*
2810 "Com neer,° thou preest, com hider, thou sir John,   *nearer*
Tel us swich thing as may oure hertes glade.°   *gladden*
Be blythe,° though thou ryde upon a jade!°   *cheerful / a poor horse*
What though thyn hors be bothe foule and lene?°   *lean*
If he wol serve thee, rekke nat a bene.°   *don't care a bean*
2815 Look that thyn herte be mery evermo."
     "Yis, sir," quod he, "yis, Host, so mote I go,°   *as I may thrive*
But° I be mery, ywis,° I wol be blamed."   *Unless / truly*
And right anon° his tale he hath attamed,°   *right away / begun*
And thus he seyde unto us everichon,°   *every one*
2820 This sweete preest, this goodly man sir John.

The Tale

A povre widwe, somdel stape in age,[5]
Was whylom° dwelling in a narwe° cotage,   *once / small*
Bisyde a grove, stondinge in a dale.°   *valley*
This widwe of which I telle yow my tale,
2825 Sin thilke° day that she was last a wyf,   *Since that same*
In pacience ladde° a ful simple lyf,   *led*
For litel was hir catel° and hir rente.°   *property / income*
By housbondrye° of such as God hire sente   *careful management*
She fond° hirself and eek° hir doghtren° two. *provided for / also / daughters*
2830 Three large sowes hadde she and namo,°   *no more*
Three kyn,° and eek a sheep that highte° Malle.   *cows / was called*
Ful sooty was hire bour, and eek hir halle,[6]
In which she eet ful many a sclendre° meel.   *lean*
Of poynaunt° sauce hir neded never a deel:°   *pungent / portion*
2835 No deyntee morsel passed thurgh hir throte.
Hir diete was accordant° to hir cote°—   *matched / small farm*
Repleccioun° ne made hir never syk.   *Surfeit*
Attempree diete was al hir phisyk,[7]
And exercyse, and hertes suffisaunce.°   *heart's contentment*
2840 The goute lette° hire nothing for to daunce,° *hindered / from dancing*
N'apoplexye shente° nat hir heed.   *Nor did apoplexy injure*
No wyn° ne drank she, neither whyt° ne reed;°   *wine / white / red*
Hir bord° was served most with whyt and blak—   *table*
Milk and broun breed—in which she fond no lak,°   *found no fault*
2845 Seynd° bacoun, and somtyme an ey or tweye,°   *Broiled / egg or two*
For she was as it were a maner deye.°   *kind of dairymaid*
     A yerd° she hadde, enclosed° al aboute   *yard / fenced*
With stikkes, and a drye dich° withoute,   *ditch*

---

5. A poor widow, somewhat advanced in years.
6. Her "bed-chamber" and her "banquet hall" were grimy with soot. (The terms are being used ironically; her humble cottage lacks such rooms, and offers implicit moral criticism of such grandeur.)
7. A temperate diet was her only medicine.

In which she hadde a cok hight° Chauntecleer: called
2850 In al the land of° crowing nas° his peer.   at / there was not
His voys was merier than the mery orgon°   organ
On messe-dayes° that in the chirche gon;°   feast days / plays
Wel sikerer° was his crowing in his logge°   more certain / lodgings
Than is a clokke or an abbey orlogge.°   (great) clock
2855 By nature knew he ech ascencioun
Of the equinoxial in thilke toun:⁸
For whan degrees fiftene were ascended,
Thanne crew he, that it mighte nat ben amended.°   improved
His comb was redder than the fyn coral,
2860 And batailed° as it were a castel wal.   notched (like battlements)
His bile° was blak, and as the jeet° it shoon;   bill / jet (semiprecious stone)
Lyk asur° were his legges and his toon;°   azure / toes
His nayles° whytter than the lilie flour,°   claws / lily flower
And lyk the burned° gold was his colour.   burnished
2865 This gentil cok hadde in his governaunce°   under his control
Sevene hennes,° for to doon al his plesaunce,   hens
Whiche were his sustres° and his paramours,   sisters
And wonder lyk to him, as of colours;
Of whiche the faireste hewed° on hir throte   hued, colored
2870 Was cleped° faire damoysele° Pertelote.   named / (ma)demoiselle
Curteys° she was, discreet, and debonaire,°   Courteous / gracious
And compaignable,° and bar hirself so faire,   sociable
Sin thilke day that she was seven night old,
That trewely she hath the herte in hold
2875 Of Chauntecleer, loken° in every lith;°   locked / limb
He loved hire so, that wel was him therwith.
But such a joye was it to here hem° singe,   them
Whan that the brighte sonne gan to springe,°   began to rise
In swete acord, "my lief is faren in londe."⁹
2880 For thilke tyme,° as I have understonde,   in those days
Bestes° and briddes° coude speke and singe.   Beasts / birds
     And so bifel that in a daweninge,¹
As Chauntecleer among his wyves alle
Sat on his perche that was in the halle,
2885 And next him sat this faire Pertelote,
This Chauntecleer gan gronen° in his throte   did groan
As man that in his dreem is drecched sore.°   severely troubled
And whan that Pertelote thus herde him rore,
She was agast,° and seyde, "Herte dere,   afraid
2890 What eyleth° yow to grone in this manere?   ails
Ye been a verray sleper,° fy for shame!"   You're a fine sleeper
     And he answerde and seyde thus, "Madame,

8. By natural instinct he knew each revolution of the equinoctial circle—the celestial equator—in that same town (a complicated astronomical description of how the hours pass and are numbered).
9. In sweet harmony, "my love has gone to the country" (a popular song).
1. And so it happened, one morning at dawn.

I pray yow, that ye take it nat agrief:°   amiss
By God, me mette° I was in swich meschief°   I dreamed / trouble
2895   Right now, that yet myn herte is sore afright.
Now God," quod he, "my swevene recche aright,[2]
And keep my body out of foul prisoun!
Me mette how that I romed° up and doun   roamed
Withinne our yerde, wher as I saugh° a beste,   saw
2900   Was lyk an hound and wolde han maad areste°   laid hold
Upon my body, and wolde han had me deed.°   dead
His colour was bitwixe yelow and reed,°   red
And tipped was his tail and bothe his eres°   ears
With blak, unlyk the remenant° of his heres;°   rest / hair(s)
2905   His snowte° smal, with glowinge eyen tweye.°   snout / two eyes
Yet° of his look for fere° almost I deye:°   Still / fear / die
This caused me my groning, douteless."
    "Avoy!"° quod she, "fy on yow, hertelees!°   Go on / faint heart
Allas!" quod she, "for, by that God above,
2910   Now han ye lost myn herte and al my love.
I can nat love a coward, by my feith!
For certes, what so any womman seith,
We alle desiren,° if it mighte be,   desire
To han housbondes hardy,° wyse, and free,°   bold / generous
2915   And secree,° and no nigard, ne no fool,   discreet
Ne him that is agast° of every tool,°   afraid / weapon
Ne noon avauntour.° By that God above,   boaster
How dorste° ye seyn for shame unto your love   dare
That any thing mighte make yow aferd?°   afraid
2920   Have ye no mannes herte, and han a berd?°   beard
Allas! and conne ye been agast of swevenis?°   dreams
Nothing, God wot, but vanitee° in sweven is.   foolishness, illusion
Swevenes[3] engendren of replecciouns,°   are born of surfeits
And ofte of fume,° and of complecciouns,°   vapor(s)
2925   Whan humours been to habundant° in a wight.°   too abundant / person
Certes° this dreem, which ye han met tonight,   Certainly
Cometh of the grete superfluitee
Of youre rede colera,° pardee,   choler (a humor)
Which causeth folk to dreden° in hir° dremes   fear / their
2930   Of arwes,° and of fyr with rede lemes,°   arrows / flames
Of rede bestes, that they wol hem byte,
Of contek,° and of whelpes° grete and lyte;°   strife / pups, cubs / little
Right as the humour of malencolye°   melancholy (black bile)
Causeth ful many a man in sleep to crye
2935   For fere of blake beres,° or boles° blake,   bears / bulls
Or elles, blake develes wole hem take.

2. "Now God," he said, "(help) interpret my dream correctly."
3. Pertelote's discussion of the causes of dreams and her insistence that Chauntecleer's dream
   is of physiological rather than supernatural origin (with the conclusion that it therefore need
   not be heeded) are learned in medieval dream theory. On the humours, see n. 8, p. 13, in
   the General Prologue: "compleccioun" refers to the existing balance between them.

Of othere humours coude I telle also
That werken° many a man in sleep ful wo;°   *cause / great woe*
But I wol passe as lightly as I can.
2940   Lo Catoun,° which that was so wys a man,   *Cato*
Seyde he nat thus, 'Ne do no fors of° dremes'?   *Pay no attention to*
Now, sire," quod she, "whan we flee° fro the bemes,   *fly*
For Goddes love, as tak some laxatyf.
Up° peril of my soule and of my lyf   *On*
2945 I counseille yow the beste, I wol nat lye,
That bothe of colere and of malencolye
Ye purge yow; and for° ye shul nat tarie,°   *so that / delay*
Though in this toun is noon apothecarie,
I shal myself to herbes techen° yow,   *direct*
2950 That shul ben for youre hele° and for youre prow;°   *health / benefit*
And in oure yerd tho° herbes shal I finde   *those*
The whiche han of hire propretee by kinde°   *nature*
To purgen yow binethe and eek above.
Forget not this, for Goddes owene love!
2955 Ye been ful colerik of compleccioun.°   *temperamentally dominated by choler*
Ware° the sonne in his ascencioun   *Beware*
Ne fynde yow nat repleet° of humours hote;   *full*
And if it do, I dar wel leye° a grote,°   *bet / Dutch coin*
That ye shul have a fevere terciane,[4]
2960 Or an agu,° that may be youre bane.°   *ague / destruction*
A day or two ye shul have digestyves
Of wormes, er° ye take your laxatyves,   *before*
Of lauriol,° centaure,° and fumetere,°   *spurge laurel / centaury / fumitory*
Or elles of ellebor° that groweth there,   *hellebore*
2965 Of catapuce,° or of gaytres beryis,°   *caper spurge / dogwood's berries*
Of erbe yve,° growing in oure yerd, ther mery is.°   *ivy / where it is pleasant*
Pekke hem° up right as they growe, and ete° hem in.   *Peck them / eat*
Be mery, housbond, for youre fader kin!°   *father's kin*
Dredeth no dreem: I can say yow namore."
2970   "Madame," quod he, "*graunt mercy*° of youre lore.   *many thanks*
But nathelees, as touching daun Catoun,
That hath of wisdom swich a greet renoun,°   *such great fame*
Though that he bad° no dremes for to drede,   *commanded*
By God, men may in olde bokes rede
2975 Of many a man, more of auctoritee
Than ever Catoun was, so mote I thee,°   *as I may thrive*
That al the revers° seyn of his sentence,   *reverse, opposite*
And han wel founden° by experience,   *established*
That dremes ben significaciouns°   *meaningful signs*
2980 As wel of joye° as tribulaciouns   *joy*
That folk enduren in this lyf present.
Ther nedeth make of this noon argument:
The verray preve° sheweth it in dede.   *true proof*

4. A fever recurring every third day.

Oon of the gretteste auctours° that men rede   *authorities, writers*
2985 Seith thus, that whylom° two felawes° wente   *once / companions*
On pilgrimage, in a ful good entente;
And happed so thay come into a toun,
Wher as° ther was swich congregacioun°   *Where / such a gathering*
Of peple, and eek so streit of herbergage,°   *such scarcity of lodgings*
2990 That they ne founde as muche as o° cotage   *one*
In which they bothe mighte y-logged° be.   *lodged*
Wherfor thay mosten° of necessitee,   *had to*
As for that night, departen° compaignye;   *part*
And ech of hem goth° to his hostelrye,°   *goes / lodging place*
2995 And took his logging as it wolde falle.
That oon of hem° was logged in a stalle,   *The one of them*
Fer° in a yerd, with oxen of the plough;   *Far off*
That other man was logged wel ynough,
As was his aventure° or his fortune,   *chance*
3000 That us governeth alle as in commune.°   *in general*
  And so bifel that, longe er° it were day,   *before*
This man mette° in his bed, ther as he lay,   *dreamed*
How that his felawe gan° upon him calle,   *began*
And seyde, 'Allas! for in an oxes stalle
3005 This night I shal be mordred ther° I lye.   *murdered where*
Now help me, dere brother, or I dye;
In alle haste com to me,' he sayde.
This man out of his sleep for fere abrayde,°   *started up*
But whan that he was wakened of his sleep,
3010 He turned him, and took of this no keep:°   *heed*
Him thoughte his dreem nas but a vanitee.[5]
Thus twyes° in his sleping dremed he;   *twice*
And atte thridde° tyme yet his felawe   *at the third*
Cam, as him thoughte, and seide, 'I am now slawe.°   *slain*
3015 Bihold my blody woundes, depe and wyde!
Arys° up erly in the morwe tyde,°   *Arise / morning*
And at the west gate of the toun,' quod he,
'A carte ful of donge° ther shaltow° see,   *dung / shalt thou*
In which my body is hid ful prively:°   *secretly*
3020 Do thilke carte aresten° boldely.   *Have that cart stopped*
My gold caused my mordre, sooth to sayn;'°   *the truth to tell*
And tolde him every poynt how he was slayn,
With a ful pitous face, pale of hewe.
And truste wel, his dreem he fond ful trewe,
3025 For on the morwe, as sone as it was day,
To his felawes in° he took the way;   *companion's inn*
And whan that he cam to this oxes stalle,
After his felawe he bigan to calle.
  The hostiler° answered him anon,°   *innkeeper / immediately*
3030 And seyde, 'Sire, your felawe is agon:°   *gone*

---

5. It seemed to him his dream was nothing but foolishness.

As sone as day he wente out of the toun.'
   This man gan fallen in suspecioun,°   *became suspicious*
Remembringe on his dremes that he mette,
And forth he goth, no lenger wolde he lette,°   *delay*
3035 Unto the west gate of the toun, and fond
A dong-carte, wente as it were to donge lond,[6]
That was arrayed in the same wyse°   *way*
As ye han herd the dede man devyse.°   *describe*
And with an hardy° herte he gan to crye,   *bold*
3040 'Vengeaunce and justice of this felonye!
My felawe mordred is this same night,
And in this carte he lyth° gapinge upright.°   *lies / face up*
I crye out on the ministres,'° quod he,   *officers*
'That sholden kepe and reulen° this citee,   *care for and rule*
3045 Harrow!° allas! heer lyth my felawe slayn!'   *Help*
What sholde I more unto this tale sayn?
The peple out sterte,° and caste the cart to grounde,   *came forth*
And in the middel of the dong they founde
The dede man, that mordred was al newe.°   *just recently*
3050 O blisful God, that art so just and trewe!
Lo, how that thou biwreyest° mordre alway!   *revealest*
Mordre wol out, that see we day by day.
Mordre is so wlatsom° and abhominable   *loathsome*
To God, that is so just and resonable,
3055 That he ne wol nat suffre it heled be.°   *to be concealed*
Though it abyde° a yeer, or two, or three,   *remain (hidden)*
Mordre wol out, this my conclusioun.
And right anoon,° ministres of that toun   *right away*
Han hent° the carter and so sore him pyned,°   *seized / tortured*
3060 And eek the hostiler so sore engyned,°   *racked*
That thay biknewe° hir wikkednesse anoon,   *acknowledged*
And were anhanged by the nekke-boon.°   *neck (bone)*
   Here may men seen that dremes been to drede.°   *are to be feared*
And certes,° in the same book I rede,   *certainly*
3065 Right in the nexte chapitre after this—
I gabbe° nat, so have I° joye or blis—   *lie / as I may have*
Two men that wolde han passed° over see,   *wished to travel*
For certeyn cause, into a fer° contree,   *far-off*
If that the wind ne hadde been contrarie:
3070 That made hem in a citee for to tarie
That stood ful mery upon an haven° syde.   *harbor*
But on a day, agayn the even-tyde,°   *toward evening*
The wind gan chaunge, and blew right as hem leste.°   *just as they wished*
Jolif° and glad they wente unto hir reste,   *Jolly*
3075 And casten hem° ful erly for to saille;   *they planned*
But herkneth! To that oo° man fil° a greet mervaille.   *one / befell*
That oon of hem, in sleping as he lay,

---

6. A dung-cart, going out as if to manure the land.

Him mette° a wonder dreem, agayn the° day: — *He dreamed / toward*
Him thoughte° a man stood by his beddes syde, — *It seemed to him*
3080 And him comaunded that he sholde abyde,° — *wait*
And seyde him thus, 'If thou tomorwe wende,° — *travel*
Thou shalt be dreynt:° my tale is at an ende.' — *drowned*
He wook,° and tolde his felawe what he mette, — *awoke*
And preyde him his viage for to lette;[7]
3085 As° for that day, he preyde him to byde. — *Just*
His felawe, that lay by his beddes syde,
Gan for° to laughe, and scorned him ful faste.° — *Began / very hard*
'No dreem' quod he, 'may so myn herte agaste° — *frighten*
That I wol lette° for to do my thinges.° — *leave off / business*
3090 I sette not a straw by thy dreminges,
For swevenes° been but vanitees and japes.° — *dreams / follies*
Men dreme alday of owles or of apes,
And eke° of many a mase° therwithal; — *also / maze, bewilderment*
Men dreme of thing that nevere was ne shal.° — *nor shall (be)*
3095 But sith° I see that thou wolt heer abyde, — *since*
And thus forsleuthen° wilfully thy tyde,° — *slothfully waste / time*
God woot it reweth me;[8] and have good day.'
And thus he took his leve, and wente his way.
But er that° he hadde halfe his cours y-seyled,° — *before / sailed*
3100 Noot° I nat why, ne what mischaunce it eyled,° — *Know not / ailed*
But casuelly° the shippes botme rente,° — *by chance / tore open*
And ship and man under the water wente
In sighte of othere shippes it byside,° — *alongside it*
That with hem seyled at the same tyde.
3105 And therfore faire Pertelote so dere,
By swiche ensamples olde maistow lere[9]
That no man sholde been to recchelees° — *heedless*
Of dremes, for I sey thee, doutelees,
That many a dreem ful sore° is for to drede.° — *greatly / to be dreaded*
3110 Lo, in the lyf° of Seint Kenelm I rede, — *life*
That was Kenulphus sone,[1] the noble king
Of Mercenrike,° how Kenelm mette° a thing — *Mercia / dreamed*
A lyte er° he was mordred on a day. — *A little before*
His mordre in his avisioun° he say.° — *vision / saw*
3115 His norice° him expouned every del° — *nurse / part of*
His sweven, and bad him for to kepe him wel° — *guard himself carefully*
For traisoun;° but he nas but° seven yeer old, — *Against treason / was only*
And therfore litel tale hath he told° — *he took little note*
Of any dreem, so holy was his herte.
3120 By God, I hadde lever than my sherte

---

7. And begged him to put off his voyage.
8. God knows it makes me sorry.
9. By such ancient examples thou mayest learn.
1. When King Cenwulf of Mercia died in 821, his seven-year-old son Kenelm became his heir but was murdered by agents of his aunt. Shortly before death, Kenelm had a warning dream in which he climbed a tree, was cut down by a friend, and saw himself fly to heaven in the shape of a bird.

That ye had rad his legende as have I.[2]
  Dame Pertelote, I sey yow trewely,
Macrobeus,[3] that writ the avisioun°   *vision*
In Affrike° of the worthy Cipioun,°   *Africa / Scipio*
3125 Affermeth° dremes, and seith that they been   *Affirms (the validity of)*
Warninge of thinges that men after seen.°   *afterward see*
And forthermore, I pray yow loketh wel
In the Olde Testament, of Daniel,
If he held dremes any vanitee.
3130 Reed eek of Ioseph,[4] and ther shul ye see
Wher dremes ben somtyme (I sey nat alle)
Warninge of thinges that shul after falle.°   *occur*
Loke of Egipte the king, daun Pharao,°   *Sir Pharaoh*
His bakere and his boteler° also,   *butler*
3135 Wher° they ne felte noon effect° in dremes.   *Whether / significance*
Whoso wol seken actes of sondry remes[5]
May rede of° dremes many a wonder thing.   *about*
Lo Cresus,° which that was of Lyde° king,   *Croesus / Lydia*
Mette he nat° that he sat upon a tree,   *Did he not dream*
3140 Which signified he sholde anhanged° be?   *hanged*
Lo heer Andromacha,° Ectores° wyf,   *Andromache / Hector's*
That day that Ector sholde lese° his lyf,   *was to lose*
She dremed on the same night biforn,
How that the lyf of Ector sholde be lorn°   *lost*
3145 If thilke° day he wente into bataille;   *that same*
She warned him, but it mighte nat availle;
He wente for to fighte nathelees,°   *nevertheless*
But he was slayn anoon° of Achilles.   *immediately*
But thilke tale is al to long° to telle,   *all too long*
3150 And eek it is ny° day, I may nat dwelle.   *near*
Shortly I seye, as for conclusioun,
That I shal han of this avisioun°   *vision*
Adversitee; and I seye forthermore,
That I ne telle of laxatyves no store,[6]
3155 For they ben venimous,° I woot° it wel;   *poisonous / know*
I hem defye,° I love hem never a del.°   *defy them / not a bit*
  Now let us speke of mirthe and stinte° al this;   *stop*
Madame Pertelote, so have I blis,
Of o° thing God hath sent me large° grace: *one / bounteous*
3160 For whan I see the beautee of your face—
Ye ben so scarlet reed about your yën—°   *eyes*
It maketh al my drede° for to dyen.   *fear*
For, also siker° as *In principio*,   *just as sure*

2. By God, I'd give my shirt if you had (could have) read his story, as I have. ["Lever": rather.]
3. At the end of the fourth century, Macrobius wrote a commentary on Cicero's *Dream of Scipio* that became for the Middle Ages a standard authority on the nature of dreams. See pp. 461–62.
4. For the story of Joseph, see Genesis 37, 40, and 41.
5. Whosoever wishes to seek (knowledge of) the histories of various realms.
6. That I set no store by laxatives.

Mulier est hominis confusio.[7]

3165 Madame, the sentence° of this Latin is   *meaning*
'Womman is mannes joye and al his blis.'
For whan I fele° a-night° your softe syde,   *feel / at night*
Al be it that I may nat on you ryde,
For that° our perche is maad° so narwe,° alas!   *Because / made / narrow*
3170 I am so ful of joye and of solas°   *comfort*
That I defye bothe sweven° and dreem."   *vision*
And with that word he fley° doun fro the beem,   *flew*
For it was day, and eek° his hennes alle,   *i.e., so did*
And with a chuk° he gan hem for to calle,°   *cluck / called them*
3175 For he had founde a corn° lay° in the yerd.   *grain / (which) lay*
Real° he was, he was namore aferd;°   *Regal / afraid*
He fethered° Pertelote twenty tyme, *covered with outspread wings*
And trad hir eke as ofte, er it was pryme.[8]
He loketh as it were° a grim leoun,°   *as if he were / lion*
3180 And on his toos° he rometh up and doun—   *toes*
Him deyned° not to sette his foot to grounde.   *deigned*
He chukketh whan he hath a corn y-founde,
And to him rennen thanne° his wyves alle.   *run then*
Thus royal, as a prince is in his halle,
3185 Leve I this Chauntecleer in his pasture;°   *feeding*
And after wol I telle his aventure.
    Whan that the month in which the world bigan,
That highte° March, whan God first maked man,   *is called*
Was complet, and passed were also,
3190 Sin° March bigan, thritty dayes and two,   *Since*
Bifel° that Chauntecleer, in al his pryde,   *It came to pass*
His seven wyves walkinge by his syde,
Caste up his eyen to the brighte sonne,
That in the signe° of Taurus hadde y-ronne°   *zodiacal sign / run*
3195 Twenty degrees and oon, and somwhat more;
And knew by kynde,° and by noon° other lore,° *nature / no / learning*
That it was pryme, and crew with blisful stevene.°   *voice*
"The sonne," he sayde, "is clomben° up on hevene   *has climbed*
Fourty degrees and oon, and more, ywis.
3200 Madame Pertelote, my worldes blis,
Herkneth° thise blisful briddes° how they singe, *Harken to / birds*
And see the fresshe floures how they springe;
Ful is myn herte of revel and solas."°   *joy*
But sodeinly him fil° a sorweful cas,°   *befell / happening*
3205 For ever the latter ende of joye is wo.
God woot° that worldly joye is sone ago;° *knows / soon gone*
And if a rethor° coude faire endyte,° *rhetorician / write well*
He in a cronique° saufly° mighte it wryte *chronicle / safely*

---

7. "In the beginning" (the opening of the Gospel of St. John); "woman is man's ruin" (a much-used Latin proverb). Chauntecleer tactfully mistranslates it for Pertelote.
8. And trod (i.e., copulated with) her just as often, before it was nine o'clock (the canonical hour of prime).

As for a sovereyn notabilitee.°	*supremely noteworthy fact*
3210 Now every wys° man, lat him herkne me:	*wise*
This storie is also° trewe, I undertake,°	*just as / declare*
As is the book of Launcelot de Lake,⁹	
That wommen holde in ful gret reverence.	
Now wol I torne agayn° to my sentence.°	*turn again / main subject*
3215 A col-fox,¹ ful of sly iniquitee,	
That in the grove hadde woned° yeres three,	*dwelt*
By heigh imaginacioun forncast,²	
The same night thurghout° the hegges brast°	*through / burst*
Into the yerd, ther° Chauntecleer the faire	*where*
3220 Was wont,° and eek his wyves, to repaire;°	*accustomed / to retire to*
And in a bed of wortes° stille he lay,	*herbs*
Til it was passed undren° of the day,	*midmorning*
Waytinge° his tyme on Chauntecleer to falle,	*Watching for*
As gladly doon° thise homicydes° alle,	*usually do / murderers*
3225 That in awayt liggen° to mordre men.	*lie in wait*
O false mordrour, lurkinge in thy den!	
O newe Scariot, newe Genilon!³	
False dissimilour,° O Greek Sinon,⁴	*dissembler*
That broghtest Troye al outrely° to sorwe!	*quite utterly*
3230 O Chauntecleer, acursed be that morwe,°	*morning*
That thou into that yerd flough° fro the bemes!	*flew*
Thou were ful wel y-warned by thy dremes	
That thilke day was perilous to thee.	
But what that God forwoot mot	
nedes be,°	*that which God foreknows must needs be*
3235 After the opinioun of certeyn clerkis.°	*scholars*
Witnesse on him° that any perfit clerk is	*Let him be witness*
That in scole° is gret altercacioun	*in (the) school(s)*
In this matere, and greet disputisoun,°	*disputation*
And hath ben of an hundred thousand men.	
3240 But I ne can not bulte it to the bren,⁵	
As can the holy doctour Augustyn,°	*St. Augustine*
Or Boece,° or the bishop Bradwardyn,°	*Boethius / Bradwardine (of England)*
Whether that Goddes worthy forwiting°	*excellent foreknowledge*
Streyneth° me nedely° for to doon a thing	*Constrains / necessarily*
3245 ("Nedely" clepe° I simple necessitee);	*call*
Or elles, if free choys° be graunted me	*choice, will*
To do that same thing or do it noght,	
Though God forwoot° it er° that I was wroght;	*foreknows / before*
Or if his witing° streyneth never a del°	*knowing / not at all*

9. Launcelot was the lover of Guinevere, wife to King Arthur—an entirely fictitious story.
1. A coal-fox, i.e., one with black markings (like the animal Chauntecleer saw in his dream).
2. Foreseen (preordained) by a supreme (divine) intelligence (an idea much too grand for the fate of a chicken). It leads to the problem of free will within the context of divine foreknowledge that is worried over in ll. 3234–50).
3. Oh, new (Judas) Iscariot, new Ganelon (the traitor in the *Chanson de Roland*).
4. Sinon devised the wooden horse in which the Greeks entered Troy.
5. But I cannot sift it down to the bran (i.e., argue the fine points).

3250 But by necessitee condicionel.[6]
I wol not han to do of swich matere;
My tale is of a cok, as ye may here,
That took his counseil of° his wyf, with sorwe,   *advice from*
To walken in the yerd upon that morwe°   *morning*
3255 That he had met° the dreem that I yow tolde.   *dreamt*
Wommennes counseils been ful ofte colde;°   *fatal*
Wommannes counseil broghte us first to wo,
And made Adam fro Paradys to go,[7]
Ther as° he was ful mery and wel at ese.   *There where*
3260 But for I noot° to whom it mighte displese,   *since I know not*
If I counseil of wommen wolde blame,
Passe over, for I seyde it in my game.
Rede auctours,° wher they trete° of swich matere,   *the authorities / treat*
And what thay seyn of wommen ye may here.
3265 Thise been the cokkes wordes, and nat myne;
I can noon harm of no womman divyne.[8]
      Faire in the sond,° to bathe hire merily,   *sand*
Lyth° Pertelote, and alle hire sustres° by,°   *Lies / sisters / nearby*
Agayn° the sonne; and Chauntecleer so free   *In*
3270 Song° merier than the mermayde in the see—   *Sang*
For Phisiologus[9] seith sikerly
How that they singen wel and merily—
And so bifel that, as he caste his yë°   *eye*
Among the wortes,° on a boterflye,   *herbs*
3275 He was war° of this fox that lay ful lowe.   *became aware*
Nothing ne liste him thanne for to crowe,[1]
But cryde anon, "Cok cok!" and up he sterte,°   *leaped*
As man° that was affrayed° in his herte.   *Like someone / frightened*
For naturelly a beest desyreth flee°   *desires to flee*
3280 Fro his contrarie,° if he may it see,   *opposite*
Though he never erst° had seyn it with his yë.°   *before / eye*
      This Chauntecleer, whan he gan him espye,°   *caught sight of him*
He wolde han fled, but that the fox anon°   *immediately*

---

6. Except by conditional necessity ("e.g., the sort of 'necessity' found in such a conditional sentence as 'If I see him standing, he must of necessity be standing' "—R. A. Pratt). The perplexity, at its simplest, might be put so: if God is all-knowing (that is, having a perfect knowledge of what *was, is, and will be*), He must know in advance every man's every moral choice. But if He knows how a man will choose, that man is not free to choose the alternative, for then God would be wrong (in a condition of ignorance, not omniscience). Theologians have struggled with the problem for centuries. The Middle Ages, for the most part, agreed to Boethius's resolution of it in *The Consolation of Philosophy*—that same "conditional necessity" here named: to know is not necessarily to cause, particularly if you postulate a complex difference between the orders of time and eternity. After devoting a considerable time to the question, the Nun's Priest announces with a certain ironic glee (in ll. 3251–52): I will not have anything to do with such a subject; my story concerns a rooster.
7. The fall of Adam and Eve was, naturally, the central event in discussions concerning man's free will.
8. I cannot conceive of harm in any woman (with a possible secondary meaning, "I know nothing to the discredit of any holy woman," referring to the Prioress whom he accompanies).
9. Physiologus was the supposed author of a Greek work on natural history, which was a distant source of the numerous medieval *bestiaries*: popular compilations of lore concerning animals and other creatures, some (as here with the mermaids) imaginary. In the medieval version, almost every description was moralized.
1. He had no wish at all to crow then.

Seyde, "Gentil sire, allas! wher wol ye gon?
3285   Be ye affrayed of me that am your freend?
Now certes, I were worse than a feend,°   *devil*
If I to yow wolde° harm or vileinye.°   *wished / wrong*
I am nat come your counseil for t'espye,[2]
But trewely, the cause of my cominge
3290   Was only for to herkne° how that ye singe.   *listen to*
For trewely ye have as mery a stevene°   *pleasant a voice*
As eny° aungel hath that is in hevene;   *any*
Therwith ye han in musik more feelinge
Than hadde Boece,[3] or any that can singe.
3295   My lord your fader (God his soule blesse!)
And eek your moder, of° hire gentilesse,   *because of*
Han in myn hous y-been, to my gret ese;°   *satisfaction*
And certes, sire, ful fayn° wolde I yow plese.   *very willingly*
But for° men speke of singing, I wol saye,   *since*
3300   So mote I brouke° wel myn eyen tweye,°   *profit by / two eyes*
Save° yow, I herde never man so singe   *Except*
As dide your fader in the morweninge.°   *morning*
Certes,° it was of herte,° al that he song.   *Truly / from the heart*
And for to make his voys the more strong,
3305   He wolde so peyne him° that with bothe his yën°   *take such pains / eyes*
He moste winke,° so loude he wolde cryen,   *had to shut*
And stonden on his tiptoon therwithal,[4]
And strecche forth his nekke long and smal.°   *thin*
And eek he was of swich discrecioun°   *wisdom*
3310   That ther nas no man° in no regioun   *was no man*
That him in song or wisdom mighte passe.
I have wel rad° in 'Daun Burnel the Asse,'[5]   *read*
Among his vers,° how that ther was a cok,   *its (the book's) verses*
For that° a preestes sone yaf° him a knok°   *Because / gave / blow*
3315   Upon his leg, whyl he was yong and nyce,°   *foolish*
He made him for to lese° his benefyce.   *lose*
But certeyn, ther nis no° comparisoun   *is not any*
Bitwix the wisdom and discrecioun
Of youre fader, and of his° subtiltee.   *i.e., that other rooster's*
3320   Now singeth, sire, for seinte° charitee!   *holy*
Let see, conne ye your fader countrefete?"°   *imitate*
This Chauntecleer his winges gan to bete,°   *did beat*
As man° that coude his tresoun° nat espye,° *one / betrayal / perceive*
So was he ravisshed with his flaterye.
3325   Allas! ye lordes, many a fals flatour°   *flatterer*

---

2. I've not come to spy on your private affairs.
3. Boethius, in addition to *The Consolation of Philosophy* referred to above, wrote a work on the theory of music that was used as a text in the schools.
4. And stand on (his) tiptoes at the same time.
5. *Burnellus*, or the *Speculum Stultorum*, a twelfth-century Latin satire in verse by Nigel Wireker: in one episode, a cock takes revenge on a certain Gundulfus, who injured him in his youth, by crowing so late on the morning that Gundulfus is to be ordained that he oversleeps and loses his benefice.

Is in your courtes, and many a losengeour,°   *liar*
That plesen° yow wel more, by my feith,   *Who please*
Than he that soothfastnesse° unto yow seith.   *truthfulness*
Redeth Ecclesiaste of° flaterye;   *Ecclesiasticus on*
3330 Beth war,° ye lordes, of hir trecherye.   *Beware*
     This Chauntecleer stood hye° upon his toos,   *high*
Strecching his nekke, and heeld his eyen cloos,°   *closed*
And gan to crowe loude for the nones;°   *for the occasion*
And daun Russel the fox sterte up at ones°   *once*
3335 And by the gargat° hente° Chauntecleer,   *throat / seized*
And on his bak toward the wode° him beer,°   *woods / bore*
For yet ne was ther no man that him sewed.°   *pursued*
     O destinee, that mayst nat been eschewed!°   *avoided*
Allas, that Chauntecleer fleigh° fro the bemes!   *flew*
3340 Allas, his wyf ne roghte nat° of dremes!   *took no heed*
And on a Friday fil° al this meschaunce.   *befell*
     O Venus, that art goddesse of plesaunce,°   *(amorous) pleasure*
Sin° that thy servant was this Chauntecleer,   *Since*
And in thy service dide al his poweer,°   *expended all his force*
3345 More for delyt than world to multiplye,
Why woldestow° suffre him on thy day⁶ to dye?   *wouldst thou*
     O Gaufred,⁷ dere mayster soverayn,
That whan thy worthy king Richard° was slayn   *Richard I*
With shot,° compleynedest his deth so sore,   *an arrow*
3350 Why ne hadde I now thy sentence° and thy lore,   *wisdom*
The Friday for to chide, as diden ye?
(For on a Friday soothly° slayn was he.)   *truly*
Than wolde I shewe yow how that I coude pleyne°   *lament*
For Chauntecleres drede, and for his peyne.
3355   Certes,° swich cry ne lamentacioun   *Truly*
Was never of ladies maad° when Ilioun°   *made by ladies / Ilium (Troy)*
Was wonne, and Pirrus° with his streite° swerd,   *Pyrrhus / drawn*
Whan he hadde hent° king Priam by the berd,   *seized*
And slayn him (as saith us *Eneydos*),°   *the Aeneid*
3360 As maden alle the hennes in the clos,°   *enclosure, yard*
Whan they had seyn of Chauntecleer the sighte.
But sovereynly° dame Pertelote shrighte°   *above all / shrieked*
Ful louder than dide Hasdrubales° wyf,   *Hasdrubal's*
Whan that hir housbond hadde lost his lyf,
3365 And that the Romayns hadde brend Cartage:°   *burned Carthage*
She was so ful of torment and of rage
That wilfully into the fyr she sterte,°   *leaped*
And brende hirselven° with a stedfast herte.   *i.e., to death*
     O woful hennes, right so° cryden ye   *in like manner*
3370 As, whan that Nero brende the citee

---

6. Friday is Venus's day.
7. Geoffrey de Vinsauf, author of a treatise on the writing of poetry, the *Poetria Nova* (ca. 1210). Chaucer refers to one of Geoffrey's examples of how to lament in a rhetorically elaborate style, printed on pp. 463–64.

Of Rome, cryden senatoures wyves,
For that hir° housbondes losten alle hir lyves;   *their*
Withouten gilt this Nero hath hem° slayn.   *them*
Now wol I torne to my tale agayn.
3375   This sely° widwe and eek hir doghtres two   *good, simple*
Herden thise hennes crye and maken wo,
And out at dores sterten they anoon,°   *they leap at once*
And syen° the fox toward the grove goon,°   *saw / go*
And bar° upon his bak the cok away;   *bore, carried*
3380 And cryden, "Out! harrow!° and weylaway!°   *help / alas*
Ha, ha, the fox!" and after him they ran,
And eek with staves° many another man;   *sticks*
Ran Colle our dogge, and Talbot, and Gerland,[8]
And Malkin, with a distaf° in hir hand;   *for spinning*
3385 Ran cow and calf, and eek the verray hogges,
So fered° for the berking of the dogges   *frightened*
And shouting of the men and wimmen eke,
They ronne so hem thoughte hir herte breke.[9]
They yelleden as feendes° doon in helle;   *fiends*
3390 The dokes° cryden as° men wolde hem quelle;°   *ducks / as though / kill*
The gees for fere° flowen° over the trees;   *fear / flew*
Out of the hyve cam the swarm of bees;
So hidous was the noyse, a! *benedicite!*°   *bless us*
Certes, he Jakke Straw and his meynee[1]
3395 Ne made nevere shoutes half so shrille
Whan that they wolden any Fleming kille,
As thilke° day was maad upon the fox.   *that same*
Of bras thay broghten bemes,° and of box,°   *trumpets / boxwood*
Of horn, of boon,° in whiche they blewe and pouped,°   *bone / puffed*
3400 And therwithal thay shryked° and they houped:°   *shrieked / whooped*
It seemed as that heven sholde falle.
Now, gode men, I pray yow herkneth° alle!   *listen*
     Lo, how Fortune turneth° sodeinly   *overturns*
The hope and pryde eek of hir enemy!
3405 This cok, that lay upon the foxes bak,
In al his drede unto the fox he spak,
And seyde, "Sire, if that I were as ye,
Yet sholde I seyn,° as° wis God helpe me,   *say / may*
'Turneth agayn, ye proude cherles° alle!   *churls*
3410 A verray° pestilence upon yow falle!   *real*
Now I am come unto this wodes syde,
Maugree your heed,° the cok shal heer abyde;   *Despite your efforts*
I wol him ete° in feith, and that anon.' "   *eat*
     The fox answerde, "In feith, it shal be don,"
3415 And as he spak that word, al sodeinly

8. All are common names for dogs.
9. They ran so (hard), it seemed to them their hearts would burst.
1. Jack Straw was a leader of the Peasants' Revolt ("his meynee" or company) in 1381; many
   Flemish, most of them weavers, were killed in London in that uprising (see l. 3396).

This cok brak° from his mouth deliverly,°   *broke / nimbly*
And heighe upon a tree he fleigh° anon.   *flew*
And whan the fox saugh that the cok was gon,
"Allas!" quod he, "O Chauntecleer, allas!
3420 I have to yow," quod he, "y-doon trespas,°   *wrong*
In as muche as I maked yow aferd
When I yow hente° and broghte out of the yerd.   *seized*
But, sire, I dide it in no wikke ententè;°   *with no wicked intent*
Com doun, and I shal telle yow what I mente.
3425 I shal seye sooth° to yow, God help me so."   *tell the truth*
    "Nay, than," quod he, "I shrewe° us bothe two,   *curse*
And first I shrewe myself, bothe blood and bones,
If thou bigyle° me ofter° than ones.°   *deceive / more / once*
Thou shalt namore, thurgh thy flaterye,
3430 Do° me to singe and winke with myn yë.°   *Cause / shut my eyes*
For he that winketh whan he sholde see,
Al wilfully, God lat° him never thee!"°   *let / prosper*
    "Nay," quod the fox, "but God yeve° him meschaunce,   *give*
That is so undiscreet of governaunce°   *self-control*
3435 That jangleth° whan he sholde holde his pees."°   *chatters / peace, silence*
    Lo, swich it is for to be recchelees°   *reckless*
And necligent, and truste on flaterye.
    But ye that holden this tale a folye,°   *silly thing*
As of a fox, or of a cok and hen,
3440 Taketh the moralitee,° goode men.   *moral (of it)*
For Seint Paul seith that al that writen is,
To our doctryne° it is y-write, ywis.°   *instruction / indeed*
Taketh the fruyt,° and lat the chaf° be stille.   *i.e., grain / husks*
    Now, gode God, if that it be thy wille,
3445 As seith my lord,° so make us alle good men,   *my bishop*
And bringe us to his heighe° bliss. Amen.   *high*

The Epilogue

"Sir Nonnes Preest," our Hoste seyde anoon,[2]
"Y-blessed by thy breche° and every stoon!°   *breech, thighs / stone, testicles*
This was a mery tale of Chauntecleer.
3450 But by my trouthe, if thou were seculer,°   *a layman*
Thou woldest been a trede-foul[3] aright.
For if thou have corage° as thou hast might,°   *spirit / strength*
Thee were nede of° hennes, as I wene,°   *You would need / suppose*
Ya, mo° than seven tymes seventene.   *more*
3455 See, whiche braunes° hath this gentil preest,   *what brawn, muscles*
So greet a nekke, and swich a large breest!
He loketh as a sperhauk° with his yën;°   *sparrow hawk / eyes*
Him nedeth nat his colour° for to dyen°   *complexion / dye*

---

2. This epilogue occurs in nine manuscripts only: it is not in Ellesmere, for example, and may have been rejected by Chaucer at some later stage in his work on the *Tales*.
3. "Tread-fowl," a potent rooster.

With brasile, ne with greyn of Portingale.⁴
3460 Now sire, faire falle° yow for youre tale!"   *may good befall*

* * *

The Manciple's Prologue and Tale

The Prologue

Woot° ye nat wher ther stant° a litel toun   *Know / stands*
Which that y-cleped is Bob-up-and-doun,
Under the Blee in Caunterbury weye?¹
Ther gan our Hoste for to jape° and pleye,   *jest, joke*
5 And seyde, "Sirs, what! Dun is in the myre!²
Is ther no man for preyere° ne for hyre°   *prayer / wages, money*
That wol awake our felawe° al bihinde?°   *companion / (lagging) behind*
A theef mighte him ful lightly° robbe and binde.   *very easily*
See how he nappeth!° See how, for cokkes bones,³   *naps, dozes*
10 That he wol falle from his hors atones.°   *at once*
Is that a cook of Londoun, with meschaunce?°   *bad luck to him*
Do him° come forth. He knoweth his penaunce,   *Have him*
For he shal telle a tale, by my fey,°   *faith*
Although it be nat worth a botel hey.°   *small clump of hay*
15 Awake, thou Cook," quod he, "God yeve° thee sorwe!°   *give / sorrow*
What eyleth° thee to slepe by the morwe?°   *ails / through the morning*
Hastow° had fleen° al night, or artow° dronke,   *Hast thou / fleas / art thou*
Or hastow with som quene° al night y-swonke,°   *quean, prostitute / labored*
So that thou mayst nat holden up thyn heed?"
20   This Cook, that was ful pale and no thing reed,°   *not at all red, ruddy*
Seyde to our Host, "So God my soule blesse,
As ther is falle on me swich hevinesse,°   *drowsiness*
Noot I nat° why, that me were lever° slepe   *I know not / I would rather*
Than° the beste galoun wyn° in Chepe."° *Than (have) / gallon of wine / Cheapside*
25 "Wel," quod the Maunciple, "if it may doon ese°   *bring comfort*
To thee, sir Cook, and to no wight° displese   *person*
Which that heer rydeth in this companye,
And that our Host wol,° of his curteisye,   *wills (it), is agreeable*
I wol as now excuse thee of thy tale.
30 For, in good feith, thy visage is ful pale,
Thyn eyen daswen eek,° as that me thinketh,   *are dazed also*
And wel I woot° thy breeth ful soure stinketh.   *know*
That sheweth wel thou art not wel disposed.°   *not in good health*
Of me, certein, thou shalt nat been y-glosed.°   *glossed (over), flattered*

---

4. With red powder or red dye from Portugal.
1. Which is called Bob-up-and-Down (probably a playful reference to Harbledown, two miles from Canterbury), by the Blean Forest on the Canterbury road.
2. Dun (name for a horse) is stuck in the mud. The Host uses this refrain from a popular game to say that things are at a standstill, it's time to get the tale-telling restarted.
3. For cock's bones, a euphemistic oath just this side of "for God's bones."

35 Se how he ganeth,° lo, this dronken wight,   *yawns*
    As though he wolde swolwe° us anonright.°   *swallow / immediately*
    Hold cloos° thy mouth, man, by thy fader° kin.   *Keep shut / father's*
    The devel of helle sette his foot therin!
    Thy cursed breeth infecte wol us alle.
40 Fy, stinking swyn,° fy! Foule moot thee falle!°   *swine / May evil befall thee*
    A! taketh heed, sirs, of this lusty man.
    Now, swete sir, wol ye justen atte fan?[4]
    Therto° me thinketh ye been wel y-shape°—   *For that / in good shape*
    I trowe° that ye dronken han wyn ape,   *believe*
45 And that is whan men pleyen with a straw."[5]
    And with this speche the Cook wex wrooth and wraw,°   *angry*
    And on the Maunciple he gan nodde° faste   *shook his head*
    For lakke of speche—and doun the hors him caste,
    Wher as he lay, til that men up him took.
50 This was a fayr chivachee° of a cook!   *feat of horsemanship*
    Allas, he nadde holde him by his ladel![6]
    And er° that he agayn were in his sadel,   *before*
    Ther was greet showving° bothe to and fro   *shoving, pushing*
    To lifte him up, and muchel care° and wo,   *much trouble*
55 So unweldy° was this sory palled gost.°   *unwieldy / pallid ghost*
    And to the Maunciple thanne spak our Host.
        "Bycause drink hath dominacioun
    Upon this man, by my savacioun,°   *salvation*
    I trowe he lewedly° wolde telle his tale.   *ignorantly, crudely*
60 For—were it° wyn or old or moysty° ale   *whether it were / new*
    That he hath dronke—he speketh in° his nose,   *through*
    And fneseth° faste, and eek he hath the pose.°   *sneezes / head cold*
    He hath also to do more than ynough
    To kepe him and his capel° out of the slough;°   *cart horse / mud*
65 And if he falle from his capel eftsone,°   *again*
    Than shul we alle have ynough to done°   *do*
    In lifting up his hevy dronken cors.°   *body*
    Telle on thy tale. Of him make I no fors.°   *I.e., I've had enough of him*
    But yet, Maunciple, in feith thou art to nyce°   *too foolish*
70 Thus openly repreve him of° his vyce.   *reprove, reproach him for*
    Another day he wol, peraventure,°   *perhaps, by chance*
    Reclayme thee and bringe thee to lure.[7]
    I mene, he speke wol of smale thinges,
    As for to pinchen at thy rekeninges,°   *find fault with thy accounts*
75 That were not honeste, if it cam to preef."°   *to proof, to the test*
        "No," quod the Maunciple, "that were a greet
            mescheef!°   *misfortune*

---

4. Joust at the quintain, a demanding jousting exercise far beyond the station and condition of
   the drunken Cook.
5. "Win ape" probably refers to a medieval classification of different types of drunkenness. The
   Maunciple says the Cook has drunk wine that renders him apelike, capable only of silly play
   with straw rather than being able to joust.
6. Alas, that he hadn't stuck to his cooking ladle.
7. Call thee back with a lure (as one does a hawk); i.e., get back at you.

So mighte he lightly° bringe me in the snare.   *easily*
Yet hadde I lever° payen for the mare   *I would rather*
Which he rit° on than he sholde with me stryve.°   *rides / strive, quarrel*
80 I wol nat wratthe° him, also mote I thryve.°   *anger / so may I thrive, prosper*
That that° I spak, I seyde it in my bourde.°   *That which / jesting*
And wite° ye what? I have heer in a gourde°   *know / gourd-shaped flask*
A draught of wyn—ye,° of a rype grape—   *yes (indeed)*
And right anon ye shul seen a good jape.°   *joke*
85 This Cook shal drinke therof, if I may.°   *if I may (offer him some)*
Up peyne° of deeth, he wol nat seye me nay."   *Upon pain*
        And certeinly, to tellen as it was,
Of this vessel the cook drank faste. Allas,
What neded him? He drank ynough biforn.
90 And whan he hadde pouped° in this horn,   *puffed, blown (i.e. taken a gulp)*
To the Maunciple he took the gourde agayn;°   *gave the gourd back*
And of that drinke the Cook was wonder fayn,°   *wonderfully happy*
And thanked him in swich wyse° as he coude.   *in such a way*
        Than gan our Host to laughen wonder loude,
95 And seyde, "I see wel it is necessarie,
Wher that we goon,° good drink we with us carie,   *Wherever we go*
For that wol turne rancour° and disese°   *rancor / dis-ease, discomfort*
T'acord° and love, and many a wrong apese.°   *To accord / appease, remedy*
        O Bachus,° y-blessed be thy name,   *Bacchus, god of wine*
100 That so canst turnen ernest into game.
Worship and thank be to thy deitee!°   *deity, godship*
Of that matere° ye gete namore of° me.   *On that subject / from*
Tel on° thy tale, Maunciple, I thee preye."   *forth*
        "Wel, sir," quod he, "now herkneth° what I seye."   *listen to*

The Tale

105   Whan Phebus° dwelled here in this erthe adoun,   *Phoebus Apollo*
As olde bokes maken mencioun,
He was the moste lusty bachiler°   *vigorous young knight*
In al this world and eek° the beste archer.   *also*
He slow Phitoun,° the serpent, as he lay   *slew the Python*
110 Slepinge agayn the sonne° upon a day,   *in the sun*
And many another noble worthy dede
He with his bowe wroghte,° as men may rede.   *worked, performed*
        Pleyen he coude on every minstralcye°   *musical instrument*
And singen, that it was a melodye°   *sweet music*
115 To heren of his clere vois the soun.°   *sound*
Certes° the king of Thebes, Amphioun,   *Certainly*
That with his singing walled° that citee,   *built the walls of*
Coude never singen half so wel as he.
Therto° he was the semelieste° man   *In addition / most handsome*
120 That is or was, sith° that the world bigan.   *since*
What nedeth it his fetures to discryve?°   *describe*
For in this world was noon so fair on lyve.°   *alive*

He was therwith° fulfild of gentillesse,° — *also / full of nobility*
Of honour, and of parfit° worthinesse. — *perfect*
125   This Phebus, that was flour of bachelrye° — *the flower of knighthood*
As wel in fredom° as in chivalrye,° — *generosity / knightly deeds*
For his desport,° in signe eek of victorie — *amusement, delight*
Of Phitoun,° so as telleth us the storie, — *Over Python*
Was wont to beren° in his hand a bowe. — *accustomed to carrying*
130   Now had this Phebus in his hous a crowe,
Which in a cage he fostred° many a day, — *fostered, cared for*
And taughte it speke° as men teche a jay. — *to speak*
Whyt was this crowe, as is a snow-whyt swan,
And countrefete° the speche of every man — *imitate (lit., counterfeit)*
135 He coude, whan he sholde telle a tale.
Therwith in al this world no nightingale
Ne coude, by an hondred thousand deel,° — *thousandth part*
Singen so wonder merily and weel.
    Now had this Phebus in his hous a wyf,
140 Which that he lovede more than his lyf,
And night and day dide ever his diligence
Hir for to plese and doon hir reverence,° — *show her respect*
Save° only (if the sothe° that I shal sayn) — *Except / truth*
Jalous° he was and wolde have kept hir — *Jealous*
    fayn,° — *was eager to keep her guarded*
145 For him were looth° byjaped° for to be. — *he did not like / deceived*
And so is every wight° in swich degree,° — *person / in such a situation*
But al in ydel,° for it availleth noght.° — *in vain / does not help*
A good wyf that is clene of werk° and thoght — *pure in action*
Sholde nat been kept in noon await,° certayn; — *under any surveillance*
150 And trewely the labour is in vayn
To kepe a shrewe, for it wol nat be.° — *cannot be done*
This holde I for a verray nycetee:° — *true folly*
To spille° labour for to kepe° wyves. — *waste / trying to guard*
Thus writen olde clerkes° in hir lyves. — *scholars, learned men*
155   But now to purpos, as I first bigan:
This worthy Phebus dooth all that he can
To plesen hir, weninge° by swich plesaunce,° — *thinking / pleasure*
And for° his manhede° and his governaunce,° — *because of / manliness / behavior*
That no man sholde han put him from hir grace.° — *out of favor with her*
160 But God it woot,° ther may no man embrace° — *knows / i.e., succeed*
As to destreyne° a thing which that nature — *restrain*
Hath naturelly set in a creature.
    Tak any brid° and put it in a cage, — *bird*
And do al thyn entente° and thy corage° — *give all thy attention / energy*
165 To fostre° it tendrely with mete° and drinke — *foster, raise / food*
Of alle deyntees° that thou canst bithinke,° — *delicacies / imagine*
And keep it also clenly° as thou may: — *as cleanly, neatly*
Although his cage of gold be never so gay,° — *i.e., ever so splendid*
Yet hath° this brid, by twenty thousand fold,° — *would / times*
170 Lever° in a forest that is rude° and cold — *Rather / wild*

Gon ete° wormes and swich wrecchednesse.   *Go eat*

For ever this brid wol doon his bisinesse°   *busy himself*

To escape out of his cage if he may.

His libertee this brid desireth ay.°   *always*

175 Lat take° a cat, and fostre him wel with milk   *Take (for instance)*

And tendre flesh,° and make his couche° of silk,   *meat / bed*

And lat him seen a mous go by the wal:

Anon° he weyveth° milk and flesh and al,   *Immediately / abandons*

And every deyntee that is in that hous,

180 Swich appetyt hath he to ete a mous.

Lo, here hath lust° his dominacioun,   *desire*

And appetyt flemeth discrecioun.°   *drives out (rational) judgment*

A she-wolf hath also a vileins kinde:°   *churlish, base nature*

The lewedeste° wolf that she may finde,   *lowest, most uncouth*

185 Or leest° of reputacion, wol she take   *least*

In tyme whan hir lust to han a make.°   *she desires to have a mate*

Alle thise ensamples speke I by° thise men   *concerning*

That been untrewe, and no thing° by wommen.   *not at all*

For men han ever a likerous° appetyt   *lecherous*

190 On lower thing to parfourne hir delyt°   *take their pleasure*

Than on hir wyves, be they never so faire,

Ne never so trewe ne so debonaire.°   *kind, gracious*

Flesh is so newefangel,° with meschaunce,°   *fond of novelty / a curse upon it*

That we ne conne in no thing han plesaunce°   *take pleasure*

195 That souneth into° vertu any whyle.°   *is in accord with / to any extent*

This Phebus, which that thoghte upon no gyle,°   *who suspected no deceit*

Deceyved was, for al his jolitee,°   *pleasing nature*

For under° him another hadde she,   *in addition to*

A man of litel reputacioun,

200 Noght worth° to Phebus in comparisoun.   *Worth nothing*

The more harm is° it happeth ofte so,   *is (that)*

Of which ther cometh muchel harm and wo.

And so bifel, whan Phebus was absent,

His wyf anon hath for hir lemman° sent.   *lover*

205 Hir "lemman"? Certes,° this is a knavish   *Certainly*

speche!°   *vulgar language*

Foryeveth it me, and that I yow biseche.°   *beseech, beg*

The wyse Plato seith, as ye may rede,

The word mot nede° accorde with the dede.   *ought to*

If men shal telle proprely a thing,

210 The word mot cosin° be to the werking.°   *cousin / deed*

I am a boistous° man, right thus seye I: *plain, uncultivated*

Ther nis no difference, trewely,

Bitwixe a wyf that is of heigh degree,°   *high social rank*

If of hir body dishonest° she be,   *unchaste, immoral*

215 And a povre wenche,° other than this—   *poor lower-class woman*

If it so be they werke bothe amis°—   *they both act wrongly*

But° that the gentile,° in estaat° above,   *Only / noblewoman / class, status*

She shal be cleped° his lady, as in love.   *called*

And for° that other is a povre womman,   *because*
220 She shal be cleped his wenche or his lemman.
And God it woot,° myn owene dere brother,   *knows*
Men leyn° that oon as lowe as lyth° that other.   *lay / lies (in intercourse)*
    Right so bitwixe a titlelees tiraunt°   *i.e., a usurper tyrant*
And an outlawe or a theef erraunt,°   *roving*
225 The same,° I seye, ther is no difference.   *(They are) the same*
To Alisaundre° was told this sentence:°   *Alexander the Great / observation*
That, for° the tyrant is of gretter° might   *because / greater*
By force of meynee° for to sleen° dounright   *power of his retinue / slay*
And brennen° hous and hoom and make   *burn*
    al plain,°   *level everything to the ground*
230 Lo, therfor is he cleped° a capitain;   *called*
And for° the outlawe hath but smal meynee   *because*
And may nat doon so greet an harm as he,
Ne bringe a contree to so greet mescheef,°   *misfortune, damage*
Men clepen him an outlawe or a theef.
235 But for I am a man noght textuel,°   *book-learned*
I wol noght telle of textes° never a del.°   *authorities / (not) a bit*
I wol go to my tale, as I bigan.
    Whan Phebus wyf had sent for hir lemman,
Anon they wroghten al hir lust volage.°   *took all their reckless pleasure*
240 The whyte crowe, that heng° ay in the cage,   *lived (lit., hung)*
Biheld hir werk and seyde never a word.
And whan that hoom was come Phebus, the lord,
This crowe sang "Cokkow! Cokkow! Cokkow!"[8]
    "What, brid?"° quod Phebus. "What song   *bird*
      singestow?°   *dost thou sing*
245 Ne were thow wont° so merily to singe   *accustomed*
That to myn herte it was a rejoisinge
To here thy vois? Allas, what song is this?"
    "By God," quod he, "I singe nat amis.°   *amiss, wrongly*
Phebus," quod he, "for al thy worthinesse,
250 For al thy beautee and thy gentilesse,
For al thy song and al thy minstralcye,°   *music making*
For al thy waiting°—blered° is thyn ye°   *watching / blurred (tricked) / eye*
With oon° of litel reputacioun,   *By one*
Noght worth to thee as in comparisoun
255 The mountance° of a gnat, so mote I thryve.°   *value / so may I prosper*
For on thy bed thy wyf I saugh° him swyve."°   *saw / copulate with*
    What wol ye more? The crowe anon° him tolde,   *at once*
By sadde tokenes° and by wordes bolde,   *trustworthy evidence*
How that his wyf had doon hir lecherye,
260 Him to° gret shame and to gret vileinye,°   *To his / dishonor*
And tolde him ofte he saugh it with his yën.°   *eyes*
This Phebus gan aweyward for to wryen.°   *to turn away*
Him thoughte his sorweful herte brast a-two.°   *had burst in two*

---

8. The word "cuckold" is derived from the cry of the cuckoo, which lays its eggs in other birds'
nests and thus long symbolized sexual infidelity.

His bowe he bente and sette therinne a flo,°   *arrow*
265 And in his ire° his wyf thanne hath he slayn.   *anger*
This is th'effect,° ther is namore to sayn,   *outcome*
For sorwe of which he brak° his minstralcye,°   *broke / musical instruments*
Bothe harpe and lute and giterne° and   *cittern*
      sautrye;°   *psaltery (stringed instruments)*
And eek° he brak° his arwes° and his bowe.   *also / arrows*
270 And after that thus spak he to the crowe:
"Traitour," quod he, "with tonge of scorpioun,
Thou hast me broght to my confusioun!°   *destruction*
Allas, that I was wroght!° Why nere I   *made, created*
      deed?°   *Why should I not be dead*
O dere wyf, o gemme of lustiheed,°   *delight*
275 That were to me so sad° and eek so trewe,   *steadfast*
Now lystow deed,° with face pale of hewe,   *thou liest dead*
Ful giltelees, that dorste° I swere, ywis.°   *dare / indeed*
O rakel° hand, to doon so foule amis!   *rash, impetuous*
O trouble wit,° o ire recchelees,°   *troubled mind / reckless*
280 That unavysed° smytest giltelees!°   *thoughtless / kills the innocent*
O wantrust,° ful of fals suspecioun,   *distrust*
Where was thy wit and thy discrecioun?
O every man, be war° of rakelnesse.°   *beware / rash action*
Ne trowe° no thing withouten strong witnesse.   *believe*
285 Smyt nat to sone,° er that ye witen°   *Strike not too quickly / before you know*
      why,
And beeth avysed° wel and sobrely   *take thought*
Er ye doon any execucioun°   *take any action*
Upon° your ire, for suspecioun.   *Because of*
Allas, a thousand folk hath rakel ire°   *rash anger*
290 Fully fordoon,° and broght hem° in the mire.   *destroyed / them*
Allas, for sorwe I wol myselven slee."°   *slay*
      And to the crowe, "O false theef," seyde he,
"I wol thee quyte anon° thy false tale!   *repay at once*
Thou songe whylom° lyk a nightingale.   *sang formerly*
295 Now shaltow,° false theef, thy song forgon°   *thou shalt / lose*
And eek° thy whyte fetheres everichon,°   *also / every one*
Ne never in al thy lyf ne shaltou speke.
Thus shal men on a traitour been awreke.°   *avenged*
Thou and thyn ofspring ever° shul be blake,°   *forever / black*
300 Ne never swete noise° shul ye make,   *sound*
But ever crye agayn° tempest and rayn,   *in anticipation of*
In tokeninge° that thurgh thee my wyf is slayn."   *As a sign*
And to the crowe he stirte,° and that anon,°   *leaped / at once*
And pulled° his whyte fetheres everichon,   *plucked*
305 And made him blak, and refte him° al his song,   *deprived him of*
And eek his speche, and out at dore him slong°   *slung, threw*
Unto the devel, which I him bitake.°   *to whom I commend him*
And for this caas° ben alle crowes blake.   *cause*
      Lordings, by this ensample I yow preye,

310 Beth war° and taketh kepe° what I seye.   *Be alert / heed*
Ne telleth never no man in your lyf
How that another man hath dight° his wyf.   *had intercourse with*
He wol yow haten mortally, certeyn.
Daun° Salomon, as wyse clerkes seyn,   *Master (a title of respect)*
315 Techeth a man to kepe his tonge° wel.   *hold his tongue (cf. Proverbs 21:23)*
But as I seyde, I am noght textuel.°   *learned in texts*
But nathelees, thus taughte me my dame:°   *mother*
"My sone, thenk on the crowe, a° Goddes name!   *in*
My sone, keep wel thy tonge and keep thy freend.
320 A wikked tonge is worse than a feend,°   *fiend, demon*
My sone: from a feend men may hem blesse.°   *cross (protect) themselves*
My sone, God of° his endelees goodnesse   *out of*
Walled a tonge with teeth and lippes eke,°   *also*
For° man sholde him avyse° what he speke.   *So that / consider*
325 My sone, ful ofte for to° muche speche   *too*
Hath many a man ben spilt,° as clerkes teche,   *ruined*
But for a litel speche avysely°   *discreetly, advisedly*
Is no man shent,° to speke generally.   *hurt*
My sone, thy tonge sholdestow restreyne°   *thou shouldst restrain*
330 At alle tyme but whan° thou doost thy peyne°   *except when / devotest thyself*
To speke of God in honour and preyere.
The firste vertu,° sone, if thou wolt lere,°   *First among the virtues / learn*
Is to restreyne and kepe wel thy tonge.
Thus lerne children whan that they ben yonge.
335 My sone, of° muchel speking yvel-avysed,°   *from / ill-considered*
Ther lasse° speking hadde ynough suffysed,°   *Where less / been sufficient*
Comth muchel harm; thus was me told and taught.
In muchel speche sinne wanteth naught.°   *is not wanting, lacking*
Wostow° wherof° a rakel° tonge serveth?   *Dost thou know / for what / rash*
340 Right as a swerd° forcutteth and forkerveth°   *sword / cuts and hacks*
An arm a-two,° my dere sone, right so   *in half*
A tonge cutteth frendship al a-two.°   *in two*
A jangler° is to God abhominable.   *tale-bearer, loose talker*
Reed° Salomon, so wys and honurable;   *Read*
345 Reed David in his psalmes; reed Senekke.°   *Seneca*
My sone, spek nat, but with thyn heed° thou bekke.°   *head / nod*
Dissimule as° thou were deef,° if that thou here°   *Pretend that / deaf / hear*
A jangler speke of perilous matere.
The Fleming seith°—and lerne it if thee   *I.e., people from Flanders say*
    leste—
350 That litel jangling causeth muchel reste.
My sone, if thou no wikked word hast seyd,
Thee thar° nat drede for to be biwreyd;°   *need / betrayed*
But he that hath misseyd,° I dar wel sayn,   *spoken wrongly*
He may by no wey clepe° his word agayn.°   *call / back*
355 Thing that is seyd is seyd, and forth it gooth,
Though him repente, or be him leef or looth.°   *whether he likes it or not*
He is his thral° to whom that he hath sayd   *slave*

A tale of which he is now yvel apayd.°   *displeased, regretful*
My sone, be war, and be non auctour° newe   *author*
360 Of tydinges,° whether they ben false or trewe.   *tidings, news, stories*
Wherso thou come, amonges hye or lowe,°   *high or low (social rank)*
Kepe wel thy tonge, and thenk upon the crowe."

From The Parson's Prologue and Tale

The Prologue

By that° the Maunciple hadde his tale al ended,   *By the time that*
The sonne fro the south lyne° was descended   *prime meridian*
So lowe, that he nas° nat, to my sighte,   *was not*
Degrees nyne and twenty as in highte.°   *height (above the horizon)*
5 Foure of the clokke it was tho,° as I gesse;   *then*
For elevene foot, or litel more or lesse,
My shadwe° was at thilke° tyme, as there,°   *shadow / that same / at that place*
Of swiche° feet as° my lengthe parted° were   *such / as if / divided*
In six feet equal of proporcioun.[1]
10 Therwith the mones exaltacioun,°   *position of greatest influence*
I mene Libra, alwey gan ascende,°   *steadily kept ascending*
As we were entring° at a thropes ende;°   *entering / village's edge*
For which oure Host, as he was wont° to gye,°   *accustomed / guide*
As in this caas,° oure joly companye,   *case*
15 Seyde in this wyse: "Lordings everichoon,°   *every one*
Now lakketh us no tales mo than oon.°   *one*
Fulfild is my sentence and my decree;
I trowe° that we han herd of ech degree.°   *believe / from each (social) rank*
Almost fulfild is al myn ordinaunce.
20 I prey to God, so yeve him° right good chaunce,°   *may He give him / fortune*
That telleth this tale to us lustily.°   *pleasantly*
   "Sire preest," quod he, "artow° a vicary?°   *art thou / vicar*
Or art a person?° Sey sooth,° by thy fey!°   *parson / Tell the truth / faith*
Be what thou be,° ne breke thou nat oure   *Whatever thou mayest be*
   pley;°   *game*
25 For every man, save thou,° hath told his tale.   *except for thee*
Unbokele,° and shewe us what is in thy male.°   *Unbuckle / bag*
For trewely, me thinketh by thy chere,°   *appearance*
Thou sholdest knitte up° wel a greet matere.°   *bring to conclusion / subject*
Telle us a fable anon,° for cokkes bones!"°   *immediately / (see n. 3, p. 285)*
30   This Persone him answerde, al at ones,°   *at once*
"Thou getest fable noon y-told for° me;   *by*
For Paul, that wryteth unto Timothee,[2]
Repreveth hem that weyven° soothfastnesse°   *put aside / truthfulness*
And tellen fables and swich wrecchednesse.°   *such miserable things*

---

1. I.e., if Chaucer's height were divided into sixths, his shadow would be roughly as long as eleven of those units.
2. Cf. 1 Timothy 1:4 and 4:7; 1 Timothy 4:4.

35 Why sholde I sowen draf° out of my fest,°   *chaff / fist (hand)*
   Whan I may sowen whete,° if that me lest?°   *wheat / it pleases me*
   For which I seye, if that yow list to here°   *it pleases you to listen to*
   Moralitee and vertuous matere,
   And thanne that ye wol yeve° me audience,°   *give / hearing*
40 I wol ful fayn,° at Cristes reverence,   *willingly*
   Do yow pleasaunce leefful, as I can.³
   But trusteth wel, I am a Southren man:
   I can nat geste—rum, ram, ruf—by lettre.⁴
   Ne, God wot,° rym° holde I but litel bettre.   *knows / rhyme*
45 And therfore, if you list, I wol nat glose.°   *be elaborate or subtle*
   I wol yow telle a mery tale in prose
   To knitte up al this feeste° and make an ende.   *feast, festival*
   And Jesu, for his grace, wit° me sende   *wisdom, intelligence*
   To shewe yow the wey, in this viage,°   *journey*
50 Of thilke° parfit° glorious pilgrimage   *that same / perfect*
   That highte° Jerusalem celestial.   *is called*
   And, if ye vouchesauf,° anon I shal   *permit*
   Biginne upon my tale, for whiche I preye
   Telle youre avys,° I can no bettre seye.   *Make known your wish*
55   But nathelees, this meditacioun
   I putte it ay° under correccioun   *ever*
   Of clerkes,° for I am nat textuel;°   *scholars / textually learned*
   I take but° the sentence,° trusteth wel.   *only / meaning*
   Therfor I make protestacioun
60 That I wol stonde to° correccioun."   *submit to*
      Upon this word we han assented sone,°   *at once*
   For, as us semed, it was for to done,⁵
   To enden in som vertuous sentence,
   And for to yeve° him space° and audience,°   *give / the time / a hearing*
65 And bade oure Host he sholde to him seye
   That alle we to telle his tale him preye.°   *ask respectfully*
      Oure Host hadde the wordes° for us alle: *was spokesman*
   "Sire preest," quod he, "now fayre yow bifalle!°   *may good (chance) befall you*
   Sey what yow list, and we wol gladly here."
70 And with that word he seyde in this manere:
   "Telleth," quod he, "youre meditacioun.
   But hasteth yow,° the sonne wol adoun;°   *hurry along / will set*
   Beth fructuous,° and that in litel space,°   *fruitful / a short time*
   And to do wel God sende yow his grace!"⁶

---

3. Give you lawful (permissible) pleasure, to the degree that I know how.
4. I do not know how to compose a romance in the alliterative style, "rum, ram, ruf" (nonsense
   syllables).
5. For, as it seemed to us, it was the thing to do.
6. All MSS agree on this order of the final lines, although modern editors generally move
   ll. 69–70 to the end.

From *The Tale*

[Note: The Parson's Tale is by far the longest of all the *Canterbury Tales*, and as the Parson says in his Prologue, it is a "meditacioun" rather than a "fable" or fiction. Translated from medieval Latin sources, the work is a treatise on penitence, discussing the three necessary elements of penitence according to Roman Catholic doctrine: contrition, oral confession, and satisfaction. Within the section on confession, to illustrate the need for penitents to understand what their sins are, Chaucer inserts a lengthy description of the seven deadly sins, their subdivisions, and their remedies (the virtues that counteract or oppose each sin). We print only the section on the sin of lechery and its remedy, which provides a strict doctrinal perspective on questions of love, sex, and marriage that are at the heart of many of the tales.]

* * *

Sequitur de Luxuria° — *Concerning Lechery*

After Glotonye° thanne comth Lecherie, — *Gluttony*
for thise two sinnes been so ny cosins° that — *such close cousins*
ofte tyme they wol nat departe.° / God woot,° — *part company / knows*
this sinne is ful displesaunt° thing to God, — *displeasing*
for He seyd Himself, "Do no lecherie." And
therfore He putte grete peynes agayns° this — *set great penalties for*
sinne in the olde lawe.° / If womman — *i.e., Old Testament*
thral° were taken° in this sinne, she sholde — *a servant woman / caught*
be beten° with staves° to the deeth; and if — *beaten / clubs*
she were a gentil° womman, she sholde be — *well-born*
slayn with stones; and if she were a bis-
shoppes doghter, she sholde been brent,° by — *burned*
Goddes comandement. / Further over,° by° — *Moreover / for*
the sinne of Lecherie God dreynte° al the — *drowned*
world at the diluge,° and after that He brente — *deluge, flood*
fyve citees with thonder-leyt[7] and sank hem
into helle. /

Now lat us speke thanne of thilke° — *that same*
stinkinge sinne of Lecherie that men clepe
avoutrie° of wedded folk, that is to seyn,° if — *call adultery / say*
840 that oon of hem° be wedded or elles bothe. / — *one of them*
Seint John seith that avoutiers shullen° — *adulterers will*
been in helle in a stank brenninge° of fyr — *burning pool*
and of brimston°—in fyr for the lecherie, in — *brimstone*
brimston for the stink of hir ordure.° / — *their defilement*
Certes° the brekinge of this sacrement is an — *Certainly*
horrible thing. It was maked of° God Him- — *by*
self in paradys and confermed by Jesu Crist,
as witnesseth Seint Mathew in the gospel:
"A man shal lete° fader and moder and — *leave*
taken him° to his wyf, and they shullen be — *betake himself*

---

7. He burned five cities with thunderbolts. The reference is to the destruction of Sodom and Gomorrah and the surrounding area in Genesis 19:24–25.

two in o° flesh." / This sacrement bitokneth°   *one / symbolizes*
the knittinge togidre° of Crist and of holy   *together*
chirche. / And nat only that God forbad°   *prohibited*
avoutrie in dede,° but eek° He comanded   *deed / also*
that thou sholdest nat coveite° thy neighe-   *covet*
bores wyf. / In this heeste,° seith Seint Au-   *commandment*
gustin, is forboden alle manere coveitise° to   *any sort of desire*
doon° lecherie. Lo what seith Seint Mathew   *commit*
in the gospel, that "whoso seeth° a wom-   *looks at*
man to coveitise of his lust,° he hath doon   *with lustful desire*
845   lecherie with hir in his herte." / Here may
ye seen that nat only the dede° of this sinne   *commission*
is forboden but eek the desyr to doon that
sinne. / This cursed sinne anoyeth° grevous-   *damages*
liche hem that it haunten.° / And first to hir   *those who practice it*
soule, for he° oblygeth° it to sinne and to   *i.e., Lechery / compels*
peyne of deeth that is perdurable.° / Unto   *eternal*
the body anoyeth it grevously also, for it
dreyeth him,° and wasteth° and shent° him,   *dries him up / wastes / ruins*
and of his blood he maketh sacrifyce to the
feend° of helle. It wasteth eek his catel° and   *devil / property*
his substaunce.° And certes, if it be a foul   *wealth*
thing a° man to waste his catel on wommen,   *(for) a*
yet is it a fouler thing whan that, for swich
ordure, wommen dispenden upon° men hir   *squander on*
catel and substaunce. / This sinne, as seith
the prophete, bireveth° man and womman   *steals from*
hir gode fame° and al hir honour, and it is   *reputation*
ful pleasant to the devel, for therby win-
850   neth he the moste partie° of this world. /   *greatest part*
And right° as a marchant delyteth him° most   *just / delights*
in chaffare° that he hath most avantage of,°   *trade / profit from*
right so delyteth the feend in this ordure. /
    This is that other hand of the devel, with
fyve fingres to cacche° the peple to° his   *catch, lure / into*
vileinye. / The firste finger is the fool
lookinge° of the fool womman and of the   *lascivious gazing*
fool man, that sleeth° right as the basilicok°   *slays, kills / basilisk*
sleeth folk by the venim° of his sighte; for   *i.e., deadliness*
the coveitise of eyen° folweth the coveitise   *desire of the eyes*
of the herte. / The second finger is the
vileyns° touchinge in wikkede manere.   *shameful, evil*
And therfore seith Salomon that whoso°   *whosoever*
toucheth and handleth a womman, he
fareth° lyk him that° handleth the scorpioun   *fares, behaves / one who*
that stingeth and sodeynly° sleeth thurgh his   *suddenly*
enveniminge;° as whoso toucheth warm   *poisonousness*
pich,° it shent° hise fingres. / The thridde is   *pitch, tar / defiles*
foule° wordes, that fareth lyk fyr that right   *dirty, sinful*

855 anon brenneth° the herte. / The fourthe fin-   quickly burns
ger is the kissinge; and trewely he were° a   would be
greet fool that wolde kisse the mouth of a
brenninge ovene or of a fourneys.° / And   furnace
more fooles been they that kissen in
vileinye,° for that mouth is the mouth of   sinfully
helle, and namely° thise olde dotardes   especially
holours:° yet° wol they kisse (though they   senile lechers / still
may nat do°) and smatre hem.° / Certes, they perform (sexually) / defile themselves
been lyk to houndes; for an hound, whan he
comth by the roser° or by othere busshes,   rosebush
though he may nat pisse, yet wole he heve°   heave, lift
up his leg and make a contenaunce° to   pretend
pisse. / And for that° many man weneth° that   while / believes
he may nat sinne for no likerousnesse° that   no matter what lecherous acts
he doth° with his wyf—certes, that opinion is   performs
fals. God woot,° a man may sleen° himself   knows / slay, kill
with his owene knyf, and make himselven
dronken of his owene tonne.° / Certes, be it   from his own wine cask
wyf, be it child, or any worldly thing that he
loveth biforn° God, it is his maumet° and he   above / idol
860 is an ydolastre.° / Man sholde loven his wyf   idolater
by discrecioun,° paciently and atemprely,°   rationally / moderately
and thanne is she as though it were his
suster. / The fifthe finger of the develes hand
is the stinkinge dede of Lecherie. / Certes,
the fyve fingres of Glotonie the feend put in
the wombe° of a man, and with hise fyve   belly
fyngres of Lecherie he gripeth° him by the   grasps
reynes° for to throwen him into the fourneys   loins
of helle, / ther as° they shul han° the fyr   there where / have, experience
and the wormes that evere shul lasten, and
wepinge and wailinge, sharp hunger and
thurst, and grimnesse° of develes that   savagery
shullen al totrede° hem, withouten respit°   trample on / relief
and withouten ende. /
Of° Lecherie, as I seyde, sourden° diverse   Out of / arise
speces,° as fornicacioun that is bitwixe man   kinds
and womman that been nat maried, and
865 this is deedly sinne and agayns° nature. / Al   against
that is enemy and destruccioun to nature is
agayns nature. / Parfay,° the resoun of a   Indeed
man telleth eek° him wel that it is deedly   also
sinne, for as muche as God forbad°   prohibited
Lecherie. And Seint Paul yeveth hem the
regne that nis dewe to no wight but to hem
that doon deedly sinne.[8] /

8. I.e., Saint Paul gives to them (lechers) the kingdom (of hell), which is reserved only for
those who commit deadly sins. See Galatians 5:19–21.

Another sinne of Lecherie is to bireve° a
mayden of hir maydenhede,° for he that so
dooth,° certes, he casteth a mayden out of
the hyeste degree° that is in this present lyf
/ and bireveth hir° thilke precious fruit that
the book clepeth° "the hundred fruit." I ne
can seye it noon otherweyes° in English,
but in Latin it highte° *centesimus fructus*.[9] /
Certes,° he that so dooth is cause of manye
damages and vileinyes,° mo° than any man
can rekene,° right as he° somtyme is cause
of alle damages that bestes° don in the feeld
that breketh° the hegge° or the closure,°
thurgh which he destroyeth that° may nat
870 been restored. / For certes, namore° may
maydenhede be restored than an arm that is
smiten° fro the body may retourne agayn to
wexe.° / She may have mercy (this woot° I
wel) if she do penitence; but nevere shal it
be that she nas corrupt.° /

And al be it so that° I have spoken
somwhat of avoutrie,° it is good to shewen
mo perils that longen to° avoutrie, for to es-
chue° that foule sinne. / Avoutrie in Latin is
for to seyn° approchinge of other° mannes
bed, thurgh which tho that whylom° weren
o° flessh abaundone° hir bodyes to othere
persones. / Of° this sinne, as seith the wyse
man, folwen° manye harmes. First,
brekinge of feith, and certes in feith is the
875 keye of Cristendom. / And whan that feith is
broken and lorn,° soothly° Cristendom
stant veyn° and withouten fruit. / This sinne
is eek a thefte, for thefte generally is for to
reve a wight his thing° agayns° his wille. /
Certes, this is the fouleste° thefte that may
be, whan a womman steleth hir body from
hir housbonde and yeveth° it to hire holour°
to defoulen° hir, and steleth hir soule fro
Crist and yeveth it to the devel. / This is a
fouler thefte than for to breke° a chirche
and stele the chalice, for thise avoutiers
breken the temple of God spiritually, and
stelen the vessel of grace (that is, the body
and the soule), for which Crist shal destroyen hem, as seith Seint Paul. / Soothly,
of this thefte douted gretly Joseph whan

deprive
virginity
does that
highest rank, status
steals from her
the Bible calls
otherwise
is called
Certainly
evils / more
reckon / just as a man
animals
break out of / hedge / fence
that which
no more

cut off
grow / know

has not been corrupted

although
adultery
more dangers inherent in
in order to avoid
means / another
those who once
one / give
From
follow

lost / truly
stands empty

take someone's possession / against

most wicked

gives / lecher, lover
defile

break into

9. The hundredfold fruit. From Matthew 13:8 in Jesus' parable of the sower, taken in medieval
exegesis of the Bible to refer to the highest state for women (virginity).

that his lordes wyf preyed him of vileinye,[1]
whan he seyde, "Lo,° my lady, how my   *Look*
lord hath take° to me under my warde° al   *given / in my charge*
that he hath in this world, ne no thing of
hise thinges is out of my power but° only ye   *except*
880 that been his wyf. / And how sholde I
thanne do this wikkednesse and sinne so
horribly agayns God and agayns my lord?
God it forbede!" Allas, al to litel° is swich   *all too seldom*
trouthe° now y-founde. / The thridde harm   *such loyalty, integrity*
is the filthe thurgh which they breken the
comandement of God and defoulen the
auctour° of matrimoine, that is Crist. / For   *creator, authorizer*
certes, in so muche as the sacrement of
mariage is so noble and so digne,° so muche   *honorable*
is it gretter° sinne for to breken it, for God   *a greater*
made mariage in paradys in the estaat° of   *state*
innocence, to multiplye mankinde to the
service of God. / And therfore is the
brekinge therof more grevous;° of° which   *serious / from*
brekinge comen false heires° ofte tyme that   *heirs*
wrongfully occupyen° folkes heritages.° And   *usurp / people's inheritances*
therfore wol Crist putte hem out of the
regne° of hevene, that is heritage to gode   *kingdom*
folk. / Of this brekinge comth eek ofte tyme
that folk unwar° wedden or sinnen with hir   *unknowingly*
owene kinrede,° and namely thilke harlottes°   *relatives / those same lechers*
that haunten bordels° of thise fool° wom-   *frequent brothels / lascivious*
men, that mowe° be lykned° to a com-   *may / compared*
mune gonge° where as° men purgen hir or-   *public latrine / where*
885 dure.° / What seye we eek of putours° that   *their excrement / pimps*
liven by the horrible sinne of putrie° and   *prostitution*
constreyne° wommen to yelden to hem a   *force*
certeyn rente of° hir bodily puterie—   *give them part of the income from*
ye,° somtyme of his owene wyf or his   *indeed*
child—as doon this baudes?° Certes, thise   *bawds, pimps*
been cursede sinnes. / Understond eek that
avoutrie is set gladly° in the ten comande-   *appropriately*
ments bitwixe thefte and manslaughtre, for
it is the gretteste thefte that may be, for it is
thefte of body and of soule. / And it is lyk to
homicyde, for it kerveth a-two° and breketh   *cuts in two*
a-two hem that first° were maked o° flesh,   *previously / one*
and therfore, by the olde lawe of God, they
sholde be slayn. / But nathelees, by the lawe
of Jesu Crist (that is, lawe of pitee°), whan   *mercy*

---

1. Truly, Joseph feared greatly (to commit) this sort of theft when his master's wife invited him
to sin (with her). The Parson is referring to the story of Joseph and Potiphar's wife in Genesis 39. Potiphar had entrusted to Joseph the management of all his land and property.

he seyde to the womman that was founden° — *discovered*
in avoutrie and sholde han been° slayn with — *about to be*
stones, after° the wil of the Jewes, as was — *by*
hir lawe: "Go," quod Jesu Crist, "and have
namore wil to sinne," or, "wille namore to
do sinne." / Soothly, the vengeaunce° of — *punishment*
avoutrie is awarded° to the peynes of helle, — *assigned*
but if so be that° it be destourbed° by peni- — *unless / prevented*
890   tence. / Yet been ther mo speces° of this — *more types*
cursed sinne, as whan that oon of hem is
religious or elles bothe; or of folk that been
entred into ordre,° as subdekne,° or dekne, — *a religious order / subdeacon*
or preest, or hospitaliers.° And evere the — *Knights Hospitallers*
hyer° that he is in ordre, the gretter is the — *higher*
sinne. / The thinges that gretly agreggen hir
sinne° is the brekinge of hir avow of chasti- — *make their sin worse*
tee whan they receyved the ordre. / And
forther over,° sooth is that holy ordre is — *furthermore*
chief of al the tresorie° of God and his espe- — *treasury*
cial signe and mark of chastitee to shewe
that they been joyned to chastitee, which
that is most precious lyf that is. / And thise
ordred folk° been specially tytled° to God — *people in orders / dedicated*
and of the special meynee° of God, for — *household*
which, whan they doon° deedly sinne, they — *commit*
been the special traytours of° God and of — *traitors to*
his peple; for they liven of° the peple to — *get their living from*
preye for the peple, and whyle they been
suche traitours, hir preyers availen nat° to — *are of no avail*
the peple. / Preestes been aungeles° as by° — *angels / through*
the dignitee of hir misterye;° but for sothe° — *profession / in truth*
Seint Paul seith that Sathanas transformeth
895   him° in° an aungel of light. / Soothly, the — *himself / into*
preest that haunteth° deedly sinne, he may — *repeatedly engages in*
be lykned to the aungel of derknesse trans-
formed in the aungel of light: he semeth
aungel of light but for sothe he is aungel of
derknesse. / Swiche° preestes been the — *Such*
sones of Helie,° as sheweth in the book of — *sons of Eli (1 Kings 2:12)*
Kinges that they weren the sones of Belial,
that is, the devel. / Belial is to seyn° "with- — *means*
outen juge,"[2] and so faren they: hem think-
eth° they been free and han° no juge, — *it seems to them / have*
namore than hath a free bole° that taketh — *bull*
which° cow that him lyketh° in the toun. / — *whichever / pleases him*
So faren they by° wommen. For right as a — *they act toward*

---

2. Without judge. The biblical source (Judges 19:22) reads in the Vulgate *absque iugo*, "without yoke." Chaucer possibly misread an intermediate French source.

free bole is ynough for al a toun,° right so is | *an entire town*
a wikked preest corrupcioun ynough for al a
parisshe or for al a contree.° / Thise | *county, district*
preestes, as seith the book, ne conne nat
the misterie° of preesthode to the peple, ne | *do not know the duties*
God ne knowe they nat. They ne helde hem
nat apayd,° as seith the book, of soden | *They were not satisfied*
flesh° that was to hem offred, but they toke | *boiled meat*
900 by force the flesh that is rawe. / Certes, so
thise shrewes° ne holden hem nat apayed of | *scoundrels*
rosted flesh and sode flesh, with which the
peple fedden hem in greet reverence, but
they wole have raw flesh of folkes wyves
and hir doghtres. / And certes° thise wom- | *surely*
men that consenten to hir harlotrie° doon | *their wickedness*
greet wrong to Crist, and to holy chirche,
and alle halwes,° and to alle soules; for they | *all the saints*
bireven alle thise him° that sholde worshipe | *deprive all these of him*
Crist and holy chirche and preye for Chris-
tene soules. / And therfore han swiche
preestes, and hir lemmanes° eek that | *lovers*
consenten to hir lecherie, the malisoun° | *curse*
of al the court Cristen,° till they come to | *ecclesiastical court*
amendement.° / The thridde spece of | *correction*
avoutrie° is somtyme bitwixe a man and his | *kind of adultery*
wyf, and that is whan they take no reward° | *pay no attention*
in hir assemblinge° but only° to hire fleshly | *coupling (sexual intercourse) / except*
delyt, as seith Seint Jerome, / and ne rekken
of nothing but° that they been assembled. | *care about nothing except*
Bycause that they been maried, al is good
905 ynough, as thinketh to hem.° But in° swich | *as it seems to them / over*
folk hath the devel power, as seyde the
aungel Raphael to Thobie;° for in hir | *Tobias (Tobit 6:17)*
assemblinge they putten Jesu Crist out of
hir herte and yeven hemself° to alle or- | *give themselves over*
dure.° / | *filth*
The fourthe spece° is the assemblee of | *kind (of lechery)*
hem that been of hire kinrede,° or of hem | *their own family*
that been of oon affinitee,° or elles with | *related by marriage*
hem with whiche° hir fadres or hir kinrede | *whom*
han deled° in the sinne of lecherie. This | *copulated*
sinne maketh hem lyk to houndes, that
taken no kepe° to kinrede./ And certes, par- | *pay no attention*
entele° is in two maneres, outher goostly° | *kinship / either spiritual*
or fleshly; goostly, as for to delen with hise
godsibbes.° / For right so as he that engen- | *godparents or spiritual siblings*
dreth a child is his fleshly fader, right so is
his godfader his fader espirituel. For which
a womman may in no lasse° sinne assem- | *with no less*

blen with hir godsib[3] than with hir owene
fleshly brother. /

The fifthe spece is thilke° abhominable   *that same*
sinne of which that no man unnethe oghte°   *scarcely any man should*
speke ne wryte. Nathelees, it is openly re-
910 herced° in holy writ. / This cursednesse   *mentioned*
doon° men and wommen in diverse en-   *perform*
tente° and in diverse manere; but though   *for various reasons*
that holy writ speke of horrible sinne, certes
holy writ may nat been defouled,° namore   *stained, polluted*
than the sonne that shyneth on the mixen.° /   *dunghill*

Another sinne aperteneth° to lecherie   *belongs*
that comth in slepinge, and this sinne
cometh ofte to hem that been maydenes°   *virgins*
and eek to hem that been corrupt; and this
sinne men clepen pollucioun,° that comth   *i.e., noctural emission*
in foure maneres: / somtyme of lan-
guissinge° of body, for the humours° been   *through weakness / bodily fluids*
to ranke° and habundaunt in the body of   *too profuse*
man; somtyme of infermetee for the feb-
lesse of the vertu retentif,[4] as phisik°   *medical science*
maketh mencioun; somtyme for surfeet° of   *excess*
mete° and drinke; and somtyme of vileyns°   *food / shameful, evil*
thoghtes that been enclosed in mannes
minde whan he goth to slepe, which may
nat been withoute sinne, for° which men   *against*
moste kepen hem wysely° or elles may men   *firmly guard themselves*
sinnen ful grevously. /

Remedium contra peccatum Luxurie.°   *The Remedy Against the Sin of Lechery*
Now comth the remedie agayns Lecherie,
and that is, generally, Chastitee and Continence, that restreyneth alle the desor-
deynee moevinges° that comen of fleshly   *disorderly stirrings*
915 talentes.° / And evere the gretter merite shal   *desires*
he han,° that most restreyneth the wikkede   *have*
eschaufinges° of the ordure° of this sinne.   *burnings / filth*
And this is in two maneres,° that is to seyn,   *kinds*
chastitee in mariage, and chastitee of wid-
wehode.° / Now shaltow° understonde that   *widowhood / shalt thou*
matrimoine is leefful° assemblinge of man   *allowable*
and of womman, that receyven by vertu of
the sacrement the bond thurgh which they
may nat be departed° in al hir lyf, that is to   *separated*
seyn, whyl that they liven bothe. / This, as
seith the book, is a ful greet sacrement.

---

3. That is, have sex with someone who is a child of her godparents or someone for whom her
parents served as godparents.
4. Sometimes through infirmity caused by weakness in the (body's) power to retain (fluids).

God maked it, as I have seyd, in paradys,
and wolde himself be born in mariage. / And
for to halwen° mariage, he was at a wed-   hallow, make holy
dinge° whereas he turned water into wyn;°   (in Cana; see John 2:1–11) / wine
which was the firste miracle that he
wroghte° in erthe° biforn hise disciples. /   performed / on earth
Trewe° effect of mariage clenseth° fornica-   True / purifies
cioun and replenisseth° holy chirche of   replenishes
good linage; for that is the ende° of mariage;   goal
and it chaungeth deedly sinne into venial
sinne⁵ bitwixe hem that been y-wedded, and
maketh the hertes° al oon° of hem that   hearts / all one
920 been y-wedded, as wel as the bodies. / This
is verray° mariage, that was establissed by   true
God er° that sinne bigan, whan naturel   before
lawe was in his right point° in paradys; and   its rightful position
it was ordeyned that o° man sholde have   one
but o womman, and o womman but o man,
as seith Seint Augustin, by manye resouns. /
     First, for mariage is figured° bitwixe Crist   symbolizes the relation
and holy chirche. And that other is, for a
man is heved° of a womman; algate,° by or-   the head / in every way
dinaunce it sholde be so. / For if a womman
had mo° men than oon,° thanne sholde she   more / one
have mo hevedes° than oon, and that were   more heads
an horrible thing biforn God; and eek° a   also
womman ne mighte nat plese° to many folk   please
at ones.° And also ther ne sholde nevere be   once
pees° ne reste amonges hem; for everich°   peace / each one
wolde axen° his owene thing. / And for-   ask for
therover,° no man ne sholde knowe his   moreover
owene engendrure,° ne who sholde have his   offspring
heritage; and the womman sholde been the
lasse° biloved, fro the time that she were   less
conioynt° to many men. /   conjoined
     Now comth, how that a man sholde bere
him° with his wyf; and namely in two   conduct himself
thinges, that is to seyn in suffraunce° and   patience
reverence, as shewed Crist whan he made
925 first womman. / For he ne made hir nat of
the heved° of Adam, for° she sholde nat   head / so that
clayme to greet° lordshipe. / For theras the   claim too much
womman hath the maistrie, she maketh to
muche desray;° ther neden none ensam-   disorder
ples° of this. The experience of day by day   examples

---

5. Deadly or mortal sins, committed in full understanding of their seriousness, are directly contrary to charity and the love of God; venial sins, less serious or less deliberately committed,
   impede or weaken charity but do not alienate a person from God. The Parson uses this distinction also in lines 939–43 in his evaluation of motives for sexual intercourse within marriage.

oghte suffyse.° / Also certes, God ne made
nat womman of the foot of Adam, for she
ne sholde nat been holden to lowe; for she
can nat paciently suffre:° but God made
womman of the rib of Adam, for womman
sholde be felawe° unto man. / Man sholde
bere him to° his wyf in feith, in trouthe,°
and in love, as seith seint Paul: that "a man
sholde loven his wyf as Crist loved holy
chirche, that loved it so wel that he deyde°
for it." So sholde a man for his wyf, if it
were nede.° /

    Now how that a womman sholde be sub-
get° to hir housbonde, that telleth seint Pe-
930 ter. First, in obedience. / And eek, as seith
the decree,° a womman that is a wyf, as
longe as she is a wyf, she hath noon auctoritee to swere° ne bere witnesse withoute
leve° of hir housbonde, that is hir lord; algate,° he sholde be so by resoun. / She
sholde eek serven him in alle honestee,°
and been attempree° of hir array.° I wot°
wel that they sholde setten hir entente° to
plesen hir housbondes, but nat by hir
queyntise° of array. / Seint Jerome seith that
wyves that been apparailled in silk and in
precious purpre° ne mowe nat clothen hem
in Jesu Crist. What seith Seint John eek in
this matere? / Seint Gregorie eek seith that
no wight° seketh precious array but only for
veyne glorie,° to been honoured the more
biforn the peple. / It is a greet folye, a womman to have a fair array outward and in hir-
935 self be foul inward.° / A wyf sholde eek° be
mesurable in lokinge and in beringe° and in
laughinge, and discreet in alle hir wordes
and hir dedes.° / And aboven alle worldly
thing she sholde loven hir housbonde with
al hir herte, and to him be trewe of hir
body; / so sholde an housbonde eek be to
his wyf. For sith° that al the body is the
housbondes, so sholde hir herte been, or
elles ther is bitwixe hem two, as in that,° no
parfit mariage. / Thanne shal men understonde that for three thinges a man and his
wyf fleshly mowen assemble.° The firste is
in entente of engendrure of° children to°
the service of God, for certes that is the
cause fynal° of matrimoine. / Another cause

ought to suffice

endure

a companion
conduct himself toward / loyalty

died

necessary

subject

ecclesiastical law

swear (legal) oaths
permission
at least
modesty, chastity
modest / clothing / know
i.e., seek, intend

refinement

purple

person
i.e., pride

within / also
bearing

deeds

since

as far as that is concerned

may have intercourse
engendering / in

ultimate purpose

is to yelden° everich of hem to other the *pay*
dette of hir bodies, for neither of hem hath
power over his owene body.[6] The thridde is
for to eschewe lecherye and vileinye. The
940 ferthe is, for sothe,° deedly sinne. / As to *in truth*
the firste, it is meritorie,° the seconde also, *meritorious*
for, as seith the decree, that she hath merite
of chastitee that yeldeth to hir housbonde
the dette of hir body, ye, though it be agayn
hir lykinge and the lust° of hir herte. / The *desire*
thridde manere is venial sinne, and, trewely,
scarsly may ther any of thise be withoute
venial sinne, for the corrupcion and for the
delyt.° / The fourthe manere is, for to *pleasure (of it)*
understonde, if they assemble° only for *i.e., have intercourse*
amorous love and for noon of the forseyde
causes, but for to accomplice° thilke bren- *accomplish, satisfy*
ninge° delyt, they rekke° nevere how ofte. *burning / care*
Sothly it is deedly sinne; and yet, with° *to their*
sorwe, somme folk wol peynen hem° more *exert themselves*
to doon than to hir appetyt suffyseth.° / *suffices for their sexual needs*

The seconde manere of chastitee is for to
been a clene° widewe, and eschue the em- *chaste*
bracinges of man, and desyren the em-
bracinge of Jesu Crist. / Thise been tho that
han been wyves and han forgoon° hir hous- *lost*
bondes, and eek wommen that han doon° *practiced*
945 lecherie and been releeved° by Penitence. / *relieved (of guilt)*
And certes, if that a wyf coude kepen hir al
chaast by licence° of hir housbonde, so that *permission*
she yeve° nevere noon occasion that he ag- *give*
ilte,° it were to hire a greet merite. / Thise *sin (with her)*
manere wommen that observen° chastitee *practice*
moste° be clene in herte as well as in body *must*
and in thoght, and mesurable° in clothinge *moderate, modest*
and in contenaunce; and been abstinent in
etinge and drinkinge, in spekinge, and in
dede.° They been the vessel or the boyste° *deed(s) / box (of ointments)*
of the blissed Magdelene, that fulfilleth° *fills*
holy chirche of° good odour. / The thridde *with*
manere of chastitee is virginitee, and it bi-
hoveth° that she be holy in herte and clene *is necessary*
of body. Thanne is she spouse to Jesu Crist,
and she is the lyf° of angeles. / She is the *beloved*
preisinge of° this world, and she is as thise *i.e., most praiseworthy in*
martirs in egalitee;° she hath in hir that° *equal to the martyrs / that which*

6. The idea of the marital debt, the selfless giving of one's body to one's spouse, is based on St. Paul's statements in 1 Corinthians 7:3–4 (see p. 381). This text is referred to by both the Wife of Bath (*WBP* ll. 154–62) and January (*MerchT* l. 1452).

tonge may nat telle ne herte thinke. / Vir-
ginitee baar° oure lord Jesu Crist, and vir-   *gave birth to*
950 gine was himselve. /
    Another remedie agayns Lecherie is spe-
cially to withdrawen° swiche thinges as yeve   *take away, avoid*
occasion to thilke vileinye, as ese,° etinge   *such as ease*
and drinkinge; for certes, whan the pot
boyleth strongly, the best remedie is to
withdrawe the fyr. / Slepinge longe in greet
quiete is eek a greet norice° to Lecherie. /   *nurse*
    Another remedie agayns Lecherie is that a
man or a womman eschue the companye of
hem by whiche he douteth° to be tempted;   *fears*
for al be it so that the dede is withstonden,°   *resisted*
yet is ther greet temptacioun. / Soothly a
whyt wal, although it ne brenne° noght fully   *burn*
by stikinge of° a candele, yet is the wal blak°   *holding against it / blackened*
of the leyt.° / Ful ofte tyme I rede that no   *by the flame*
man truste° in his owene perfeccioun, but°   *should trust / unless*
he be stronger than Sampson, and holier
955 than Daniel, and wyser than Salomon. /

Chaucer's Retraction

Here taketh the makere of this book his leve.

Now preye I to hem alle that herkne° this   *listen to*
litel tretis or rede,° that if ther be any thing   *read (it)*
in it that lyketh hem,° that therof they   *pleases them*
thanken oure lord Jesu Crist, of° whom pro-   *from*
cedeth al wit° and al goodnesse. / And if   *understanding*
ther be any thing that displese hem, I preye
hem also that they arrette° it to the de-   *attribute*
faute° of myn unconninge° and nat to my   *fault / unskillfulness*
wil, that wolde ful fayn° have seyd bettre if   *very willingly*
I hadde had conninge.° / For oure boke   *the skill*
seith, "al that is writen is writen for oure
doctrine";° and that is myn entente.° /   *instruction / purpose*
Wherfore I biseke° yow mekely,° for the   *beseech / meekly*
mercy of God, that ye preye for me, that
Crist have mercy on me and foryeve° me my   *forgive*
giltes;° / and namely of° my translacions   *sins / especially for*
and endytinges° of° worldly vanitees, the *compositions / concerning*
1085 whiche I revoke in my retracciouns: / as is
the book of Troilus; The book also of Fame;
The book of the XXV Ladies;[1] The book of
the Duchesse; The book of seint Valentynes

---

1. I.e., *The Legend of Good Women*.

day of the Parlement of Briddes;° The tales *Birds*
of Caunterbury, thilke° that sounen into° *those same / tend toward*
sinne; / The book of the Leoun;° and many *Lion*
another book, if they were in my remembrance;° and many a song and many a lech- *memory*
erous lay; that Crist for his grete mercy
foryeve me the sinne. / But of the translacion of Boece de Consolacione,² and othere
bokes of Legendes of seintes, and omelies,° *homilies*
and moralitee and devocioun, / that thanke
I oure lord Jesu Crist and his blisful moder
and alle the seintes of hevene; / bisekinge
hem that they from hennes forth,° unto my *henceforth*
lyves ende, sende me grace to biwayle° my *bewail*
giltes, and to studie to° the salvacioun of *for*
my soule; and graunte me grace of verray
penitence,° confessioun and satisfaccioun *true penance*
1090 to doon° in this present lyf, / thurgh° the *perform / through*
benigne grace of him that is king of kinges
and preest over alle preestes, that boghte° *Who redeemed*
us with the precious blood of his herte; / so
that I may been oon of hem at the day of
dome° that shulle be saved. *Qui cum patre,* *Doomsday, Judgment Day*
& c.³

Here is ended the book of the Tales of
Caunterbury, compiled by Geffrey
Chaucer, of° whos soule Jesu Crist have *on*
mercy. Amen.

---

2. Boethius's *De Consolatione [Philosophiae]*.
3. Who (lives) with the Father, etc. (the benedictional close).

SOURCES AND BACKGROUNDS

The General Prologue

The *General Prologue* is first of all a framing device for the stories that follow. Among the many story collections in the Middle Ages, the one most relevant to the *Canterbury Tales* is Giovanni Boccaccio's *Decameron*. Its long introduction describes the plague in Florence and the decision of ten young men and women to leave the city and indulge in various recreations, including storytelling. This frame narrative concludes briefly with the return of the storytellers to Florence.

Chaucer complicated Boccaccio's recreational frame by setting his storytelling game within a pilgrimage to Canterbury. The Christian idea of life as a pilgrimage to God was prominent throughout the Middle Ages, and it is expressed succinctly and eloquently in a well-known passage from St. Augustine's *On Christian Doctrine*. The spiritual implications of pilgrimage are discussed in the essay by Arthur Hoffman on pp. 492–503. But pilgrimage was also a social fact as well as a symbol, and by the late fourteenth century reformers argued that its spiritual purposes were being subverted by the worldliness of its participants; the selection from *The Examination of William Thorpe* reveals both Lollard censure and orthodox defense of pilgrimages.

The form of the portraits in the *General Prologue* is indebted to traditional rhetorical modes of character description. For many details of the pilgrims themselves, Chaucer draws heavily on what is known as estates literature: descriptions, usually satiric, of various classes and occupations. Thomas Wimbledon's sermon, probably delivered in London about the time Chaucer was beginning the *Canterbury Tales*, offers a religious perspective on the estates and their purposes. The passages from William Langland and John Gower suggest both what is conventional and what is original in Chaucer's portrait of the Monk. Much social criticism in Chaucer's time came from John Wyclif and his followers in the Lollard movement, some of whom Chaucer doubtless knew; two passages from Wycliffite tracts offer background to Chaucer's portraits of the Merchant, Pardoner, and Parson. For material relevant to the Friar, see the passage from the *Romance of the Rose*, pp. 431–36; for the source of Chaucer's treatment of the Prioress's table manners, see the *Romance* passage on pp. 348–57.

GIOVANNI BOCCACCIO

From the *Decameron*, First Day, Introduction†

Here begins the first day of The Decameron, *in which, after the author has explained why certain people (soon to be introduced) have gathered together to tell stories, they speak on any subject that pleases them most, under the direction of Pampinea.*

Whenever, gracious ladies, I consider how compassionate you are by nature, I realize that in your judgment the present work will seem to have had a serious and painful beginning, for it recalls in its opening the unhappy memory of the deadly plague just passed, dreadful and pitiful to all those who saw or heard about it. But I do not wish this to frighten you away from reading any further, as if you were going to pass all of your time sighing and weeping as you read. This horrible beginning will be like the ascent of a steep and rough mountainside, beyond which there lies a most beautiful and delightful plain, which seems more pleasurable to the climbers in proportion to the difficulty of their climb and their descent. And just as pain is the extreme limit of pleasure, so misery ends by unanticipated happiness. This brief pain (I say brief since it contains few words) will be quickly followed by the sweetness and the delight, which I promised you before, and which, had I not promised, might not be expected from such a beginning. To tell the truth, if I could have conveniently led you by any other way than this, which I know is a bitter one, I would have gladly done so; but since it is otherwise impossible to demonstrate how the stories you are about to read came to be told, I am almost obliged by necessity to write about it this way.

Let me say, then, that thirteen hundred and forty-eight years had already passed after the fruitful Incarnation of the Son of God when into the distinguished city of Florence, more noble than any other Italian city, there came the deadly pestilence. It started in the East, either because of the influence of heavenly bodies or because of God's just wrath as a punishment to mortals for our wicked deeds, and it killed an infinite number of people. Without pause it spread from one place and it stretched its miserable length over the West. And against this pestilence no human wisdom or foresight was of any avail; quantities of filth were removed from the city by officials charged with this task; the entry of any sick person into the city was prohibited; and many directives were issued concerning the maintenance of good health. Nor were the humble supplications, rendered not once but many times to God by pious people, through public processions or by other means, efficacious; for almost at the beginning of springtime of the year in

† From *The Decameron*, ed. and trans. Mark Musa and Peter E. Bondanella (New York: W. W. Norton & Company, 1977), 3–17. Copyright © 1982 by Mark Musa and Peter Bondanella. Reprinted by permission of W. W. Norton & Company, Inc. The translators' notes have been renumbered. Boccaccio wrote this account of the Black Death in Florence during or shortly after the event, ca. 1348–51.

question the plague began to show its sorrowful effects in an extra-ordinary manner. It did not act as it had done in the East, where bleeding from the nose was a manifest sign of inevitable death, but it began in both men and women with certain swellings either in the groin or under the armpits, some of which grew to the size of a normal apple and others to the size of an egg (more or less), and the people called them *gavoccioli*.[1] And from the two parts of the body already mentioned, within a brief space of time, the said deadly *gavoccioli* began to spread indiscriminately over every part of the body; and after this, the symptoms of the illness changed to black or livid spots appearing on the arms and thighs, and on every part of the body, some large ones and sometimes many little ones scattered all around. And just as the *gavoccioli* were originally, and still are, a very certain indication of impending death, in like manner these spots came to mean the same thing for whoever had them. Neither a doctor's advice nor the strength of medicine could do anything to cure this illness; on the contrary, either the nature of the illness was such that it afforded no cure, or else the doctors were so ignorant that they did not recognize its cause and, as a result, could not prescribe the proper remedy (in fact, the number of doctors, other than the well-trained, was increased by a large number of men and women who had never had any medical training); at any rate, few of the sick were ever cured, and almost all died after the third day of the appearance of the previously described symptoms (some sooner, others later), and most of them died without fever or any other side effects.

This pestilence was so powerful that it was communicated to the healthy by contact with the sick, the way a fire close to dry or oily things will set them aflame. And the evil of the plague went even further: not only did talking to or being around the sick bring infection and a common death, but also touching the clothes of the sick or anything touched or used by them seemed to communicate this very disease to the person involved. What I am about to say is incredible to hear, and if I and others had not witnessed it with our own eyes, I should not dare believe it (let alone write about it), no matter how trustworthy a person I might have heard it from. Let me say, then, that the power of the plague described here was of such virulence in spreading from one person to another that not only did it pass from one man to the next, but, what's more, it was often transmitted from the garments of a sick or dead man to animals that not only became contaminated by the disease, but also died within a brief period of time. My own eyes, as I said earlier, witnessed such a thing one day: when the rags of a poor man who died of this disease were thrown into the public street, two pigs came upon them, as they are wont to do,

---

1. *Gavoccioli*—or *bubboni*, in modern Italian—are called "buboes" in English, the source of the phrase "bubonic plague." The plague of 1348 is often known as the Black Plague because of the black spots Boccaccio describes. One of the most important casualties of this plague in literature was Laura, the woman who inspired the many sonnets and songs in the *Canzoniere* ("Songbook") by Boccaccio's friend and contemporary, Francesco Petrarca (1304–1374). Both *The Decameron* and the *Canzoniere* deal with the experience of human love, and both are set against a stark background of plague, death, and earthly mutability.

and first with their snouts and then with their teeth they took the rags and shook them around; and within a short time, after a number of convulsions, both pigs fell dead upon the ill-fated rags, as if they had been poisoned. From these and many similar or worse occurrences there came about such fear and such fantastic notions among those who remained alive that almost all of them took a very cruel attitude in the matter; that is, they completely avoided the sick and their possessions; and in so doing, each one believed that he was protecting his good health.

There were some people who thought that living moderately and avoiding all superfluity might help a great deal in resisting this disease, and so, they gathered in small groups and lived entirely apart from everyone else. They shut themselves up in those houses where there were no sick people and where one could live well by eating the most delicate of foods and drinking the finest of wines (doing so always in moderation), allowing no one to speak about or listen to anything said about the sick and the dead outside; these people lived, spending their time with music and other pleasures that they could arrange. Others thought the opposite: they believed that drinking too much, enjoying life, going about singing and celebrating, satisfying in every way the appetites as best one could, laughing, and making light of everything that happened was the best medicine for such a disease; so they practiced to the fullest what they believed by going from one tavern to another all day and night, drinking to excess; and often they would make merry in private homes, doing everything that pleased or amused them the most. This they were able to do easily, for everyone felt he was doomed to die and, as a result, abandoned his property, so that most of the houses had become common property, and any stranger who came upon them used them as if he were their rightful owner. In addition to this bestial behavior, they always managed to avoid the sick as best they could. And in this great affliction and misery of our city the revered authority of the laws, both divine and human, had fallen and almost completely disappeared, for, like other men, the ministers and executors of the laws were either dead or sick or so short of help that it was impossible for them to fulfill their duties; as a result, everybody was free to do as he pleased.

Many others adopted a middle course between the two attitudes just described: neither did they restrict their food or drink so much as the first group nor did they fall into such dissoluteness and drunkenness as the second; rather, they satisfied their appetites to a moderate degree. They did not shut themselves up, but went around carrying in their hands flowers, or sweet-smelling herbs, or various kinds of spices; and often they would put these things to their noses, believing that such smells were a wonderful means of purifying the brain, for all the air seemed infected with the stench of dead bodies, sickness, and medicines.

Others were of a crueler opinion (though it was, perhaps, a safer one): they maintained that there was no better medicine against the plague than to flee from it; and convinced of this reasoning, not caring about anything but themselves, men and women in great numbers abandoned their city, their houses, their farms, their relatives, and their possessions and sought other places, and they went at least as far away as the Florentine countryside—as if the wrath of God could not pursue them with this pestilence wherever they went but would only strike those it found within the walls of the city! Or perhaps they thought that Florence's last hour had come and that no one in the city would remain alive.

And not all those who adopted these diverse opinions died, nor did they all escape with their lives; on the contrary, many of those who thought this way were falling sick everywhere, and since they had given, when they were healthy, the bad example of avoiding the sick, they, in turn, were abandoned and left to languish away without care. The fact was that one citizen avoided another, that almost no one cared for his neighbor, and that relatives rarely or hardly ever visited each other—they stayed far apart. This disaster had struck such fear into the hearts of men and women that brother abandoned brother, uncle abandoned nephew, sister left brother, and very often wife abandoned husband, and—even worse, almost unbelievable—fathers and mothers neglected to tend and care for their children, as if they were not their own.

Thus, for the countless multitude of men and women who fell sick, there remained no support except the charity of their friends (and these were few) or the avarice of servants, who worked for inflated salaries and indecent periods of time and who, in spite of this, were few and far between; and those few were men or women of little wit (most of them not trained for such service) who did little else but hand different things to the sick when requested to do so or watch over them while they died, and in this service, they very often lost their own lives and their profits. And since the sick were abandoned by their neighbors, their parents, and their friends and there was a scarcity of servants, a practice that was almost unheard of before spread through the city: when a woman fell sick, no matter how attractive or beautiful or noble she might be, she did not mind having a manservant (whoever he might be, no matter how young or old he was), and she had no shame whatsoever in revealing any part of her body to him—the way she would have done to a woman—when the necessity of her sickness required her to do so. This practice was, perhaps, in the days that followed the pestilence, the cause of looser morals in the women who survived the plague. And so, many people died who, by chance, might have survived if they had been attended to. Between the lack of competent attendants, which the sick were unable to obtain, and the violence of the pestilence, there were so many, many people who died in the city both day and night that it was incredible just to hear this described, not to mention seeing it! Therefore, out of sheer necessity, there arose among those who remained alive customs which were contrary to the established practices of the time.

It was the custom, as it is again today, for the women, relatives, and

neighbors to gather together in the house of a dead person and there
to mourn with the women who had been dearest to him; on the other
hand, in front of the deceased's home, his male relatives would gather
together with his male neighbors and other citizens, and the clergy
also came (many of them, or sometimes just a few) depending upon
the social class of the dead man. Then, upon the shoulders of his
equals, he was carried to the church chosen by him before death with
the funeral pomp of candles and chants. With the fury of the pestilence increasing, this custom, for the most part, died out and other
practices took its place. And so, not only did people die without having
a number of women around them, but there were many who passed
away without even having a single witness present, and very few were
granted the piteous laments and bitter tears of their relatives; on the
contrary, most relatives were somewhere else, laughing, joking, and
amusing themselves; even the women learned this practice too well,
having put aside, for the most part, their womanly compassion for
their own safety. Very few were the dead whose bodies were accompanied to the church by more than ten or twelve of their neighbors, and
these dead bodies were not even carried on the shoulders of honored
and reputable citizens but rather by gravediggers from the lower
classes that were called *becchini*. Working for pay, they would pick up
the bier and hurry it off, not to the church the dead man had chosen
before his death but, in most cases, to the church closest by, accompanied by four or six churchmen with just a few candles, and often none
at all. With the help of these *becchini*, the churchmen would place the
body as fast as they could in whatever unoccupied grave they could
find, without going to the trouble of saying long or solemn burial services.

The plight of the lower class and, perhaps, a large part of the middle
class, was even more pathetic: most of them stayed in their homes or
neighborhoods either because of their poverty or their hopes for remaining safe, and every day they fell sick by the thousands; and not
having servants or attendants of any kind, they almost always died.
Many ended their lives in the public streets, during the day or at
night, while many others who died in their homes were discovered
dead by their neighbors only by the smell of their decomposing bodies.
The city was full of corpses. The dead were usually given the same
treatment by their neighbors, who were moved more by the fear that
the decomposing corpses would contaminate them than by any charity
they might have felt towards the deceased: either by themselves or
with the assistance of porters (when they were available), they would
drag the corpse out of the home and place it in front of the doorstep
where, usually in the morning, quantities of dead bodies could be seen
by any passerby; then, they were laid out on biers, or for lack of biers,
on a plank. Nor did a bier carry only one corpse; sometimes it was
used for two or three at a time. More than once, a single bier would
serve for a wife and husband, two or three brothers, a father or son, or
other relatives, all at the same time. And countless times it happened
that two priests, each with a cross, would be on their way to bury

someone, when porters carrying three or four biers would just follow along behind them; and where these priests thought they had just one dead man to bury, they had, in fact, six or eight and sometimes more. Moreover, the dead were honored with no tears or candles or funeral mourners but worse: things had reached such a point that the people who died were cared for as we care for goats today. Thus, it became quite obvious that what the wise had not been able to endure with patience through the few calamities of everyday life now became a matter of indifference to even the most simple-minded people as a result of this colossal misfortune.

So many corpses would arrive in front of a church every day and at every hour that the amount of holy ground for burials was certainly insufficient for the ancient custom of giving each body its individual place; when all the graves were full, huge trenches were dug in all of the cemeteries of the churches and into them the new arrivals were dumped by the hundreds; and they were packed in there with dirt, one on top of another, like a ship's cargo, until the trench was filled.

But instead of going over every detail of the past miseries which befell our city, let me say that the same unfriendly weather there did not, because of this, spare the surrounding countryside any evil; there, not to speak of the towns which, on a smaller scale, were like the city, in the scattered villages and in the fields the poor, miserable peasants and their families, without any medical assistance or aid of servants, died on the roads and in their fields and in their homes, as many by day as by night, and they died not like men but more like wild animals. Because of this they, like the city dwellers, became careless in their ways and did not look after their possessions or their businesses; furthermore, when they saw that death was upon them, completely neglecting the future fruits of their past labors, their livestock, their property, they did their best to consume what they already had at hand. So, it came about that oxen, donkeys, sheep, pigs, chickens and even dogs, man's most faithful companion, were driven from their homes into the fields, where the wheat was left not only unharvested but also unreaped, and they were allowed to roam where they wished; and many of these animals, almost as if they were rational beings, returned at night to their homes without any guidance from a shepherd, satiated after a good day's meal.

Leaving the countryside and returning to the city, what more can one say, except that so great was the cruelty of Heaven, and, perhaps, also that of man, that from March to July of the same year, between the fury of the pestiferous sickness and the fact that many of the sick were badly treated or abandoned in need because of the fear that the healthy had, more than one hundred thousand human beings are believed to have lost their lives for certain inside the walls of the city of Florence whereas, before the deadly plague, one would not have estimated that there were actually that many people dwelling in that city.

Oh, how many great palaces, beautiful homes, and noble dwellings, once filled with families, gentlemen, and ladies, were now emptied, down to the last servant! How many notable families, vast domains, and famous fortunes remained without legitimate heir! How many valiant men, beautiful women, and charming young men, who might have been pronounced very healthy by Galen, Hippocrates, and Aesculapius[2] (not to mention lesser physicians), dined in the morning with their relatives, companions, and friends and then in the evening took supper with their ancestors in the other world!

Reflecting upon so many miseries makes me very sad; therefore, since I wish to pass over as many as I can, let me say that as our city was in this condition, almost emptied of inhabitants, it happened (as I heard it later from a person worthy of trust) that one Tuesday morning in the venerable church of Santa Maria Novella[3] there was hardly any congregation there to hear the holy services except for seven young women, all dressed in garments of mourning as the times demanded, each of whom was a friend, neighbor, or relative of the other, and none of whom had passed her twenty-eighth year, nor was any of them younger than eighteen; all were educated and of noble birth and beautiful to look at, well-mannered and gracefully modest. I would tell you their real names, if I did not have a good reason for not doing so, which is this: I do not wish any of them to be embarrassed in the future because of the things that they said to each other and what they listened to—all of which I shall later recount. Today the laws regarding pleasure are again strict, more so than at that time (for the reasons mentioned above when they were very lax), not only for women of their age but even for those who were older; nor would I wish to give an opportunity to the envious, who are always ready to attack every praiseworthy life, to diminish in any way with their indecent talk the dignity of these worthy ladies. But, so that you may understand clearly what each of them had to say, I intend to call them by names which are either completely or in part appropriate to their personalities. We shall call the first and the oldest Pampinea and the second Fiammetta, the third Filomena, and the fourth Emilia, and we shall name the fifth Lauretta and the sixth Neifile, and the last, not without reason, we shall call Elissa.[4] Not by prior agreement, but purely by chance, they gathered together in one part of the church and were seated almost in a circle, saying their rosaries; after many sighs, they began to discuss among themselves various matters concerning the nature of the times, and after a while, as the others fell silent, Pampinea began to speak in this manner:

2. The Roman god of medicine and healing, often identified with Asclepius, Apollo's son, who was the Greek god of medicine. Galen: Greek anatomist and physician (A.D. 130?–201?). Hippocrates: Greek physician (460?–377?–B.C.), to whom the Hippocratic oath, administered to new physicians, is attributed.
3. This church, called "novella" or "new" because it replaced a preexisting structure, was begun in 1279 and was completed by Jacopo Talenti in 1348. An excellent example of Italian Gothic style, it is also noted for the Renaissance façade grafted onto its exterior by Leon Battista Alberti in the fifteenth century and for frescoes in its interior chapels done by various artists.
4. The qualities usually associated by critics with these ladies are as follows: Pampinea (a wise and confident lady, often in love and the most mature of the group); Filomena (wise and discreet and full of desire); Elissa (very young and dominated by a violent passion); Neifile (also young but ingenuous); Emilia (in love with herself); Lauretta (a jealous lover); and Fiammetta (happy to love and to be loved but afraid that she will lose her love).

"My dear ladies, you have often heard, as I have, how a proper use of one's reason does harm to no one. It is only natural for everyone born on this earth to aid, preserve, and defend his own life to the best of his ability; this is a right so taken for granted that it has, at times, permitted men to kill each other without blame in order to defend their own lives. And if the laws dealing with the welfare of every human being permit such a thing, how much more lawful, and with no harm to anyone, is it for us, or anyone else, to take all possible precautions to preserve our own lives! When I consider what we have been doing this morning and in the past days and what we have spoken about, I understand, and you must understand too, that each one of us is afraid for her life; nor does this surprise me in the least—rather I am greatly amazed that since each of us has the natural feelings of a woman, we do not find some remedy for ourselves to cure what each one of us dreads. We live in the city, in my opinion, for no other reason than to bear witness to the number of dead bodies that are carried to burial, or to listen whether the friars (whose number has been reduced to almost nothing) chant their offices at the prescribed hours, or to demonstrate to anyone who comes here the quality and the quantity of our miseries by our garments of mourning. And if we leave the church, either we see dead or sick bodies being carried all about, or we see those who were once condemned to exile for their crimes by the authority of the public laws making sport of these laws, running about wildly through the city, because they know that the executors of these laws are either dead or dying; or we see the scum of our city, avid for our blood, who call themselves *becchini* and who ride about on horseback torturing us by deriding everything, making our losses more bitter with their disgusting songs. Nor do we hear anything but "So-and-so is dead," and "So-and-so is dying"; and if there were anyone left to mourn, we should hear nothing but piteous laments everywhere. I do not know if what happens to me also happens to you in your homes, but when I go home I find no one there except my maid, and I become so afraid that my hair stands on end, and wherever I go or sit in my house, I seem to see the shadows of those who have passed away, not with the faces that I remember, but with horrible expressions that terrify me. For these reasons, I am uncomfortable here, outside, and in my home, and the more so since it appears that no one like ourselves, who is well off and who has some other place to go, has remained here except us. And if there are any who remain, according to what I hear and see, they do whatever their hearts desire, making no distinction between what is proper and what is not, whether they are alone or with others, by day or by night; and not only laymen but also those who are cloistered in convents have broken their vows of obedience and have given themselves over to carnal pleasures, for they have made themselves believe that these things are permissible for them and are improper for others, and thinking that they will escape with their lives in this fashion, they have become wanton and dissolute.

"If this is the case, and plainly it is, what are we doing here? What

are we waiting for? What are we dreaming about? Why are we slower
to protect our health than all the rest of the citizens? Do we hold ourselves less dear than all the others? Or do we believe that our own
lives are tied by stronger chains to our bodies than those of others
and, therefore, that we need not worry about anything which might
have the power to harm them? We are mistaken and deceived, and we
are mad if we believe it. We shall have clear proof of this if we just call
to mind how many young men and ladies have been struck down by
this cruel pestilence. I do not know if you agree with me, but I think
that, in order not to fall prey, out of laziness or presumption, to what
we might well avoid, it might be a good idea for all of us to leave this
city, just as many others before us have done and are still doing. Let us
avoid like death itself the ugly examples of others, and go to live in a
more dignified fashion in our country houses (of which we all have
several) and there let us take what enjoyment, what happiness, and
what pleasure we can, without going beyond the rules of reason in any
way. There we can hear the birds sing, and we can see the hills and the
pastures turning green, the wheat fields moving like the sea, and a
thousand kinds of trees; and we shall be able to see the heavens more
clearly which, though they still may be cruel, nonetheless will not
deny to us their eternal beauties, which are much more pleasing to
look at than the empty walls of our city. Besides all this, there in the
country the air is much fresher, and the necessities for living in such
times as these are plentiful there, and there are just fewer troubles in
general; though the peasants are dying there even as the townspeople
here, the displeasure is the less in that there are fewer houses and inhabitants than in the city. Here on the other hand, if I judge correctly,
we would not be abandoning anyone; on the contrary, we can honestly
say it is we ourselves that have been abandoned, for our loved ones are
either dead or have fled and have left us alone in such affliction as
though we did not belong to them. No reproach, therefore, can come
to us if we follow this course of action, whereas sorrow, worry, and
perhaps even death can come if we do not follow this course. So,
whenever you like, I think it would be well to take our servants, have
all our necessary things sent after us, and go from one place one day
to another the next, enjoying what happiness and merriment these
times permit; let us live in this manner (unless we are overtaken first
by death) until we see what ending Heaven has reserved for these horrible times. And remember that it is no more forbidden for us to go
away virtuously than it is for most other women to remain here dis-
honorably."

When they had listened to what Pampinea had said, the other
women not only praised her advice but were so anxious to follow it
that they had already begun discussing among themselves the details,
as if they were going to leave that very instant. But Filomena, who was
most discerning, said:

"Ladies, regardless of how convincing Pampinea's arguments are,
that is no reason to rush into things, as you seem to wish to do. Remember that we are all women, and any young girl can tell you that

women do not know how to reason in a group when they are without the guidance of some man who knows how to control them. We are changeable, quarrelsome, suspicious, timid, and fearful, because of which I suspect that this company will soon break up without honor to any of us if we do not take a guide other than ourselves. We would do well to resolve this matter before we depart."

Then Elissa said:

"Men are truly the leaders of women, and without their guidance, our actions rarely end successfully. But how are we to find any men? We all know that the majority of our relatives are dead and those who remain alive are scattered here and there in various groups, not knowing where we are (they, too, are fleeing precisely what we seek to avoid), and since taking up with strangers would be unbecoming to us, we must, if we wish to leave for the sake of our health, find a means of arranging it so that while going for our own pleasure and repose, no trouble or scandal follow us."

While the ladies were discussing this, three young men came into the church, none of whom was less than twenty-five years of age. Neither the perversity of the times nor the loss of friends or parents, nor fear for their own lives had been able to cool, much less extinguish, the love those lovers bore in their hearts. One of them was called Panfilo, another Filostrato, and the last Dioneo, each one very charming and well-bred; and in those turbulent times they sought their greatest consolation in the sight of the ladies they loved, all three of whom happened to be among the seven ladies previously mentioned, while the others were close relatives of one or the other of the three men. No sooner had they sighted the ladies than they were seen by them, whereupon Pampinea smiled and said:

"See how Fortune favors our plans and has provided us with these discreet and virtuous young men, who would gladly be our guides and servants if we do not hesitate to accept them for such service."

Then Neifile's face blushed out of embarrassment, for she was one of those who was loved by one of the young men, and she said:

"Pampinea, for the love of God, be careful what you say! I realize very well that nothing but good can be said of any of them, and I believe that they are capable of doing much more than that task and, likewise, that their good and worthy company would be fitting not only for us but for ladies much more beautiful and attractive than we are, but it is quite obvious that some of them are in love with some of us who are here present, and I fear that if we take them with us, slander and disapproval will follow, through no fault of ours or of theirs."

Then Filomena said:

"That does not matter at all; as long as I live with dignity and have no remorse of conscience about anything, let anyone who wishes say what he likes to the contrary: God and Truth will take up arms in my defense. Now, if they were just prepared to come with us, as Pampinea says, we could truly say that Fortune was favorable to our departure."

When the others heard her speak in such a manner, the argument was ended, and they all agreed that the young men should be called over, told about their intentions, and asked if they would be so kind as to accompany the ladies on such a journey. Without further discussion, then, Pampinea, who was related to one of the men, rose to her feet and made her way to where they stood gazing at the ladies, and she greeted them with a cheerful expression, outlined their plan to them, and begged them, in everyone's name, to keep them company in the spirit of pure and brotherly affection.

At first the young men thought they were being mocked, but when they saw that the lady was speaking seriously, they gladly consented; and in order to start without delay and put the plan into action, before leaving the church they agreed upon what preparations must be made for their departure. And when everything had been arranged and word had been sent on to the place they intended to go, the following morning (that is, Wednesday) at the break of dawn the ladies with some of their servants and the three young men with three of their servants left the city and set out on their way; they had traveled no further than two short miles when they arrived at the first stop they had agreed upon.

The place was somewhere on a little mountain, at some distance away from our roads, full of various shrubs and plants with rich, green foliage—most pleasant to look at; at the top there was a country mansion with a beautiful large inner courtyard with open collonades, halls, and bedrooms, all of them beautiful in themselves and decorated with cheerful and interesting paintings; it was surrounded by meadows and marvelous gardens, with wells of fresh water and cellars full of the most precious wines, the likes of which were more suitable for expert drinkers than for sober and dignified ladies. And the group discovered, to their delight, that the entire palace had been cleaned and the beds made in the bedchambers, and that fresh flowers and rushes had been strewn everywhere. Soon after they arrived and were resting, Dioneo, who was more attractive and wittier than either of the other young men, said:

"Ladies, more than our preparations, it was your intelligence that guided us here. I do not know what you intend to do with your thoughts, but I left mine inside the city walls when I passed through them in your company a little while ago; and so, you must either make up your minds to enjoy yourselves and laugh and sing with me (as much, let me say, as your dignity permits), or you must give me leave to return to my worries and to remain in our troubled city."

To this Pampinea, who had driven away her sad thoughts in the same way, replied happily:

"Dioneo, you speak very well: let us live happily, for after all it was unhappiness that made us flee the city. But when things are not organized they cannot long endure, and since I began the discussions which brought this fine company together, and since I desire the continuation of our happiness, I think it is necessary that we choose a leader from among us, whom we shall honor and obey as our superior and whose every thought shall be to keep us living happily. And in order that each one of us may feel the weight of this responsibility together with the pleasure of its authority, so that no one of us who has not experienced it can envy the others, let me say that both the weight and the honor should be granted to each one of us in turn for a day; the first will be chosen by election; the others that follow will be whomever he or she that will have the rule for that day chooses as the hour of vespers[5] approaches; this ruler, as long as his reign endures, will organize and arrange the place and the manner in which we will spend our time."

These words greatly pleased everyone, and they unanimously elected Pampinea queen for the first day; Filomena quickly ran to a laurel bush, whose leaves she had always heard were worthy of praise and bestowed great honor upon those crowned with them; she plucked several branches from it and wove them into a handsome garland of honor. And when it would be placed upon the head of any one of them, it was to be to all in the group a clear symbol of royal rule and authority over the rest of them for as long as their company stayed together.[6]

After she had been chosen queen, Pampinea ordered everyone to refrain from talking; then, she sent for the four servants of the ladies and for those of the three young men, and as they stood before her in silence, she said:

"Since I must set the first example for you all in order that it may be bettered and thus allow our company to live in order and in pleasure, and without any shame, and so that it may last as long as we wish, I first appoint Parmeno, Dioneo's servant, as my steward, and I commit to his care and management all our household and everything which pertains to the services of the dining hall. I wish Sirisco, the servant of Panfilo, to act as our buyer and treasurer and follow the orders of Parmeno. Tindaro, who is in the service of Filostrato, shall wait on Filostrato and Dioneo and Panfilo in their bedchambers when the other two are occupied with their other duties and cannot do so. Misia, my servant, and Licisca, Filomena's, will be occupied in the kitchen and will prepare those dishes which are ordered by Parmeno. Chimera, Lauretta's servant, and Stratilia, Fiammetta's servant, will take care of the bedchambers of the ladies and the cleaning of those places we use. And in general, we desire and command each of you, if you value our favor and good graces, to be sure—no matter where you go or come from, no matter what you hear or see—to bring us back nothing but pleasant news."

---

5. According to church practice, special forms of prayers were prescribed by canon law for recitation at specified times during the day. As a result, people often told the time according to these seven canonical hours: matins (dawn); prime (about 6:00 A.M.); tierce (the third hour after sunrise, about 9:00 A.M.); sext (noon); nones (the ninth hour after sunrise, or about 3:00 P.M.); vespers (late afternoon); and compline (in the evening just before retiring).

6. The leaves of the laurel bush were traditionally used in ancient times to fashion crowns or garlands not only for warriors and heroes but also for outstanding poets, musicians, and artists. Laura, the inspiration of Petrarca's *Canzoniere*, was so named because of her association with the laurel and, therefore, with excellence in poetry. Most medieval and Renaissance illustrations of the great Italian poets Dante, Petrarca, and Boccaccio picture them with such laurel crowns, implying that they have equaled and perhaps even excelled the poets of classical antiquity.

And when these orders, praised by all present, were delivered, Pampinea rose happily to her feet and said:

"Here there are gardens and meadows and many other pleasant places, which all of us can wander about in and enjoy as we like; but at the hour of tierce let everyone be here so that we can eat in the cool of the morning."

After the merry group had been given the new queen's permission, the young men, together with the beautiful ladies, set off slowly through a garden, discussing pleasant matters, making themselves beautiful garlands of various leaves and singing love songs. After the time granted them by the queen had elapsed, they returned home and found Parmeno busy carrying out the duties of his task; for as they entered a hall on the ground floor, they saw the tables set with the whitest of linens and with glasses that shone like silver and everything decorated with broom blossoms; then, they washed their hands and, at the queen's command, they all sat down in the places assigned them by Parmeno. The delicately cooked foods were brought in and very fine wines were served; the three servants in silence served the tables. Everyone was delighted to see everything so beautiful and well arranged, and they ate merrily and with pleasant conversation. Since all the ladies and young men knew how to dance (and some of them even knew how to play and sing very well), when the tables had been cleared, the queen ordered that instruments be brought, and on her command, Dioneo took a lute and Fiammetta a viola, and they began softly playing a dance tune. After the queen had sent the servants off to eat, she began to dance together with the other ladies and two of the young men; and when that was over, they all began to sing carefree and gay songs. In this manner they continued until the queen felt that it was time to retire; therefore, at the queen's request, the three young men went off to their chambers (which were separate from those of the ladies), where they found their beds prepared and the rooms as full of flowers as the halls; the ladies, too, discovered their chambers decorated in like fashion. Then they all undressed and fell asleep.

Not long after the hour of nones, the queen arose and had the other ladies and young men awakened, stating that too much sleep in the daytime was harmful; then they went out onto a lawn of thick, green grass, where no ray of the sun could penetrate; and there, with a gentle breeze caressing them, they all sat in a circle upon the green grass, as was the wish of their queen. Then she spoke to them in this manner:

"As you see, the sun is high, the heat is great, and nothing can be heard except the cicadas in the olive groves; therefore, to wander about at this hour would be, indeed, foolish. Here it is cool and fresh and, as you see, there are games and chessboards with which all of you can amuse yourselves to your liking. But if you take my advice in this matter, I suggest we spend this hot part of the day not in playing games (a pastime which of necessity disturbs the player who loses without providing much pleasure either for his opponents or for those who watch) but rather in telling stories, for this way one person, by telling a story, can provide amusement for the entire company. In the time it takes for the sun to set and the heat to become less oppressive, you will each have told a little story, and then we can go wherever we like to amuse ourselves; so, if what I say pleases you (and in this I am willing to follow your pleasure), then, let us do it; if not, then let everyone do as he pleases until the hour of vespers."

The entire group of men and women liked the idea of telling stories.

"Then," said the queen, "if this is your wish, for this first day I order each of you to tell a story about any subject he likes."

And turning to Panfilo, who sat on her right, she ordered him in a gracious manner to begin with one of his tales; whereupon, hearing her command, Panfilo, while everyone listened, began at once as follows.

* * *

GIOVANNI BOCCACCIO

From the *Decameron*, Tenth Day, Conclusion†

Dioneo's tale had ended, and the ladies, some taking one side and some taking the other, some criticizing one thing about it and some praising another, had discussed the story at great length when the King, looking up at the sky and seeing that the sun had already sunk low toward the hour of vespers, began, without getting up, to speak in this fashion:

"Lovely ladies, as I believe you know, human wisdom does not consist only in remembering past events or in knowing about present ones, but rather in being able, with a knowledge of both one and the other, to predict future events, which wise men consider the highest form of intelligence. As you know, it will be fifteen days tomorrow that we left Florence in order to find some means of amusement, to preserve our health and our lives, and to escape from the melancholy, suffering, and anguish which has existed continuously in our city since the beginning of the plague. This goal, in my opinion, we have virtuously achieved; for, as far as I have been able to observe, even if the stories we have told were amusing, and possibly of the sort conducive to arousing our carnal appetites, and though we have continually eaten and drunk well, played and sung (all things which may well incite weaker minds to less proper behavior), neither in word nor in deed nor in any other way do I feel that either you or ourselves are worthy of criticism. Constant decorum, constant harmony, and constant fraternal friendship are, in fact, what I have seen and felt here— something which, of course, pleases me, for it redounds to both your honor and merit and mine. And therefore, to prevent an overly practiced custom from turning into boredom as well as to prevent anyone

† From *The Decameron* by Giovanni Boccaccio, translated by Mark Musa and Peter Bondanella. Pp. 682–84. Copyright © 1982 by Mark Musa and Peter Bondanella. Used by permission of Dutton Signet, a division of Penguin Group (USA) Inc.

from criticizing our having stayed here too long, I now think it proper, since each of us has, with his own day of storytelling, enjoyed his share of the honor that still resides in me, that, with your approval, we return to the place from where we came. Not to mention the fact that, if you consider the matter carefully, since our company is already known to many others in these parts, our numbers could increase in such a way as to destroy all our pleasure. Therefore, if you approve of my suggestion, I shall retain the crown given me until our departure, which I propose should be tomorrow morning; if you decide otherwise, I am already prepared to crown someone else for the next day."

The discussion between the ladies and the young men was long, but finally, having decided that the King's advice was sensible and proper, they all decided to do as he had said; and so, having sent for the steward, the King discussed with him the arrangements that had to be made for the following morning and then, having given the group their leave until suppertime, he rose to his feet.

The ladies and the other young men got up too, and as they usually did, some turned their attention to one amusement and others to another; and when it was time for supper, with the greatest of delight they went to the table; and after supper they began to sing and play and dance; and while Lauretta was leading a dance, the King ordered Fiammetta to sing a song. * * *

* * *

After this song, they sang many others; and when it was nearly midnight, they all, at the King's request, went to bed.

By the time they arose at dawn of the new day, the steward had already sent all of their possessions on ahead, and so, under the guidance of their prudent King, they returned to Florence; and having taken their leave of the seven ladies at Santa Maria Novella, from where they had all set out together, the three young men went off to see to their other pleasures, while the ladies, when they felt it was time, returned to their homes.

ST. AUGUSTINE

[Human Life as a Pilgrimage]†

* * *

There are some things which are to be enjoyed, others which are to be used, others still which enjoy and use. Those things which are objects of enjoyment make us happy. Those things which are objects of use assist and (so to speak) support us in our efforts toward happiness, so

† From *On Christian Doctrine* I.3–4. Adapted from the translation of J. F. Shaw in *A Select Library of the Nicene and Post-Nicene Fathers of the Christian Church*, First Series, v. 2 (Buffalo: Christian Literature Co., 1887), p. 523.

that we can attain the things that make us happy and rest in them. We ourselves, who enjoy and use these things, being placed among both kinds of objects, if we set ourselves to enjoy those which we ought to use, are hindered in our course and sometimes even led away from it; so that, getting entangled in the love of lower gratifications, we lag behind in or even altogether turn back from the pursuit of the real and proper objects of enjoyment.

For to enjoy a thing is to rest with satisfaction in it for its own sake. To use, on the other hand, is to employ whatever means are at one's disposal to obtain what one desires, if it is a proper object of desire; for an unlawful use ought rather to be called an abuse. Suppose, then, we were wanderers in a strange country and could not live happily away from our fatherland, and that we felt wretched in our wandering and, wishing to put an end to our misery, determined to return home. We find, however, that we must make use of some mode of conveyance, either by land or water, in order to reach that fatherland where our enjoyment is to commence. But the beauty of the country through which we pass and the very pleasure of the motion charm our hearts, and turning these things which we ought to use into objects of enjoyment, we become unwilling to hasten the end of our journey; and becoming engrossed in a factitious delight, our thoughts are diverted from that home whose delights would make us truly happy. Thus in this mortal life, wandering from God [see 1 Cor. 5:6], if we wish to return to our Father's home, this world must be used, not enjoyed, so that the invisible things of God may be clearly seen, being understood by the things that are made [see Rom. 1:20]—that is, that by means of what is material and temporary we may take hold of that which is spiritual and eternal.

* * *

SIR WILLIAM THORPE

[On Pilgrimage]†

* * *

And than he [Archbishop Arundel] said to me, "What saist thou to the thirde poynte that is cer-

---

† Text based on *The examinacion of master W. Thorpe* [1530]. The work is William Thorpe's own account of the inquiry conducted against him by Thomas Arundel, archbishop of Canterbury, for preaching Lollard doctrines in a sermon in Shrewsbury in 1407. The only manuscript in English of Thorpe's account has been edited by Anne Hudson in *Two Wycliffite Texts*, EETS o.s. 301 (Oxford: Oxford UP, 1993). The manuscript is closer to Thorpe's original, but the [1530] printing possesses independent authority, and its updating of spelling and vocabulary makes it more accessible for students. Where needed, we have adapted and put in brackets some readings from Hudson's edition to emend or clarify the meaning of the [1530] text. For background on the Lollard movement see Anne Hudson, *The Premature Reformation: Wycliffite Texts and Lollard History* (Oxford: Clarendon P, 1988).

tified° against the:° preching openly in Shrewis-   *officially testified / thee*
bery that pilgrimage is not lefull?° And over° this   *lawful / beyond*
thou saidist that those men and women that go
on pilgrimagis to Canturbery, to Beverley, to
[Bridlington], to Walsingame° and to ony soche   *Walsingham*
other placis, ar acursed and made foolisch,
spending their goodes in waste."

And I said, "Sir, by this certificacion° I am   *official testimony*
accused to you that I sholde teache that no pil-
grimage is lefull. But I said never thus, for I
knowe that ther be trew pilgrimagis and lefull and
full plesaunt to God. And therfore, sir, how so
ever myne enemies have certified you of me, I
tolde at Shrewisbery of two maner of pilgrimagis,
[saying that ther be trew pilgrimes and fals pil-
grimes]."

And the Archebisshop said to me, "Whome
callest thou trewe pilgrimes?"

And I said, "Sir, with my protestacion,° I call   *solemn, public affirmation*
them trew pilgremis travelyng toward the blisse of
heven which—in the state, degre, or ordre that
God calleth them [to]—doo besy them° feithfully   *busy themselves*
for to occupie all their wittes, bodely and gostely,°   *spiritual*
to knowe trewly and to keape feithfully the bid-
dinges of God, hatyng and fleyng all the seven
dedely synnes and every braunche of them;
reulyng them° verteuously, as it is said before,   *governing themselves*
with all their wittes; doyng discretely, wilfully, and
gladly all the werkis of mercy, bodely and gostely,[1]
after° their connyng° and power; ablyng them   *according to / knowledge*
to° the gyftes of the Holy Goste; disposing them   *preparing themselves for*
to receyve in their soules and to holde therin
the eight blessinges of Christe;° beseyng   *the beatitudes (Matt. 5:3–11)*
them° to knowe and to kepe the sevene principall   *busying themselves.*
vertues. And so than° they shall obteyne   *then*
herethorow° grace for to use thankfully to God all   *through these (actions)*
the condicions of charite; and than they shall be
moovyd with the good spirite of God for to examyne ofte and diligently their conscience that
nother wilfully nor wittingly they erre° in ony arti-   *err*
cle of beleve,° havyng continually, as frailte will   *faith*
suffer,° all their besinesse to drede and to flee the   *allow*
offence of God, and to loove over all thing and to
seke ever to doo his plesaunt will.

---

1. Thorpe is referring to the traditional categories of the seven corporal acts of mercy (feeding
the hungry, giving drink to the thirsty, clothing the naked, helping the sick, visiting the prisoner, sheltering the homeless, burying the dead) and the seven spiritual acts of mercy (admonishing the sinner, instructing the ignorant, counseling the doubtful, comforting the
afflicted, bearing wrongs patiently, forgiving injuries, praying for the living and the dead).

"Of these pilgremis," I said, "what so ever goode thoughte that they ony tyme thinke, what verteuous worde that they speake, and what frutefull worke that they worke: every soche thoughte, worde, and werke is a steppe noumbered of° God *by* toward hym into hevene. Thes forsaid pilgremis of God delyte sore° whan they heare of seyntis or of *greatly* verteuous men and women: how they forsoke wilfully the prosperite of this lyfe; how they withstode the suggestion of the fende; how they restreined their fleschly lustes; how discrete they wer in their penaunce doying; how pacient they wer in all their adversites; how prudent they wer in counseling of men and women, moovyng them to hate all synnes and to flye° them, and to *flee, avoid* shame° ever greatly thereof, and to love all *be ashamed* vertues and to drawe to them, ymaginyng how Christe and his folowers—by example of hym— suffered skornis and sclaunders; and how paciently they abode° and toke the wrongfull *endured* manasyng° of tyrauntis; how homely° they wer *hostility / kindly, modest* and servisable to poore men to relieve and comforte them, bodely and gostely,° after their power *spiritually* and connyng; and how devote they wer in praiers, how fervent they wer in hevenly desyres, and how they absented them fro spectacles of veyne seyngis° and hearingis; and how stable [of conte- *idle sights* naunce they were, how heartely they wailed and sorrowed for synne, how besy] they wer to lett° *prevent, hinder* and to destroye all vices, and how laborious and joifull they wer to sowe and to plante vertues. Thes hevenly condicions and soche other have the pilgremis, or endever them for to have, whose pilgrimagie God acceptith."

"And ageyne[ward],"° I saide, "as their werkis *on the contrary* shew, the moste parte of men and women that go now on pilgrimagis have not thes forsaid condicions, nor loveth to besy them feithfully for to have. For as I well know syns I have full ofte assaide:° examyne who so ever will twentie of thes *tested (it)* pilgremis, and he shall not fynde thre men or women that knowe surely° a commaundment of *correctly* God,° nor can say their Pater Noster and Ave *one of the Ten* Maria nor their Credo redely, in ony maner of lan- *Commandments* gage.[2] And as I have learnid and also know somwhat by experience of thes same pilgremis tellying the cause why that many men and women

---

2. I.e., either in Latin or in the vernacular.

go hither and thither now on pilgrimagis, it is
more for the helthe of their bodies than of their
soules, more for to have richesse and prosperite of
thys worlde than for to be enryched with vertues
in their soules, more to have here worldely and
fleschely frendship than for to have frendship of
God and of his seintis in heven. For what so ever
thing man or woman dothe, the frendship of God
nor of ony other seynt can not be hadde without
keaping of Goddis commaundementis.

"Forther with my protestacion, I say now as I
said in Shrewisbery: though they that have
fleschely willes travell [sore]° their bodies and   *greatly exert*
spende mekill° money to seake and to visite the   *much*
bonys or ymagis (as they say they do) of this
seynte or of that, soche pilgrimage-goyng is
nother praisable nor thankefull to God nor to ony
seinte of God, syns in effect all soche pelgrimes
despise God and all his commaundmentis and
seyntis. For the commaundmentis of God they
will nother knowe nor keape, nor conforme them°   *themselves*
to lyve verteously by example of Christe and of his
seyntis. Wherfor, syr, I have prechid and taucht
openly [and privately]—and so I purpose all my
lyfetime to do, with Gods helpe—saing that soche
fonde° people wast° blamefully Gods goods in   *foolish / waste*
their veyne pilgrimagis, spending their goodes
upon vicious hostelars° [and upon tapsters]°   *innkeepers / barmaids*
which ar ofte unclene° women of their bodies,   *unchaste*
and at the leste those goodes with the which thei
sholde doo werkis of mercie, after° Goddis bid-   *according to*
ding, to poore nedy men and women.

"Thes poore mennis goodes and their lyvelode°   *livelihood, sustenance*
thes runnars about° offer to riche priestis, which   *wanderers*
have mekill more lyvelode than they neade. And
thus those goodes they waste wilfully and spende
them unjustely, ageinst Goddis bidding, upon
straungers, with which thei sholde helpe and
releve, after° Goddis will, their poore nedy neigh-   *according to*
bours at home. Ye, and over° this foly, ofte tymes   *beyond*
diverse men and women of thes runners° thus   *"runners about"*
madly hither and thither in to pilgrimage borowe
hereto° other mennis goodes—ye, and some tyme   *for this (purpose)*
they stele mennis goodes hereto—and they pay
them never agein.

"Also, sir, I know well that whan diverse men
and women will go thus after their own willes,
and fynding out one pilgrimage, they will orden°   *arrange*
with them before° to have with them bothe men   *in advance*

and women that can well synge wanton songes;
and some other pilgremis will have with them
baggepipes, so that every towne that they come
throwe°—what with the noyse of their syngyng, *through*
and with the sounde of their piping, and with the
jangelyng of their Canterbery bellis, and with the
barkyng out of doggis after them—that they make
more noyse than if the kyng came there awaye° *along that route*
with all his clarions° and many other menstrelles. *trumpeters*
And if thes men and women be a monethe° out in *month*
their pilgrimage, many of them shall be, an halfe
yeare after, greate jangelers,° tale tellers, and *chatterers*
lyers."° *liars*

And the Archebishop said to me, "Leude
losell,° thou seest not ferre ynough in this mater, *Ignorant scoundrel*
for thou considerest not the great travell° of pil- *travail*
gremys, therfore thou blamest that thing that is
praisable. I say to the° that it is right well done *thee*
that pilgremys have with them bothe syngers and
also pipers, that whan one of them that goeth
barfote striketh his too° upon a stone and hurteth *toe*
hym sore and maketh hym to blede, it is well
done that he or his felow begyn than° a songe, or *then*
els take out of his bosome a baggepype, for to
dryve away with soche myrthe the hurte of his
felow. For with soche salace° the travell and weri- *solace*
nesse off pylgremes is lightely and merily
broughte forthe."° *relieved*

And I said, "Sir, Seynt Paule teacheth men to
wepe with them that wepe [Romans 12:15]."

And the Archebishoppe [scorned me and]
saide, "What janglist thou° ageinst mennis devo- *Why dost thou chatter*
cion? Whatsoever thou or soch other say, I say
that the pilgrimage that now is used° is to them *practiced*
that doo it a praysable and a good meane to come
the rather° to grace. But I holde the unable to *sooner, more readily*
know this grace, for thou enforsest the to lett° the *attemptest to hinder*
devocion of the people, syns by authorite of Holy
Scripture men maye lefully° have and use soche *lawfully*
solace as thou reprovest. For David in his laste
psalme teacheth men to have diverse instrumentes of musike for to prayse therwith God."

And I saide, "Sir, by the sentence° of diverse *according to the understanding*
doctours expounding the psalmes of David, the
musike and menstrelcy that David and other
seyntes of the olde lawe spake of owe° now *ought*
nother to be taken nor used by the letter.° But *literally*
thes instrumentes with theire musike ought to be
interpreted gostely,° for all those figures are called *spiritually*

vertues and grace, with which vertues men shold please God and prayse his name. For Saynt Paule saith, 'All soche thynges befell to them in figure.'[3] Therfore, sir, I understonde that the letter of this psalme of David, and of soche other psalmes and sentences, dothe slee them that take them now letterally. This sentence I understond, sir, Christ approveth him self, putting out the menstrelles or° that he wolde quycken° the deade damsell."

before / bring to life

And the Archebishop saide to me, "Leude losell, is it not lefull to us to have organes in the chirche for to worship therwithall God?"

And I said, "Ye, syr, by mannys ordynaunce;° but by the ordinaunce of God a goode sermonne to the peoples understondying were mekill more plesaunt to God."

decree

And the Archebisshoppe sayde that organes and goode delectable songe quyckened° and sharpened more mennys wyttes than sholde ony sermonne. But I said, "Sir, lusty° men and worldly lovers delyte and covete and travell to have all theire wittes quickened and sharpened with diverse sensible° solace; but all the feithfull lovers and folowers of Christe have all their delyte to heare Goddis worde, and to understond it truely, and to worke therafter faithfully and continually. For no doute, to dreade to offende God and to love to please him in all thing quyckeneth and sharpeneth all the wittes of Christes chosen people, and ableth° them so to grace that they joye greatly to withdrawe [their eyes], their eares and all their wittes and membres frome all worldly delyte and frome all fleschly solace. For Seynt Jerome, as I thinke, saith, 'Nobody may joye with this worlde and reigne with Christe.' "[4]

(have) awakened

pleasure-loving

sensual

aids

And the Archebishop, as yf he had ben displeased with myne answere, said to his clerkes, "What gesse ye this ydiote will speke ther wher he hath none dreade, syns he speaketh thus nowe, here in my presence? Well, well, by God thou shalt be ordened for!"°

dealt with

* * *

3. By "figures" Thorpe means the details in Psalm 150 that invite an allegorical rather than a literal reading. His interpretation is consistent with those of many medieval "doctours," such as St. Augustine, who in his *Enarrationes in psalmos* explains that the instruments named in the psalm refer to various aspects of the human soul or the community of souls that worship God. They are "figures" of virtues. After citing 1 Corinthians 10:11, Thorpe alludes to Paul's famous teaching that "the letter killeth, but the spirit giveth life" (2 Corinthians 3:6). His allusion to Christ putting out the minstrels refers to Matthew 9:23–25, part of the story of Jairus's daughter, which is told more fully but without the mention of minstrels in Mark 5:22–43.
4. As Hudson's note explains, this quotation is actually from St. Gregory.

THOMAS WIMBLEDON

[On the Estates]†

My dere ferendis, ye shullen undirstonde that
Crist Jesus, auctour and doccour° of trewthe, in   *teacher*
his book of the gospel liknyng° the kyngdom of   *comparing*
hevene to an housholdere, seith on this maneres:°   *in this way*
"Lik is the kyngdom of hevene to an hous-
holdynge man that wente out first on the morwe°   *morning*
to hire werkemen into his vine.° Also aboute the   *vineyard*
thridde,° sixte, nyenthe, and elevene houris he   *third*
wente out and fond men stondynge ydel° and sey   *idle*
to hem: Go yee into my vyne and that right is° I   *what is just*
wole yeve° yow. Whanne the day was ago, he   *give*
clepid° his styward and heet° to yeve eche man a   *called / commanded (him)*
peny."

To spiritual undirstondyng this housholdere is
oure lord Jesu Crist, that "is heed of the houshold
of holi chirche."[1] And thus he clepith men in diverse houris of the day, that is in diverse ages of
the world; os° in tyme of lawe of kynde° he   *as / nature*
clepide by enspirynge Abel, Ennok, Noe,° and   *Noah*
Abraham; in tyme of the olde lawe Moyses,
David, Ysaye,° and Jeremie;° and in tyme of grace   *Isaiah / Jeremiah*
apostelis, martiris, and confessoures,[2] and vir-
gines. Also he clepeth men in diverse ages:
summe in childhood, as Jon Baptist; summe on
stat° of wexenge,° as Jon the Evangelist; summe   *in the process / maturing*
in stat of manhod, as Petir and Andrew; and
summe in old age, as Gamaliel and Josep of Ara-
mathie.° And alle these he clepith to travayle on   *Joseph of Arimathea*
his vyne, that is the chirche, and that on diverse
maneres.

For right as yee seeth that in tilienge° of the   *tilling*
material vine there beeth diverse laboreris: for
summe kuttyn awey the voyde° braunchis; summe   *unproductive*
maken forkes° and rayles to beren up the veyne;   *forked stakes*
and summe diggen awey the olde erthe fro the
rote and leyn° there fattere.° And alle theise of-   *put / richer (soil)*

---

† Text based on *Wimbledon's Sermon "Redde Rationem Villicationis Tue": A Middle-English
Sermon of the Fourteenth Century*, ed. Ione Kemp Knight (Pittsburgh: Duquesne UP, 1967),
61–66. Reprinted with permission of the publisher. This opening passage of the sermon is
based on the parable of the vineyard (Matthew 20:1–10).
1. Colossians 1:18.
2. Christians who heroically affirm their faith in the face of persecution but escape martyrdom.

fices° *duties* ben so nescessarie to the veyne that yif eny of hem fayle° *are lacking* it schal harme gretly or distroye the vyne. For but yif° the vine be kut, he° schal wexe *unless / it* wilde; but yif she be rayled, she shal be overgoo° *overrun* with netles and wedis; and but yif the rote be fettid° *enriched* with donge, she for feblenesse shold wexe barayne.

Ryght so in the chirche beeth nedeful° *necessary* thes thre offices: presthod, knyghthod, and laboreris. To prestis it fallith° *it is proper* to kutte awey the voide braunchis of synnis with the swerd of here tonge. To knyghtis it fallith to lette° *stop* wrongis and theftis to be do,° *from being done* and to mayntene Goddis lawe and hem that ben techeris ther-of, and also to kepe the lond fro enemyes of other londes. And to laboreris it falleth to travayle bodily and with here sore swet geten out of the erthe bodily liflode° *sustenance* for hem and for other parties. And these statis° beth also° *estates / so* nedeful to the chirche that non may wel ben withouten other. For yif presthod lackede,° *were missing* the puple for defaute° *lack* of knowyng of Goddis lawe shulde wexe wilde on vices and deie gostly.° *die spiritually* And yif the knythod lackid and men to reule the puple by lawe and hardnesse,° *resoluteness* theves and enemies shoden so encresse that no man sholde lyven in pes.° *peace* And yif the laboreris weren not, bothe prestis and knyghtis mosten bicome acremen° *plowmen* and heerdis,° and ellis° they sholde for defaute of *shepherds / or otherwise* bodily sustenaunce deie.

And herfore seith a gret clerk,° Avycenne,[3] that *scholar* every unresonable beest, yif he have that that kynde° hath ordeyned for hym as kynde hath *nature* ordeyned it, he is sufficiaunt to lyve by hymself withouten eny other of the same kynde.° As yif *species* there were but one hors other° oon sheep in the *or* world, yit yif he hadde graas and corn° as kynde *grain* hath ordeyned for suche bestes, he shulde lyve wel inow.° But yif ther were but oon man in the *enough* world, though he hadde all that good that is therin, yit for defaute he scholde die, or his life shulde be worse than yif he were nought.° And *did not exist* the cause is this: for thyng that kynde ordeyneth for a mannis sustinaunce, withoutyn other arayinge° than it hath of kynde, acordith° nought to *preparation / suits* hym. As though a man have corn as it cometh fro the erthe, yit it is no mete acordynge to° hym *suitable food for*

---

3. This paragraph follows closely the beginning of Avicenna's *Liber de anima seu sextus de naturalibus*, part 5, chapter 1.

into° it be by mannis craft chaungid into bred. *until*
And though he have flesche other fissche, yit
while it is raw, as kynde ordeyneth it, forto° it be *until*
by mannis travayle sothen,° rosted, other bake, it *boiled*
acordith not to mannis liflode. And ryght so
wolle° that the sheep berith mot,° by many di- *wool / must*
verse craftis and travaylis, be chaungid er° it be *before*
able to clothe eny man. And certis° o° man bi *certainly / one*
hymsilf shulde nevere don alle thise labouris. And
therfore seith this clerk, it is nede that summe
beth acremen,° summe bakeris, summe makeris *plowmen*
of cloth, and summe marchaundis to fecche that
that o lond fauteth° from another ther it is plente. *lacks*

And certis this shulde be o cause why every
staat shul love other and men of o craft shulde
neither hate ne despise men of another craft,
sith° they beth so nedeful everych to other. And *since*
ofte thilke° craftis that semen most unhonest *those*
myghthen worst° be forbore.° And o thyng y dar *least well / dispensed with*
wel seye: that he that is neither traveylynge in this
world on prayeris and prechynge for helpe of the
puple, as it fallith to prestis; neither° in fyghtinge *nor*
ayenis tyrauntis and enemyes, as it fallith to
knyghtis; neither travaylynge on the erthe, as it fallith to laboreris—whanne the day of his rekenyng° *accounting*
cometh (that is, the ende of this lif), ryght as he
lyvede here withoutyn travayle, so he shal there
lacke the reward of the peny (that is, the endeles
joye of hevene). And as he was here lyvynge aftir
noon staat° ne ordre, so he shal be put thanne "in *according to no stability*
that place that noon ordre is inne, but evere-
lastynge horrour"[4] and sorwe (that is, in helle).

WILLIAM LANGLAND

[On Monks]†

* * *

Amonges rightful religiouse,° this reule schulde *righteous*
    be holde: *members of religious orders*
Gregorie, the grete clerke° and the goed pope, *scholar*
Of religioun the reule reherseth° in his morales,[1] *expounds*

---

4. Job 10:22.
† Text based on *The Vision of William concerning Piers the Plowman,* ed. Walter W. Skeat, 2 vols. (1886; London: Oxford UP, 1965), I. 308–10: B-text, Passus X, 291–320. This version of the poem is thought to have been written ca. 1377–79.
1. The *Moralia,* one of the best-known works of Pope Gregory the Great (d. 604).

And seyth it in ensaumple° for° thei schulde do° *as an example / so that / act*
there-after;

5 "Whenne fissches failen° the flode° or the *lack / stream*
fresche water,

Thei deyen for drouthe° whanne thei drie ligge.° *drought / lie*

Right so," quod Gregorie, "religioun roileth,° *roams about*

Sterveth° and stynketh and steleth lordes *Dies*
almesses,° *alms*

That oute of covent° and cloystre coveyten° to *convent / desires*
libbe."° *live*

10 For if hevene be on this erthe and ese° to any *ease, rest*
soule,

It is in cloistere or in scole, be° many skilles° I *for / reasons*
fynde.

For in cloistre cometh no man to chide ne to
fighte,

But alle is buxumnesse° there and bokes to rede *obedience*
and to lerne.

In scole there is scorne but if° a clerke wil lerne, *unless*

15 And grete love and lykynge, for eche of hem
loveth other.

Ac° now is Religioun a ryder, a rowmer° *But / roamer*
bi° stretes, *through*

A leder of lovedayes[2] and a lond-bugger,° *land buyer*

A priker° on a palfray fro manere° to manere, *rider / manor*

An heep of houndes at his ers,° as° he a lorde *arse / as if*
were.

20 And but if his knave° knele, that shal his cuppe *servant*
brynge,

He loureth on° hym and axeth him who taughte *scowls at*
hym curteisye.

Litel had lordes to done to gyve londe fram her
heires[3]

To religious, that have no reuthe° though it reyne *do not care*
on her auteres.° *altars*

In many places ther hii persones ben° be° *where they are parsons / by*
hemself at ese,

25 Of the pore have thei no pite—and that is her
charite—

Ac thei leten hem as° lordes, her londe lith° so *behave like / extends*
brode.° *widely*

Ac there shal come a kyng and confesse° yow *be a confessor to*
religiouses,

And bete° yow, as the Bible telleth, for brekynge *chastise*
of yowre reule,

---

2. A judge on lovedays, days when disputes were settled out of court. Cf. *General Prologue*,
l. 258.
3. Lords have little reason to transfer property from their heirs.

And amende monyales,° monkes and chanouns,°   *nuns / canons*
30 And putten hem to her penaunce, *ad pristinum*
    statum ire.[4]

* * *

JOHN GOWER

[On Monks]†

We now consider the estate of the religious orders, and first those that
hold property. They should be attentive in praying to the glorious God,
within their cloisters and monasteries, for us secular people. That is
the function of their order, for which they are abundantly endowed
with a full measure of goods so that they do not desire to seek elsewhere for money. St. Augustine says in his teaching that just as a fish
lives only in water, so Religion must lead its life according to the rule
of the convent, fully obedient and cloistered. For if it lives in the
world, then it alters the nature of the order that was first established,
and consequently respect for the profession is lost.

    In following the original order, monks took vows against the plea-
sures of the flesh and endured the pain of a harsh life. But now those
observances have been completely abandoned. Gluttony guards all the
doors so that hunger and thirst do not enter in there to make the fat
paunches lean. With fur cloaks they have kept out the agonies of cold
weather, for they do not wish to make its acquaintance. The old rule
regularly ate fish, but this one wants to change that: when meat that
has been finely chopped or well pounded in a mortar is prepared and
served, the new rule maintains that such ground meat is not flesh. It
hopes to deceive God but is itself deceived, for it cherishes the belly so
much that rather than lose a single meal, which might make the body
grow thinner, it neglects the well-being of the soul. I do not know if
the monks dance or joust, but I know well that when one of them
takes his large flagon filled with wine, he downs it with great boister-
ousness and says that is the proper rule. I do not mean St. Augustine's:
it is the rule of Robin,[1] who leads the life of a raven, searching first for
what he can gulp down to fill himself and giving no thought to his

---

4. In order to return (them) to their former state (within the Rule).
† Translated by Glending Olson, from *Mirour de l'omme*, lines 20833–92 and 20953–1060,
   The Works of John Gower, ed. G. C. Macaulay (Oxford: Clarendon P: 1899–1902),
   I.235–37. There is a complete English translation by William Burton Wilson (East Lansing:
   Colleagues P, 1992). These two excerpts contain the closest parallels to Chaucer's portrait of
   the Monk; they constitute about half of Gower's criticism of the monastic orders. The poem,
   whose title means *Mirror of Man*, is a didactic one in French, of which 29,444 lines survive;
   it was written ca. 1376–78. It begins with an allegory on the origins of sin, treats at length
   the seven vices and seven virtues, and then offers a critical survey of London life in the
   1370s. Chaucer was a close friend of Gower, naming him as one of two persons legally authorized to act on his behalf during his second trip to Italy in 1378 and codedicating the
   Troilus and Criseyde to him ("O moral Gower") and the "philosophical Strode."
1. Robin is a standard medieval name for a man of the lower classes and often carries the suggestion of low morals as well. It is the name of Chaucer's Miller and, in the *Miller's Tale*, of
   John's servant.

neighbor, just the way a mastiff devours everything down to the crumbs and crust. * * *

The monk who has been made guardian or steward of any outside property is not a good cloisterer, for then he needs a horse and saddle to get around the countryside, and he spends lavishly. He takes the best part of the grain for himself and leaves the chaff for others, such as peasants; and thus the foolish, proud monk behaves like a lord. But an empty barn and a full belly do not yield an even balance. When he is guardian of an estate, the monk says "Everything is ours" out of twisted charity; he speaks the truth in part, but only a little, for with his wicked appetite he wants for himself more than what seven others get. Surely the cloister is better for such a guardian than ownership of property, which only takes income away from others. As St. Bernard says, it is repugnant to see an overseer in a monk's habit. The monk who acts this way is half worldly, and he comes close to apostasy when he has taken possession of the world again and dispossessed himself of the cloister. I do not know how he can justify himself for this failure of rule, nor do I think that his control of land and income can be security for him before God, to whom he first pledged his faith when he became a monk.

St. Jerome tells us that the filthiness of the habit a monk wears is an outward sign that he is without pride and haughtiness, that his inner spirit is of a pure white spotlessness. But our monk of today regularly seeks fancy adornment for his body and disfigures his soul. Although he wears the habit of suffering, he also has, in his vanity, a coat adorned with fur. There is a story that a great nobleman loved by God dressed himself in wretched haircloth when King Manasses married his daughter; even on that occasion he would not sacrifice his simplicity but rather directed his actions more to pleasing God than man. Thus he set an example for others: one should not attend to the body so much that he becomes proud. I do not know how monks will react to this story, but the example should disquiet that monk who behaves luxuriously because of worldliness. He seeks not haircloth but the very best wool he can find, trimmed with gray squirrel fur, for he disdains fleece. Nor does he forget a silver pendant but gaily displays it hanging from his hood on his breast. That is the kind of simplicity we see now in monks and their dress.

A monk should nurture his religion through discretion, humility, and simplicity; but ours does not want to do that. He hates to hear the name of monk, which he vowed to take, even though his mother was a shepherdess and his father without high rank, perhaps a servant. But when those of low status rise to the heights, and poverty becomes wealthy, there is nothing in the world so villainous. The monk who seeks property sins greatly against the rule, but he has nevertheless amassed great sums for himself, wealth which he procured from the world just like a merchant. And moreover, to entertain himself, he goes along the river with game birds, falcon and molted hawk, with swift greyhounds as well, and fine high-spirited horses—all that is missing is a wife. And on the subject of wives, what can I do but

wonder, for I have heard about the children that our monk accumu-
lated while he was running around here and there, day after day. But
they cannot inherit from him, so he must pass along great sums in order to enrich them. I leave it to you to decide if this is the way charity
acts.

* * *

Wycliffite Estates Criticism†

[On Merchants]

* * *

Also marchauntis and riche men of this wikked
world fallen in moche ypocrise; for thei traveilen
nyght and day, bi watir and lond, in cold and in
hete, bi false sotilis° and cautelis° and grete   *tricks / wiles*
sweringes nedles° and false, for to gete muche   *needless*
drit° or muk of this world, to gete riche wyves,   *dirt, filth*
and purchase° londis and rentis,° and dewelle° in   *acquire / revenues / linger*
pore mennus dette after that thei han desceyved
hem in byynge of here catel.° And yit ben° so bisi   *goods / they are*
in thought and speche, in goyng and rydyng
abouten this muk, that unnethe° may thei onys°   *scarcely / once*
thenke on God and han mynde of° here false rob-   *reflect on*
berie that thei usen° bi false wettes° and mesures   *practice / weights*
to amende hem.° Yif alle here° bisinesse and love   *prosper / their*
goo thus wrongly to the world and nought or to
litel to hevene and hevenely thingis, thei failen
foule of° holy lif; and yit holden hem self holy and   *in*
coveiten to ben holden holy of° other men, and   *by*
ben wode° yif men speken treuly ayenst here   *mad, angry*
cursed synnes. But certes this is ypocrisie.

† Text based on *The English Works of John Wyclif Hitherto Unprinted*, ed. F. D. Matthew, 2nd
ed., EETS o.s. 74 (London, 1902), 24–25, 154. Reprinted with permission of the Council of
the Early English Text Society. Wyclif (ca. 1329–1384) was briefly Master of Balliol College,
Oxford (1361) and, as philosopher, theologian, and reformer, a most controversial figure in
his time. He was first prosecuted for heresy in 1377 and again in 1382, when he was condemned for ten heresies and fourteen errors. But his criticism of corruption in the church
and in the estates expressed attitudes shared by many of his contemporaries, including
those—a majority—who did not necessarily interest themselves in, or subscribe to, his views
on the powers of the pope, "dominion by Grace," or his denial of the truth of Transubstanti-
ation. He was responsible for the first translation of the Bible into English, a work accomplished in the last quarter of the fourteenth century.

[On Pardoners and Priests]

Thei [curates, clergymen in charge of a parish] assenten° to pardoners disceyvynge the peple in feith and charite and worldly goodis for to have part of here gederynge,° and letten° prestis to preche° the gospel for drede laste° here synne and ypocrisie be knowen and stoppid. For whanne there cometh a pardoner with stollen bullis and false relekis,° grauntynge mo yeris of pardon than comen bifore domes day for yevynge° of worldly catel° to riche placis where is no nede, he schal be sped° and resceyved of° curatis for to have part of that° he getith. But a preste that wole telle the trewthe to alle men withouten glosynge° and frely withouten beggynge of° the pore peple, he schal be lettid by sotil cavyllacions° of mannus lawe, for drede last° he touche the sore of here conscience and cursed lif. And this pardoner schalle telle of more power than evere Crist grauntid to Petir or Poul or ony apostle, to drawe the almes fro pore bedrede° neigheboris that ben knowen feble and pore, and to gete it to hem self and wasten it ful synfulli in ydelnesse and glotonye and lecherie, and senden gold out of oure lond to riche lordis and housis where is no nede, and make oure lond pore by many sotile weies. And here bi° the peple is more bold to lien° stille in her synne, and weneth° not to have as myche thank and reward of Crist for to do° here almes to pore feble men— as Crist biddith in the gospel—as whanne thei don here almes to riche housis aftir graunt° of synful foolis. And this is opyn errour ayenst Cristene feith.

consent

winnings / prevent
from preaching / lest

relics

giving
goods
aided / received by
what
glossing, distorting
from
subtle cavils
lest

bedridden

hereby
remain
think
give

following the advice

The Miller's Prologue and Tale

Although there are a number of analogues to individual motifs in the *Miller's Tale*, only one story that survives from Chaucer's age contains all the major plot elements. It is a Flemish fabliau, titled *The Three Guests of Heile of Bersele* in Constance B. Hieatt's translation. Chaucer's source may well have been a French fabliau now lost, but the *Miller's Tale* is rich with detail and nuance usually lacking in the genre, of which *Heile* is a fairly typical representative.

The Three Guests of Heile of Bersele†

You have often heard tales of all manner of things, told or sung to the tune of a fiddle or harp; but I think few will have heard of such a strange case as one which happened here in Antwerp some time ago. I will tell you about it at the request of a boon companion of mine; he wouldn't let me off.

Here in the market street in Antwerp, there lived, I recall, a fine wench, and she was called Heile of Bersele. She often made love, for a price, with good fellows to whom she displayed her arts. It fell out once, as I heard the story, that three such fellows came to her on the same day, one after the other, all three asking her that for the sake of friendship she would let them come where she lived: each wanted to speak to her alone, in secret. This was good business for Heile, who determined to satisfy all three.

The first one she made an appointment with was a miller called William Hoeft. She told him to come as soon as evening fell. The second was a priest; she told him to come when the curfew-bell rang. She told the third, a smith who was a neighbor of hers, to come when the clock struck midnight. This satisfied all three, and they all went their way happily, awaiting the proper time.

At twilight, William came promptly. Heile received him graciously and made him quite at home. They played the game of love—she knew that business well—and thus they lay taking their pleasure until it was time for curfew.

As the bell rang out for curfew, the priest came, all eagerness, saying, "Heile, let me in! I am here: you know who."

† From Constance B. Hieatt, ed., *The Miller's Tale*, by Geoffrey Chaucer (New York: The Odyssey Press, 1970), 51–54. The Flemish text is printed in *Sources and Analogues of Chaucer's* Canterbury Tales, ed. W. F. Bryan and Germaine Dempster (Chicago: U of Chicago P, 1941), pp. 112–18. It was written in the late fourteenth century.

"Good heavens, Heile," said William, "who is that there?"

"I don't know, William," she answered, "but it seems to me it's the priest. He is supposed to instruct me and mend my faults."

"Oh, dear Heile," William cried, "quick—where can I run so that the priest can't see me?"

Heile said, "Up above there is a trough which I have found useful at various times before. It is tied to the rafters with a good sound rope. You'll be better off there than anywhere else."

William hid himself in the trough and told her to let the priest in. Heile then made her second guest comfortable. After they had done the wide-awake dance three times, the priest began to discourse on the gospels. He said that the time would soon come when God would bring judgment upon the world, coming with water and fire; and that everyone—high and low, young and old—should drown.

William, sitting overhead in the trough, heard all this, and believed that it might well be true: the priests taught it, and the gospel bore witness to it.

But meanwhile Hugh, the smith, came; he thought he had waited quite long enough, and a good deal longer than he had wished. He gave a soft knock at the door. Heile said, "Who is there?"

"Why indeed, Heile, it's me," he replied.

Heile answered, "You can't come in."

"But Heile, my love, are you going to break your promise? I have to speak to you!"

"That you shall not," said Heile, "right now, for I am unwell. You cannot come in at this time."

"Ah, dear Heile, then I beg you, let me at least kiss your mouth right now."

Then Heile said to the priest, "Now, sir, let this fellow kiss your behind: he will certainly think it's me, and nobody else."

"Marvelous!" said the priest. "A splendid jest!" And he jumped right up and quickly put his tail out the window. Hugh, thinking that it was Heile, kissed the priest's arse with such ardour that his nose pushed right inside and he was caught, it seemed to him, like a mouse in a trap. He was thrown into a frenzy of rage: he was not so dull that he could not tell, from the feel and smell of the thing, that he had kissed an arse, for the mouth seemed to be set the wrong way between cheeks above and below.

"By Christ," he said to himself, "I'll come back!"

He ran as though he were mad to his house nearby and quickly picked up a huge iron. He thrust it into the fire until it was so hot that it glowed brightly, then ran with it to Heile's door, crying, "Heile, my love, let me in now, or at least let me kiss your little mouth: one or the other, or I'll stand here all night. The strength of my love for you forces me to it!"

The priest, hearing his cue, again put his hind passage out where it had been before. Without hesitating, the smith struck the glowing iron into his arse. Then the priest sang his verse loud and clear: "Water,

water! Oh, I am dead," he cried at length, until the words died out in his mouth.

William, who lay hidden above, was greatly alarmed for he thought, "What the priest predicted tonight has now come true—surely the water has come and all the earth shall now be drowned! But if I can float away from here, the trough will save my life." Grasping his knife, he cut through the rope by which the trough was hanging, and said, "Now may God and good fortune aid William Hoeft in his voyage!"

Down to the ground came William, trough and all, with such a crash that he was badly hurt—both his arm and his thigh were broken. Now the priest, thinking that the devil had come, scooted off into a corner, where he fell into a privy. They say that he came home covered with filth, burned in the arse, and held up to scorn and shame. It would have been far better for him if he had stayed home and said his prayers!

That was what happened to Heile's guests. The smith had a setback, but he found good consolation for that in burning the priest's hole— he was well revenged.

Saving your dignity, let it be said that whoever keeps company with whores will surely find strife, harm, shame, and sorrow coming upon him. The guests of Heile found this out.

The Reeve's Prologue and Tale

The cradle-trick story that forms the central episode of the *Reeve's Tale* was popular throughout the later Middle Ages and Renaissance, and a number of analogues survive. *The Miller and the Two Clerics*, a thirteenth-century French fabliau, is the closest to Chaucer. For texts and translations of other medieval versions, including a story from Boccaccio's *Decameron*, see *The Literary Context of Chaucer's Fabliaux*, ed. Larry D. Benson and Theodore M. Andersson (Indianapolis: Bobbs-Merrill, 1971), pp. 79–201, and Peter G. Beidler's chapter on the *Reeve's Tale* analogues in *Sources and Analogues of The Canterbury Tales, Vol. I*, ed. Robert M. Correale and Mary Hamel (Cambridge: D. S. Brewer, 2002), pp. 23–73.

The Miller and the Two Clerics†

There were once two poor fellows of the minor clergy who were born in the same region and in the same city. They were friends and deacons of a woodland church, where they found a living, until, as happens often and again, they fell on hard times, which is a great pity for poor people. They were heavy at heart when they considered their state of affairs, nor did they see any way out of it. For they did not know how to earn their living, either in their own country or anywhere else, and they were ashamed to beg their bread out of regard for their order, as well as for other reasons. They had no possessions by which they might keep themselves alive, and they didn't know where to turn.

One Sunday they met outside the church, and they went for a walk about the town in order to talk things over. "Listen to me," one of them said to the other, "we are helpless because we cannot earn our livings; and now hunger, which vanquishes everything, has got hold of us. Nobody can defend us against it, and we have nothing to draw upon. Have you put by anything at all by which we might keep ourselves going?" The other one answered: "By Saint Denis, I can't think of anything except that I have a friend to whom I suggest we go and ask for a bushel of wheat at the current price; he will very willingly give me credit, and at long term, until Saint John's Day, to tide us over this bad year." Then the first one said: "That's a piece of luck for us; for I have a brother who owns a fat mare. I'll go get her while you get the wheat, and we'll become bakers. There is no load too shameful to

† From *Fabliaux: Ribald Tales from the Old French*, translated by Robert Hellman and Richard O'Gorman, 51–57. Copyright © 1965 by Robert Hellman and Richard O'Gorman. Reprinted by permission of HarperCollins Publishers Inc.

bear if it will get us through this bad year." And they did this without further delay.

Then they brought their wheat to the mill, which was at a great distance, more than two leagues away. It was a mill with a millrace near a little wood. There was no town or farm or any house nearby except the house of the miller, who knew his trade only too well. The clerics undid the gate at once and threw their sacks inside. Then they put their mare in a meadow by the millrace. One of them remained outside to keep an eye on things, and the other went in to get the miller started at their work. But the miller had gone into hiding. He had indeed seen the clerics coming, and I think he wanted a part of their wheat.

When the cleric came running into the miller's house, he found his wife at her spinning. "Lady," he said, "by Saint Martin, where is the owner of the mill? He ought to come and help us." "Sir cleric," said she, "it's no trouble at all. You will find him in that wood right near the mill, if you will be so kind as to go there." And the cleric set out quickly to find him. His friend, who was waiting for him, grew impatient that he stayed so long and came running into the house. "Lady," he said, "for the love of God, where has my companion gone?" "Sir," said she, "on my honor, he went in search of my husband who has just left the house." So she sent one cleric after the other, while the miller came around quickly to the mill. With his wife's help he took both sacks and mare and hid them in his barn. Then he returned to the mill.

The two clerics looked everywhere, and finally they also returned to the mill. "Miller," they said, "God be with you! For the love of God, help us out." "My lords," said he, "how may I do so?" "In faith, with the wheat we have here." But, when they went to get the wheat, they found neither sacks nor mare. They looked at one another. "What's this?" said one. "We are robbed!" "Yes," said the other, "so it seems to me. For our sins we are undone!" Then both cried out: "Alas! Alas! Help us, Nicholas!" "What's wrong with you?" said the miller. "Why do you cry so loud?" "Miller, we have surely lost everything. A misfortune has befallen us, for we have neither mare nor anything. And that was our whole fortune." "Lords," said the miller, "I know nothing about this." "Sir," they said, "there's nothing you can do except to tell us where we may go to look for what we have lost." "Lords," he said, "I can't help you very much, but go look in that wood there near the mill." The two clerics set out and at once went into the woods; and the miller went his way.

They looked high and low until the sun had set; and then one of the clerics said to the other: "Surely it is truly said that he's a fool who puts himself out for nothing. Wealth comes and goes like straws blown by the wind. Let's go find a lodging for the night." "And where shall we go?" "To the miller's, in whose mill we were. May God grant us lodging in Saint Martin's name!"

They went straight to the miller's house; but he was not pleased at their coming. At once he asked them: "What has Saint Nicholas done

for you?" "Miller," they said, "not one thing or another." "Then," said
he, "you'd better earn other goods. For what you've lost is a long way
off; you won't have it for present needs." "Miller," they said, "that may
well be. But put us up for Saint Sylvester's sake. We don't know where
else to go at this hour." The miller took thought and decided that he
would be worse than a dog if he didn't provide something for them out
of their own belongings, as he was well able. "My lords," he said, "I
have nothing but the floor to offer you; that you shall have and nothing more." "Miller," they said, "that is enough."

The peasant did not have many in his household. With himself
there were only four: his daughter, who deserves to be mentioned first,
his wife, and a little baby. The daughter was beautiful and charming,
and to protect her against her own warmth, the miller put her in a
cupboard every night, and there she slept. The miller would lock her
in and pass her the key through an opening, and then he would go to
bed.

But let us return to our clerics. In the evening at suppertime, the
miller brought bread and milk and eggs and cheese, country fare, and
he gave each of the clerics a good share. One of them supped with the
maiden and the other with the miller and his wife. In the hearth was a
little andiron with a ring on it that could be taken off and put back
again. The cleric who ate with the maiden took the ring from the andiron and hid it well. That night, when they went to bed, the cleric
watched the daughter carefully and saw how the miller locked her in
the cupboard and threw her the key.

When they had settled down for the night, the cleric nudged his
companion and said: "Friend, I want to go and speak to the miller's
daughter, who is locked up in the cupboard." "Do you want to start a
quarrel," said the other, "and stir up a tempest in the house? Truth is
you are a rogue. Evil can soon come of this." "Even if I die," said the
first, "I must go and see if I can make anything of her." He quickly
jumped out of bed and went straight to the cupboard. He drew near it
and scratched on it a little, and she heard him. "Who is it out there?"
she said. "It is he who for your sake is so grieved and so unhappy that,
unless you have pity on him, he will never feel joy again. It is he with
whom you supped and who brings you a gold ring—you never had
such a treasure. It is known and proved that its stone has such power
that any woman, no matter how light she may be or how she may wanton about, will remain a virgin if she has it on her finger in the morning. Here, I make you a gift of it." At once she held out the key to him;
and he quickly unlocked the chest. He got in and she squeezed over.
And so they could take their pleasure, for there was no one to disturb
them.

Before daybreak the miller's wife got up from beside her husband
and all naked went into the courtyard. And she passed before the
cleric where he lay abed. When he saw her go by, he thought of his
friend who was taking his pleasure in the cupboard, and he had a
great longing for the same kind of pleasure. He thought he would trick
the wife on her way back. But then he thought he would not, for fear

of what mad consequences might ensue. And then again he thought of a new stratagem. He jumped out of bed and went straight to the bed where the miller lay. He carried away the child in its cradle; and when the wife came in the door, the cleric pinched the baby's ear, whereupon it awoke and cried out. The wife, who had been going to her own bed, when she heard the cry turned about and went in that direction. When she found the cradle she was reassured, and she lifted the cover and lay down beside the cleric, who hugged her tight. He drew her to him and squeezed her so tight in his pleasure that he quite crushed her. In amazement she allowed him to do what he liked.

Meanwhile, the other cleric, when he heard the cock crow, felt he had been lingering too long. He made himself ready, took his leave of the maiden, and slipped out of the chest. He went straight to his own bed where his companion lay, but when he found the cradle he was dismayed, and no wonder. He was frightened, but nonetheless he felt a little further; and when he came on two heads he knew he must be wrong. So he went quickly to the bed where the miller was lying and lay down beside him. The miller had not yet awakened and noticed nothing. "Comrade," said the cleric, "what are you doing? He who never has anything to say is worth nothing. On my word, I've had a fine night, God save me! She's a warm little girl, the miller's daughter. That kind of pleasure is very wicked indeed, but there is great pleasure in the cupboard. Go, my friend, slip in now yourself and get your share of the bacon. There's plenty left before you get to the rind. I've bent her back seven times tonight, but she still hasn't got her fill. All she got in return was the ring from the andiron. I've done a good job."

When the miller heard this trick, he seized the cleric by the collar; and the cleric, when he saw what was up, grabbed the miller and treated him so roughly that he almost strangled him. The wife began to kick the other cleric who was lying beside her. "Husband," she said, "what's going on? Please, let's get up at once. Those clerics are strangling each other over there." "Never you mind," said the cleric, "let them be, let the fools kill each other." (He knew very well that his companion was the stronger of the two.)

When the miller managed to break loose, he ran at once to light the fire. And when he saw his wife lying with the cleric, he shouted: "Get up, you brazen whore. How did you get in there? Now it's all up with you." "Husband," she said, "it's not quite as you say. For if I am a brazen whore, I was tricked into it. But you're a bold-faced thief, for you have made away with these clerics' sacks of wheat and their mare, for which you will be hanged. It's all stuck away in your barn."

The two clerics took hold of the miller and came little short of milling him like wheat, so hard did they beat and bruise him. They kicked and cuffed him until he gave them back all their wheat. Then they went to another mill to get their wheat ground. They got Saint Martin's lodging, and they worked so well at their new trade that they got through the bad year and gave thanks up and down to God and to Saint Nicholas.

The Wife of Bath's Prologue and Tale

The Wife of Bath is inimitable but not unprecedented. She is one of a number of sexually experienced older women in classical and medieval literature. Chaucer's largest debt to this tradition may be seen in the long speech of the Old Woman in the *Romance of the Rose*, from which he derived many of the Wife's traits and even a few of her lines.

The Wife's prologue is also built up from a vast medieval repertoire of antifeminist literature and debate. We include A. G. Rigg's translation of sections from the principal sources: Theophrastus, St. Jerome, and Walter Map. Various passages from the Bible, used not only by Jerome but by the Wife herself, are the central authorities for medieval ideas on marriage, remarriage, and widowhood. Further commentary may be found in Chaucer's Parson's own treatment of the sin of lechery and its remedy, which appears on pp. 295–306.

There are a number of analogues to the Wife's tale, the closest being the *Tale of Florent*, one of many *exempla* in the *Confessio Amantis* by Chaucer's friend John Gower. It has been argued that Chaucer based his tale on Gower's treatment alone, but many scholars believe he had a source now lost.

JEAN DE MEUN

From the *Romance of the Rose*†

[The Old Woman's Speech]

* * *

"Know then, that if only, when I was your age, I had been as wise about the games of Love as I am now! For then I was a very great beauty, but now I must complain and moan when I look at my face,

---

† From Guillaume de Lorris and Jean de Meun, *The Romance of the Rose*, trans. Charles Dahlberg (Princeton: Princeton UP, 1971), pp. 222–33, 241–42, 247–48. Copyright © 1971 by Princeton University Press. Excerpts reprinted by permission of Princeton University Press. The Old Woman (La Vieille) is advising a young lady on how to deal with men; the "son" she addresses is Fair Welcoming (Bel Accueil), a personification of part of the lady's psyche. This episode occurs in Jean de Meun's part of the poem, written ca. 1275. We know from the prologue to the *Legend of Good Women* that Chaucer had himself "translated the Romaunce of the Rose"; but the surviving Middle English version is in three fragments, not all of them thought to be by Chaucer, and together they amount to only about one-third of the French poem. The Old Woman's speech translated here is not represented in the extant Middle English text, though we may be certain Chaucer knew it in its original French and nearly as certain he had once translated it himself.

which has lost its charms; and I see the inevitable wrinkles whenever I remember how my beauty made the young men skip. I made them so struggle that it was nothing if not a marvel. I was very famous then; word of my highly renowned beauty ran everywhere. At my house there was a crowd so big that no man ever saw the like. At night they knocked on my door: I was really very hard on them when I failed to keep my promises to them, and that happened very often, for I had other company. They did many a crazy thing at which I got very angry. Often my door was broken down, and many of them got into such battles as a result of their hatred and envy that before they were separated they lost their members and their lives. If master Algus, the great calculator, had wanted to take the trouble and had come with his ten figures, by which he certifies and numbers everything, he could not, however well he knew how to calculate, have ascertained the number of these great quarrels. Those were the days when my body was strong and active! As I say, if I had been as wise then as I am now, I would possess the value of a thousand pounds of sterling silver more than I do now, but I acted too foolishly.

"I was young and beautiful, foolish and wild, and had never been to a school of love where they read in the theory, but I know everything by practice. Experiments, which I have followed my whole life, have made me wise in love. Now that I know everything about love, right up to the struggle, it would not be right if I were to fail to teach you the delights that I know and have often tested. He who gives advice to a young man does well. Without fail, it is no wonder that you know nothing, for your beak is too yellow. But in the end, I have so much knowledge upon which I can lecture from a chair that I could never finish. One should not avoid or despise everything that is very old; there one finds both good sense and good custom. Men have proved many times that, however much they have acquired, there will remain to them, in the end, at least their sense and their customs. And since I had good sense and manners, not without great harm to me, I have deceived many a worthy man when he fell captive in my nets. But I was deceived by many before I noticed. Then it was too late, and I was miserably unhappy. I was already past my youth. My door, which formerly was often open, both night and day, stayed constantly near its sill.

" 'No one is coming today, no one came yesterday,' I thought, 'unhappy wretch! I must live in sorrow.' My woeful heart should have left me. Then, when I saw my door, and even myself, at such repose, I wanted to leave the country, for I couldn't endure the shame. How could I stand it when those handsome young men came along, those who formerly had held me so dear that they could not tire themselves, and I saw them look at me sideways as they passed by, they who had once been my dear guests? They went by near me, bounding along without counting me worth an egg, even those who had loved me most; they called me a wrinkled old woman and worse before they had passed on by.

"Besides, my pretty child, no one, unless he were very attentive or had experienced great sorrows, would think or know what grief gripped my heart when in my thought I remembered the lovely speeches, the sweet caresses and pleasures, the kisses and the deeply delightful embraces that were so soon stolen away. Stolen? Indeed, and without return. It would have been better for me to be imprisoned forever in a tower than to have been born so soon. God! Into what torment was I put by the fair gifts which had failed me, and how wretched their remnants had made me! Alas! Why was I born so soon? To whom can I complain, to whom except you, my son, whom I hold so dear? I have no other way to avenge myself than by teaching my doctrine. Therefore, fair son, I indoctrinate you so that, when instructed, you will avenge me on those good-for-nothings; for if God pleases, he will remind you of this sermon when he comes. You know that, because of your age, you have a very great advantage in retaining the sermon so that it will remind you. Plato said: 'It is true of any knowledge that one can keep better the memory of what one learns in one's infancy.'

"Certainly, dear son, my tender young one, if my youth were present, as yours is now, the vengeance that I would take on them could not rightly be written. Everywhere I came I would work such wonders with those scoundrels, who valued me so lightly and who vilified and despised me when they so basely passed by near me, that one would never have heard the like. They and others would pay for their pride and spite; I would have no pity on them. For with the intelligence that God has given me—just as I have preached to you—do you know what condition I would put them in? I would so pluck them and seize their possessions, even wrongly and perversely, that I would make them dine on worms and lie naked on dunghills, especially and first of all those who loved me with more loyal heart and who more willingly took trouble to serve and honor me. If I could, I wouldn't leave them anything worth one bud of garlic until I had everything in my purse and had put them all into poverty; I would make them stamp their feet in living rage behind me. But to regret it is worth nothing; what has gone cannot come. I would never be able to hold any man, for my face is so wrinkled that they don't even protect themselves against my threat. A long time ago the scoundrels who despised me told me so, and from that time on I took to weeping. O God! But it still pleases me when I think back on it. I rejoice in my thought and my limbs become lively again when I remember the good times and the gay life for which my heart so strongly yearns. Just to think of it and to remember it all makes my body young again. Remembering all that happened gives me all the blessings of the world, so that however they may have deceived me, at least I have had my fun. A young lady is not idle when she leads a gay life, especially she who thinks about acquiring enough to take care of her expenses.

* * *

"O fair, most sweet son," said the Old Woman, "O beautiful tender flesh, I want to teach you of the games of Love so that when you have learned them you will not be deceived. Shape yourself according to my art, for no one who is not well informed can pass through this course of games without selling his livestock to get enough money. Now give your attention to hearing and understanding, and to remembering everything that I say, for I know the whole story.

"Fair son, whoever wants to enjoy loving and its sweet ills which are so bitter must know the commandments of Love but must beware that he does not know love itself. I would tell you all the commandments here if I did not certainly see that, by nature, you have overflowing measure of those that you should have. Well numbered, there are ten of them that you ought to know. But he who encumbers himself with the last two is a great fool; they are not worth a false penny. I allow you eight of them, but whoever follows Love in the other two wastes his study and becomes mad. One should not study them in a school. He who wants a lover to have a generous heart and to put love in only one place has given too evil a burden to lovers. It is a false text, false in the letter. In it, Love, the son of Venus, lies, and no man should believe him; whoever does will pay dearly, as you will see by the end of my sermon.

"Fair son, never be generous; and keep your heart in several places, never in one. Don't give it, and don't lend it, but sell it very dearly and always to the highest bidder. See that he who buys it can never get a bargain: no matter how much he may give, never let him have anything in return; it were better if he were to burn or hang or maim himself. In all cases keep to these points: have your hands closed to giving and open to taking. Certainly, giving is great folly, except giving a little for attracting men when one plans to make them one's prey or when one expects such a return for the gift that one could not have sold it for more. I certainly allow you such giving. The gift is good where he who gives multiplies his gift and gains; he who is certain of his profit cannot repent of his gift. I can indeed consent to such a gift. * * *

"But I can tell you this much: if you want to choose a lover, I advise you to give your love, but not too firmly, to that fair young man who so prizes you. Love others wisely, and I will seek out for you enough of them so that you can amass great wealth from them. It is good to become acquainted with rich men if their hearts are not mean and miserly and if one knows how to pluck them well. Fair Welcoming may know whomever he wishes, provided that he gives each one to understand that he would not want to take another lover for a thousand marks of fine milled gold. He should swear that if he had wanted to allow his rose, which was in great demand, to be taken by another, he would have been weighed down with gold and jewels. But, he should go on, his pure heart was so loyal that no man would ever stretch out his hand for it except that man alone who was offering his hand at that moment.

"If there are a thousand, he should say to each: 'Fair lord, you alone will have the rose; no one else will ever have a part. May God fail me if I ever divide it.' He may so swear and pledge his faith to them. If he perjures himself, it doesn't matter; God laughs at such an oath and pardons it gladly.

"Jupiter and the gods laughed when lovers perjured themselves; and many times the gods who loved *par amour* perjured themselves. When Jupiter reassured his wife Juno, he swore by the Styx to her in a loud voice and falsely perjured himself. Since the gods give them, such examples should assure pure lovers that they too may swear falsely by all the saints, convents, and temples. But he is a great fool, so help me God, who believes in the oaths of lovers, for their hearts are too fickle. Young men are in no way stable—nor, often times, are the old—and therefore they belie the oaths and faith that they have given.

"Know also another truth: he who is lord of the fair should collect his market-toll everywhere; and he who cannot at one mill—Hey! to another for his whole round! The mouse who has but one hole for retreat has a very poor refuge and makes a very dangerous provision for himself. It is just so with a woman: she is the mistress of all the markets, since everyone works to have her. She should take possessions everywhere. If, after she had reflected well, she wanted only one lover, she would have a very foolish idea. For, by Saint Lifard of Meun, whoever gives her love in a single place has a heart neither free nor unencumbered, but basely enslaved. Such a woman, who takes trouble to love one man alone, has indeed deserved to have a full measure of pain and woe. If she lacks comfort from him, she has no one to comfort her, and those who give their hearts in a single place are those who most lack comfort. In the end, when they are bored, or irritated, all these men fly from their women.

* * *

"Briefly, all men betray and deceive women; all are sensualists, taking their pleasure anywhere. Therefore we should deceive them in return, not fix our hearts on one. Any woman who does so is a fool; she should have several friends and, if possible, act so as to delight them to the point where they are driven to distraction. If she has no graces, let her learn them. Let her be haughtier toward those who, because of her hauteur, will take more trouble to serve her in order to deserve her love, but let her scheme to take from those who make light of her love. She should know games and songs and flee from quarrels and disputes. If she is not beautiful, she should pretty herself; the ugliest should wear the most coquettish adornments.

* * *

"If she has a lovely neck and white chest, she should see that her dressmaker lower her neckline, so that it reveals a half foot, in front and back, of her fine white flesh; thus she may deceive more easily. And if her shoulders are too large to be pleasing at dances and balls, she should wear a dress of fine cloth and thus appear less ungainly. And if, because of insect bites or pimples, she doesn't have beautiful, well-kept hands, she should be careful not to neglect them but should remove the spots with a needle or wear gloves so that the pimples and scabs will not show.

"If her breasts are too heavy she should take a scarf or towel to bind them against her chest and wrap it right around her ribs, securing it with needle and thread or by a knot; thus she can be active at her play.

"And like a good little girl she should keep her chamber of Venus tidy. If she is intelligent and well brought up, she will leave no cobwebs around but will burn or destroy them, tear them down and sweep them up, so that no grime can collect anywhere.

"If her feet are ugly, she should keep them covered and wear fine stockings if her legs are large. In short, unless she's very stupid she should hide any defect she knows of.

"For example, if she knows that her breath is foul she should spare no amount of trouble never to fast, never to speak to others on an empty stomach, and, if possible, to keep her mouth away from people's noses.

"When she has the impulse to laugh, she should laugh discreetly and prettily, so that she shows little dimples at the corners of her mouth. She should avoid puffing her cheeks and screwing her face up in grimaces. Her lips should be kept closed and her teeth covered; a woman should always laugh with her mouth closed, for the sight of a mouth stretched like a gash across the face is not a pretty one. If her teeth are not even, but ugly and quite crooked, she will be thought little of if she shows them when she laughs.

"There is also a proper way to cry. But every woman is adept enough to cry well on any occasion, for, even though the tears are not caused by grief or shame or hurt, they are always ready. All women cry; they are used to crying in whatever way they want. But no man should be disturbed when he sees such tears flowing as fast as rain, for these tears, these sorrows and lamentations flow only to trick him. A woman's weeping is nothing but a ruse; she will overlook no source of grief. But she must be careful not to reveal, in word or deed, what she is thinking of.

"It is also proper to behave suitably at the table. Before sitting down, she should look around the house and let everyone understand that she herself knows how to run a house. Let her come and go, in the front rooms and in back, and be the last to sit down, being sure to wait a little before she finally takes her seat. Then, when she is seated at table, she should serve everyone as well as possible. She should carve in front of the others and pass the bread to those around her. To deserve praise, she should serve food in front of the one who shares her plate. She should put a thigh or wing before him, or, in his presence, carve the beef or pork, meat or fish, depending upon what food there happens to be. She should never be niggardly in her servings as long as there is anyone unsatisfied. Let her guard against getting her fingers wet up to the joint in the sauce, against smearing her lips with soup, garlic, or fat meat, against piling up too large morsels and stuffing her mouth. When she has to moisten a piece in any sauce, either *sauce verte, cameline,* or *jauce,* she should hold the bit with her fingertips and bring it carefully up to her mouth, so that no drop of soup, sauce, or pepper falls on her breast. She must drink so neatly that she doesn't spill anything on herself, for anyone who happened to see her spill would think her either very clumsy or very greedy. Again, she must take care not to touch her drinking cup while she has food in her mouth. She should wipe her mouth so clean that grease will not stick to the cup, and should be particularly careful about her upper lip, for, when there is grease on it, untidy drops of it will show in her wine. She should drink only a little at a time, however great her appetite, and never empty a cup, large or small, in one breath, but rather drink little and often, so that she doesn't go around causing others to say that she gorges or drinks too much while her mouth is full. She should avoid swallowing the rim of her cup, as do many greedy nurses who are so foolish that they pour wine down their hollow throats as if they were casks, who pour it down in such huge gulps that they become completely fuddled and dazed. Now a lady must be careful not to get drunk, for a drunk, man or woman, cannot keep anything secret; and when a woman gets drunk, she has no defenses at all in her, but blurts out whatever she thinks and abandons herself to anyone when she gives herself over to such bad conduct.

"She must also beware of falling asleep at the table, for she would be much less pleasant; many disagreeable things can happen to those who take such naps. There is no sense in napping in places where one should remain awake, and many have been deceived in this way, have many times fallen, either forward or backward or sideways, and broken an arm or head or ribs. Let a woman beware lest such a nap overtake her; let her recall Palinurus, the helmsman of Aeneas's ship. While awake, he steered it well, but when sleep conquered him, he fell from the rudder into the sea and drowned within sight of his companions, who afterward mourned greatly for him.

"Further, a lady must be careful not to be too reluctant to play, for she might wait around so long that no one would want to offer her his hand. She should seek the diversion of love as long as youth deflects her in that direction, for, when old age assails a woman, she loses both the joy and the assault of Love. A wise woman will gather the fruit of love in the flower of her age. The unhappy woman loses her time who passes it without enjoying love. And if she disbelieves this advice of mine, which I give for the profit of all, be sure that she will be sorry when age withers her. But I know that women will believe me, particularly those who are sensible, and will stick to our rules and will say many paternosters for my soul, when I am dead who now teach and comfort them. I know that this lesson will be read in many schools.

"O fair sweet son, if you live—for I see well that you are writing down in the book of your heart the whole of my teaching, and that, when you depart from me, you will study more, if it please God, and will become a master like me—if you live I confer on you the license to teach, in spite of all chancellors, in chambers or in cellars, in meadow, garden, or thicket, under a tent or behind the tapestries, and to inform the students in wardrobes, attics, pantries, and stables, if you find no more pleasant places. And may my lesson be well taught when you have learned it well!

"A woman should be careful not to stay shut up too much, for while she remains in the house, she is less seen by everybody, her beauty is less well-known, less desired, and in demand less. She should go often to the principal church and go visiting, to weddings, on trips, at games, feasts, and round dances, for in such places the God and Goddess of Love keep their schools and sing mass to their disciples.

"But of course, if she is to be admired above others, she has to be well-dressed. When she is well turned out and goes through the streets, she should carry herself well, neither too stiffly nor too loosely, not too upright nor too bent over, but easily and graciously in any crowd. She should move her shoulders and sides so elegantly that no one might find anyone with more beautiful movements. And she should walk daintily in her pretty little shoes, so well made that they fit her feet without any wrinkles whatever.

* * *

"And what I say about the black mare, about the sorrel horse and mare and the gray and black horses, I say about the cow and bull and the ewe and ram; for we do not doubt that these males want all females as their wives. Never doubt, fair son, that in the same way all females want all males. All women willingly receive them. By my soul, fair son, it is thus with every man and every woman as far as natural appetite goes. The law restrains them little from exercising it. A little! but too much, it seems to me, for when the law has put them together, it wants either of them, the boy or the girl, to be able to have only the other, at least as long as he or she lives. But at the same time they are tempted to use their free will. I know very well that such a thing does rise up, only some keep themselves from it because of shame, others because they fear trouble; but Nature controls them to that end just as she does the animals that we were just speaking of. I know it from my own experience, for I always took trouble to be loved by all men. And if I had not feared shame, which holds back and subdues many hearts, when I went along the streets where I always wanted to go—so dressed up in adornments that a dressed-up doll would have been nothing in comparison—I would have received all or at least many of those young boys, if I had been able and if it had pleased them, who pleased me so much when they threw me those sweet glances. (Sweet God! What pity for them seized me when those looks came toward me!) I wanted them all one after the other, if I could have satisfied them all. And it seemed to me that, if they could have, they would willingly have received me. I do not except prelates or monks, knights, burgers, or canons, clerical or lay, foolish or wise, as long as they were at the height of their powers. They would have jumped out of their orders if they had not thought that they might fail when they asked for my love; but if they had known my thought and the whole of our situations they would not have been in such doubt. And I think that several, if they had dared, would have broken their marriages. If one of them had had me in private he would not have remembered to be faithful. No man would have kept his situation, his faith, vows, or re-

ligion unless he were some demented fool who was smitten by love
and loved his sweetheart loyally. Such a man, perhaps, would have
called me paid and thought about his own possessions, which he
would not have given up at any price. But there are very few such
lovers, so help me God and Saint Amand; I certainly think so. If he
spoke to me for a long time, no matter what he said, lies or truth, I
could have made him move everything. Whatever he was, secular, or
in an order, with a belt of red leather or of cord, no matter what headdress he wore, I think that he would have carried on with me if he
thought that I wanted him or even if I had allowed him. Thus Nature
regulates us by inciting our hearts to pleasure. For this reason Venus
deserves less blame for loving Mars.

* * *

"By my soul, if I had been wise, I would have been a very rich lady,
for I was acquainted with very great people when I was already a coy
darling, and I certainly was held in considerable value by them, but
when I got something of value from one of them, then, by the faith
that I owe God or Saint Thibaut, I would give it all to a rascal who
brought me great shame but pleased me more. I called all the others
lover, but it was he alone that I loved. Understand, he didn't value me
at one pea, and in fact told me so. He was bad—I never saw anyone
worse—and he never ceased despising me. This scoundrel, who didn't
love me at all, would call me a common whore. A woman has very poor
judgment, and I was truly a woman. I never loved a man who loved
me, but, do you know, if that scoundrel had laid open my shoulder or
broken my head, I would have thanked him for it. He wouldn't have
known how to beat me so much that I would not have had him throw
himself upon me, for he knew very well how to make his peace, however much he had done against me. He would never have treated me
so badly, beaten me or dragged me or wounded my face or bruised it
black, that he would not have begged my favor before he moved from
the place. He would never have said so many shameful things to me
that he would not have counseled peace to me and then made me
happy in bed, so that we had peace and concord again. Thus he had
me caught in his snare, for this false, treacherous thief was a very hard
rider in bed. I couldn't live without him; I wanted to follow him always. If he had fled, I would certainly have gone as far as London in
England to seek him, so much did he please me and make me happy.
He put me to shame and I him, for he led a life of great gaiety with the
lovely gifts that he had received from me. He put none of them into
saving, but played everything at dice in the taverns. He never learned
any other trade, and there was no need then for him to do so, for I
gave him a great deal to spend, and I certainly had it for the taking.
Everybody was my source of income, while he spent it willingly and always on ribaldry; he burned everything in his lechery. He had his
mouth stretched so wide that he did not want to hear anything good.
Living never pleased him except when it was passed in idleness and
pleasure. In the end I saw him in a bad situation as a result, when
gifts were lacking for us. He became poor and begged his bread, while

I had nothing worth two carding combs and had never married a lord. Then, as I have told you, I came through these woods, scratching my temples. May this situation of mine be an example to you, fair sweet son; remember it. Act so wisely that it may be better with you because of my instruction. For when your rose is withered and white hairs assail you, gifts will certainly fail."

* * *

THEOPHRASTUS

From *The Golden Book on Marriage*†

[Theophrastus was a Greek philosopher (371–287 B.C.E.), who succeeded Aristotle as head of the Peripatetic school. He wrote many works on philosophy but is best known for his *Characters*, brief sketches of types of men. His work *On Marriage* has not survived in the original but has been preserved in translation into Latin in Jerome's treatise *Against Jovinian* (see pp. 359–73). It is better to treat it as a separate work from Jerome's in that it presents a purely pagan attitude toward the subject of marriage. The introductory words are by Jerome.]

* * *

[JEROME] I feel that in my catalogue of women [see p. 370], I have exceeded the customary space given to examples, and may rightly be censured by a critical reader. But what else can I do, when women of our own time attack the authority of Paul, and, when the funeral of their first husband is not yet over, start to recite arguments for a second marriage?[1] As they despise belief in Christian chastity, let them at any rate learn chastity from the pagans. There is a book by Theophrastus on the subject of marriage, called *The Golden Book*, in which he discusses whether the wise man should take a wife. After concluding that if the woman is beautiful and virtuous, her parents noble, and the husband healthy and rich, then a wise man may sometimes marry, he immediately adds:

[THEOPHRASTUS] However, it is very unusual for all these conditions to be present in a marriage, and therefore the philosopher[2] ought not to take a wife. Firstly, the pursuit of Philosophy is impeded: no one can serve both books and a wife at the same time.[3] There are many things which women require—fine clothes, gold, jewels, money, maidservants, all kinds of furniture, litters, and gilded coaches. And then

---

† This excerpt and the ones from St. Jerome and Walter Map following were prepared for this Norton Critical Edition by A. G. Rigg. Because of the length and complexity of these texts, Professor Rigg has used a combination of summary, translation, and annotation to present them to the reader.
1. Cf. the *Wife of Bath's Prologue* 587 ff. (hereafter cited as *WBP*) and Deschamps, *Miroir de Mariage* (cited in *Sources and Analogues of Chaucer's* Canterbury Tales, ed. W. F. Bryan and Germaine Dempster [Chicago: U of Chicago P, 1941], p. 220).
2. In all these discussions, "wise man, philosopher," etc. (Lat. *sapiens*) are equivalent to the Middle English *clerk* (i.e., Jankyn, the Wife's fifth husband).
3. The remark is echoed by Cicero, cited by both Jerome and Walter Map (below pp. 370, 376).

there is the ceaseless chatter and grumbling all through the night—
"So-and-so has smarter clothes to go out in than I do. Everyone admires *her*, but when I meet other women they all look down on me,
poor thing. Why were you looking at the girl next door? What were you
saying to our serving girl? What did you bring me from the market?"[4]

We are not allowed a friend or companion, for she suspects that
friendship for another means hatred of her.[5] If a learned lecturer is at
some nearby city, we can neither leave our wives behind nor burden
ourselves with them. It is difficult to look after a poor wife, but torture
to put up with a rich one.[6]

Moreover, there is no choice in the matter of a wife: one has to take
whatever comes along. If she's nagging, stupid, ugly, proud, smelly—
whatever fault she has, we find out *after* marriage. Now a horse, an
ass, a cow, a dog, the cheapest slaves, clothes, kettles, a wooden chair,
a cup, a clay pot—all these are tested first, and *then* purchased. Only
a wife is not put on display—in case her faults are discovered before
we take her.[7]

We always have to be noticing her appearance and praising her
beauty, in case she thinks that we don't like her if we ever look at another woman. She has to be called "Madam"; we have to celebrate her
birthday and make oaths by her health, saying "Long may you live!"
We have to honor her nurse, her old nanny, her father's servant, her
foster son, her elegant follower, her curly-haired go-between, some eunuch (cut short for the sake of a long and carefree pleasure!)—all of
them are adulterers under another name. Whoever has her favors, you
have to love them, like it or not.[8]

If you give the whole management of the house to her, she complains "I'm just a servant"; if you keep any part of it to yourself, "You
don't trust me!"[9] She begins to hate you and quarrel with you, and
if you don't watch out she'll be mixing poison. If you allow into the
house old dames, sooth-sayers, fortune-tellers, and gem-setters and
silkworkers, she says, "You're endangering my virtue!"; but if you
don't, "Why are you so suspicious?" But what good is it to keep a
careful watch over her?—if a wife is unchaste, she can't be guarded,
and if she isn't she doesn't need guarding. In any case, the compul-
sion to be chaste is an untrustworthy guard—the woman really to
be called "chaste" is the one who could sin if she wanted to. Men
are quick to desire a beautiful woman: an ugly one is herself lecherous. It is difficult to guard what everyone is after: it is misery to
possess what no one thinks worth having. However, there's less misery
in having an ugly wife than in trying to keep a beautiful one. Nothing
is safe which the whole population has set its heart on—one man
uses his handsome figure to court her, another his intellect, another

---

4. *WBP*, 235–42.
5. Chaucer seems to have taken this as part of the woman's speech.
6. *WBP*, 248–52.
7. *WBP*, 282–92.
8. *WBP*, 293–306.
9. *WBP*, 308–10.

his witticisms, another his generosity: some day, in some way, the castle besieged on all sides must surrender.[1]

Now some people marry in order to have someone to run the home, or to cheer them up, or to avoid loneliness: but (i) a faithful servant, obedient to his master's authority and conforming to his wishes, is a better majordomo than a wife, who only considers herself mistress of the house if she goes against her husband's wishes; that is, she does what she pleases, not what she's told. (ii) At the side of a sick man friends, and servants bound by ties of old benefits, do more good than a wife: she puts her tears on our charge sheet, and sells her flood of tears in the hope of the inheritance: by her show of solicitude she upsets the sick man's temper by her despair. On the other hand, if our wife herself is sick, we have to be sick in sympathy and are never allowed to leave her bedside. Or, if she is a good and gentle wife (a rare bird!), then we suffer agony with her in her birthpangs, and are in anguish when she is in danger. (iii) The philosopher can never be alone: he has with him all men who are or ever were good, and can send his free mind where he wishes. What he cannot reach in the flesh, he embraces in contemplation. And if there is a shortage of men, he speaks with God. He will never be less lonely than when he is alone.

Further, to take a wife in order to have children, either to make sure that our name survives, or to have supports in our old age and be sure of having heirs—this is the most stupid of all. For what does it matter to us as we leave this world if someone else has the same name as we did? The son does not immediately assume his father's name (?),[2] and there are countless people who are called by the same name. Why bring up at home aids for your old age, who may either die before you, or may turn out to have bad characters (or at the least, when your son reaches maturity, he will certainly think you are taking a long time to die)? Better and more certain heirs are your friends and neighbors whom you can choose judiciously, than heirs whom you have to have, whether you like it or not. Even if your heredity is sufficiently secure, it is better to use up your wealth while you still live, rather than to abandon to uncertain uses what you have collected by your own hard work.

ST. JEROME

From *Against Jovinian*†

[This treatise, written ca. 393 C.E., was the principal source for the medieval Church in its arguments for clerical celibacy. It is referred to by the Wife of Bath thus:

---

1. *WBP*, 253–72 (with the arguments in a different order).
2. Translation doubtful.
† Prepared for this volume by A. G. Rigg; see footnote, p. 357.

And eek ther was somtyme a clerk at Rome,
A cardinal, that highte Seint Jerome,
That made a book agayn Jovinian.

                                    (673–75)

It is, however, primarily a refutation of heresy rather than an antifeminist tract: in two books (ed. J. P. Migne, *Patrologia Latina* 23, cols. 211–338), Jerome answers the following points made by the monk Jovinian:

> (i) that virgins, widows, and married women, once they have been baptized, are of the same merit, as long as they do not differ because of other actions; (ii) those who are purified by baptism cannot be overcome by the devil; (iii) there is no distinction between fasting and the grateful receiving of food; (iv) all who have been baptized and have kept the Faith obtain the same reward in heaven.

The first of these heresies is dealt with in the first book and is the only one that concerns us here. Quotations are selected below only insofar as they contribute to the general antifeminist debate, the arguments of the Wife of Bath, and the status of the Wife in the eyes of the Church. Omissions are indicated by * * * where the argument is irrelevant for the present purpose. Translations of biblical quotations (in Jerome's Latin) sometimes follow the wording of the King James Bible of 1611; often, however, the Latin presents a different sense from the original Hebrew on which the 1611 version was based—for instance, 1 Corinthians 7:3, the King James version has "Let the husband render unto the wife due benevolence," but the Latin here reads *Uxori vir debitum reddat*, "man shal yelde to his wyf hire dette" (*Wife of Bath's Prologue* 130). In all such cases I have translated Jerome's Latin.

[After some introductory remarks, Jerome presents Jovinian's arguments:]

[i, 5: col. 215-] First he says that it is God's decree that "for this reason a man shall leave his father and his mother, and shall cleave unto his wife, and the two shall be in one flesh" (Gen. 2:24). In case we object that this is only an Old Testament saying, he adds that it was confirmed by God himself in the Gospels, "What God has joined together, let no man put asunder" (Matt. 19:5–6).[1] He then adds the quotation, "Be fruitful, and multiply, and replenish the earth" (Gen. 1:28), and lists in order Seth, Enos, Cainam, Malaleel, Jared, Enoch, Mathusalem, Lamech, and Noah, all of whom had wives and produced children according to God's decree. * * * "There was Enoch, who walked with God and was snatched up into Heaven. There was Noah, who, despite all those who must have been virgins by their age, went into the ark alone with his sons and wives, and was saved in the shipwreck of the world. Again, after the flood, pairs of men and women were joined together in, as it were, a second beginning of the human race, and the blessing 'Be fruitful, and multiply, and replenish the earth' was renewed (Gen. 8:17, etc.)." * * * He runs to Abraham, Isaac, and Jacob, of whom the first had three wives, the second one, and the third

---

1. For the whole of this section, cf. the *Wife of Bath's Prologue* (hereafter cited as *WBP*), 27–29.

four. * * * He says that because of his faith Abraham received a blessing in the birth of a son. * * * [His examples include, among others] Rebecca, * * * Jacob, * * * Rachel, * * * Joseph (the most holy and chaste), * * * and all the patriarchs who had wives and were equally blessed by God. * * * [He continues with many more, e.g.,] Sampson, * * * he says that there was no difference between Jephta and his daughter who was sacrificed to God. * * * Samuel, he says, produced children, and his priestly honor was not diminished by his embracing a wife. * * * Need I mention Solomon[2] whom he places in his catalogue of married men, asserting that he was a figure of the Savior? * * *

Passing on to the New Testament, he gives us Zacharias, Elizabeth, Peter and his mother-in-law, and the rest of the Apostles, and then adds, "In case my opponents hope to put up a vain defense, and claim that all this was because the early world needed populating, let them hear what Paul has to say!" [From Paul, he quotes:] "Therefore my wish is that the younger widows marry and produce children" (1 Tim. 5:14), "Marriage is honorable in all, and the bed undefiled" (Heb. 13:4), "The wife is bound to her husband as long as he lives, but if he dies, let her marry whom she wishes, only in the Lord" (1 Cor. 7:39). * * *

Finally he makes an apostrophe to a virgin, and says, "I wish no harm to you, virgin: you chose chastity because of the present necessity (cf. 1 Cor. 7:26); it pleased you to be holy in body and spirit, but do not be proud—you are a member of the same Church as married women."

[(i, 6, col. 217-): Jerome now begins his reply. His main authority is St. Paul, 1 Cor. 7, on which his argument depends. The Christians of Corinth have written to Paul asking, among other things, whether they should remain celibate after becoming Christians and, for the sake of continence, leave their wives. Jerome begins by quoting the opening of Paul's reply, 1 Cor. 7:1–9, and then continues:]

[i, 7, col. 218-] Let us go back to the beginning of the quotation: "It is better for a man not to touch a woman." Now if it is good not to touch a woman, it is bad to do so, for the only opposite to "good" is "bad." Now if it is bad and yet pardoned, it is allowed only lest anything worse than bad results. Now what kind of "good" is that which is only allowed because of the risk of something worse? Paul would never have said "let each one have his wife" (1 Cor. 7:2) if he had not first made the premise "because of (the danger of) fornication." Remove this last phrase, and he will not then say "let each one have his wife." It is as though one were to say, "It is good to be fed on the purest wheat and to eat the finest bread, but in case anyone is forced by starvation to eat cow-dung I concede the eating of barley-bread."[3] Now does wheat lose its purity if barley is preferred to cow-dung? That thing is good by nature which does not have to be compared with evil, and which is not overshadowed by merely being preferred to something else.

2. *WBP*, 35–43.
3. Cf. *WBP*, 143–46.

Note also the wisdom of the Apostle: he did not say that it is good not to have a wife, but "it is good not to touch a woman," implying that the danger is in the act of touching: whoever touches her cannot escape, for "she snatches the precious souls of men" (cf. Prov. 6:26) and makes the hearts of young men fly. "Can a man take fire in his bosom, and not be burned? Can one go upon hot coals, and not be burned?" (Prov. 6:27–28). Just as anyone is burnt if they touch a fire, so the touch of a man and a woman senses their nature, and realizes the difference between the sexes. * * *

He did not say, "On account of fornication let each one *take* a wife"; otherwise he would by this excuse have given a free rein to lust— whenever a wife died, one would take another to avoid fornication! He said, "let each man *have* his wife." * * *[4]

> [Jerome comments on the instruction that wives taken before conversion to Christianity should not be set aside and goes on to elaborate on the implications of 1 Cor. 7:5 and 1 Peter 3:7, that prayer is impeded by sexual activities.]

Do you want to know what the Apostle favors? Then take his remark, "I would that all men were even as I myself" (1 Cor. 7:7).[5] Blessed is the man who is like Paul. Fortunate is the man who listens to Paul not when he is pardoning but when he is giving instruction. "This I want," he said, "this I long for, that you should be imitators of me, just as I am an imitator of Christ." * * *

[i, 9, col. 222-] Having conceded to married people the practice of intercourse, and having shown them what he wants (or rather, what he allows), Paul passes on to the unmarried and the widows; he sets himself as an example, and says that they are blessed if they remain in their present state. * * * He gives the reason why he said "if they cannot contain themselves, let them marry"—namely "for it is better to marry than to burn." This is why is it better to marry—because burning is worse; if you remove the fervence of passion, he will not then say "it is better to marry." He considers it better only by comparison with the worse, not because it is inherently good. It is as though one were to say, "it is better to have one eye than none; it is better to go on one foot supported by a stick, than to crawl with both one's legs broken." * * *

> [(i, 10–11, cols. 223–26): Jerome here expounds the doctrines in 1 Cor. 7:10–24. Most of this is not relevant to our purpose, but in cols. 223–24 he prophetically says:]

I know that many women will be furious with me, and that with the same lack of shame that they showed in their contempt for Christ they will rave against me, a miserable flea, the lowest Christian. Nevertheless, I shall say what the Apostle taught me, that they are on the side of iniquity, not of justice, of the dark rather than the light, of Belial

4. Cf. *WBP*, 47–52 (ignoring Jerome's argument).
5. Cf. *WBP*, 80 ff.

rather than Christ; they are not temples of the living God, but idols
and empty shrines of the dead! * * * [i, 12, cols. 226–29] After the
discussion of the married and the continent, Paul finally comes to the
subject of virgins: "On virgins, I have no order from God, but I give
advice, having obtained the mercy of the Lord to be faithful. I think,
therefore, that this is good, because of the present need, for it is good
for man to be so (virgin)" (1 Cor. 7:25–26).[6] At this our adversary
[Jovinian] goes wild with rejoicing, shattering open the wall of virginity with this powerful battering-ram: "You see," he says, "the Apostle
says that he has no order from God about virgins; he who made orders
with authority about married men and wives, dare not command what
God did not order, and rightly: what is ordered, is commanded; what is
commanded must be done; what must be done must carry some
penalty if it is not done. For a command which is left within the authority of the person to whom it is given is a useless command."

[Jerome's answer:] If God had commanded virginity, he would have
seemed to condemn marriage, and to take away the human seedbed
from which virginity itself grows.[7] If he cut away the root, how would
he get the fruit? If he did not first lay the foundations, how could he
raise up the building and set a roof over everything? Mountains are
brought down by great labor of ditch-digging: the depths of the earth
are penetrated with difficulty in the search for gold. When a necklace
is made from the finest pebbles, first in the blast of the furnace, and
then set by the skillful hand of the craftsman, it is not the man who
refined the gold from the mud who is called beautiful, but the person
who uses the beauty of the gold.

Do not be surprised if, amid all the titillations of the flesh and the
incentives to sin, we are not commanded to follow the life of the angels but merely recommended to do so. For when advice is given, the
decision is left with the person who is freely making the offering to
God [or: it is merely the authority of the suggestor],[8] but a command
is an obligation imposed on a servant. Paul said, "I do not have an order from God, but I give advice, having obtained the mercy of the
Lord." If you do not have a command from God, [one might ask,] why
do you dare to give advice? The Apostle will answer, "Do you think I
should order what God did not command, but merely suggested? He is
the creator, the potter who knows how fragile is the vessel which he
made; he left virginity in the power of the person who hears his words.
Should I, teacher of peoples, 'made all things to all men,' (1 Cor. 9:22)
attempt to win everyone, and right from the start impose a burden of
perpetual chastity on the necks of weak believers? Let them enjoy for
a while the holiday of marriage, and give some time to prayer; so that
having had a taste of chastity they may continue to long for that which
they have only delighted in for a short while."

6. WBP, 63–70, 82–86, and frequently.
7. WBP, 69–72.
8. Either is possible: the Latin is *offerentis arbitrium est.*

When Christ was tempted by the Pharisees who asked if it was right according to the Law of Moses to put aside one's wife, he forbade it entirely. His disciples, considering this, said, "If this is the case of a man and his wife, it is advisable not to marry." He replied, "All men cannot receive this saying, save they to whom it is given. For there are some eunuchs which were born this way from their mothers' wombs, some who were castrated by men, and some who castrated themselves for the sake of the kingdom of heaven. He that is able to receive it, let him receive it" (Matt. 19:2–12). This is why the Apostle says he has no command, because God had said "All men cannot receive this saying, save they to whom it is given," and "He that is able to receive it, let him receive it." He sets out the reward for the contest, he invites to the race, he holds in his hand the prize for virginity;[9] he shows the purest fountain, and says, "If any man thirst, let him come and drink (John 7:37); He who can receive, let him receive." He does not say that you *must* drink, and run the race, whether you want to or not, but that he who wishes to, and can, run and drink, will win the race and will be sated. For this reason Christ loves virgins the more, because they pay voluntarily what they were not ordered to pay. It is of greater grace to offer what you do not owe than to hand over what you are forced to pay. The Apostles considered the burdens of a wife and said, "If this is the case of a man and his wife, it is advisable not to marry." God approved their decision, and said, "You are right: marriage is not expedient for a man reaching for heaven, but it is a difficult matter, and not all receive this word, only those to whom it is given." * * *

What is the "immediate necessity" (1 Cor. 7:26) for rejecting the ties of marriage and pursuing the freedom of virginity?—"Woe on those who are pregnant and giving suck on that day!" (Matt. 24:19). Here it is not the prostitute or whore who is condemned (their damnation is not in doubt), but those whose wombs swell, the squalling children, the fruits and works of marriage. * * *

> [Jerome argues that virgins who have consecrated themselves to God are guilty of incest if they marry. Marriage is a short-term prospect, for it ends with death. He demonstrates the spiritual distinction between a virgin who thinks only of God and a wife whose thought is on how to please her husband.]

[i, 14, col. 233-] In the same way that Paul allowed virgins to marry because of the danger of fornication, excusing that which is not sought after for its own sake, so, for the same reason (the avoidance of fornication), he allowed widows to marry again, for it is better to have knowledge of one man, even if he is the second or third, than of many: that is, it is more tolerable to be prostituted to one man than to many. The Samaritan woman in the Gospel of John said that her present husband was her sixth, but Christ told her that he was not her husband (John 4:17–18), for where there was a succession of spouses,

9. WBP, 75–76.

this one ceased to be her husband, for properly speaking only one man can be the husband.[1] In the beginning one rib was turned into one wife, "and the two will be in one flesh" (Gen. 2:24)—not three, not four, for otherwise there are not two of them, if there are more.

First of all Lamech,[2] who was a man of blood and a homicide, divided one flesh into two wives; the same punishment of the flood destroyed both homicide and bigamy [Jerome means by this marrying a second time]. * * * The holiness of monogamy is illustrated by the fact that a bigamist cannot be chosen as a priest. It is for this reason that Paul writes "let a widow be chosen if she is not less than sixty years old, and has been the wife of one husband only" (1 Tim. 5:9): this instruction concerns those widows who are fed on the charity of the Church—an age limit is prescribed, so that the food of the poor can only be given to those who can no longer work. At the same time, note that a woman who has had two husbands, even if she is old and decrepit and starving, does not deserve to receive the alms of the Church. Now if she is refused the bread of alms, how much more will she lack the bread which comes from heaven—anyone who eats this unworthily is guilty of violating the body and blood of Christ! * * *

[(i, 16, col. 234-) Jerome moves away from a discussion of Paul's teachings, and demonstrates that chastity has *always* been preferred to marriage; he proceeds to take each of the figures of the Old Testament cited by Jovinian, and to show how they are variously to be interpreted. He begins with Adam:]

It should be said of Adam and Eve, that in Paradise, before their offense, they were virgins; it was after their sin, and outside the garden, that marriage took place. * * *[3]

[The Biblical instruction "Be fruitful, and multiply, and replenish the earth" (Gen. 1:28) is explained by Jerome thus:]

It was necessary first to plant trees and to increase, so that there would be something which could be cut away later. Also, consider the meaning of "replenish the earth"—marriage fills the earth, but paradise is filled by virginity.

[Jerome notes that the phrase "God saw that it was good" was not applied to the second day of Creation (Gen. 1:6–8), indicating a disapproval of the number 2, a symbol of marriage. The various married figures proposed by Jovinian are each dealt with in turn: some of them are interpreted typologically (Isaac, for instance, is a figure of the Church rather than a physical reward given to Sarah, Moses signifies the Law, etc.). Of Solomon (i, 24, col. 243) he notes that it was his wives and concubines that turned his heart from God—he built the Temple in his youth, at the beginning of the reign. Jerome asks the reader not to criticize those who lived under the Old Law—"they served their own times and conditions, and fulfilled the injunction of

1. WBP, 14–25.
2. WBP, 53–54.
3. Note that Map (below, p. 375) cites Eve as an example of disobedience *within* the garden.

the Lord to increase and multiply and fill the earth; more than this, they gave us figures of the future. * * *" Further, he notes (i, 26, col. 245) that the married Apostles, etc., all married *before* the arrival of the New Law.

At i, 28 (col. 249) Jerome moves into the attack with quotations from the Proverbs of Solomon:]

Above, when my adversary mentioned the many-wived Solomon, the builder of the Temple, I replied specifically to his arguments, so that I could quickly go through the remaining questions. Now, in case he shouts that Solomon and the other patriarchs, prophets and holy men who lived under the Old Law have been insulted by me, I will set out Solomon's sentiments on marriage—the very man who himself had so many wives and concubines—for no one can know better what a woman or wife is really like than someone who has suffered one. In Proverbs (9:13)[4] he says, "A woman is foolish and bold, and is made lacking in bread." What bread is this?—The bread of heaven! He immediately adds, "The people of earth perish in her, and rush into the depths of hell." Who are these "people of earth"?—Those who follow the first Adam, who was of earth, not the second Adam, who was from heaven. Again, in another place Solomon says, "Just as a worm in wood, so does an evil woman destroy her husband" (25:20).[5] If you argue that this was said only of *evil* women, I will reply shortly, "Why should I be compelled to wonder whether my bride is going to turn out good or bad?"

"It is better," Solomon says, "to live in the desert than with a nagging and angry woman" (21:9).[6] As to how rare it is to find a wife who lacks these vices—he knows who is married. As that fine orator Varius Geminus neatly puts it, "The man who doesn't quarrel is the single man."

"It is better to live in the corner of the roof than in a house shared with an evil-tongued woman" (Prov. 25:24). If a house shared by man and wife makes the wife proud and brings shame on her husband, how much more so if the woman is the richer, and the husband lives in *her* house! For rather than behaving as a wife, she begins to have the mastery of the house—if she takes exception to her husband, *he* has to go. "On a winter day a dripping roof drives a man from his house—so does an evil-tongued woman" (27:15)[7]—she makes the house flow with her continual abuse and daily chattering, and throws him out of his own house—that is, from the Church. * * *

We must not fail to mention the riddling saying, "The blood-sucking leech had three daughters, beloved in love, and they could not be satisfied; the fourth could never say 'Enough!': Hell, the love of a woman,

---

4. Note that the text of the *Proverbs of Solomon* used by Jerome is often very different from that used by the King James version, and sometimes even from the Vulgate (see p. 367, n. 8).
5. Not in the King James (= WBP, 376–77).
6. Not in the King James (= WBP, 778–81).
7. Chaucer (WBP, 278–80, *Melibee*, VII, 1085 ff.) used a combined version of the "three-things" proverb: see Robinson's note to *Melibee*, VII, 1086, in Chaucer, *Works* (Boston: Houghton-Mifflin, 1957), 742. I have found this "new" proverb frequently in medieval Latin texts.

the earth which cannot be sated by water, fire which never says, 'Enough!' "[8] (Prov. 30:15–16). The leech is the devil; those "beloved in love" are the devil's daughters who cannot be satisfied with the blood of those they have slain—Hell, a woman's love, dry earth, and burning fire. Here he is not talking about just a whore or an adulteress—the love of woman is accused in general: it is always insatiable; when quenched it burns; after a supply it is still hungry; it enfeebles a virile spirit and does not let it think of anything but the passion which it sustains. We read of something similar in the following proverb: "By three things is the earth moved, and the fourth cannot be tolerated: if a slave rules, if a foolish man is sated with bread, if a hateful wife has a good husband, and if a serving-wench throws out her own mistress" (Prov. 30:21–23).[9] In this heap of evils is numbered a wife; if you reply that it specifies "a *hateful* wife," I will say what I said above. * * * he who takes a wife is in doubt whether he is marrying a hateful wife or a loving one. If the former, she cannot be borne; if she is loving, her love is compared to Hell, to dry earth and to fire.

> [Jerome continues with an argument based on Ecclesiastes 3:1 ("To everything there is a season . . .") and an interpretation of the role of sex in Paradise. In i, 30 (col. 251) he digresses in order to stress the point that the highly erotic Song of Songs is not to be interpreted literally, but is a symbol of the marriage of the Old and New Law through the visitation of Christ. He emphasizes the choice of a virgin to be mother of Christ, demonstrating the importance of virginity in the Christian religion. In i, 33 (col. 255) he reverts to the topic of widows and virgins:]

If, because baptism makes a man new, there is no difference between a virgin and a widow once they are baptized, by the same argument prostitutes and whores, once baptized, will be equated with virgins. For if past marriage does not harm a baptized widow, then the past pleasures of a prostitute, the exposure of her body to everyone's lust, will after baptism obtain the same reward as virginity! It is one thing to join to God a mind which is pure and is not polluted by any memories; it is quite another thing to remember the vile necessity of the embraces of a man, and to simulate in one's memory what one does not do physically.

> [In i, 34 (col. 256-), he says that the early church was given lighter instructions by Paul because it was still weak, like a child that can drink only milk. To be perfect, however, is more difficult: he cites the story of the man who was told by Christ to give away all his goods.[1] Married men are only chosen as priests *faute de mieux*: there may be no one else available, or those who are celibate may have other faults. He then turns to a difficult problem:]

---

8. Jerome's Latin text of the Proverb makes little sense: it is the text neither of (his own) Vulgate Latin translation nor of the King James version. I have modified my translation according to the Vulgate version: the alteration does not affect Jerome's interpretation (= WBP, 371–75).
9. WBP, 362–67.
1. WBP, 107–11.

[i, 36, cols. 259–61] But you will say, "If everyone becomes a virgin, how is the human race to survive?" I will reply with an analogy: if all women were widows, or chaste in marriage, how would mortal progeny be propagated? According to this argument, it would cease to exist altogether.[2] Now, if everyone was a philosopher, there would be no farmers; and not only farmers—there would be no orators, no lawyers, no teachers of any subjects. If everyone was a king, who would be a soldier? If everyone were head, what would we say they were head of, if all the limbs were removed? Are you really afraid that if more people pursued virginity, prostitution and adultery would cease to exist, and that there would be no children squalling in the towns and villages? Every day the blood of lechers is spilled, acts of adultery are condemned, and in the very law-courts and tribunals lust dominates. There is no need to fear that all will become virgins: virginity is hard, and therefore rare—"many are called, but few are chosen" (Matt. 20:16, etc.). Many people can begin, but few persevere, and therefore those who do persevere win a great reward. If everyone could be a virgin, God would never have said, "Let him receive who can receive" (Matt. 19:12), and the Apostle Paul would not have hesitated in his advice when he said, "But on virgins, I have no instructions from God" (1 Cor. 7:25).

And you will say, "Why were genitals created? Why were we made in such a way by the most wise Creator, as to share passions for each other and to long for natural copulation?"[3] My modesty in replying involves me in a risk, and I am caught between two rocks, the Symplegades of necessity and modesty, pulled this way and that, fearing the loss of my case or of my honor. I flush with shame to reply to the question, but if my modesty causes me to remain silent, I shall be thought to have given up my position, and will give my opponent the chance of beating me. Better to fight with one's eyes shut, like the gladiators who are blindfolded, than not to ward off his arrows with the shield of truth. Now I *could* say, "In the same way that the posterior section of the body and bowels, through which the excrement of the belly is removed, is hidden from the eyes, and is placed as it were behind one's back, similarly God has hidden away that which is beneath the stomach for bringing out the moistures and liquids which irrigate the veins of the body."

Since, however, the organs themselves and the construction of the genitals, the distinction between men and women, and the receptacles of the womb made to receive and nourish the foetus—since all these indicate the difference between the sexes, I will make this brief reply: Are we, then, never to cease from lust, so that we shouldn't have these limbs to no purpose? Why should a man abstain from his wife? Why should a widow keep herself chaste, if we were born only in order to live like animals? or, What harm will it do me, if my wife sleeps with

---

2. Exact translation uncertain. The Latin is *Hac ratione nihil omnino erit, ne aliud esse desistat.*
3. *WBP*, 115 ff. The Wife seems to accept Jerome's argument but with a slightly different emphasis.

someone else? For in the same way that the job of teeth is to chew, and to transmit what is chewed into the stomach, and there is no harm in anyone giving my wife bread, similarly, if it is the job of genitals always to follow their nature, then let someone else's virility surpass my lassitude, and let any chance lust quench my wife's eager appetite. What does the Apostle mean by exhorting continence, if it is against nature? Or God himself, by prescribing kinds of eunuchs (cf. Matt. 19:12)? The Apostle, who recommended his chastity to us, should constantly be assailed by this question, "Why do *you* have a tool, Paul? Why are you distinguished from the female sex by beard, hair, and other physical characteristics? Why don't your breasts swell, your hips spread out, your chest narrow? Your voice is older, your tone more fierce, and your brow shaggier. There is no point in your having all these male characteristics, if you do not have sexual intercourse." I have had to descend to a ridiculous kind of argument, but it was you who forced me to make this bold reply.

Our Lord and Savior, although in the form of God, deigned to take on the form of a servant, obedient to his Father, obedient till his death on the Cross. Why, then, was it necessary for him to be born with these limbs which he was not going to use?[4] For he was circumcised in order to indicate his sex. Why in his love did he castrate John the Apostle and John the Baptist, whom he had created as men? Therefore, let us, who believe in Christ, follow the example of Christ. * * * Certainly, at the Resurrection of the flesh our bodies will be of the same substance as now, though increased in glory. For the Savior had the same body after death as he had when he was crucified, to the extent that he showed his hands perforated by nails and the wound in his side. * * * "In the resurrection of the dead, they neither marry nor are given in marriage, but will be like angels" (Matt. 22:30). What others are going to be in heaven, virgins have already begun to be on this earth. If we are promised the likeness of angels (who are not distinguished into sexes), either we shall lack sex, like the angels, or, what is clearly proved to be the case, we shall arise in our own sex, but not perform the offices of sex.

> [He continues with an exposition of various statements of the Apostles, directed mainly to show that "living by the spirit" precludes marriage, and that the opposite is the way of death. In i, 39 (col. 265), he lists various precepts to chastity in the writings of other Apostles (notably 2 Pet. 2:9–22). In i, 40 (col. 267), he gives a description of the vicious life and habits of Jovinian himself, "a dog returning to his vomit" (2 Pet. 2:22). He summarizes the teachings of the early church:]

[i, 40, col. 270] The church does not condemn marriage, it relegates it; it does not reject it, but weighs it, knowing that in a great house there are not only gold and silver containers, but ones of wood and clay;[5] some are to our honor, some to our shame; whoever purifies

---

4. *WBP*, 139.
5. *WBP*, 99–101.

himself will be an honorable container, prepared as is necessary for every good work.

> [(i, 41, col. 270) Jerome realizes that his opponents may argue that this "new religion" (Christianity) is recommending a dogma which runs counter to nature; he therefore turns to pagan history and literature to produce examples of the honor in which virginity is held even by non-Christians. His examples include Atalanta, Harpalice, Camilla, Leo, Iphigeneia, the Sibyl, pagan priestesses and Vestal Virgins, the sign of the Zodiac, etc. He lists examples of women who have committed suicide rather than lose their virginity. (i, 42, col. 273-) He gives examples of pagan stories of virgin birth, including the Buddha, Athene, Bacchus, Plato (born of Apollo by Perictione), etc.
>
> (i, 43, col. 273) He continues with examples of famous widows from pagan literature who would not take a second husband, including Dido (!), etc. (i, 46, col. 275) He lists famous Roman women, beginning with Lucretia. After this he quotes at length from Theophrastus in i, 47, cols. 276–78 (see above, pp. 357–59).]

[i, 48, cols. 278–80] Does the co-heir of Christ really want a human heir?[6] Does he long to have children, and to delight in a succession of descendants who may be seized by Antichrist? We read that Moses and Samuel set others before their own sons, and did not regard as their own children those whom they saw offending God.

After his divorce from Terentia Cicero was asked by Hirtius to marry the latter's sister; Cicero refused, and said that it was not possible to give attention both to philosophy and a wife. This fine wife, who had drunk wisdom from the Ciceronian spring, then married Sallust, his enemy, and her third husband was Messala Corvinus—she devolved down the ladder of eloquence, so to speak.

Socrates had two wives, Xantippe and Myron, niece of Aristeides. They used to quarrel frequently, and Socrates used to laugh at them because they quarreled over such a terrible picture of a man, snub-nosed, bald-headed, shaggy-armed, and bow-legged; finally they turned their rage on him, and made him pay heavily—from then on he was put to flight and persecuted by them. On one occasion Xantippe was standing above him and wouldn't stop shouting at him; suddenly he found himself deluged by dirty water; he merely wiped his head and said, "I knew this thunder was sure to be followed by rain."[7]

Lucius Sylla the Lucky (if he hadn't been married) had a wife Metella who was openly unfaithful, and, because we are always the last to hear of our own misfortunes, Sylla didn't know about it even when it was common gossip in Athens; he finally learnt the secrets of his own home through the abuse of an enemy.

Pompey also had an unfaithful wife, Mutia, who was always surrounded by Easterners and crowds of eunuchs from the Pontus; everyone thought he knew about her and was suffering in silence, but a

---

6. This picks up the final remarks of Theophrastus (see above, p. 359).
7. WBP, 727–32.

fellow-soldier mentioned it to him on an expedition, and by this sad message shook the conqueror of the world.

Cato the Censor had a lowly born wife, Actoria Paula, who was a drunkard, violent, and, what is hard to credit, arrogant towards Cato: I mention this in case anyone thinks that by marrying a poor woman he ensures married bliss for himself.

Philip, King of Macedon (the object of Demosthenes' tirades, the *Philippics*) was once shut out of his bedroom by his angry wife: he suffered in silence, and consoled himself for his misfortune with tragic verses. At Olympia the orator Gorgias once recited a book "On Concord" to the Greeks who were quarreling amongst themselves. His opponent Melanthius retorted: "Here is a man preaching to us about concord, who can't get concord in one house between his wife, his serving-wench and himself!"—his wife was jealous of the serving-girl's good looks, and was continually abusing her husband (in fact the most pure of men).

All Euripides' tragedies are indictments of women: Hermione, for instance, says "the counsels of evil women deceived me." * * *[8] We read of a noble at Rome who was defending himself among his friends for divorcing a rich, chaste, and beautiful wife; he stretched out his foot, and said, "This shoe that you see here looks fine and new to you: I alone know where my own shoe pinches." Herodotus writes that a woman takes off her chastity with her clothes.[9] Our Comic says that no one is fortunate who has married. Need I mention Pasiphae, Clytemnestra, Eriphyle?[1] The first was deep in luxury, being a king's wife, but is said to have sought the embrace of a bull; the second killed her husband for the love of her paramour; the third betrayed Amphiareus, by putting a golden necklace above her husband's safety. The tragedies are full of it, cities, kingdoms, homes are overthrown by it—the quarrel between wives and sweethearts. Parents take up weapons against their children; poisonous feasts are set out; for the rape of one woman Europe and Asia endured a ten-year war. We hear of some women married one day, divorced on the second day, and married again on the third: both husbands deserve censure, the one for being too quickly displeased, the other for being too quickly pleased. Epicurus, the prophet of pleasure (although his pupil Metrodorus married Leontia), said that few wise men should undertake marriage, because there were many disadvantages in it. In the same way that riches, honors, bodily health, and the other things which we call "morally indifferent" are in themselves neither good nor bad, and become good or bad only according to the way they are used and their result, so women are in this category of "both good and bad." Now it is a serious thing for a wise man to be in doubt whether he is going to marry a good wife or a bad one! Jokingly Chrysippus told the Romans

8. The omitted passage explains the point of a somewhat obscure mother-in-law joke by Terence.
9. *WBP*, 782–83.
1. *WBP*, 733–46.

to marry in order not to offend the "Jupiter of Marriage and Birth," for
by this they would not marry at all, because they do not have a "Jupiter
of Marriage"! * * *2

[i, 49, col. 280] Some of the above remarks are taken from writings
on marriage by Aristotle, Plutarch, and Seneca. I here add some more:
Love of beauty is loss of reason, and is the neighbor to insanity, a foul
and inappropriate blemish on a blessed spirit. It destroys wise counsel,
breaks high and noble spirits, drags them down from the loftiest to the
meanest thoughts; it makes men quarrelsome, angry, rash, roughly imperious, servilely fawning, useless to everyone, and finally useless to
love itself; for when it rages insatiably in the lust for enjoyment, it
wastes many hours in suspicions, tears, and complaints. It makes one
hate oneself, and finally hate love itself. The whole condemnation of
love is set out by Plato [in the *Phaedro*], and Lysias expounds all its
disadvantages—one takes a wife in madness, not in judgment; above
all, the beauty of women needs the most strict guard. Further, Seneca
tells us that he knew a fine man, who, when he was going out used to
wrap his wife's girdle round his breast; not for a moment could he do
without her presence; husband and wife would not drink anything unless both their lips had touched it; they did many equally foolish
things, into which the sudden passion of burning love forced them.
The origin of their love was honorable, but its size became monstrous.
But in any case it makes no difference from what fine cause a man
goes insane. Xystus says in his *Sentences* "the too eager lover of his
own wife is an adulterer."3 All love for another man's wife is disgrace-
ful, but so is too great love for one's own wife[?].4 A wise man should
take a wife out of careful consideration, not out of love. He should
keep a check on the urge of pleasure, not be rushed headlong into
intercourse. Nothing is worse than to love a wife as one would a mistress. There are some who say that they couple with their wives and
produce children for the sake of the state and the human race; they
should at any rate imitate the animals, and not destroy their sons once
their wife's womb has begun to swell. Let them behave to their wives
as husbands, not as lovers. * * *5 Thus satiety dissolves marriage of
that sort swiftly. As soon as the pander of lust has gone, what once
pleased is now cheapened. "What," says Seneca, "should I say of the
poor men who for the most part marry to acquire the name of 'husband' in order to avoid the laws against celibacy?"

How can a married man control morals, order chastity, and keep the
authority of a husband? The wisest of men says that chastity should be
kept above all: once it is lost, all virtue tumbles. In this consists the
chief of women's virtues. Chastity honors the poor woman, extolls the
rich, redeems the ugly, adorns the beautiful: she deserves well of her
ancestors because she has not soiled their line with a furtive conception; she deserves well of her children, who need have no shame of

---

2. Jerome's comment on this joke is obscure.
3. See C. S. Lewis, *The Allegory of Love* (London: Oxford UP, 1936), p. 15 and n. 5.
4. Translation uncertain.
5. The omitted passage is difficult and obscure.

their mother nor doubt about who their father is, and most of all from herself, since she protects herself from insults on her outer body [?].[6] Captivity brings no greater misfortune than to be the object of another's lust. Men are honored by the consulship, eloquence extols their name forever, military glory and the triumph over a new people ennobles them. There are many things which bring glory to fine minds: a woman's virtue is properly her chastity. This made Lucretia the equal of Brutus—or even his superior, for he learnt from this woman that it is not possible to be a slave. It made Cornelia equal of Gracchus, Portia of the second Brutus. Tanaquilla is more famous than her husband—age has buried him among the names of kings, but her virtue (rare among all women) has fixed her name too firmly in the memory of all ages ever to be erased. Therefore let married women imitate Theano, Celobulina, Gorguntes, Timoclia, the Claudias and the Cornelias, and although they may see Paul pardoning evil women for their bigamy, let them read that even before the Christian religion shone forth in the world, faithful wives had glory among their sex: through virgins it was the custom to honor the goddess Fortune; no priest married twice or committed bigamy. Even today the High Priests at Athens are still castrated by a draught of hemlock; after they have been selected for the priesthood, they cease to be men.

End of Book One

WALTER MAP

From *The Letter of Valerius to Ruffinus, against Marriage*†

[This letter was written by the celebrated Walter Map, archdeacon of Oxford, probably before 1180; it was an early work and was not at first credited to him (because of the pseudonyms). Map therefore inserted it in his much longer work *De Nugis Curialium* (1181–93) ed. M. R. James (Anecdota Oxoniensia 14, 1914); the letter is on pp. 142–58. Here he firmly asserted his authorship. The tone of the antifeminism is more akin to that of Theophrastus than of Jerome: it is philosophical rather than religious. It is referred to by the Wife of Bath as *Valerie*. I have made a few omissions.]

* * *

I had a friend who lived the life of a philosopher; after many visits over a long time I once noticed that he had changed in his dress, his bearing and his expression: he sighed a lot, his face was pale and his dress

6. Translation uncertain.
† Prepared for this volume by A. G. Rigg; see footnote, p. 357. The present translation is based on the 1914 edition by M. R. James. Since then the James edition has been revised by C. M. L. Brooke and R. A. B. Mynors as Walter Map, *De nugis curialium; Courtiers' Trifles* (Oxford: Clarendon P, 1983). The new edition includes a revised translation and will be useful to anyone desiring access to the full text.

vulgarly ostentatious; he said little and was sombre, but was arrogant in a strange way; he had lost his old wit and jollity. He said he was not well, and indeed he wasn't. I saw him wandering about alone, and in so far as respect for me allowed he refused to speak to me. I saw a man in the grip of Venus's paralysis: he seemed all suitor, not at all a philosopher. However, I hoped that he would recover after his lapse: I pardoned what I didn't know; I thought it was a joke, not something brutally serious: he planned not to be loved but to be wived—he wanted to be not Mars but Vulcan. My mind failed me; because he was bent on death, I began to die with him. I spoke to him, but was repulsed. I sent people to talk to him, and when he wouldn't listen to them I said "An evil beast hath devoured him" (Gen. 37:33). To fulfill all the good turns of friendship I sent him a letter in which I altered the names, and called myself (Walter) Valerius and him (John, a redhead [Lat. *rufus*]) Ruffinus, and called the letter "the letter of Valerius to Ruffinus the philosopher, against marrying."

I am forbidden to speak, and I cannot keep silent. I hate the cranes, the voice of the night-owl, the screech-owl and the other birds which gloomily predict with their wails the sadness of foul winter, and you mock the prophesies of disaster which will surely come true if you continue as you are. Therefore I am forbidden to speak, for I am a prophet not of pleasure but of truth.

I love the nightingale and the blackbird, for with their soft harmony they herald the joy of the gentle breeze, and above all the swallow,[1] which fills the season of longed-for joy with its fulness of delights, and I am not deceived. You love parasites and hangers-on with their sweet flatteries, and above all Circe who pours on you joys full of sweet-scented delight, to deceive you: I cannot keep silent, lest you are turned into a pig or an ass.[2]

The servant of Babel pours out for you honeyed poison, which "moveth itself aright" (Prov. 23:31) and delights and leads astray your spirit: therefore I am forbidden to speak. I know that "at the last it biteth like a serpent" (ibid.) and will give a wound which will suffer no antidote: therefore I cannot keep silent.

You have many to persuade you to pleasure, and they are pleasant to hear; I am a stumbling speaker of bitter truth which makes you vomit: therefore I am forbidden to speak. The voice of the goose among swans is held to be a poor delight for men to hear, but it taught the senators to save the city from fire, the treasure-houses from plunder, and themselves from the arrows of their foes. Perhaps you too will realize with the senators, for you are no fool, that the swans sing death, and the goose screeches safety: therefore I cannot keep silent.

You are all afire with longing, and, seduced by the nobility of its fine head do not realize that you are seeking the chimaera,[3] you refuse to

---

1. This word also usually means "nightingale," but clearly Map had a different bird in mind from the first.
2. I.e., by Circe.
3. The image of the Chimaera (ultimately from Lucretius V. 903) was developed as an example against prostitutes by Marbod of Rennes (fl. 1100 C.E.) in his *Liber Decem Capitulorum*, ed. W. Bulst (Heidelberg, 1947), 3. 45–49, and came to be almost a proverb. The passage from

recognize that that three-formed monster is graced with the face of a noble lion, is sullied by the belly of a stinking goat, and is armed in its tail with a poisonous serpent: therefore I am forbidden to speak.

Ulysses was enticed by the harmony of the Sirens, but, because he knew the voices of the sirens and the drinks of Circe, he restrained himself with the chains of virtue, so that he avoided the whirlpool. I trust in the Lord and hope that you will imitate Ulysses, not Empedocles who was overcome by his philosophy (or rather, melancholy), and chose Etna as his tomb. In order that you may take notice of the parable you hear, I cannot keep silent.

But your present flame, by which the worse choice pleases you, is stronger than the flame which draws you to me; therefore, lest the greater flame draws the lesser to it, and I myself perish, I am forbidden to speak. That I may speak with the spirit by which I am yours, let the two flames be weighed in any scale, equal or not, and let your decision, whatever it is, be at my risk: you must pardon me, for the impatience of the love I have for you will not let me keep silent.

After the first creation of man the first wife of the first Adam sated the first hunger by the first sin, against God's command. The sin was the child of Disobedience, which will never cease before the end of the world to drive women tirelessly to pass on to the future what they learned from their mother. Friend, a disobedient wife is dishonor to a man: beware.

The Truth which cannot be deceived said of the blessed David, "I have found a man according to my heart" (1 Sam. 13:14). But by love of a woman he fell conspicuously from adultery to homicide, to fulfil the saying "scandals never come singly" (Matt. 18:7). For every iniquity is rich in followers, and whatever house it enters, it hands over to be soiled by abuse. Friend, Bathsheba was silent, and has never been criticized for anything; yet she became the spur which caused the fall of her perfect husband, the arrow of death for her innocent spouse. Is she innocent who strives with both eloquence, like Sampson's Delilah, and beauty, like Bathsheba, when the latter's beauty triumphed alone, even without intending to? If you are no closer than David to the heart of God, do not doubt that you too can fall.

Solomon, Sun of men, treasure of God's delights, singular home of wisdom, was clouded over by the cloud of darkness and lost the light of his soul, the smell of his glory, and the glory of his house by the witchery of women: finally, he bowed down before Baal, and from a priest of the Lord was turned into a servant of the Devil, so that he can be seen to have fallen from a higher precipice than Phoebus in the fall of Phaeton, when he became Admetus's shepherd instead of Jupiter's Apollo. Friend, if you are not wiser than Solomon—and no man is—you are not too great to be bewitched by a woman. Open your eyes and see.[4]

Map was used by Lydgate, *Reson & Sensualyte*, 11. 3370–78, and is quoted in the margin of one MS at this point.

4. Cf. Chaucer, *Parson's Tale*, X, 955: "Ful ofte tyme I rede that no man truste in his owene perfeccioun, but he be stronger than Sampson, and hoolier than David, and wiser than Salomon." See also *Sir Gawain & the Green Knight*, 2416–19. The list was used often: Map may be the direct source of many of the occurrences.

[Map continues his argument with a pun on *amare* "love" and *amarus* "bitter"; he says that chastity perished with Lucretia, Penelope, and the Sabine women. As examples of women's viciousness, he cites Scilla and Mirra. He quotes the stories of Jupiter, who became a bull in order to love Europa ("a woman will make you roar too"); Phoebus Apollo, whose light was eclipsed because of Leucithoe; Mars, who was put in chains by Vulcan when he was found sleeping with Venus, Vulcan's wife ("consider the chains which you cannot see but are beginning to feel, and tear yourself free while they can still be broken"). He notes that Paris passed an unfavorable judgment on Pallas Athene (when he preferred Helen), because she promised profit not pleasure ("would you make the same decision?"). He reminds his friend of the fate of Julius Caesar, who did not heed the advice of the soothsayer on the day of his assassination. He then gives a series of anecdotes:]

King Phoroneus [famous for his legal innovations] on the day on which he went the way of all flesh said to his brother Leontius, "I would not have fallen short of the highest summit of good fortune, if only I had never had a wife." Leontius said, "How has a wife impeded you?" He replied, "All married men know!" Friend, would that you had experienced marriage, but were not married, so that you would know what an impediment it is to felicity!

The Emperor Valentius, eighty years old and still a virgin, when on the day of his death he heard the praises of his triumphs recounted—and he had had many—said that he was only proud of one victory. Asked "Which?" he said, "When I conquered my worst enemy, my own flesh." Friend, this emperor would have left the world without glory, if he had not boldly resisted that with which you have now made a pact.

After his divorce from Terentia, Cicero would not marry again; he said it was not possible to give one's attention both to a wife and to philosophy. * * *

Canius of Cadiz, a poet of a light and pleasant wit, was reproved by the sombre hen-pecked historian Livy of Phoenicia, because he enjoyed the loves of many women: "You cannot share in our philosophy when you yourself are shared by so many: Tityus does not love Juno with a liver torn into so many pieces by vultures!" Canius replied: "Whenever I slip, I get up more cautiously; when I am pushed down a little, I come up for air more quickly. The alternations of my nights make my days happier: a perpetuity of darkness is like hell. The first lilies of the springtime sun spread with a more effusive joy if they enjoy winds both from the South-east and the South-west—more than those which are blown over by the single blast of the fiery South wind. Mars broke his chains and sits at the heavenly banquet, from which hen-pecked Vulcan is excluded, held back by a long rope. Many threads bind less firmly than one chain: from philosophy I obtain pleasure—you go to it for relief!" Friend, I approve the words of both, but the lives of neither, but it is true that many diseases, which continually interrupt health, do less harm than a single disease which continually afflicts one with incurable illnesses.

Weeping, Pacuvius said to his neighbor Arrius, "Friend, I have in my garden an unlucky tree: my first wife hanged herself on it, then my second wife, and now the third." Arrius replied, "I'm surprised you find yourself able to weep in all these successes"; then he said, "Good Lord, think how many sorrows that tree has saved you!" Thirdly he said, "Friend, let me have some shoots of that tree to plant for myself." Friend, I'm afraid you may have to beg shoots of that tree when you won't be able to find any.[5]

Sulpicius, who had divorced a noble and chaste wife, knew where his own shoe pinched him. Friend, be careful that you don't have a pinching shoe which you can't take off.

Cato of Utica said, "If the world could exist without women, our company would not differ from that of the gods." Friend, Cato said nothing that he hadn't experienced and known; none of these men who attacked the deceits of women did so without having themselves been deceived—they were fully experienced and aware. You should believe them, for they tell the truth: they know that love pleases and then the loved one stabs [or: and stabs the loved one]; they know that the flower of Venus is a rose, but under its bright colour lie hidden many thorns.

Metellus would not marry the daughter of Marius, although she was rich in dowry, beautiful to look at, famous in birth, and of good reputation; he said, "I prefer to be mine than hers"; Marius said, "But she will be yours"; Metellus retorted, "A man has to be a woman's, because it is a point of logic that the predicates are only what the subject allows."[6] Thus by a joke Metellus turned away a load from his back. Friend, even if it is fitting to take a wife, it is not expedient. May it be love (and not blind love) that is in question, not income; may you choose beauty, not clothes; her mind, not her gold; may your bride be a wife, not a dowry. If it can possibly happen in this way, you may be able to be a predicate in such a way that you do not derive anger from the subject!

Lais of Corinth, a renowned beauty, only deigned to accept the embraces of kings and princes, but she tried to share the bed of the philosopher Demosthenes, so that she would seem, by breaking his notorious chastity, to have made rocks move by her beauty (as Amphion did with his lyre), and having attracted him by her blandishments treat him at her pleasure. When Demosthenes was enticed to her bedroom, Lais asked him for a hundred talents for the privilege; he looked up to heaven and said "I don't pay so much to feel penitent!" Friend, would that you might lift your attention to heaven, and avoid that which can only be redeemed by penitence.

Livia killed her husband whom she hated greatly; Lucilia killed hers, whom she loved to excess.[7] The former intentionally mixed poison, the latter was deceived and poured out madness as a cup of love. Friend, these women strove with opposite intentions, but neither was cheated

---

5. *WBP*, 757–64 (with *Latumyus* inexplicably for *Pacuvius*).
6. Puns on *predicate* and *subject* (that which is literally "placed underneath" but logically governs the predicate) abound in Medieval Latin antifeminist writers, both serious and frivolous.
7. *WBP*, 747–56 (with *Lucye* for *Lucilia*).

of the end of female treachery, that is, their natural evil. Women walk by varying and diverse paths, but whatever the paths they wander, whatever the by-ways they take, there is one result, one finishing-post for all their routes, one head and point of agreement of all their ways—mischief. Take the example of these two women as evidence that woman, whether she loves or hates, is bold in everything—crafty, when she wants to do harm (which is always), and when she tries to help frequently gets in the way, and so turns out to do harm even unintentionally. You are placed in the furnace: if you are gold, you will come out gold.

Deianeira clothed Hercules in a shirt, and brought vengeance on the "hammer of monsters" with the blood of a monster: what she had contrived to bring her happiness resulted in her tears * * * [women always look to their own pleasure, and never think of its effect on other people]. Hercules fulfilled twelve inhuman labors, but by the thirteenth, which surpassed all inhumanity, he was consumed. Thus the bravest of men lay dead, to be lamented like the most pitiful man,—he who had held up on his shoulders the span of the world without a groan.

Finally, what woman, among so many thousand thousands, ever saddened the eager and consistent suitor by a permanent refusal? Which one ever invariably cut off the words of a wooer? Her reply always savors of her favor, and however hard she may be she will always have hidden in her words some hint of encouragement for your plea. Any woman may say "No," but none say "No" for ever.

> [His examples of unchastity[8] are inappropriately Jupiter's visit to Danae in a shower of gold and Perictione's virgin-birth of Plato out of Apollo: they are taken from Jerome (see above, p. 370) where they are used more appropriately. Map concludes his letter with a justification of his use of pagan examples, which may offer even a Christian a good example—in any case one should note that the pagans applied themselves to learning even without the promise of eternal felicity, simply to avoid ignorance—how much more should we pay attention to Scripture! He wants Ruffinus to marry not Venus but Pallas. The hand of the surgeon is hard, but it cures; the way to life is narrow and difficult, as was Jason's to the Golden Fleece. . . . Hard beginnings are rewarded by a sweet result. If you need any more evidence, read Theophrastus, or Seneca's *Medea*.]

8. Cf. *WBP*, 765 ff.

From the Gospel According to St. John†

Chapter 4

* * *

5 He cometh therefore to a city of Samaria, which is called Sichar, near the land which Jacob gave to his son Joseph.

6 Now Jacob's well was there. Jesus therefore being wearied with his journey, sat thus on the well. It was about the sixth hour.

7 There cometh a woman of Samaria, to draw water. Jesus saith to her: Give me to drink.

8 For his disciples were gone into the city to buy meats.

9 Then that Samaritan woman saith to him: How dost thou, being a Jew, ask of me to drink, who am a Samaritan woman? For the Jews do not communicate with the Samaritans.

10 Jesus answered, and said to her: If thou didst know the gift of God, and who he is that saith to thee, Give me to drink; thou perhaps wouldst have asked of him, and he would have given thee living water.

11 The woman saith to him: Sir, thou hast nothing wherein to draw, and the well is deep; from whence then hast thou living water?

12 Art thou greater than our father Jacob, who gave us the well, and drank thereof himself, and his children, and his cattle?

13 Jesus answered, and said to her: Whosoever drinketh of this water, shall thirst again; but he that shall drink of the water that I will give him, shall not thirst for ever:

14 But the water that I will give him, shall become in him a fountain of water, springing up into life everlasting.

15 The woman saith to him: Sir, give me this water, that I may not thirst, nor come hither to draw.

16 Jesus saith to her: Go, call thy husband, and come hither.

17 The woman answered, and said: I have no husband. Jesus said to her: Thou hast said well, I have no husband:

18 For thou hast had five husbands: and he whom thou now hast, is not thy husband. This thou hast said truly.

19 The woman saith to him: Sir, I perceive that thou art a prophet.

20 Our fathers adored on this mountain, and you say, that at Jerusalem is the place where men must adore.

21 Jesus saith to her: Woman, believe me, that the hour cometh, when you shall neither on this mountain, nor in Jerusalem, adore the Father.

22 You adore that which you know not: we adore that which we know; for salvation is of the Jews.

23 But the hour cometh, and now is, when the true adorers shall adore the Father in spirit and in truth. For the Father also seeketh such to adore him.

---

† For this and the following Bible selections, we print the Douay/Rheims translation of the Latin Vulgate Bible, first published in 1582 and 1609, from the edition published by P. J. Kenedy and Sons (New York, 1914).

24 God is a spirit, and they that adore him, must adore him in spirit and in truth.

25 The woman saith to him: I know that the Messias cometh (who is called Christ); therefore, when he is come, he will tell us all things.

26 Jesus saith to her: I am he, who am speaking with thee.

27 And immediately his disciples came; and they wondered that he talked with the woman. Yet no man said: What seekest thou? or, why talkest thou with her?

28 The woman therefore left her water-pot, and went her way into the city, and saith to the men there:

29 Come, and see a man who has told me all things whatsoever I have done. Is not he the Christ?

30 They went therefore out of the city, and came unto him.

31 In the mean time the disciples prayed him, saying: Rabbi, eat.

32 But he said to them: I have meat to eat, which you know not.

33 The disciples therefore said one to another: Hath any man brought him to eat?

34 Jesus saith to them: My meat is to do the will of him that sent me, that I may perfect his work.

35 Do not you say, There are yet four months, and then the harvest cometh? Behold, I say to you, lift up your eyes, and see the countries; for they are white already to harvest.

36 And he that reapeth receiveth wages, and gathereth fruit unto life everlasting: that both he that soweth, and he that reapeth, may rejoice together.

37 For in this is the saying true: That it is one man that soweth, and it is another that reapeth.

38 I have sent you to reap that in which you did not labour: others have laboured, and you have entered into their labours.

39 Now of that city many of the Samaritans believed in him, for the word of the woman giving testimony: He told me all things whatsoever I have done.

40 So when the Samaritans were come to him, they desired that he would tarry there. And he abode there two days.

41 And many more believed in him because of his own word.

42 And they said to the woman: We now believe, not for thy saying: for we ourselves have heard him, and know that this is indeed the Saviour of the world.

* * *

From St. Paul to the Corinthians 1

Chapter 7

Now concerning the things whereof you wrote to me: It is good for a man not to touch a woman.

2 But for fear of fornication, let every man have his own wife, and let every woman have her own husband.

3 Let the husband render the debt to his wife, and the wife also in like manner to the husband.

4 The wife hath not power of her own body, but the husband. And in like manner the husband also hath not power of his own body, but the wife.

5 Defraud not one another, except, perhaps, by consent, for a time, that you may give yourselves to prayer; and return together again, lest Satan tempt you for your incontinency.

6 But I speak this by indulgence, not by commandment.

7 For I would that all men were even as myself: but every one hath his proper gift from God; one after this manner, and another after that.

8 But I say to the unmarried, and to the widows: It is good for them if they so continue, even as I.

9 But if they do not contain themselves, let them marry. For it is better to marry than to be burnt.

10 But to them that are married, not I but the Lord commandeth, that the wife depart not from her husband.

11 And if she depart, that she remain unmarried, or be reconciled to her husband. And let not the husband put away his wife.

12 For to the rest I speak, not the Lord. If any brother hath a wife that believeth not, and she consent to dwell with him, let him not put her away.

13 And if any woman hath a husband that believeth not, and he consent to dwell with her, let her not put away her husband.

14 For the unbelieving husband is sanctified by the believing wife; and the unbelieving wife is sanctified by the believing husband: otherwise your children should be unclean; but now they are holy.

15 But if the unbeliever depart, let him depart. For a brother or sister is not under servitude in such *cases*. But God hath called us in peace.

16 For how knowest thou, O wife, whether thou shalt save thy husband? Or how knowest thou, O man, whether thou shalt save thy wife?

17 But as the Lord hath distributed to every one, as God hath called every one, so let him walk: and so in all churches I teach.

18 Is any man called, being circumcised? let him not procure uncircumcision. Is any man called in uncircumcision? let him not be circumcised.

19 Circumcision is nothing, and uncircumsion is nothing: but the observance of the commandments of God.

20 Let every man abide in the same calling in which he was called.

21 Wast thou called, being a bondman? care not for it; but if thou mayest be made free, use it rather.

22 For he that is called in the Lord, being a bondman, is the freeman of the Lord. Likewise he that is called, being free, is the bondman of Christ.

23 You are bought with a price; be not made the bondslaves of men.

24 Brethren, let every man, wherein he was called, therein abide with God.

25 Now concerning virgins, I have no commandment of the Lord; but I give counsel, as having obtained mercy of the Lord, to be faithful.

26 I think therefore that this is good for the present necessity, that it is good for a man so to be.

27 Art thou bound to a wife? seek not to be loosed. Art thou loosed from a wife? seek not a wife.

28 But if thou take a wife, thou hast not sinned. And if a virgin marry, she hath not sinned: nevertheless, such shall have tribulation of the flesh. But I spare you.

29 This therefore I say, brethren; the time is short; it remaineth, that they also who have wives, be as if they had none;

30 And they that weep, as though they wept not; and they that rejoice, as if they rejoiced not; and they that buy, as though they possessed not;

31 And they that use this world, as if they used it not: for the fashion of this world passeth away.

32 But I would have you to be without solicitude. He that is without a wife, is solicitous for the things that belong to the Lord, how he may please God.

33 But he that is with a wife, is solicitous for the things of the world, how he may please his wife: and he is divided.

34 And the unmarried woman and the virgin thinketh on the things of the Lord, that she may be holy both in body and in spirit. But she that is married thinketh on the things of the world, how she may please her husband.

35 And this I speak for your profit: not to cast a snare upon you; but for that which is decent, and which may give you power to attend upon the Lord, without impediment.

36 But if any man think that he seemeth dishonoured, with regard to his virgin, for that she is above the age, and it must so be: let him do what he will; he sinneth not, if she marry.

37 For he that hath determined being steadfast in his heart, having no necessity, but having power of his own will; and hath judged this in his heart, to keep his virgin, doth well.

38 Therefore, both he that giveth his virgin in marriage, doth well; and he that giveth her not, doth better.

39 A woman is bound by the law as long as her husband liveth; but if her husband die, she is at liberty: let her marry to whom she will; only in the Lord.

40 But more blessed shall she be, if she so remain, according to my counsel; and I think that I also have the spirit of God.

From St. Paul to the Ephesians

Chapter 5

Be ye therefore followers of God, as most dear children;

2 And walk in love, as Christ also hath loved us, and hath delivered himself for us, an oblation and a sacrifice to God for an odour of sweetness.

3 But fornication, and all uncleanness, or covetousness, let it not so much as be named among you, as becometh saints:

4 Or obscenity, or foolish talking, or scurrility, which is to no purpose; but rather giving of thanks.

5 For know you this and understand, that no fornicator, or unclean, or covetous person (which is a serving of idols), hath inheritance in the kingdom of Christ and of God.

6 Let no man deceive you with vain words. For because of these things cometh the anger of God upon the children of unbelief.

7 Be ye not therefore partakers with them.

8 For you were heretofore darkness, but now light in the Lord. Walk then as children of the light.

9 For the fruit of the light is in all goodness, and justice, and truth;

10 Proving what is well pleasing to God.

11 And have no fellowship with the unfruitful works of darkness, but rather reprove them.

12 For the things that are done by them in secret, it is a shame even to speak of.

13 But all things that are reproved, are made manifest by the light; for all that is made manifest is light.

14 Wherefore he saith: *Rise, thou that sleepest, and arise from the dead: and Christ shall enlighten thee.*

15 See therefore, brethren, how you walk circumspectly: not as unwise,

16 But as wise: redeeming the time, because the days are evil.

17 Wherefore become not unwise, but understanding what is the will of God.

18 And be not drunk with wine, wherein is luxury; but be ye filled with the holy Spirit,

19 Speaking to yourselves in psalms, and hymns, and spiritual canticles, singing and making melody in your hearts to the Lord;

20 Giving thanks always for all things, in the name of our Lord Jesus Christ, to God and the Father:

21 Being subject one to another, in the fear of Christ.

22 Let women be subject to their husbands, as to the Lord:

23 Because the husband is the head of the wife, as Christ is the head of the church. He *is* the saviour of his body.

24 Therefore as the church is subject to Christ, so also let the wives be to their husbands in all things.

25 Husbands, love your wives, as Christ also loved the church, and delivered himself up for it:

26 That he might sanctify it, cleansing it by the laver of water in the word of life:

27 That he might present it to himself a glorious church, not having spot or wrinkle, or any such thing; but that it should be holy, and without blemish.

28 So also ought men to love their wives as their own bodies. He that loveth his wife, loveth himself.

29 For no man ever hated his own flesh; but nourisheth and cherisheth it, as also Christ doth the church:

30 Because we are members of his body, of his flesh, and of his bones.

31 *For this cause shall a man leave his father and mother, and shall cleave to his wife, and they shall be two in one flesh.*

32 This is a great sacrament; but I speak in Christ and in the church.

33 Nevertheless let every one of you in particular love his wife as himself: and let the wife fear her husband.

From St. Paul to Timothy 1

Chapter 2

* * *

9 In like manner women also in decent apparel: adorning themselves with modesty and sobriety, not with plaited hair, or gold, or pearls, or costly attire,

10 But as it becometh women professing godlines, with good works.

11 Let the woman learn in silence, with all subjection.

12 But I suffer not a woman to teach, nor to use authority over the man: but to be in silence.

13 For Adam was first formed; then Eve.

14 And Adam was not seduced; but the woman being seduced, was in the transgression.

15 Yet she shall be saved through child-bearing; if she continue in faith, and love, and sanctification, with sobriety.

Chapter 5

* * *

3 Honour widows, that are widows indeed.

4 But if any widow have children, or grandchildren, let her learn first to govern her own house, and to make a return of duty to her parents: for this is acceptable before God.

5 But she that is a widow indeed, and desolate, let her trust in God, and continue in supplications and prayers night and day.

6 For she that liveth in pleasures, is dead while she is living.

7 And this give in charge, that they may be blameless.

8 But if any man have not care of his own, and especially of those of his house, he hath denied the faith, and is worse than an infidel.

9 Let a widow be chosen of no less than threescore years of age, who hath been the wife of one husband.

10 Having testimony for her good works, if she have brought up children, if she have received to harbour, if she have washed the saints' feet, if she have ministered to them that suffer tribulation, if she have diligently followed every good work.

11 But the younger widows avoid. For when they have grown wanton in Christ, they will marry:

12 Having damnation, because they have made void their first faith.

13 And withal being idle they learn to go about from house to house: and are not only idle, but tattlers also, and busy-bodies, speaking things which they ought not.

14 I will therefore that the younger should marry, bear children, be mistresses of families, give no occasion to the adversary to speak evil.

15 For some are already turned aside after Satan.

16 If any of the faithful have widows, let him minister to them, and let not the church be charged: that there may be sufficient for them that are widows indeed.

* * *

From St. Paul to Timothy 2

Chapter 2

* * *

14 Of these things put them in mind, charging them before the Lord. Contend not in words, for it is to no profit, but to the subverting of the hearers.

15 Carefully study to present thyself approved unto God, a workman that needeth not to be ashamed, rightly handling the word of truth.

16 But shun profane and vain babblings: for they grow much towards ungodliness.

17 And their speech spreadeth like a canker: of whom are Hymeneus and Philetus:

18 Who have erred from the truth, saying, that the resurrection is past already, and have subverted the faith of some.

19 But the sure foundation of God standeth firm, having this seal: the Lord knoweth who are his; and let every one depart from inquity who nameth the name of the Lord.

20 But in a great house there are not only vessels of gold and of silver, but also of wood and of earth: and some indeed unto honour, but some unto dishonour.

21 If any man therefore shall cleanse himself from these, he shall be a vessel unto honour, sanctified and profitable to the Lord, prepared unto every good work.

22 But flee thou youthful desires, and pursue justice, faith, charity, and peace, with them that call on the Lord out of a pure heart.

23 And avoid foolish and unlearned questions, knowing that they beget strifes.

24 But the servant of the Lord must not wrangle: but be mild towards all men, apt to teach, patient,

25 With modesty admonishing them that resist the truth: if peradventure God may give them repentance to know the truth,

26 And they may recover themselves from the snares of the devil, by whom they are held captive at his will.

JOHN GOWER

The Tale of Florent†

* * *

Mi Sone, and I thee rede° this,		*advise*
What so befalle of other weie,°		*otherwise*
That thou to loves heste° obeie		*command*
Als ferr as thou it myht suffise;°		*be able*
1400 For ofte sithe° in such a wise°		*oftentimes / way*
Obedience in love availeth,		
Wher al a mannes strengthe faileth.		
Wherof, if that the list to wite°		*it pleases thee to know*
In a cronique° as it is write,		*chronicle*
1405 A gret ensample° thou myht fynde,		*example*
Which now is come to my mynde.		
Ther was whilom° be° daies olde		*once upon a time / in*
A worthi knyht, and as men tolde		
He was nevoeu° to th'emperour		*nephew*
1410 And of his court a courteour.°		*courtier*
Wifles° he was, Florent he hihte,°		*Wifeless / was called*
He was a man that mochel myhte.°		*could (do) a great deal*
Of armes he was desirous,		
Chivalerous and amorous,		
1415 And for the fame of worldes speche,°		*worldly reputation*
Strange aventures forto seche,°		*seek*
He rod the Marches al aboute.		
And fell° a time, as he was oute,		*there befell*

---

† *Confessio Amantis* 1.1396–1871. Text based on *The English Works of John Gower*, ed. G. C. Macaulay EETSe.s. 81–82 (London, 1900–01; rpt. 1969), I.74–86. Reprinted with permission of the Council of the Early English Text Society. The framing device in the *Confessio* is the lover-narrator's confession to Genius, who instructs him with many exempla organized according to the seven deadly sins. *The Tale of Florent* is told to counteract disobedience, one of the subdivisions of Pride. Gower completed the first version of the *Confessio* in 1390, having begun it some four years earlier. A revised version was completed in 1392–93. On Gower's relationship to Chaucer, see footnote, p. 337.

Fortune, which may every thred
1420 Tobreke° and knette° of mannes sped,°   *Break apart / knit up / success*
Schop,° as this knyht rod in a pas,°   *Arranged / at a walk*
That he be strengthe° take was,   *by force*
And to a castell thei him ladde,°   *led*
Wher that he fewe frendes hadde;
1425 For so it fell that ilke stounde°   *at that same time*
That he hath with a dedly wounde,
Feihtende, his oghne hondes slain°   *Fighting, (with) his own hands slew*
Branchus, which to the Capitain
Was sone and heir, wherof ben wrothe°   *angry*
1430 The fader and the moder bothe.
That knyht Branchus was of his hond
The worthieste of al his lond,
And fain° thei wolden do vengance°   *willingly / take revenge*
Upon Florent, bot° remembrance   *except for*
1435 That thei toke of his worthinesse
Of knyhthod and of gentilesse,
And how he stod of cousinage°   *was related*
To th'emperour, made hem° assuage,°   *them / abate (their anger)*
And dorsten° noght slen° him for fere.°   *(they) dared / slay / out of fear*
1440 In gret desputeisoun° thei were   *argumentation*
Among hemself, what was the beste.
    Ther was a lady, the slyheste°   *most clever*
Of alle that men knewe tho,°   *then*
So old sche myhte unethes go,°   *could scarcely walk*
1445 And was grantdame° unto the dede;°   *grandmother / dead (man)*
And sche with that began to rede,°   *counsel*
And seide how sche wol bringe him inne,
That° sche schal him to dethe winne°   *So that / bring to*
Al only of his oghne grant,°   *by his own consent*
1450 Thurgh strengthe of verray° covenant   *a true*
Withoute blame of eny wiht.°   *person*
Anon° sche sende for this kniht,   *Immediately*
And of hire sone sche alleide°   *alleged, cited*
The deth, and thus to him sche seide:
1455 "Florent, how so thou be to wyte°   *blame*
Of Branchus deth, men schal respite°   *delay*
As now° to take vengement,°   *Just now / revenge*
Be so° thou stonde in juggement   *If*
Upon certein condicioun—
1460 That thou unto a questioun
Which I schal axe° schalt ansuere;   *ask*
And over this thou schalt ek° swere,   *also*
That if thou of the sothe° faile,   *truth*
Ther schal non other thing availe,
1465 That thou ne schalt thi deth receive.
And for men schal thee noght deceive,
That thou therof myht ben avised,°   *take counsel*

Thou schalt have day and tyme assised°   *fixed, appointed*
And leve° saufly° forto wende,°   *permission / safely / depart*
1470 Be so that° at thi daies ende   *If*
Thou come ayein° with thin avys."°   *again / conclusion*
    This knyht, which worthi was and wys,
This lady preith° that he may wite,°   *beseeches / know*
And have it under seales write,
1475 What question it scholde be,
For which he schal in that degree
Stonde of his lif in jeupartie.°   *jeopardy*
With that sche feigneth compaignie,°   *friendliness*
And seith: "Florent, on love it hongeth°   *depends, concerns*
1480 Al that to myn axinge° longeth:°   *asking, question / belongs*
What alle wommen most desire,
This wole I axe, and in th'empire
Wher as° thou hast most knowlechinge°   *Where / largest acquaintance*
Tak conseil upon this axinge."
1485   Florent this thing hath undertake,
The day was set, the time take;
Under his seal he wrot his oth°   *oath*
In such a wise,° and forth he goth   *way*
Hom to his emes° court ayein;°   *uncle's / again*
1490 To whom his aventure plein
He tolde, of that him is befalle.
And upon that thei weren alle
The wiseste of the lond asent,°   *sent for*
Bot natheles° of on° assent   *nevertheless / one*
1495 Thei myhte noght acorde plat.°   *plainly*
On° seide this, an othre that.   *One*
After° the disposicioun   *According to*
Of naturel complexioun,°   *temperament*
To som womman it is plesance°   *a pleasure*
1500 That to an other is grevance;°   *a vexation*
Bot such a thing in special,°   *particular*
Which to hem alle in general
Is most plesant, and most desired
Above alle othre and most conspired,°   *sighed after*
1505 Such o thing conne° thei noght finde   *could*
Be constellacion ne kinde.°   *Through astrological or natural investigation*
And thus Florent withoute cure°   *remedy*
Mot stonde upon his aventure,°   *Must endure his fortune*
And is al schape° unto the lere,°   *prepared / loss*
1510 As in defalte of his answere.
    This knyht hath levere° forto dye   *rather*
Than breke his trowthe° and forto lye   *vow*
In place ther as he was swore,
And schapth him gon ayein° therfore.   *prepares himself to return again*
1515 Whan time cam he tok his leve,
That lengere° wolde he noght beleve,°   *longer / remain*

And preith° his em he be noght wroth,   *begs*
For that is a point of his oth,
He seith, that noman schal him wreke,°   *avenge*
1520 Thogh afterward men hiere speke°   *hear (it) said*
That he par aventure° deie.°   *by chance / die*
And thus he wente forth his weie°   *way*
Alone as knyht aventurous,
And in his thoght was curious
1525 To wite° what was best to do;   *know*
And as he rod al one° so,   *all alone*
And cam nyh° ther° he wolde be,   *nigh (near) / where*
In a forest under a tre
He syh° wher sat a creature,   *saw*
1530 A lothly° wommannysch figure,   *loathly*
That forto speke of fleisch and bon°   *flesh and bone*
So foul yit° syh° he nevere non.   *yet, until then / saw*
This knyht behield hir redely,°   *intently*
And as he wolde have passed by,
1535 Sche cleped° him and bad abide;   *called*
And he his horse heved° aside   *pulled*
Tho° torneth, and to hire he rod,   *Then*
And there he hoveth° and abod,   *remained*
To wite° what sche wolde mene.°   *know / say*
1540 And sche began him to bemene,°   *speak*
And seide: "Florent, be° thi name,   *by*
Thou hast on honde such a game,
That bot° thou be the betre avised,   *unless*
Thi deth is schapen° and devised,   *arranged*
1545 That al the world ne mai the save,
Bot if that° thou my conseil have."   *Unless*
     Florent, whan he this tale herde,
Unto this olde wyht° answerde   *person*
And of hir conseil° he hir preide.°   *advice / begged*
1550 And sche ayein° to him thus seide: *again, in turn*
"Florent, if I for the° so schape,   *thee*
That thou thurgh me thi deth ascape°   *escape*
And take worschipe of° thi dede,   *receive honor for*
What schal I have to my mede?"°   *for my reward*
1555 "What° thing," quod he, "that thou wolt axe."°   *Whatever / ask*
"I bidde° nevere a betre taxe,"°   *ask / no better fee*
Quod sche, "bot ferst, er° thou be sped,°   *before / have hastened off*
Thou schalt me leve° such a wedd,°   *leave / pledge*
That I wol have thi trowthe° in honde   *troth, promise*
1560 That thou schalt be myn housebonde."
"Nay," seith Florent, "that may noght be."
"Ryd thanne forth thi wey," quod sche,
"And if thou go withoute red,°   *advice*
Thou schalt be sekerliche° ded."   *surely*
1565   Florent behihte° hire good ynowh—°   *promised / goods enough*

Of lond, of rente,° of park,° of plowh—°   *income / forest / plowland*
Bot al that compteth sche at noght.°   *she considers worth nothing*
Tho° fell this knyht in mochel° thoght;   *Then / much*
Now goth he forth, now comth ayein,
1570 He wot° noght what is best to sein,°   *knows / say*
And thoghte, as he rod to and fro,
That chese he mot on of the tuo,°   *That he must choose one of the two*
Or° forto take hire to his wif   *Either*
Or elles° forto lese° his lif.   *else / lose*
1575 And thanne he caste° his avantage,   *considered*
That sche was of so gret an age,
That sche mai live bot a while,
And thoghte° put hire in an ile,°   *thought to / on an island*
Wher that noman hire scholde knowe,
1580 Til sche with deth were overthrowe.
And thus this yonge lusti° knyht   *vigorous*
Unto this olde lothly° wiht°   *loathly / person*
Tho seide: "If that non other chance
Mai make° my deliverance,   *bring about*
1585 Bot only thilke same° speche   *that same*
Which, as thou seist, thou schalt me teche,
Have hier myn hond, I schal thee wedde."
And thus his trowthe° he leith to wedde.°   *troth, pledge / sets forth*
With that sche frounceth° up the browe: *wrinkles*
1590 "This covenant I wol allowe,"°   *accept*
Sche seith: "if eny other thing
Bot° that° thou hast of my techyng   *Except / what*
Fro deth thi body mai respite,°   *delay, put off*
I woll thee of thi trowthe acquite,°   *release*
1595 And elles° be non other weie.   *otherwise*
Now herkne me what I schal seie:°   *say*
Whan thou art come into the place,
Wher now thei maken gret manace°   *show great hostility*
And upon thi comynge abyde,
1600 Thei wole anon° the same tide°   *at once / time*
Oppose thee of° thin answere.   *Demand from thee*
I wot° thou wolt nothing° forbere°   *know / not at all / hold back*
Of that° thou wenest° be thi beste,°   *With what / thinkest / best (answer)*
And if thou myht so finde reste,°   *peace*
1605 Wel is,° for thanne is ther nomore.   *it is*
And elles this schal be my lore,°   *teaching*
That thou schalt seie, upon this molde°   *earth*
That alle wommen lievest° wolde   *most dearly*
Be soverein of° mannes love;   *sovereign over, master of*
1610 For what° womman is so above,   *whatever*
Sche hath, as who seith,° al hire wille;   *as it is said*
And elles may sche noght fulfille
What thing hir were lievest have.

With this answere thou schalt save
1615 Thiself, and other wise noght.
And whan thou hast thin ende wroght,
Com hier ayein, thou schalt me finde,
And let nothing out of thi minde."°   escape thy memory
    He goth him forth with hevy chiere,°   sad countenance, mood
1620 As he that not° in what manere   knows not
He mai this worldes joie atteigne;°   attain
For if he deie,° he hath a peine,   die
And if he live, he mot him binde
To such on° which of alle kinde°   a one / the species
1625 Of wommen is th'unsemlieste.°   the unseemliest, ugliest
Thus wot° he noght what is the beste,   knows
Bot be him lief° or be him loth,°   dear, desirable / loath, distasteful
Unto the castell forth he goth,
His full answere forto yive,°   give
1630 Or° forto deie° or forto live.   Either / die
Forth with his conseil° cam the lord,   council
The thinges° stoden of record;°   Everything / as previously arranged
He sende up for the lady sone,°   immediately
And forth sche cam, that olde mone.°   crone
1635 In presence of the remenant°   rest
The strengthe of al the covenant
Tho° was reherced openly,   Then
And to Florent sche bad forthi°   therefore
That he schal tellen his avis,°   conclusion
1640 As he that woot° what is the pris.   knows
Florent seith al that evere he couthe,°   knew
Bot such word cam ther non to mowthe,°   mouth
That he for yifte° or for beheste°   by any gift / promise
Mihte eny wise° his deth areste.°   in any way / prevent
1645 And thus he tarieth longe and late,
Til that this lady bad° algate°   commanded / finally, at last
That he schal for the dom° final   judgment
Yive° his answere in special°   Give / particular
Of that sche hadde him ferst opposed:°   first put to him
1650 And thanne he hath trewly supposed
That he him may of nothing yelpe,°   boast
Bot if° so be tho° wordes helpe   Unless / those
Whiche as the womman hath him tawht°   taught
Whereof he hath an hope cawht°   caught, conceived
1655 That he schal ben excused so,
And tolde out plein° his wille tho.°   plainly / then
And whan that this matrone herde
The manere how this knyht ansuerde,
Sche seide: "Ha, treson!° Wo thee be,°   treason / Woe be to thee
1660 That hast thus told the privite,°   the secret knowledge
Which° alle wommen most desire!   What

I wolde that thou were afire!"
Bot natheles° in such a plit°   *nevertheless / plight*
Florent of° his answere is quit,°   *for / released*
1665 And tho° began his sorwe newe,   *then*
For he mot gon, or ben untrewe,
To hire which his trowthe hadde.
Bot he, which alle schame dradde,°   *feared*
Goth forth in stede of° his penance,   *to the place of*
1670 And takth the fortune of his chance,
As he that was with trowthe affaited.°   *governed by truth*
This olde wyht° him hath awaited   *person*
In place wher as° he hire lefte.   *where*
Florent his wofull heved° uplefte°   *head / uplifted*
1675 And syh° this vecke° wher sche sat,   *saw / hag, old woman*
Which was the lothlieste what°   *thing*
That evere man caste on his yhe:°   *eye*
Hire nase° bass,° hire browes hyhe,°   *nose / low, long / high*
Hire yhen° smale and depe set,   *eyes*
1680 Hire chekes ben with teres wet
And rivelen° as an emty skyn°   *shriveled / skin*
Hangende doun unto the chin;
Hire lippes schrunken ben for age,
Ther was no grace in the visage;
1685 Hir front° was nargh,° hir lockes°   *forehead / narrow / locks (of hair)*
        hore,°   *hoary*
Sche loketh forth° as doth a More;°   *looks / Moor*
Hire necke is schort, hir schuldres courbe,°   *stooped*
That myhte a mannes lust destourbe;°   *trouble, destroy*
Hire body gret° and nothing° smal,   *large / not at all*
1690 And schortly to descrive° hire al,   *describe*
Sche hath no lith° withoute a lak,°   *limb / defect, fault*
Bot lich° unto the wollesak°   *like / woolsack*
Sche proferth hire° unto this knyht,   *proffers herself*
And bad him, as he hath behyht,°   *promised*
1695 So as° sche hath ben his warrant,°   *Since / protection*
That he hire holde covenant,°   *keep the covenant with her*
And be° the bridel sche him seseth.°   *by / seizes*
Bot Godd wot how that sche him pleseth
Of ° suche wordes as sche spekth.   *By*
1700 Him thenkth° welnyh° his herte brekth   *It seems to him / almost*
For° sorwe that he may noght fle,   *Out of*
Bot if° he wolde untrewe be.   *Unless*
    Loke how° a sek° man for his hele°   *Just as / sick / health*
Takth baldemoine° with canele,°   *gentian (a medicinal root) / cinnamon*
1705 And with the mirre° takth the sucre,°   *myrrh / sugar*
Ryht upon such a maner lucre°   *kind of profit, reward*
Stant° Florent, as in this diete: *Stands*
He drinkth the bitre° with the swete,   *bitter*
He medleth° sorwe with likynge,°   *mixes / pleasure (at being alive)*

1710 And liveth, as who seith, deyinge;
      His youthe schal be cast aweie°   *away*
      Upon such on,° which as the weie°   *a one / like the road*
      Is old and lothly° overal.   *loathly*
      Bot nede he mot that nede schal:°   *i.e., there's no denying necessity*
1715 He wolde algate his trowthe holde,°   *keep his troth, promise*
      As every knyht therto is holde,°   *beholden, bound*
      What happ° so evere him is befalle.   *fortune, chance*
      Thogh sche be the fouleste of alle,
      Yet to th'onour of wommanhiede°   *womanhood*
1720 Him thoghte he scholde taken hiede,°   *heed*
      So that for pure gentilesse,°   *nobility, courtesy*
      As he hire couthe best adresce,°   *knew best how to position her*
      In ragges as sche was totore°   *all torn*
      He set hire on his hors tofore°   *before (him)*
1725 And forth he takth his weie° softe;°   *way / gently*
      No wonder thogh he siketh° ofte.   *sighs*
      Bot as an oule° fleth° by nyhte   *owl / flies*
      Out of alle othre briddes syhte,°   *sight*
      Riht so° this knyht on daies brode° *Just so / in broad daylight*
1730 In clos° him hield, and schop° his rode°   *hiding / arranged / ride*
      On nyhtes time, til the tyde°   *time*
      That he cam there° he wolde abide.   *there where*
      And prively° withoute noise   *secretly*
      He bringth this foule grete coise°   *hag (lit., rump, thigh)*
1735 To his castell in such a wise°   *way*
      That noman myhte hire schappe° avise,°   *form / discern*
      Til sche into the chambre cam:
      Wher he his prive conseil° nam°   *private counsel / took*
      Of suche men as he most troste,°   *trusted*
1740 And tolde hem that he nedes moste°   *needs must*
      This beste° wedde to his wif,   *beast*
      For elles hadde he lost his lif.
         The prive° wommen were asent,°   *confidential / sent for*
      That scholden ben of his assent.
1745 Hire ragges thei anon of drawe,°   *take off*
      And, as it was that time lawe,
      She hadde bath, sche hadde reste,
      And was arraied to the beste;
      Bot with no craft of combes brode°   *wide combs*
1750 Thei myhte hire hore lockes schode,°   *part*
      And sche ne wolde noght be schore°   *shorn*
      For no conseil;° and thei therfore,   *On anyone's advice*
      With such atyr° as tho° was used,   *attire / then*
      Ordeinen° that it was excused,   *Ordained*
1755 And hid so crafteliche° aboute,   *skillfully*
      That noman myhte sen hem oute.° *discern them (the locks of her hair)*
      Bot when sche was fulliche arraied
      And hire atyr was al assaied,°   *examined, inspected*

Tho was sche foulere on to se;°   *fouler to look on*
1760 Bot yit° it may non other° be,   *yet / not otherwise*
Thei were wedded in the nyht.
So wo begon° was nevere knyht   *woebegone*
As he was thanne of mariage.
And sche began to pleie° and rage,°   *play / carry on wantonly, foolishly*
1765 As who° seith, I am wel ynowh;°   *Like one who / happy enough*
Bot he thereof nothing ne° lowh,°   *not at all / laughed*
For° sche tok thanne chiere on honde°   *So / became more cheerful*
And clepeth° him hire housebonde,   *calls*
And seith, "My lord, go we to bedde,
1770 For I to that entente° wedde,   *for that reason*
That thou schalt be my worldes blisse";
And profreth° him with that to kisse,   *proffers*
As° sche a lusti° lady were.   *As if / jolly*
His body myhte wel be there,
1775 Bot as of° thoght and of memoire°   *for / memory*
His herte was in purgatoire.°   *purgatory*
Bot yit for strengthe of matrimoine
He myhte make non essoine,°   *excuse*
That he ne mot algates plie°   *could not in any way comply*
1780 To gon to bedde of° compaignie.   *in*
And whan thei were abedde naked,
Withoute slep he was awaked;°   *Sleepless, he lay awake*
He torneth on that other side,
For that he wolde hise yhen° hyde   *eyes*
1785 Fro lokynge on that foule wyht.°   *creature*
The chambre was al full of lyht,
The courtins were of cendal° thinne;   *a kind of silk*
This newe bryd° which lay withinne,   *bride*
Thogh it be noght with his acord,
1790 In armes sche beclipte° hire lord,   *embraced*
And preide,° as° he was torned fro,°   *begged / since / away*
He wolde him torne ayeinward° tho;   *around*
"For now," sche seith, "we ben bothe on."°   *one*
And he lay stille as eny ston,
1795 Bot evere in on° sche spak and preide,   *continually*
And bad him thenke on that° he seide,   *what*
Whan that he tok hire be the hond.
   He herde and understod the bond,
How he was set to his penance,
1800 And as it were a man in trance
He torneth him al sodeinly,°   *suddenly*
And syh° a lady lay him by   *saw*
Of eyhtetiene wynter age,°   *i.e., eighteen years old*
Which was the faireste of visage°   *appearance*
1805 That evere in al this world he syh.
And as he wolde have take hire nyh,°   *nigh, close*
Sche put hire hand and be his leve°   *by his leave, with his permission*

Besoghte him that he wolde leve,°   *leave off*
And seith that forto wynne or lese°   *lose*
1810 He mot on of tuo thinges chese:°   *choose*
Wher° he wol have hire such on nyht,°   *Whether / at night*
Or elles upon daies lyht,°   *by day's light*
For he schal noght have bothe tuo.
And he began to sorwe tho
1815 In many a wise, and caste his thoght,°   *pondered*
Bot for al that yit cowthe he noght°   *he didn't know how to*
Devise himself° which was the beste.   *Decide (for) himself*
And sche, that wolde his hertes reste,
Preith° that he scholde chese algate,°   *Begs / nevertheless*
1820 Til ate laste longe and late
He seide: "O ye my lyves hele,°   *health, prosperity*
Sey what you list° in my querele,°   *pleases you / on my behalf*
I not° what ansuere I schal yive;°   *know not / give*
Bot evere whil that I may live,
1825 I wol that ye be my maistresse,
For I can noght miselve gesse°   *guess, determine*
Which is the beste unto my chois.
Thus grante I yow myn hole vois:°   *my whole voice, my full assent*
Ches for ous bothen,° I you preie,   *both*
1830 And what as evere that ye seie,
Riht as ye wole,° so wol I."   *Just as you wish*
     "Mi lord," sche seide, "grant merci,°   *many thanks*
For of this word that ye now sein,°   *say*
That ye have made me soverein,
1835 Mi destine° is overpassed,°   *destiny, fate / overcome*
That° nevere hierafter schal be lassed°   *So that / lessened*
Mi beaute, which that I now have,
Til I be take into my grave;
Bot nyht and day as I am now
1840 I schal alwey be such to yow.
The kinges dowhter of Cizile°   *Sicily*
I am, and fell bot siththe awhile,°   *it happened but a while ago*
As I was with my fader late,°   *recently*
That my stepmoder for an hate,°   *hatred*
1845 Which toward me sche hath begonne,°   *established, nurtured*
Forschop me,° til I hadde wonne   *Changed my shape*
The love and sovereinete
Of what knyht that in his degre
Alle othre passeth of good name.
1850 And, as men sein,° ye ben the same;   *say*
The dede proeveth it is so—
Thus am I youres evermo."
Tho was plesance° and joye ynowh,°   *delight / enough*
Echon° with other pleide° and lowh;°   *Each one / played / laughed*
1855 Thei live longe and wel thei ferde,°   *fared*
And clerkes that this chance° herde   *happening, story*

Thei writen it in evidence,
To teche how that obedience
Mai wel fortune° a man to love   *bring about*
1860 And sette him in his lust above,°   *give him happiness, delight*
As it befell unto this knyht.
    Forthi,° my Sone, if thou do ryht,   *Therefore*
Thou schalt unto thi love obeie,
And folwe hir will be alle weie.°   *in all ways*
1865   Min holy fader, so I wile:
For ye have told me such a skile°   *reason*
Of° this ensample° now tofore,°   *By / example / foregoing*
That I schal evermo therfore
Hierafterward myn observance
1870 To love and to his obeissance°   *obedience*
The betre kepe.

* * *

The Friar's Prologue and Tale

Many analogues to the *Friar's Tale* exist in many countries of Europe, not only from the Middle Ages but from later centuries as well. All of them feature an evil protagonist who meets and converses with a devil; the protagonist then encounters someone he has wronged, one whose heartfelt curse permits the devil to seize the evildoer. The story functioned as an illustrative moral tale or exemplum and appears both in medieval sermons and in collections of exempla. We print one of the closest analogues to Chaucer's version, from a sermon by Robert Rypon, an English Benedictine monk, probably composed around the turn of the fifteenth century.

ROBERT RYPON

A Greedy Bailiff†

* * * Thirdly, in the first main part [of this sermon], it remains to say in what way sin is observed in the devil. But some good men and women might perhaps dislike hearing the devil named. But it should be noted that there are two ways to speak about the devil, one of which is pleasing to him and the other displeasing. They displease him who preach about and expose the evils that he inflicts upon mankind so that these can be avoided. But those who name the name of the one whose naming pleases him, either by cursing out of negligence or rancor or in conjurations and such, give him pleasure with their speech, and more often than it is sought, the devil is permitted to carry out such curses and oaths.

So it is told of a certain bailiff, who in collecting rents for his lord was excessively greedy and eager for his own profit, being less merciful to the poor in particular. One day as he was riding to a certain village because of his duties, it happened that the devil in the form of a young man became his companion on his journey. The devil asked him, "Where are you going?", and he replied, "To the next village, on the business of my lord." The devil asked, "Is it true that you wish to gain for yourself and for your lord as much as you can and to take whatever they might wish to give to you?" The bailiff answered, "Yes, so I wish, if the gift is free." "Good," the devil said to him; "you do justly." "And

---

† Translated for this Norton Critical Edition by Peter Nicholson. For the Latin original and a more literal translation see Professor Nicholson's chapter on analogues to the *Friar's Tale* in *Sources and Analogues of The Canterbury Tales, Vol. I*, ed. Robert M. Correale and Mary Hamel (Cambridge: D. S. Brewer, 2002), pp. 87–99.

who are you?" the bailiff asked, "and where do you come from?" "I," said his companion, "am the devil, and I go about for my profit just as you do for yours and for yours lord's. And I too do not wish to take just anything that men might give to me, but only what they give me freely with heart and will will I accept." "You do most justly," the bailiff replied. Going on together, they approached the village, and they saw coming towards them some nearly untamed oxen pulling a plough, and since they were going more often crookedly and off the track, the farmer commended them to the devil. "Here," said the bailiff; "these are yours." "No," was the response, "because they are not given from the heart." Then coming into the village, they heard a baby cry, and the angry mother, not able to calm it down, said, "Be quiet or let the devil have you!" The bailiff said, "This is yours." The devil answered, "Not at all, because she has no wish to give up her child." Finally reaching the edge of the village, they saw a poor widow whose only cow the bailiff had seized the day before, and when she saw the bailiff, she fell on her knees and stretched out her hands and cried, "To all the devils of hell I commend you!" Then said the devil, "Surely this one is mine, because it is given to me sincerely. And so I wish to have you." And he led the bailiff that he had received off to hell.

    This story, though partly humorous, also provides a warning against certain evils. For it teaches first that one should not name the devil out of negligence or rancor, and second, that one should never commend anything to him, for such an offer might be carried out. Third, it teaches that the officers of lords should not be too greedy, and fourth, that they should do no wrong to the poor or to others either by harming their persons or extorting their goods, lest perhaps it happen to them in the end as it happened to this bailiff.

The Clerk's Prologue and Tale

The *Clerk's Tale* is a close translation of Petrarch's Latin version of the story of Griselda, although Chaucer also relied on a French translation of Petrarch as well. Petrarch had expanded the story from the final tale of Boccaccio's *Decameron*, and his narrative became highly popular in the late fourteenth century. Petrarch wrote to Boccaccio about his interest in the story and also recorded the responses of some friends. Further evidence of medieval reaction to it can be found in the comments of an anonymous Parisian citizen (probably like the Franklin in social status) who included a French translation of the tale in a book that he wrote for his fifteen-year-old bride to instruct her in the duties of a good wife.

GIOVANNI BOCCACCIO

From the *Decameron*, Tenth Day, Tenth Tale†

The marquis of Saluzzo, by the requests of his vassals, is urged to take a wife, and in order to have his own way in the matter, he picks the daughter of a peasant from whom he has two children; he pretends to her that he has had them killed; then, under the pretense that she has displeased him, he pretends to have taken another wife, and has their own daughter brought into the house as if she were his new wife once he has his real wife driven out in nothing more than her shift; after he discovers that she has patiently endured it all, he brings her back home, more beloved than ever, shows their grown children to her, and honors her, and has others honor her, as the marchioness.

* * *

A long time ago, among the various marquises of Saluzzo, there was the first-born son of the family, a young man named Gualtieri who, having no wife or children, spent his time doing nothing but hawking and hunting, and never thought of taking a wife or of having children—and this was very wise on his part. This did not please his vassals, and they begged him on many an occasion to take a wife so that he would not be without an heir and they left without a master; they offered to find him a wife born of the kind of mother and father that might give him good expectations of her and who would make him happy. To this Gualtieri answered:

† From *The Decameron*, ed. and trans. Mark Musa and Peter E. Bondanella (New York: W. W. Norton & Company, 1977), pp. 133–42. Copyright © 1982 by Mark Musa and Peter Bondanella. Reprinted by permission of W. W. Norton & Company, Inc. With this story—the one hundredth—the tale-telling ends, and the young people return to Florence. See the tenth-day conclusion, pp. 325–26.

"My friends, you are urging me to do something that I was determined never to do, for you know how difficult it is to find a woman with a suitable character, and how plentiful is the opposite kind of woman, and what a wretched life a man would lead married to a wife that is not suitable to him. And to say that you can judge the character of a daughter by examining those of her father and mother is ridiculous (which is the basis of your argument that you can find a wife to please me), for I do not believe that you can come to know all the secrets of the father or mother; and even if you did, a daughter is often unlike her father and mother. But since you wish to tie me up with these chains, I will do as you request; and so that I shall have only myself to blame if things turn out badly, I want to be the one who chooses her; and I tell you now that if she is not honored by you as your lady—no matter whom I choose—you will learn to your great displeasure how serious a matter it was to compel me with your requests to take a wife against my will!"

His worthy men replied that they would be happy if he would only choose a wife. For some time Gualtieri had been pleased by the manners of a poor young girl who lived in a village near his home, and since she seemed very beautiful to him, he thought that life with her could be quite pleasant; so, without looking any further, he decided to marry her, and he sent for her father, who was extremely poor, and made arrangements with him to take her as his wife. After this was done, Gualtieri called all his friends in the area together and said to them:

"My friends, you wished and continue to wish that I take a wife, and I am ready to do this, but I do so more to please you than to satisfy any desire of mine to have a wife. You know what you promised me: to honor happily anyone I chose for your lady; therefore, the time has come for me to keep my promise to you, and for you to do the same for me. I have found a young girl after my own heart, very near here, whom I intend to take as my wife and bring home in a few days; so, make sure that the wedding celebrations are splendid and that you receive her honorably, so that I may consider myself as content with your promise as you are with mine."

The good men all happily replied that this pleased them very much and that, whoever she was, they would treat her as their lady and honor her in every way they could; and soon after this, they all set about preparing for a big, beautiful, and happy celebration, and Gualtieri did the same. He had a great and sumptuous wedding feast prepared, and he invited his friends and relatives and the great lords and many others from the surrounding countryside; and besides this, he had beautiful and expensive dresses cut out and tailored to fit a young girl who he felt was about the same size as the young girl he had decided to marry; he also saw to it that girdles and rings were purchased and a rich, handsome crown, and everything else a new bride might require. When the day set for the wedding arrived, Gualtieri mounted his horse at about the middle of tierce, and all those who had come to honor him did the same; when all was arranged, he said:

"My lords, it is time to fetch the new bride."

Setting out on the road with the entire company, they arrived at the little village; they came to the house of the girl's father and found her returning from the well in great haste in order to be able to see the arrival of Gualtieri's bride in time with the other women; when Gualtieri saw her, he called her by name—that is, Griselda—and asked her where her father was; to this she replied bashfully:

"My lord, he is in the house."

Then Gualtieri dismounted and ordered all his men to wait for him; alone, he entered that wretched house, and there he found Griselda's father, who was called Giannucolo, and he said to him:

"I have come to marry Griselda, but before I do, I should like to ask her some things in your presence."

And he asked her, if he were to marry her, would she always try to please him, and would she never become angry over anything he said or did, and if she would always be obedient, and many other similar questions—to all of these she replied that she would. Then Gualtieri took her by the hand, led her outside, and in the presence of his entire company and all others present, he had her stripped naked and the garments he had had prepared for her brought forward; then he immediately had her dress and put on her shoes, and upon her hair—as disheveled as it was—he had a crown placed; then, while everyone was marveling at the sight, he announced:

"My lords, this is the lady I intend to be my wife, if she will have me as her husband."

And then, turning to Griselda who was standing there blushing and perplexed, he asked her:

"Griselda, do you take me for your husband?"

To this she answered: "Yes, my lord."

And he replied: "And I take you for my wife."

In the presence of them all he married her; then he had her set upon a palfrey and he led her with an honorable company to his home. The wedding feast was great and sumptuous, and the celebration was no different from what it might have been if he had married the daughter of the king of France. The young bride seemed to have changed her soul and ways along with her garments: she was, as we have already said, beautiful in body and face, and as she was beautiful before, she became even more pleasing, attractive, and well-mannered, so that she seemed to be not the shepherdess daughter of Giannucolo but rather the daughter of some noble lord, a fact that amazed everyone who had known her before; moreover, she was so obedient and indulgent to her husband that he considered himself the happiest and the most satisfied man on earth, and she was also so gracious and kind towards her husband's subjects that there was no one who was more beloved or willingly honored than she was; in fact, everyone prayed for her welfare, her prosperity, and her further success. Whereas everyone used to say that Gualtieri had acted unwisely in taking her as his wife, they now declared that he was the wisest and the cleverest man in the world, for none other than he could have ever recognized her noble character hidden under her rude garments and her peasant dress.

In short, she knew how to comport herself in such a manner that before long, not only in her husband's marquisate but everywhere, her virtue and her good deeds became the topic of discussion, and for anything that had been said against her husband when he married her, she now caused the opposite to be said. Not long after she had come to live with Gualtieri, she became pregnant, and in the course of time she gave birth to a daughter, which gave Gualtieri much cause for rejoicing. But shortly afterwards, a new thought entered his mind: he wished to test her patience with a long trial and intolerable proofs. First, he offended her with harsh words, pretending to be angry and saying that his vassals were very unhappy over her because of her low birth and especially now that they saw her bear children; they were most unhappy over the daughter that had been born and did nothing but mutter about it. When the lady heard these words, without changing her expression or her good intentions in any way, she answered:

"My lord, do with me what you believe is best for your honor and your happiness, and I shall be completely happy, for I realize that I am of lower birth than they and am not worthy of this honor which your courtliness has bestowed upon me."

This reply was very gratifying to Gualtieri, for he realized that she had not become in any way haughty because of the respect which he or others had paid her. A short time later, after he had told his wife in vague terms that his subjects could not tolerate the daughter to whom she had given birth, he spoke to one of her servants and sent him to her, and with a very sad expression, he said to her:

"My lady, since I do not wish to die, I must do what my lord commands. He has commanded me to take this daughter of yours and to . . ." And he could say no more.

When the lady heard these words and saw her servant's face, she remembered what her husband had said to her and understood that her servant had been ordered to murder the child; therefore, she quickly took the girl from the cradle, kissed her and blessed her, and although she felt a great pain in her heart, without changing her expression she placed her in her servant's arms and said to him:

"There, do exactly what your lord and mine has ordered you to do; but do not abandon her body to be devoured by the beasts and birds unless he has ordered you to do so."

The servant took the child and told Gualtieri what the lady had said, and he was amazed at her perseverance; then he sent the servant with his daughter to one of his relatives in Bologna, begging her to raise and educate the girl carefully but without ever telling whose daughter she was. Shortly after this, the lady became pregnant again, and in time she gave birth to a male child, which pleased Gualtieri very much; but what he had already done did not satisfy him, and he wounded the lady with even a greater hurt, telling her one day in a fit of feigned anger:

"Lady, since you bore me this male child, I have not been able to live with my vassals, for they bitterly complain about a grandson of Giannucolo's having to be their lord after I am gone; because of this, I am very much afraid that unless I want to be driven out, I must do what I did the other time, and must eventually abandon you and take another wife."

The lady listened to him patiently and made no other reply than this:

"My lord, think only of making yourself happy and of satisfying your desires and do not worry about me at all, for nothing pleases me more than to see you contented."

After a few days, Gualtieri sent for his son in the same way he had sent for his daughter, and he again pretended to have the child killed, actually sending him to be raised in Bologna as he had his daughter; and the lady's face and words were no different from what they were when her daughter had been taken, and Gualtieri was greatly amazed at this and remarked to himself that no other woman could do what she had done: if he had not seen for himself how extremely fond she was of her children as long as they found favor in his sight, he might have believed that she acted as she did in order to be free of them, but he realized that she was doing it out of obedience.

His subjects, believing he had killed his children, criticized him bitterly and regarded him as a cruel man, and they had the greatest of compassion for the lady; but she never said anything to the women with whom she mourned the deaths of her children. Then, not many years after the birth of their daughter, Gualtieri felt it was time to put his wife's patience to the ultimate test: he told many of his vassals that he could no longer bear having Griselda as a wife and that he realized he had acted badly and impetuously when he had taken her for his wife, and that he was going to do everything possible to procure a dispensation from the pope so that he could marry another woman and abandon Griselda; he was reprimanded for this by many of his good men, but to them he answered that it was fitting that this be done.

When the lady heard about these matters and it appeared to her that she would be returning to her father's house (perhaps even to guard the sheep as she had previously done) and that she would have to bear witness to another woman possessing the man she loved, she grieved most bitterly; but yet, as with the other injuries of Fortune which she had suffered, she determined to bear this one too with a stern countenance. Not long afterwards, Gualtieri had forged letters sent from Rome, and he showed them to his subjects, pretending that in these letters the pope had granted him the dispensation to take another wife and to abandon Griselda; and so, having his wife brought before him, in the presence of many people he said to her:

"Lady, because of a dispensation which I have received from the pope, I am able to take another wife and to abandon you; and since my ancestors were great noblemen and lords of these regions while yours have always been peasants, I wish you to be my wife no longer and to return to Giannucolo's home with the dowry that you brought me, and I shall then bring home another more suitable wife, whom I have already found."

When the lady heard these words, she managed to hold back her tears only with the greatest of effort (something quite unnatural for a woman), and she replied:

"My lord, I have always realized that my lowly origins were not suitable to your nobility in any respect, and the position I have held with you, I always recognized as having come from God and yourself; I never made it mine or considered it given to me—I always kept it as if it were a loan; if you wish to have it back again, it must please me (as it does) to return it to you: here is your ring with which you married me—take it. You order me to take back with me the dowry I brought you, and to do this no accounting on your part, nor any purse or beast of burden, will be necessary, for I have not forgotten that you received me naked; and if you judge it proper that this body which bore your children should be seen by everyone, I shall leave naked; but I beg you, in the name of my virginity which I brought here and which I cannot take with me, that you at least allow me to carry away with me a single shift in addition to my dowry."

Gualtieri, who felt closer to tears than anyone else there, stood nevertheless with a stern face and said:

"You may take a shift."

Many of those present begged him to give her a dress, so that this woman who had been his wife for more than thirteen years would not be seen leaving his home so impoverished and in such disgrace as to leave clad only in a shift; but their entreaties were in vain, and in her shift, without shoes or anything on her head, the lady commended him to God, left his house, and returned to her father, accompanied by the tears and the weeping of all those who witnessed her departure.

Giannucolo, who had never believed that Gualtieri would keep his daughter as his wife, and who had been expecting this to happen any day, had kept the clothes that she had taken off that morning when Gualtieri married her; he gave them back to her, and she put them on, and began doing the menial tasks in her father's house as she had once been accustomed to doing, suffering the savage assaults of a hostile fortune with a brave spirit.

After Gualtieri had done this, he led his vassals to believe that he had chosen a daughter of one of the counts of Panago for his new wife; and as he was making great preparations for the wedding, he sent for Griselda to come to him, and when she arrived he said to her:

"I am bringing home the lady I have recently chosen as my wife, and I intend to honor her at her first arrival; you know that I have no women in my home who know how to prepare the bedchambers or to do the many chores that are required by such a grand celebration; you understand these matters better than anyone in the house; therefore, I want you to arrange everything: invite those ladies whom you think should be invited, and receive them as if you were the lady of the house; then when the wedding is over, you can return to your home."

These words were like a dagger in Griselda's heart, for she had not yet been able to extinguish the love that she bore for him (as she had learned to do without her good fortune), and she answered:

"My lord, I am ready and prepared."

And so in a coarse, peasant dress she entered that house which a short time before she had left dressed only in a shift, and she began to clean and arrange the bedchambers, to put out hangings and ornamental tapestries on the walls, to make ready the kitchen, and to put her hands to everything, just as if she were a little servant girl in the house; and she never rested until she had organized and arranged everything as it should be. After this, she had invitations sent in Gualtieri's name to all the ladies of the region and then waited for the celebration; when the day of the wedding came, in the poor clothes she had on and with a pleasant expression on her face and a noble manner, she courageously received all the ladies who arrived for the celebration.

Gualtieri had had her children carefully raised in Bologna by one of his relatives who had married into the family of the counts of Panago; the daughter was already twelve years of age and the most beautiful thing anyone had ever seen, and the boy was already six; he sent a message to his relative in Bologna, requesting him to be so kind as to come to Saluzzo with his daughter and his son, and to organize a handsome and honorable retinue to accompany them, and not to reveal her identity to anyone but to tell them only that he was bringing the girl as Gualtieri's bride.

The nobleman did what the marquis had asked him: he set out, and after several days he arrived at Saluzzo at about suppertime with the young girl, her brother, and a noble company, and there he found all the peasants and many other people from the surrounding area waiting to see Gualtieri's new bride. She was received by the ladies and then taken to the hall where the tables were set, where Griselda, dressed as she was, met her cheerfully and said to her:

"Welcome, my lady!"

Many of the women had begged Gualtieri (but in vain) either to allow Griselda to stay in another room or that she be permitted to wear some of the clothing that had once been hers so that she would not have to meet his guests in such clothing. Everyone sat down at the table and was served, and they all stared at the young girl and agreed that Gualtieri had made a good exchange; but it was Griselda who praised her and her little brother more than any of the others did.

Gualtieri finally felt that he had seen as much evidence as he needed to of his wife's patience; he observed that the new arrangement had not changed Griselda one bit, and since he was certain that her attitude was not due to stupidity, for he knew her to be very wise, he felt that it was time to remove her from the bitterness which he felt she must be concealing under her impassive face; so, he had her brought to him, and in the presence of everyone, he said to her with a smile:

"What do you think of my new bride?"

"My lord," replied Griselda, "she seems very beautiful to me; and if she is as wise as she is beautiful (which I believe to be the case), I have no doubt that you will live with her as the happiest lord in the world; but I beg you as strongly as I can not to inflict those wounds upon her which you inflicted upon the other woman who was once your wife, for I believe that she could scarcely endure them, both because she is younger and because she has been brought up in a more delicate fashion, while the other woman was used to continuous hardships from the time she was a little girl."

When Gualtieri saw that she firmly believed the girl was to be his wife, yet in spite of this said nothing but good about her, he made her sit beside him, and he said:

"Griselda, it is time now for you to reap the fruit of your long patience, and it is time for those who have considered me cruel, unjust, and bestial to realize that what I have done was directed toward a preestablished goal, for I wanted to teach you how to be a wife, to show these people how to know such a wife and how to choose and keep one, and to acquire for myself lasting tranquility for as long as I was to live with you; when I went to take you for my wife, I greatly feared that this tranquility I cherished would be lost, and so, to test you, I submitted you to the pains and trials you have known. But since I have never known you to depart from my wishes in either word or deed, and since I now believe I shall receive from you that happiness which I always desired, I intend to return to you now what I took from you for a long time and to soothe with the greatest of delight the wounds that I inflicted upon you; therefore, with a happy heart receive this girl, whom you suppose to be my bride, and her brother as your very own children and mine; they are the ones you and many others have long thought I had brutally murdered; and I am your husband, who loves you more than all else, for I believe I can boast that no other man exists who could be so happy with his wife as I am."

After he said this, he embraced and kissed her, and she was weeping for joy; they arose and together went over to their daughter who was listening in amazement to these new developments; both of them tenderly embraced first the girl and then her brother, thus dispelling their confusion as well as that of many others who were present. The ladies arose from the tables most happily, and they went with Griselda to her bedchamber, and with a more auspicious view of her future, they took off her old clothes and dressed her in one of her noble garments, and then they led her back into the hall as the lady of the house, which she had, nonetheless, appeared to be even in her tattered rags.

Everyone was most delighted about how everything had turned out, and Griselda with her husband and children celebrated in great style, with the joy and feasting increasing over a period of several days; and Gualtieri was judged to be the wisest of men (although the tests to which he had subjected his wife were regarded as harsh and intolerable) and Griselda the wisest of them all.

The count of Panago returned to Bologna several days later, and Gualtieri took Giannucolo away from his work, setting him up as his father-in-law in such a way that he lived the rest of his life honorably and most happily. After giving their daughter in marriage to a noble-man, Gualtieri lived a long and happy life with Griselda, always honor-ing her as much as he could.

What more can be said here, except that godlike spirits do some-times rain down from heaven into poor homes, just as those more suited to governing pigs than to ruling over men make their appear-ances in royal palaces. Who besides Griselda could have endured the severe and unheard-of trials that Gualtieri imposed upon her and re-mained with a not only tearless but happy face? It might have served Gualtieri right if he had run into the kind of woman who, once driven out of her home in nothing but a shift, would have allowed another man to shake her up to the point of getting herself a nice-looking dress out of the affair!

* * *

FRANCIS PETRARCH

The Story of Griselda (*Historia Griseldis*)†

In the chain of the Apennines, in the west of Italy, stands Mount Viso, a very lofty mountain, whose summit towers above the clouds and rises into the bright upper air. It is a mountain notable in its own na-ture, but most notable as the source of the Po, which rises from a small spring upon the mountain's side, bends slightly toward the east, and presently, swollen with abundant tributaries, becomes, though its downward course has been but brief, not only one of the greatest of streams but, as Vergil called it, the king of rivers. Through Liguria its raging waters cut their way, and then, bounding Aemilia and Flaminia and Venetia, it empties at last into the Adriatic sea, through many mighty mouths. Now that part of these lands, of which I spoke first, is sunny and delightful, as much for the hills which run through it and the mountains which hem it in, as for its grateful plain. From the foot of the mountains beneath which it lies, it derives its name; and it has many famous cities and towns. Among others, at the very foot of Mount Viso, is the land of Saluzzo, thick with villages and castles. It is ruled over by noble marquises, the first and greatest of whom, accord-ing to tradition, was a certain Walter, to whom the direction of his own estates and of all the land pertained. He was a man blooming with youth and beauty, as noble in his ways as in his birth; marked

† From Robert Dudley French, *A Chaucer Handbook*, 2/e, © 1947, pp. 291–311. Reprinted by permission of Prentice-Hall, Inc., Englewood Cliffs, New Jersey. French's translation, origi-nally made from a much earlier text of Petrarch's story, was changed in his second edition to reflect the more accurate version edited by J. Burke Severs, which appears both in *Sources and Analogues of Chaucer's* Canterbury Tales, ed. W. F. Bryan and Germaine Dempster (Chicago: U of Chicago P, 1941), pp. 296–330, and in Severs's own *The Literary Relation-ships of Chaucer's* Clerkes Tale (New Haven: Yale UP, 1942). As the letters on pp. 417–20 make clear, Petrarch translated and adapted Boccaccio's story in 1373. New texts and trans-lations of the chief sources of the *Clerk's Tale*, by Thomas J. Farrell and Amy W. Goodwin, are available in *Sources and Analogues of the Canterbury Tales, Vol. I*, ed. Robert M. Correale and Mary Hamel (Cambridge: D. S. Brewer, 2002), pp. 101–67.

out, in short, for leadership in all things,—save that he was so contented with his present lot that he took very little care for the future. Devoted to hunting and fowling, he so applied himself to these arts that he neglected almost all else; and—what his subjects bore most ill—he shrank even from a hint of marriage. When they had borne this for some time in silence, at length they came to him in a company; and one of their number, who had authority and eloquence above the rest and was on more familiar terms with his overlord, said to him, "Noble Marquis, your kindness gives us such boldness that we come separately to talk with you, with devoted trust, as often as occasion demands, and that now my voice conveys to your ears the silent wishes of us all; not because I have any especial privilege, unless it be that you have shown by many signs that you hold me dear among the others. Although all your ways, then, justly give us pleasure and always have, so that we count ourselves happy in such an overlord, there is one thing in which we should assuredly be the happiest of all men round about, if you would consent to it and show yourself susceptible to our entreaties; and that is, that you should take thought of marriage and bow your neck, free and imperious though it be, to the lawful yoke; and that you should do this as soon as possible. For the swift days fly by, and although you are in the flower of your youth, nevertheless silent old age follows hard upon that flower, and death itself is very near to any age. To none is immunity against this tribute given, and all alike must die; and just as that is certain, so is it uncertain when it will come to pass. Give ear, therefore, we pray you, to the entreaties of those who have never refused to do your bidding. You may leave the selection of a wife to our care, for we shall procure you such an one as shall be truly worthy of you, and sprung of so high a lineage that you may have the best hope of her. Free all your subjects, we beseech you, of the grievous apprehension that if anything incident to our mortal lot should happen to you, you would go leaving no successor to yourself, and they would remain deprived of a leader such as their hearts crave."

Their loyal entreaties touched the man's heart, and he made answer: "My friends, you constrain me to that which never entered my thoughts. I have had pleasure in complete liberty, a thing which is rare in marriage. Nevertheless, I willingly submit to the wishes of my subjects, trusting in your prudence and your devotion. But I release you from the task, which you have offered to assume, of finding me a wife. That task I lay on my own shoulders. For what benefit can the distinction of one confer upon another? Right often, children are all unlike their parents. Whatever is good in a man comes not from another, but from God. As I entrust to Him all my welfare, so would I entrust to Him the outcome of my marriage, hoping for His accustomed mercy. He will find for me that which shall be expedient for my peace and safety. And so, since you are resolved that I should take a wife, so much, in all good faith, I promise you; and for my part, I will neither frustrate nor delay your wishes. One promise, in your turn, you must make and keep: that whosoever the wife may be whom I shall choose, you will yield her the highest honor and veneration; and let there be none among you who ever shall dispute or complain of my decision. Yours it was that I, the freest of all the men you have known, have submitted to the yoke of marriage; let it be mine to choose that yoke; and whoever my wife may be, let her be your mistress, as if she were the daughter of a prince of Rome."

Like men who thought it hardly possible that they should see the wished-for day of the nuptials, they promised with one accord and gladly that they should be found in nothing wanting; and with eager alacrity they received the edict from their master, directing that the most magnificent preparations be made for a certain day. So they withdrew from conference; and the marquis, on his part, laid care upon his servants for the nuptials and gave public notice of the day.

Not far from the palace, there was a village, of few and needy inhabitants, one of whom, the poorest of all, was named Janicola. But as the grace of Heaven sometimes visits the hovels of the poor, it chanced that he had an only daughter, by name Griseldis, remarkable for the beauty of her body, but of so beautiful a character and spirit that no one excelled her. Reared in a frugal way of living and always in the direst poverty, unconscious of any want, she had learned to cherish no soft, no childish thoughts; but the vigor of manhood and the wisdom of age lay hidden in her maiden bosom. Cherishing her father's age with ineffable love, she tended his few sheep, and as she did it, wore her fingers away on the distaff. Then, returning home, she would prepare the little herbs and victuals suited to their fortune and make ready the rude bedchamber. In her narrow station, in fine, she discharged all the offices of filial obedience and affection. Walter, passing often by that way, had sometimes cast his eyes upon this little maid, not with the lust of youth, but with the sober thoughts of an older man; and his swift intuition had perceived in her a virtue, beyond her sex and age, which the obscurity of her condition concealed from the eyes of the common throng. Hence it came about that he decided, at one and the same time, to take a wife—which he had never before wished to do—and to have this woman and no other.

The day of the nuptials drew on, but no one knew whence the bride should come, and there was no one who did not wonder. Walter himself, in the meanwhile, was buying golden rings and coronets and girdles, and was having rich garments and shoes and all necessities of this kind made to the measure of another girl, who was very like Griseldis in stature. The longed-for day had come, and since not a word about the bride was to be heard, the universal bewilderment had risen very high. The hour of the feast arrived; and already, the whole house was in a great ferment of preparation. Then Walter came out of the castle, as if he were setting out to meet his approaching bride, and a throng of noble men and matrons followed in his train.

Griseldis, ignorant of all the preparations which were being made on her account, had performed what was to be done about her home; and now, with water from the distant well, she was crossing the threshold of her father's house, in order that, free from other duties, she might hasten, with the girls who were her comrades, to see her master's bride. Then Walter, absorbed in his own thoughts, drew near and, calling her by name, asked her where her father was; and when she had replied, reverently and humbly, that he was within, "Bid him," he said, "come hither."

When the old man was come, Walter took him by the hand and drew him a little aside; and lowering his voice, he said, "Janicola, I know that I am dear to you. I have known you for my faithful liege- man, and I believe you wish whatever suits my pleasure. One thing in particular, however, I should like to know: whether you would take me, whom you have as your master, for a son-in-law, giving me your daughter as a wife?"

Stupefied at this unlooked-for matter, the old man went rigid. At length, hardly able to stammer out a few words, he replied, "It is my duty to wish or to deny nothing, save as it pleases you, who are my master." "Let us, then, go in alone," said the marquis, "that I may put certain questions to the girl herself in your presence." They entered the house, therefore, while the populace stood expectant and wonder- ing, and found the maiden busying herself about her father's service and abashed by the unexpected advent of so great a throng of strangers. Walter, approaching her, addressed her in these words: "It is your father's pleasure and mine that you shall be my wife. I believe that this will please you, too. But I have one thing to ask you: when that is done which shortly shall take place, will you be prepared, with consenting mind, to agree with me in all things; so that you dispute my wish in nothing, and permit me, with mind consenting, and with- out remonstrance of word or look, to do whatever I will with you?"

Trembling at this marvelous thing, the girl made answer: "I know myself unworthy, my lord, of so great an honor; but if it be your will, and if it be my destiny, I will never consciously cherish a thought, much less do anything, which might be contrary to your desires; nor will you do anything, even though you bid me die, which I shall bear ill."

"It is enough," said he; and so, leading her out before the throng, he showed her to the people, and said, "This is my wife, this is your lady; cherish her and love her; and if you hold me dear, hold her most dear of all." Then, lest she carry into her new home any relic of her former fortune, he commanded her to be stripped, and clad from head to heel with new garments; and this was done, reverently and swiftly, by ma- trons who stood around her and who embraced her each in turn. So this simple peasant girl, new clad, with her dishevelled tresses col- lected and made smooth, adorned with gems and coronet, was as it were suddenly transformed, so that the people hardly knew her. And Walter solemnly plighted her his troth with a precious ring, which he had brought with him for that purpose; and having placed her on a snow-white horse, he had her conducted to the palace, the populace accompanying her and rejoicing. In this way, the nuptials were cele- brated, and that most happy day was passed.

Shortly thereafter, so much did God's favor shine upon the lowly bride, it seemed she was reared and bred, not in a shepherd's cottage, but in the imperial court; and to all she became dear and venerable beyond belief. Even those who had known her from her birth could hardly be persuaded she was Janicola's daughter; such was the graciousness of her life and of her ways, the gravity and sweetness of her speech, by which she had bound the hearts of all the people to her with the bond of a great love. And already her name, heralded by frequent rumor, had spread abroad, not only within the confines of her fatherland, but through every neighboring province; so that many men and matrons, with eager desire, came flocking to see her. So, graced by a marriage, which, however humble, was distinguished and prosperous, Walter lived in the highest peace and honor at home; and abroad he was held in the highest esteem; and because he had so shrewdly discovered the remarkable virtue hidden under so much poverty, he was commonly held to be a very prudent man. Not only did his wife attend adroitly to those domestic matters which pertain to women; but when occasion demanded, in her husband's absence, she undertook state affairs, settling and composing the country's law-suits and disputes among the nobles, with such weighty opinions and so great a maturity and fairness of judgment, that all declared this woman had been sent down from heaven for the public weal.

Not long time had passed ere she became pregnant; and after she had held her subjects for a time in anxious expectation, at length she bore the fairest of daughters. Though they had preferred a son, nevertheless she made both her husband and her country happy by this proof of the fertility they longed for. In the meanwhile, it so happened, when his little daughter had been weaned, that Walter was seized with a desire more strange than laudable—so the more experienced may decide—to try more deeply the fidelity of his dear wife, which had been sufficiently made known by experience, and to test it again and again. Therefore, he called her alone into his chamber and addressed her thus, with troubled brow:

"You know, Griseldis—for I do not think that amid your present good fortune you have forgotten your former state—you know, I say, in what manner you came into this house. To me, indeed, you are dear enough and well beloved; but to my nobles, not so; especially since you have begun to bear children. For they take it most ill that they should submit to a low-born mistress. Since, therefore, I desire peace with them, I must follow another's judgment, not my own, in the case of your daughter, and do that which is most grievous to me. But I would never do it without letting you know, and I wish you to accommodate your will to mine and to show that obedience which you promised at the outset of our married life."

She listened without a protesting word or glance. "You are our master," she said, "and both this little girl and I are yours. Do, therefore, as you will with your own; for nothing can please you which would displease me. There is absolutely nothing which I wish to have or fear to lose, save you. This is fixed in the very center of my heart, and never, either by lapse of years or by death, will it be torn away. Anything can happen ere I shall change my mind."

Happy in her reply, but feigning sadness in his looks, he left her; and a little later, he sent to her one of his underlings, a most faithful man, whose services he was wont to use in his most weighty affairs, and whom he instructed in the task before him. The fellow, coming to Griseldis by night, said to her, "Spare me, my lady, and do not lay to my blame what I am forced to do. You are right knowing, and you understand what it is to be subject to a master; nor is the harsh necessity of obedience unknown to one endowed with so much sense, though inexperienced. I am bidden to take this little baby girl, and—" Here, breaking off his speech, he ceased, as if he would indicate his cruel business by his silence. Suspect was the reputation of the man, suspect his face, suspect the hour, suspect his words. By these tokens, she clearly knew her sweet daughter was to be killed; yet she shed no tear, she breathed no sigh,—a thing most hard, even for a nurse, much more so for a mother. But taking up the little girl, with tranquil brow, she looked at her a little, and kissing her, blessed her and made the sign of the Holy Cross upon her. Then she gave the child to the fellow, and said, "Go; and whatever our lord hath laid upon you, see that you perform it. One thing I beg of you: take care lest beasts or birds tear her little body; and this, only if no contrary orders have been laid upon you."

The fellow returned to his master and told him what he had said and how Griseldis had replied; and when he had given him his daughter, paternal pity touched the marquis to the heart. Nevertheless, he did not relax the rigor of his purpose. He ordered his slave to wrap the child in cloths, to place it in a wickerwork basket upon a beast of burden, and carry it, secretly and with all the diligence he could command, to Bologna, to Walter's sister, who had married the Count of Panago. He should hand the child over to her, to be cherished with maternal care, to be reared in gentle ways, and to be concealed, moreover, with so much care that no one could know whose daughter she was. The slave journeyed thither and fulfilled with care what had been laid upon him.

Walter, in the meanwhile, though he often studied his wife's face and words, never detected any sign of a change of feeling: equal alacrity and diligence, her accustomed complaisance, the same love, no sadness, no mention of her daughter! Never did the girl's name fall from her mother's lips, either by design or by chance. In this way, four years went by; and being again with child, behold she brought forth a most excellent son, a great delight to his father and all their friends. But when, after two years, this child had been weaned, the father fell back into his former caprice. And again he said to his wife, "Once before you have heard that my people bear our marriage ill, especially since they knew you capable of bearing children; but it has never been so bad as since you gave birth to a son. For they say—and the murmur of it comes often to my ears, 'So, when Walter dies, Janicola's grandson shall rule over us, and so noble a land will be subject to such a

master.' Each day many things of this tenor are current among my
people; and I, eager for peace and—to say sooth—fearing for myself,
am therefore moved to dispose of this infant as I disposed of his sister.
I tell you this beforehand, lest the unexpected and sudden grief disturb you."

To which she made answer: "I have said, and I say again, that I can
have no wishes save yours. In these children, indeed, I have no share,
beyond the pangs of labor. You are my master and theirs: use your
power over your own. Nor seek my consent; for when I entered your
house, as I put off my clothes, so I put off my wishes and desires, and
put on yours. Whatever you wish to do, therefore, about anything
whatsoever, that is what I wish, too. Nay, if I could foresee your future
wishes, I should begin beforehand, whatever it might be, to wish and
desire what you wish. Now I gladly follow your desire, which I cannot
anticipate. Suppose it pleased you that I should die, I would die gladly;
nor is there any other thing—not death itself—to equal our love."

Marvelling at the steadfastness of the woman, he took his departure, his face agitated with emotion; and straightway he sent to her
the servant whom he had sent before. The latter, with many a plea of
the necessity of obedience, and with many an entreaty for forgiveness,
if he had done or was doing her a wrong, demanded her child, as one
who is about to commit a monstrous crime. But she, with unchanged
mien, whatever might be passing in her mind, took up in her arms the
son who was so well beloved, not only by his mother but by everyone,
for the beauty of his body and his disposition; and she made upon him
the sign of the Cross, blessing him, as she had blessed her daughter,
clinging to him just a little while with her eyes, and bending down to
kiss him; but she gave absolutely no other sign of her grief. Then she
gave him to the fellow who had come to seek him, and she said, "Take
him, too, and do what you are bidden. But one thing I beg of you: that
if it can be done, you will protect the tender limbs of my beautiful
baby against the ravages of birds and beasts."

The man, returning to his master with these words of hers, drove
him to yet greater wonder, so that if he had not known her for the
most loving of mothers, he might have had some faint suspicion that
the strength of the woman came from a certain hardness of heart; but
while she was strongly attached to all that were hers, she loved no one
better than her husband. The servant was then bidden to set out for
Bologna and to take the boy where he had taken his sister.

These trials of conjugal affection and fidelity would have been sufficient for the most rigorous of husbands; but there are those who,
when once they have begun anything, do not cease; nay, rather, they
press on and cling to their purpose. Keeping his eyes upon his wife,
therefore, Walter watched continually for any change in her behavior
toward him, and he was not able to find any at all, save that she became each day more devoted and more obedient to his wishes; so that
it seemed there was but one mind between them, and that not common to them both, but, to say truth, the husband's alone; for the wife
had declared, as has been said, that she had no wishes of her own.

Little by little, an ugly rumor about Walter had begun to spread abroad; namely, that with savage and inhuman cruelty, out of regret and shame for his humble marriage, he had ordered his children slain; for neither did his children appear, nor had anyone heard where in the world they were. Wherefore, he who had once been a man of spotless reputation, dear to his people, had become in the eyes of many men infamous and hateful. Not on that account, however, was his stern purpose altered, but he persevered in the severity which he had assumed and in his harsh caprice of testing his wife. And so, when twelve years had passed since the birth of his daughter, he sent envoys to Rome to bring back thence documents bearing the appearance of a papal bull, which should cause the rumor to circulate among the people that license had been granted him by the Roman pontiff, with a view to his own peace and that of his people, to annul his first marriage and to take another wife; nor was it difficult, in fact, to convince those untutored Alpine folk of anything you pleased. When this rumor reached Griseldis, she was sad, I think; but as one who had made her decision, once and for all, about herself and her destiny, she stood unshaken, awaiting what should be decreed for her by him to whom she had submitted herself and all that was hers.

Walter had already sent to Bologna and had asked his kinsman to send him his children, spreading the story in every quarter that this maiden was to be Walter's bride. His kinsman faithfully performed these orders and set out upon his journey on the appointed day, bringing with him, amid a brilliant throng of noblemen, the young maiden, who was now of marriageable age, of excellent beauty, and adorned with magnificent attire; and with her he brought her brother, who was now in his seventh year.

Walter, in the meanwhile, with his accustomed inclination to try his wife, even to the heights of grief and shame, led her forth before the multitude and said, "I have been wont to take ample delight in our marriage, having regard for your character, not your lineage; but now, since I perceive that great place is always great servitude, it is not permitted me to do what any peasant may. My people compel me—and the Pope consents—to take another wife. Already my wife is on her way, and presently she will be here. Therefore, be of stout heart, and yielding your place to another, take back your dowry and return to your former home with equal mind. No good fortune lasts forever."

She made answer: "My lord, I have always known that there was no proportion between your greatness and my lowly station. I have never considered myself worthy to be—I will not say, your wife, but your servant; and in this house, in which you have made me mistress, I call God to witness that I have remained in spirit as a handmaid. For these years, therefore, that I have dwelt with you in honor far beyond my deserts, I give thanks to God and you. For the rest, I am ready, with good heart and peaceful mind, to return to my father's house, to pass my age and to die where I have passed my youth, always happy in the honorable estate of widowhood, since I have been the wife of such a man. I readily yield place to your new bride—and may her coming bring you joy!—and I will not take away any ill feeling from this place, where I was wont to live most happily, while it so pleased you. But as for my dowry, which you bid me take back with me, I see of what sort it is, and it has not been lost; for as I came to you long since, stripped at my father's threshold of all my clothes and clad in yours, I had no other dowry but nakedness and devotion. Lo, therefore, I strip off this dress and restore this ring, with which you wed me. And the other rings and finery, with which your gifts have enriched me to the point of envy, are in your chamber. Naked I came from my father's house, and naked shall I return again—save that I think it unseemly that this belly, in which the children you begot were shaped, should appear naked before the people. Wherefore, if it please you—but not other-wise—I pray and beseech you, as the price of the maidenhood which I brought hither and do not take hence, bid me keep one shift, out of those I have been wont to wear, that I may cover therewith the belly of her who was once your wife."

The tears welled into her husband's eyes, so that they could no longer be restrained; and so, turning his face aside, "Take your one shift," he said, and his voice trembled so that he could scarcely say it. So, weeping, he took his departure. Before them all, she stripped off her clothes, keeping upon her only her shift; and covered with that alone, she went forth before them with feet and head quite bare. Fol-lowed by many, who wept and railed at fortune, she alone dry-eyed and to be honored for her noble silence, returned to her father's house. The good man, who had always held his daughter's marriage in suspicion and had never allowed himself high hopes, ever expecting it to turn out that so high-born a husband, proud after the fashion of noblemen, would one day be sated with so lowly a bride and send her home, had kept her coarse and well-worn gown hidden away in some corner of his narrow dwelling. Hearing the uproar, not of his daughter, who returned in silence, but of the accompanying throng, he ran to meet her at the threshold and covered her, half naked as she was, with the old gown. She remained with her father a few days, showing mar-velous equanimity and kindness; for she gave no sign of the sadness of her heart and showed no trace of her more favorable lot, since, for-sooth, she had always dwelt amid riches with lowly and humble spirit.

Now the Count of Panago was drawing near; and, on every hand, rumors of the new nuptials were rife. Sending forward one of his train, he announced the day on which he would arrive at Saluzzo. The day before, therefore, Walter sent for Griseldis, and when she had come with all fidelity, he said to her, "It is my desire that the maiden who is coming on the morrow to dine with us should be received sumptu-ously, as well as the men and matrons who come with her and such of our own people as are present at the feast, so that honor of place and welcome may be preserved unspotted, according to the dignity of each and all. But I have no women in the house who are suited to cope with this task; therefore, though your garments are but poor, you may best assume the duty of receiving and placing my guests, for you know my ways."

"I will do this," said she, "and whatever else I see will please you, not only willingly, but eagerly. Nor shall I grow weary or sluggish in this labor, so long as the least remnant of my spirit shall last." And when she had said this, straightway she caught up the implements of servant's toil and set to work, sweeping the house, setting the tables, making the beds, and urging on the others, like the best of handmaids.

At the third hour of the next day, the count arrived; and all the people vied in commending the manners and the beauty of the maiden and her youthful brother. There were those who said that Walter had been fortunate and prudent in the change he made, since this bride was more delicate and of nobler breeding, and had so fine a kinsman into the bargain. So, while the preparations for the feast went feverishly on, Griseldis, who had been present everywhere and solicitous of all—not cast down by so grievous a lot nor confused with shame for her old-fashioned clothing, but serene of countenance—came to meet the maiden as she entered. Bending the knee before her, after the manner of servants, with eyes cast reverently and humbly down, she said, "Welcome, my lady." Then she greeted others of the guests with cheerful face and marvelous sweetness in her words, and she managed the vast household with great skill; so that everyone greatly wondered—especially the newcomers—whence came that dignity of manner and that discretion beneath such a dress. She, in her turn, could not grow weary of praising the maiden and the boy: now she extolled the maiden's beauty, now the boy's.

Just as they were to sit down at the tables, Walter turned toward her and said before them all, as if he were making game of her, "What think you, Griseldis, of this bride of mine? Is she pretty and worthy enough?"

"Surely," said she, "no prettier or worthier could be found. Either with her or with no one, can you lead a life of tranquillity and happiness; and that you may find happiness is my desire and my hope. One thing, in all good faith, I beg of you, one warning I give you: not to drive her with those goads with which you have driven another woman. For since she is younger and more delicately nurtured, I predict she would not be strong enough to bear so much."

Walter, seeing the cheerfulness with which she spoke, and turning over in his mind the steadfastness of the woman, who had been so often and so bitterly injured, took pity on the unworthy fate that had befallen her so unjustly. Able to bear it no longer, he cried out, "It is enough, my Griseldis! Your fidelity to me is made known and proved; nor do I think that under heaven there is another woman who has undergone such trials of her conjugal love." And saying this, with eager arms he embraced his dear wife, who stood all overcome with stupor and as if waking from a troubled sleep. "And you," he said, "are my only wife. I have no other, nor ever shall have. This maiden, whom you think to be my bride, is your daughter; and he, who is thought to be my kinsman, is your son. They whom you believed you had lost, each in turn, you get back both together. Let all know, who thought the contrary, that I am curious and given to experiments, but am not impious: I have tested my wife, not condemned her; I have hidden my children, not destroyed them."

Almost out of her wits for joy and beside herself with maternal love, on hearing these words, Griseldis rushed into her children's arms, shedding the most joyous tears. She wearied them with kisses and bedewed them with her loving tears. And straightway the ladies gathered about her with alacrity and affection; and when her vile apparel had been stripped off her, they clothed her in her accustomed garments and adorned her. The most joyous plaudits and auspicious words from all the throng resounded all about; and the day was the most renowned that ever was for its great joy and sorrow,—more renowned, even, than the day of her nuptials had been.

Many years thereafter they lived in great peace and concord; and Walter, who had appeared to neglect his father-in-law, lest he should stand in the way of the experiment he had conceived, had the old man moved into his palace and held him in honor. His own daughter he gave in noble and honorable marriage, and his son he left behind him as his heir, happy in his wife and in his offspring.

This story it has seemed good to me to weave anew, in another tongue, not so much that it might stir the matrons of our times to imitate the patience of this wife—who seems to me scarcely imitable—as that it might stir all those who read it to imitate the woman's steadfastness, at least; so that they may have the resolution to perform for God what this woman performed for her husband. For He cannot be tempted by evil, as saith James the Apostle, and He himself tempts no man. Nevertheless, He often proves us and suffers us to be vexed with many a grievous scourage; not that He may know our spirit, for that He knew ere we were made, but that our own frailty may be made known to us through notable private signs. Therefore I would assuredly enter on the list of steadfast men the name of anyone who endured for his God, without a murmur, what this obscure peasant woman endured for her mortal husband.

FRANCIS PETRARCH

[Two Letters to Boccaccio]†

I

Your book, written in our mother tongue and published, I presume, during your early years, has fallen into my hands, I know not whence or how. If I told you that I had read it, I should deceive you. It is a very

† From *Petrarch: The First Modern Scholar and Man of Letters*, trans. James Harvey Robinson and Henry Winchester Rolfe (New York: G. P. Putnam's Sons, 1914), pp. 191–96. Although Robinson and Rolfe print these two selections as parts of one letter, the first was written in 1373 as the preface to Petrarch's translation, the second in 1374, when Petrarch found that his original letter had not reached Boccaccio and sent him another copy of his translation. He begins by referring to the *Decameron* as a whole.

big volume, written in prose and for the multitude. I have been, moreover, occupied with more serious business, and much pressed for time. You can easily imagine the unrest caused by the warlike stir about me, for, far as I have been from actual participation in the disturbances, I could not but be affected by the critical condition of the state. What I did was to run through your book, like a traveller who, while hastening forward, looks about him here and there, without pausing. I have heard somewhere that your volume was attacked by the teeth of certain hounds, but that you defended it valiantly with staff and voice. This did not surprise me, for not only do I well know your ability, but I have learned from experience of the existence of an insolent and cowardly class who attack in the work of others everything which they do not happen to fancy or be familiar with, or which they cannot themselves accomplish. Their insight and capabilities extend no farther; on all other themes they are silent.

My hasty perusal afforded me much pleasure. If the humour is a little too free at times, this may be excused in view of the age at which you wrote, the style and language which you employ, and the frivolity of the subjects, and of the persons who are likely to read such tales. It is important to know for whom we are writing, and a difference in the character of one's listeners justifies a difference in style. Along with much that was light and amusing, I discovered some serious and edifying things as well, but I can pass no definite judgment upon them, since I have not examined the work thoroughly.

As usual, when one looks hastily through a book, I read somewhat more carefully at the beginning and at the end. At the beginning you have, it seems to me, accurately described and eloquently lamented the condition of our country during that siege of pestilence which forms so dark and melancholy a period in our century. At the close you have placed a story which differs entirely from most that precede it, and which so delighted and fascinated me that, in spite of cares which made me almost oblivious of myself, I was seized with a desire to learn it by heart, so that I might have the pleasure of recalling it for my own benefit, and of relating it to my friends in conversation. When an opportunity for telling it offered itself shortly after, I found that my auditors were delighted. Later it suddenly occurred to me that others, perhaps, who were unacquainted with our tongue, might be pleased with so charming a story, as it had delighted me ever since I first heard it some years ago, and as you had not considered it unworthy of presentation in the mother tongue, and had placed it, moreover, at the end of your book, where, according to the principles of rhetoric, the most effective part of the composition belongs. So one fine day, when, as usual, my mind was distracted by a variety of occupations, discontented with myself and my surroundings, I suddenly sent everything flying, and, snatching up my pen, I attacked this story of yours. I sincerely trust that it will gratify you that I have of my own free-will undertaken to translate your work, something I should certainly never think of doing for anyone else, but which I was induced to do in this instance by my partiality for you and for the story. Not neglecting the precept of Horace in his *Art of Poetry*, that the careful translator should not attempt to render word for word, I have told your tale in my own language, in some places changing or even adding a few words, for I felt that you would not only permit, but would approve, such alterations.

Although many have admired and wished for my version, it seemed to me fitting that your work should be dedicated to you rather than to anyone else; and it is for you to judge whether I have, by this change of dress, injured or embellished the original. The story returns whence it came; it knows its judge, its home, and the way thither. As you and everyone who reads this knows, it is you and not I who must render account for what is essentially yours. If anyone asks me whether this is all true, whether it is a history *[historia]* or a story *[fabula]*, I reply in the words of Sallust, "I refer you to the author"—to wit, my friend Giovanni. With so much of introduction, I begin.

* * *

II

My affection for you has induced me to write at an advanced age what I should hardly have undertaken even as a young man. Whether what I have narrated be true or false I do not know, but the fact that you wrote it would seem sufficient to justify the inference that it is but a tale. Foreseeing this question, I have prefaced my translation with the statement that the responsibility for the story rests with the author; that is, with you. And now let me tell you my experiences with this narrative *[historia]*, or tale *[fabula]*, as I prefer to call it.

In the first place, I gave it to one of our mutual friends in Padua to read, a man of excellent parts and wide attainments. When scarcely half-way through the composition, he was suddenly arrested by a burst of tears. When again, after a short pause, he made a manful attempt to continue, he was again interrupted by a sob. He then realized that he could go no farther himself, and handed the story to one of his companions, a man of education, to finish. How others may view this occurrence I cannot, of course, say; for myself, I put a most favourable construction upon it, believing that I recognise the indications of a most compassionate disposition; a more kindly nature, indeed, I never remember to have met. As I saw him weep as he read, the words of the Satirist came back to me:

> Nature, who gave us tears, by that alone
> Proclaims she made the feeling heart our own;
> And 't is our noblest sense.[1]

Some time after, another friend of ours, from Verona (for all is common between us, even our friends), having heard of the effect produced by the story in the first instance, wished to read it for himself. I readily complied, as he was not only a good friend, but a man of abil-

---

1. Juvenal, xv., 131–33, as translated by William Gifford [*Translators*].

ity. He read the narrative from beginning to end without stopping
once. Neither his face nor his voice betrayed the least emotion, nor a
tear or a sob escaped him. "I too," he said at the end, "would have
wept, for the subject certainly excites pity, and the style is well adapted
to call forth tears, and I am not hard-hearted; but I believed, and still
believe, that this is all an invention. If it were true, what woman,
whether of Rome or any other nation, could be compared with this
Griselda? Where do we find the equal of this conjugal devotion, where
such faith, such extraordinary patience and constancy?" I made no reply to this reasoning, for I did not wish to run the risk of a bitter debate in the midst of our good-humoured and friendly discussion. But I
had a reply ready. There are some who think that whatever is difficult
for them must be impossible for others; they must measure others by
themselves, in order to maintain their superiority. Yet there have been
many, and there may still be many, to whom acts are easy which are
commonly held to be impossible. Who is there who would not, for example, regard a Curtius, a Mucius, or the Decii, among our own people, as pure fictions; or, among foreign nations, Codrus and the
Philæni; or, since we are speaking of woman, Portia, or Hypsicratia, or
Alcestis, and others like them?[2] But these are actual historical persons. And indeed I do not see why one who can face death for another,
should not be capable of encountering any trial or form of suffering.

* * *

From *Le Ménagier de Paris*†

* * *

Dear sister [dear wife], this story was translated by master Francis Petrarch, the poet crowned at Rome,[1] not in order to move good women
to have patience amid the tribulations which their husbands cause
them solely because of their love for those husbands. It was translated
to show that since God, the Church, and Reason would have them be
obedient; and since their husbands would have them endure a great

---

2. All these examples from classical history and legend involve stories of acts of extraordinary
   courage or self-sacrifice. The first three are Roman: Marcus Curtius leapt into a chasm in
   order to close it; Caius Mucius Scaevola, captured by enemies, put his hand into a fire to
   show that he did not fear their threats; the Decii—father, son, and grandson—all died in
   battle for Rome. Codrus was the last king of Athens and sacrificed himself because of a
   prophecy that success in battle would come to the side whose king died. The Philæni were
   two brothers who consented to being buried alive in order to secure extended territory for
   Carthage. The three women Petrarch cites are more directly related to his story of wifely devotion: Portia killed herself when she learned of the death of Brutus; Hypsicratia so loved
   Mithridates that she accompanied him everywhere, even in battle; Alcestis gave up her life
   so that Admetus could live.
† Translated for this volume by Glending Olson and V. A. Kolve: *Le Ménagier de Paris*, ed.
   Jérôme Pichon, 2 vols. (Paris: Crapelet, 1846), I. 124–26. The book was written by a
   wealthy householder of Paris—a member of the upper bourgeoisie—for the instruction of
   his young wife, sometime between 1392 and 1394. His paraphrase of Petrarch's version of
   the Griselda story is one of several tales through which he discusses the obedience and humility a wife should show her husband.
1. In 1341, Petrarch was given the laurel crown for poetry, in imitation of ancient custom. Cf.
   Clerk's Prologue, ll. 31–33.

deal; and since, to avoid worse, it is necessary that they submit themselves completely to their husbands' wills, enduring patiently whatever their husbands desire; and what is more, since these good women must conceal such troubles, keep silent about them, and indeed come to terms with them while seeking always, with a happy spirit, to draw closer to the favor and love of those mortal husbands: how much greater then the reason for which men and women ought to suffer in patience the tribulations which God, who is immortal and eternal, sends to them. Whether it be the death of friends; the loss of goods, children, or kinfolk; the distress brought about by enemies, captures, slaughters, destruction, fire, tempest, thunderstorms, floods or other unexpected disasters: one ought always to endure it patiently and turn oneself again, with love and solicitude, to the love of the immortal Sovereign, eternal and everlasting God. This we may learn by the example of this pitiable woman, born into poverty among simple people without rank or learning, who suffered so much for her mortal husband [*ami*].

I have set down this story here only in order to instruct you, not to apply it directly to you, and not because I wish such obedience from you. I am in no way worthy of it. I am not a marquis, nor have I taken in you a shepherdess as my wife. Nor am I so foolish, arrogant, or immature in judgment as not to know that I may not properly assault or assay you thus, nor in any such fashion. God keep me from testing you in this way or any other, under the color of lies and dissimulations. Nor do I wish to test you in yet some other manner, for I am fully satisfied by the proof already established through the good name of your ancestors and of yourself, along with what I feel and see and know from direct experience.

I apologize if this story deals with too great cruelty—cruelty, in my view, beyond reason. Do not credit it as having really happened; but the story has it so, and I ought not to change it nor invent another, since someone wiser than I composed it and set it down. Because other people have seen it, I want you to see it too, so that you may be able to talk about everything just as they do.

* * *

The Merchant's Prologue and Tale

Chaucer draws upon a great variety of literary texts and genres in the making of this tale, as its many allusions suggest. Here we print only the closest analogue for its concluding action, one of several medieval versions of what is known as the pear-tree story. It is taken from the *Novellino*, the first major collection of tales and anecdotes in Italian, whose earliest version dates from late in the thirteenth century (ca. 1280). For other material relevant to the tale's treatment of women, marriage, and the battle of the sexes, see the Sources and Backgrounds we provide for the *Wife of Bath's Prologue and Tale* and the section on lechery and its remedy in Chaucer's *Parson's Tale*, also printed in this Norton Critical Edition.

The Woman and the Pear-Tree†

There was once a rich man who had a very beautiful woman as his wife; he loved her ardently and was very jealous of her. Now, as God would have it, an illness befell this man's eyes and made him blind; he saw the light of day no more. And so it happened that this man would not leave his wife nor ever let her out of his reach, for he feared she might go astray.

Now it chanced that a man of the neighborhood fell in love with this woman, and not seeing how he could find an opportunity to converse with her—for her husband was always at her side—he made signs indicating he was dying of love. The woman, seeing him so enamored, felt sorry for him, and gave him to understand in return, "You see I can do nothing, for this man never leaves me." So the good man did not know what to do or say, and looked as thought he wanted to die. He could find no way of meeting the woman alone.

The woman, seeing this behavior, took pity on him and thought of a way of helping him. She had a long tube made from a reed, and put it to the ear of this man, and by that means spoke to him so that her husband could not hear. She said to the gentleman, "I am sorry for you, and have thought of a way of helping you. Go into our garden and

† Translation freely adapted from *Il Novellino, the Hundred Old Tales*, trans. Edward Storer (New York: Dutton, 1925), pp. 130–33; for the original see *Le novelle antiche dei codici panciatichiano-palatino 138 e laurenziano-gaddiano 193*, ed. Guido Biagi (Florence: Sansoni, 1880), pp. 199–201. Biagi's text is reprinted in *Sources and Analogues of Chaucer's Canterbury Tales*, ed. W. F. Bryan and Germaine Dempster (Chicago: U of Chicago P, 1941), pp. 342–43, and (with a more literal translation) in *The Literary Context of Chaucer's Fabliaux*, ed. Larry D. Benson and Theodore M. Andersson (Indianapolis: Bobbs-Merrill, 1971), pp. 238–41. This story appears in only one manuscript of the *Novellino*, dating from the fourteenth century, and is not thought to be part of the original collection.

climb up a pear-tree that has many fine pears, and wait for me there, and I will come up to you." The good man went at once into the garden and climbed up the pear-tree, and waited for the woman.

Now came the time when the woman was in the garden, wishing to help the good man—but her husband was still by her side. And so she said, "I feel a desire for those pears at the top of that pear-tree, for they are very fine." The husband said, "Call someone to pick them for you." And the woman said, "I will pick them myself—otherwise I would not enjoy them." Then the woman went to the tree to climb it, and her husband came with her to its foot, putting his arms around its trunk so that no one could follow her up it.

Thus it happened that the woman climbed up the pear-tree to the friend who was awaiting her. They gave each other great happiness, and the pear-tree shook with their weight, and the pears fell down on top of the husband. Then he said, "What are you doing, woman, that you don't come back down? You are knocking down all the pears!" And the woman replied, "I wanted the pears off a certain branch, and that was the only way I could get them."

Now you should know that the Lord God and Saint Peter saw this happening, and Saint Peter said to the Lord God, "Do you not see the trick that woman is playing on her husband? Lord, cause the husband to see the light again, so he may see what his wife is doing." And the Lord God said, "I tell you, Saint Peter, no sooner will he see the light than the woman will find an explanation—an excuse. And so I will make the light return to his eyes, and you shall see what she will say."

Then the light returned to him, and he looked up and saw what the woman was doing. "What are you doing with that man? You honor neither yourself nor me, nor is this the loyalty proper in a woman." And the woman replied at once, "If I had not done so with him, you would not have seen the light." And the husband, hearing this, was satisfied. So you see how women and females are loyal, and how quick they are to find an excuse.

The Franklin's Prologue and Tale

The story told in the *Franklin's Tale* appears twice in Boccaccio: first in Book 4 of the *Filocolo* as one of the questions of love debated by a group of young men and women at their leisure; second in the *Decameron*, in a shorter version told on the final day as one of the tales illustrating the theme of generosity. Critics have argued for Chaucer's indebtedness to one or the other, or both, of these stories. We print the *Decameron* version here, along with Boccaccio's description, at the start of the following tale, of the listeners' responses to the issues posed by the narrative. We also include as background to some of the Franklin's thinking about love and marriage a passage discussing these topics from a fourteenth-century English translation of a popular thirteenth-century Latin encyclopedia, Bartholomaeus Anglicus's *De proprietatibus rerum*. Some of the biblical and antifeminist material printed above as background to the *Wife of Bath's Prologue and Tale* is also pertinent to this one; for example, Dorigen's long soliloquy about women who have preferred death to dishonor is drawn from St. Jerome's *Against Jovinian*.

GIOVANNI BOCCACCIO

From the *Decameron*, Tenth Day, Fifth Tale†

Madonna Dianora asks Messer Ansaldo to give her a garden that would be as beautiful in January as in May; by hiring a magician, Messer Ansaldo manages to grant her wish; her husband agrees that she must fulfill Messer Ansaldo's desires, but when Messer Ansaldo hears of her husband's generosity, he frees her from her promise, and the magician, refusing to accept anything from him, also frees Messer Ansaldo from his.

Every member of the merry company had already praised Messer Gentile to the skies, when the King ordered Emilia to continue, and she, longing to speak, self-confidently began as follows:

Tender ladies, no one can reasonably say that Messer Gentile did not act generously, but if anyone were to claim that it would be impos-

† From *The Decameron* by Giovanni Boccaccio, translated by Mark Musa and Peter Bondanella. Pp. 623–27. Copyright © 1982 by Mark Musa and Peter Bondanella. Used by permission of Dutton Signet, a division of Penguin Group (USA) Inc. For texts and translations of both this tale and the *Filocolo* version, as well as other source material, see Robert R. Edwards' chapter in *Sources and Analogues of The Canterbury Tales, Vol. I*, ed. Robert M. Correale and Mary Hamel (Cambridge: D. S. Brewer, 2002), pp. 211–65.

sible to act more generously, it would not be hard to show the contrary, as I mean to show you in this little tale of mine.

In Friuli, a rather cold province but one which boasts of beautiful mountains, many rivers, and clear springs, there is a town called Udine, in which there once lived a beautiful and noble lady named Madonna Dianora, the wife of a very wealthy man named Gilberto, a very pleasant and amiable person. Such was this lady's worth that she was greatly loved by a famous and noble baron of high rank, whose name was Messer Ansaldo Gradense and who was known everywhere for his feats of arms and chivalry. And while Messer Ansaldo loved Madonna Dianora passionately and did everything he could to be loved in return by her, often sending her numerous messages with this end in mind, he labored in vain. And when the lady, having become weary of the knight's entreaties, realized that no matter how much she denied him everything he requested, he nevertheless continued to love her and to implore her, she decided to rid herself of him by making a strange and, in her judgment, impossible request.

And so she said the following to a woman who often came to her on his behalf:

"Good woman, you have assured me many times that Messer Ansaldo loves me above all other things, and you have, on his behalf, offered me marvelous gifts; he may keep these gifts, for they could never bring me to love him or to fulfill his pleasure. But if I could be certain he loved me as much as you say he does, I would be moved without a doubt to love him and to do whatever he wished. And so, whenever he is willing to provide me with proof by doing what I request, I shall be ready to do whatever he wants."

The good woman said: "What is it, my lady, that you wish him to do?"

The lady replied:

"What I desire is this: in the month of January which is soon to come, I want there to be on the outskirts of town a garden full of green grass, flowers, and leafy trees no different from one in the month of May; if he is unable to do this, he should never again send you or anyone else to me, for if he continues to bother me, just as until now I have completely concealed everything from my husband and my relatives, I shall, by complaining to them about him, seek to get rid of him."

When the knight heard his lady's request and offer, no matter how difficult or rather impossible a task he felt it was to fulfill, and in spite of the fact that he realized the lady had made this request for no other reason than to destroy his hope, nevertheless, he made up his mind to try to do what he could. He sent word to all parts of the world to find out if there was someone who might provide him with assistance or advice, and a certain man came to him who offered to do it by means of magic, provided he was well paid. Messer Ansaldo came to an agreement with him for an enormous sum of money and then happily awaited the time the lady had set for him. When it arrived and the weather was bitter cold and everything was covered with snow and ice, in a most beautiful meadow near the town, the worthy man, on the night before the first day of January, employed his magic to such effect that on the following morning there appeared, according to the testimony of those who saw it for themselves, one of the most beautiful gardens that had ever been seen, with grass, trees, and fruit of every kind. As soon as Messer Ansaldo saw the garden, with great joy he had gathered some of the most beautiful fruits and flowers growing there and then secretly had them presented to the lady, inviting her to come and see the garden she had requested so that she would not only realize how much he loved her but would also recall the promise she had made to him, sealed with her oath, and in so doing would seek, as a woman of good faith, to keep her promise.

The lady had heard much talk about the marvelous garden, and when she saw the flowers and fruit, she began to regret her promise. In spite of her regret, curious as she was to see so unusual a thing, she went with many other ladies of the town to have a look at the garden; after praising it very highly, and not without amazement, she returned home the most sorrowful of women, thinking about what she was obliged to do because of it. So intense was her grief that she was unable to conceal it, and her husband, who could not help noticing it, insisted on knowing the cause of it. Out of shame, the lady kept silent for a long time; then, finally compelled to speak, she revealed everything to him.

When Gilberto heard all this, at first he was very much disturbed; but then, when he considered his wife's pure intentions, he put aside his anger and said:

"Dianora, it is not proper for a wise or virtuous woman to pay attention to messages of that sort or to fix a price on her chastity with anyone, under any circumstances. Words received by the heart through the ears have more power than many would believe, and almost everything becomes possible for lovers. Hence, you did wrong first by listening and then by bargaining, but since I know the purity of your heart, I shall allow you, in order to absolve you of the obligation of your promise, to do something which perhaps no other man would allow, being also moved by my fear of the magician, whom Messer Ansaldo, if we were to disappoint him, would perhaps have do us harm. I want you to go to him, and by any means possible, short of your chastity, seek to be released from this promise, and if that is impossible, then this one time you must give him your body, but not your heart."

When the lady heard her husband, she wept and refused to accept such a favor from him. But no matter how much the lady objected, Gilberto insisted that she do it, and so, the following morning, around daybreak, without dressing up too much, the lady, preceded by two of her retainers and followed by one of her maidservants, went to Messer Ansaldo's home.

When he heard that the lady had come to him, he was quite amazed, and so, rising, he sent for the magician, and said to him: "I want you to see how much good your art has procured me." And then he went to greet her, and with no display of unbridled passion, with reverence he received her courteously, after which he had everyone go into a beautiful room where a big fire was burning, and after arranging for her to be seated, he said:

"My lady, I beg you, if the long love which I have borne you deserves any reward, be good enough to tell me the real reason why you have come here at such an hour and with such an escort."

Ashamed and with tears welling in her eyes, the lady replied:

"Sir, neither because I love you, nor because of my promise do I come here, but rather, because of my husband's orders. Having more consideration for the labors of your unbridled passion than for his or my honor, he has made me come here; and it is at his command that I am disposed, this one time, to fulfill your every desire."

If Messer Ansaldo was astonished when she began speaking, he was even more so after she finished. Moved by Gilberto's generosity, his passion began to change into compassion, and he said:

"My lady, since things are as you say, God forbid that I should soil the honor of a man who has taken pity on my love, and so, as long as you wish to stay here, you will be treated just as if you were my sister, and whenever you like, you are free to leave, provided that you give your husband such thanks as you deem befitting such courtesy as his, and that henceforth you always consider me as a brother and your servant."

When the lady heard these words, happier than ever before, she said:

"Nothing could ever make me believe, considering your manners, that anything else could have resulted from my coming here than what I see you have made of it, and I shall always be obliged to you for this."

And having taken her leave, honorably escorted, she returned to Gilberto and reported to him what had happened; and as a result, a very close and loyal friendship grew up between Gilberto and Messer Ansaldo.

When Messer Ansaldo was ready to give the magician his promised fee, the magician, having witnessed the generosity of Gilberto toward Messer Ansaldo and that of Messer Ansaldo toward the lady, said:

"God forbid that having seen Gilberto so generous with his honor and you with your love, I should not be just as generous with my reward; and so, recognizing the justice of leaving the reward with you, it is my intention that you keep it."

The knight was embarrassed and tried to make him take if not all of the money, at least a part of it; but he labored in vain, and after the third day, when the magician had removed his garden and wanted to depart, Messer Ansaldo bid him Godspeed. And with his sensual passion for the lady extinguished in his heart, there remained the honest flame of affection.

What shall we say of this, loving ladies? Shall we place the lady who was almost dead and the love already grown lukewarm through lost hope above the generosity of Messer Ansaldo, who was more warmed with love than ever and kindled with even more hope, who held in his

very hands the catch he had pursued for so long a time? It seems foolish to me to believe that his kind of generosity could ever be compared
to the other.

* * *

Who could possibly recount in full the various discussions taking
place among the ladies as to which man, Gilberto, Messer Ansaldo, or
the magician, had shown the greatest generosity in Madonna Dianora's regard? It would take too long. But after the King had allowed
them to debate for a while, looking at Fiammetta, he ordered her to
end their discussions by telling a story. Without further delay, she began.

BARTHOLOMAEUS ANGLICUS

[On Love and Marriage]†

De viro.

A man hatte° *vir* in latyn, and hath that name	*is called*
of° myght and vertu° and strengthe. So seith	*because of / power*
Isidre.[1] For in myght and strengthe a man pas-	
sith° a womman, and a man is the hed of a wom-	*surpasses*
man, as the apostil seith.[2] Therfore a man is	
holde° to rule his wif, as the heed hath the cure°	*bound / care*
and reule of al the body. And a man hatte *maritus*,	
as it were wardinge° and defendinge the modir,	*keeping*
for he taketh so the charge, the warde,° and the	*guardianship*
kepinge of his wif that is modir of children, and	
hatte *sponsus* also, and hath that name of *spondere*,°	*from "to betroth"*
for a behotith° and oblegith himsilf. For in the	*he promises*
contract of weddinge he plightith his treuthe,°	*troth*
and oblegith himsilf to lede his lif with his wif	
withoute departange,° and to paye dettis to here°	*parting from her /*
and to kepe to here feith and companie, and that	*pay his (sexual) debts to her*
he schal leve hire for none othir. A man hath so	
gret love to his wif that because of here he aven-	
turith him° to al perilus,° ande settith [here] love	*himself / perils*
tofore his modir love,° and for to dwelle with	*love for his mother*
his wif he forsaketh his fadir and modir and	
his contray, as oure lord seith: Herefore a man	

---

† Text based on *On the Properties of Things: John Trevisa's Translation of Bartholomaeus Anglicus de Proprietatibus Rerum,* ed. M. C. Seymour et al. 2 vols. (Oxford: Oxford UP, 1975),
I. 307–309. Reprinted by permission of Oxford University Press.
1. Isidore of Seville (d. 636), author of a popular medieval encyclopedia, the *Etymologies.* The
explanations of the meanings of the Latin words *vir* (man), *maritus* (husband), and *sponsus*
(bridegroom) in this paragraph are based on Latin etymologies that the English translation
cannot reproduce.
2. St. Paul, in Ephesians 5:23; see p. 383.

schal forsake fadir and modir and abide with his wif.[3]

Tofore° the weddinge the spouse fondith° to winne the love of hise spouse that° he wowith° with giftis, and certifieth of his wille° with lettres and messingeres and with divers sondes,° and geveth many giftis and meche good and catelle,° and behotith° wel more. And to plese hire he puttith hym° to divers pleyes and games among gederinge° of puple, and usith° ofte dedis of myght and of maistrie,° and maketh hym gay° and semeliche° in divers clothinge and aray. And alle that he is i-prayed° to geve othir° to doo for here love he geveth and doth anon with alle his myght, and werneth none bone° that is i-prayed in here name and for here love. He spekith to here plesingeliche,° and beholdith hire in the face with plesinge and glad chere° and with a scharp eye, and assentith° to hire at the laste, and tellith openliche his wille and his assent° in presence of hire frendes, and spousith° hire with a ring and taketh hire to wif, and geveth hire grete giftis in tokene of the contract of weddinge, and maketh to hire chartres and dedes° of graunt° and of giftis, and maketh revels and festis of spousailes,° and geveth many goode giftis to frendis and gestis, and comfortith and gladith his gestis with songis and pipis and with instrumentis of musik. And hereaftir he bryngith his spouse into the privetees° of his chambre, and fongith hire to felawe° and maketh hire felawe in bedde and at bourde.[4] And thanne he maketh hire lady of his money and of his meyne.° Thanne he hath hire cause as moche to herte as his owne, and taketh the charge and keping of here. And for special love he amendith° hire yif sche doth amys,° and taketh hede° of here beringe and goynge,° of spekinge and lokynge, and of here passinge° and agencomynge° and entringe.

No man hath more welthe than he that hath a good womman to wif. Ne no man is more wrecche nothir° hath woo and sorwe than he that hath an yvel wif, crienge, jangelinge,° chidinge and skoldinge, drunkelew° and unstedefast and contrarye° to hym, costlew,° stoute and gay,[5] envyous,

Before / strives
whom / woos
makes known his intentions
messages
many goods and possessions
promises
himself
gathering / practices
prowess / well dressed
comely
asked / or

refuses no boon, request

pleasantly
countenance
submits
intent
espouses, marries

deeds / allowance
wedding feasts

privacy
takes her as a companion

household

corrects
wrong / heed
behavior
departing / returning

nor
chattering
prone to drunkenness
hostile / extravagant

3. Ephesians 5:31; see p. 384.
4. Literally "at table," but the phrase "bed and board" refers to the full range of a wife's sexual and domestic responsibilities and privileges.
5. Haughty and ostentatiously dressed.

noyful,° and lepinge ouer londes and contrayes, *troublesome*
and mychinge,° suspicious, and wrethful. Fulgen- *thieving*
cius touchith al this matere in a certeyn sermon
*de nupciis in Chana Galile.*⁶ And so he likneth° *likens, compares*
Crist to the goode man, and holy chirche to a
goode wif, and the synagoge to an evel wif that
breketh spousehode.° In a goode spouse and wif *commits adultery*
nedith thes condicions: that sche be busy and de-
voute in goddes servyse; meke° and servisable to *meek*
here housbonde, and faire spekinge and goodlich° *kind*
to here meyne;° merciable and good to wrecchis *household*
that beth nedy; esi° and pesible° to here neigh- *agreeable / peaceful*
bores; redy, ware,° and wys in thinges that schal *wary, careful*
be i-voided; rightful and pacient in soffringe;° besi *suffering*
[and] diligent in here doinge and dedis; maner-
liche in clothinge; sobre in movinge; ware in
spekinge; chast° in lokinge; honest in beringe; *chaste, modest*
sad° in goynge,° schamfast° among the puple; *steady / behavior / modest*
meri and glad with here housbonde; and chast in
privete. Such a wif is worthi to be i-preised,° that *praised*
fondith° more to plese here housbonde with heer° *strives / hair*
homliche i-wounde° than with heer gailiche *simply braided*
i-pinchid,° and i-wrolled° more with vertues than *gaily curled / wrapped*
with faire and gay clothinge. Sche usith the
goodnes of matrimoni more bicause of children
than of fleischliche likynge,° and hath more *physical pleasure*
likinge in spousehod in children of grace than
of kynde.⁷ Of a goode wif be this inowgh° at this *enough*
tyme.

6. We have not been able to find a sermon on the marriage at Cana (John 2:1–11) in the extant works of either Fulgentius, bishop of Ruspe, or Fulgentius the mythographer.
7. For spiritual than for earthly reasons.

The Pardoner's Prologue and Tale

As in the case of the Wife of Bath, the relationship between the Pardoner's prologue and his tale is exceptionally provocative. The Pardoner's open revelation of his own hypocrisy and avarice, which frames the narrative, has precedent in the speech of False Seeming (*Faus Semblant*) from *The Romance of the Rose*. The basis of the story of the rioters and the treasure is an exemplum found in various forms in the Middle Ages and Renaissance, known in its fullest version as *The Hermit, Death, and the Robbers*. The Pardoner's discussion of the tavern sins owes much to traditional lore, such as Thomas of Cantimpré's exemplum about swearing. The grim atmosphere of death and its arbitrariness that permeates the tale is due in great part to the impact of the plague on late medieval consciousness, and the most substantial contemporary description of the Black Death is in the introduction to Boccaccio's *Decameron*, printed on pp. 312–25.

JEAN DE MEUN

From *The Romance of the Rose*†

[False Seeming's Speech]

* * *

* * * False Seeming began his lecture and said to all in hearing:

"Barons, hear my theme: he who wants to become acquainted with False Seeming must seek him in the world or in the cloister. I dwell in no place except these two, but more in one and less in the other. Briefly, I am lodged where I think that I am better hidden. The safest hiding place is under the most humble garment. The religious are very covert, the worldly more open. I do not want to blame or defame the religious calling, in whatever habit one may find it. I shall not, as I may, blame the humble and loyal religious life, although I do not love it.

† From Guillaume de Lorris and Jean de Meun, *The Romance of the Rose*, trans. Charles Dahlberg (Princeton: Princeton UP, 1971), pp. 194–98, 202–205, 208–209. Copyright © 1971 by Princeton University Press. Excerpts reprinted by permission of Princeton University Press. Jean de Meun wrote his vast conclusion to Guillaume's poem ca. 1275. In this passage, False Seeming (*Faus Semblant*) offers his service to the God of Love in an assault upon the Castle wherein Jealousy has imprisoned the Rose and Fair Welcoming (*Bel Accueil*), the object of the Lover's quest. False Seeming (who personifies an aspect of the Lover's mind and a part of his erotic strategy) here presents his credentials—an extended self-portrait of hypocrisy exultant—to the God of Love and his assembled barons. On Chaucer's knowledge of this poem, see p. 348 of this volume.

"I have in mind the false religious, the malicious criminals who want to wear the habit but do not want to subdue their hearts. The religious are all compassionate; you will never see a spiteful one. They do not care to follow pride, and they all want to live humbly. I never dwell with such people, and if I do, I pretend. I can indeed assume their habit, but I would rather let myself be hanged than desert my main business, whatever face I put on it.

"I dwell with the proud, the crafty, the guileful, who covet worldly honors and who carry out large dealings, who go around tracking down large handouts and cultivating the acquaintance of powerful men and becoming their followers. They pretend to be poor, and they live on good, delicious morsels of food and drink costly wines. They preach poverty to you while they fish for riches with seines and trammel nets. By my head, evil will come of them. They are neither religious nor worldly. To the world they present an argument in which there is a shameful conclusion: this man has the robe of religion; therefore he is a religious. This argument is specious, not worth a knife of privet; the habit does not make the monk. Nevertheless no one knows how to reply to the argument, no matter how high he tonsures his head, even if he shaves with the razor of the *Elenchis*, that cuts up fraud into thirteen branches.[1] No man knows so well how to set up distinctions that he dare utter a single word about it. But whatever place I come to, no matter how I conduct myself, I pursue nothing except fraud. No more than Tibert the cat has his mind on anything but mice and rats do I think of anything except fraud. Certainly by my habit you would never know with what people I dwell, any more than you would from my words, no matter how simple and gentle they were. You should look at actions if your eyes have not been put out; for if people do something other than what they say, they are certainly tricking you, whatever robes they have or whatever estate they occupy, clerical or lay, man or woman, lord, sergeant, servant, or lady.

* * *

"But indeed I want to promise you to further the causes of all your friends, provided that they want my companionship. They are dead if they don't receive me, and they will serve my friend, or, by God, they will never succeed! Without fail, I am a traitor, and God has judged me a thief. I am perjured, but one hardly knows before the end what I am bringing to an end, for several who never recognized my fraud have received their deaths through me, and many are receiving them and will receive them without ever recognizing it. The man who does so, if he is wise, protects himself from it, or it will be his great misfortune. But the deception is so strong that it is very difficult to recognize it. For Proteus, who was accustomed to change into whatever form he wished, never knew as much fraud or guile as I practice; I never entered a town where I was recognized, no matter how much I was heard

---

1. The allusion is to scholastic subtlety in argumentation; an *elenchus* is a procedure of refutation.

or seen. I know very well how to change my garment, to take one and then another foreign to it. Now I am a knight, now a monk; at one time I am a prelate, at another a canon; at one hour a clerk, at another a priest; now disciple, now master, now lord of the manor, now forester. Briefly I am in all occupations. Again I may be prince or page, and I know all languages by heart. At one hour I am old and white, and then I have become young again. Now I am Robert, now Robin, now Cordelier, now Jacobin. And in order to follow my companion, Lady Constrained Abstinence, who comforts me and goes along with me, I take on many another disguise, just as it strikes her pleasure, to fulfill her desire. At one time I wear a woman's robe; now I am a girl, now a lady. At another time I become a religious: now I am a devotee, now a prioress, nun, or abbess; now a novice, now a professed nun. I go through every locality seeking all religions. But, without fail, I leave the kernel of religion and take the husk. I dwell in religion in order to trick people; I seek only its habit, no more. What should I tell you? I disguise myself in the way that pleases me. The time is very much changed in me; my deeds are very different from my words."

At this point False Seeming wanted to stay silent, but Love did not pretend that he was annoyed at what he heard; instead, to delight the company, he said to him:

"Tell us more especially in what way you serve disloyally. Don't be ashamed to speak of it, for, as you tell us of your habits, you seem to be a holy hermit."

"It is true, but I am a hypocrite."

"You go around preaching abstinence."

"True, indeed, but I fill my paunch with very good morsels and with wines such as are suitable for theologians."

"You go around preaching poverty."

"True, abundantly richly. But however much I pretend to be poor, I pay no attention to any poor person. I would a hundred thousand times prefer the acquaintance of the King of France to that of a poor man, by our lady, even though he had as good a soul. When I see those poor devils all naked, shivering with cold on those stinking dunghills, crying and howling with hunger, I don't meddle in their business. If they were carried to the Hôtel-Dieu, they wouldn't get any comfort from me, for they wouldn't feed my maw with a single gift, since they have nothing worth a cuttlefish. What will a man give who licks his knife? But a visit to a rich usurer who is sick is a good and pleasant thing. I go to comfort him, for I expect to bring away money from him. And if wicked death stifles him, I will carry him right up to his grave. And if anyone comes to reprove me for avoiding the poor, do you know how I escape from him? I give out behind my cloak that the rich man is more stained with sin than the poor, and has greater need of counsel, and that that is the reason that I see him and advise him.

* * *

"Working can give me no pleasure: I have nothing to do with it, for there is too great difficulty in working. I prefer to pray in front of people and cover my foxlike nature under a cloak of pope-holiness."

"What's this?" said Love. "The devil! What are your words? What have you said here?"

"What?"

"Great and open disloyalty. Don't you fear God then?"

"Certainly not. The man who wants to fear God can hardly attain anything great in this world, for the good, who avoid evil, live legitimately on what they have, and keep themselves according to God, scarcely get from one loaf to the next. Such people drink too much discomfort; there is no life that displeases me so much.

"But consider how usurers, counterfeiters, and loan sharks have money in their storehouses. Bailiffs, beadles, provosts, mayors, all live practically by rapine. The common people bow to them, while they, like wolves, devour the commoners. Everybody runs over the poor; there isn't anyone who does not want to despoil them, and all cover themselves with their spoil. They all snuff up their substance and pluck them alive without scalding. The strongest robs the weakest. But I, wearing my simple robe and duping both dupers and duped, rob both the robbed and the robbers.

"By my trickery I pile up and amass great treasure in heaps and mounds, treasure that cannot be destroyed by anything. For if I build a palace with it and achieve all my pleasures with company, the bed, with tables full of sweets—for I want no other life—my money and my gold increases. Before my treasure can be emptied, money comes to me again in abundance. Don't I make my bears tumble? My whole attention is on getting. My acquisitions are worth more than my revenues. Even if I were to be beaten or killed, I still want to penetrate everywhere. I would never try to stop confessing emperors, kings, dukes, barons, or counts. But with poor men it is shameful; I don't like such confession. If not for some other purpose, I have no interest in poor people; their estate is neither fair nor noble.

"These empresses, duchesses, queens, and countesses; their high-ranking palace ladies; these abbesses, beguines, and wives of bailiffs and knights; these coy, proud bourgeois wives, these nuns and young girls; provided that they are rich or beautiful, whether they are bare or well turned out, they do not go away without good advice.

"For the salvation of souls, I inquire of lords and ladies and their entire households about their characteristics and their way of life; and I put into their heads the belief that their parish priests are animals in comparison with me and my companions. I have many wicked dogs among them, to whom I am accustomed to reveal people's secrets, without hiding anything; and in the same way they reveal everything to me, so that they hide nothing in the world from me.

"In order that you may recognize the criminals who do not stop deceiving people, I will now tell you here the words that we read of Saint Matthew, that is to say, the evangelist, in the twenty-third chapter: 'Upon the chair of Moses' (the gloss explains that this is the Old Testament), 'the scribes and pharisees have sat.' These are the accursed false people that the letter calls hypocrites. 'Do what they say, but not what they do. They are not slow to speak well, but they have no desire to do so. To gullible people they attach heavy loads that cannot be carried; they place them on their shoulders, but they dare not move them with their finger.' "

"Why not?" asked Love.

"In faith," replied False Seeming, "they don't want to, for porters' shoulders are often accustomed to suffer from their burdens, and these hypocrites flee from wanting to do such a thing. If they do jobs that may be good, it is because people see them. They enlarge their phylacteries and increase their fringes; since they are haughty, proud, and overbearing, they like the highest and most honorable seats at tables and the first in the synagogues. They like people to greet them when they pass along the street, and they want to be called 'master,' when they shouldn't be called, for the gospel goes against this practice and shows its unlawfulness.

"We have another custom toward those that we know are against us. We want to hate them very strongly and attack them all by agreement among ourselves. He whom one hates, the others hate, and all are bent on ruining him. If we see that he may, through certain people, win honor in the land, income, or possessions, we study to find out by what ladder he may mount up, and the better to capture and subdue him, we treacherously defame him to those people, for we do not love him. We cut the rungs from his ladder, and we strip him of his friends in such a way that he will never know by a word that he has lost them. If we troubled him openly, we would perhaps be blamed for it and thus miss out in our calculation; if he knew our worst intention, he would protect himself against it so that we would be reprimanded for it.

"If one of us has done something very good, we consider that we have all done it. Indeed, by God, if he was pretending it, or if he no more than condescends to brag that he has advanced certain men, we make ourselves partners in the deed and, as you should well know, we say that these people have been helped on by us. In order to win people's praise we tell lies to rich men and get them to give us letters bearing witness to our goodness, so that throughout the world people will think that every virtue abounds in us. We always pretend to be poor, but no matter how we complain, we are the ones, let me tell you, who have everything without having anything.

"I also undertake brokerage commissions, I draw up agreements, I arrange marriages, I take on executor's duties, and I go around doing procurations. I am a messenger and I make investigations, dishonest ones, moreover. To occupy myself with someone else's business is to me a very pleasant occupation. And if you have any business to do with those whom I frequent, tell me, and the thing is done as soon as you have told me. Provided that you have served me well, you have deserved my service. But anyone who wanted to punish me would rob himself of my favor. I neither love nor value the man by whom I am reproved for anything. I want to reprove all the others, but I don't want to hear their reproof, for I, who correct others, have no need of another's correction.

* * *

"But to you I dare not lie. However, if I could feel that you would not recognize it, you would have a lie in hand. Certainly I would have tricked you, and I would never have held back on account of any sin. And I would indeed desert you if you were to treat me poorly."

The god smiled at this wonder, and everyone laughed with amazement and said, "Here is a fine sergeant, of whom people should indeed be proud!"

"False Seeming," said Love, "tell me: since I have brought you so near to me that your power in my court is so great that you will be king of camp followers here, will you keep your agreement with me?"

"Yes, I swear it and promise you; neither your father nor your forefathers ever had sergeants more loyal."

"How! It is against your nature."

"Take your chances on it, for if you demand pledges, you will never be more sure, in fact, not even if I gave hostages, letters, witnesses, or security. I call on you as witness of the fact that one can't take the wolf out of his hide until he is skinned, no matter how much he is beaten or curried. Do you think that I do not deceive and play tricks because I wear a simple robe, under which I have worked many a great evil? By God! I shall never turn my heart from this kind of life. And if I have a simple, demure face, do you think that I may cease doing evil? My sweetheart Constrained Abstinence has need of my providence. She would long ago have been dead and in a bad plight if she hadn't had me in her power. Grant that we two, she and I, may carry out the task."

"So be it," said Love, "I believe you without guarantee."

And the thief with the face of treachery, white without and black within, knelt down on the spot and thanked him.

* * *

The Hermit, Death, and the Robbers†

Here is the story of a hermit who, walking through a forest, found a very great treasure.

One day a hermit, walking through a forest, found a cave that was very large and well hidden, and went toward it to rest for he was very tired. Just as he reached the cave, he saw at a certain place within it a great brightness, because there was much gold there. As soon as he recognized what it was, he swiftly took his leave, and began running through the desert as fast as he could go. While running thus, this

---

† Translated for this volume by V. A. Kolve. The tale survives in a Renaissance collection of stories—Borghini's 1572 *Libro di novelle e di bel parlar gentile*—but materials in that collection have been traced back to the thirteenth century. For the Italian text and reference to the antecedents, see *Sources and Analogues of Chaucer's* Canterbury Tales, ed. W. F. Bryan and Germaine Dempster (Chicago: U Chicago P, 1941), pp. 416–19. This and other relevant texts are now edited and translated by Mary Hamel in *Sources and Analogues of The Canterbury Tales, Vol. I*, ed. Robert M. Correale and Mary Hamel (Cambridge: D. S. Brewer, 2002), pp. 267–319.

hermit happened upon three bold thieves who haunted that forest to rob anyone who passed through it, and who had not yet realized that this gold was there. As they stood in hiding, they saw this man running away with no one in pursuit, and were a little frightened. But they came out of hiding nevertheless, in order to learn why he was fleeing, for they marveled greatly at it. And he answered, "My brothers, I flee death, who comes after me, pursuing me." Seeing neither man nor beast chasing him, they said, "Show us who is pursuing you, and lead us to the place where he is." Then the hermit said to them, "Come with me, and I will show him to you," while begging them every step of the way not to go seeking death, whom he himself was fleeing. But they, wishing to find death, and to see how he was made, would not settle for anything else. The hermit, seeing he could not do otherwise, and being frightened of them, led them to the cave from which he had fled, and said to them, "Here is death, which pursued me," and showed them the gold that was there.

They immediately knew what it was, and began to rejoice greatly and to make merry together. They dismissed the good man, who went away about his own affairs, and remarked to each other on what a great simpleton he was. The three robbers stayed together, guarding the treasure and discussing what they wished to do with it. One said, "It seems to me, since God has given us this great good fortune, that we should not leave here until we carry away all this treasure." Another said, "Let us do otherwise. Let one of us take a part of it and go to town and sell it, and get some bread and some wine and whatever else is necessary; and let him be as clever about this as he can, until he has obtained what we need." All three agreed to this together.

Now the Devil, who is crafty and inclined always to do as much evil as he can, put this thought into the heart of him who was going into town for provisions: "As soon as I am in town," he said to himself, "I want to eat and drink my fill, provide myself with certain things that have become necessary to me, and then poison the food which I carry back to my fellows. Once they are both dead, I shall be Lord of all that treasure. It seems so great, I think I shall be the richest man in this whole region." He did all those things, just as they had come into his mind. He took as much food for himself as he needed, poisoned all the rest, and brought it thus to his friends.

But while he went to town in the fashion I have told you, thinking evil and plotting to kill his friends so that everything would remain to himself, they were thinking no better of him. They said to each other, "As soon as this friend of ours returns with the bread and the wine and the other things we need, we will murder him, and then eat as much as we want, and afterward we'll have this great treasure just between the two of us. Since there will be fewer of us, each one will have a larger part of the treasure." When the one who had gone to town to buy the things they needed came back, his friends attacked him, as soon as they saw him, with lances and knives, and murdered him. When he was dead, they ate what he had brought, and as soon as they were full, both fell dead. And thus they died all three, for each killed the other, as you have heard, and did not possess the treasure.

Thus does our Lord God repay traitors: they went seeking death, and found it in such manner as they deserved. The wise man fled from it wisely. The gold remained free as before.

THOMAS OF CANTIMPRÉ

From *Liber de Apibus*†

Exemplum 103

In the city of Louvain, within the boundaries of Brabant we saw a noble and worthy citizen who, rising to go to matins on the holy night of Good Friday, passed in front of a tavern in which dissolute young men were sitting, playing at dice and vying with one another in blasphemies and oaths. Continuing on his way, this citizen found men in the street near the tavern who were making loud lamentation over a certain stranger who was badly wounded and bleeding. When he asked the men who had inflicted these wounds they answered: "Those young men who are playing dice." Entering the tavern, the citizen upbraided the young men for playing on that night and asked them sternly why they had so cruelly beaten the stranger who had been with them. Much astonished, the young men denied that anyone had come in since they had sat down, and protested that they had wounded no one either by word or blow. Going forth quickly with the citizen, they sought for the bleeding stranger but could not find him. Having now recovered their senses, each of them realized that by their terrible oaths they had again insulted the Lord Christ and by their taunts had crucified him afresh.

---

† Trans. Carleton Brown, *The Pardoner's Tale*, by Geoffrey Chaucer (Oxford: Oxford UP, 1935), pp. xvii–xviii. Reprinted by permission of Oxford University Press. Thomas Cantimpré (or Chantimpré) was born in Brabant ca. 1200 and died ca. 1270; the story here translated was written sometime before 1263. As an exemplum, it is less a tale in its own right than a narrative abstract that a preacher could use to illustrate and make vivid his theme and that he would characteristically expand in the telling through further dialogue and detail to the level of his ability and the needs of his sermon audience.

The Prioress's Prologue and Tale

Stories of the miracles performed by the Virgin Mary constitute one of the most familiar genres in medieval literature, and there are many analogues, in a variety of languages, to the *Prioress's Tale*. The richest and in many ways the closest to Chaucer is a fifteenth-century Latin version, here translated into English for the first time by A. G. Rigg. We also include a verse analogue from the Vernon manuscript, an important fourteenth-century collection of English religious and didactic literature. The song sung by Chaucer's "litel clergeoun," the *Alma Redemptoris Mater*, is printed both in Latin and in Cardinal Newman's English translation. Finally, the historical context of the tale's anti-Semitism is illustrated by a thirteenth-century papal bull concerned with claims of Jewish murder of Christian children, such as the one described by the Prioress in her story.

The Story of the *Alma Redemptoris Mater*†

The Mother of Grace never forgets those who remember her, and so the memory of her should be continually brought to mind; praise should be lavished upon her, and we should preach her mighty works as often as possible. Although the treasure-chest of all goodness has no need of our good offices, nevertheless it is beneficial and salutary for us to heap praises on her goodness. I have, therefore, decided to take care to entrust the following chapter to writing, so that the story may come to the notice of future generations, and so that those who hear it may be inspired all the more deeply and firmly to remember the Virgin.

There was once a certain boy born and bred in the city of Toledo; by the diligence of his mother he was sent to be instructed at school; he learned to dot his "i"s and to make the forms of letters; he learned the

† Translated and annotated for this volume by A. G. Rigg. The original Latin is printed in *Sources and Analogues of Chaucer's* Canterbury Tales, ed. W. F. Bryan and Germaine Dempster (Chicago: U Chicago P, 1941), pp. 480–85, from the unique MS Trinity College, Cambridge 0.9.38. The MS was compiled ca. 1450, mainly from material written much earlier; on the other hand, several stylistic features of this story resemble those of another Latin narrative in the MS, and both of them may have been "retouched" by the scribe with his own rhetorical embellishments (such as frequent biblical quotation for purely literary effect, not always aptly). There is, however, no a priori reason for saying that Chaucer could not have known the story in a version very close to this. The punctuation in SA is frequently deficient, and the following corrections should be made: 480/28 for *precanere* read *precauere*; 481/n.3 MS reads *diffitetur*; 481/22 delete *animis*; 482/41 *cunque* read *scilicet*; 483/22 *quanto* read *quanta*; 483/32 *suo* read *sue*; 484/20 *monumentum* read *monimentum*. Several unneccessary emendations of typical MS spellings are made in SA. The following emendations are necessary: 480/11 for *figura* read *figuram*; 481/6–7 *doctam* read *docta*; 483/22 *que* read *qui*; 484/9 *excitato* read *excitatus*.

alphabet, and how to marry letter to letters and figure to figures properly. When he had learned how to join letters, he gladly passed on to
music, in order that the understanding of the voice might be open to
him as well as knowledge acquired by words.

Every day he dutifully made his reading, according to what the authority of his teacher required of him. Each day, when he had fulfilled
his educational duty, the hour of mealtime followed, and this little boy
then used to go to the house of a canon of Mother Church; by the
help of this canon the boy relieved his hunger and cheated the demands of that most importunate of debt-collectors, his stomach. He
went there in hope of satisfying his hunger with the rich man's
crumbs; every day he was given a measure of the crumbs which fell
from the table of his masters and of the fragments left over by those
who had eaten. He carefully collected everything that was given him,
not in a shepherd's bag but in a little pocket at his breast; for his own
use he kept the smallest and most worthless scraps, setting aside the
bigger and better portions for his mother. O Lord, you who look into
and know our hearts—you know what lies within man!

One day the boy was assigned as his daily schoolwork that sweet and
delightful antiphon in praise of the Virgin Mother, whose opening line
is "Alma Redemptoris Mater."[1] The boy was anxious not to suffer the
terrifying taunts of his schoolmaster, and so he carefully learned the
antiphon by heart, and meditated on it, both because it was difficult to
learn and because it is a delightful song to sing. In my opinion, however, he learned and sang the antiphon so often not so much because
of the sweetness of the song as because of the memory and love of the
Virgin Mother. For more worthy than the string of the harp is the heart
of the player who prays out of love.[2] The judge who judges the hearts of
men is more affected by the love from the heart than by the loudness of
the harp, more by the prayer than by the voice which makes the prayer:
when one learns to pray in faith one also learns to speak with beauty.
Why is this? Because the voice never sounds pleasant unless the spirit
leads the voice and prayer in the singing.

One day, when the hour of breakfast had arrived, the boy, who had
earned rest by his hard work, was released from school; he practiced
with effect what he had learned from usage, like the calf of Ephraim
who was taught to love treading.[3] He proceeded in the direction of the
house of the canon by whose mercy he used to relieve his own misfortune. By chance he happened to go into the courtyards of Jewry
where that stiffnecked race lives, that detestable family—the race
which objects to the fruitfulness of the Virgin Mary and denies that
the Son of God was made incarnate in her womb. A great number of
the sons of the synagogue had gathered together in a house there,

1. The hymn was probably composed in the eleventh century; for text and translation, see
   p. 448.
2. *Sources and Analogues* notes the presence of a rhyme on which this conceit is based in another MS, but in fact a later hand has added it in this text also; the rhyme puns on *amor,
   clamor, vox, votum*, etc.
3. Hosea 10:11 (all quotations are from the Vulgate): the line is not clarified by the biblical
   passage.

strengthening by their number that brotherhood of iniquity, that oppressive branch of sin. The boy arrived close by the house, singing the antiphon we have mentioned above, the *Alma Redemptoris Mater*. His intention was to pass through the area, but he did not get through unharmed. Among the Jews was a certain young Hebrew boy who had been taught a little Latin and understood the Latin idiom. They heard the song, and wondered what it was; Satan came among them, and one of them asked the Hebrew who knew Latin what the Christian boy was singing. The Hebrew replied that the boy was singing an antiphon composed in praise of the Virgin Mary; its delightful sweetness was intended to inspire the minds of the listeners to the memory of Mary. At the mention of the name of the Virgin, the Jew cried out; Satan put it into his heart to betray and kill the innocent boy.

He therefore treacherously asked his colleague to bring the boy in: if he couldn't do what was required simply by asking, he was to offer the boy a bribe. So the innocent boy was summoned and brought in, introduced—or, rather, traduced. They took firm hold of him; "their rejoicing was as that of him who eats the poor in secret."[4] Without delay they made themselves ready for the murder, and prepared to condemn the innocent boy to death. The lamb was seized by the wolves; one of them set a knife to his throat, and his tongue was cruelly cut out; his stomach was opened and his heart and liver taken out. They imagined that they were offering a double sacrifice, firstly by cutting the throat from which emerged the voice of praise, and secondly by tearing out the heart which incessantly meditated on the memory of the Virgin. They thought they were obeying God, but in fact they were making a sacrifice not to God but to the devils of hell. It is usual for malice to cease after death, but although they had killed the boy, their malice did not come to an end: they threw his corpse into a place of the coarsest filth, where nature purges itself in secret.

Immediately the blessed mother of the Redeemer arrived by his side; her gracious mercy was present; she appeared to place a pebble (which looked very like a stone) on and within the mouth of the dead boy. When the pebble had been put in place, the boy's heart and throat opened up; his voice and power of speech returned, and he began to sing the *Alma Redemptoris Mater*.

In the meantime the boy's mother was anxious at his delay: he was her only son. She was alarmed at his unusually long delay, and suddenly began to be afraid and frightened at his daylong absence. For a mother does not easily forget the child of her womb and the joy that a man is born into the world. Thus, scarcely in control of herself, she set aside her domestic task, and went out into the courtyards and walked through the streets of the town; everywhere she looked at the passersby, and carefully scrutinized everyone she met. But nowhere did she see the face of her son. She walked on and on, into the Jewish quarter, scarcely able to support herself for her grief: her soul slept for weariness when she pictured as dead the child whom she had loved in

4. Habakkuk 3:14.

life. She was now close to the house where the progeny of vipers had committed the crime. Suddenly she heard her son singing the *Alma Redemptoris Mater*: that is, she heard his voice, but she saw no one. She stopped in amazement, but just as a sheep recognizes its lamb by its bleat alone, so this mother recognized her own son by the uniqueness of his singing voice: she was in labour close to death when she bore him, and so now she was in labour again, shouting and not sparing her voice. She could not put a guard on her mouth; however hoarse her throat became through her shouting, she incessantly cried out at the doors of her bloody enemies, "Give me back my son! Give me back my son!" As she repeated the words again and again, her grief was opened up. Time and again, as she stood outside the house she begged the Jews for her son, but the cruel and treacherous Jews would not give her any satisfaction; on stumbling feet she went to the house of the canon, and told him the whole sequence of events. In great grief and sorrow for the boy, the canon came to the house and demanded back the body from the murderers, but the perfidious Jews still refused to satisfy his demand in any way. Nevertheless he also heard and recognized the voice of the innocent child sweetly singing the *Alma Redemptoris Mater*.

Together they ran to the Archbishop of the city of Toledo and told him the sequence of events. He gathered a huge company of men and quickly went to investigate. He entered the guilty and treacherous house, breaking down the doors in his way, and roughly ordered the killer to produce the remains of the murdered innocent as quickly as possible—for he was sure that the boy was dead, in view of the great secrecy with which the malicious Jews had hidden him. All of them had conspired in the murder, but the main culprit in the murder, fearing the majesty of the Archbishop, confessed the truth of all his wickedness— how, out of envy at the mother of the Redeemer, he had extinguished the life of an innocent child, just because he had sung such a sweet song in honour of the Virgin Mother. After his confession of the crime— or rather his conviction—he put himself under the judgment of the Archbishop, and asked him for his mercy rather than his condemnation. He led the Archbishop by the hand, for all was darkness and gloom where the boy lay dead in the depths. The singing voice was their leader and guide, and at last they arrived where the dead boy miraculously continued to sing the *Alma Redemptoris Mater* without ceasing—for when the dead boy's voice had finished the end of the antiphon, it would begin the same song over again throughout the whole day.

The boy was lifted out, like a second Joseph out of the pit;[5] with speed and rejoicing he was taken to the church. The song to the Virgin did not leave his lips; continually he sang the *Alma Redemptoris Mater*. The people were summoned, and the clergy sat down in complete devotion. The Archbishop began to celebrate the divine office in honour of the blessed Virgin. The moment came when the congregation was ordered to be silent; the preacher began to speak, bringing a

5. Genesis 37:28.

message of salvation through the gospel. At this moment the boy also became quiet, and placed "a door of circumstance"[6] on his lips, so that the words of the gospel would not be misheard or misunderstood because of the sound of his voice.

The congregation listened with faith and devotion to the reading, and when the message of salvation was over, once again the boy miraculously began to sing the antiphon. How great then was the pious devotion of the clergy's prayers! How great was the effusion of tears among the congregation in its place, when the dead boy began again what he had just stopped, going through in his song what he had just passed over in silence! The health-giving Host was offered devoutly on the altar and the memory of the Lord's Passion worshipped, and all this time the boy's voice continued to sing of the purity of Mary. When the mysteries of our Redemption had been performed, the Archbishop turned to the congregation and delivered a sermon in praise of the innocence of the Virgin—though while he reverently called to memory the mother, of course he did not neglect to honour Christ as well. At the end of the sermon he wept and encouraged the clergy and people altogether to beseech the Virgin's son with the aroma of devotion and the sweet scent of pious prayer, and to pray by the merits of his mother and the prayers of the precious Virgin that Christ should deign to restore the boy to life, and breathe the breath of life into the dead corpse.

The clergy and the people poured out their souls within themselves, giving out their hearts like water in the sight of the Lord, letting their tears flow in a willing shower in the evening, a shower of tears, for their tears "were on their cheeks."[7] They prayed in supplication; in faith they beseeched; they were not beset by a cloud of mistrust about the efficacy of their prayer, for it went straight up to the Trinity: their faith swiftly penetrated to heaven, and their blessed trust was faithfully and joyfully repaid. In reply to their public and private prayers, the Virgin Mother (as I imagine) looked into the face of Christ and beseeched him in what I picture as a familiar fashion; and immediately the boy's cut throat was allowed to breathe again, his previously torn flesh was restored fully, and his tongue, which sang divine praise, was given back to him; his heart and liver which had been removed were put back again, or were created anew by divine aid. His soul was summoned back again into its vessel and vehicle, and the boy became whole again; the immortal spirit was again married to the dead flesh. He who was dead came to life again and returned; the boy awoke, aroused, as it were, from a deep sleep. Even now he did not cease his praise of Mary, and his sweet voice continued to sing the *Alma Redemptoris Mater*. Truly blessed are you, Mother of the Redeemer, for coming to the help of the dead boy who lacked the power to rise again: she who, to the amazement of Nature,[8] gave birth to her own creator,

6. Psalms 140:3.
7. Lamentations 1:2; cf. Joel 2:23.
8. The phrase *Natura mirante*, "to Nature's amazement," is taken from the antiphon *Alma Redemptoris Mater*.

again astonished Nature by pouring back the vital spirit into the dead child through the intercession of her prayer.

At the sight of this amazing miracle, the congregation of the faithful rejoiced, and at the sight they dissolved into tears: they still wondered if it was an illusion. When they looked at the revived boy's face, they discovered the pebble which Mary had placed in his mouth; they removed it, and immediately he stopped his singing of the antiphon. He lost the impelling power of speech which before had not allowed him to be silent. The pebble was placed as a sign in the cathedral church, to act as a monument of the event and as evidence of the miracle, to be kept there for ever.

The Archbishop now asked the boy to tell him the whole sequence and order of the affair, and he answered the pontiff to his satisfaction, giving him a full and true account of the whole series of events—the crime of the Jews, his own martyrdom and the assistance of the Virgin Mary. He attributed everything to the Mother of God: whatever had happened to him was done by the Mother of Grace, who had thus aided his wretchedness from the abundance of her mercy. As he told his story, he pointed with his finger at the murderer, but this boy, who had been raised from death, prayed humbly but insistently that his murderer should not be condemned to die for the crime. At last the boy rose, and gave thanks fully to his saviour, the Virgin, and, now made whole in every particular, lived long after in the city of Toledo.

The Jew was more sure of his punishment than hopeful for mercy, but after seeing the miracle he confessed himself guilty and worthy of execution; nevertheless, he asked first to be bathed by the saving water of baptism. The Archbishop was more eager for the saving of a soul than for the punishment of the crime; he baptized the Jew and entrusted him to the church; having marked him with the sign of our faith, he remitted the penalty and pardoned the crime. Afterward the Jew, who had before been the most impious persecutor of the name of the Virgin, became her most pious devotee. There was also an infidel who witnessed the miracle and who became a member of the Christian faith. Thus, in the faith of Christ, the two walls of the cornerstone, from both circumcised and uncircumsised,[9] were joined together. The second man, now a believer instead of an infidel, was prosperous and very rich: he built a church in honour of the Virgin Mother, where her memory is memorably celebrated. Thus the kindly Mother of the Redeemer helps everyone with success; by her deserts may she commend to God those of us who are mindful of her, and help them by her good actions. AMEN.

---

9. The image of the two walls meeting at the cornerstone comes from Ephesians 2:11–22 and Psalms 117:22, the antiphon for the Magnificat on December 22. The passage was interpreted in this way, as the union of circumcised and uncircumcised, by Gregory: see *The Christ of Cynewulf*, ed. A. S. Cook (1900; Hamden: Archon Books, 1964), p. 75.

A Miracle of Our Lady†

"Hou the Jewes, in despit° of Ure Lady, threwe   scorn
    a chyld in a gonge"°   privy

Wose° loveth wel Ure Ladi,   Whoever
Heo° wol quiten his wille wel whi,[1]   She
Othur° in his lyf or at his ende,   Either
The ladi is so freo° and hende.°   generous / gracious
5 Hit fel sumtyme° in Parys,°   It happened once / Paris
As witnesseth in Holy Writ storys,
In the cite bifel this cas:°   case, adventure
A pore child was° of porchas,°   there was / income
That with the beggeri that he con wynne[2]
10 He fond° sumdel what of° his kinne—   supported / certain of
His fader, his moder, and eke himself.
He begged in cite bi everi half.°   in every section
    The child non othur craftus° couthe°   skills / knew
But winne hys lyflode° with his mouthe.   livelihood
15 The childes vois was swete and cler;
Men lusted° his song with riht good cher.   listened to
With his song that was ful swete
He gat mete° from strete to strete.   obtained food
Men herked° his song ful likyngly°   listened to / pleasurably
20 Hit was an antimne° of Ure Lady;   anthem
He song that antimne everiwher,
I-called Alma Redemptoris Mater,
That is forthrightly° to mene°   plainly, simply / mean
"Godus° moder, mylde and clene,°   God's / chaste
25 Hevene gate and sterre of se,°   star of the sea
Save thi peple from synne and we."°   woe
That song was holden deynteous;°   considered precious
The child song hit from hous to hous.
For° he song hit so lykynglye,°   Because / pleasingly
30 The Jewes hedde° alle to hym envye.   had
Til hit fel on a Setersday°   Saturday
The childes wey thorw the Jewerie° lay;   the Jewish quarter
The Jewes hedden that song in hayn,°   hate
Therfore thei schope° the child be slayn.   made plans that
35 So lykingly the child song ther,
So lustily song he never er.°   before
    On° of the Jewes malicious   One

† Text based on *The Minor Poems of the Vernon MS*, ed. Carl Horstmann and F. J. Furnivall, EETS o.s. 98, 117 (London, 1892, 1901), I. 141–45. Reprinted with permission of the Council of the Early English Text Society. The MS was made in the late fourteenth century, sometime after 1382, and is a vast miscellany of religious or didactic pieces written in Middle English and Anglo-Norman. It once included a comprehensive collection of Miracles of the Virgin—the index lists forty-two—but most of that part of the MS was destroyed long ago. Only eight Miracles, of which this is the second, survive in full; a ninth is fragmentary.
1. She will for that (reason) repay well his determination.
2. Who with the money that he earned by begging.

Tilled° the child in to his hous. — *Enticed*
His malice there he gan to kuythe:° — *show*
40 He cutte the childes throte alswithe.° — *quickly*
The child ne spared nout° for that wrong — *did not cease*
But never-the-latere° song forth his song. — *nevertheless*
Whon he hedde endet, he eft° bigon; — *again*
His syngyng couthe stoppe no mon.° — *no man knew how to stop*
45 Therof the Jeuh was sore anuyet,° — *annoyed, troubled*
Leste his malice mihte ben aspyet.° — *spied out, discovered*
The Jeuh bithouhte him of a gynne:° — *stratagem*
Into a gonge-put° fer withinne — *privy-pit*
The child adoun therinne he throng;° — *thrust*
50 The child song evere the same song.
So lustily the child con crie,
That song he never er so hyghe.° — *loudly*
Men mihte him here fer and neer,
The childes vois was so heigh and cleer.
55 The childes moder was wont to abyde° — *wait (for him)*
Every day til the non-tyde;° — *noontime*
Then was he wont to bring heom° mete — *them*
Such as he mihte with his song gete.
Bote that day was the tyme apast;
60 Therfore his moder was sore agast.° — *afraid*
With syk° and serwe° in everi strete — *sighing / sorrow*
Heo souhte wher° heo mihte with him mete. — *She sought (the place) where*
Bote whon heo com in to the Jewery,
Heo herde his vois so cler of cry.
65 Aftur that vois his modur dreuh;° — *drew, followed*
Wher he was inne, therbi heo kneuh.° — *knew*
Then of hire child heo asked a siht.° — *sight*
The Jew withnayted° him anon-riht° — *denied / promptly*
And seide ther nas non such child thrinne.° — *therein*
70 The childes moder yit nolde not blinne,° — *cease*
But ever the moder criede in on.° — *continually*
The Jeuh seide evere ther nas such non.
Then seide the wommon, "Thou seist wrong.
He is herinne, I knowe his song."
75 The Jeuh bigon to stare° and swere — *glare*
And seide ther com non such child there.
But never-the-latere men mihte here
The child song evere so loude and clere,
And ever the lengor, herre° and herre, — *higher, louder*
80 Men mihte him here bothe fer and nerre.
The modur coude° non othur won:° — *knew / hope*
To meir° and baylyfs° heo is gon. — *mayor / bailiffs*
Heo pleyneth° the Jeuh hath don hire wrong — *complains*
To stelen hire sone so for his song.
85 Heo preyeth to don hire lawe and riht,° — *justice*
Hire sone don° come bifore heore siht. — *To cause her son to*

Heo preyeth the meir par charite°   *in the name of charity*
Of him to have freo lyveré.°   *to take legal custody*
Thenne heo telleth the meir among°   *the mayor along with others*
90 Hou heo lyveth bi hire sone song.
The meir then hath of hire pite,
And sumneth° the folk of that cite.   *summons*
He telleth hem of that wommons sawe°   *story*
And seith he mot don° hire the lawe,   *enforce (for)*
95 And hoteth° hem with hym to wende,°   *orders / go*
To bringe this wommons cause to ende.
      Whon thei cum thider, for al heore noyse
Anon thei herde the childes voyse.
Riht as an angeles vois hit were,
100 Thei herde him never synge so clere.
Ther the meir maketh entré,
And of the child he asketh lyveré.°   *delivery (into his possession)*
The Jeuh may nought the meir refuse,
Ne of the child hym wel excuse;
105 But nede he moste knouleche° his wrong,   *acknowledge*
Ateynt° bi the childes song.   *Convicted*
      The meir let serchen hym° so longe   *had him searched for*
Til he was founden in the gonge,°   *privy*
Ful depe i-drouned in fulthe° of fen.°   *filth / muck, dung*
110 The meir het drawe the child° up then,   *ordered the child raised*
With fen and fulthe riht foule biwhorven,°   *bespattered*
And eke the childes throte i-corven.°   *carved, cut*
Anon-riht, er thei passede forthere,
The Jeuh was jugget° for that morthere.°   *judged / murder*
115 And er the peple passede in sonder,°   *dispersed*
The bisschop was comen to seo that wonder.
      In presence of bisschop and alle ifere,°   *together*
The child song evere iliche° clere.   *continually*
The bisschop serchede with his hond;
120 Withinne the childes throte he fond
A lilie flour, so briht and cler,
So feir a lylie nas nevere seyen er,
With guldene° lettres everiwher: *golden*
"Alma Redemptoris Mater."
125 Anon° that lilie out was taken,   *As soon as*
The childes song bigon to slaken.
That swete song was herd no more,
But as a ded cors° the child lay thore.°   *corpse / there*
      The bisschop with gret solempnete°   *ceremony*
130 Bad bere the cors° thorw al the cite;   *Ordered the body carried*
And hymself with processioun
Com with the cors thorw al the toun,
With prestes and clerkes that couthen° syngen.   *knew how to*
And alle the belles he het hem ryngen,
135 With torches brennynge and clothus riche;

With worschipe thei ladden that holi liche.°   *body*
In to the munstre° whon thei kem,°   *minster, church / came*
Bigonne the masse of requiem,°   *Requiem Mass*
As for the dede men is wont.°   *customary*
140   But thus sone thei weren i-stunt:°   *astounded*
The cors aros in heore° presens,   *their*
Bigon then "Salve sancta parens."°   *"Hail, holy parent" (antiphon)*
Men mihte wel witen° the sothe° therbi: *know / truth*
The child hedde i-servet Ur Swete Ladi,
145   That worschipede° him so on erthe her°   *honored / here*
And broughte his soule to blisse al cler.
      Therfore I rede° that everi mon   *advise*
Serve that ladi wel as he con,
And love hire in his beste wyse.°   *way*
150   Heo wol wel quite° him his servise.   *repay*
Now, Marie, for thi muchele° miht,   *great*
Help us to hevene that is so briht!

Alma Redemptoris Mater†

Alma Redemptoris Mater quae pervia coeli
Porta manes, et stella maris, succurre cadenti,
Surgere qui curat, populo; tu quae genuisti,
Natura mirante, tuum sanctum Genitorem,
Virgo prius ac posterius, Gabrielis ab ore,
Sumens illud Ave, peccatorum miserere.

Kindly Mother of the Redeemer, who art ever of heaven
The open gate, and the star of the sea, aid a fallen people,
Which is trying to rise again; thou who didst give birth,
While Nature marveled how, to thy Holy Creator,
Virgin both before and after, from Gabriel's mouth
Accepting the All hail, be merciful toward sinners.
                              (trans. John Henry Newman)

† This is one of four antiphons of the Blessed Virgin Mary used to conclude Compline, the final hour of the canonical day. Each is assigned to a different portion of the church year, the
present antiphon being sung from Saturday before the first Sunday of Advent through Feb-
ruary 1. Cardinal Newman's translation is printed from *Tracts for the Times* 75 (3.23 in the
bound editions of 1840–42, rpt. New York: AMS Press, 1969).

POPE GREGORY X

[On Christian Mistreatment of Jews]†

Gregory, bishop, servant of the servants of God, extends greetings and the apostolic benediction to the beloved sons in Christ, the faithful Christians, to those here now and to those in the future. Even as it is not allowed to the Jews in their assemblies presumptuously to undertake for themselves more than that which is permitted them by law, even so they ought not to suffer any disadvantage in those [privileges] which have been granted them. Although they prefer to persist in their stubbornness rather than to recognize the words of their prophets and the mysteries of the Scriptures, and thus to arrive at a knowledge of Christian faith and salvation; nevertheless, inasmuch as they have made an appeal for our protection and help, we therefore admit their petition and offer them the shield of our protection through the clemency of Christian piety. In so doing we follow in the footsteps of our predecessors of blessed memory, the popes of Rome—Calixtus, Eugene, Alexander, Clement, Celestine, Innocent, and Honorius.

We decree moreover that no Christian shall compel them or any one of their group to come to baptism unwillingly. But if any one of them shall take refuge of his own accord with Christians, because of conviction, then, after his intention will have been manifest, he shall be made a Christian without any intrigue. For, indeed, that person who is known to have come to Christian baptism not freely, but unwillingly, is not believed to possess the Christian faith.

Moreover no Christian shall presume to seize, imprison, wound, torture, mutilate, kill, or inflict violence on them; furthermore no one shall presume, except by judicial action of the authorities of the country, to change the good customs in the land where they live for the purpose of taking their money or goods from them or from others.

In addition, no one shall disturb them in any way during the celebration of their festivals, whether by day or by night, with clubs or stones or anything else. Also no one shall exact any compulsory service of them unless it be that which they have been accustomed to render in previous times.

Inasmuch as the Jews are not able to bear witness against the Christians, we decree furthermore that the testimony of Christians against Jews shall not be valid unless there is among these Christians some Jew who is there for the purpose of offering testimony.

Since it happens occasionally that some Christians lose their Christian children, the Jews are accused by their enemies of secretly

† From Jacob Rader Marcus, *The Jew in the Medieval World. A Source Book: 317–1791*, rev. ed., intro. Marc Saperstein (Cincinnati: Hebrew Union College P, 1999), pp. 170–72. Reprinted with the permission of Hebrew Union College Press. We have omitted Marcus's historical commentary. Gregory's bull is dated 7 October 1272. The first four paragraphs repeat language from earlier papal bulls that attempted to protect Jews. For the historical context of this letter and an edition of the Latin text, see Solomon Grayzel, *The Church and the Jews in the XIIIth Century*, vol. II, ed. Kenneth R. Stow (New York: Jewish Theological Seminary of America, 1989), pp. 1–45, 116–20.

carrying off and killing these same Christian children and of making sacrifices of the heart and blood of these very children. It happens, too, that the parents of these children or some other Christian enemies of these Jews secretly hide these very children in order that they may be able to injure these Jews, and in order that they may be able to extort from them a certain amount of money by redeeming them from their straits. And most falsely do these Christians claim that the Jews have secretly and furtively carried away these children and killed them, and that the Jews offer sacrifice from the heart and the blood of these children, since their law in this matter precisely and expressly forbids Jews to sacrifice, eat, or drink the blood, or to eat the flesh of animals having claws. This has been demonstrated many times at our court by Jews converted to the Christian faith: nevertheless very many Jews are often seized and detained unjustly because of this.[1]

We decree, therefore, that Christians need not be obeyed against Jews in a case or situation of this type, and we order that Jews seized under such a silly pretext be freed from imprisonment, and that they shall not be arrested henceforth on such a miserable pretext, unless—which we do not believe—they be caught in the commission of the crime. We decree that no Christian shall stir up anything new against them, but that they should be maintained in that status and position in which they were in the time of our predecessors, from antiquity till now.

We decree, in order to stop the wickedness and avarice of bad men, that no one shall dare to devastate or to destroy a cemetery of the Jews or to dig up human bodies for the sake of getting money. Moreover, if any one, after having known the content of this decree, should—which we hope will not happen—attempt audaciously to act contrary to it, then let him suffer punishment in his rank and position, or let him be punished by the penalty of excommunication, unless he makes amends for his boldness by proper recompense. Moreover, we wish that only those Jews who have not attempted to contrive anything toward the destruction of the Christian faith be fortified by the support of such protection. . . .

---

1. On the child-murder libel, see Gavin I. Langmuir, *Toward a Definition of Antisemitism* (Berkeley: U of California P, 1990), chaps. 9–11, and esp. chap. 12; also *The Blood Libel Legend: A Casebook in Anti-Semitic Folklore*, ed. Alan Dundes (Madison: U of Wisconsin P, 1991). It should be noted that this papal bull, like others before it, had little effect overall on Christian attitudes toward Jews in the Middle Ages.

The Prologue and
Tale of Sir Thopas

Chaucer's *Tale of Sir Thopas* is a parody of popular Middle English romances, particularly those written in tail-rhyme stanzas (rhyming couplets
bound together by shorter lines ending in a single repeated rhyme). Almost every feature of *Thopas*—its metrics, its conventional diction, its
scenes of the hero's questing, arming, encountering a giant, and falling in
love—can be found in one or another of the many romances that it sports
with. As an example of this genre, we print a very small portion of a very
long poem, *Guy of Warwick*, alluded to in line 899 of Chaucer's tale. Guy's
military and amorous successes represent the typical exploits of romance
heroes and thus suggest a norm against which to consider how Thopas
conducts himself in battle and in love.

From *Guy of Warwick*†

God graunt hem heven blis to mede°	*heaven's bliss as a reward*
That herken to mi romaunce rede,°	*Who listen to my tale readily*
Al of a gentil° knight.	*noble*
The best bodi° he was at nede°	*person / in (times of) need*
5 That ever might bistriden stede,°	*sit on a horse*
And freest° founde in fight.	*most valorous*
The word of him ful wide it ran.	
Over al this warld the priis he wan°	*he took the prize*
As man most° of might.	*greatest*
10 Balder bern° was non in bi.°	*A bolder man / in any place (lit., in town)*
His name was hoten sir Gii°	*called Sir Guy*
Of Warwick, wise and wight.°	*valiant*
Wight he was, for sothe to say,°	*to tell the truth*
And holden for priis° in everi play°	*considered worthy / i.e., activity*
15 As knight of gret bounte.°	*goodness*
Out of this lond he went his way	

† Text adapted from *The Romance of Guy of Warwick*, ed. Julius Zupitza, EETS e.s. 49 (London, 1887; rpt. 1966), pp. 384–88, 394–96. Reprinted with permission of the Council of
the Early English Text Society. There are various Middle English versions of this thirteenth-
century Anglo-Norman historical romance. We print a passage from the tail-rhyme portion
of the version in the Auchinleck manuscript, written in the 1330s in London and conceiv-
ably read by Chaucer. This passage occurs in the second half of the poem; Guy is returning
to England after many displays of heroism in adventures overseas, thus proving his worthiness to marry the woman he loves, Felice, daughter of the Earl of Warwick.

Thurch° mani divers cuntray°   *Through / countries*
  That was biyond the see.°   *sea*
Sethen° he com into Inglond   *Afterward*
20 And Athelston° the king he fond,°   *Athelstan / sought*
  That was bothe hende° and fre.°   *courteous / generous*
For his love, ich° understond,   *I*
He slough° a dragoun in Northumberlond,   *slew, killed*
  Ful fer in the north cuntre.°   *region*

25 He and Herhaud,[1] for sothe to say,
  To Wallingforth° toke the way,   *Wallingford (in south-central England)*
    That was his faders toun.°   *father's town*
Than was his fader, sothe to say,
Ded and birid° in the clay.   *buried*
30   His air was sir Gioun.°   *Sir Guy was his heir*
Alle that held of° him lond or fe°   *received from / payment for service*
Deden him omage° and feute°   *Gave him homage / fealty (feudal loyalty)*
  And com to his somoun.°   *came (to court) at his summons*
He tok alle his faders lond
35 And yaf it hende Herhaud in hond°   *gave it to courteous Herhaud to control*
  Right to his warisoun.°   *As a proper reward (for Herhaud's service)*

And alle that hadde in his servise be°   *been*
He yaf hem gold and riche fe°   *splendid payment*
  Ful hendeliche° on honde.   *courteously*
40 And sethen° he went with his meyne°   *afterward / retinue*
To th'Erl Rohaud° that was so fre.°   *Earl Rohaud (Guy's feudal lord) / noble*
  At Warwike° he him fond.   *Warwick*
Alle than were thai glad and blithe
And thonked God a thousand sithe°   *times*
45   That Gii was comen° to lond.   *had returned*
Sethe on hunting thai gun ride°   *did ride*
With knightes fele° and miche pride   *many*
  As ye may understond.

On a day Sir Gii gan fond,°   *decided to act*
50 And feir Felice he tok bi hond
  And seyd to that bird° so blithe:°   *lady / glad, merry*
"Ichave,"° he seyd, "thurch Godes sond°   *I have / gift*
Won the priis° in mani lond   *Taken the honors*
  Of° knightes strong and stithe,°   *From / valiant, stalwart*
55 And me is boden gret anour°   *great honor has been offered me*
Kinges douhter and emperour°   *emperor's*
  To have to mi wive.°   *take as my wife*
Ac,° swete Felice," he seyd than,°   *But / then*
"Y no schal never spouse wiman°   *I shall never marry (any other) woman*
60   Whiles thou art olive."°   *alive*

---

1. Guy's foster-father, teacher, and constant companion on his adventures.

Than answerd that swete wight°   *person*
And seyd ogain° to him ful right:°   *in reply / directly*
  "Bi him that schope mankinne,°   *created mankind*
Icham° desired day and night   *I am*
65 Of° erl, baroun, and mani a knight,   *By*
  For nothing wil thai blinne.°   *They will not cease for anything*
Ac Gii," sche seyd, "hende and fre,
Al mi love is layd on the;°   *given to thee*
  Our love schal never twinne.°   *be parted*
70 And bot ich have the to make°   *unless I have thee as my mate*
Other lord nil y non take,°   *I will accept no other lord*
  For al this warld to winne."

Anon to hir than answerd Gii,
To fair Felice that sat him bi,°   *sat by him*
75   That semly was of sight.°   *Who was pleasing to look upon*
"Leman,"° he seyd, "gramerci."°   *Lover / thank you*
With joie and with melodi
  He kist° that swete wight.   *kissed*
Than was he bothe glad and blithe.°   *merry*
80 His joie couthe he noman kithe
  For that bird so bright.[2]
He no was never therbiforn°   *He had never before been*
Half so blithe sethe° he was born,   *since*
  For nought that man him hight.°   *For anything anyone had promised him*

                          * * *

85 When he hadde spoused° that swete wight,   *married*
The fest° lasted a fourtennight,°   *feast / fortnight (two weeks)*
  That frely° folk in fere°   *noble / together*
With erl, baroun, and mani a knight,
And mani a levedy° fair and bright,   *lady*
90   The best in lond that were.
Ther wer giftes for the nones,°   *for the occasion*
Gold and silver and precious stones
  And druries° riche and dere.°   *treasures / valuable*
Ther was mirthe and melody
95 And al maner menstracie°   *every sort of minstrelsy (i.e., entertainment)*
  As ye may fortheward here:°   *hear next*

Ther was trumpes° and tabour,°   *trumpets / drum*
Fithel, croude, and harpour,
  Her craftes for to kithe;[3]
100 Organisters° and gode stivours,°   *Organ players / bagpipers*
Minstrels of mouthe° and mani dysour°   *I.e., singers / storytellers*
  To glade tho bernes blithe.°   *To gladden those merry folk*

---

2. He knew no way of expressing to anyone the joy he took in such a beautiful lady.
3. Fiddle, crowd [a stringed instrument played with a bow], and harper, (all) showing their skill.

Ther nis no tong° may telle in tale   *tongue*
The joie that was at that bridale°   *wedding party (lit., bride-ale)*
105   With menske° and mirthe to mithe,°   *courtesy / to be seen*
For ther was al maner of gle°   *music, entertainment*
That hert might thinke other eyghe se,°   *or the eye see*
    As ye may list and lithe.°   *As it may please and soothe you*

Herls,° barouns hende and fre   *Earls*
110   That ther war gadred° of mani cuntre,   *Who were gathered there*
    That worthliche were in wede,°   *Who were nobly dressed*
Thai yoven glewemen° for her gle   *They gave to the entertainers*
Robes riche, gold, and fe.°   *fee (payment)*
    Her giftes were nought gnede.°   *stingy*
115   On the fiften° day, ful yare,°   *fifteenth / fully prepared*
Thai toke her leve for to fare°   *journey*
    And thonked hem her gode dede.°   *i.e., for their hospitality*
Than hadde Gii, that gentil knight,
Feliis° to his wil day and night,   *Felice*
120   In gest also we rede.°   *As we read in the story*

The Nun's Priest's
Prologue and Tale

Beast fables were popular throughout the Middle Ages. The preface to
William Caxton's translation of Aesop's fables provides a summary of conventional views about the genre and its purposes. Sometime around 1200
Marie de France wrote a collection of fables in Anglo-Norman; one of
them, "The Cock and the Fox," tells the story that is the nucleus of the
Nun's Priest's Tale. For the expansion of fable into beast-epic, Chaucer
knew of the tales of Reynard the Fox, which circulated widely in France
and elsewhere. Robert A. Pratt has argued that the confrontation of Reynard and Chanteclere in branch 2 of the *Roman de Renart* is one of
Chaucer's direct sources. The learned and mock-heroic inflations of the
Nun's Priest's Tale derive from many places; we include Macrobius's authoritative chapter on dreams and Geoffrey of Vinsauf's rhetorical lament
on the death of King Richard I. The courtly elements of Chaucer's story
may even have been suggested by the encyclopedic tradition, as may be
seen in a portion of Bartholomaeus Anglicus's description of the cock,
here printed in John of Trevisa's fourteenth-century English translation.

WILLIAM CAXTON

From *Aesop's Fables*†

[Book I]

Here begyneth the preface or prologue of the fyrst
book of Esope.

I, Romulus, son of Thybere[1] of the cyte of
Atyque,° gretyng. Esope, man of Grece, subtyll   *Attica*
and ingenyous, techeth in his fables how men
ought to kepe and rewle them° well. And to   *themselves*
th'ende that he shold shewe the lyf and customes
of al maner of men, he induceth° the byrdes, the   *introduces*
trees and the beestes spekynge, to th'ende that
the men may knowe wherfore the fables were
found.° In the whiche he hath wreton the malyce   *invented*

---

† Text based on Caxton's 1484 edition as printed in *The Fables of Aesop*, ed. Joseph Jacobs,
2 vols. (London: David Nutt, 1889), 2.3.
1. Tiberius. The "Romulus" version of Aesop's fables circulated widely in the Middle Ages; the
author is unknown, but it was certainly not the Roman emperor's son.

of the evylle people and the argument of the im-
probes.° He techeth also to be humble and for to   *wicked*
use wordes, and many other fayr ensamples re-
herced and declared here after, the whiche I,
Romulus, have translated oute of Grekes tongue
in to Latyn tongue, the which yf thou rede them,
they shalle aguyse° and sharp thy wytte and shal   *adorn*
gyve to the cause of joye.

MARIE DE FRANCE

The Cock and the Fox†

This is the story of a cock, who was standing on a dunghill, singing. A
fox came up alongside and spoke to him with pleasant words: "How
very handsome you are, sir," he said. "I've never seen such a noble
bird; you have the clearest voice of any creature. Except for your father, whom I knew well, no bird has sung better—but he was better at
it than you, because he kept his eyes closed." "I can do it that way,"
said the cock. He flapped his wings and shut his eyes, thinking that he
would sing all the more beautifully. The fox jumped, seized him, and
fled toward the forest with him.

As the fox passed through a field, all the shepherds ran to catch
him, and the dogs all around ran barking after him. So here is the fox
holding the cock: he will lose what he's won if he comes too close to
them. "Go ahead," the cock said, "call out to them that you've got me
and will never let me go." The fox was determined to shout loudly, at
which point the cock bolted out of his mouth and flew up to a tall
trunk of a tree. When the fox realized what had happened, he knew he
had been completely fooled by the cock's clever trickery. In vexation
and sheer anger at himself he began to curse his own mouth for
speaking when it should have been silent. The cock said in response:
"I should do likewise: curse the eye that would close when it ought to
keep watch and be alert that no evil comes to its lord."

This is how many foolish people act: they speak when they should
be silent and stay silent when they should speak.

---

† Translated by Glending Olson from Marie de France, *Les Fables*, 2d ed., ed. and trans.
Charles Brucker (Paris and Louvain: Peeters, 1998), pp. 238–41. For a complete text and
English translation, see Marie de France, *Fables*, ed. and trans. Harriet Spiegel (Toronto:
U of Toronto P, 1987).

FROM *LE ROMAN DE RENART*, BRANCH 2†

How Chanteclere Makes a Fool of Reynard

It happened on a day that Reynard the Fox, well-versed in evil arts and guile, came trotting up to a farm set in the woods. The farm possessed many chickens, ducks, and geese. The lord of that land was Constantine of Noyes, a farmer of great wealth. His house was full to the bursting with fowl and bacon and salted meat. He also had plenty of grain set by, and the orchards bore their many and various fruits in season. It was here that Reynard came for his own amusement.

The courtyard was enclosed by a palisade of sharp oak stakes and spiny hawthorn, and there Sir Constantine had placed his hens, as in a kind of fortress. Reynard addressed himself to the palisade, but though his resourcefulness was great, the spines were sharper still. At last he squatted in the road, angry and upset, yet not wanting to abandon the hens. If he tried to leap the stockade wall, he would be seen, and the hens that pecked the dirt not two feet beyond would disappear. The fox paced angrily up and down, until he spied a broken stake. At once he plunged through the wall. Where the stockade was broken, the farmer had planted cabbages, and Reynard dropped down among them, hoping he had not been seen. But the chickens had heard the noise of his fall, and every one of them took flight.

Master Chanteclere the Cock, who had been scratching in a dusty path, came toward the band of chickens. Plumes spread and neck outstretched, he demanded haughtily why they had fled. Pinte of the Large Eggs, who roosted at the cock's right hand, was the wisest, and she told him what had happened: "We were all terrified," she said.

"But why?" the rooster demanded. "What have you seen?"

"Some kind of wild beast, who would have done great harm, if we hadn't fled the garden."

"I beg your pardon," Chanteclere replied, "but this is just a trifle. Don't worry yourself about it further."

"By my faith," said Pinte, "I loyally swear to you I saw him clearly."

"And how did you catch sight of whatever it was?"

"How? I saw the enclosure shake and the cabbage leaf tremble where he lies in wait."

"Pinte," exclaimed the cock, "you're a fool! I don't know of any fox or polecat strong enough to breach our walls. I promise you by the loyalty I owe you, there is nothing there. Go on back!" And the rooster returned to his dust.

He who fears nothing, except a dog or fox, will always be quite confident—as long as he thinks himself safe. And thus Chanteclere acted quite disdainfully, for he feared nothing but the fox.

---

† Translated for this volume by Elizabeth Hanson-Smith from *Le Roman de Renart*, ed. Ernest Martin (Strasbourg: Trübner, 1882), 1. 91–104. For texts and translations of this and other sources of the *Nun's Priest's Tale*, see Edward Wheatley's chapter in *Sources and Analogues of The Canterbury Tales, Vol. I*, ed. Robert M. Correale and Mary Hamel (Cambridge: D. S. Brewer, 2002), pp. 449–89.

As one bored with both singing and scratching, one eye open, the other shut, the cock at last flew up under the eaves and took his rest. Roosting there in delicious sleep, Chanteclere began to dream. (Now don't think I'm making this up—it's the whole truth, and you can find it written down.) He dreamed that something entered the courtyard, although it was securely locked, and came up to him, face to face. Chanteclere shuddered at this. The creature had a fur mantle of red and white, its collar trimmed in bone. Here Chanteclere tossed and turned in his sleep. Suddenly the cloak was wrapped about him, by force. And most strange, he was forced into it through the narrow collar, so that his head was at the creature's tail. Great was the pain that Chanteclere suffered for that dream, and he thought himself cursed in that vision. At last he struggled into wakefulness and heaved a sigh, saying "Holy Spirit, save my body from that prison, and keep me safe!" Off he rushed, no longer quite so secure, and came upon the hens, who pecked beside the hawthorn. He did not cry out to them at once, but called Pinte aside to take counsel with her first.

"Pinte," he said, for he trusted her, "I can't hide my sorrow and despair. And fear. I think some bird of prey or wild beast is going to harm us."

"Dear sweet lord," cried Pinte, "never say that aloud! For shame! You'll frighten us all. You betray yourself in saying you are afraid. By all the saints to whom we pray, you're like the dog who whines before the stone is cast. Why are you frightened? What's the matter with you?"

"You don't know," he answered, "what a strange dream I've had. It seemed to me there was an evil apparition within the enclosure of this very farm. That is why you see me pale and trembling. It seemed to me some animal came in, wearing a mantle of red fur, sown together without scissors or seam, trimmed in bone, all white and hard. He forced me to dress in his mantle, and I had to put it on over my head, collar first. When I awoke I was no longer wrapped up in fur, but I marvel still at the tightness of that collar, and at the tail that seemed to be in front of my face. That is why I despair. Pinte, I am tormented by this dream. By the loyalty you owe me, tell me, do you know what this signifies?"

Pinte, his trusted one, answered then, "You have told me your dream, but please God, it won't come true. If you wish an explanation of it, I know well what it is, for what you have seen while dreaming, that thing dressed in a red cloak—that is the fox. He's easily known by his red fur coat. The trim of bone, that was his teeth, by which he forced you inside him. The collar that did not fit, that was so horribly tight for you—that is the gullet of the beast, that's how you entered his belly. The tail means, no doubt—by all the saints in all the world!— that when the fox has swallowed you, his tail will be before your nose! Now you know the meaning of your dream, God help me. Gold and silver can't save you. And it will all come to pass before high noon. But if you still don't believe me, take a look over there, for he lies in wait, quietly, in the cabbage patch, ready to betray and deceive you."

When Chanteclere had heard this interpretation of his dream, he said, "Pinte, these are traitorous words! You say I'll be conquered by a beast who is even now inside our stockade. Cursed is the man who believes that! You've told me nothing I care to hear. No matter what, I won't believe I'll suffer for this dream."

"Sire," she answered, "God forbid it should be so, but I swear to you, if things don't turn out as I've predicted, I am no longer your true love."

"Oh, Pinte," said Chanteclere, "never mind!"

Chanteclere considered that interpretation a wild tale, and walked back to take his pleasure in his patch of dust, where he soon began to slumber again.

Meanwhile, Reynard had waited patiently and looked on, much amused. Once certain the cock had fallen asleep, Reynard crept up, one paw after another, soundlessly. If once the fox had Chanteclere in his teeth, he would make a meal of him. He longed for chicken dinner, but when he sprang, heavy-handed, he missed. While Chanteclere flew to the top of a dung-heap, well out of reach, Reynard cursed himself for failing. But at once the fox began again to plot a way to trick poor Chanteclere. If he did not eat that rooster, his time was wasted.

"Dear Chanteclere," he called, "don't fly away for this trifle. After all, you and I are first cousins, quite closely related."

Chanteclere gained confidence at this, and sang a little song for joy.

Reynard said to his cousin, "Do you remember Chanteclin, your dear father, who begot you? No other cock could sing the way he did. The country folk miles away could hear him. When he sang, he took a good deep breath and closed his eyes tight. Ah, but his voice was grand. He wasn't always peering about him, when he let go in the pleasures of song."

"Reynard, cousin," said Chanteclere, "are you trying to pull a trick?"

"Of course . . ." answered Reynard, "I am not. But now, please sing! Shut those eyes and go to it! You know we are of one flesh, one blood—and I would rather lose a leg than see you come to grief."

Said Chanteclere, "I don't believe you. Remove yourself a little way before I sing a song. There won't be a neighbor far or near who cannot hear my falsetto!"

Reynard smiled broadly: "Well, do it loudly, then! Sing, cousin! Let it be known you were born of my uncle Chanteclin."

The cock began quite loudly, letting out a terrific din, but with only one eye closed, and the other open, watching Reynard, whom he strongly suspected of mischief.

Reynard said, "This is nothing. Chanteclin sang far differently. He'd close his eyes tight and his great crowing could be heard for miles beyond the palisade."

Chanteclere at last believed him, and screwing his eyes up tight in the effort, he sent forth his melody. Reynard did not hesitate a moment, but seized the cock by the neck, and off he raced in high spirits, for he'd won his prey.

Pinte saw that Reynard had her love, and she fell into a frenzied despair when she saw the cock being carried off. She wailed after them,

"Sire, I told you so! But you scorned my words and called me a fool. Now those words are proven true and it is your own reasoning that brought you to ruin. I was a fool to cry 'fox' before you had actually seen him. Now Reynard has you and bears you off. Alas! Misery! I shall die! For if I lose my lord and master, my honor too is lost forever!"

The good old woman of the manor opened the door to her yard, for it was evening, and she wished to put her hens back in the coop. "Come, Pinte, Bise, Rosette!" she called, but none of them answered. She wondered what was wrong, until she heard her cock yelling, as best he could, and saw the fox running off with him. She knew she couldn't catch them and raised a cry for help. All the peasants on the farm came running when they heard her bawling so. They asked her what was wrong.

"Alas," she sighed heavily, "what a wicked thing has happened!"

"But what is it?" they demanded.

"I have lost my rooster—the fox has him!"

"You foul old hag!" shouted Constantine. "Didn't you stop him?"

"Sire," she replied, "You do me wrong. By holy God, I couldn't catch him. He wouldn't wait for me."

"Why didn't you hit him?"

"I couldn't find a stick. But anyway, he ran so fast, a Breton hound couldn't have caught up with him."

"Where did he go?"

"That way."

And off the peasants ran in great haste, shouting, "Over there, he's over there!"

Reynard leaped through the hole in the palisade and bore the cock to earth with him, but the noise he made was heard by all. "After him!" Constantine shouted, and called his mastiffs: "Mauvoisin! Bardol! Travers! Humbaut! Rebors! After him! After Renard the Red!"

Now Chanteclere was in great peril if he didn't think of some trick. And so he said, "Lord Reynard, don't you hear the shameful things those peasants say? Constantine recognized you and called you all sorts of names. When he shouts, 'Reynard is stealing my rooster!' you should say, 'In spite of all your efforts!' There's nothing that would annoy him more."

No one is so wise that he can't be fooled sometime: Reynard had tricked all the world, but this time he himself was deceived. The peasants raised the cry again, and Reynard turned to shout back, "In spite of all your efforts! I'll steal him any time I please!"

But with these words, Chanteclere felt those terrible jaws go slack, and beating his wings with all his might, he flew into an apple-tree. Reynard sat down on a dung-heap below him, chagrined, enraged, tormented by the cock who had escaped. Chanteclere just laughed: "Reynard," he said, "how's the world treating you these days?"

The traitor shook with rage and in sheer bad humor said, "Cursed be the mouth that speaks when it should be silent."

"Amen, amen," said the rooster. "Yes, and I wish him every evil who shuts his eyes and goes to sleep when he should stay awake. Cousin Reynard," he continued, "no one should ever trust you. Cursed be your cousinage! It almost ruined me. Reynard, you liar, get out of here! If you wait around, you'll lose your hide!"

Reynard was always very careful of his fur coat. He spoke not a word more, but turned at once and ran. Through the hedge beside the plain, straight down the road he fled. But his heart was heavy because of the rooster, who had escaped when he'd had him in his hands.

MACROBIUS

[On Dreams]†

* * *

After these prefatory remarks, there remains another matter to be considered before taking up the text of *Scipio's Dream*. We must first describe the many varieties of dreams recorded by the ancients, who have classified and defined the various types that have appeared to men in their sleep, wherever they might be. Then we shall be able to decide to which type the dream we are discussing belongs.

All dreams may be classified under five main types: there is the enigmatic dream, in Greek *oneiros*, in Latin *somnium*; second, there is the prophetic vision, in Greek *horama*, in Latin *visio*; third, there is the oracular dream, in Greek *chrematismos*, in Latin *oraculum*; fourth, there is the nightmare, in Greek *enypnion*, in Latin *insomnium*; and last, the apparition, in Greek *phantasma*, which Cicero, when he has occasion to use the word, calls *visum*.

The last two, the nightmare and the apparition, are not worth interpreting since they have no prophetic significance. Nightmares may be caused by mental or physical distress, or anxiety about the future: the patient experiences in dreams vexations similar to those that disturb him during the day. As examples of the mental variety, we might mention the lover who dreams of possessing his sweetheart or of losing her, or the man who fears the plots or might of an enemy and is confronted with him in his dream or seems to be fleeing him. The physical variety might be illustrated by one who has overindulged in eating or drinking and dreams that he is either choking with food or unburdening himself, or by one who has been suffering from hunger or thirst and dreams that he is craving and searching for food or drink or has found it. Anxiety about the future would cause a man to dream that he is gaining a prominent position or office as he hoped or that he is being deprived of it as he feared.

Since these dreams and others like them arise from some condition or circumstance that irritates a man during the day and consequently

† From *Commentary on the Dream of Scipio*, trans. William Harris Stahl (New York: Columbia UP, 1952), pp. 87–90. Copyright © 1952 Columbia University Press. Reprinted by permission of the publisher. Stahl's notes have been omitted.

disturbs him when he falls asleep, they flee when he awakes and vanish into thin air. Thus the name *insomnium* was given, not because such dreams occur "in sleep"—in this respect nightmares are like other types—but because they are noteworthy only during their course and afterwards have no importance or meaning.

Virgil, too, considers nightmares deceitful: "False are the dreams (*insomnia*) sent by departed spirits to their sky." He used the word "sky" with reference to our mortal realm because the earth bears the same relation to the regions of the dead as the heavens bear to the earth. Again, in describing the passion of love, whose concerns are always accompanied by nightmares, he says: "Oft to her heart rushes back the chief's valour, oft his glorious stock; his looks and words cling fast within her bosom, and the pang withholds calm rest from her limbs." And a moment later: "Anna, my sister, what dreams (*insomnia*) thrill me with fears?"

The apparition (*phantasma* or *visum*) comes upon one in the moment between wakefulness and slumber, in the so-called "first cloud of sleep." In this drowsy condition he thinks he is still fully awake and imagines he sees specters rushing at him or wandering vaguely about, differing from natural creatures in size and shape, and hosts of diverse things, either delightful or disturbing. To this class belongs the incubus, which, according to popular belief, rushes upon people in sleep and presses them with a weight which they can feel. The two types just described are of no assistance in foretelling the future; but by means of the other three we are gifted with the powers of divination.

We call a dream oracular in which a parent, or a pious or revered man, or a priest, or even a god clearly reveals what will or will not transpire, and what action to take or to avoid. We call a dream a prophetic vision if it actually comes true. For example, a man dreams of the return of a friend who has been staying in a foreign land, thoughts of whom never enter his mind. He goes out and presently meets his friend and embraces him. Or in his dream he agrees to accept a deposit, and early the next day a man runs anxiously to him, charging him with the safekeeping of his money and committing secrets to his trust. By an enigmatic dream we mean one that conceals with strange shapes and veils with ambiguity the true meaning of the information being offered, and requires an interpretation for its understanding. We need not explain further the nature of this dream since everyone knows from experience what it is. There are five varieties of it: personal, alien, social, public, and universal. It is called personal when one dreams that he himself is doing or experiencing something; alien, when he dreams this about someone else; social, when his dream involves others and himself; public, when he dreams that some misfortune or benefit has befallen the city, forum, theater, public walls, or other public enterprise; universal, when he dreams that some change has taken place in the sun, moon, planets, sky, or regions of the earth.

* * *

GEOFFREY OF VINSAUF

[Lament on the Death of Richard I]†

Once defended by King Richard's shield, now undefended, O England, bear witness to your woe in the gestures of sorrow. Let your eyes flood with tears, and pale grief waste your features. Let writhing anguish twist your fingers, and woe make your heart within bleed. Let your cry strike the heavens. Your whole being dies in his death; the death was not his but yours. Death's rise was not in one place only but general. O tearful day of Venus! O bitter star! That day was your night; and that Venus your venom. That day inflicted the wound; but the worst of all days was that other—the day after the eleventh—which, cruel stepfather to life, destroyed life. Either day, with strange tyranny, was a murderer. The besieged one pierced the besieger; the sheltered one, him without cover; the cautious one pierced the incautious; the well-equipped soldier pierced an unarmed man—his own king! O soldier, why, treacherous soldier, soldier of treachery, shame of the world and sole dishonour of warfare; O soldier, his own army's creature, why did you dare this against him? Why did you dare this crime, this hideous crime? O sorrow! O greater than sorrow! O death! O truculent death! Would you were dead, O death! Bold agent of a deed so vile, how dare you recall it? You were pleased to remove our sun, and condemn day to darkness. Do you realize whom you snatched from us? To our eyes he was light; to our ears, melody; to our minds an amazement. Do you realize, impious death, whom you snatched from us? He was the lord of warriors, the glory of kings, the delight of the world. Nature knew not how to add any further perfection; he was the utmost she could achieve. But that was the reason you snatched him away: you seize precious things, and vile things you leave as if in disdain. And Nature, of you I complain: for were you not, when the world was still young, when you lay new-born in your cradle, giving zealous attention to him? And that zeal did not flag before your old age. Why did such strenuous effort bring this wonder into the world, if so short an hour stole the pride of that effort away? You were pleased to extend your hand to the world and then to withdraw it; to give thus, and then to recall your gift. Why have you vexed the world? Either give back to us him who is buried, or give us one like him in excellence. But you have not resources for that; whatever you had that was wondrous or precious was expended on him. On him were exhausted your stores of delight. You were made most wealthy by this creature you made; you see yourself, in his fall, most impoverished. If you were happy before, in proportion to happiness then is your misery now. If heaven allow it, I chide even God. O God, most excellent of beings, why do you fail in your nature here? Why, as an enemy would, do you strike down a friend? If you

---

† From the *Poetria Nova of Geoffrey of Vinsauf*, trans. Margaret F. Nims (Toronto: Pontifical Institute of Mediaeval Studies, 1967), 29–31. Copyright © 1967 by Pontifical Institute of Mediaeval Studies, Toronto. Reprinted by permission of the publisher. This passage is one of several examples given by Geoffrey to illustrate the use of apostrophe as a device of amplification.

recall, your own Joppa gives evidence for the king—alone he defended it, opposed by so many thousands. Acre, too, gives evidence—his power restored it to you. The enemies of the cross add their witness—all of them Richard, in life, inspired with such terror that he is still feared now he is dead. He was a man under whom your interests were safe. If, O God, you are, as befits your nature to be, faithful and free of malice, just and true, why then did you shorten his days? You could have shown mercy to the world; the world was in need of him. But you choose to have him with you, and not with the world; you would rather favour heaven than the world. O Lord, if it is permissible to say it, let me say— with your leave—you could have done this more graciously, and with less haste, if he had bridled the foe at least (and there would have been no delay to that end; he was on the verge of success). He could have departed more worthily then to remain with you. But by this lesson you have made us know how brief is the laughter of earth, how long are its tears.

BARTHOLOMAEUS ANGLICUS

[On the Cock]†

* * * Also the kok is hoot and drie of complexioun,° and therfore he is ful bolde and hardy, and so fightith boldeliche for his wyfes agenst his adversaries and assaileth and resith on° hem and tereth and woundeth ham with bile° and with spores.° And whan he hath the maistrie he singeth anon, and or° he singeth he betith himself with his wynges to make him the more able to singe. And he usith° fer in the nyght to singe moost cleereliche and strongliche, and aboute the morwetyde° he schapith° lyght voys and song, as Ambrose saith. The cok bereth a comb on his hede in stede of a crowne, and yif he lesith° his comb he lesith his hardinesse and is the more slow and coward to assaile his adversarie. And he loveth cherliche° his wyves. And whenne he fyndeth mete° he clepith his wifes togedres with a certeyn voys and spareth his owne mete to fede therwith his wifes. And settith next to him on rooste the henne that is most fatte and tendre and loveth hire best and desireth most to have hire presence. In the morwetide whanne he fleeth° to gete his mete, furst he leith his side to hire side

i.e., temperament

attacks
beak
spurs

before

is accustomed

morning / produces

loses

tenderly
food

flies

† Text based on *On the Properties of Things: John Trevisa's Translation of Bartholomaeus Anglicus De Proprietatibus Rerum*, ed. M. C. Seymour et al., 2 vols. (Oxford: Oxford UP, 1975), 1. 627. Reprinted by permission of Oxford University Press.

and bi certeyne tokenes and beckes,° as it were   *gestures*
love tacchis,° a woweth° and prayeth hire to   *indications / he woos*
tredinge;° and fightith for hire specialliche as   *copulation*
though he were jelous, and with byle and spores
he chacith and dryveth awey from him cokkes
that cometh nyghe° his wifes. And in fightinge he   *near*
smytith the grounde with his bile and rereth up
the weyes° aboute his necke to maken him the   *feathers*
more bolde and hardy, and meveth the fetheres of
his taile upwarde and donwarde that he mowe so
the more abilliche° come to the bataile.   *ably*

* * *

The Manciple's Prologue and Tale

Ovid's *Metamorphoses* is the most important source for western medieval versions of the story about the punishment of a truth-telling bird. We print a translation of Ovid's story of Phoebus, Coronis, and the raven. The *Metamorphoses* was widely translated, adapted, and commented on in the Middle Ages; these texts usually treat the story of Phoebus and Coronis as a lesson about the dangers of indiscreet speech. It is not certain which, if any, of these medieval versions Chaucer relied on. We include a brief adaptation by his acquaintance John Gower as an example of how the tale could be reworked for didactic purpose.

OVID

[The Story of Phoebus and Coronis]†

[At that time] the shining white wings of the chattering raven had been suddenly changed to dusky black.

This bird was once of a silvery hue, with such snowy feathers that it could rival any spotless dove. It was no less white than the geese who were one day to save the Capitol with their wakeful voices, as white as the swan that haunts rivers. But its tongue brought about the raven's downfall. Thanks to its chattering tongue, its plumage, once white, is now the very opposite.

In all Thessaly there was no one lovelier than Coronis of Larissa. At any rate, she won the heart of the god of Delphi [i.e., Phoebus Apollo], while she remained true to him, or at least while her faults passed unobserved. But the bird of Phoebus detected her in wrongdoing, and, a pitiless informer, hurried to its master, determined to reveal her guilt. . . . [It] went and told its master, Phoebus, that it had seen Coronis lying with a young Thessalian.

When her lover heard this charge against Coronis, the wreath of laurel slipped from his head, his face changed, his colour ebbed away, and the plectrum fell from his fingers. His heart was in a fever of swelling rage. Seizing his customary weapons, he strung his bow, bending it from its horns, and, with the arrow that none can avoid, pierced the breast he had so often clasped to his own. As the shaft

---

† *Metamorphoses* 2. 534–57, 598–632. From *The Metamorphoses of Ovid*, trans. Mary M. Innes (London: Penguin Books Ltd.) pp. 64–67. © Mary M. Innes, 1955. We have omitted a tale embedded within the story of Phoebus and Coronis that includes another instance of a truthful revelation angrily received.

466

struck home, Coronis groaned; when she drew it out, scarlet blood welled over her fair white limbs. "O Phoebus," she cried, "you could have let me bear your child, and then have punished me. Now, in my one person, two will perish." That was all she said, before her spirit ebbed out with her blood. A deathly chill crept over her lifeless body.

Too late, the lover repented of the cruel punishment he had exacted, and hated himself for listening to the tale, for allowing his anger to blaze up in such a way. He hated the bird, whose officiousness had forced him to learn of Coronis' guilt, forced him to know that he had cause for indignation; and no less did he hate his bow, his hands, his arrows too, shafts he had so rashly launched. Fondling her lifeless frame, he tried to thwart the fates, but he employed his healing art without avail: his aid came too late.

When he saw that his attempts were vain, that the pyre was being got ready, and that her limbs were about to be consumed by the funeral fires, then indeed Apollo groaned from the very depths of his heart—tears are forbidden to the gods. Even so does a heifer mourn when, before her eyes, the mallet is poised close to the slaughterer's right ear, and then brought crashing down with a resounding blow upon the hollow forehead of her unweaned calf. Then he poured upon Coronis' breast perfumes which she could never enjoy, clasped her to him for the last time, and performed all too soon the rites that death demands.

That his own seed should perish in those same ashes was more than he could bear. He snatched his son from his mother's womb, saved him from the flames, and carried him to the cave of Chiron, the centaur.

As for the raven, which was hoping for a reward for revealing the truth, Phoebus decreed that never again should it be numbered among white birds.

JOHN GOWER

The Tale of Phoebus and Cornide†

* * *

775 And over this, my sone diere,°	*furthermore, my dear son*
Of° othre men, if thou might hiere°	*Concerning / hear, learn of*
In privete° what thei have wroght,°	*Privately, secretly / done*
Hold conseil° and descoevere° it noght,	*Be silent / reveal*
For Cheste° can no conseil hele°	*Chiding / conceal no secret*
780 Or be it wo or be it wele.°	*Whether it be bad or good*
And tak a tale into thi mynde,°	*memory*
The which of olde ensample I finde.°	*Which I derive from (an) old story*
Phebus,° which makth the daies lihte,	*Phoebus Apollo (god of the sun)*
A love he hadde, which tho hihte°	*who then was called*
785 Cornide,° whom aboven alle	*Coronis*
He pleseth. Bot° what schal befalle°	*But / befall, happen*
Of° love ther is noman° knoweth,	*In regard to / no person (who)*
Bot° as fortune hire happes throweth.°	*Except / disposes by chance*
So it befell upon a chaunce°	*by chance*
790 A yong kniht° tok hire aqueintance°	*knight / made her acquaintance*
And hadde of hire al that he wolde;°	*all that he desired (sexually)*
Bot a fals bridd,° which sche hath holde	*false, untrustworthy bird*
And kept in chambre of pure yowthe,°	*i.e., because she was young*
Discoevereth° all that ever he cowthe.°	*Reveals / knew*
795 This briddes name was as tho°	*at that time*
Corvus,° the which was thanne also	*Raven (Latin)*
Welmore° whyt than eny swan,	*Much more*
And he, that schrewe,° al that he can°	*scoundrel / knows*
Of° his ladi to Phebus seide.°	*About / spoke, revealed*
800 And he for wraththe° his swerd outbreide,°	*in anger / drew out*
With which Cornide anon° he slowh.°	*immediately / slew*
Bot after him was wo ynowh,°	*But afterwards he was very sorrowful*
And tok a full gret repentance,	
Wherof—in tokne° and remembrance	*as a sign*
805 Of hem whiche usen wicke speche°—	*those who engage in evil speech*
Upon this bridd he tok this wreche.°	*vengeance*
That ther° he was snow whyt tofore,°	*whereas / before*

---

† *Confessio Amantis* 3.775–835. Text based on *The English Works of John Gower*, ed. G. C. Macaulay EETS e.s. 81–82 (London, 1900–1901; rpt. 1969), 1.247–48. Reprinted with permission of the Council of the Early English Text Society. The speaker of this passage is the priest and counsellor Genius, who instructs his "son" Amans, the lover-protagonist, about the sins he should avoid. Here Genius discusses a subdivision of the sin of wrath, Cheste (chiding, contentiousness), personified as a creature whose mouth is always open, spewing forth whatever bad things he knows, fomenting strife. After telling the story of the raven, Genius adds a second short example of ill-fated tale-bearing (ll. 818–27), drawn from Ovid's *Fasti* 2.585–616. On the *Confessio* see further the note on p. 386, and on Chaucer's relationship to Gower see the note on p. 337. It is not certain that Chaucer knew Gower's version, though some critics think that the Manciple's repetitious invocation of his mother's advice to "my sone" is a parody of the way Genius addresses Amans throughout the *Confessio* and, by implication, of an approach to fiction that is purely instructional.

Ever afterward colblak° therfore   *coal black*
He was transformed, as it scheweth.°   *is evident*
810 And many a man yit° him beschreweth°   *still / curses*
And clepen° him into° this day   *call(s) / to*
A raven, be° whom yit° men mai   *by / still*
Take evidence° whan he crieth   *Take as a sign*
That som mishapp it signefieth.°   *it signifies some misfortune*
815 Be war° therfore and sei° the beste   *Be careful / speak*
If thou wolt be thiself° in reste,   *keep thyself*
My goode sone, as I the rede.°   *advise thee*
    For in an other place I rede°   *read*
Of thilke Nimphe which Laar hihte.°   *that nymph called Lara*
820 For° sche the privete be nyghte°   *Because / the nighttime secret*
(How Jupiter lay be Jutorne°)   *with Juturna (a naiad)*
Hath told, god° made hire overtorne.°   *i.e., Jupiter / come to grief*
Hire tunge he kutte, and into helle
For evere he sende° hir forto duelle,   *sent*
825 As sche that was noght worthi hiere°   *here (on earth)*
To ben of love a chamberere,°   *chambermaid, servant*
For sche no conseil couwthe hele.°   *could keep no secret*
And suche adaies be now fele°   *(there) are many such nowadays*
In loves court, as it is seid,
830 That lete here tunges gon unteid.°   *let their tongues go untied, loose*
    Mi sone, be thou non of tho°   *do not be one of those*
To jangle° and telle tales so,°   *speak indiscreetly / in such a way*
And namely that thou ne chyde,°   *chide, reproach (someone else)*
For Cheste° can no conseil hide,   *Chiding*
835 For Wraththe seide nevere wel.°   *Since Anger never spoke well (of another)*

CRITICISM

CRITICISM

F. R. H. Du BOULAY

The Historical Chaucer†

The world in which Chaucer lived was small in terms of people but large in terms of geography. A magical journey backwards in time would place us in an England where the most terrifying noise would not be made by bomb or jet but the yelling of a murderous crowd, and where for every twenty people on today's streets there would be only one. The south-east was already more heavily populated than the rest of the country, but the London throngs would have seemed comparatively thin. Perhaps the age-structure of the population would also have appeared different. Many children died, and to be fifty was to be quite old. When Chaucer began his literary career the bubonic plague had recently taken a specially heavy toll of the very young, so that by modern standards English life was carried on by a large majority of people who were between twenty and forty years old. The children, as was customary, fitted into the work of the adult world without the doting attention of today. Above all, the effective leadership of society was in the hands of relatively few men. The historian who reads the records of government, law and commerce between 1340 and 1400 is constantly surprised by meeting the same people and noticing how often they knew each other and were connected with the same affairs. In his brilliant *Some New Light on Chaucer*, Professor J. M. Manly tried to identify some of the characters in *The Canterbury Tales* with real people, and even if he does not always carry conviction it is a remarkable sign of society's smallness that such attempts at identification could be made. Another illustration of this close community is furnished by the account-book of Gilbert Maghfeld, a London merchant and money-lender. His customers between 1390 and 1395 included nobles, knights, clerks and merchants from England and abroad, and of these no less than thirty to forty are known to have been associated in some way with Chaucer.[1]

Though lightly peopled, the world of Chaucer was mobile. War, diplomacy, trade, administration and the impulses of religion shifted men and women of even humble station about the country and far beyond its shores. The framework of a pilgrimage from Southwark to Canterbury which Chaucer chose for his best-known collection of tales is not out of keeping with historical truth, but the theme of the journey appears even more clearly after a closer look at the pilgrims. There were thirty-two of them, and out of these at least thirteen not counting Chaucer himself were regular travellers by profession or taste. The knight as a chivalric crusader had seen Granada, North

---

† Reprinted from *Writers and Their Background: Geoffrey Chaucer*, edited by Derek Brewer. Athens, Ohio: Ohio UP, 1974, pp. 33–57. Reprinted by permission of the author.
1. J. M. Manly, *Some New Light on Chaucer*, New York, 1926; for remarks on Maghfeld's account-book and excerpts from it see *Chaucer's World*, compiled by Edith Rickert, ed. Clair C. Olson and Martin M. Crow, New York, 1948, pp. 185–93.

Africa, Armenia, Russia, Lithuania and Prussia.[2] The squire like his literary creator had fought in Flanders, Artois and Picardy. The monk coursed over the countryside with a string of hunters. Unlike the monk the friar belonged to a religious order in which travel was part of the vocation itself, necessary for study, preaching and organized begging. The merchant's business trips to the Low Countries were a commonplace activity upon which depended the export-import trade and credit transactions of Merchant Venturers and other groups from English towns. The Serjeant-at-Law made his assize-circuits just as his modern counter-part does and incidentally helped by so doing to bring to remoter shires the English of the king 'that is lord of this langage'.[3] As a well-to-do landowner the franklin had been commissioned as sheriff and justice of the peace and elected as a parliamentary 'knight' for his shire, so that he was familiar with constant journeying, at least within the realm. The shipman like the friar was so much a medieval byword for rootlessness that he was regarded as a good spy in war and a bad surety in the courts.[4] Chaucer's example was evidently experienced on both the Bordeaux and Baltic routes. The reeve was an agricultural overseer from Norfolk and accustomed to presenting biannual accounts to his lord's auditors. The summoner was a specialized postman whose round covered an entire diocese and made him an embarrassingly familiar figure. The pardoner was one of a whole crowd of 'Rome-runners', and the manciple, if he were like many other estate-officials, was probably the servant of more than one lord and liable to serve in several parts of England in any one year.

The rustic members of this company have been called the manorial aristocracy, and it is true that we do not meet the poorest villagers among them, nor did Chaucer write about the mass of small-holders as did Langland about the cottage-dwellers he felt to be his neighbours. But even Langland envisaged pilgrimage, and the estate-documents of the time leave no doubt that the manorial poor travelled too, bound on errands or carrying-services for their masters, service in wars, or in search of wage labour.

Of course this pilgrimage to Canterbury was a literary construct, yet behind it lay a constant historical reality which can to some extent be measured. Offerings at the shrine of Becket in Canterbury Cathedral amounted during the fourteenth century to some £300 or £400 a year, more during the second half of the century, and they only declined permanently after 1420.[5] If aristocratic pilgrims were more noticed in the monks' records they sometimes cost the cathedral more than they gave: most of the donors were the anonymous, humble people who were doubtless often able to make the journey because their fortunes were improving through the forces of economic change.

2. For maps of the crusading journeys to Prussia and Lithuania undertaken in the 1390s by Henry of Derby and his knightly companions, see *Richard II*, ed. F. R. H. Du Boulay and Caroline M. Barron, 1971, pp. 163, 166.
3. *The Works of Geoffrey Chaucer*, ed. F. N. Robinson, 2nd edn. 1957, p. 546.
4. *The Paston Letters, 1422–1509*, ed. James Gairdner, 1900–08, I, Nos. 146, 195.
5. C. Eveleigh Woodruff, 'The financial aspect of the cult of St. Thomas of Canterbury', *Archaeologia Cantiana* XLIV, 1932, esp. pp. 18–25.

For Chaucer's lifetime spanned a period of economic transition so important that neither his career nor his writing can be properly understood without some brief reference to it. It is basically a question of demography. The first and most lethal epidemic of plague occurred in 1348–49, when Chaucer was a small boy. During his middle years there were further epidemics, so that within a generation the population of Britain like that of Europe as a whole had been severely reduced. Historians often argue that the horrors of pestilence made late medieval men and women preoccupied with death and filled their art and literature with fantasies of mortality, but the most striking historical consequence seems to have been a sharper appetite for a better life. As people died the pressure of population on land was relieved. The survivors inherited property more quickly. Poorer fields could go out of cultivation, leaving men in possession of the most productive arable. In general the price of basic foodstuffs remained low while the wages of labourers rose. The unskilled man who got 1d a day in 1300 got 4d or 5d by 1400. In short, labouring men benefited from the very fewness of their numbers and could expect to have more to spend after rents had been paid and food bought or grown. It is not surprising that lords and knights thought their inferiors were becoming uppish and attempted, though without success, to control wages and prevent the flaunting of fine clothes and personal possessions by folk whose fathers had known better how to keep to their station.

Chaucer's age was consequently one of unusual tension, born of betterment rather than oppression. The Great Revolt of 1381 was only the biggest explosion in a fire of change. Up the ladder of society inferior answered back to superior with sharp criticism and occasional blows, whether it was bondmen against lords and lawyers, commons against the tax-men, middling townsmen against the big financiers, laymen against rich, endowed clergy, or warlike nobles against a young king who wanted peace with France and respectful acquiescence for his tactless spending on personal friends. These conflicts sometimes merged into each other and are in any case too complex for full discussion here, but a word must be given to the problem of social class which clearly coloured Chaucer's own assumptions.

The fundamental distinction in English society was between those who were *gentils* and those who were not, in very much the same way as this was true at least up until the early twentieth century. A squire in a noble household was usually *gentilhomme* no less than the king himself. By about 1425 this simple class distinction was being frequently expressed in the English language by the word 'gentleman' which was taking the place of the older Latin *generosus* and French *gentil*. This is not to say that more numerous gradations in rank were of no account. It was an aristocratic society in which king, nobles, prelates and knights all received particular expressions of deference. It was also a world of social mobility which in fact sharpened the sense of status. Merchants who had just climbed into *gentilesse* could be de-

spised by those who had forgotten any remoter taint of trade. Even the
de la Poles, dukes of Suffolk and most splendid of medieval *arrivistes*,
could now and then be reminded without much delicacy how they
were 'worshipful men grown to fortune of the world.'[6] But the bi-
section of society into gentle and simple was understood clearly
enough and is the basic historical reality of late medieval class structure. It makes no difference that Chaucer wrote moralizing lines to
the effect that a real gentleman is a man who behaves decently. 'Handsome is as handsome does' is an acceptable motto to the most snob-
bish societies, just as in our own somewhat more relaxed days 'nature's
gentleman' remains a wholly intelligible alternative for a rough dia-
mond. To this extent the social historian must differ from the literary
scholar who sees equal reality in literary statements of fourteenth-
century class distinction.[7] The idea of 'degree', according to which
men were ranked by their function in society, was certainly attractive
to the theological cast of mind that understood society's God-given ar-
chitecture in terms of men's vocations and mutual dependence. But it
was of no more social significance than are ranks and regiments in the
armed services of today. As to the theoretical division of men into
those who fight, those who pray and those who work (such as the
knight, the clerk and the ploughman), this was only a more primitive
version of 'degree': if it is 'the only class system known to medieval
theory', then it must be answered that the class distinctions which
possess the greatest everyday importance are those least subject to
theory.

Hence, when we enquire about Chaucer's place in Society (which
must have been of more account to him than society), we may accept
that he was a gentleman because he had a courtly upbringing and
worked, behaved and wrote like one. True, his origins were mercantile,
his position modest, his ambitions even a trifle eccentric in their artistic solitariness. But he was not a hired craftsman who came in at the
back door and downed his ale with the life-long servants. He 'com-
muned with gentle wights'.

The sort of people who gathered for their entertainment round a
public reader would have been aware of changes that were taking
place in language. Three of these changes were leaving their mark
upon the fourteenth century. English was moving towards a standard-
ized form. French was being forgotten, and the ability to read and
write in English was becoming more widespread amongst lay people.
In a well-known passage of *Troilus* Chaucer alludes to the variations
which still existed in English and hopes that what he is writing will be
understood.

6. For all this, see the present writer's *An Age of Ambition*, 1970, chap. 4.
7. A skilful literary analysis is by D. S. Brewer, 'Class distinctions in Chaucer', *Speculum* XLIII,
   1968, pp. 290–308.

And for ther is so gret diversite
In Englissh and in writyng of oure tonge,
So prey I God that non myswrite the,
Ne the mysmetre for defaute of tonge . . .

Yet the very apostrophe suggests the marvellous possibility of a wider comprehension:

And red wherso thow be, or elles songe,
That thou be understonde, God I biseche!
                                        (V, 1793–98).

And no one who has glanced at the provincial literature of the same age can doubt that the future lay on the sophisticated London tongues of Chaucer and his friends, not with the up-country authors of *Pearl*, *Gawayne* or *Sir Orfeo*. There is a historical point here too. In the mid-fourteenth century the richer classes of London society were being reinforced by immigrants from the east midlands who brought their speech with them and fused it with existing London language as the vehicle of communication between Englishmen of position. These people were merchants who dealt in major commodities like wool and wine, so that the economic drift to the south-east accomplished changes in society and speech as well as in production and government. Once more, the de la Poles of Hull provide a leading in-stance, but so too does the Chaucer family of Ipswich whose migra-tion to the capital helped the victory of the very language used by its most famous member. The fact that French was concurrently becoming a foreign tongue is probably a parallel development ra-ther than a consequence of this slowly forming linguistic identity. En-mity with France never stopped the interchange of ideas and people across the Channel, but the standardization of speech into its modern shapes was occurring none the less, and indeed in France and Ger-many as well as England. It was encouraged the more vigorously in England because London stood as a capital city in a relatively small country, whereas France was larger and even more regionalized, and Germany had no capital at all. So to London wealth and substantial people were drawn, and thence flowed the torrent of administration and law, expressed in the dialect of Europe's most centralized govern-ment. All the standard history books tell how English began to be used in London courts and parliaments in the 1360s. French was becoming an accomplishment rather than a habit, and a sidelight on this comes from the will of James de Peckham, a Kentish gentleman who died in the same year as Chaucer. His codicil of 30 September 1400 ordering the bequest of 10 oxen and 200 sheep added that 'my executors shall distribute all my books in French to those who know how to use them'.[8]

With language went literacy in the sense of an ability to read and even write in the mother tongue. The great collections of private cor-

---

8. Lambeth Palace Library, Register of Archbishop Arundel, I, fos. 176b–177a: *. . . volo ut ex-ecutores mei distribuant omnes libros meos gallicos scientibus illos occupare . . .'*

respondence like the Paston Letters begin to survive from about this time. If Chaucer himself had been an exception as a literate layman it would hardly have made sense for him to describe so naturally the exchange of love-letters between Troilus and Criseyde:

> The lettres ek that she of olde tyme
> Hadde hym ysent he wolde allone rede,
> An hondred sithe atwixen noon and prime . . .
> (V, 470–72).

So too does his midnight remedy invite a flash of sympathy from fellow insomniacs: 'to rede, and drive the night away'. (*The Booke of the Duchess* 49).

Evidence does not exist to make possible any geography of literacy, though we may guess that more people who could read and write lived in the southeast and east of England than elsewhere. But certainly the most advanced institutions of government had their home in and about London. The king himself was often on the move, accompanied by friends and counsellors. But the established departments of state were organized in permanent buildings spread out over the metropolis, like the Exchequer and Chancery at Westminster, and the Wardrobe's permanent offshoots, the Great and Privy Wardrobe which housed bulk supplies and armaments in Baynard's Castle and the Tower within the City walls. Household departments both stationary and itinerant possessed seals as the essential instruments to authenticate orders, commissions and grants of property and privilege. To remove the seals from the effective control of the king was an organized baronage's chief answer to his supposed misrule, yet at the same time the action most likely to arouse the king's vengeful anger. During the reigns of Edward III (1327–77) and Richard II (1377–99), the internal politics of England turned principally round the problem of controlling such commissions and grants, in peace and in war, and of how the groups of politically influential men combined with and against each other in ever-changing factions: nobles, parliamentary knights, bishops and merchants; king's friends and king's critics, allies or enemies of each other according to a thousand personal interests, but never parties in a modern sense. There is no place here for a detailed chronicle, but it may be helpful to explain two basic characteristics of political life. Medieval government at every level was organized through households; and the disposition of property was the stuff of politics.

Public affairs in modern times are carried on in offices and committees which operate for the most part in office hours and rely heavily upon administrative standing orders and the services of secretaries. In the fourteenth century the household of an important man was also to a great extent the place where political decisions were taken. Private and public life were not yet clearly distinguished. This is true of insignificant country lords with small estate councils and a handful of armed retainers, of merchants who slept near their bales and accounts, and of the king himself whose advisers might talk gravely with their master in a private room whilst his immense entourage prepared the meals, mended the waggons, or rollicked in halls and yards. Our imaginative picture of minstrels and large-scale catering is sound enough if we remember also that the household was a moving centre of government where messengers to and from the outside world sped like bees. Charters, letters and writs drawn up with professional care in Chancery or Exchequer often awaited their ultimate authority from this pell-mell dwelling.

The subject-matter of public business was in a curious way equally private. At tense moments educated men might speak of the crown in distinction from the king, or of 'the law and course of parliament', but the underlying realities were cornfields, flocks of sheep, rents, pensions from the Exchequer, rake-offs from customs houses or judicial courts, and, perhaps above all, the capital gains that accrued from rich marriages. The king's task was to walk on the knife-edge between all-round generosity and the insolvency which left him desperate.

One of the medieval historian's greatest difficulties is to discover in detail the jealousies and ambitions which set men at daggers drawn or brought them for a time into sworn friendship, but the generalized picture is quite a simple one. The royal household and noble households were the same in kind but different in degree. Their outward form was a family structure of men and women living according to rank yet with a good deal of of informality, and in a milieu where kindness to a young knight or an unexpected flirtation might have the most serious political undertones. Everybody wanted security and income, and these things were in the gift of the dynasts: offices, pensions, manors or the hand of a girl with an inheritance whence might spring another young family to struggle and jockey in its turn for livelihood and power. All this is quite different from modern family life of which the function at its best is fulfilled by twenty years of intimate parental care. The medieval *familia* embraced other people's children as well who from early adolescence shared in the work of the adult world, whether they were apprentices, religious postulants or pages.

To call Chaucer's age violent is not very illuminating as this is true of almost all epochs, but the particular forms violence took are of interest. In the first place there was endemic warfare. When Chaucer was born the young Edward III had just reopened the war with France which was fundamentally about the king of England's lands and status across the Channel. The 'Hundred Years War' (1337–1453) sounds like a distinct episode but was in fact a fresh series of phases in a conflict so old that it was part of the folk-memory. In the middle years of the fourteenth century war took the form of sea fights, raids across the Scottish border and, more centrally, long-range expeditions or *chévauchées* into France under a king with unusual gifts of affability and comradeship with his own nobility. Thousands of people were involved besides the knights, men-at-arms and archers, from the clothiers who made uniforms for the retinues to the craftsmen who supplied bowstrings and the shipmen who ferried grain for the armies overseas.[9] But war is never a unifying activity for long, and cracks soon widened in the fabric of English society. These were of two kinds: the little fissures of outrage committed by men habituated to the violent seizure of what they wanted; and the crevasses which opened when the dramatic victories of Crécy and Poitiers were over and the slog had to be paid for by taxation, when financiers were caught profiteering, and (worst of all) when a new young king, wilful, cliquish and extravagant, actually wanted to make peace with his ancient adversary and use his soldiers nearer home. Two examples of political shock may be chosen for their bearing on Chaucer's life.

In 1376 a group of highly placed courtiers and London financiers was impeached in parliament for peculation, at the instigation of Peter de la Mare, knight of the shire for Herefordshire and the earliest known Speaker of the Commons. The incident is complex because it was part of an aristocratic wrangle, and is also especially famous for the earliest eyewitness account of a debate amongst the parliamentary Commons. But to the point here is the person of Richard Lyons, the chief merchant culprit, for he was a man of similar background to Chaucer's and a London neighbour, though he had made himself of much greater political importance. Little is known of Lyons's origins apart from the fact that he was illegitimate. But by 1359 he was buying houses and shops in London and in the 1360s was a prominent vintner with a group of taverns which sold sweet wine. He had a country property in Essex as well and was to represent Essex in the parliament of 1380. In the 1370s he was lessee of much of the petty custom and subsidy in English ports and able to lend the government money and buy the government's debts at a heavy discount. Professor Myers calls him 'not so much a thief as a rich individual who could help to rescue a virtually bankrupt government'.[1] After his impeachment his wealth was confiscated, but he soon got it back. The present interest lies in seeing how an obscure vintner could become so rich and how his heart lay where his treasure was. His confiscated possessions were worth nearly £2500 and he owned a fairly large ship. In 1380 he bought exemption for life from being made sheriff, escheator, coroner, J.P. or collector of taxes against his will. Probably these tasks would have interfered too much with business, and the exemption is suggestive of the fact that these important offices were not always either desired or voluntary. Lyons's end was neither happy nor dignified, for he was murdered in Cheapside by the rebels of 1381, his house at Overhall in Essex was wrecked and a woman called Isabella spent fruitless years of litigation in claiming to be his widow, though the executors argued that the marriage had been annulled in 1363. Stow saw his tomb in St. James Garlickhithe, with his effigy showing 'hair rounded by his ears and curled, and a little beard forked', like the king he

---

9. H. J. Hewitt, *The Organization of War under Edward III*, 1966.
1. A. R. Myers, 'The Wealth of Richard Lyons' in *Essays in Medieval History presented to Bertie Wilkinson*, ed. T. H. Sandquist and M. R. Powicke, Toronto 1969.

served. Compared with Lyons, we may reflect that Chaucer had the better part in remaining a politically modest figure.

Ten years after the Good Parliament the court was again attacked, this time by the impeachment of Michael de la Pole, earl of Suffolk and Chancellor. The opposition of the autumn and winter of 1386 was led by Thomas of Woodstock (duke of Gloucester since 1385) and the earl of Arundel. The most recent research has shown that it was indeed the king himself, not yet twenty, who was the real target of attack,[2] for his extravagance and political partisanship; and the crisis of the next two years during which many of the king's friends were executed or exiled was a most violent confrontation in which the king's possession of the throne and perhaps of his life itself hung in balance. It has proved all too tempting for scholars to argue that Chaucer's surrender of his post in the customs was a minor consequence of this massive political purge, but as we shall see this seems on balance unlikely. The events of 1386–88 are more useful as a prominent instance of political upheaval which help to explain the prudence of Chaucer's life but did not involve any punishment for his associations.[3]

The Church which might have stood as a city of peace in so unquiet a world shared in fact in all that world's frictions and political malice. This is not to deal out the almost total disapproval bestowed upon late medieval Catholicism by disdainful critics like G. M. Trevelyan. In parishes, monasteries and even in the lives of certain bishops there are examples of fidelity, study and the works of charity. But the deep connections between secular and ecclesiastical government involved the Church in precisely the same imperfections as the world itself of which it was part, and attracted criticisms which reasonably condemned many blemishes. It may at the same time be remembered that the criticisms themselves are a sign of grace, and that not every revolted conscience belonged to a heretic or cynic.

In 1305 the papacy had moved to Avignon, and fourteenth-century Englishmen had grown accustomed to thinking of a *curia* where the cardinals were mostly French as an institution hostile to English interests. Papal taxation had been loudly resented even in the early thirteenth century; the resentment did not abate even after kings in the fourteenth century had moderated its impact upon their subjects. The claims of popes to provide their direct nominees to church benefices and the unremitting hostility of English parliaments to such papal provisions are prominent in the records of the fourteenth century. If this was material enough for an English political anti-papalism, the Great Schism which began in 1378 was an enormous aggravation. It is arguable that before 1378 the popes had the will of peace-makers between England and France, but afterwards the divided papacy was yet another *casus belli*.

Perhaps a gaze too firmly fixed on Rome or Avignon causes optical

---

2. J. J. N. Palmer, 'The Impeachment of Michael de la Pole in 1386', *Bulletin of the Institute of Historical Research* XLII, 1969, pp. 96–101.
3. This is the place to applaud the general sound historical sense displayed in a now quite old work: J. R. Hulbert, *Chaucer's Official Life* (Ph.D. dissertation), Chicago 1912.

illusions in students of Chaucer. Understanding of Englishmen's attitudes must in the best analysis be sought in England itself. Here was a society both religious and anti-clerical, and to miss the fact that both these attitudes co-existed is to misread the age. Indeed, it is doubtful whether anti-clericalism can occur in an irreligious society.

In the fourteenth century there were at least three different kinds of hostility to clergy. Occasionally there was anger against senior prelates who were also high government officials, like the bishops of Chichester and Lichfield, Chancellor and Treasurer respectively, who were dismissed for inefficiency by Edward III in 1340 and replaced by laymen on the grounds that their clerical order gave them undue protection against punishment. Similarly, William of Wykeham, bishop of Winchester, was thrown out of the Chancellorship in 1371, and Simon of Sudbury, archbishop of Canterbury and Treasurer of England, had his head cut off by the rebels in 1381. Secondly, bitter feelings were often shown towards the friars. The *Summoner's Tale* is a well-known joke in this vein, but the belief that the friars had betrayed their ministry to the poor is expressed with more solemn indignation in *The Vision of Piers the Plowman*. Yet hatred of the mendicants was more keenly felt by other kinds of clergyman than by laymen. The friars were competitors with the secular clergy for the alms and esteem of parishioners and for academic privileges in the universities. No amount of literary vilification can hide the fact that lay men and women continued to leave bequests of money to the orders of friars right up until the Reformation, so that friar-baiting was in a sense a clerical variety of anticlericalism. Third, and most important, was a disgust with the wealthy, established, sacerdotal Church which was felt with varying intensity by a wide range of people, from outright Lollard heretics to those who were entirely orthodox in fundamental belief and practice, yet devoted in their hearts to the simplicities of the New Testament and the application of moral principles to everyday life. It is difficult to avoid the conclusion that Chaucer himself moved in these circles, and equally difficult to show that in Richard II's reign there was any clear dividing line between Lollards and what, for lack of a better term, may be called orthodox evangelicals.

The careers of the so-called Lollard knights reflect these ambiguities. In the chronicles at least ten distinguished laymen are named and portrayed as supporters of heresy and heretics themselves. The interpretation of their activities is still controversial but any account of Chaucerian society must at least face the same problem.[4] Seven of these men formed a closely knit group of friends, namely, the knights Richard Stury, Lewis Clifford, Thomas Latimer, William Nevill, John Clanvowe, John Montagu (earl of Salisbury from 1397) and John Cheyne. All were courtiers and members of the king's household. Stury,

---

4. W. T. Waugh, 'The Lollard Knights' in *Scottish Historical Review* XI, 1914, pp. 55–92, held that most of them were never serious Lollards and all made orthodox ends. Conversely, the genuine and lasting Lollardy of these knights was argued by the late K. B. McFarlane in a paper read to the *Canterbury and York Society* on 13 December 1962 and now published in fuller form in *Lancastrian Kings and Lollard Knights*, Oxford 1972.

Clifford, Nevill and Clanvowe were knights of the king's Chamber and thus members of an intimate circle of which Chaucer, as an esquire of the Chamber, was also part. In 1372 when Chaucer was certainly occupying this position he was about 30 years old; Stury would then have been about 45, Clifford about 40, Nevill and Clanvowe roughly Chaucer's age. They were therefore more or less contemporaries, and they lived the same kind of life. By 1378 they were mostly veteran campaigners who knew other lands and had also, except for Latimer, travelled on diplomatic missions. In September 1385 the same Wardrobe account records the issue of black cloth for mourning the king's mother to Clanvowe, Clifford, Clifford's son-in-law, La Vache, and Chaucer. Several of this circle had literary tastes. Clifford had brought Chaucer a copy of a poem written in his honour by Eustache Deschamps, praising him for his wisdom and his ability as translator of the *Roman de la Rose*, which is, incidentally, more a satire in its English form against false love and corrupt morals than a work of courtly love.[5] Stury also owned a copy. Montagu was a versifier praised by Christine de Pisan. Clanvowe was himself a sincerely moralizing author who will be referred to again. The group were also knights, and individually much more well-to-do than Chaucer. Although Clifford began as an almost landless man in a Devonshire village, by 1389 he had nearly £400 a year in annuities and was exchanging them quickly for land, an intelligent business move which Chaucer too may have been making when in 1388 he granted his Exchequer annuities to John Scalby. Several of the knights married heiresses and some invested in the English lands of Norman abbeys confiscated by the king, and thus had an interest in the disendowment of the Church at a time when Lollards were demanding the same thing. But financial success formed no barrier between these men and Chaucer. Nevill and Clanvowe acted as witnesses to a deed in Chaucer's interest.[6] Clifford was his close friend and the father-in-law of Sir Philip La Vache whom Chaucer in his popular poem *Truth* advised to shun the servitude of this world. Whether the knights were Lollards in any exact sense must remain an open question. They were called such in the chronicles, but chroniclers were emotionally hostile even to implicit criticisms of the Church. True, Latimer was accused of heresy before the king's council, and when Wycliff's disciple, master Nicholas Hereford, was arrested Nevill asked to have his custody 'because of the honesty of his person'. Clifford, Latimer and Cheyne drew up wills which used phrases dear to Lollards, like referring to their bodies as 'stinking carrion', and requesting burial in cheap cloth and without funeral pomp, and to supervise the execution of these wills they chose Lollard overseers. Yet it remains possible that as a group they showed in exaggerated form the sentiments felt by many orthodox contemporaries. What betrays this attitude to the historian is less the ambiguous record of action than the common feeling behind Chaucer's own poem *Truth* (before 1390?) and the English tract by Clanvowe

5. D. W. Robertson, *Chaucer's London*, New York 1968, p. 209.
6. *Chaucer Life-Records*, ed. M. M. Crow and C. C. Olson, Oxford 1966, p. 343.

later entitled *The Two Ways* (1391?).[7] The message of Chaucer is that the world is a wilderness, not a home, through which the wise man goes as a pilgrim in dread of avarice and self-advancement:

> *Hold the heye wey, and lat thy gost thee lede:*
> *And trouthe thee shal delivere, it is no drede.*

In Clanvowe's pamphlet the meaning is the same and even the imagery similar. No more than Chaucer does he attack or defend the Church's institutions, but begs Christians to avoid the 'broad way' that leads to hell and enter the 'narrow way' to heaven. Insistent that salvation lies through a life in which scriptural teaching is observed he speaks with the same voice as Chaucer in his moments of direct simplicity or, for the matter of that, of Langland when he uses the metaphor of pilgrimage and prefers Do-Wel to triennials. It is an authentic English voice of late fourteenth-century spirituality.

> For that that is cleped richesse it is greet trauail to geten it and it is greet drede to keepen it and to departe therfro it is greet heuynesse, so that fro the first getynge to the laste forgoying it is alle sorewe . . .

Nothing in the rhythmic phrases of Clanvowe is wholly out of accord with what little of his private mind Chaucer himself permits us to hear. So we come from the world of Chaucer to the man himself.

There can be no intention here to rehearse in detail the well-known fragments of Chaucer's biography, but rather to offer the view of a single historian about what in that life is important to understanding the poet. His life indeed begins and ends in historical obscurity, and even the extraordinary labours which have culminated in the *Life-Records* leave us in a twilight unimaginable to students of post-Plantagenet England. The first frustration is of a natural wish to know about the domestic life of a poet who wrote so much of marriage and children. The most that can be said is that Chaucer was probably married to Philippa de Roet from about 1366 to 1387, by which time she was dead, and that he had a son called Thomas who rose higher in the world than his father, probably also a son called Lewis, and just possibly a surviving daughter called Elizabeth. To attempt deductions from the poetry about Chaucer's happiness or otherwise in the married state seems a waste of time like so much other effort which, unsupported by real evidence, has been put into the Chaucer industry. Yet enough is known of the fourteenth-century milieu to allow a reflection that Chaucer was lucky in having legitimate parents, a settled home, a father who did not die till his son was about 22, and a marriage which lasted some 21 years. Despite the Christian teaching about monogamy and fidelity it was an age when family life was often brief and fragile. Parents frequently died young, leaving the survivor to

---

7. V. J. Scattergood, 'The two ways: an unpublished religious treatise by Sir John Clanvowe', in *English Philological Studies* X, 1967, pp. 33–56.

re-marry quickly. Bastardy was exceedingly common. Children were likely to be shunted off to fend for themselves at quite an early age. Chaucer's own maternal grandmother Mary was married three times. His father John was abducted by an aunt who tried to marry him off at the age of about 11. In fact, many of Chaucer's contemporaries had a rough youth, such as Langland who was illegitimate and resented it, or Boccaccio legitimized after his birth and estranged from a father 'old, coarse and mean'.[8] Richard Lyons was also illegitimate; Dante and Petrarch exiles; Boccaccio, Dante and Petrarch had step-mothers; Boccaccio and Petrarch had many illegitimate children. Even Chaucer's sister-in-law was a mistress for many years before she became John of Gaunt's third wife, and her very marriage attracted sneers rather than rejoicing.

Like the great Italians, Chaucer started from a mercantile background and was educated in letters—we do not know where—at an early age. Literary originality was rare among the old landed families. But he did not have the advantages or disadvantages of being a tonsured cleric and in this he was unlike Langland, Froissart, Boccaccio, Petrarch, Hoccleve and Lydgate. Although the literate layman was becoming quite a common figure as a reader it was still exceptional for a layman to be a professional poet, let alone a great one. In this he is perhaps to be compared only with Dante.

Undoubtedly the career of Chaucer was made possible by his acceptance into courtly households. It is not necessary to suppose either that he was a faintly bourgeois usher or the partisan of any longlasting political faction. He had a foot in several worlds: the courtly; the mercantile and the literary, but as already explained he lived naturally as a gentleman, like many other Englishmen of the governing class, with jobs to do and the usual rewards in return. Further, it was easy to pass from one household to another. Chaucer began as an adolescent in the household of Elizabeth, countess of Ulster, wife of Lionel, duke of Clarence, who was the second son of Edward III and one of Richard II's uncles. By 1367 he was in Edward III's household and from then on until his death he was connected with the royal court in one way or another even though he did not always travel about with the king as one of his personal entourage. Another point is worth making. There were times when political and personal hostility (much the same thing) existed between some of the magnates and the king, and even between Richard II and his uncle John of Gaunt, and as everyone knows Gaunt's son Henry ultimately deposed his cousin. But factions however savage were transient, and although royal or noble servants connected with unpopular policies might on occasion be dismissed or even destroyed, there were whole substrata of courtiers, officials and servants who did not suffer if they did not seem to pose any political threat or to have committed any political crime. Guilt by association was not taken very far. It is hard to believe that Chaucer was not liked and valued, and not because he was a wary trimmer but for his genial

8. John Lamer, *Culture and Society in Italy, 1290–1420*, 1971, p. 216.

skill in bringing 'mirth and solas' to his neighbours and a personal inability to get seriously diverted from practising his gift. This seems the
explanation of his professional and financial survival. Doubtless he was
welcome in the great Lancastrian family. In 1386 his wife was admitted
to the fraternity of Lincoln Cathedral in the presence of Gaunt and
along with Henry of Derby and a galaxy of Lancastrian luminaries. It
was both a distinguished occasion and a family affair. This sort of thing
did not prevent Chaucer continuing in the service of Richard II, and
even riding through England on his urgent business within a year of
Derby's landing. On the day of Henry IV's coronation Chaucer, still
king's esquire, received a handsome rise in his pension.[9] There is no
contradiction in all this, for it is a sequence of rewards for uncompli-
cated service and friendship, the bright lining of political storm-clouds.

Much of Chaucer's employment was too fleeting, too ordinary or of
too little significance in his life to merit discussion in a short essay,
but his work at the London Customs House is worth a moment's attention. He was appointed Controller of the wool custom, the wool
subsidy and the petty custom in London in 1374, increasingly allowed
deputies to do the work at the wool quay, and replaced in these posts
in December 1386. It is sometimes said that these were important
posts from which he was dismissed when the Wonderful Parliament
placed the king's government in commission under the power of
Gloucester, Arundel and Warwick. Neither of these suppositions is
likely. It is true that the wool custom was one of the chief props of the
crown's finances despite the decline in exports of raw wool, by reason
of the high tariff and the relative efficiency of its collection by the best
civil service in Christendom. But the really important officials were
the Collectors and not the Controllers. The Collector was usually a
London merchant-financier who lent the crown money and spent his
time in the customs service in repaying himself out of the £18,000 or
so annual revenue which flowed through his hands. His work was in
the technicalities of the credit system while the actual collecting was
done by deputies. The Controller (*contrarotulator*) was intended to act
as a check on the Collector, returning to the Exchequer his own
counter-roll which detailed the exports and imports. In fact, of course,
he was so inferior in wealth and status that he was no effective check.
The idea was that the Collector had one half of the customs seal (the
cocket) and the Controller the other half, and that the application of
this seal to documents of consignment would show that the customs
had been paid. But the Controller's half had to be surrendered to the
king's creditors, and when this happened the Controller was virtually
deprived of office and the creditor was made Controller in all but
name. In 1379, for instance, the City of London held half the cocket
seal, which meant that the great financier John Philipot held one
half of the seal as Collector and the other as Mayor.[1] No doubt the job
of Controller needed expertise, especially in accounting at the Ex-

9. *Life-Records*, pp. 91, 62, 525.
1. An expert study is Olive Coleman's 'The Collectors of Customs in London under Richard II'
   in *Studies in London History presented to P. E. Jones*, 1969, pp. 181–96.

chequer, and it yielded a salary equivalent to the income of a simple country knight. But it was 'a modest office for a modest man'. Nor, despite parliamentary petitions that life-holders of Controllerships should have their appointments annulled, is there evidence that any of them was discharged after investigations or purges. Chaucer's service for 12½ years had in 1386 already run beyond the usual term. Once more the attempt to dramatize the events of his external life must fail.

The years 1385–86 saw the beginning of serious political disturbance in England, and at the same time a number of changes occurred in Chaucer's life, so that scholars have naturally assumed some connection between the two. The changes are interesting, but the assumption does not carry strong conviction. In 1385 Chaucer got a permanent deputy at the wool quay and also became one of the J.P.'s for Kent. In the late summer of 1386 he was elected knight of the shire for Kent in the parliament that was to meet at Westminster on 1 October, he gave up his house at Aldgate, and by December had ended his employment at the Customs House altogether. No direct evidence survives to tell us what property he acquired in Kent, but what most likely happened is that now, past his fortieth year and perhaps with a sick wife, he went to live in north Kent and hoped to give more time to his writing in agreeable surroundings. Of course the idealization of May and the cult of the daisy were stock literary forms. But it is hard to reject as mere devices the expressed delight at the tranquillity of gardens in the Prologue to the *Legend of Good Women*, whether that poem was written before or after Chaucer's exit from the city. At this point it will be timely to say something of Chaucer's connection with Kent. The county was as much the scene of his life as London. On occasion he uses Kentish dialect forms, the road to Canterbury he knew in actuality as well as imagination, and close investigation shows that many of the people he knew lived near Greenwich, the Cray valley or within sight of the North Downs, then a prosperous residential area and even now offering a certain freshness to the London worker.

As early as 1375 Chaucer had a considerable financial profit out of Kent through the custody of a Canterbury heir called Edmund Staplegate,[2] but by the time he was appointed J.P. for the county in 1385 he probably possessed property in the part of Kent nearest to London.[3] When in 1387 he was placed on a commission to enquire into the abduction of a young heiress, the session was held at Dartford and the other three commissioners possessed land and interests in the same area. The centre of the enquiry was indeed Bexley, North Cray, Sidcup and Chislehurst, whence came plaintiff, defendant and jurors as well as commissioners, and the wills of some of their descendants are ex-

---

2. *Life-Records*, chap. 12.
3. The only other esquires in this list of Kentish J.P.'s were Hugh Fastolf who was Deputy Constable of Dover Castle and William Topcliffe who was a lifelong servant of the archbishop and probably lived in Maidstone, F. R. H. Du Boulay, *The Lordship of Canterbury*, 1966, pp. 394, 396, 398.

tant and derive from the same region.[4] Again in 1388 the transfer of a small action for debt against Chaucer suggests that the Exchequer considered Kent to be his home. Frequently during the 1390s official records hint at Chaucer's association with the Woolwich and Greenwich areas, and a manuscript of 'Lenvoy a Scogan' dating from c. 1393 has a marginal note which says that Chaucer was then living in Greenwich. This is made virtually certain by the series of deeds dated 1395–96 transferring Spittlecombe in East Greenwich from Archbishop Arundel to Gregory Ballard. The technical details do not matter here, but the witness-list fairly clearly numbers Chaucer among the Greenwich residents. Chaucer was also one of the attorneys appointed by Ballard to take possession in his behalf which would have been most conveniently done by a local inhabitant. There is an additional point. Gregory Ballard was a busy official who during his life served both the king and Archbishop Arundel, the king's enemy. He was butler to Richard II in the 1390s (a post later held by Thomas Chaucer) and both Treasurer (1398–1401) and Steward of the estates (1400–12) to the archbishop. His will made in October 1415 shows him a well-to-do inhabitant of Greenwich, accustomed to travel, and leaving a widow, one son and at least four menservants.[5] When Arundel suffered forfeiture in 1397 Ballard received this property from the king, yet again became the archbishop's counsellor when Arundel was restored to favour. His career illustrates the kind of friend Chaucer had in prosperous north Kent: a modest landholder with professional skills, accustomed to riding over southern England and giving official orders, and surviving the cross-winds of political fortune.

The years 1385–6 formed a dividing-point in Chaucer's life. Hitherto his work had been carried on in contact with communities, whether in great households or in the bustle of city life. Thereafter his appointments required him to travel about but to live less closely surrounded by his fellow men. From 1389 to 1391 he was Clerk of the King's Works with responsibilities for buildings and repairs at various royal residences; from at latest 1391 till the end of his life he was one of the deputy foresters of North Petherton, Somerset. There is no evidence that as Clerk of the Works he was unsatisfactory, and his duties in Somerset, if any, are quite obscure. The impression is that as he grew older he continued to be favoured on all sides, received posts which made decreasing demands on him, and was granted emoluments to maintain him at a decent standard of living. The debts which have attracted such attention were nothing unusual, but rather indi-

---

4. William Hall (1512) and Thomas Hall (1526), yeomen of Bexley (Public Record Office, filed will and Prerogative Court of Canterbury (PCC) Will Register 20 Porch); William Swetesyre (1527), yeoman of North Cray (ibid., 23 Porch). For these, see my pamphlet *Medieval Bexley*, Bexley Corporation Public Libraries 1961. The case clearly concerned the Bexley Halls, so *Life-Records* p. 379, n. 3, is wrong, but p. 381 is on the right lines. Rickhill, the chief commissioner and a man connected with the death of the duke of Gloucester in 1397, was from Rochester, where his second wife, Rose, died in 1418 or 1419 (*Register of Henry Chichele, archbishop of Canterbury, 1414–43*, ed. E. F. Jacob, II, Oxford 1938, pp. 161–62). Thomas Carshill (Cressell), one of the defendants, had a descendant, Richard Cressell, gent., still living in Chislehurst in 1508 (PCC Will Register 12 Bennett).

5. *The Lordship of Canterbury*, pp. 394, 398; *Register Chichele* II, pp. 114–15. These works add to the information in *Life-Records*, p. 509, n. 2.

cate a certain affluence, for his income tended to rise and was paid with remarkable regularity for the times, and the ability to borrow money was then as now a sign of creditworthiness. His service as Justice of the Peace for Kent in 1385–89 has left no trace of any personal activities, nor does the commission mark him out from scores of country gentry who were thus associated with magnates in the shires, but his election to parliament in 1386 merits comment. It was the last time that Chaucer found himself at the centre of public affairs. Any personal part played by him is quite unknown (again, the same is true of many others) but the occasion can be made to illustrate with some satisfying detail the society in which he found himself.

During the thirteenth and fourteenth centuries the king's government was always trying to persuade men of suitable substance to take up knighthood and thus formally qualify themselves for various kinds of public duty in their localities. This is true of Londoners as well as of rural landholders, but resistance to so expensive a distinction was stubborn. Consequently, many of the parliamentary 'knights of the shire' were not true knights at all, ceremonially girt with the sword and styled *chivaler*, but squires and gentlemen more interested in their estates than in the warrior pursuits so admired by monastic chroniclers and other desk-romantics who liked to deplore the softness of the times. Likewise, election to parliament was not always the prized honour it later became. Absence from one's domestic concerns might be awkward; travel had its risks, and so too did business among the powerful and demanding men who surrounded the king; and four shillings a day would not seem much when faced with the need to furbish accommodation, as were the four citizens of London who travelled to the Cambridge parliament of 1389 and had to spend £112 7s 0d restoring and equipping a ruined house for their stay.[6]

In any parliament there were men who had never been there before and some who would serve once only. For all that, the parliamentary knights were becoming an influential body in petitioning the king, arguing about taxation and at critical moments supporting the king's aristocratic opponents. Politics were still 'lords' matters', and the political leaders were the higher nobility. Between the ordinary run of barons and knights there was no very sharp social division. It was a strongly held opinion that the knights in parliament ought to have some property in the shires they represented. The rule of primogeniture in aristocratic inheritance meant that a knight could well be a lord's close kinsman and even if he were not many knights were followers and retainers of the lords. Likewise, a knight could have ties of business or relationship with a burgess, although the townsmen enjoyed less prestige than the knights when they met in parliamentary sitting. In brief, the Commons in parliament were by Chaucer's day becoming a homogeneous group, yet one in which wide differences of career and importance could be found.[7]

---

6. *English Historical Documents, 1327–1485*, ed. A. R. Myers, 1969, pp. 451–52.
7. The following biographical details have been made available before their official publication by courtesy of the *History of Parliament Trust*, London, and special thanks are due to its Secretary, Mr. E. L. C. Mullins.

In the parliament which met on 1 October 1386 only 38 out of the 71 shire representatives present were real knights.[8] No pattern can be discerned. Both representatives for Sussex and Buckinghamshire happened to be knights, but neither for Kent or Bedfordshire. If anything, the north, the east midlands and the west country produced on this occasion more knights than the south-east. But there was a tendency for men of greater wealth to be knights, whether they had inherited it, married it or been granted it for good service. A constant feature in the lives of shire knights is that they also at some time acted as sheriff, Justice of the Peace and commissioner for the various tasks of local government. A few instances must suffice to show how diverse were the men whose characteristics might seem at first glance so similar. Ralph Carminew of Cornwall was elected but never sat in the parliament at all because he was pulled over a cliff on 9 October by a pair of greyhounds he was leading. He had been to parliament twice before, but his fellow Cornishman, John Bevyle, sat only the once even though he was unusually young at this time; as sheriff of Cornwall he complained of his 'great losses and costs in office', but he married an heiress and became richer than his father. Walter atte Lee of Hertfordshire sat for parliament eleven times and was a king's knight and vigorous soldier, but Thomas atte Lee, esquire, his colleague and probable kinsman, never came to parliament again although he was a favoured retainer of the king. Sir Thomas Broke of Somerset, who sat twelve times, owed his position largely to marriage with the rich widow of a Bristol merchant who had sixteen manors in the west country. They lived in a stone mansion at Holditch (now in Dorset) where they had a deer-park. The family became connected with the Cobhams, notorious for Lollardy, and Broke himself requested in his will (1415) a simple grave that might be trampled by people going to church, and left no bequests to religious institutions. The knights for Northumberland were quite different again: Sir Bertram de Montboucher and Sir Robert de Claveryng were both campaigners much occupied with the unremitting border struggle against the Scots. Chaucer's Kentish colleagues were less distinguished. Hardly anything is known of the Rochester burgesses, Piers Pope and John Fleming, not even their connection with Rochester. One of the Canterbury burgesses, called L. H. Holt, was in 1387 a trustee for the property of Edmund Staplegate, former ward of Chaucer.[9] The other shire representative was William Bettenham of Hawkhurst who owed large sums of money, including £13s 4d to Sir Richard Stury. He must have been related to Stephen Bettenham, esquire of Cranbrook, and it is interesting that whereas William obtained a papal licence to have a private altar, Stephen showed signs of the evangelical views that were common in Kent, for he asked in his will that money should be given to the poor rather than spent on a funeral feast 'which is rather called

---

8. *Calendar of Close Rolls, 1385–89*, H.M.S.O., pp. 298–99.
9. See p. 487 above. Edmund Staplegate was also a landlord of James de Peckham who arranged masses to be said for him. See the will referred to on p. 477, n. 8.

the solace of the living and dissipation of goods than refreshment and salvation of souls'. He cannot have been a wholehearted Lollard as he did not forbid obsequies but merely wished to avoid a multiplicity of masses for his soul.[1] Chaucer could almost have made a variegated pilgrimage out of his fellow-parliamentarians.

Nothing is more natural than the wish to give genius a human face. Yet five hundred documents excavated with monumental labour and printed in the *Life-Records* still leave the figure veiled. There can be little surprise at the exasperation of scholars with Chaucer's habit of slipping into the background of historical events. Some have preferred the most fearful precision of conjecture rather than a blurring of the biographical edges and have argued for almost anything but the commonplace: domestic misery, political cowardice, insolvency, incompetence, rape, or even a *diseur*'s subjection to the patronizing tolerance of courtiers. Criticism is disfigured by such rash dramatizations; nor does Chaucer's fame need the aid of worldly distinction. There is indeed a biographical singularity about him if we will see it. It is, I dare to say, in a personal modesty which was real and not simply a device of rhetoric designed to charm an audience. Geoffrey Chaucer did not struggle for the kind of advancement which his son Thomas achieved. There is no question of an actual poverty or public neglect (though the absence of his last will is one of the worst gaps in the evidence), for his financial means never failed and his son cannot have begun a well-heeled life on nothing. But the poet's own life-work was truly in poetry which he generated in quiet reading and expressed as professional entertainment. To a society not surfeited with mental recreation he brought mirth and solace. Implicit in the solace was an assumption that even a story has a 'signification', a morality that assured his hearers of values beyond mere storytelling. In the fourteenth century it was impossible that it should be otherwise, and Chaucer did not speak a language wholly different from that of Langland or the preachers, mystics, or religious lyricists. In a sense his outlook was a spiritual one, while entirely compatible with the conventions of courtly love, mild pessimism, irony, a sense of destiny and pleasurable indecency. For the historian the literature's integrity is matched by that of the man when he is compared with the great Italians he admired and used. Despite similarities in mercantile origins, life at courts, public position and dedication to letters, we miss in Chaucer the spiritual violence of Dante, the bitterness of Boccaccio, the vanity of Petrarch. It is a dubious excuse to argue that he did not suffer as they did; that he was able to stand outside the pain of his own utterances, unlike Boccaccio for whom *Il Filostrato* was a shield 'for his secret and amorous grief'. If Troy was London, the *Troilus* is incredible as a mere entertainment, indited without sentiment as the author claimed.[2] The fifth book of *Troilus and Criseyde* is the Everest of Chaucer's Himalayas and cannot have been climbed without cost.

1. *Register Chichele*, II, pp. 33–36.
2. *Troilus*, II, 13, and, for the closing of the gate, V, 1177–80.

When at nightfall the warden of the gates began to call in the townsmen and their beasts, and Troilus at last gave up his gazing for the
woman who did not come, the poet was communicating an experience
satisfying to the historian, who is fiction's enemy, and the historian
must be silent and content.

ARTHUR W. HOFFMAN

Chaucer's Prologue to Pilgrimage: The Two Voices†

Criticism of the portraits in Chaucer's General Prologue to *The Canterbury Tales* has taken various directions: some critics have praised the
portraits especially for their realism, sharp individuality, adroit psychology, and vividness of felt life; others, working in the genetic direction,
have pointed out actual historical persons who might have sat for the
portraits; others, appealing to the light of the medieval sciences, have
shown the portraits to be filled, though not burdened, with the lore of
Chaucer's day, and to have sometimes typical identities like case histories. Miss Bowden,[1] in her recent study of the Prologue, assembles the
fruits of many earlier studies and gives the text an impressive resonance
by sketching historical and social norms and ideals, the facts and the
standards of craft, trade, and profession, so that the form of the portraits can be tested in the light of possible conformities, mean or noble,
to things as they were or to things as they ought to have been.

It is not unlikely that the critics who have explored in these various
directions would be found in agreement on one commonplace, a
metaphor which some of them indeed have used, the designation of
the portraits in the General Prologue as figures in a tapestry. It is less
likely that all of the critics would agree as to the implications of this
metaphor, but it seems to me that the commonplace deserves to be explored and some of its implications tested. The commonplace implies
that the portraits which appear in the General Prologue have a designed togetherness, that the portraits exist as parts of a unity.

Such a unity, it may be argued, is partly a function of the exterior
framework of a pilgrimage to Canterbury; all the portraits are portraits
of pilgrims:

> At nyght was come into that hostelrye
> Wel nyne and twenty in a compaignye,
> Of sondry folk, by aventure yfalle
> In felaweshipe, and pilgrimes were they alle,   (23–26)[2]

† From *ELH* 21 (1954): 1–16. Copyright © The Johns Hopkins University Press. Reprinted
  with permission of The Johns Hopkins University Press.
1. Muriel Bowden, *A Commentary on the General Prologue to the Canterbury Tales* (New York,
   1948).
2. All references to the text of *The Canterbury Tales* are to *The Poetical Works of Chaucer*, ed.
   F. N. Robinson (Cambridge, Mass., 1933).

But the unity of the Prologue may be also partly a matter of internal relationships among the portraits, relationships which are many and various among "sondry folk." One cannot hope to survey all of these, but the modest objective of studying some of the aesthetically important internal relationships is feasible.

If one begins with the unity that is exterior to the portraits, the unity that contains them, one faces directly the question of the nature of pilgrimage as it is defined in this dramatic poem. What sort of framework does the Prologue in fact define? Part of the answer is in the opening lines, and it is not a simple answer because the definition there ranges from the upthrust and burgeoning of life as a seasonal and universal event to a particular outpouring of people, pilgrims, gathered briefly at the Tabard Inn in Southwark, drifting, impelled, bound, called to the shrine of Thomas a Becket at Canterbury. The pilgrimage is set down in the calendar of seasons as well as in the calendar of piety; nature impels and supernature draws. "Go, go, go," says the bird; "Come," says the saint.

In the opening lines of the Prologue springtime is characterized in terms of procreation, and a pilgrimage of people to Canterbury is just one of the many manifestations of the life thereby produced. The phallicism of the opening lines presents the impregnating of a female March by a male April, and a marriage of water and earth. The marriage is repeated and varied immediately as a fructifying of "holt and heeth" by Zephirus, a marriage of air and earth. This mode of symbolism and these symbols as parts of a rite of spring have a long background of tradition; as Professor Cook[3] once pointed out, there are eminent passages of this sort in Aeschylus and Euripides, in Lucretius, in Virgil's *Georgics*, in Columella, and in the *Pervigilium Veneris*, and Professor Robinson cites Guido delle Colonne, Boccaccio, Petrarch, and Boethius. Zephirus is the only overt mythological figure in Chaucer's passage, but, in view of the instigative role generally assigned to Aphrodite in the rite of spring, she is perhaps to be recognized here, as Professor Cook suggested, in the name of April, which was her month both by traditional association and by one of the two ancient etymologies.[4] Out of this context of the quickening of the earth presented naturally and symbolically in the broadest terms, the Prologue comes to pilgrimage and treats pilgrimage first as an event in the calendar of nature, one aspect of the general springtime surge of human energy and longing. There are the attendant suggestions of the renewal of human mobility after the rigor and confinement of winter, the revival of wayfaring now that the ways are open. The horizon extends to distant shrines and foreign lands, and the attraction of the strange and faraway is included before the vision narrows and focusses upon its English specifications and the pilgrimage to the shrine at Canterbury with the vows and gratitude that send pilgrims there. One way of regarding the structure of this opening passage would empha-

---

3. Albert S. Cook, "Chaucerian Papers—1: 1. Prologue 1–11," *Transactions of the Connecticut Academy of Arts and Sciences*, XXIII (New Haven, 1919), pp. 5–21.
4. Cook, pp. 5–10.

size the magnificent progression from the broadest inclusive generality
to the firmest English specification, from the whole western tradition
of the celebration of spring (including, as Cook pointed out, such
a non-English or very doubtfully English detail as "the droghte of
March") to a local event of English society and English Christendom,
from natural forces in their most general operation to a very specific
and Christian manifestation of those forces. And yet one may regard
the structure in another way, too; if, in the calendar of nature, the passage moves from general to particular, does it not, in the calendar of
piety, move from nature to something that includes and oversees nature? Does not the passage move from an activity naturally generated
and impelled to a governed activity, from force to *telos*? Does not the
passage move from Aphrodite and *amor* in their secular operation to
the sacred embrace of "the hooly blisful martir" and of *amor dei*?

The transition from nature to supernature is emphasized by the
contrast between the healthful physical vigor of the opening lines and
the reference to sickness that appears in line 18. On the one hand, it
is physical vitality which conditions the pilgrimage; on the other hand,
sickness occasions pilgrimage. It is, in fact, rather startling to come
upon the word "seeke" at the end of this opening passage, because it is
like a breath of winter across the landscape of spring. "Whan that they
were seeke" may, of course, refer literally to illnesses of the winter just
past, but, in any event, illness belongs symbolically to the inclement
season. There is also, however, a strong parallelism between the beginning and end of this passage, a parallelism that has to do with
restorative power. The physical vitality of the opening is presented as restorative of the dry earth; the power of the saint is presented as
restorative of the sick. The seasonal restoration of nature parallels a
supernatural kind of restoration that knows no season; the supernatural kind of restoration involves a wielding and directing of the
forces of nature. The Prologue begins, then, by presenting a double
view of the Canterbury pilgrimage: the pilgrimage is one tiny manifestation of a huge tide of life, but then, too, the tide of life ebbs and
flows in response to the power which the pilgrimage acknowledges,
the power symbolized by "the hooly blisful martir."

After line 18 the process of particularizing is continued, moving
from "that seson" just defined to a day and to a place and to a person
in Southwark at the Tabard, and thence to the portraits of the pilgrims. The double view of pilgrimage is enhanced and extended by the
portraits where it appears, in one aspect, as a range of motivation.
This range of motivation is from the sacred to the secular and on to
the profane—"profane" in the sense of motivations actually subversive
of the sacred. All the pilgrims are, in fact, granted an ostensible sacred
motive; all of them are seeking the shrine. The distances that we are
made aware of are both *within* some of the portraits, where a gulf
yawns between ostensible and actual motivation, and *between* the portraits, where the motivation of the Knight and the Parson is near one
end of the spectrum, and the motivation of the Summoner and the
Pardoner near the other end. There is such an impure but blameless

mixture as the motivation of the Prioress; there is the secular pilgrimage of the Wife of Bath, impelled so powerfully and frankly by Saint
Venus rather than drawn by Saint Thomas, and goaded by a Martian
desire to acquire and dominate another husband; in the case of the
Prioress, an inescapable doubt as to the quality of *amor* hesitates between the sacred and secular, and in the case of the thoroughly secular Wife of Bath, doubt hesitates between the secular and the profane
while the portrait shows the ostensible motive that belongs to all the
pilgrims shaken without ever being subverted, contradicted perhaps,
brazenly opposed, but still acknowledged and offered, not, at any rate,
hypocritically betrayed. In the area of motivation, the portraits seem to
propose, ultimately, a fundamental, inescapable ambiguity as part of
the human condition; prayer for the purification of motive is valid for
all the pilgrims. And the pilgrims who move, pushed by impulse and
drawn by vows, none merely impelled and none perfectly committed,
reflect, in their human ambiguity, the broad problem of origins and
ends, the stubbornness of matter and the power of spirit, together
with ideas of cosmic resolution and harmony in which source and end
are reconciled and seem to be the same, the purposes of nature and
supernature found to be at one, the two restorative powers akin, the
kinds of love not discontinuous, Saint Venus and Saint Thomas different and at odds yet not at war, within the divine purpose which contains both.

The portraits of the Knight and the Squire have a particular interest. The relationships between these two portraits are governed by and
arise out of the natural relationship of father and son. Consanguinity
provides the base for a dramatic relationship, and at the same time is
the groundwork for a modestly generalized metaphor of age and youth.
Each portrait is enhanced and defined by the presence of the other:
the long roll of the Knight's campaigns, and the Squire's little opportunity ("so litel space"), a few raids enumerated in one line; a series of
past tenses, a history, for the Knight, and for the Squire a present
breaking forth in active participles; the Knight not "gay," wearing fus-
tian soiled by his coat of mail, "bismotered," the Squire bright and
fresh and colorful; the Knight meek and quiet,—or so the portrait
leaves him—beside the Squire, who sings and whistles all the day. The
Knight's love is an achieved devotion, a matter of pledges fulfilled and
of values, if not completely realized, yet woven into the fabric of experience (ideals—"trouthe," "honour," "fredom," "curteisie"). The Squire
is a lover, a warm and eager lover, paying court to his lady and sleeping no more than the nightingale. In the one, the acquired, tutored,
disciplined, elevated, enlarged love, the piety; and in the other, the
love channelled into an elaborate social ritual, a parody piety, but still
emphatically fresh and full of natural impulse. One cannot miss the
creation of the Squire in conventional images of nature, and meadow,
the flowers, the freshness like May, the lover like the nightingale,—
comparisons that are a kind of re-emergence of the opening lines of
the Prologue, the springtime surge of youthful, natural energy that an-
imates the beginning. "Go, go, go," the bird's voice, is a major impulse

in the portrait of the Squire and in the Squire's pilgrimage; the Knight's pilgrimage is more nearly a response to the voice of the saint. Yet the Squire is within the belt of rule, and learning the calendar of piety. The concluding couplet of the portrait

> Curteis he was, lowely and servysable,
> And carf biforn his fader at the table.   (99–100)

has the effect of bending all the youth, energy, color, audibleness, and high spirit of the Squire to the service of his father, the Knight, and to attendance on his pilgrimage, with perhaps a suggestion of the present submitting to the serious and respected values served and communicated by the past, the natural and the imposed submitting of the son to his natural father, and beyond him to the supernatural goal, the shrine to which the father directs his pilgrimage.

The portraits of the Knight and the Squire represent one of the ways in which portraiture takes into account and develops the double definition of pilgrimage which is established at the beginning. The double definition of pilgrimage is involved in a different way in the portrait of the Prioress; there it appears as a delicately poised ambiguity. Two definitions appear as two faces of one coin. Subsequently, when the portrait of the Prioress is seen together with the portraits of the Monk and the Friar, a sequence is realized, running from ambiguity to emphatic discrepancy, and the satire that circles the impenetrable duality of sacred and secular impulse in the case of the Prioress knifes in as these impulses are drawn apart in the case of the Monk and strikes vigorously in the still wider breach that appears in the case of the Friar. What is illustrated within the portraits is amplified by a designed sequence.

The delicate balance in the picture of the Prioress has been generally recognized and has perhaps been only the more clearly exhibited by occasional seesawing in the critical interpretation of the portrait in which the satiric elements are sometimes represented as heavy, sometimes as slight, sometimes sinking the board, and sometimes riding light and high. There is, perhaps, no better illustration of the delicacy of the balance than the fact that the Prioress's very presence on a pilgrimage, as several commentators have pointed out, may be regarded as the first satiric touch. The very act of piety is not free from the implication of imperfection; the Prioress is obligated to a cloistered piety that serves and worships God without going on a journey to seek a shrine, and prioresses were specifically and repeatedly enjoined from going on pilgrimages. Prioresses did, nevertheless, go as pilgrims, so that Chaucer's Prioress is not departing from the norm of behavior of persons in her office so much as she is departing from the sanctioned ideal of behavior.[5] In the case of the Prioress, the blemish is sufficiently technical to have only faint satiric coloring; it is not the notable kind of blemish recognized in all times and all places. Never-

---

5. The relevance of the ideal sanctioned character of an office to the portrait of a person will appear again strikingly in the case of the Summoner and the Pardoner.

theless, it is precisely this kind of hint of a spot that places the Prioress at one end of a sequence in which the more obviously blemished Monk and Friar appear. If we pose a double question—What kind of woman is the Prioress, and what kind of prioress is the woman?—the portrait responds more immediately to the first part of the question, and leaves the answer to the second part largely in the area of implication. The portrait occupies forty-five lines, and more than three-fourths of the lines have to do with such matters as the Prioress's blue eyes, her red mouth, the shape of her nose and width of her forehead, her ornaments and dress, her table manners, her particular brand of French, her pets and what she fed them, and her tenderness about mice. It is, of course, one of the skilful arts of these portraits to work with surfaces and make the surfaces convey and reveal what lies beneath, but it should be observed that in the case of the Parson—or even in the case of the Knight—a character is arrived at almost entirely without physical and superficial detail. One need not take the emphatic surface in the portrait of the Prioress as necessarily pejorative in its implication; it need not follow that the Prioress is a shallow and superficial person, and, in consequence, sharply satirized. But the portrait does seem, by means of its emphasis on surfaces, to define the Prioress as woman, and strongly enough so that tension between the person and her office, between the given human nature and the assumed sacred obligation is put vividly before us, and rather as the observation of a fact than as the instigation of a judgment. In the cases of the Monk and the Friar, the tension is so exacerbated that judgment is, in the case of the Monk, incited, and in the case of the Friar, both incited and inflamed to severity.

In the portrait of the Prioress the double view of pilgrimage appears both in an ambiguity of surfaces, and in an implied inner range of motivation. In the surfaces there is a sustained hovering effect: the name, Eglentyne, is romance, and "simple and coy" is a romance formula, but she *is* a nun, by whatever name, and "simple" and "coy," aside from their romance connotations have meanings ("simple" and "modest") appropriate enough to a nun; there are the coral beads and the green gauds, but they *are* a rosary; there are the fluted wimple and the exposed forehead, but the costume *is* a nun's habit; there is the golden brooch shining brightly, but it *is* a religious emblem. Which shall be taken as principal, which as modifying and subordinate? Are the departures or the conformities more significant of her nature? Are her Stratford French and her imitation of court manners more important than the fact that she sings well and properly the divine service? Do we detect vanity in her singing well, or do we rely on what she sings and accept her worship as well performed—to the glory of God? The ambiguity of these surface indications leads into the implied range of motivation; this implied range has been generally recognized in the motto—"*Amor vincit omnia*"—on the Prioress's golden brooch, and the implications set up in the portrait as a whole seem to be clustered and tightly fastened in this ornament and symbol.

The motto itself has, in the course of history, gone its own double

pilgrimage to the shrine of Saint Venus and to sacred shrines; the
original province of the motto was profane, but it was drawn over to a
sacred meaning and soon became complexly involved with and com-
pactly significant of both. Professor Lowes comments on the motto as
it pertains to the Prioress:

> Now is it earthly love that conquers all, now heavenly; the
> phrase plays back and forth between the two. And it is precisely
> that happy ambiguity of the convention—itself the result of
> an earlier transfer—that makes Chaucer's use of it here . . . a
> master stroke. *Which of the two loves does "amor" mean to the Pri-
> oress?* I do not know; but I think she thought she meant love ce-
> lestial.[6]

Professor Lowes, presumably, does not really expect to see the matter
concluded one way or the other and finds this very inconclusiveness,
hovering between two answers, one of the excellences of the portrait.
There is, however, a certain amount of illumination to be gained,
though not an answer to the question as formulated by Professor
Lowes, by asking the question another way and considering an answer
in terms that lie outside of the Prioress's motivation. Put the question
in this form: Which of the two loves does the *portrait* in the context of
the Prologue mean by *amor*? The answer to this question, of course, is
both. On the one hand, profane love or the love of earthly things does
overcome all; the little vanities and pretensions, the love of color and
decoration and dress, the affection squandered in little extravagances
toward pets, the pity and tender emotion wasted upon a trapped
mouse—the multiplicity of secular, impulsive loves threatens to and
could ultimately stifle the dedication to the celestial love. This answer
is, in fact, a version of the Prioress's character and motivation sometimes offered. It actually implies one half of the view of pilgrimage—
the natural powers that move people and that may usurp the whole
character. But the other answer—celestial love conquers all things—
also applies to the portrait, though it is not very easily arrived at in
terms of the Prioress's motivation. Here we are dealing with the ostensible meaning of the motto, the ideal meaning of the motto as worn by
a prioress—what it ought to mean in terms of her office. And, no matter what the impurity of the Prioress's motives, no matter what she
means or thinks she means by the motto, the motto does, in the calendar of piety, mean that God's love is powerful over all things, powerful
in this case over the vanity that may be involved in the wearing of the
brooch, powerful over all the shallowness and limitation and reduction
and misdirection of love that the Prioress may be guilty of, powerful
over all her departures from or misunderstandings of discipline and
obligation and vow, powerful over all inadequacy, able to overcome the
faults of God's human instruments and make this woman's divine office valid. The motto and the portrait of which it is the conclusion
appreciate both the secular impulses and the sacred redemptive will,

---

6. John Livingston Lowes, *Convention and Revolt* (Boston and New York, 1919), p. 66.

but there is no doubt which love it is that is crowned with ultimate power.

Chaucer has found ways, as in the case of the Prioress, of making an ideal or standard emerge within a portrait. The standard may be ambiguously stated or heavily involved in irony, but it is almost always present, and nowhere with greater effectiveness than in the most sharply satiric portraits. This, I take it, is the effect of the formula of worthiness which is applied to so many of the pilgrims. A character is declared to be "worthy" or "the best that ever was" of his craft or profession or office, and frequently under circumstances that make the statement jarring and the discrepancy obvious. There is a definite shock, for example, when Friar Huberd is declared to be a "worthy lymytour," or the Pardoner "a noble ecclesiaste." Even when the satiric thrust has two directions, striking both at the individual and at the group to which he belongs, the implication has nevertheless been lodged in the portrait that there could be, for example, a worthy friar, or a pardoner who was indeed a noble ecclesiastic. The reader is, as it were, tripped in the act of judging and reminded that if he condemns these figures, if they appear culpable, there must be some sort of standard by which they are so judged, by which they appear so.

Chaucer has also adopted the method of including ideal or nearly ideal portraits among the pilgrims. There are, for example, the Knight and the Plowman, figures at either end of the secular range, and among the clerical figures there is the Parson. A host of relative judgments, of course, are set up by devices of sequence and obvious pairing and contrasting of portraits. It is the ideal portraits, however, that somehow preside over all these judgments and comparisons, and it is to them that the relative distinctions are presented for a kind of penultimate judgment. Prioress, Monk, and Friar, and all the other clerical figures are reckoned with the Parson who is, in fact, made to speak in an accent of judgment upon the clerical figures who go astray—". . . if gold ruste, what shal iren do?" (We may remember the Prioress's shining gold brooch, the Monk's gold pin, and, among the secular figures, the Physician who so doubly regarded gold as a sovereign remedy.)

Chaucer has used an interesting device for undergirding the ideal portrait of the Parson. He employs consanguinity with metaphorical effect. After the assertions which declare that the Parson "first . . . wroghte, and afterward . . . taughte," the actualizing of Christian ideals is supported by the representation of the Parson as brother to the Plowman. It is the Parson's Christian obligation to treat men as brothers, and the portrait abundantly affirms that he does so. Making him actually the brother of the Plowman brilliantly insists that what supernature calls for is performed by the Parson and, more than that, comes by nature to him.[7] The achieved harmony both comes from above and rises out of the ground; sacred and secular are linked, the shepherd of souls and the tiller of the soil. This is a vantage point from

---

7. There is, of course, plenty of actual basis for representing a parson as a son of the soil; the connection is not merely an artistic and symbolic device.

which the conflicts of secular and sacred, of nature and supernature, are seen in a revealing light, a point at which one sees reflected in the clear mirror of ideal characters and an actual-ideal relationship the fundamental double view of pilgrimage established in the beginning.

The double definition of pilgrimage is differently but nonetheless revealingly illuminated by the portraits of another fraternizing pair, the Summoner and Pardoner, who conclude the sequence of pilgrims. The illumination here is not clarified by way of ideal characters but somehow refracted and intensified by the dark surfaces upon which it falls. The darkness is most visible in connection with the theme of love, which appears here in a sinister and terrible distortion. The hot and lecherous Summoner, the type of sexual unrestraint, is represented as harmonizing in song with the impotent Pardoner, the eunuch; the deep rumbling voice and the thin effeminate voice are singing, "Com hider, love, to me!" The song, in this context, becomes both a promiscuous and perverted invitation and an unconscious symbolic acknowledgment of the absence of and the need for love, love that comes neither to the grasping physical endeavor of the Summoner nor to the physical incapacity of the Pardoner—nor to their perverted spirits. Love has been treated in the Prologue from the beginning as dual in character, a matter both of the body and the spirit, the *amor* symbolized by Venus, sung by the Squire, equivocally illustrated by the Prioress, lustily celebrated by the Wife of Bath; and the *amor dei*, the love shadowily there beyond all the secular forms of love, a hovering presence among the pilgrims and sometimes close, as to the Knight and the Parson and the Plowman, and symbolized in the saint's shrine which is the goal of all of them. On this view, the song of the Summoner and the Pardoner is a superb dramatic irony acknowledging the full extent of their need and loss, the love of God which they ought to strive for, the love which they desperately need.

The office which each of these men is supposed to fulfill should be taken into account. The Summoner is, ostensibly, an instrument through whom divine justice, in a practical way, operates in the world. There are, in the portrait, a few touches that may be reminders of the ultimate source of his authority and function: his "*Questio quid iuris,*" though it is represented satirically as the sum and substance of his knowledge, and posed as a question, *is* legitimately the substance of his knowledge—his province is law, especially the divine law; "*Significavit*" is the opening word of a legal writ, a dreaded worldly pronouncement of divine judgment, excommunication; he is physically a fearful figure from whom children run (not the divine love which suffers them to come), and some of the physical details may be reminders of noble and awesome aspects of divine justice—his "fyr-reed cherubynnes face" and the voice described in a significant analogy as like a trumpet, "Was nevere trompe of half so greet a soun." The Pardoner, on the other hand, is the ostensible instrument of divine mercy and love. Many of the pardoners, as Miss Bowden points out, went so far as to pretend to absolve both *a poena* and *a culpa*, thereby usurping, in the pretended absolution *a culpa*, a function which theological doctrine reserved to God and His grace. In any case, their legitimate functions were an appeal for charity and an extension of God's mercy and love. The Pardoner, it should be observed, is, compared to the Summoner, an attractive figure. We may be reminded of the superior affinity of the Pardoner's office by the veil which he has sewed upon his cap, the copy of St. Veronica's veil which is supposed to have received the imprint of Christ's face.[8]

The justice and love[9] of which the Summoner and Pardoner are emissaries are properly complementary and harmoniously, though paradoxically and mysteriously, related, so that the advances that are being made both of persons and of values are, in a very serious sense, proper to this pair. The radical physical distinctness of Summoner and Pardoner is at this level the definition of two aspects of supernature; there is the same employment of physical metaphor here that there is in the portraits of the Parson and the Plowman, but with the difference that light comes out of darkness, and out of the gravest corruption of nature the supernatural relationship emerges clarified in symbol. The Summoner cannot finally pervert, and the Pardoner's impotence cannot finally prevent; the divine justice and love are powerful even over these debased instruments—*Amor vincit omnia*. Beyond their knowing, beyond their power or impotence, impotently both Pardoner and Summoner appeal for the natural love—melody of birdsong and meadows of flowers—and both pray for the celestial love, the ultimate pardon which in their desperate and imprisoned darkness is their only hope: "Com hider, love, to me!"

The exterior unity achieved by the realistic device and broadly symbolic framework of pilgrimage is made stronger and tighter in the portraits, partly by local sequences and pairings, but most impressively by the illustration, the variation and enrichment by way of human instances, of a theme of love, earthly and celestial, and a general complex intermingling of the consideration of nature with the consideration of supernature. The note of love is sounded in different keys all through the portraits:

The Knight
> . . . he loved chivalrie,
> Trouthe and honour, fredom and curteisie (45–46)

The Squire
> A lovyere and a lusty bacheler . . . (80)
> So hoote he lovede that by nyghtertale
> He sleep namoore than dooth a nyghtyngale. (97–98)

8. Later, in telling his story, the Pardoner acknowledges that his pardons are inferior versions of the supreme pardon which is Christ's. See *The Pardoner's Tale*, 915–18.

9. This statement of the symbolic values behind the Summoner and the Pardoner is not a disagreement with, but merely an addition to, the point made by Kellogg and Haselmayer (Alfred L. Kellogg and Louis A. Haselmayer, "Chaucer's Satire of the Pardoner," *PMLA* LXVI [March 1951], 215–77) when they assert: "In this paradox, this ironic portrait of justice and crime singing in close harmony, we reach the center of Chaucer's satire" (p. 275). There is, indeed, the strongest satiric impact in this affiliation of the man who should apprehend the wrong-doer with the criminal. In addition, however, if we are to see beyond the Summoner's disabilities to his representation of justice, we see in parallel vision beyond the Pardoner's disabilities a representation of love.

The Prioress
> . . . *Amor vincit omnia.* (162)

The Monk
> A Monk . . . that lovede venerie, . . . (166)
> He hadde of gold ywroght a ful curious pyn;
> A love-knotte in the gretter ende ther was. (196–97)
> A fat swan loved he best of any roost. (206)

The Friar
> In love-dayes ther koude he muchel help . . . (258)
> Somewhat he lipsed, for his wantownesse, . . . (264)

The Clerk
> For hym was levere have at his beddes heed
> Twenty bookes, clad in blak or reed,
> Of Aristotle and his philosophie,
> Than robes riche, or fithele, or gay sautrie. (293–96)

The Frankelyn
> Wel loved he by the morwe a sop in wyn;
> To lyven in delit was evere his wone,
> For he was Epicurus owene sone . . . (334–36)

The Physician
> He kepte that he wan in pestilence.
> For gold in phisik is a cordial,
> Therefore he lovede gold in special. (442–44)

The Wife of Bath
> Of remedies of love she knew per chaunce,
> For she koude of that art the olde daunce. (475–76)

The Parson
> But rather wolde he yeven, out of doute,
> Unto his povre parisshens aboute
> Of his offryng and eek of his substaunce. (487–89)
> . . . Cristes loore and his apostles twelve
> He taughte, but first he folwed it hymselve. (527–28)

The Plowman
> With hym ther was a Plowman, was his brother, . . . (529)
> Lyvynge in pees and parfit charitee.
> God loved he best with al his hoole herte
> At alle tymes, thogh him gamed or smerte,
> And thanne his neighebor right as hymselve. (532–35)

The Summoner and The Pardoner
> . . . "Com hider, love, to me!" (672)

The theme of restorative power attends upon the theme of love. It is, of course, announced at the beginning and defined in terms both of nature and supernature. Both the Physician, concerned with natural healing, and the Pardoner, the agent of a supernatural healing, appear under the rubric of "Physician, heal thyself." The worldly Physician is disaffected from God; the Pardoner is naturally impotent. Serious inadequacy in either realm appears as counterpart of inadequacy in the other. It is the Parson who both visits the sick and tends properly to the cure of souls; he works harmoniously in both realms, and both realms are in harmony and fulfilled in him.

The pilgrims are represented as affected by a variety of destructive and restorative kinds of love. Their characters and movement can be fully described only as mixtures of the loves that drive and goad and of the love that calls and summons. The pilgrims have, while they stay and when they move, their worldly host. They have, too, their worldly Summoner and Pardoner who, in the very worst way, move and are moved with them. Nevertheless, the Summoner and Pardoner, who conclude the roll of the company, despite and beyond their appalling personal deficiency, may suggest the summoning and pardoning, the judgment and grace which in Christian thought embrace and conclude man's pilgrimage and which therefore, with all the corrosions of satire and irony, are also the seriously appropriate conclusion to the tapestry of Chaucer's pilgrims.

E. TALBOT DONALDSON

Chaucer the Pilgrim†

Verisimilitude in a work of fiction is not without its attendant dangers, the chief of which is that the responses it stimulates in the reader may be those appropriate not so much to an imaginative production as to an historical one or to a piece of reporting. History and reporting are, of course, honourable in themselves, but if we react to a poet as though he were an historian or a reporter, we do him somewhat less than justice. I am under the impression that many readers, too much influenced by Chaucer's brilliant verisimilitude, tend to regard his famous pilgrimage to Canterbury as significant not because it is a great fiction, but because it seems to be a remarkable record of a fourteenth-century pilgrimage. A remarkable record it may be, but if we treat it too narrowly as such there are going to be certain casualties among the elements that make up the fiction. Perhaps first among these elements is the fictional reporter, Chaucer the pilgrim, and the role he plays in the Prologue to the *Canterbury Tales* and in the links between them. I think it time that he was rescued from the comparatively dull record of history and put back into his poem. He is not really Chaucer the poet—nor, for that matter, is either the poet, or the poem's protagonist, that Geoffrey Chaucer frequently mentioned in contemporary historical records as a distinguished civil servant, but never as a poet. The fact that these are three separate entities does not, naturally, exclude the probability—or rather the certainty—that they bore a close resemblance to one another, and that, indeed, they frequently got together in the same body. But that does not excuse us from keeping them distinct from one another, difficult as their close resemblance makes our task.

† Reprinted by permission of the Modern Language Association from *Speaking of Chaucer* (New York: W. W. Norton and Company, 1970), pp. 1–12. Donaldson's essay originally appeared in *PMLA* 69 (1954): 928–36.

The natural tendency to confuse one thing with its like is perhaps best represented by a school of Chaucerian criticism, now outmoded, that pictured a single Chaucer under the guise of a wide-eyed, jolly, rolypoly little man who, on fine Spring mornings, used to get up early, while the dew was still on the grass, and go look at daisies. A charming portrait, this, so charming, indeed, that it was sometimes able to maintain itself to the exclusion of any Chaucerian other side. It has every reason to be charming, since it was lifted almost *in toto* from the version Chaucer gives of himself in the Prologue to the *Legend of Good Women*, though I imagine it owes some of its popularity to a rough analogy with Wordsworth—a sort of *Legend of Good Poets*. It was this version of Chaucer that Kittredge, in a page of great importance to Chaucer criticism, demolished with his assertion that 'a naïf Collector of Customs would be a paradoxical monster'. He might well have added that a naïve creator of old January would be even more monstrous.

Kittredge's pronouncement cleared the air, and most of us now accept the proposition that Chaucer was sophisticated as readily as we do the proposition that the whale is a mammal. But unhappily, now that we've got rid of the naïve fiction, it is easy to fall into the opposite sort of mistake. This is to envision, in the *Canterbury Tales*, a highly urbane, literal-historical Chaucer setting out from Southwark on a specific day of a specific year (we even argue somewhat acrimoniously about dates and routes), in company with a group of persons who existed in real life and whom Chaucer, his reporter's eye peeled for every idiosyncrasy, determined to get down on paper—down, that is, to the last wart—so that books might be written identifying them. Whenever this accurate reporter says something especially fatuous—which is not infrequently—it is either ascribed to an opinion peculiar to the Middle Ages (sometimes very peculiar), or else Chaucer's tongue is said to be in his cheek.

Now a Chaucer with tongue-in-cheek is a vast improvement over a simple-minded Chaucer when one is trying to define the whole man, but it must lead to a loss of critical perception, and in particular to a confused notion of Chaucerian irony, to see in the Prologue a reporter who is acutely aware of the significance of what he sees but who sometimes, for ironic emphasis, interprets the evidence presented by his observation in a fashion directly contrary to what we expect. The proposition ought to be expressed in reverse: the reporter is, usually, acutely unaware of the significance of what he sees, no matter how sharply he sees it. He is, to be sure, permitted his lucid intervals, but in general he is the victim of the poet's pervasive—not merely sporadic—irony. And as such he is also the chief agent by which the poet achieves his wonderfully complex, ironic, comic, serious vision of a world which is but a devious and confused, infinitely various pilgrimage to a certain shrine. It is, as I hope to make clear, a good deal more than merely fitting that our guide on such a pilgrimage should be a man of such naïveté as the Chaucer who tells the tale of *Sir Thopas*. Let us accompany him a little distance.

It is often remarked that Chaucer really liked the Prioress very much, even though he satirized her gently—very gently. But this is an understatement: Chaucer the pilgrim may not be said merely to have liked the Prioress very much—he thought she was utterly charming. In the first twenty-odd lines of her portrait (A118 ff.) he employs, among other superlatives, the adverb *ful* seven times. Middle English uses *ful* where we use *very*, and if one translates the beginning of the portrait into a kind of basic English (which is what, in a way, it really is), one gets something like this: 'There was also a Nun, a Prioress, who was very sincere and modest in the way she smiled; her biggest oath was only "By saint Loy"; and she was called Madame Eglantine. She sang the divine service very well, intoning it in her nose very prettily, and she spoke French very nicely and elegantly'—and so on, down to the last gasp of sentimental appreciation. Indeed, the Prioress may be said to have transformed the rhetoric into something not unlike that of a very bright kindergarten child's descriptive theme. In his reaction to the Prioress Chaucer the pilgrim resembles another—if less—simple-hearted enthusiast: the Host, whose summons to her to tell a tale must be one of the politest speeches in the language. Not 'My lady Prioresse, a tale now!' but, 'as curteisly as it hadde been a maide',

> My lady Prioresse, by youre leve,
> So that I wiste I sholde you nat greve,
> I wolde deemen that ye telle sholde
> A tale next, if so were that ye wolde.
> Now wol ye vouche sauf, my lady dere? (B² 1636–41)

Where the Prioress reduced Chaucer to superlatives, she reduces the Host to subjunctives.

There is no need here to go deeply into the Prioress. Eileen Power's illustrations from contemporary episcopal records show with what extraordinary economy the portrait has been packed with abuses typical of fourteenth-century nuns. The abuses, to be sure, are mostly petty, but it is clear enough that the Prioress, while a perfect lady, is anything but a perfect nun; and attempts to whitewash her, of which there have been many, can only proceed from an innocence of heart equal to Chaucer the pilgrim's and undoubtedly directly influenced by it. For he, of course, is quite swept away by her irrelevant *sensibilité*, and as a result misses much of the point of what he sees. No doubt he feels that he has come a long way, socially speaking, since his encounter with the Black Knight in the forest, and he knows, or thinks he knows, a little more of what it's all about: in this case it seems to be mostly about good manners, kindness to animals, and female charm. Thus it has been argued that Chaucer's appreciation for the Prioress as a sort of heroine of courtly romance *manquée* actually reflects the sophistication of the living Chaucer, an urbane man who cared little whether amiable nuns were good nuns. But it seems a curious form of sophistication that permits itself to babble superlatives; and indeed, if this is sophistication, it is the kind generally seen in the least experienced people—one that reflects a wide-eyed wonder at the glamour of the great world. It is just what one might expect of a bourgeois exposed to the splendours of high society, whose values, such as they are, he eagerly accepts. And that is precisely what Chaucer the pilgrim is, and what he does.

If the Prioress's appeal to him is through elegant femininity, the Monk's is through imposing virility. Of this formidable and important prelate the pilgrim does not say, with Placebo,

> I woot wel that my lord can more than I:
> What that he saith, I holde it ferm and stable, (E1498–99)

but he acts Placebo's part to perfection. He is as impressed with the Monk as the Monk is, and accepts him on his own terms and at face value, never sensing that those terms imply complete condemnation of Monk *qua* Monk. The Host is also impressed by the Monk's virility, but having no sense of Placebonian propriety (he is himself a most virile man) he makes indecent jokes about it. This, naturally, offends the pilgrim's sense of decorum: there is a note of deferential commiseration in his comment, 'This worthy Monk took al in pacience' (B3155). Inevitably when the Monk establishes hunting as the highest activity of which religious man is capable, 'I saide his opinion was good' (A183). As one of the pilgrim's spiritual heirs was later to say, Very like a whale; but not, of course, like a fish out of water.

Wholehearted approval for the values that important persons subscribe to is seen again in the portrait of the Friar. This amounts to a prolonged gratulation for the efficiency the deplorable Hubert shows in undermining the fabric of the Church by turning St Francis's ideal inside out:

> Ful swetely herde he confessioun
> And plesant was his absolucioun.
>
> For unto swich a worthy man as he
> Accorded nat, as by his facultee,
> To have with sike lazars aquaintaunce. (A221–22, 243–45)

It is sometimes said that Chaucer did not like the Friar. Whether Chaucer the man would have liked such a Friar is, for our present purposes, irrelevant. But if the pilgrim does not unequivocally express his liking for him, it is only because in his humility he does not feel that, with important people, his own likes and dislikes are material: such importance is its own reward, and can gain no lustre from Geoffrey, who, when the Friar is attacked by the Summoner, is ready to show him the same sympathy he shows the Monk (see D1265–67).

Once he has finished describing the really important people on the pilgrimage the pilgrim's tone changes, for he can now concern himself with the bourgeoisie, members of his own class for whom he does not have to show such profound respect. Indeed, he can even afford to be a little patronizing at times, and have his little joke at the expense of the too-busy lawyer. But such indirect assertions of his own superiority do not prevent him from giving substance to the old cynicism that the only motive recognized by the middle class is the profit motive, for his interest and admiration for the bourgeois pilgrims is centred mainly in their material prosperity and their ability to increase it. He starts, properly enough, with the out-and-out moneygrubber, the Merchant, and after turning aside for that *lusus naturae*, the non-profit-motivated Clerk, proceeds to the Lawyer, who, despite the pilgrim's little joke, is the best and best-paid ever; the Franklin, twenty-one admiring lines on appetite, so expensively catered to; the Gildsmen, cheered up the social ladder, 'For catel hadde they ynough and rente' (A373); and the Physician, again the best and richest. In this series the portrait of the Clerk is generally held to be an ideal one, containing no irony; but while it is ideal, it seems to reflect the pilgrim's sense of values in his joke about the Clerk's failure to make money: is not this still typical of the half-patronizing, half-admiring *un*understanding that practical men of business display towards academics? But in any case the portrait is a fine companion-piece for those in which material prosperity is the main interest both of the characters described and of the describer.

Of course, this is not the sole interest of so gregarious—if shy—a person as Chaucer the pilgrim. Many of the characters have the additional advantage of being good companions, a faculty that receives a high valuation in the Prologue. To be good company might, indeed, atone for certain serious defects of character. Thus the Shipman, whose callous cruelty is duly noted, seems fairly well redeemed in the assertion, 'And certainly he was a good felawe' (A395). At this point an uneasy sensation that even tongue-in-cheek irony will not compensate for the lengths to which Chaucer is going in his approbation of this sinister seafarer sometimes causes editors to note that *a good felawe* means 'a rascal'. But I can find no evidence that it ever meant a rascal. Of course, all tritely approbative expressions enter easily into ironic connotation, but the phrase *means* a good companion, which is just what Chaucer means. And if, as he says of the Shipman, 'Of nice conscience took he no keep' (A398), Chaucer the pilgrim was doing the same with respect to him.

Nothing that has been said has been meant to imply that the pilgrim was unable to recognise, and deplore, a rascal when he saw one. He could, provided the rascality was situated in a member of the lower classes and provided it was, in any case, somewhat wider than a barn door: Miller, Manciple, Reeve, Summoner, and Pardoner are all acknowledged to be rascals. But rascality generally has, after all, the laudable object of making money, which gives it a kind of validity, if not dignity. These portraits, while in them the pilgrim, prioress-like conscious of the finer aspects of life, does deplore such matters as the Miller's indelicacy of language, contain a note of ungrudging admiration for efficient thievery. It is perhaps fortunate for the pilgrim's reputation as a judge of men that he sees through the Pardoner, since it is the Pardoner's particular tragedy that, except in Church, every one can see through him at a glance; but in Church he remains to the pilgrim 'a noble ecclesiaste' (A708). The equally repellent Summoner, a practising bawd, is partially redeemed by his also being a good fellow, 'a gentil harlot and a kinde' (A647), and by the fact that for a moderate bribe he will neglect to summon: the pilgrim apparently subscribes to the popular definition of the best policeman as the one who acts the least policely.

Therefore Chaucer is tolerant, and has his little joke about the Summoner's small Latin—a very small joke, though one of the most amusing aspects of the pilgrim's character is the pleasure he takes in his own jokes, however small. But the Summoner goes too far when he cynically suggests that purse is the Archdeacon's hell, causing Chaucer to respond with a fine show of righteous respect for the instruments of spiritual punishment. The only trouble is that his enthusiastic defence of them carries *him* too far, so that after having warned us that excommunication will indeed damn our souls—

> But wel I woot he lied right in deede:
> Of cursing oughte eech gilty man him drede,
> For curs wol slee right as assoiling savith— (A659–61)

he goes on to remind us that it will also cause considerable inconvenience to our bodies: 'And also war him of a *Significavit*' (A662). Since a *Significavit* is the writ accomplishing the imprisonment of the excommunicate, the line provides perhaps the neatest—and most misunderstood—Chaucerian anticlimax in the Prologue.

I have avoided mentioning, hitherto, the pilgrim's reactions to the really good people on the journey—the Knight, the Parson, the Plowman. One might reasonably ask how his uncertain sense of values may be reconciled with the enthusiasm he shows for their rigorous integrity. The question could, of course, be shrugged off with a remark on the irrelevance to art of exact consistency, even to art distinguished by its verisimilitude. But I am not sure that there is any basic inconsistency. It is the nature of the pilgrim to admire all kinds of superlatives, and the fact that he often admires superlatives devoid of—or opposed to—genuine virtue does not inhibit his equal admiration for virtue incarnate. He is not, after all, a bad man; he is, to place him in his literary tradition, merely an average man, or mankind: *homo*, not very *sapiens* to be sure, but with the very best intentions, making his pilgrimage through the world in search of what is good, and showing himself, too frequently, able to recognize the good only when it is spectacularly so. Spenser's Una glows with a kind of spontaneous incandescence, so that the Red Cross Knight, mankind in search of holiness, knows her as good; but he thinks that Duessa is good, too. Virtue concretely embodied in Una or the Parson presents no problems to the well-intentioned observer, but in a world consisting mostly of imperfections, accurate evaluations are difficult for a pilgrim who, like mankind, is naïve. The pilgrim's ready appreciation for the virtuous characters is perhaps the greatest tribute that could be paid to their virtue, and their spiritual simplicity is, I think, enhanced by the intellectual simplicity of the reporter.

The pilgrim belongs, of course, to a very old—and very new—tradition of the fallible first person singular. His most exact modern counterpart is perhaps Lemuel Gulliver who, in his search for the good, failed dismally to perceive the difference between the pursuit of reason and the pursuits of reasonable horses: one may be sure that the pilgrim would have whinnied with the best of them. In his own century he is related to Long Will of *Piers Plowman*, a more explicit seeker after the good, but just as unswerving in his inability correctly to evaluate what he sees. Another kinsman is the protagonist of the *Pearl*, mankind whose heart is set on a transitory good that has been lost—who, for very natural reasons, confuses earthly with spiritual values. Not entirely unrelated is the protagonist of Gower's *Confessio Amantis*, an old man seeking for an impossible earthly love that seems to him the only good. And in more subtle fashion there is the teller of Chaucer's story of *Troilus and Criseide*, who, while not a true protagonist, performs some of the same functions. For this unloved 'servant of the servants of love' falls in love with Criseide so persuasively that almost every male reader of the poem imitates him, so that we all share the heartbreak of Troilus and sometimes, in the intensity of our heartbreak, fail to learn what Troilus did. Finally, of course, there is Dante of the *Divine Comedy*, the most exalted member of the family and perhaps the immediate original of these other first-person pilgrims.

Artistically the device of the *persona* has many functions, so integrated with one another that to try to sort them out produces both over-simplification and distortion. The most obvious, with which this paper has been dealing—distortedly, is to present a vision of the social world imposed on one of the moral world. Despite their verisimilitude most, if not all, of the characters described in the Prologue are taken directly from stock and recur again and again in medieval literature. Langland in his own Prologue and elsewhere depicts many of them: the hunting monk, the avaricious friar, the thieving miller, the hypocritical pardoner, the unjust stewards, even, in little, the all-too-human nun. But while Langland uses the device of the *persona* with considerable skill in the conduct of his allegory, he uses it hardly at all in portraying the inhabitants of the social world: these are described directly, with the poet's own voice. It was left to Chaucer to turn the ancient stock satirical characters into real people assembled for a pilgrimage, and to have them described, with all their traditional faults upon them, by another pilgrim who records faithfully each fault without, for the most part, recognizing that it is a fault and frequently felicitating its possessor for possessing it. One result—though not the only result—is a moral realism much more significant than the literary realism which is a part of it and for which it is sometimes mistaken; this moral realism discloses a world in which humanity is prevented by

its own myopia, the myopia of the describer, from seeing what the daz-
zlingly attractive externals of life really represent. In most of the analogues mentioned above the fallible first person receives, at the end of
the book, the education he has needed: the pilgrim arrives somewhere.
Chaucer never completed the *Canterbury Tales*, but in the Prologue to
the Parson's Tale he seems to have been doing, rather hastily, what his
contemporaries had done: when, with the sun nine-and-twenty degrees from the horizon, the twenty-nine pilgrims come to a certain—
unnamed—*thropes ende* (112), then the pilgrimage seems no longer to
have Canterbury as its destination, but rather, I suspect, the Celestial
City of which the Parson speaks.

   If one insists that Chaucer was not a moralist but a comic writer (a
distinction without a difference), then the device of the *persona* may
be taken primarily as serving comedy. It has been said earlier that the
several Chaucers must have inhabited one body, and in that sense the
fictional first person is no fiction at all. In an oral tradition of literature the first person probably always shared the personality of his creator: thus Dante of the *Divine Comedy* was physically Dante the
Florentine; the John Gower of the *Confessio* was also Chaucer's friend
John Gower; and Long Will was, I am sure, some one named William
Langland, who was both long and wilful. And it is equally certain that
Chaucer the pilgrim, 'a popet in an arm t'enbrace' (B1891), was in
every physical respect Chaucer the man, whom one can imagine reading his work to a courtly audience, as in the portrait appearing in one
of the MSS of *Troilus*. One can imagine also the delight of the audience
which heard the Prologue read in this way, and which was aware of
the similarities and dissimilarities between Chaucer, the man before
them, and Chaucer the pilgrim, both of whom they could see with si-
multaneous vision. The Chaucer they knew was physically, one gath-
ers, a little ludicrous; a bourgeois, but one who was known as a
practical and successful man of the court; possessed perhaps of a certain diffidence of manner, reserved, deferential to the socially imposing persons with whom he was associated; a bit absent-minded, but
affable and, one supposes, very good company—a good fellow; saga-
cious and highly perceptive. This Chaucer was telling them of another
who, lacking some of his chief qualities, nevertheless possessed many
of his characteristics, though in a different state of balance, and each
one probably distorted just enough to become laughable without
becoming unrecognizable: deference into a kind of snobbishness, affability into an over-readiness to please, practicality into Babbittry,
perception into inspection, absence of mind into dimness of wit; a
Chaucer acting in some respects just as Chaucer himself might have
acted but unlike his creator the kind of man, withal, who could mistake a group of stock satirical types for living persons endowed with all
sorts of superlative qualities. The constant interplay of these two
Chaucers must have produced an exquisite and most ingratiating humour—as, to be sure, it still does. This comedy reaches its superb climax when Chaucer the pilgrim, resembling in so many ways Chaucer
the poet, can answer the Host's demand for a story only with a rhyme

he 'lerned longe agoon' (B1899)—*Sir Thopas*, which bears the same complex relation to the kind of romance it satirizes and to Chaucer's own poetry as Chaucer the pilgrim does to the pilgrims he describes and to Chaucer the poet.

Earlier in this paper I proved myself no gentleman (though I hope a scholar) by being rude to the Prioress, and hence to the many who like her and think that Chaucer liked her too. It is now necessary to retract. Undoubtedly Chaucer the man would, like his fictional representative, have found her charming and looked on her with affection. To have got on so well in so changeable a world Chaucer must have got on well with the people in it, and it is doubtful that one may get on with people merely by pretending to like them: one's heart has to be in it. But the third entity, Chaucer the poet, operates in a realm which is above and subsumes those in which Chaucer the man and Chaucer the pilgrim have their being. In this realm prioresses may be simultaneously evaluated as marvellously amiable ladies and as prioresses. In his poem the poet arranges for the moralist to define austerely what ought to be and for his fictional representative—who, as the representative of all mankind, is no mere fiction—to go on affirming affectionately what is. The two points of view, in strict moral logic diametrically opposed, are somehow made harmonious in Chaucer's wonderfully comic attitude, that double vision that is his ironical essence. The mere critic performs his etymological function by taking the Prioress apart and clumsily separating her good parts from her bad; but the poet's function is to build her incongruous and inharmonious parts into an inseparable whole which is infinitely greater than its parts. In this complex structure both the latent moralist and the naïve reporter have important positions, but I am not persuaded that in every case it is possible to determine which of them has the last word.[1]

BARBARA NOLAN

"A Poet Ther Was": Chaucer's Voices in the General Prologue to *The Canterbury Tales*†

Chaucer gives us no explicit portrait headed "A Poet ther was" in the General Prologue to *The Canterbury Tales*. Yet the entire Prologue, like so many vernacular invitations to narrative from the twelfth century on, is designed to introduce the poet, describe his task, and gain the goodwill of the audience. Scholars generally agree that the later

---

1. Books referred to or cited in this paper are G. L. Kittredge, *Chaucer and His Poetry* (Cambridge, Mass., 1915), p. 45; Eileen Power, *Medieval People* (London, 1924), pp. 59–84. Robinson's note to A650 records the opinion that *a good felawe* means a 'rascal'. The medieval reader's expectation that the first person in a work of fiction would represent mankind generally and at the same time would physically resemble the author is commented on by Leo Spitzer in an interesting note in *Traditio*, iv. (1946), 414–22.

† Reprinted by permission of the Modern Language Association of America from *PMLA* 101 (1986): 154–69. We have renumbered the notes, omitting those providing the Latin texts translated within the article.

medieval practice of composing prologues depended on the grammar school study of rhetorical handbooks and classical poetry. By the fourteenth century a self-reflexive prologue conforming to handbook definitions had become more or less de rigueur for aristocratic narrative, both secular and religious.[1] Chaucer's Prologue, though longer and more complex than most, is no exception. It raises expectations in just the areas the handbooks propose, promising to take up important matters of natural and social order, moral character, and religion and outlining the organization the work will follow. Above all, the poet *presents himself*, as the handbooks direct, to ingratiate himself with his listeners or readers and render them receptive to his argument.

Chaucer's Prologue, however, meets these generic expectations in entirely unexpected ways. Most recent critics have recognized that it does not provide a neat, straightforward portrait of the poet. Chaucer's authority remains elusive, exceeding the requirements of the humility topos. Furthermore, whatever potential there may be for coherence in his self-presentation tends to be undermined by the several abrupt changes of style and subject. In fact, the parts of the General Prologue seem to function as several attacks on a beginning, each of them probing from a different angle a problem that traditionally belonged to prologues, "How shall I begin and to what purpose?" At first the various styles and subjects juxtaposed in the Prologue appear to suggest no clear answer. Moreover, the parts, or attempts at beginning, are governed not by a single, cumulatively enriched and deepened figure of the poet but, as I argue, by a series of impersonations. None of these taken alone reveals the poet's presence fully. Nor, taken together, do they reveal the poet literary tradition might have led readers to expect.

The General Prologue, I suggest, contains not one voice of the poet but three major attempts at authorial voicing. Each constitutes part of a complex argument about the nature of the poet and poetry in terms authorized by well-known medieval theory and practice. The first of these voices declaims the April opening with the learned assurance and scientific attention of a clerk deliberating in venerable literary formulas on the causes of things. The last is a tavern keeper's, urging good cheer and play for material profit. In between we hear the modest, devout "I" of Chaucer the pilgrim, intent on giving systematic order to his experience. But the voices of the other pilgrims so intrude on his own that he is left at last simply with genial apologies for failing to do what he had promised. All the voices are finally Chaucer's, of course, all of them impersonations. And all participate in the poet's complex, unexpected argument concerning his character(s) and purpose.[2]

For the most part, only the voice of the pilgrim has been related to Chaucer's self-presentation. In his well-known and brilliantly persua-

---

1. Hunt provides a useful history of this medieval genre, including an outline of its characteristics. See also Arbusow 97–103; Curtius 83–89; Porqueras Mayo; Cunningham; and Baldwin 32–35.
2. For a valuable discussion of Chaucer's creative engagement with classical notions of the orator, see Payne.

sive essay, E. Talbot Donaldson urges a separation of the pilgrim from the poet. He argues that the pilgrim persona is a comic device that the poet manipulates as an ironic foil for his own incisive wit. The poet, he says, "operates in a realm which is above and subsumes those in which Chaucer the man and Chaucer the pilgrim have their being" (936).

Few critics have questioned the isolation of the pilgrim persona as Chaucer's principal foil in the Prologue, though several have challenged Donaldson's way of explaining the relationship between the persona and the poet or the man. In an important article and in his book, Donald Howard argues for a more complex and mysterious relationship between the pilgrim and the poet than Donaldson proposes. The pilgrim, he suggests, gives a tantalizingly partial sense of the man behind the work; the limitations invite us to create Chaucer finally in our own image ("Chaucer the Man").[3]

More recently, Marshall Leicester has objected to all interpretations that separate the pilgrim from the poet, contending that the poet's presence is to be discovered not beyond the work but in the voicing of the text. Positing a separation, he argues, gives us the comfortable (and false) sense that we can know who is speaking at any given moment and what position each speaker holds on the matter presented. In his view, it is "just this sense of knowing where we are, with whom we are dealing, that the General Prologue deliberately and calculatedly denies us" (219). Instead of a pilgrim persona juxtaposed with an unimpersonated poet, Leicester proposes the model of a "prologal voice" that belongs to an impersonator preparing to take on the character of each pilgrim in turn. This thesis is provocative, important because it insists that we listen to the text's voicings of character rather than read from preconceived character to text.

But Leicester assumes that such attention to voices should aim at discovering the "personality" of the poet and his pilgrims. This concern for "personality," as also for the presence of the "man," misses the essentially rhetorical, ideologically oriented character of the poet's self-presentation. Heeding Leicester's warning against positing more speakers than necessary and casting Howard's concern for the man in different terms, I argue that Chaucer as a single author projects three major "authorial" voices in his Prologue to examine several possibilities for poetry, all of them empowered by well-known medieval theory and all of them useful for his tales. The three voices lead us not to the poet's "personality" or to Chaucer the man in a general sense but rather to the problem of being a poet in the late fourteenth century. Instead of giving us a single image of the poet and a single definition of the poet's authority, Chaucer juxtaposes images of himself as three possible kinds of poet. The pilgrim is only one of these, though he holds a privileged position among the rest. He is the "I" from whom the others take their being, and he provides a moral center from which

---

3. Other helpful studies on this issue include Malone; Duncan; Hoffman; Woolf; Bronson; Major; Nevo; Jordan, "Chaucer's Sense" and *Chaucer* 111–31.

to judge the other voices. But an impersonal voice pronounces the opening third-person narration, and Harry's "boold" voice finally replaces the pilgrim's to announce the literary theory and design of the fictive order that follows.

Poetry and poets occupy an uncertain position in medieval theory. Some writers—among them the twelfth-century Platonists, Dante, Petrarch, and Boccaccio—contend that the poet can express truth under the veil of "beautiful lies." In this well-known argument, the reader is to take the fruit, or sentence, and discard the rhetorical chaff of the poet's fictive covering. Another, less generous position—put forward by the Parson in *The Canterbury Tales*—refuses to traffic in "fables" at all. In this view, poetry is frivolity, diversion, false consolation; poets, the perpetrators of falsehood. Chaucer's three voices in the General Prologue form dramatic images of several theories, carrying us from a notion of poetry as philosophy to Harry's view of poetry as distracting merriment.

The argument Chaucer makes about the poet and poetry is neither mechanical nor detached. In the Prologue and in the tales, he explores the whole range of medieval positions regarding poetry, not so much to establish a "true" position as to emphasize his sense of the ambiguities and contradictions surrounding fiction's valuation, and also to turn these difficulties to his advantage. The pilgrim-poet deliberately places himself in the midst of the questions he poses—and he has his pilgrims take up the problem again and again in their prologues and tales. In his many voices, he invites readers to share intimately his quest for a radically new, personal (and ultimately comic, provisional) poetic, one true to his sense of the ironies and limitations inherent in his art of fiction.

1. Multiple Voicing in Medieval Theory and Practice

Multiple voicing as a mode of argument was essential to later medieval narrative, whether in allegorical debate or exemplary private conversation or interior monologue framed by first- or third-person narration. Indeed, romance and allegory, the two dominant narrative forms of the later Middle Ages, positively required multiple voicing. These essentially dialectical forms typically pose challenging social or moral or spiritual questions to be solved by means of the narrative process. Nearly always, the subjectivity of such texts—their grounding in the poet's authority—is presented through two or more voices. Beatrice, Vergil, Raison, Gracedieu, a hermit, a grotesque maiden may serve in the poet's place as a guide to wisdom at various moments in the narrative. By putting on a number of voices, the poet can mask his position and thus draw the audience into an exacting, unpredictable process of discovery.

When we listen to Chaucer's several voices in the General Prologue (and in the tales), therefore, we hear the master of an art cultivated by generations of French and Italian writers. To be sure, in Chaucer the art of playing voice against voice assumes a decisive new direction predictive of the novel's complexities. Yet his invention depended absolutely on the prior discoveries of those major poets who had most influenced him—among them, Benoit de Sainte-Maure, Guillaume de Lorris, Jean de Meung, Boccaccio, Dante, and Machaut.

To find the main theoretical bases for multiple voicing in the Middle Ages, we must turn to the rhetorical handbooks universally used in the grammar schools and to schoolroom exegesis of the curriculum authors. Handbook discussions give primary attention to calculated voicing and impersonation in the orator's self-presentation and in the acting out of the client's attitudes, feelings, and experiences in order to build a convincing case.

When Quintilian describes the orator's self-presentation in the exordium, or prologue, he recommends an artful management of voice, style, and manner:

> [W]e should . . . give no hint of elaboration in the *exordium*. . . . But to avoid all display of art in itself requires consummate art. . . . The style of the *exordium* . . . should . . . seem simple and unpremeditated, while neither our words nor our looks should promise too much. For a method of pleading which conceals its art . . . will often be best adapted to insinuate its way into the minds of our hearers. (4.1.56–60; 2: 36–39)

If artifice and adjustments of voice are to be used even in the defense of honorable cases, they become all the more important for doubtful or discreditable ones.

In this regard, the rhetorical handbooks distinguish between a direct prologue (*principium*) for good causes and a subtle approach (*insinuatio*) for doubtful ones. The *Ad Herennium*, for example, a popular rhetoric attributed to Cicero, defines the difference as follows:

> The direct opening should be such that by . . . straightforward methods . . . we immediately make the hearer well-disposed or attentive or receptive; whereas the Subtle Approach should be such that we effect all these results covertly, through dissimulation, and so can arrive at the same vantage-point in the task of speaking. (1.7; 20–21)

As the classroom handbooks suggest, the assumption of a persona to mask intentions and win favor in the exordium has to do with pragmatic manipulation and strategic dissimulation quite separate from issues of truth and falsehood.

There was also, however, another, larger theory of multiple voicing, propounded in well-known scriptural and literary exegesis. This theory supports the indirect pursuit of true understanding in and through narrative discourse that dramatically represents several opinions, including the author's. Commentators on a variety of texts describe the ways in which a writer can use personae or characters to represent various positions on a given subject. These discussions are rich with suggestion for understanding Chaucer and other vernacular poets. Servius, for example, explaining Vergil's first eclogue, writes:[4]

> A certain shepherd is introduced lying safe and at leisure under a tree in order to make a musical composition; another, indeed, has been expelled from his homelands with his flock, who, when he has seen Tityrus reclining, speaks. And in this place we must understand Vergil under the character [persona] of Tityrus; however, not everywhere, but wherever the argument demands it. (1: 4)

Here, according to Servius, the author presents himself through his characters, not to reveal his personality, but to serve his argument. Tityrus does not always represent Vergil, but speaks for him only when the argument requires it. In this dispensation the author is present not as a distinctive personality but, rather, as a writer strictly speaking, arranging characters and voices in relation to the large argument being made.

In terms still more suggestive for medieval poetry, commentators regularly identify dialogical self-dramatization as a formal feature of some of the most important and influential works of the period, including Augustine's *Soliloquies* and Boethius's *De consolatione*. Of these two texts Peter Abelard says:

> [It is] as if someone, speaking with himself, set up his argument as if two [were speaking], just as Boethius in his book, the *Consolation of Philosophy*, or Augustine in his *Book of Soliloquies*. (760)

And Conrad of Hirsau writes of the *Consolatio*:

> Three characters [personae] are brought forward by Boethius: miserable Boethius seeking to be consoled; Philosophia who consoles; Boethius the author who speaks about both of them. (Huygens 108)

There can be no doubt that such dialogical forms as the *Consolation* and the *Soliloquies*, together with the commentaries surrounding them, provided powerful models for multiple voicing in many kinds of texts throughout the medieval period, but particularly from the twelfth century on.

Gregory the Great's comments on Ecclesiastes offer us yet another full and well-known discussion of the writer's manipulative use of personae and voices in philosophical argument. His description of Solomon's authorial strategies might well have served as a headnote for many a medieval text, including *The Canterbury Tales*. Emphasizing the orator's role in bringing together and reconciling the opinions of a contentious audience, Gregory explains how Solomon impersonates the characters and views of many people as if to pacify a cantankerous crowd:

---

4. All translations from works not cited in translation are my own.

This book is called "The Orator" because Solomon takes up there the thinking of a crowd which is in disagreement: under the form of questions he expresses what the man on the street is tempted to think. All the ideas that he takes up in his inquiry correspond to the various characters he impersonates. (4.1; 3: 26–27)

According to Gregory, Solomon ends his multivoiced discourse by addressing his listeners in his own voice and drawing them into unity. After he has assumed the many characters and positions leading away from salvation, he argues for the necessity of fearing God and understanding the world's vanity.[5]

Hugh of St. Victor's homily on Ecclesiastes improves on Gregory's description of impersonation and sheds further light on Chaucer's art of multiple voicing:

[A] many-sided disputation is signified, and [one that has] elicited diverse opinions. For since, in this book, the moral conduct, aspirations, and achievements of many are described, it is necessary for the speaker to assume the voices of many speakers, to express the opinions of many in his discourse, so that he has the power to present the characters of many in his own person, when he who speaks is nonetheless only one. For at the end of the book, having spoken in many [voices], he himself testifies that he has been many [characters] in himself, saying: Let us all equally hear the end of the speaking: "Fear God, and obey his commandments. This is every man." For this is why he wanted to be called "Ecclesiastes" in his work, namely, because his discourse is directed here not to a certain person particularly but to the whole Church—that is, the assembly or multitude of people—and the argument in this book serves at once to portray the conduct of many and to form an image of it. (115)

Of course, Chaucer's art of voicing is far more complex than the kind described by Gregory and Hugh. Among other things it involves a detailed dramatic action so compelling that some eminent critics have assumed that the drama itself was Chaucer's principal concern.

But medieval theorizing about multiple voicing, both the rhetoricians' and the exegetes', suggests a different emphasis, and one well suited to the intricate play of Chaucer's Prologue and tales. While the exegetical comments I have quoted do not explain precisely how multiple voicing works in medieval poetry or in Chaucer, they do provide a rationale for its use and encourage us to examine Chaucer's complex management of voicing with a closer scrutiny than it has generally been given. As I have already suggested, critics propose a false problem when they try to determine who is speaking in a Chaucerian passage—whether, for example, we are to hear the poet or the pilgrim or

5. Gregory's description of Ecclesiastes was well known and popular in the later Middle Ages. It appears, for example, in a truncated form in Wyclif's English commentary on Ecclesiastes. I am indebted to Eric Eliason for this reference to Wyclif.

the man at a particular moment in the General Prologue (see also Christianson). The real question is not autobiographical but rhetorical and dialectical.[6] For what rhetorical purpose does the poet assume the pilgrim's voice? How and why is this voice juxtaposed with others in the Prologue and in the tales?

In the General Prologue, we must listen closely to all the voices—the impersonal voice of the opening lines, the pilgrim's, the Host's—as aspects of an argument in which the poet himself participates through his juxtaposition of tonally and stylistically different voices. The poet's presence and his self-definition inhere in his acts of manipulation and his multiple impersonation. Seen in this light, Chaucer emerges from the Prologue, as from the tales, a quick-change artist, a shape shifter, a prestidigitator, a player with voices.

Chaucer's play, however, is more like Solomon's than like Harry Bailly's. It takes the form of an exacting dialectic that dramatically articulates various positions on the human condition. If one attends only to the linear, temporal, narrative process of the Prologue and tales, the play is a source of rich comedy. But for those who assume the poet's perspective as master player and look to the form, the many voices also offer a way to philosophical clarification. By experiencing the voices as parts in a complex argument, the reader, like the poet, may avoid commitment to the misplaced seriousness, the ego attachments, and the foolishness that govern most of the characters. Chaucer's deft juxtapositions of one position with another point in a wise, deep way to the absurdities, the pain, the poignancy, the pretensions, the limited perspectives of the human condition. The poet's own fully conscious play, expressed through his multivoiced dialectic, allows him to acknowledge his fiction making, and that of his characters, for what it is. In this way, he can vindicate the muses of poetry as Boethius could not. Chaucer's play with voices does not issue in a resolution as clear or univocal as Solomon's in Ecclesiastes. Yet the Parson's Tale and the Retraction offer images of finality and closure that *may* bring the Canterbury fictions to an end by an appeal to an order of being beyond the tales.

II. Chaucer's Voices in the General Prologue

As I have suggested, three voices and three attitudes toward poetic authority vie for control in the Prologue—the "clerk's," the pilgrim's, and the Host's.[7] While the first and last are diametrically opposed, the important central voice of the pilgrim mediates between them and explains the unavoidable "fall" from the first to the last in the deliberate

---

6. For useful discussions of the medieval rhetorical "I," see Spitzer; Bethurum; Kellogg; Bevington; and Kane. See also Anne Middleton's excellent description of the public voice (and public "I") developed by certain English poets, including Langland and Gower, during Richard II's reign. Derek Brewer offers important observations about Chaucer's dramatized tellers.

7. These three voices coincide interestingly with T. S. Eliot's description of the poet's three voices. Chaucer's articulation of the theory, however, grows out of rhetorical tradition and serves a philosophical argument, while Eliot is describing his own writing experience (4).

absence of a truth-telling allegorical guide. Harry Bailly becomes the necessary muse for *The Canterbury Tales* because no Philosophia or Raison or Gracedieu or Holichurche provides a graceful alternative. But Harry's worldly theory of poetry does not prevail entirely. The other two major prologal voices encourage the possibility of higher poetic aspirations. "Authors" in search of philosophical or spiritual wisdom—like the Knight, the Oxford Clerk, the Second Nun, and the Parson—imitate the clerkly or pilgrim voice in one way or another. In this respect they counter the fictions of others—like the Miller, the Reeve, the Merchant, and the Pardoner—who in one way or another follow the Host in his purely secular play. In addition, the higher voices remain available as alternative models of authority and purpose for readers who will "rewrite" the tales in their private quests for a saving doctrine.

III. The Clerk's Voice

The first of the Chaucerian voices we hear—the first impersonation—gives us the learned poet of the schools. Versed in the literary topoi of the Latin tradition and skilled in rhetorical composition, he is also a scientist of sorts who knows precisely how plants grow and a philosopher who looks into the nature of things.

The rhetorical description of spring spoken in Chaucer's clerkly voice occurs over and over in classical and medieval poets, philosophers, and encyclopedists alike. It belongs to no particular genre or poetic form but appears in a wide variety of contexts—in Lucretius, in Vergil and Boethius, in Carolingian and Goliardic poetry, in encyclopedias like the one by Bartholomeus Anglicus, in scientific manuals like the *Secreta secretorum*, in vernacular lyric and narrative poetry.[8] Whether philosophic or lyrical, the spring topos usually serves as a synecdoche, pointing to the whole order of creation. In medieval lore, spring, as the first of the four seasons, signals the regularity of nature and implies the causal presence of the Creator. In love poetry the arrival of spring may explain the beginnings of erotic feeling and the lover's joyful discovery of his beloved. Or the regularity of spring's appearance may be shown to be at odds with a lover's unseasonal dejection at the loss of his lady.

Like his predecessors, Chaucer in his clerkly guise uses the synecdoche of spring to imply a hierarchy in the universe, one that points inevitably to God as the source of love and order. Within this cosmic scheme Chaucer emphasizes the erotic movement of all creation, imperfect and incomplete, inherently synecdochic, toward completion and the fulfillment of longing. The "when . . . then" construction of the long opening monologue, full of "gret and high sentence," underscores the poet's philosophical urge to explain the causes and laws of

---

8. Numerous studies trace the history of the spring topos. Among the most important for Chaucer are Cook; Hankins; Tuve, *Seasons* and "Spring"; and Baldwin 19–28. See also Curtius 185–202 and Ross. For a discussion of the *Secreta secretorum* and Chaucer's spring opening, see esp. Tuve, *Seasons* 52–58.

things (including human behavior). Within this tight syntactic construction the speaker's facile descent from pilgrimages in general to the Canterbury pilgrimage—from genus to species—exemplifies schoolroom habits of logical thought. Furthermore, the highly literary beginning exactly coincides with its subject, the cosmic beginnings of things, whether in lower nature or in human life. The outer garb of poetry in the high style suits its philosophical subject perfectly, as if the poet could explore and explain the deep matter of natural and human and divine causality.

This sort of beginning sums up a dominant medieval tradition of narrative authority. Just such a voice might well have initiated an allegorical vision of the kind written by Raoul de Houdenc or Dante or Deguileville. Or it might have generated a rewriting of the *Roman de la rose*, exploring the philosophical distinctions between secular and religious love. Allegories like these presuppose the poet's (and humanity's) power to know causes, to give cosmic explications of the kind the first Chaucerian "beginning" seems to promise.[9] The heightened, philosophizing voice is the voice of authoritative literary tradition. It articulates a general longing—shared by poet and readers alike—for a wise, full vision of the human condition and even for entrance into the recesses of divine privity. Yet Chaucer's clerkly articulation of the poet's task is abruptly truncated. It remains a fragment, a possibility unexploited. In the very next section of the Prologue a second voice definitively denies access to the high mysterious realm of causes—a realm that had been confidently explored by medieval poets of the greatest importance, including Bernard Silvestris, Alain de Lille, and Dante.

IV. The Pilgrim's Voice

The poet's startling shift from a clerk's voice to a pilgrim's turns on the important word *bifil*. It is a word that, together with *bifalle, falle*, and *fil* in the same sense, occurs often in the course of *The Canterbury Tales*. It typically signifies chance happenings, unexpected events occurring at random. The order of time governed by *bifil* and *fil* is radically different from the mythic, cyclic time of the spring topos. It is, in fact, the "order" of the fallen historical world, in which chance, change, unpredictability hold sway. Nor is this time synecdochic; unlike the springtime imagery, it does not point beyond itself. By its nature it does not lend itself to allegory and the wise explication of causes but, rather, supports the more modest claims of chronicle, storytelling, and confession.

The abrupt break in Chaucer's introductory monologue, initiated by the word *bifil* and dominated by a personal "I," constitutes just the sort of "semantic reversal" that the Czech critic Jan Mukarovsky has singled out as a sign of "dialogic discourse."[1] We are unexpectedly

9. For a suggestive discussion of the relations among allegory, explorations of causality, and the language of truth, see Quilligan, esp. 156–223. See also Brewer 222–23.
1. See chap. 3, "Two Studies of Dialogue" (81–115). I am grateful to Ralph Cohen for directing me to Mukarovsky and other modern theorists who deal with the question of voicing in fiction.

jolted from the monologic structure of the clerkly discourse, largely free of involvement in specific time or space, to the pilgrim's direct dialogic address to the other pilgrims and to the readers. Mukarovsky's description of this kind of discourse precisely suits the complex interplay in the pilgrim's speech as the "I" introduces himself and the other pilgrims: "by a sleight of hand the listener becomes the speaker, and the function of the carrier of the utterance constantly jumps from participant to participant" (113).

We observe immediately that the character into which the poet has "fallen" defines him as essentially imperfect, incomplete, on the way: "I lay / Redy to wenden on my pilgrymage / To Caunterbury with ful devout corage" (1.20–22). Through his pilgrim "I" as the central voice in the Prologue, Chaucer exploits to the full the humility topos the rhetorical handbooks recommend for the exordium. He genially claims incompetence in the art of making arguments, and he speaks directly and personally to his audience with the same ingratiating deference he had evidently used in insinuating himself into the fellowship of pilgrims. As we follow Chaucer's development of the pilgrim's character, however, we discover that the device is no mere device. The pilgrim persona is not just a mask but a central fact of this and every poet's existence. Chaucer's genius here, as elsewhere, lies in his ability to transform a familiar topos into a precise metaphor.

The image of the pilgrim is heavy with meaning, though critics have had a tendency to pass lightly over it, settling for its function as a comically ironic front for the poet. In fact, this assumption leaves us with an incomplete understanding of Chaucer's point in having his central persona and voice develop as they do. Chaucer gives us not a poet assuming the guise of a pilgrim but a pilgrim attempting the poet's task. His "I" persona identifies the speaker as *first* a pilgrim. The priority thus defined is an important one because it establishes an ontological perspective from which to measure all the rhetorical play recorded in the portraits.

How are we to interpret this voice, this image, if we take it seriously as a necessary replacement for the clerkly voice? As pilgrim, the poet participates in "corrumpable" nature, acknowledging by his pilgrimage that his nature takes its beginning from a being greater than himself and finds its end beyond himself in a "thyng that parfit is and stable" (1.3009). The pilgrim, like Everyman, proceeds at least to some extent "dronke . . . as is a mous" who "noot which the righte wey is thider" (1.1261, 1263). Of course the pilgrim Chaucer is not the lovesick Arcite or the drunken Miller or any of the other "sondry folk" in and out of the tales. But he claims fellowship with them. His identity and his voice are intimately bound up with theirs, and he discovers his own powers and limits by investigating theirs.[2]

The pilgrim insists that his investigation be made not from the superior vantage point assumed by the clerkly voice but from within: "I was

---

2. For discussions of Chaucer's involvement with his pilgrims, see Malone 40–45; Green; and Mandel.

of hir felaweshipe anon, / And made forward erly for to ryse, / To take *oure* wey ther as I yow devyse" (1.32–34). Chaucer the pilgrim submits himself explicitly to the demands and limits of the occasion "in *that* seson on *a* day" (19). And he makes an immediate accord with the motley crowd of travelers who have come together at the Tabard "by aventure" (25). Accepting their chance fellowship as a matter of course, he assumes the responsibility of telling us about them and their plans. Instead of casting about in old books and authorities for material, as his clerkly and courtly predecessors had typically done, Chaucer simply "finds" the matter that has fallen in his way—the flesh and blood (and words) of his fellows at the Tabard. Instead of remaining apart from this matter to infuse it with wise meaning, the pilgrim joins the group, becomes a part of the matter he proposes to investigate and invest with form.

Now from the point of view of literary history such involvement is not unprecedented. Dante had, after all, admitted his own participation in the sins of his purgatorial ascent—particularly lust and pride. Yet he had also styled himself a visionary, blessed with a higher understanding of his matter, able to transcend his mortal blindness by intellect and grace. Chaucer the pilgrim, by contrast, eschews the perspective of the allegorist and the comforts of enlightenment. The relationship he establishes with his pilgrim characters and their stories is rather the historian's than the visionary's.

Indeed, in his self-defining art of portraiture in the General Prologue and in the imitation he proposes to undertake, the pilgrim as *auctor* probably owes his greatest debt to the literary example of Dares, the self-styled eyewitness chronicler of the Trojan War. Dares, perhaps chiefly through his medieval "translators," had profoundly influenced Chaucer in writing the *Troilus*. In the General Prologue, the influence of Dares and his progeny appears once again, this time as part of the poet's complex defense of his art. Chaucer the pilgrim, like Dares, claims direct, personal observation as the basis for his "true" writing.[3] But in the Prologue, the historian's voice is absorbed into the character of the pilgrim-poet and linked to a game of storytelling.

The connection Chaucer makes in linking the pilgrim persona, historiographic mimesis, and the Canterbury fictions is deep and important, for it crystallizes one of the most painful lessons of medieval Christianity: that human beings in their condition of exile must depend for their knowledge on limited powers of observation, an imperfect understanding of events, and a language essentially different from, and inadequate to, the truths it seeks to express.

The pilgrim-poet acknowledges his metaphysical condition most directly at the end of his "historiographic" portrait gallery in the well-known declaration "My wit is short, ye may wel understonde" (1.746).

3. R. M. Lumiansky and Jill Mann have rightly observed a connection between the portrait gallery in Benoit de Sainte-Maure's *Roman de Troie*, based on Dares, and Chaucer's portraits in the General Prologue. Even more important is Chaucer's borrowing of the authorial perspective of the eye-witness historian that supports the portraits in Dares and Benoit. See Lumiansky, "Benoit's"; Mann 179–81.

This disclaimer is most often interpreted as a tongue-in-cheek gesture, the calculated stance of a brilliant bourgeois before his social betters. And it probably is an opportune rhetorical strategy. But, as is often true in Chaucer, the surface significance may be shown to belie a deeper, or even opposite, sense. If we consider the apology not only a ploy but also a straightforward, nonironic statement of fact—and the language, as well as medieval theology, allows us to do so—then Chaucer's self-definition as poet assumes a new direction in this central voice. The pilgrim seeks to authorize himself not by his brilliance or learning or moral perspicuity but by his common humanity. If we read *wit* in its central medieval acceptation as "power of knowing and understanding" rather than as "ingenuity" only, the clause "My wit is short" assumes a philosophical sense.[4] Absolute shortness of wit supplies a principle of organization whereby the poet may bypass high cultural literary order in favor of a larger, ironic inquiry into the sorry but also comic plight of the human spirit in this world's exile.[5]

V. The Pilgrim's Portrait Gallery

In every aspect of his self-presentation, Chaucer's pilgrim persona practices a comically incomplete power of "devysyng," one that reveals the *humana fragilitas* in the historian's stance. He begins his portrait series with the confident formula "A Knyght ther was" (1.43), as if he intends to uncover the nature of each social type by giving a full, precise, ordered example. The formula proposes rhetorical and philosophical plenitude by way of synecdoche; yet the text fails to deliver fullness or completeness. Individual characters systematically escape from or evade the expected formulas, leaving us with a sense not only of the social "obsolescence" Donald Howard has suggested but also of an essential partiality and eccentricity (*Idea* 94–106).

Through his voice as pilgrim-historian, Chaucer structures the portraits so as to deny us a clear, total representation of the individuals as types related to transcendent ideals. The portraits fail to arrange themselves in a recognizable hierarchical order, an order that would call our attention to the expected, or "proper," order of society. Nor, for the most part, do the eccentric characters who claim nominal participation in the various estates fully clarify their preordained roles, ei-

---

4. In Middle English the word *wit* has several more or less related meanings: "mind," "faculty or power of thinking and reasoning," "bodily and spiritual powers of perception," "sanity," "genius, talent, or cleverness." When the pilgrim says, "My wit is short," he is usually thought to be referring to his ingenuity or power of invention. In the immediate context, he is speaking about his inability to set the rest of the pilgrims in their proper order. Because this task is, technically speaking, an act of rhetorical invention, the reading "my ingenuity is short" is not improbable. Then we have only the simple irony of the brilliant poet's "humility." If, however, the deeper meaning, "my power to know is limited," is the central one, then Chaucer is affirming the metaphysical irony of absolute human limitation and acknowledging his necessary participation in this condition.

5. Two centuries later Cervantes would choose a similar ploy to explore similar questions. His *Don Quixote*, he tells us, emanated from a shriveled brain. From this comic vantage point he can reveal high literary romances as elegant (falsifying) fabrications designed, consciously or unconsciously, to obscure the sad, sordid reality of quotidian life. For Cervantes and Chaucer alike a self-critical posture coincides with an ironic critique of all linguistic efforts—particularly efforts by courtly poets—to express truth or to describe reality accurately.

ther negatively or positively. The ideal knight, the ideal monk and friar, the ideal wife (or their systematically developed opposites) remain notions partly beyond the horizon of the text.

What is important in the fictions of the portrait gallery is that the pilgrim participates in them, allowing his "exemplary" figures to overtake his own voice dialogically through indirect discourse. As rhetor and historian, Chaucer delights in his pilgrims as dramatis personae. He observes, often with admiration, the details of their self-dramatization—the fictions they project to fool themselves or to impress, cajole, or exploit others.

Yet, if the pilgrim-poet were *homo rhetoricus* and secular historian only, there would be no moral center against which to measure the wanderings and eccentricities of those he describes.[6] And the portraits would lack just the tension that gives them their lasting power and point. In fact, the amorality of the historian's rhetorical stance is pervasively countered by reminders of a nonrhetorical, suprahistorical mode of existence. Not only the "ful devout corage" of the pilgrim himself but also the figure of the Parson provides a point of reference for this alternative mode. The Parson's "pose"—or, more properly, "role"—as a shepherd conscientiously caring for his flock approximates his central identity. He imitates Christ the Good Shepherd in every detail of his life and thereby identifies himself exclusively as a son of God. Indeed, our *only* image of the Parson's physical presence is that of a Christian shepherd of souls with staff in hand. What Chaucer emphasizes in the Parson's portrait is the coincidence of word and deed, of Christian teaching and high moral conduct. There is in the Parson's life little matter for "troping," little rhetorical distance between his soul's self and his outward presentation.

From the perspective of Christian pilgrimage, the social or religious roles of most of the other characters appear to be added onto them, like their costumes, often accompanied by distorting or falsifying elaborations. The Knight's remarkable achievements in battle, the Pardoner's fashionable cape, the Friar's girlfriends, the Wife of Bath's old and young husbands—all distract the pilgrims more or less from their single proper concern, the destiny of their souls. In rhetorical terms, the lives and speech of most of the pilgrims are "troped," turned in one way or another away from transcendent truth in the direction of Harry Bailly's kind of worldly fiction making.

Both the Parson's life and the poet's brilliant juxtapositions of detail call attention to the artifices the pilgrims practice. The obvious contradictions between pretension and fact encourage us to recognize the fictions for what they are. Yet we do not hear in the pilgrim's portraits the voice of the strict moralist anatomizing human folly with clerical rigor. In his rendering, the fictions of daily life in the temporal world of "bifil" coincide with the fictions of art, and the poet exploits, even as he delights in, the coincidence.

6. For a thought-provoking discussion of *homo rhetoricus* in Western tradition, see Lanham, esp. chap. 1, "The Rhetorical Ideal of Life" (1–35).

For an anagogically "true" reading of the poem's matter we must wait for the Parson. It is he who will insist on a definitive separation of fact and truth from fiction:

> Thou getest fable noon ytoold for me;
> For Paul, that writeth unto Thymothee,
> Repreveth hem that weyven soothfastnesse,
> And tellen fables and swich wrecchednesse.
>
> (10.31–34)

Chaucer might have given the Parson's voice to himself as "I" from the beginning. Had he done so, however, he would have had to reject all the "pley," all the voices, of *The Canterbury Tales*. Boethius's Lady Philosophy, it will be remembered, had rejected the muses of falsifying, consolatory poetry at the start of his *Consolation*. In pointed (and I think calculated) contrast, Chaucer's Retraction comes only at the end of his work. The very existence of the tales depends on his deliberately *not* beginning as Boethius had, not rejecting the sweet venom of fiction until its pleasures and possibilities have been fully explored as well as exposed.

VI. The Pilgrim Voice and the Question of Truth

The pilgrim broaches the question of truth, and broaches it explicitly, in the General Prologue. Yet when he invokes a Platonic theory to support his tale-telling, he misapplies the theory and thereby brilliantly defers the question of a transcendent truth beyond the truth of historical reportage:

> Whoso shal telle a tale after a man,
> He moot reherce as ny as evere he kan
> Everich a word, if it be in his charge,
> Al speke he never so rudeliche and large,
> Or ellis he moot telle his tale untrewe,
> Or feyne thyng, or fynde wordes newe.
> . . . .
> Eek Plato seith, whoso that kan hym rede,
> The wordes moote be cosyn to the dede.
>
> (1.731–36; 741–42)

Here, in a flagrant misreading, the pilgrim comically conflates his own "historiographic" notion of truth as the imitation of passing life with Plato's theory relating words to the transcendent truth of things. We may pass lightly over the conflation and assume that the poet is simply pleading for a new kind of artistic freedom. But Chaucer seems to intend something deeper by deliberately juxtaposing the pilgrim's and Plato's ideas of imitation. In placing his theory cheek by jowl with Plato's, he aims, I think, to provide a mortal correction for what he considers an impossible dream.

The pilgrim's description of his language is straightforwardly *anti*-allegorical in an age that generally revered allegorical poetry: his words

will not, at least easily or directly, point to things (or truth or doctrine)
as words were said to do in allegorical poems like the *Roman de la
rose*. They will simply imitate the words and "chiere" of the other pilgrims, which are neither Platonic "things" nor stable ideas, but transient phenomena. The text as a collection of unstable, ambiguous
signs will mark the beginning rather than the completion of specula-
tion about the nature of things. The poet in his pilgrim voice will not
be a philosopher or a repository of high wisdom, at least not in a traditional sense. Instead he will simply be an earthly maker and historian,
putting idiosyncratic words and actions together according to his limited powers of observation and invention and the unpredictable demands of the matter.[7] Chaucer the pilgrim, like Dares the historian,
thus turns the text over to the audience, who will have to interpret or
translate the signs into meaning, discerning the "true" inner structure
informing the ensemble of outward manifestations. While this
management of the poet's and the audience's roles may appear modern, or even postmodern, it is in fact thoroughly explicable as a logical
(though also brilliantly original) development from dominant medieval
theories concerning fiction and the limits of human knowledge.

The Platonic theory Chaucer's pilgrim invokes originated in the
Timaeus (29B), and versions of it appear in many a medieval text, including Boethius's *Consolation* (3, pr. 12) and Jean de Meung's *Roman
de la rose* (Guillaume, lines 6943–78 and 15159–94). Underlying all
the arguments from Plato to Jean is a confidence that words describe
objective, knowable, nameable reality, whether that reality is the mo-
tions of the will (Plato) or ideas in the mind (Chalcidius) or God
(Boethius) or testicles (Jean de Meung). For writers of fictions, the
theory provided some assurance that poetic narratives—"beautiful
lies" according to the dominant learned tradition—could legitimately
explore the causes of things and teach truth. In Boethius and Jean,
voices of authority—Philosophia, Raison, the Poet—speak the theory.
Their authority is in a certain sense absolute. They grant the poet and
therefore the reader power to cut through the artifices of allegorical
fabrication to touch the secrets of philosophy.

What distinguishes Chaucer from earlier poets is that he refuses to
give the Platonic doctrine to an authority figure. Instead of speaking it
through Philosophia or Raison or Gracedieu, he presents it through
his pilgrim voice. The pilgrim as historian proposes to use words not to
represent things or truth or doctrine or ideas, as a clerk would have
done, but to mimic the transient words and gestures of others. These
acts belong to the sundry folk of the fallen world, who are not likely,
by and large, to speak or behave philosophically. Some of them are
counterfeiters. Some are professional (lying) rhetoricians. Others are
professional cheaters or tricksters or swindlers. Of course all of them
are finally given voice by Chaucer. All are part of his grand masquer-
ade, and all represent aspects of his self-presentation as pilgrim-poet.

Paradoxically, the pilgrim's very act of mimicry bespeaks an oblique

7. See Olson for a useful discussion of the poet as maker.

recognition of the truth about his poetry. On one side of his equation are the stories he and his subjects offer—the fictions they construct about themselves as well as those they construct for the game's sake. On the other is his own *humana fragilitas*, yearning for, needing transcendent truth, the explanation of causes, but bound by the necessities of limited wit, imperfect observation, ambiguous language, and inevitable mortality. The pilgrim-poet can do no more than endeavor to record and illustrate these limitations, using trope and omission at every turn to acknowledge his distance from truth and wholeness. As a sort of magician, an illusion maker, he—like the Orleans clerk of the Franklin's Tale, or the Fiend of the Friar's Tale—can only make free with necessities. His tellers, in presenting themselves as "characters" and telling their tales, will propose causal explanations for themselves and try to elucidate the events of their stories. But the explanations will be limited finally by their fictiveness. Only the Parson's Tale will probe the true causes of things directly, but his "tale" is not a fiction. The language of the tales is deliberately and designedly the language of error, as judged by an unrealized, extratextual language of transcendent truth.

In the pilgrim's argument, fiction, like history, is a necessity imposed by the Fall. Chaucer's pilgrim voice as it mingles with the voices of the other Canterbury pilgrims proclaims the delights of tale-telling. The poet willingly, even willfully, engages the fallen world's illusions, opinions, and beliefs, questioning by his play their relations to truth.

Is there, then, any "truth" to be found in the pilgrim's report of the Canterbury adventure? And, if so, where and how? As the orchestrator of all the artifices, all the falsifications, all the voices of the *Tales*, the pilgrim Chaucer unashamedly encourages his fictive surrogates in their mendacious enterprises. A shapeshifter and a trickster, he himself thrives on lying. Yet because he styles himself a pilgrim, his lying, like that of the Fiend of the Friar's Tale, may be read as part of God's service. The Fiend, as he tells the summoner, lies partly because human "wit is al to bare" to understand the truth (3.1480). Even when he tells the summoner the transcendent truth about himself—recessed within the fiction of his bailiff disguise and voice—the summoner fails to grasp it. In a parallel way, Chaucer gives his tellers matters of truth in their stories, but the truth more often than not remains unobserved by the tellers and their characters within the fictive frames.

Of course, as the Fiend says, some withstand "oure temptacioun"— see through the disguises—and this act is "cause of [their] savacioun" (3.1497–98). Multiple (and wrong) interpretation must be the rule in reading the "divers art and . . . diverse figures" of the Fiend and the pilgrim-poet alike (3.1486). Yet Chaucer, like the Fiend, holds out the possibility of "right" interpretation. Such interpretation, however, will depend more on the reader's intention than on the fiction itself—the individual's personal concern for truth and salvation.

Chaucer provides this saving extraliterary definition of fiction and interpretation not through his pilgrim but through his final voice and final image in *The Canterbury Tales.* In his Retraction after the Parson's Tale, he says, " 'Al that is writen is writen for oure doctrine,' and that is myn entente" (10.1083). The poet in this last voice also begs pardon for any of his tales that "sownen into synne" and apologizes for his "enditynges of worldly vanitees" (10.1085, 1084). Yet, while he, like the Fiend, warns of the dangers of fiction, he knows that his audience may not heed the warning. In fact, he himself has succumbed to temptation in allowing his many fictive voices to enjoy the delights of Harry's game.

VII. The Host's Voice

Harry Bailly's voice, which dominates the final movement of the General Prologue, follows directly from the pilgrim's declaration "My wit is short." From that point on, another "I," another character, empowered by the pilgrim voice, assumes control over the design of the tales. Like most Chaucerian transitions, the juxtaposition of the apologetic voice with Harry's portrait and his "boold" speech requires more than cursory attention. It is as if Harry were born of the pilgrim-poet's essential limitation.

Yet, as a child of insufficiency, Harry lacks the self-critical awareness of his parent. Like the pilgrim, he espouses a theory of fiction. But while his notion of "making"—the third in Chaucer's series in the General Prologue—coincides with the pilgrim's in fundamental ways, it lacks the pilgrim's acknowledgment of partiality, limitation, and absence. Despite Harry's pious bow to "sentence" in the General Prologue, his fiction is essentially fiction for the sake of play and mirth and also for financial profit. As such, it is a fiction unmoored in ideas about truth or the quest for truth.[8]

Harry, the fourteenth-century bourgeois innkeeper, has often been regarded as an "original," having no clear literary antecedents. Manly even identifies him with a historical Henry Bailly, thus establishing his credentials as a "realistic" character (78–79). Like so many other Chaucerian characters, however, Harry owes his originality not only to his apparently idiosyncratic, realistic "condicioun" and "chiere" but also to the poet's complex manipulation of well-established literary and theoretical formulations. Understood as the latter-day spokesman for an ancient tradition, Harry assumes a climactic place in Chaucer's dialectical argument concerning the character of the poet and the functions of poetry.

We first meet Harry Bailly in the dining room of his inn after he has served supper to his guests and collected their bills. For this third major voice in Chaucer's complex introductory defense of his fiction, the context has narrowed significantly. The vast panorama of the exter-

---

8. Alan Gaylord offers one of the fullest, most helpful discussions of Harry Bailly's involvement in the theory of storytelling. He rightly observes that Harry's principal concern in the tales proper is solace and not the "sentence" he piously invokes in the General Prologue. For other discussions of Harry's theoretical commitments and significance, *see* Lumiansky, *Of Sondry Folk* 85–95; Ruggiers 6; David 75–76; Richardson; Scheps; and Bloomfield 49.

nal, seasonal world served as locus for the clerkly voice. An entire inn treated *as* an inn—a place on the way—framed the pilgrim. By contrast, a single public room designed for drinking and eating encloses Harry's authority and poetic theory. And Harry is at home in the Tabard. As the scene narrows, so too do the possibilities for poetry as an art of wise interpretation. In the dining room of a tavern we listen to the host's limited and limiting notions about the poet and poetry.

As the innkeeper "reads" poetry, it fully deserves the notoriety assigned to it by the stricter antique and medieval theorists, from Paul, Augustine, and Boethius to Chaucer's Parson. Harry sponsors fiction for reasons very like those of Boethius's muses—the "scaenicas meretriculas" 'theatrical whores'—at the beginning of the *Consolation*. The Muses that Lady Philosophy dismisses from Boethius's chamber are those Plato and Cicero had also condemned, those who inspire laments over bad fortune and celebrate pleasure as the proper goal of poetry (and life). Some medieval commentators widened Philosophia's condemnation to include all secular poetry. As one exegete puts it, Boethius's "theatrical whores" are the "Musas quas inuocant illi qui saeculariter scribunt Horatius Virgilius et alii qui nouem Musas nouem deas fingunt et inuocant" 'The Muses whom those invoke who write in a worldly way: Horace, Vergil, and others who depict the nine Muses as nine goddesses and invoke them' (Silk 7).[9] In the environment of philosophy, so the medieval commentator's argument goes, all worldly poetry is to be recognized as falsifying fiction. Later theorists—among them Petrarch and Boccaccio—fully aware of such religiously based opposition to secular poetry, took pains to redress the criticisms.[1] They insisted with humanist zeal on the correctness of ancient definitions that allow poetry both its fictive covering and its truth. Chaucer, by contrast, turns over the direction of his poetry making to Harry Bailly and thereby gives a hearing to a notion of poetic fiction divorced from the philosophical search for truth.

Despite his brief, perfunctory bow to Horatian "sentence," Harry prefers poetry as mirthful distraction from the hard realities and pain of the human condition. His interest in tale-telling coincides with his pleasure in drinking and, covertly, his desire for money. This last use of fiction for profit aligns him particularly with Boethius's theatrical strumpets. As Nicholas Trivet puts it in his commentary on the *Consolation*, "the poetic muses are called theatrical whores—[because] just as a whore copulates with those [lovers] for love not of procreation but of lucre, so poets were writing about those [things]—for the love not of wisdom but of praise, that is to say, of money" (fol. 6v). Harry's ultimate goal in generating the fictions of the Canterbury journey is to collect the price of twenty-nine suppers, minus his own small contribution to the winner's meal at the end of the trip.

As a master of mirth, Harry is also kin to the all-important figure of

9. For the attribution of this commentary, see Courcelle 304.
1. See Petrarch's coronation speech in Godi; also, his *Invective contra medicum* in Petrarch 648–93.

Déduit in Guillaume de Lorris's *Roman de la rose*.[2] This character, whom Chaucer called "Sir Mirth" in his translation of the *Roman*, is the courtly proprietor of the garden into which the poet enters as a young lover (about to be trapped by erotic desire). In this garden Déduit acts as choragus for a troop of jongleurs, jugglers, musicians, singers, and dancers. In a parallel way, Harry in his dining room proposes himself as the leader of a band of fiction makers. As Déduit's followers are distracted by the garden's "siren" birds and the music of his players, Harry's pilgrims succumb without demur to the innkeeper's strong wine and promises of mirth through storytelling.

Above all, both Déduit and Harry traffic in "divertissement." In Chaucer's translation of the *Roman*, Sir Mirth in the garden "walketh to solace . . . for sweeter place / to pleyen ynne he may not find" (lines 621–23). Like Guillaume's allegorical figure, Harry, who seeks play for the sake of solace, is essentially mirthful. The words *mirth, myrie, pley, disport,* and *comfort* appear twelve times in twenty-six lines as Chaucer gives us Harry's portrait and has him explain his game. The very name Déduit suits both characters exactly, containing as it does the two senses "having a good time" and "turning away from a [right] course" (Dahlberg 361, line 590n). To be sure, Harry and his followers leave the Tabard and walk out into the world engaged to play a diversionary game, whereas Déduit remains at home in his symbolic garden. Yet Harry sees to it that his pilgrim subjects never forget that they have contracted to remain within the bounds of his play and his notions of solace. The fictions themselves, together with Harry's framing commentary, become the pilgrims' "pleasure garden" for the duration of the Canterbury journey. At the same time, however, the inescapable fact of the pilgrimage serves as an ever-present critique of the game, reminding us that there is another, "right" course.

While Harry, in framing his game, shares Déduit's concern for mirth and solace, his image of diversionary art is richer and more philosophically complex than his French counterpart's. In his avowed antipathy for silence and his intended use of fiction for financial profit, he sums up Boethius's whole argument concerning the conflict between distracting fictions and the search for philosophical truth. Harry's kind of fiction explicitly opposes the silence of spiritual introspection proper to the life of true pilgrimage. Poetry is, for him, a pleasant noise that keeps the mind conveniently distracted from any pilgrim sense of the need for truth or meditation on the *lacrimae rerum*. "And wel I woot," he says,

> as ye goon by the weye,
> Ye shapen yow to talen and to pleye;
> For trewely, confort ne myrthe is noon
> To ride by the weye doumb as a stoon;
> And therfore wol I maken yow disport,

2. Alan Gaylord points out the connections between Harry's interest in mirth and its importance in the *Roman de la rose* (230), but he does not observe the direct relation between Déduit and Chaucer's innkeeper.

As I seyde erst, and doon yow som confort.

(1.771–76)

Harry's interest in distraction coincides with his pervasive urge to rush from one tale to another. Gaps in diversionary discourse, like the absence of mirth, may allow introspection to enter, and this Harry cannot bear.[3]

Why, we must ask, does Chaucer turn over the important last place in his prologal argument to so disreputable a voice and position? He does so at least in part, I believe, to give a full, unabridged account of all aspects of the fiction he proposes to write. Like Dante in the *Commedia*, he intends to include—and even praise—the impure, infernal element in his poetry as well as its potential for philosophical vision. Indeed, poetry as rhetorical bedazzlement may have seemed to him the most evident, accessible, attractive aspect of his art, the one most likely to charm his audience into paying attention. By way of Harry's voice, Chaucer, unlike many of his critics, defends (though with the substantial reservations imposed by the other prologal voices) the delights of puzzlement, diversion, and absorption in the illusions wrought by rhetorical coloring.

Through Harry, Chaucer also calls attention to the common tendency, in which the tavern keeper's notion of fiction making participates, to miss or set aside contemplation of the providential design of the universe and humanity's place within it. Storytelling, at least at one level, affords a pleasure not unlike the Wife's putative joy in wealthy and virile husbands, the Friar's enjoyment of rich patrons and comfortable taverns, the Monk's pleasure in hunting, January's delight in his love garden, and the myriad other diversions by which the Canterbury characters live. Chaucer the poet does not exempt himself or his writing from this pleasurable, spiritually subversive function of fiction. But he admits his involvement in so disreputable a cause only indirectly, as a good orator should, using Harry's voice and character to mask his own. In his last voice, Chaucer slyly celebrates poetry in just the terms that the strictest theorists had used to condemn it.

In doing so, however, Chaucer is not giving Harry's ideas about poetry precedence over other, higher notions. Like the opening formulations of the clerkly voice, the Host's game provides a framing contrast for the central, dynamic notion of the poetic enterprise in the General Prologue—the one articulated by the pilgrim's voice. The voices of the clerk and the innkeeper offer relatively fixed, static images of poetry: one is concerned with causality, hierarchy, and order, the other with the disorders, sexual exploits, and trivialities of quotidian life. Both positions are curiously abstracted, though in opposite ways, from the complex central subject of poetry as the pilgrim voice proposes it—human consciousness of a universe that emanates from God but also participates in entropy, mortality, disintegration.

---

3. Harry's notions of tale-telling as a source of mirth align his poetry with the sphere of "curiositas"—"a fastidious, excessive, morally diverting interest in things and people" (Zacher 20). Zacher's discussion of "curiositas" is full and illuminating.

Neither the first nor the last notion of poetry entertained in the General Prologue allows for the rich, active, tentative, dialogic exploration of that difficult subject as the pilgrim voice engages it. The pilgrim Chaucer may reach upward toward the clerk's philosophical formulations or downward to Harry's bourgeois laughter. He is bound by neither, though he may play with both. His deeply human engagement with his flawed, mortal subject and art precludes direct statements of transcendent truth in his fiction. By the same token, his storytelling will rise above the category of fictions made simply for the sake of rhetorical play and distracting frivolity. What remains—the poetry at the center—is fictive, certainly. But it is as richly various and morally dense and stubbornly inconclusive as its total subject. Its self-conscious fictionality will press well-disposed readers toward a new awareness of the nature of illusion and self-deception, whether in literature or in life. The truths the tales uncover have to do mainly with human ways of knowing (and not knowing) the self and the mortal world.

To find the truths of Christian doctrine, however, one must set the tales aside. Transcendent truth remains largely absent from the Chaucerian narratives, and it must. In Chaucer's argument, this is just the kind of truth that makes all secular fiction untenable. Nonetheless, Chaucer the poet in his several voices points directions, marks boundaries, poses questions and puzzles that bear heavily on the truths beyond his fictions.

WORKS CITED

Abelard, Peter. *Expositio in hexameron*. Migne 178: 731–84.

Arbusow, Leonid. *Colores rhetorici*. 1948. Geneva: Slatkin, 1974.

Baldwin, Ralph. *The Unity of* The Canterbury Tales. Copenhagen: Rosenkilde, 1955.

Benoit de Sainte-Maure. *Roman de Troie*. Ed. L. Constans. 6 vols. Paris: Firmin-Didot, 1904–12.

Bethurum, Dorothy. "Chaucer's Point of View as Narrator in the Love Poems." *PMLA* 74 (1959): 511–20.

Bevington, D. M. "The Obtuse Narrator in Chaucer's *House of Fame*." *Speculum* 36 (1961): 288–98.

Bloomfield, Morton W. "*The Canterbury Tales* as Framed Narratives," *Leeds Studies in English* ns 14 (1983): 44–56.

Boccaccio, Giovanni. *Genealogie deorum gentilium libri*. Ed. V. Romano Bari: Laterza, 1951.

Boethius, Anicius Manlius Severinus. *Philosophiae consolationis in libri quinque*. Leipzig, 1871.

Brewer, Derek S. "Towards a Chaucerian Poetic." *Proceedings of the British Academy* 60 (1974): 219–52.

Bronson, B. H. *In Search of Chaucer*. Toronto: U of Toronto P, 1960.

Chaucer, Geoffrey. *Works*, Ed. F. N. Robinson. 2nd ed. Boston: Houghton, 1957.

Christianson, Paul. "Chaucer's Literacy." *Chaucer Review* 11 (1976): 112–27.

[Cicero]. *Ad C. Herennium. De ratione dicendi*. Ed. and trans. Harry Caplan. Cambridge: Harvard UP; London: Heinemann, 1964.

Cicero. *De oratore*. Ed. and trans. E. W. Sutton and H. Rackham. Cambridge: Cambridge UP; London: Heinemann, 1967.

Cook, A. S. "Chaucerian Papers: I." *Transactions of the Connecticut Academy of Arts and Sciences* 23 (1919): 5–10.

Courcelle, P. *La consolation de philosophie dans la tradition littéraire*. Paris: Studies Augustiniennes, 1967.

Cunningham, J. V. "The Literary Form of the Prologue to *The Canterbury Tales*." *Modern Philology* 49 (1951–52): 172–81.

Curtius, E. R. *European Literature and the Latin Middle Ages*. Trans. R. W. Trask. New York: Pantheon, 1953.

Dahlberg, Charles, ed. and trans. *Le roman de la rose*. By Guillaume de Lorris and Jean de Meun. Princeton: Princeton UP, 1971.

Dares Phrygius. *De excidio Troiae historia*. Ed. F. O. Meister. Leipzig, 1873.

David, Alfred. *The Strumpet Muse*. Bloomington: Indiana UP, 1976.

Donaldson, E. Talbot. "Chaucer the Pilgrim." *PMLA* 69 (1954): 928–36.

Duncan, E. H. "The Narrator's Point of View in the Portrait-Sketches, Prologue to *The Canterbury Tales*." *Essays in Honor of Walter Clyde Curry*. Nashville: Vanderbilt UP, 1954. 77–101.

Eliot, T. S. *The Three Voices of Poetry*. Cambridge: Cambridge UP, 1953.

Gaylord, Alan. "Sentence and *Solaas* in Fragment VII of *The Canterbury Tales*: Harry Bailly as Horseback Editor." *PMLA* 82 (1967): 226–33.

Godi, Carlo. "La 'Collatio laureationis' del Petrarca." *Italia mediovate e umanistica* 13 (1970): 1–27.

Green, Eugene. "The Voices of the Pilgrims in the General Prologue to *The Canterbury Tales*," *Style* 9 (1975): 55–81.

Gregory the Great. *Dialogues*. Ed. A. de Vogüé, Trans. into French P. Antin. 3 vols. Paris: Cerf, 1980.

Guillaume de Lorris and Jean de Meun. *Le roman de la rose*. Ed. Ernest Langlois. 5 vols. Paris: Firmin-Didot, 1914–24.

Hankins, John E. "Chaucer and the *Per Virgilium veneris*." *Modern Language Notes* 44 (1934): 80–83.

Hoffman, A. "Chaucer's Prologue to Pilgrimage: The Two Voices." *ELH* 21 (1954): 1–16.

Howard, Donald. "Chaucer the Man." *PMLA* 80 (1965): 337–43.

———. *The Idea of the* Canterbury Tales. Berkeley: U of California P, 1976.

Hugh of St. Victor. "Homilia prima." *In Salomonis Ecclesiasten. Homiliae XIX*. Migne 175: 115–33.

Hunt, Tony. "The Rhetorical Background to the Arthurian Prologue: Tradition and the Old French Vernacular Prologues." *Forum for Modern Language Studies* 6 (1970): 1–23.

Huygens, R. B. C., ed. *Accessus ad auctores. Bernard d'Utrecht. Conrad d' Hirsau*. Leiden: Brill, 1970.

Jordan, R. M. *Chaucer and the Shape of Creation*. Cambridge: Harvard UP, 1967.

———. "Chaucer's Sense of Illusion: Roadside Drama Reconsidered." *Journal of English and Germanic Philology* 29 (1962): 19–33.

Kane, George. *The Autobiographical Fallacy in Chaucer and Langland Studies*. London: Lewis, 1965.

Kellogg, A. L. "Chaucer's Self-Portrait and Dante's." *Medium Ævum* 29 (1960): 119–20.

Lanham, Richard. *The Motives of Eloquence*. New Haven: Yale UP, 1976.

Leicester, Marshall. "A General Prologue to the *Canterbury Tales*." *PMLA* 95 (1980): 213–24.

Lumiansky, R. M. "Benoit's Portraits and Chaucer's General Prologue." *Journal of English and Germanic Philology* 55 (1956): 431–38.

———. *Of Sondry Folk*. Austin: U of Texas P, 1955.

Major, John. "The Personality of Chaucer the Pilgrim." *PMLA* 75 (1960): 160–62.

Malone, Kemp. "Style and Structure in the Prologue to the *Canterbury Tales*." *ELH* 13 (1946): 38–45.

Mandel, Jerome. "Other Voices in the *Canterbury Tales*." *Criticism* 19 (1977): 338–49.

Manly, John. *Some New Light on Chaucer*. New York: Holt, 1926.

Mann, Jill. *Chaucer and Medieval Estates Satire*. Cambridge: Cambridge UP, 1973.

Middleton, Anne. "The Idea of Public Poetry in the Reign of Richard II." *Speculum* 53 (1978): 94–114.

Migne, J. P., ed. *Patrologia Latina*. 221 vols. Paris, 1844–64.

Mukarovsky, Jan. *The Word and Verbal Art*. New Haven: Yale UP, 1977.

Nevo, Ruth. "Chaucer: Motive and Mask in the General Prologue." *Modern Language Review* 58 (1963): 1–9.

Olson, Glending. "Making and Poetry in the Age of Chaucer." *Comparative Literature* 31 (1979): 272–90.

Payne, R. O. "Chaucer's Realization of Himself as Rhetor." *Medieval Eloquence*. Ed. J. J. Murphy. Berkeley: U of California P, 1978. 270–87.

Petrarch. *Prose*. Ed. G. Martellotti et al. Milano: Ricciardi, 1955.

Plato. *The Timaeus*. Trans. F. M. Cornford. Indianapolis: Bobbs, 1959.

Porqueras Mayo, A. *El prólogo como género literario*. Madrid: Consejo Superior de Investigaciones Científicas, 1957.

Quilligan, Maureen. *The Language of Allegory*. Ithaca: Cornell UP, 1979.

Quintilian. *Institutio oratoria*. Ed. and trans. H. E. Butler. 4 vols. London: Heinemann; New York: Putnam, 1921.

Richardson, Cynthia. "The Function of the Host in the *Canterbury Tales*." *Texas Studies in Literature and Language* 12 (1970): 325–44.

Ross, Werner. "Über den Sogennanten Natureingang der Trobadors." *Romanische Forschungen* 65 (1953): 49–68.

Ruggiers, Paul. *The Art of the* Canterbury Tales. Madison: U of Wisconsin P, 1965.

Scheps, Walter. " 'Up Roos Oure Hoost, and Was Oure Aller Cok': Harry Bailly's Tale-Telling Competition." *Chaucer Review* 10 (1975–76): 113–28.

Servius. *In Vergilii carmina commentarii*. Ed. G. Thilo and H. Hagen. 3 vols. Leipzig, 1897.

Silk, Edmund T., ed. *Saeculi noni auctoris in Boetii* Consolationem philosophiae *commentarius*. Rome: American Acad. in Rome, 1935.

Spitzer, Leo. "A Note on the Poetic and the Empirical 'I' in Medieval Authors." *Traditio* 4 (1946): 414–22.

Trivet, Nicholas. Commentary on Boethius's *Consolation of Philosophy*. Latin ms. 18424. Bibliothèque Nationale.

Tuve, Rosamond. *Seasons and Months*. Paris: Librairie Universitaire, 1933.

———. "Spring in Chaucer and before Him." *Modern Language Notes* 52 (1937): 9–16.

Virgil. *The Eclogues and Georgics*. Ed. Robert D. Williams. New York: St. Martin's, 1979.

Woolf, Rosemary. "Chaucer as a Satirist in the General Prologue to the *Canterbury Tales*." *Critical Quarterly* 1 (1959): 150–57.

Zacher, Christian. *Curiosity and Pilgrimage*. Baltimore: Johns Hopkins UP, 1976.

GEORGE LYMAN KITTREDGE

[The Dramatic Principle of the *Canterbury Tales*]†

The Canterbury Tales exists in fragments, which no one has ever succeeded in fitting together. Different manuscripts arrange them in different ways, and modern scholars have exhibited much ingenuity in trying to make out the right order of the several stories. Of late, there has been a disposition amongst the learned to believe either that Chaucer made more than one tentative arrangement, or that he never settled the matter in his mind at all. These are questions, however, that need not now detain us. The plan is clear enough for our immediate purposes. We may profitably study the tales in groups, without regard to disputed problems of order.

We know, at least, that the series begins with the Knight, the Miller, the Reeve, and the Cook, and ends with the Manciple and the Parson. Within these extremities, we can make out several groups, each of which holds together. One of the longest of these begins with the Shipman's Prologue and ends with the Nun's Priest's Epilogue, containing the tales of the Shipman, the Prioress, Chaucer himself (namely, two, Sir Thopas and the Melibee), the Monk, and the Nun's Priest. This group is admirably organized. Another, still longer, which is called the Marriage Group, begins with the Wife of Bath's Prologue and ends with the Franklin's Tale: the order is Wife, Friar, Sumner, Clerk, Merchant, Squire, Franklin. The Physician's Tale and the Pardoner's also form a group; so do the Second Nun's and the Canon's Yeoman's. The Tale of the Man of Law stands, in a manner, by itself, with an elaborate introduction which makes it clear that it was to begin the day. By common consent it is placed after the Cook's fragment. It will not be possible, in the limited time at my disposal, to consider every group of tales. I shall make a selection, therefore, with a view to illustrate Chaucer's art in the two main points of character and dramatic method.

There has been a rather active discussion, for more than a hundred years, concerning the probable source of Chaucer's scheme of the Canterbury Pilgrimage. The result is a *non liquet*. Several possible models have been pointed out, and others are turning up continually.

† From *Chaucer and His Poetry*, by George Lyman Kittredge (Cambridge, Massachusetts: Harvard University Press, 1970), pp. 146–56. Copyright © 1915 by George Lyman Kittredge; © 1970 by the President and Fellows of Harvard College. Reprinted by permission of the publisher.

The *pros* and *cons* in every case have been argued with learning and ingenuity. So far as I can see, however, the advocates of each new source, though they have found it easy to demolish the arguments of their predecessors, have not been quite so successful in constructing acceptable theories of their own. There is, then, no single collection of tales to which we can point, with any confidence, as that which gave Chaucer the hint.

This condition of things should not surprise us. It is what we ought to expect, and the inference is easy. The plan of attaching stories together so as to make a collection is very old, very widespread, and very obvious. It was a traditional bit of technique, both in literature and in folklore, ages before Chaucer was born, and in all four quarters of the world. And furthermore, it was a bit of technique that accorded with actual practice. What could people do, in old times, but tell stories, when they were assembled and had plenty of leisure? The practice, indeed, has not died out, even in these days of novels and newspapers, and it was universal and inevitable, under all sorts of circumstances, when these time-killing but unsociable inventions did not yet exist. Chaucer's problem was not, to hunt through literature for an idea which confronted him, unsought, at every turn in life. That he knew collections of tales may be taken for granted; that he often followed convention is a matter of course. He had some knowledge of the literary device, and much knowledge of the immemorial habit of mankind.

That the particular frame which Chaucer adopted resembles this or that frame which preceded it in literary history, signifies nothing— except that some things in life are more or less like other things. Chaucer had no need to borrow or to invent: he needed only to observe. His genius appears, in the first place, in making a good choice among his several observations, in perceiving the advantages of one particular frame over all others. Pilgrims were as familiar sights to Chaucer as commercial travellers are to us. There is not one chance in a hundred that he had not gone on a Canterbury pilgrimage himself. And pilgrims did, for a fact, while away the time in story-telling. Newton did not learn that apples fall by reading treatises on pomology.

The most tantalizing of all the parallels, by the way, is Sercambi's *Novelle*, for which the frame is likewise a pilgrimage. But it is hard to get an historical point of contact. Dates are right enough, and geography does not interfere. It is even conceivable that Chaucer and Sercambi met in Italy, though there is no evidence either way. The difficulties are less tangible than dates and places; but, such as they are, they cannot be surmounted. Yet, after all, Sercambi's scheme is a precious document in the case, though not in proof of imitation. What it does show, is that it was possible for a writer of far less originality than Chaucer to hit upon the device of a pilgrimage as a convenient frame for a collection of stories.

Before the idea of a pilgrimage occurred to him, Chaucer had twice undertaken to compose a series of tales. The results lie before us in the Tragedies, afterwards assigned to the Monk, and the Legend of Cupid's Saints, otherwise known as Good Women. Both works exhibit, in the most striking fashion, the orderly habits of mediæval literature. They likewise prove, beyond cavil, the docility of Chaucer himself, the instinctive readiness with which he deferred to technical authority and bowed his neck to the rhetorical yoke. The lesson is salutary. We perceive, in this great poet, not a vast, irregular, untaught genius,—an amiable but terrible infant, impatient of regulation, acknowledging no laws of structure, guided by no canons of criticism. Quite the contrary! Chaucer was a conscientious student of literary form. He submitted with patient eagerness to the precepts of his teachers. Schematism was the governing principle of their instruction, and he had no wish to rebel. Thus he got the training which enabled him, when the time came, to give free rein to his vivacious originality without losing his self-control.

From these considerations there emerges a rule of judgment that is of some value for our guidance in interpreting Chaucer's final masterpiece, the Canterbury Tales. It may be stated in the simplest language: *Chaucer always knew what he was about.* When, therefore, he seems to be violating dramatic fitness,—as in the ironical tribute of the Clerk to the Wife of Bath, or the monstrous cynicism of the Pardoner's confessions,—we must look to our steps. Headlong inferences are dangerous. We are dealing with a great literary artist who had been through the schools. The chances are that such details are not casual flourishes. Somehow, in all likelihood, they fall into decorous subordination to his main design.

This design, as we know, is a pilgrimage to Canterbury. I have spoken of it, for convenience, as a "frame." That, indeed, is the light in which it is commonly regarded. We read each tale by itself, as if it were an isolated unit; often, indeed, as if Chaucer were telling it in his own person. At most, we inquire, in a half-hearted fashion, whether it is appropriate to the character of the Knight, or the Sumner, or the Franklin. Very seldom do we venture to regard the several stories from the dramatic point of view. Yet that is manifestly our paramount duty.

Many and great were the advantages that Chaucer discerned in his plot of a Canterbury pilgrimage. They stand out in sharp contrast against the monotonous background of his two earlier experiments, the Tragedies and the Legend, to which we may return for a moment.

Each of these is unified not by structure but by subject matter. The unity, therefore, is not organic, but mechanical. In the Tragedies,—for the idea of which Chaucer was indebted in equal measure to the Romance of the Rose and Boccaccio's *De Casibus*,—we have a number of sombre sketches, rather declamatory than narrative, of exalted personages whom Fortune brought low. In the Good Women,—a singular cross between the *Legenda Aurea* and Ovid's *Heroides*, with a charming prologue, which reverts for its machinery to the French love-visions,—we read the lives of famous ladies of ancient days who suffered death, or worse, for love of faithless men. In both works the plan is absolutely rigid. Variety in form or matter is excluded by the convention adopted (tragedy, in the one; legend in the other) and by the limitations of the theme. Movement is impossible, for there is no connection between the parts. Dramatic presentation is not attempted, or even thought of, all the stories being told by one person, the poet himself.

Turn now to the Canterbury Tales, and the change is startling. It results, in the last analysis, from Chaucer's adopting the scheme of a Canterbury pilgrimage. The stories are no longer alike in form or subject, nor are they all in one key. There is infinite variety, because they are told by a variety of persons. Every reader may discover something to his taste, both in style and substance, as Chaucer himself protests in his apology for the Miller, "who tolde his cherles tale in his manere." Those who do not fancy low comedy may find enough of polite history, as well as of morality and religion.

> And therfore, whoso list it nat yheere,
> Turne over the leef and chese another tale;
> For he shal fynde ynowe, grete and smale,
> Of storial thyng that toucheth gentillesse,
> And eek moralitee and hoolynesse.
> Blameth nat me if that ye chese amys.
>
> (A. 3176–81)

But this is not all. Chaucer's adoption of a Canterbury pilgrimage was not a mere excuse for story-telling. Most readers, I am aware, treat this great masterpiece simply as a storehouse of fiction, and so do many critics. Yet everybody feels, I am sure, that Chaucer was quite as much interested in the Pilgrims themselves as in their several narratives. This, no doubt, is what Dryden had in mind when he wrote, comparing Chaucer with Ovid: "Both of them understood the manners, under which name I comprehend the passions, and, in a larger sense, the descriptions of persons, and their very habits. For an example, I see Baucis and Philemon as perfectly before me, as if some ancient painter had drawn them; and all the pilgrims in the Canterbury Tales,—their humors, their features, and the very dress, as distinctly as if I had supped with them at the Tabard in Southwark; yet even there too the figures in Chaucer are much more lively, and set in a better light."

I am much deceived if Dryden is not here treading on the verge of the proposition that the Canterbury Tales is, to all intents and purposes, a Human Comedy. Certainly he is calling our attention to something that distinguishes Chaucer's work from every collection of stories that preceded it. It was much, as we have seen, that Chaucer had the judgment, among the infinite doings of the world, to select a pilgrimage, and to parcel out his tales to the miscellaneous company that met at the Tabard on the way to Canterbury. It was more, far more, that he had the genius to create the Pilgrims, endowing each of them with an individuality that goes much beyond the typical. If we had only the Prologue, we might, perhaps, regard the Pilgrims as types. The error is common, and venial. But we must not stop with the Prologue: we must go on to the play. The Pilgrims are not static: they move and live. The Canterbury Pilgrimage is, whether Dryden meant it or not, a Human Comedy, and the Knight and the Miller and the Pardoner and the Wife of Bath and the rest are the *dramatis personae.* The Prologue itself is not merely a prologue: it is the first act, which sets the personages in motion. Thereafter, they move by virtue of their inherent vitality, not as tale-telling puppets, but as men and women. From this point of view, which surely accords with Chaucer's intention, the Pilgrims do not exist for the sake of the stories, but *vice versa.* Structurally regarded, the stories are merely long speeches expressing, directly or indirectly, the characters of the several persons. They are more or less comparable, in this regard, to the soliloquies of Hamlet or Iago or Macbeth. But they are not mere monologues, for each is addressed to all the other personages, and evokes reply and comment, being thus, in a real sense, a part of the conversation.

Further,—and this is a point of crucial significance,—the action of the plot, however simple, involves a great variety of relations among the Pilgrims. They are brought together by a common impulse, into a casual and impermanent association, which is nevertheless, for the time being, peculiarly intimate. They move slowly along the road, from village to village and inn to inn, in groups that are ever shifting, but ever forming afresh. Things happen to them. They come to know each other better and better. Their personalities act and react. Friendships combine for the nonce. Jokes are cracked, like the Host's on the Pardoner, which are taken amiss. Smouldering enmities of class or profession, like that between the Sumner and the Friar, which was proverbial, blaze into flaming quarrels. Thus the story of any pilgrim may be affected or determined,—in its contents, or in the manner of the telling, or in both,—not only by his character in general, but also by the circumstances, by the situation, by his momentary relations to the others in the company, or even by something in a tale that has come before. We lose much, therefore, when we neglect the so-called prologues and epilogues, and the bits of conversation and narrative that link the tales together. Many more of these would have been supplied if Chaucer had not left his work in so fragmentary a condition; but such as we have are invaluable, both for their own excellence, and for the light they throw upon the scope and details of the great design.

* * *

GEORGE LYMAN KITTREDGE

[The Marriage Group]†

* * *

One other act of Chaucer's Human Comedy is complete (but for the
story of Cambuscan) and highly finished. It begins with the Wife of
Bath's Prologue and ends with the Tale of the Franklin. The subject is
Marriage, which is discussed from several points of view, as the most
important problem in organized society. The solution of the problem
brings the act to an end.

The dominant figure in this act of the Comedy is the Wife of Bath.
It is she who starts the debate, and the participants keep her steadily
in mind, and mention her and her doctrines more than once. Even the
comic interlude which breaks into the discussion is occasioned by
her prologue. Nowhere is the dramatic spirit of the Canterbury Pilgrimage more evident than in this Marriage group of tales. Nowhere
is it more important to heed the relations of the Pilgrims to each
other. Neglect of this precaution has led to a good deal of misunder-
standing.

The Wife's ostensible subject is Tribulation in Marriage. On this,
she avers, she can speak with the authority of an expert, for she has
outlived five husbands, worthy men in their degree, and she is ready to
welcome a sixth when God shall send him.

> "Yblessed be God that I have wedded fyve!
> Welcome the sixte, whan that evere he shal." [44–45]

Somebody—was it one of the clerics in the party?—has told her lately
that she should have married but once. This dictum rankles: she finds
no warrant for it in Scripture, and certainly none in her inclinations.
Accordingly, she breaks forth in a vehement defense of her own principles and practices. The celibate life, she admits, may be a high and
holy thing, well fitted for the Apostle Paul and other saints. Out of deference to them, she accords it the palm, for form's sake; but, at the
same time, she makes her own position perfectly clear. She despises
the ideal of the Church in this regard, and looks down with contempt
upon all who aspire to it. Human nature is good enough for her. This
is her first heresy; but she is so jovial in proclaiming it that no one
takes offence, however strongly some of the Pilgrims may reprobate
her principles in their hearts.

* * *

† From *Chaucer and His Poetry*, by George Lyman Kittredge (Cambridge, Massachusetts: Harvard University Press), pp. 185–203, 205–10. Copyright © 1915 by George Lyman Kittredge; © 1970 by the President and Fellows of Harvard College. Reprinted by permission of
the publisher. We have abridged Kittredge's argument by omitting his discussion of tales not
directly related to marriage, some of his lengthy citations from Chaucer, and a few shorter
references. His ideas were first and most fully presented in "Chaucer's Discussion of Marriage," *Modern Philology* 9 (1911–12): 435–67.

The Wife proceeds, with infinite zest, to give the history of her married life, unfolding, as she does so, another heretical doctrine of a startling kind, which, in fact, is the real subject of her discourse. This is nothing less than the dogma that the wife is the head of the house. Obedience is not her duty, but the husband's. Men are no match for women, anyway. Let them sink back to their proper level, and cease their ridiculous efforts to maintain a position for which they are not fit. Then marriages will all be happy. Otherwise there is no hope for anything but misery in wedlock. She supports her contention with much curious learning, derived, of course, from her fifth and latest husband, who was a professional scholar; and she overbears opposition by quoting her own experience, which is better testimony than the citation of authorities. She had always had her own way. Sometimes she cowed her husbands, and sometimes she cajoled them; but none of the five could resist her government. And it was well for them to yield. This is happy marriage. Who should know so well as she? Once, indeed, she rises almost to sublimity, as she looks back on the joy of her life:

> "But, Lord Crist! whan that it remembreth me
> Upon my yowthe, and on my jolitee,
> It tikleth me aboute myn herte roote.
> Unto this day it dooth myn herte boote
> That I have had my world as in my tyme." [469–73]

This is one of the great dramatic utterances of human nature, as the Wife of Bath is one of the most amazing characters that the brain of man has ever yet conceived.

The Pilgrims, we may be sure, are not inattentive to the Wife's harangue. To the Prioress, her complete antithesis, it means little, either good or bad. She does not understand the language of the worldly widow. The Parson and the Clerk of course are scandalized: such heresies cannot pass unchallenged, even as a jest. Of the two, the Clerk has the greater cause for resentment, for the Wife has aimed her shafts at him directly, not in malice, but in mischievous defiance. Not only has she entered the lists as a disputant in theology, but she has gone out of her way to attack his order, railing at them especially for their satire on women. "No clerk," she declares, "can speak well of wives. It is an impossibility." And, worse than all, she has told how she had married a clerk of Oxford, an alumnus of our modest scholar's own university, and had reduced him to shameful subjection. The Wife is an heresiarch after her own boisterous fashion. She is not to be taken too seriously, but she deserves a rebuke; and who is so fit to administer it as the Clerk himself, whose orthodoxy is unflinching, and whose every word is "sownynge in moral vertu"? It is not our Clerk's way, however, to thrust himself forward. His turn will come, and meanwhile he rides quietly along, listening without comment, and biding his time.

* * *

The Wife's tale of What Women most Desire is a famous old story, which is extant in several versions. As she tells it, it becomes an illustrative exemplum, to enforce the moral of her sermon. Sovereignty over men is a woman's ambition, and the knight of the Round Table, who found himself in a strange dilemma, submitted his judgment to his wife's choice, with the happiest result. He lived with her in perfect joy till their life's end,—and so "I pray," concludes the Wife of Bath, "that those may die early who will not yield themselves entirely to petticoat government." Mediæval feminism has had its say. The sermon is finished, and the moral is driven home.

Thus far the Wife of Bath has had plain sailing. She has proved her case to her own satisfaction, by experience, by authority, and by an illustrative story; and nobody seems inclined to take her to task.

The Friar compliments her in a non-committal fashion, but turns off, with a clever transition, to assail the Sumner, at whom he had been looking "with a louring chere" ever since that worthy had reproved him for laughing at the Wife's preamble. What follows, then, is a comic interlude, like that between Miller and Reeve at an earlier stage of the pilgrimage. The Friar tells a tale of a sumner who was carried off by the devil, and the Sumner, so angry that he stood up in his stirrups, retorts with an incomparable satire on begging friars, worked up on the basis of a trivial and sordid fabliau. Nowhere in the pilgrimage is the dramatic interplay of character more remarkable. For the Wife is the moving cause of the quarrel, though quite involuntarily. Harry Bailly, we note, has been content to drop the reins. The drama guides itself, moving on by virtue of the relations of the *dramatis personae*, their characters, and the logic of the situation. To all appearances the discussion of marriage has ended with the speaker who began it. The day's journey closes with the Sumner's Tale. The Host, at all events, has no thought of reopening the debate on matrimony when he calls upon the Clerk of Oxford to begin the entertainment next morning.

The Clerk has made no sign. He is as demure, the Host remarks, as a bride at her wedding breakfast. "Cheer up!" cries Harry, "this is no time to study. Tell us some merry tale, not in the high style, of which you are doubtless a master, but in plain language, so that we may all understand it." * * * The Oxford scholar yields a courteous assent, and begins the tale of Griselda, taught him at Padua by a noble clerk of Italy, one Francis Petrarch, who is now dead and buried. God rest his soul!

The story starts quite innocently. Not until it is well underway do the Pilgrims perceive the Clerk's drift. He is telling the tale of a patient and obedient wife, whose steadfast devotion to her husband was proof against every trial. With consummate art he is answering the Wife of Bath without appearing to take any notice either of her arguments or of her boisterous assault upon his order. "Clerks," she has declared, "cannot possibly speak well of wives." Yet here is one clerk, repeating the tale told him by another, and its theme is wifely fidelity and woman's fortitude under affliction.

We should not forget that the Clerk's Tale, like the Wife's long sermon, is addressed to the Canterbury Pilgrims, not to us, though we
are privileged to overhear. We must not only listen, but look. In our
mind's eye, we must see the Pilgrims, and watch their demeanor. Naturally, they are interested, and, equally of course, they understand
what the Clerk is doing. He is replying to the Wife of Bath,—confut-
ing her heresies, and at the same time vindicating his own order from
her abusive raillery.

One can hardly conceive a more skilful method of replying. Its in-
directness and deliberation are alike masterly. The Clerk is not talking
about the Wife of Bath. His tale contains no personal allusions. It is,
on the face of it, simply an affecting narrative which he chanced to
hear from a learned friend in Italy, and which he supposes may interest his fellow-travellers. But, as the picture of Griselda grows slowly
on the canvas, no Pilgrim can fail to recognize the complete antithesis
to the Wife of Bath. Besides, however you and I may feel about it, to
Chaucer's contemporaries the story was infinitely pathetic. One of Petrarch's friends broke down while reading it aloud, and could not continue, so deep was his emotion, but had to hand the manuscript to one
of his retinue to finish. Another read it through unmoved, but only because he did not believe that there ever lived a wife so loving, so submissive, and so patient under affliction.

This point, in truth,—the incredibility of the example,—might have
weakened its force as an answer to the Wife of Bath, if she were logically in a position to take advantage of such an objection. But this she
cannot well do without abandoning her main thesis, that women are
vastly superior to men. She might, to be sure, retort that the story proves
too much, that it shows that men are unfit to have dominion over
their wives, since they abuse it so abominably. But, before she can
frame any retort whatever,—if, indeed, she is not too much affected by
the pathos to be mistress of her argumentative faculties,—the Clerk,
who is a professional logician and a conscientious moralist, makes all
debate impossible by explaining, in Petrarch's words, the true lesson.
"This story is not meant as an exhortation to wives to be as patient as
Griselda, for that would transcend the powers of human nature. It
teaches all of us, men and women alike, how we should submit ourselves to the afflictions that God sends. The Marquis Walter was a
ruthless experimenter with souls. God is not like that. The trials He
sends are for our good, and we should accept them with Christian res-
ignation."

* * *

Here is a remarkable situation. The Clerk has vindicated his order
by praising women, and he has set up again the orthodox tenet of
wifely obedience. But he has not said a word to the Wife of Bath, and,
in the moral, he has expressly removed the story from the domain of
controversy by asserting, in the plainest terms, that it is not a lesson
for wives, but for Christians in general. If he drops the subject now, he
has left the Wife of Bath unanswered after all.

But he does not drop the subject. He has a surprise in store for the would-be feminist heresiarch and for the whole company. Suddenly, without a moment's warning, he turns to the Wife of Bath, and, with an air of serene and smiling urbanity, offers to recite a song that he has just composed in her honor, and in honor of the sect which she represents and of which she has proved herself so doughty a champion:—"May God establish both her way of life and her principles; for the world would suffer if they should not prevail":—

> "Whos lyf and al hire secte God mayntene
> In heigh maistrie, and elles were it scathe." [1171–72]

And so he declaims his Envoy in praise of feminism. It is an address to all wise and prudent married women, exhorting them to follow the precepts and the practice of the Wife of Bath. [Here Kittredge quotes all of the Clerk's Envoy, ll. 1163–1212.]

* * *

The moment is completely dramatic. It is not Chaucer who speaks, but the Clerk of Oxenford, and every word is in perfect character. His mock encomium is not only a masterpiece of sustained and mordant irony; it is a marvellous specimen of technical skill in metre, in diction, and in vigorous and concentrated satire. None but the Clerk, a trained rhetorician, could have composed it. None but the Clerk, a master of logic and a practised disputant, could have turned upon an opponent so adroitly. The home thrust comes when the guard is down. The Clerk is a moral philosopher, and he has proved both his earnestness and his competence. It is one of the humors of literature that this Envoy is traditionally judged a violation of dramatic propriety, as being out of accord with the Clerk's character. On the contrary, as we have seen, it is adjusted, with the nicest art, not only to his character, but also to the situation and the relations among the *dramatis personae*.

Heedless criticism has thrown the Wife's Prologue into the huge heap of satires on woman piled up by successive generations of mediæval poets. This indiscriminate procedure ignores the essential element that distinguishes the Canterbury Tales from the ordinary narrative and didactic poetry of the middle ages. The Wife of Bath is an individual expressing herself in character, not a stalking horse for a satirist's poisoned arrows. Her revelations apply to herself. To extend them to wives or women in general, is as ludicrous as it would be to interpret Iago's cynical speeches as Shakspere's satire on men and husbands. We may even take the Miller to witness:—

> Ther been ful goode wyves many oon,
> And evere a thousand goode ayeyns oon badde.
> That knowestow wel thyself, but if thou madde. [3154–56]

Similarly, the ironical Envoy is not to be taken as Chaucer's revolt against the false morality of Griselda's parable, but as the utterance of the Clerk, under quite particular circumstances. Nor is it, even on the Clerk's part, an attack on wives or women. It is simply a satirical encomium on a particular person, the obstreperous widow of Bath, and on any others who may choose to adopt her principles or join her heretical sect.

The dramatic connection between the Clerk's Envoy and the Merchant's Tale is especially close. The last line of the Clerk's ironical advice to wives—to let their husbands "care and weep and wring and wail"—is picked up by the Merchant in a despairing echo:—

> "Wepyng and waylyng, care and oother sorwe
> I knowe ynogh, on even and a-morwe,"
> Quod the Marchant, "and so doon other mo
> That wedded been."   [1213–16]

"There is no likeness between my wife and Griselda! I have been married only two months, and I have suffered more than any bachelor in a lifetime!"

The tale that follows is one of the most remarkable in the whole collection,—not for the plot, which is an old indecorous jest, but for the savage and cynical satire with which the Merchant has loaded the story. We need not respect him, for he no longer respects himself; but we cannot be angry. He is a stately and dignified personage, the last man from whom so furious an outburst would be expected; but his disillusion has been sudden and complete. Habitually cautious, both in word and act, he has played the fool by marrying the wrong woman, and, now that excitement loosens his tongue, he goes all lengths, for he is half-mad with rage and shame.

Let us not mistake the purpose of the Merchant's satire. May, the young wife, is not so much its object as the dotard January, who has not a single redeeming feature. Man's folly is the Merchant's text, rather than woman's frailty; and all the time he is really castigating himself. Yet the tale is also, in substance, another reply to the Wife of Bath and her heresies. It is as if one of her many husbands had come back to earth to confute her by giving his own side of the case. Above all things, we must avoid the error of those critics who treat the Merchant as if he were Chaucer. Here, if ever, it is vitally necessary to bear the drama in mind.

The Host is somewhat startled at the Merchant's story. His own wife, he is glad to say, is true as any steel, shrew though she may be. But he goes on jestingly to express, in strict confidence—with all the Pilgrims listening—his wish that he were out of wedlock bonds. He will not tell all his wife's faults, for fear some woman in the company may blab when they all get back to Southwark. Besides, his wit would not suffice. The list would "dizzy the arithmetic of memory." Obviously, Harry Bailly, too, is having his little fling at the Wife of Bath, who still holds the centre of the stage as the only begetter of the whole discussion.

* * *

The Franklin, like the Clerk before him, has a surprise ready for Harry Bailly and the Pilgrims. He resumes the debate on Matrimony, which had lapsed, to all appearances, with the Host's calling upon the Squire for a tale of love; and he not only resumes it, but carries it to a triumphant conclusion by solving the problem. He solves it, too, by an appeal to precisely that quality which he so much admires in the Squire, and which the Host has scoffed at him for mentioning—the quality of "gentillesse."

This procedure on the Franklin's part is manifestly deliberate; it is not accident, but belongs to Chaucer's plan.

The Franklin, as we have noted, feels a wistful interest in "gentillesse"—a delightful old term which includes culture, good breeding, and generous sentiments, or, to borrow Osric's words to Hamlet, "the continent of what part a gentleman would see." Naturally, therefore, he selects a story that illustrates this quality. It involves a graceful compliment to two of the Pilgrims who have held the stage in this act of Chaucer's Human Comedy, for the plot turns on the competing generosity of a husband (who is a knight), a lover (who is a squire), and a magician (who is a clerk), the appraisal of merit being left to the audience.

In itself, this tale, which is an old one, throws no light on the problem of sovereignty in marriage. At the outset, however, the Franklin makes a definite application. Arveragus, a noble knight of Brittany, wins the love of the lady Dorigen, who "takes him for her husband and her lord." Out of pure gentillesse, he promises that he will never assert his authority after they are married, but will continue to be her humble servant, as a lover ought to be to his lady. In return for this gentillesse, Dorigen vows never to abuse her sway, but to be his true and obedient wife. Thus the married lovers dwell together in perfect accord, each deferring to the other, and neither claiming the sovereignty; and it is this relation of mutual love and forbearance, the outcome of gentillesse, that carries them safely through the entanglements of the plot and preserves their wedded happiness unimpaired as long as they live.

Love and marriage, according to the courtly system, were held to be incompatible, since marriage involves mastery on the husband's part, and mastery drives out love. * * * This theory the Franklin utterly repudiates. In true marriage, he argues, there should be no assertion of sovereignty on either side. Love must be the controlling principle,— perfect, gentle love, which brings forbearance with it. Such is his solution of the whole problem, and thus he concludes the long debate begun by that jovial heresiarch, the Wife of Bath. [Here Kittredge quotes ll. 760–805 of the Franklin's Tale.]

* * *

There is no mistaking Chaucer's purpose in this, the final scene of that act of the Canterbury Pilgrimage which deals with the problem of husband and wife. He does not allow the Franklin to tell a tale without a moral expressed and to leave the application to our powers of inference. On the contrary, the Franklin's discussion of the subject is both definite and compendious. It extends to nearly a hundred lines, without a particle of verbiage, and occupies a conspicuous position at the very beginning of the story, so that the tale is utilized to illustrate and enforce the principle. And in the course of this discussion the

Franklin alludes, in a way that cannot have escaped his fellow-travellers, to the Wife of Bath's harangue on the thraldom of husbands, to the patience of Griselda and the theories of the Marquis Walter as described by the Clerk of Oxford, and to the grimly ironical praise of wedlock which makes lurid the frenzied satire of the disillusioned Merchant. It is clear, therefore, that Chaucer means us to regard the Franklin as "knitting up the matter," as summarizing the whole debate and bringing it to a definitive conclusion which we are to accept as a perfect rule of faith and practice.

In assigning to the Franklin this supremely important office, Chaucer acted with his usual perspicacity. Marriage, when all is said and done, is an affair of practical life. Theorists may talk about it,—divines, philosophers, men of law, harpers harping with their harps, —but we listen with a certain skepticism when they take high ground, or shut their eyes to the weakness of human nature. To the Franklin, on the contrary, we lend a credent ear. He is no cloistered rhetorician, but a ruddy, white-bearded vavasour, a great man in his neighborhood, fond of the good things of life and famous for his lavish hospitality. He has been sheriff of his county and Member of Parliament, and is perpetual presiding justice at the sessions of the peace. Such a man lies under no suspicion of transcendental theorism or vague heroics. When *he* speaks of mutual forbearance and perfect gentle love between husband and wife, we listen with conviction. The thing is possible. The problem need puzzle us no longer.

> Who koude telle, but he hadde wedded be,
> The joye, the ese, and the prosperitee
> That is bitwixe an housbonde and his wyf? [803–05]

* * *

LEE PATTERSON

From The *Parson's Tale* and the Quitting of the *Canterbury Tales*†

* * *

In closing the *Canterbury Tales* with a work of this generality [i.e., the *Parson's Tale*], * * * Chaucer forces us to look beyond the specific world that has so far occupied our attention. He concludes, in other words, with something of the same dismissive withdrawal to a higher, more inclusive perspective as occurs at the end of the *Troilus*. In both cases Chaucer himself emerges at the end, replacing the narratorial voice, dramatic, engaging, and multivalent, with his own identifiably

† Pp. 370–80 of "The *Parson's Tale* and the Quitting of the *Canterbury Tales*," *Traditio* 34 (1978): 331–80. Reprinted with permission of Fordham University Press. We have renumbered the notes and in some cases added publication information provided earlier in the article.

historical tone. In the *Troilus* he invokes the judgment of his friends Gower and Strode and in the *Canterbury Tales* he provides us with an account of his past and a promise for the future. The effect of this gradual withdrawal from fiction to history is to devalue fiction, and the specific reductions occasioned by these endings are in effect extensions of the larger reduction implied by the form itself. The elaborately contrived fictional world is brought into contact with a reality, both divine and human, which exposes simply by its presence the factitiousness of what has preceded it. The effect, then, is not to invite a reinterpretation or even revaluation of the fiction but to declare it transcended. Having once been granted his vision of the insignificance of earth, Troilus can hardly return, and the certainties of the *Parson's Tale* render the complexities of the tales inconsequential and even sophistical. Indeed, to argue that the Parson's view of human character provides the standard by which we should measure what we have just read is to encourage us to reread precisely that which Chaucer now dismisses as unworthy.

Yet while the *Parson's Tale* issues into the clear light of reality it takes its beginning in the imprecision of fiction, and it is itself a part of the whole it dismisses. This is the paradox the Parson himself expresses when he promises to 'telle a myrie tale in prose' that will 'knytte up al this feeste, and make an ende' (46–47). On the one hand, the *Parson's Prologue* stands securely within the limited dramatic world of the pilgrimage; but on the other, despite its air of agreeable consensus, it radically redefines the nature of the taletelling itself. As the sun descends and the shadows lengthen the Host moves confidently toward the completion, oddly enough, not of the journey but of the tale-telling game he has initiated and presided over:

> Lordynges everichoon,
> Now lakketh us no tales mo than oon.
> Fulfilled is my sentence and my decree;
> I trowe that we han herd of ech degree;
> Almoost fulfild is al myn ordinaunce.   (15–19)

The note of self-satisfaction is clearly heard here, and it is continued in his direction to the final participant in the game. 'Be what thou be, ne breke thou nat our pley' (24), he warns him, and advises him that in order to 'knytte up wel a greet mateere' he should 'Telle us a fable anoon' (28–29). In rejecting fables the Parson rejects more than the Ovidian form chosen by the Manciple and more than the 'gesta, poemata vel fabulas extra corpus scripturae' [stories, verses or fables outside Scripture] that (according to Wyclif) infected the popular preaching of the day.[1] He rejects both the Host's game and its tales,

---

1. On *fabula* as designating specifically a beast fable, see Vincent of Beauvais, *Speculum doctrinale* 3.113 in *Bibliotheca Mundi* (Douai 1624) II col. 289; and Bromyard, *Summa praedicantium* 6.14 (Antwerp 1614). Wyclif's strictures are quoted by H. Simon in 'Chaucer a Wycliffite: An Essay on Chaucer's Parson and *Parson's Tale*,' *Essays on Chaucer* Part 3 (Chaucer Society, 2nd series 16; London 1876), 239.

the *fabulae Chauceri*, as one manuscript labels them.[2] The Parson invokes Paul's exhortation to Timothy: 'preach the word, be urgent in season and out of season, convince, rebuke, and exhort, be unfailing in patience and in teaching. For the time is coming when people will not endure sound teaching'—*sanam doctrinam*, the Parson's 'moralitee and vertuous mateere' (38)—'but having itching ears they will accumulate for themselves teachers to suit their own likings, and will turn away from listening to the truth and wander into myths [*fabulas*]. As for you, always be steady, endure suffering, do the work of an evangelist, fulfil your ministry' (2 Timothy 4.2–5). When the Host proposed the tale-telling game in the *General Prologue* he presented it as a pastime 'to shorte with oure weye' (791), a means of 'confort' and 'myrthe' (773) to while away the journey. Far from an extension or expression of the pilgrimage, the tale-telling is in fact an alternative, a distraction from both the tedium of the journey and, inevitably and even deliberately, its significance. As we approach the end the Host is proud of the fulfillment of 'my sentence and my decree,' of 'al myn ordinaunce.' But as he fails to realize, this completion is possible only because the tale-telling has been simply 'pley,' a game that is by definition enclosed and delimited. The Parson rightly understands that their journey is linear and not circular, and that it extends further than they can easily see, into a darkness of which the approaching night is a mere symbol. In its ultimate terms, the opposition between Host and Parson is between literalist and symbolist, between an attitude that accepts the here and now as a sufficient reality and one that perceives human experience as only the foreground to a larger horizon. In literary terms it is an opposition between *fabulae* and *sana doctrina*, and between two concepts of form: an additive, self-generating, and almost extemporaneous seriality on the one hand, and on the other a carefully organized action with beginning, middle, and end.[3]

Everybody agrees that the *Canterbury Tales* has a coherent beginning and end, but the large, undistributed middle remains to challenge the ingenuity of the exegete. Any reading that presents the tales as providing, as a recent writer puts it, 'most of all a way of expressing the developing pilgrimage,' is compromised by several unavoidable facts.[4] First, it is not enough to show that there is a beginning, middle, and end, to all of which the concept of pilgrimage is relevant, since it is indeed relevant to all medieval action. Rather, we must show how the middle develops from the beginning and requires the end: we can go from A to Z easily enough, but how are all the other letters to be fitted into their appropriate order? To my knowledge, nobody has even attempted this kind of progressive reading of the tales; but if one is to

2. See John Norton-Smith, *Geoffrey Chaucer* (London 1974), 146.
3. These two kinds of medieval narrative form are discussed by Charles Singleton, 'Meaning in the *Decameron*,' *Italica* 21 (1944): 117–24; in *The Unity of the* Canterbury Tales (*Anglistica* 5; Copenhagen 1955), Ralph Baldwin discusses Singleton's distinction in relation to the *Canterbury Tales* and attempts to see the pilgrimage frame as providing a *sovrasenso* equivalent to that of the *Divine Comedy*.
4. The phrase is used by Edmund Reiss, 'The Pilgrimage Narrative and the *Canterbury Tales*,' *Studies in Philology* 67 (1970): 295–305.

argue that they are meaningful primarily ('most of all') in terms of pilgrimage, then this timely and specific relevance must be demonstrated.[5] Second, a reading that invokes the pilgrimage metaphor as continuously relevant must confront the fact that it is never explicitly invoked throughout the tales. It is present at the beginning of the *General Prologue*, momentarily in Egeus' speech in the *Knight's Tale*, and in the *Parson's Prologue and Tale*, but it is absent from everything in between. Professor Donaldson is surely right when he reminds us that the medieval reader would have been most struck by Chaucer's 'avoidance throughout most of the Canterbury Tales of the expected implications of the pilgrimage.'[6] For Chaucer's poem bears only an oblique relationship to pilgrimage allegories such as Deguileville's *Pèlerinage de la vie humaine* or Jean de Coucy's *Chemin de vaillance*, and to describe the *Canterbury Tales* as 'linked a priori to the great body of pilgrimage literature written during the late Middle Ages'[7] is to allow one contingent and carefully limited theme to become the sole determinant of genre.[8] It would of course be excessive on the other side to say that the pilgrimage theme is irrelevant. One of the major differences between Chaucer's formal conception and those of Boccaccio and Sercambi is that Chaucer's travellers are not simply wandering in an effort to escape from reality but actually journeying toward it. But the tale-telling game in which they engage is in a radical way opposed to the concerns of their journey. Indeed, that the game comes so near to completion is a testimony to the success with which the meaning of the pilgrimage has been repressed throughout.

The degree of this repression can be gauged by recalling how narrow is the scope granted to the tales of 'moralitee and devocioun' in the course of the narrative. The narrator's division of the tales into 'sentence' and 'solaas,' despite its limitations, has the advantage of sorting out Chaucer's complicated blendings of *utile dulci* [profit and pleasure] into opposed categories. The serious tales of the Knight, Man of Law, Clerk, Physician, Prioress, Monk, and Second Nun, and the *Tale of Melibee*, provide not merely recreation for those sophisticated enough to enjoy them but absolutes that are uplifting and urgent. They present to their audience imperatives that go beyond appreciation to self-scrutiny and moral action. In this sense, each of the serious tales is at odds with the holiday mood that is the context and foundation of the tale-telling, and much of the *Canterbury Tales* is concerned with disarming this threat to its continuance. Hence we

5. Paul Ruggiers, 'The Form of The Canterbury Tales: Respice Fines,' *College English* 17 (1956): 439–44, does discuss the relevance of the *Knight's Tale* and the *Man of Law's Tale* as providing, respectively, a philosophical and religious guide for the pilgrimage, with the *Parson's Tale* then as a final admonition to those who have not followed this advice and have gone astray; see also his comments in *The Art of the Canterbury Tales* (Madison 1965), 5–11, 247–57. There are many discussions of the appropriateness of beginning with the classical values of the *Knight's Tale*, e.g., Joseph Westlund, 'The *Knight's Tale* as an Impetus for Pilgrimage,' *Philological Quarterly* 43 (1964): 526–37.
6. *Chaucer's Poetry* (2nd ed.; New York, 1975), 1113.
7. Reiss 297.
8. In responding to Reiss's article, Siegfried Wenzel, 'The Pilgrimage of Life as a Late Medieval Genre,' *Mediaeval Studies* 35 (1973): 370–88, discusses these, and other, pilgrimage allegories and shows to just how substantial a degree Chaucer's poem differs from them.

should notice that the serious tales are never allowed to impose their tone or perspective upon the pilgrimage but are consistently countered and limited.

The most obvious instances of this limitation are the refusals by the comic characters to allow the sober Knight and Man of Law to be followed by the equally sober Monk and Parson. These interruptions are perhaps judgment enough, but a finally more telling critique is provided by the new and severely limiting contexts which the interjected comic tales establish for their dour predecessors. This limitation is enforced by the narrative strategy of the *Canterbury Tales* itself: the inclusion of the teller with the tale personalizes the meanings that emerge and encourages a dramatic reading that discounts any authoritative significance. The Truth that each teller labors to express is rendered simply as an individual truth or the truth for an individual. The total effect, then, of the *Miller's Tale* on the Knight's is to suggest that the Knight's Boethian wisdom is as much a function of his class consciousness as are his preferred ways of making love and war. Similarly, while the uncertainties of order make it difficult to provide the same context for the *Man of Law's Tale*, it is easy enough to see how the faithless wife of the *Shipman's Tale* or the Wife of Bath herself provides a sufficient foil for the otherworldly Constance. Further, in reinvoking the dominant dramatic and psychological mode of the *Tales* either of these succeeding tales serves to foreground the unseemly personal qualities of the Man of Law that have been allowed a presence in his tale. The same kind of deflation and even satiric dismissal is brought to bear upon the Physician, Prioress, and Monk, whose personalities stand in awkward contrast to their proffered values and indecorously intrude into their tales. Finally, the *Second Nun's Tale*, while secure in its anonymity, is revealed as providing at best only a partial antidote to the problem of sloth and despair when set next to the hectic confession of the Canon's Yeoman; and the *Clerk's Tale*, by far the most assured of Chaucer's creations in this mode, carries an epilogue that ironically limits its relevance. In sum, the *Canterbury Tales* provides various prospects on and versions of the truth, but no one is allowed authority or even an unchallenged assertion. Indeed it seems that truth fares best when, as in the *Nun's Priest's Tale*, it is pared down to the limitations of a proverb and hidden within the sharp perspectives of irony.

While this circumscription of the serious and the demanding is characteristic of Chaucer's urbane good humor, it also implies an unorthodox and even subversive poetics. The full range of medieval literary theory can hardly be dealt with on this occasion, but we should note that Chaucer's poetic practice more often reflects the internally determined values of a rhetorical poetics than the external strategies prescribed by the allegorists. As the exegete discovers when he tries to specify the full meaning of a Chaucerian poem, Chaucerian *sententiae* are less the conclusion which all the elements of the text express than occasions for writing which the complexities of the text rapidly transcend. Theme figures as only one element among many, not the *res* [things, realities] which the *verba* [words] labor to express but a ground of significance upon which the variables of fable, personality, and language display themselves. Like the Pardoner's sermon, Chaucer's poems use traditional truths as *themae* upon which to play variations, and we can no more define the significance of the whole by reference to its rhetorical origins than we can say that the *Pardoner's Tale* means *radix malorum est cupiditas* [avarice is the root of all evil; see *PardT* 333–34]. When located within a rhetorical perspective, then, the *Canterbury Tales* reveals itself not as a progression toward a goal—parts that signify a unifying whole—but as a series of poetic experiments in various styles, a witty compendium of late medieval literary fashion embellished with the appropriate personalities.

Indeed, not only does the progressive and coherent form of the pilgrimage frame not extend to the inner organization of the tales, but the form this great, undistributed middle *does* display is minimal, additive, and arbitrary. It is a form required by the tale-telling game; the Host, in his role of *magister ludi*, defines it as *quitting* (I.3119). Its workings are demonstrated in Fragment I: Miller quits Knight, Reeve quits Miller, Cook (presumably) quits Reeve, but not before warning the Host, 'But er we parte, ywis, thou shalt be quit' (4362) in turn. The form is thus one of the most common of medieval narrative structures, bipartition or binarism.[9] The tales proceed two-by-two, and a mere listing of the pairs (appropriately annotated) is sufficient to indicate the binary form: Man of Law/Wife of Bath; Friar/Summoner; Wife of Bath/Clerk; Clerk/Merchant; Squire/Franklin; Physician/Pardoner; Shipman/Prioress; *Tale of Sir Thopas/Tale of Melibee*; Monk/Nun's Priest; Second Nun/Canon's Yeoman; Manciple/Parson.[1]

9. An account of the bipartite or 'diptych' form, with examples, is provided by William W. Ryding, *Structure in Medieval Narrative* (The Hague 1971): 116–137. Donald Howard, *The Idea of the Canterbury Tales* (Berkeley 1976), 224–25, 322–24, discusses binary structure, with interesting comments on its source in the relationship of the Old to the New Testament. It is worth remembering that the single most important source for the *Canterbury Tales*, the *Roman de la Rose*, is itself binary, the second part functioning as a revision and hence a gloss on the first: Jean de Meun promises 'si la chose espondre / que riens ne s'i porra repondre' [to explain the matter so that none of it can stay concealed] (10573–574); ed. Félix Lecoy (CFMA 95; Paris 1966), II 72.

1. My list assumes the Ellesmere order, convincingly defended by E. Talbot Donaldson, 'The Ordering of the *Canterbury Tales*,' in *Medieval Literature and Folklore Studies: Essays in Honor of Francis Lee Utley*, ed. Jerome Mandel and Bruce A. Rosenberg (New Brunswick 1970), 193–204; but it can easily be accommodated to the Bradshaw shift. Indeed, nothing could more tellingly demonstrate the absence of a coherent, sequential order in the tales than the fact that readers are still arguing about the proper placement of over 3000 lines. What other masterpiece could survive such uncertainty? The point is that the different placements require only local adjustments, i.e., they make no difference to the total meaning of the poem because the 'poem' has no total meaning. Hence Donaldson is right to argue that the question of order is properly an editorial one, and to opt for Ellesmere because it has greater manuscript authority.

The thematic connections between the Man of Law and the Wife of Bath have often been discussed: see, e.g., Lee Sheriden Cox, 'A Question of Order in the *Canterbury Tales*,' *Chaucer Review* 1 (1966–67): 228–52. More important is the formal pairing: these two tales are the first of four pairs that are generically linked by the pattern of hagiography and confession, the other three being Clerk/Merchant, Physician/Pardoner and Second Nun/Canon's Yeoman. For discussions of this pattern in the last pair of the sequence, see Joseph E. Grennen, 'Saint Cecillia's "Chemical Wedding": The Unity of the *Canterbury Tales*, Fragment VIII,' *Journal of English and Germanic Philology* 65 (1966): 466–81, and Bruce A. Rosenberg, 'The Contrary Tales of the Second Nun and the Canon's Yeoman,' *Chaucer Review* 2 (1967–68): 278–91. Of the other pairs listed, the only problematical one is

Certainly larger thematic patterns exist, but in relying upon binarism for his basic narrative structure Chaucer reduces form to a bare minimum. Indeed, as the tales proceed even the use to which this form is put is simplified. Fragment I displays a relatively sophisticated use, in which the second member of each pair provides the first member of the next (Knight/Miller, Miller/Reeve), and this pattern is repeated, with an interruption, in Fragments II–IV: Man of Law/Wife of Bath, Wife of Bath/Clerk, Clerk/Merchant. Is the *Franklin's Tale* then the conclusion to the Marriage Group? Perhaps, but the Franklin is in the first instance responding to the Squire, a tale-teller who has, his gracious opponent admits, 'yquit' himself well (V.673).[2] The quitting pattern is thus explicitly reinvoked in Fragment V, and from then on the binary form continues in its simplest mode. It is the *first instance* that is crucial: the binary pattern provides Chaucer with a clearly defined structure upon which to play variations, but it also enforces the discreteness of each pair and so foregrounds their merely sequential relationship. Tied to each other, they look inward rather than out to the tales as a whole. As our reading proceeds, then, the variations fall away to reveal the repetitive pattern beneath. Uncontrolled by any larger purpose, there is no reason the pattern should not repeat itself endlessly, extending itself even beyond the one hundred and twenty tales envisioned by the Host: any ending is arbitrary for a form that is merely additive. The form itself, in other words, is no more meaningful than the ten-by-ten scheme of the *Decameron*. Nor should we expect it to be: the rules of every game are arbitrary.[3]

The Parson's final contribution to the game is thus a formal alternative that in effect renders the game unplayable: the monolithic articulation of his *summa* reveal how inconsequent and even random are the self-generated oppositions of the tales. But there are compensations, for it is only by such an interruption that the tales can be brought to any conclusion. The Parson destroys the poem, in other words, in order to release the poet from his fiction-making, to turn him finally from shadows to reality. The beneficence the Parson offers can be fully appreciated only when we recognize how persistently Chaucer has asked the moral questions raised by his kind of poetry, and how persistently he has refused to answer them. Of course poetry can never tell the truth in quite the way that the allegorical literary theory of Chaucer's day prescribed, and his conventionalized gestures toward authenticity, whether moral or historical, are more appeasements of this expectation than real claims to truthfulness.[4] The traditional justifications are of-

the Shipman/Prioress, a difficulty that arises, I suppose, because of the incompleteness of the revisions. For the Squire/Franklin, see below, n. 2.

2. For this linking of Squire and Franklin, see Harry Berger, Jr., 'The F-Fragment of the *Canterbury Tales*,' *Chaucer Review* 1 (1966–67): 88–102, 135–56.

3. The reader will have noticed that the brevity of my discussion has allowed me to beg several important questions. The most recent and most ambitious attempt to demonstrate that a premeditated and fully articulated form lies 'behind' the *Canterbury Tales* is Donald Howard's *The Idea of the Canterbury Tales*; I have offered a fuller critique of this project, both particularly and in general, in the *University of Toronto Quarterly* 48 (1978–9).

4. As Robert O. Payne, *The Key of Remembrance: A Study of Chaucer's Poetics* (New Haven 1963), has shown, Chaucer is fascinated with the relation of poetry to scientific and moral

fered but they are never pressed home, for Chaucer's unwillingness to
define a poetics that is anything more than *ad hoc* is a prerequisite for
his most striking formal innovations. But it leaves him vulnerable to
moralistic attacks, such as that which (as Alfred David has shown) lies
behind the autobiographical comments in the *Man of Law's Prologue*.[5]
Chaucer's response to these Gower-like criticisms is typically delimited.
Rather than providing a comprehensive defense of his stylistic eclecti-
cism and complex *modus significandi*, Chaucer is content with an *ad
hominem* and local victory. He gently parodies Gower in the fussy
moral narrowness of the Man of Law and then out-Gowers Gower by
retelling, more effectively, one of his opponent's own stories. This is not
a defense, in short, but an avoidance of attack, and the problem of the
morality of Chaucer's kind of poetry remains unresolved. It is raised
again, in a particularly telling form, by the *Manciple's Tale*. Indeed, the
Manciple prepares for the Parson not just by rehearsing one of the fables the Parson is going to reject but by casting doubt upon the whole
poetic enterprise. Superficially, his tale is simply a bitter commentary
on the contretemps of his prologue: the crow is to Phoebus as he himself is to the Cook. Just as he was rebuffed in his attempt to admonish
a public drunkard, so the crow is a truth-teller who is punished for
his honesty. The concluding litany of homely saws and proverbial
wisdom serves then as the Manciple's mocking celebration of the
trimmer's motto that silence is the best policy. The disdain and self-
regard of his rebuke to the Cook, mirrored in the tale by the crow's
cruelly elaborate account to Phoebus of his wife's adultery, allows
the reader to see the Manciple's pose as an injured moralist in an ironic
light. But the severity of the charge implicitly levelled against poetry
is not diminished by the Manciple's own moral inadequacy. On the
contrary, the *Manciple's Prologue and Tale* provides a bitter parody
of the tale-telling game. The festivity in which it began and by which
it has been sustained has by this time degenerated into the Bacchic
excesses of the Cook, and the balancing pressure of a larger vision,
never granted its full scope throughout the course of the tales, is
now reduced to the querulous cynicism of the Manciple.[6] Further,
the Manciple implicitly calls into question the artful use of language it-

---

wisdom, to dreams, and to experience itself. But none of these relationships is anything less
than complex and ambiguous, and in no case does the poem resolve itself into one pole of
the dialectic. At the end of the *General Prologue*, for instance, the narrator defends the salty
language he is going to use by reference to the demands of *mimesis* (731–36). Far from being a statement of theoretical intent, however, this passage is in fact a way of assuring a
courtly audience that the bourgeois literature they are about to enjoy is authentic and grati-
fyingly vulgar. Chaucer is asserting not a realistic relationship of life to literature but defining the relation of one form of literature to another. Similarly local purposes are served by
the other quasi-theoretical statements in the *Canterbury Tales*. The Physician's boast that
the tale of Virginia 'is no fable, / But knowen for historical thyng notable' (155–56) is part of
his larger effort at self-authorization; and when the Second Nun says that she is simply
recording 'the wordes and sentence / Of hym that at the seintes reverence / The storie wroot'
(81–83) she is defining a stance of spiritual humility rather than a poetics relevant to
Chaucer, as the subtlety and elegance of the tale suggest.
5. 'The Man of Law vs. Chaucer: A Case in Poetics,' *Publications of the Modern Language Association* 82 (1967): 217–25.
6. Norton-Smith, 150–51, connects the Cook to Bacchus, but sees the relationship as wholly
comic. As a further link, see the passage quoted by Pamela Gradon, *Form and Style in Early
English Literature* (London 1971), 54, from Holcot, *In Librum Sapientiae*: 'Someone feigns

self.[7] His tale is a set of evasions that offers an opinion only to withdraw it and that mouths moralisms but remains in fact deeply cynical. He asserts with harsh realism that man is dominated by an animal nature, but the only redemption he offers is expediency dressed as integrity—the verbal equivalent to the wine with which the Cook is put back to sleep and a version of the poetic encomium by which the self-deluded Phoebus reconciles himself to the wife he has murdered. In sum, the Manciple's refusal to give a serious answer to the complex moral issues raised by his tale stands as a dark parody of Chaucer's dispassionate withdrawal from assertion, and we are invited to see in the cynical Manciple a sour self-portrait of the ironic poet.[8]

These doubts about the moral integrity of poetic language have been raised throughout the *Canterbury Tales*. The dismissal of the tales that the *Parson's Tale* effects consists not merely in the reduction of the rich complexity of personality to seven types of misbehavior, nor in the transcendence of the various truths of the preceding tales with an authoritative Truth. Rather, by choosing as his final work a treatise on confession Chaucer redefines in an irremediable way the very act of speaking. Poetic speech in its largest definition, as the artful use of language, is the most general target of this redefinition, and the *Manciple's Tale* exists precisely to present poetic speech in its most morally offensive form. But there is as well a more local target, specific to the *Canterbury Tales*, in the self-expressiveness that runs through the tales and that in characters such as the Wife of Bath, Pardoner, and Canon's Yeoman becomes virtually confessional.[9] While the degree of this self-expressiveness is a matter of critical dispute, the very form of the narrative forces the issue upon us. By including within his poem the tellers as well as their tales, Chaucer manages to achieve the same poetic range as in his dream visions: the total meaning of each tale extends beyond its narrative to include its relationship with its teller, just as the experience of the poet-dreamer provides a crucial element of the total significance of those poems. To some extent, then, each of the tales is self-expressive, and it is this process of self-expression that the *Parson's Tale* serves to redefine. For his sober and prosaic treatise is a rejection of all personal speaking that does not confront, in

the image of Drunkenness to have been thus depicted, the image of a child, having in his hand a horn and on his head a crown of [vine]. He was a boy in token that (drunkenness) makes a man speechless and senseless, in the manner of a child. He had a horn in his hand as a token that (the drunken man) conceals no secret but reveals (it) with clamour and clangour. He has a [vine] crown, because he considers himself glorious and wealthy, he who is drunk, whereas he has nothing.'

7. V. J. Scattergood, 'The Manciple's Manner of Speaking,' *Essays in Criticism* 24 (1974): 124–46.

8. Scattergood points out the parallel between the Manciple as a servant to lawyers and Chaucer as patronized by the court, and adds: 'Chaucer is particularly interested in the Manciple because the Manciple's way of using words bears some relation to the strategies he himself uses as a poet' (143).

9. See my 'Chaucerian Confession: Penitential Literature and the Pardoner,' *Medievalia et Humanistica* 7 (1976): 153–73, and Lawrence V. Ryan, 'The Canon's Yeoman's Desperate Confession,' *Chaucer Review* 8 (1973–74): 297–310. The paratactic and digressive style in which these confessional prologues are couched provides a paradigm for the form of the *Canterbury Tales* as a whole, and, as the extent of the critical literature suggests, the Wife of Bath and Pardoner express literary values that are recognized as quintessentially Chaucerian.

the sacramental language of penance, the sinfulness of the human condition. It is not merely the qualifying complexities of the personality that are to be abandoned, but any language that does not deal with sin in the terms defined by the Parson. 'Why sholde I sowen draf out of my fest, / Whan I may sowen whete, if that me lest?' (35–36): his question draws its authority less from medieval arguments about the validity of literature than from its immediate context, the shadows that lengthen about him. The tales were told as a pastime to 'shorte with the weye,' but now the time has passed and the way must be attended to. So the Parson redefines not only the journey but the tale-telling itself: he gives not so much directions to the heavenly Jerusalem as the prior and more radical knowledge that 'this viage' itself, the specific journey to Canterbury, can be so undertaken that it can itself become a 'parfit glorious pilgrymage,' a pilgrimage that does not merely lead to but in fact constitutes—'is highte'—'Jerusalem celestial.' And for this to happen the various voices of the tales must give way to the penitential speaking defined by the Parson.

It is necessary, then, that the *Parson's Tale* should provide not a fulfillment to the tales but an alternative, a complete and exclusive understanding of character, action, and even language. But in concluding we must return to the paradox in which the tale is grounded. If it cancels out rather than completes that which precedes, its position at once enforces and weakens its authority. His tale takes its origin in the very dramatic and realistic context which it will dismiss, and it is a denial of the tale-telling game that in the first instance quits the Manciple. In sum, while the Parson has the last word he must wait until last to say it, and although the transcendence of his message is never in doubt he must wait until the imperfect and even immoral expressions of merely verbal art have been passed in review. Chaucer and the pilgrims have it both ways, but this should lead us to question neither their nor Chaucer's sincerity. The evidence is that the *Parson's Tale* was written late in the poet's career, and there seems no reason not to accept the obvious biographical implication that it was his last work. Furthermore, its very nature is terminal. It begins within the fictional construct but becomes the tale to end all tales, and its conclusion inevitably escapes from the narrative frame and now refers to the larger context of biography. The tale becomes not simply the last element of a sustained poetic enterprise but a crucial and even decisive piece of evidence about the moral worth of Chaucer himself. As the *licentia auctoris* [authorial license] informs us, it is to be measured by the standards not of literary fame but of eternal salvation. Indeed, the *Parson's Tale* itself shows Chaucer already beginning to respond to these new imperatives. The writing of an edifying treatise as an act of penance is a not uncommon medieval habit. Chaucer would certainly have known the treatise on *The Two Ways* written by his friend Sir John Clanvowe just before he died in 1391, and would probably also have been familiar with *Le Livre de seyntz medicines* by Henry, Duke of Lancaster, written in 1354. Both the *licentia* and the medieval habit of the repentance of old age encourage us to see the *Parson's Tale* as another instance of literary penance. This is a penance that is neither perfunctory, as the care with which the tale is composed suggests, nor unexpected. Rather it is a part of the fitting shape of the Christian life, hardly a hypocritical *volte-face* but an inevitable and gratifying process of change and fulfillment. 'Young devil, old saint' runs one of the proverbs that express this conception, and its cynicism is tempered with a benign assurance that each man's history is concluded with a reversal that is both fulfillment and justification. It is in this radically linear awareness of the range of human action in its response to divine requirements that we should locate the paradox of a tale that can at once 'knytte up al this feeste, and make an ende.'

PAUL STROHM

From *Social Chaucer*:
"A Mixed Commonwealth of Style"†

A Literary Model of Social Diversity

* * *

A special property of the *Canterbury Tales* is the extent to which its generic and stylistic variety is couched in polyvocality, in its embrace of separate and distinctive voices as a means of asserting social difference. Chaucer's poetry was always polyphonic, permitting the juxtaposition of separate themes and generic structures within the external form of a given work, but it becomes increasingly polyvocalic in its capacity to contain unreconciled voices as we move from the avian disputants of the *Parliament* to the distinctive and ultimately incompatible voices of Troilus and Pandarus and Criseyde to the yet fuller degree of autonomy assigned to the diverse Canterbury speakers. The Canterbury tales are richly polyphonic *and* polyvocalic, in the sense that, like medieval music, they pursue autonomous lines of development, and in the twentieth-century sense that they remain independent and unmerged. The principal theorist of this latter sense is of course Bakhtin, who argues that the precondition for true polyphony is that its voices are never subject to dialectical resolution, but remain unmerged in "unceasing and irreconcilable quarrel."[1] Chaucer critics

† From *Social Chaucer*, by Paul Strohm (Cambridge, Massachusetts: Harvard University Press, 1989), pp. 168–9, 171–78, 179–82, 225–27. Copyright © 1989 by the President and Fellows of Harvard College. Reprinted by permission of the publisher. This selection is from the chapter titled "A Mixed Commonwealth of Style." We have renumbered the notes, with some additions to and subtractions from them.
1. *Problems of Dostoevsky's Poetics* (Minneapolis: U of Minnesota P, 1984), p. 30. Bakhtin would restrict total polyvocality, in which "every thought" is represented as "the position of a personality" (p. 9) to the capitalist era (pp. 20–21), and he may be correct in this most rigorous application of his term. But, even while recognizing that many passages of the *Canterbury Tales* bear meanings that cannot be attributed to their imaginary speakers, I would nevertheless argue for the general applicability of his concept to works by Chaucer, Langland, and other pre-nineteenth-century authors.

have long appreciated the senses in which his commitment to autonomous voices inspires debate, though critics of an earlier day
regarded the principal debates of the *Canterbury Tales* as subject to
dialectical resolution.[2] In recent years critics have moved to embrace more fully the concept of Chaucer's polyphony, as defined both
by medieval practice and modern theory, and his poetry is now characterized by such terms as "contrastive," "exploratory," a repository of
"partial truths," "pluralistic," "inconclusive," "plurivalent," and "disjunctive."[3]

Rather than repeating the work of the many critics who have set out
to demonstrate the polyphonic presuppositions of the *Canterbury
Tales*,[4] I wish instead to pose a related question: in what sense is
Chaucer's commitment to polyvocality *itself* a socially significant gesture? I have asserted that the stylistic and generic variety sustained by
Chaucer's varied speakers is a figure for social variety, within the more
conciliatory sphere of literary language, and Bakhtin's own description
of polyphony in Dostoevsky's novels specifies the dynamics of this
process. Bakhtin argues that Dostoevsky's polyphony is a refraction,
through available literary possibilities, of the "contradictory multi-
leveledness" of his own society. He argues that, had Dostoevsky perceived multi-leveledness as residing only in the human spirit, he could
have created an ultimately monologic novel that took as its subject the
contradictory evolution of the human spirit; instead, since he found
multi-leveledness in the objective social world, he brought it into his
novels as an equivalent for irreducible social contradiction.[5] Bakhtin
here points to the possibility of an ultimately monologic portrayal of
diversity, as opposed to a portrayal of diversity that is polyphonic
through and through and could not have been otherwise because of
divisions in the author's experience of society. The *Canterbury Tales* is,
I believe, polyphonic in this latter sense, and the polyphony is bound
up in its identity as a social text.

* * *

Helen Cooper describes Chaucer's "house of fiction" as one that offers vantages through various windows, each presenting a perspective
peculiar to a particular genre and each with its own partial truth,[6] and
her metaphor is apt in its emphasis on Chaucer's rejection of a single,
univalent "truth" and preference for truths embodied in multiple
voices. This is not to say that the claims of different Canterbury narratives to validity go unchallenged. The Wife of Bath's inversion of tradi-

---

2. Especially in the influential formulation of G. L. Kittredge, who believed the *Franklin's Tale*
to propose a solution with which "the whole debate has been brought to a satisfactory conclusion." "Chaucer's Discussion of Marriage," *MP* (1911–12): 467.
3. See Helen Cooper, *The Structure of the Canterbury Tales* (London: Duckworth, 1983), pp.
54–55; Larry Sklute, *Virtue of Necessity: Inconclusiveness and Narrative Form in Chaucer's
Poetry* (Columbus: Ohio State U, 1984), pp. 3–12; Jesse M. Gellrich, *The Idea of the Book
in the Middle Ages* (Ithaca: Cornell UP, 1985), pp. 213–14.
4. For example, those critics listed in the previous note, together with David A. Lawton,
Chaucer's Narrators (Cambridge: D. S. Brewer, 1985), and Paul Strohm, "Form and Social
Statement in *Confessio Amantis* and the *Canterbury Tales*," *SAC*, 1 (1979): 17–40.
5. Bakhtin, *Dostoevsky's Poetics*, p. 27.
6. Cooper, p. 55.

tional authority is promptly challenged by the Clerk's reassertion of
the necessity for submissiveness, the Merchant's disenchanted account of an abuse of human trust is promptly challenged by the
Franklin's assertion of human trustworthiness to do the right thing
once freed of sterile agreements. But, just as no claims are permitted
to stand unchallenged, so is no claim—however overidealized on the
one hand or jaundiced on the other—presented to us as devoid of any
truth at all. The polyphonic work is, as Bakhtin has reminded us, "dialogic through and through,"[7] and it is grounded not simply in a per-
verse human nature that refuses to recognize transcendent truth, but
in an experience of a society constituted by various groups, each with
its own version of reality.

Like Bakhtin's Dostoevsky, Chaucer may be viewed as having "par-
ticipated in the contradictory multi-leveledness of his own time,"[8] and
the form of his work as the expression of a socially determined view
that presupposes irreconcilable difference. The form of the *Canterbury Tales* is not, of course, to be regarded as a direct reflection of a
society riven by faction and socially based disagreement, but rather as
a mediation of that view. "Mediation" is here taken not in its most traditional Marxist sense, in which the contradictions inherent in a given
situation are restated at different cultural levels with added conceal-
ment but without any progress toward resolution. Mediation is, rather,
conceived in an alternative—though, I would argue, still Marxist—
sense, as a positive social process, which does not simply restate in-
tractable situations but restates them *in terms more amenable to
resolution.*[9] The potential of this restatement for socially constructive
resolution lies in the receptivity of Chaucer's chosen form to the language of conflict. The socially creative form of the *Canterbury Tales*
permits a relatively untroubled contemplation of extreme difference, a
degree of difference that could not be acknowledged in the social
sphere without danger to the participants. The literary language of the
Canterbury Tales is thus "conciliatory" in the sense proposed by
Macherey, in its ability to restate and to accommodate extremes of
opinion as great as those of Chaucer's social reality, but to accommodate them "avec moins de risque," undangerously.[1] This accommodation is, as Macherey would be quick to point out, imaginary, since it
has no necessary effect on social reality. Yet, in its literary reproduc-
tion of a social reality that embraces varied social tendencies for the
good of all, Chaucer's work itself becomes a social agent in the constructive possibilities it imagines and poses.

---

7. Bakhtin, *Dostoevsky's Poetics*, p. 40.
8. Ibid., p. 27.
9. As in Claude Lévi-Strauss, "The Structural Study of Myth," *Structural Anthropology* (New
   York: Anchor Books, 1967), esp. pp. 217–27.
1. Etienne Balibar and Pierre Macherey, "On Literature as an Ideological Form," in *Untying
   the Text: A Post-Structuralist Reader*, ed. Robert Young (London: Routledge and Kegan Paul,
   n.d.).

The Silent Plowman and the Talkative Parson

Chaucer has used the vehicle of a temporally and socially defined pilgrimage to inscribe a community of mixed discourse that models the possible harmony of a mixed state. The space within which he imagines his discursive community has, however, been precariously maintained. It has, on the one hand, required an extreme stylization of actual social conditions in late fourteenth-century English society, including near erasure of the numerical preponderance (and the sometimes threatening claims) of those agricultural workers who comprised over nine tenths of the English populace. It has, on the other hand, required deferral of the claims of an authoritative spiritual system that minimizes the importance of secular society even as it somewhat paradoxically insists on the organization of secular society according to divinely ordained hierarchy. The complicated exclusions that render Chaucer's mixed commonwealth possible are epitomized in the silence of the Plowman, the single peasant participating in the pilgrimage. The deferral of a system of spiritual transcendence inimical to the natural and mixed temporal state is brought to an end by his suddenly loquacious brother, the Parson, with his rejection of the "draf" of fabulation in favor of the "whete" of unmediated doctrine (X. 35–36).

The Plowman is admitted to the *compaignye* of pilgrims, but without a tale. In this regard, Chaucer's practice is consistent with that of most commentators on the natural state, among whom even the relative democrats emphasize the participation of a *gravior pars* [more dignified part of society], noting the importance of the peasantry but assigning it no consequential role. John of Salisbury is typical in his praise of the *agricolae* he calls the *pedes* or feet of the commonwealth, classing them among those who are useful or profitable to the commonwealth but who have nothing to do with its governance ("quae nec ad praesidendi pertinent auctoritatem et uniuersitati rei publicae usquequaque proficiunt"—VI. 20). And even the democratic Marsilius[2] classes agricultural workers among the *officia* rather than the *partes* of the state—with the former exercising necessary functions and belonging to the *vulgi* and the latter participating in civic rule and belonging to the *honorabilitates* (I. 5). Hierarchical theory tended to demand a single thing of these workers—obedient service or *obsequium*—while suggesting that this service would be repaid with other kinds of benign assistance ("Debent autem obsequium inferiora superioribus quae omnia eisdem uicissim debent necessarium subsidium prouidere"—*Polycraticus*, VI. 20). Organic theory tended to conceal this demand within broader assertions of reciprocity ("singula sint quasi aliorum ad inuicem membra"—*Polycraticus*, VI. 20). Often commingled, each justified major exactions from agricultural producers, while simultaneously expecting servitude and denying a consequential civic role. In this regard Chaucer's silent servitor is fully assimilated to an ideology that asks much of him in the way of willing work (he is a

---

2. Marsilius of Padua (d. 1342), an important political theorist. John of Salisbury, for several years secretary to Archbishop Thomas Becket, sent him the *Polycraticus* in 1159 [*Editors*].

"trewe swynkere"—I.531), cheerful relinquishment of the surplus value of his toil ("His tithes payde he ful faire and wel"—I.539), and acceptance of broad communal obligation ("He wolde thresshe . . . for every povre wight"—I.536–37).

All preliminary indications suggest that the voice of the Plowman, when Chaucer came to give him one, would not have been a voice of complaint, as was the Plowman of the Chaucer apocrypha who decries clerical theories of agricultural labor ("They make us thralles at hir lust"[3]). But we are not finally to know. For, as Patterson has argued, the voice of peasant protest is effectively erased within the *Canterbury Tales*.[4] He finds that this voice is given limited articulation in the Miller's prologue and tale, and even more limited articulation in the case of the Wife of Bath, but that it is progressively suppressed in favor of a depoliticized and transhistorical subjectivity. Patterson's argument is plainly essentially correct, although one wonders if the exclusion of the peasantry might not be even more thoroughgoing than he supposes; the Miller and the Wife of Bath are rural small producers, but hardly peasants or *agricolae* in any meaningful sense of the word.[5]

But I agree that, certain traces notwithstanding, Chaucer has virtually excluded the peasantry and rural small production from the *Canterbury Tales*. Just as the peasantry is slighted both descriptively and functionally in medieval political theory, so does Chaucer suppress its numerical and economic importance in the process of establishing his commonwealth of mixed literary discourse. Briefly to venture an absurd reduction: just as Chaucer would have been unlikely to imagine a commonwealth that admitted to full participation the 90 or so percent of the populace in various states of peasantry or villeinage, so could he hardly have created a literary counterpart to his own civic experience while drawing some two dozen of his speakers from the ranks of peasants and villeins. A price has certainly been paid, in regard to accurate representation of the peasantry and to direct articulation of the voice of peasant protest. Yet this devaluation of peasant concerns is an act of exclusion that, paradoxically, opens a narrative space within which the mixed middle strata produce a literary model of social diversity.

Chaucer's literary model of social diversity is itself increasingly threatened by forces hostile to those practices of fabulation and artificial use of language on which his discursive community is founded. The reliability of fabulation as a means of embodying the truth is questioned as early as the Pardoner's prologue and tale. The dilemma is posed in the Pardoner's contention that a "vicious man" can nevertheless tell a "moral tale" (VI.459–460)—a dilemma that, as we have seen, creates

3. "The Plowman's Tale," in Chaucer, *Works*, ed. W. W. Skeat, vol. 7, 11. 41–42.
4. Lee Patterson, " 'No man his reson herde': Peasant Consciousness, Chaucer's Miller, and the Structure of the *Canterbury Tales*," *South Atlantic Quarterly* 86 (1987): 457–95.
5. The Miller would, for example, be considered a prosperous "yoman" in the terms of the 1363 statute; an "artificer" in the 1379 poll tax; a "man of craft" in the Norwich guild ordinance.

discomfort for the pilgrim audience and for subsequent audiences as well. This mistrust of what might be called the uses of fabulation is extended in the *Manciple's Tale* to the act of tale telling itself (cautionarily represented in the silencing of the song of the crow as punishment for indiscriminate conversation or "false tale"—IX.293) and to the narrator's mistrust of language in relation to its referent (in his acknowledgment of the "loaded" judgment implied in his choice of the word "lemman" to describe Apollo's wife's lover—IX.205–222). That the *Manciple's Tale* is about "the failure of words" has been mentioned on several occasions.[6] What remains to be added here is that the failure in question is not only a general failure of reference but a failure of *socially charged* reference, of language in its capacity justly to represent the social implications of human action. *Lemman* is one of those courtly terms that, as Donaldson reminded us, slipped a good deal between the thirteenth and fourteenth centuries.[7] The narrator accordingly pauses to note its harsh, or at least drab and ordinary, connotations, informing us that nothing separates the misconduct of a "wyf" of "heigh degree" and a "povre wenche" except the words by which we describe their behavior:

> . . . the gentile, in estaat above,
> She shal be cleped his lady, as in love;
> And for that oother is a povre womman,
> She shal be cleped his wenche or his lemman. (IX.217–20)

Then follows a crude and assertively male observation, driving home the point that beneath the words the behavior is the same:

> And, God it woot, myn owene deere brother,
> Men leyn that oon as lowe as lith that oother. (IX.221–22)

Called into question here is the meaningfulness of social specification in language: "lady" (in the sense of "beloved") versus "lemman," and by implication the broader categories of "wyf" and "lady" versus "wenche" and "womman." The *swyving* is all the same, regardless of social category, and the categories have begun to blur a bit too. But the idea that different discourses are appropriate to different social levels, that certain genres and even certain styles may be assigned to persons of certain social levels, has been one of the crucial enabling ideas of the *Canterbury Tales*. Once this equation of social level and discourse is called seriously into question, Chaucer's creation of a community of discourse as a figure for a mixed commonwealth loses a crucial underpinning. That this wound to Chaucer's narrative enterprise is essentially self-inflicted suggests a crucial shift in the status of narrative itself, and this shift is shortly to be confirmed in the words with which the Parson prefaces the penitential treatise that will be his "tale."

6. Most notably, James Dean, "Dismantling the Canterbury Book," *PMLA* 100 (1985): 746–59.
7. E. Talbot Donaldson, "Idiom of Popular Poetry in the Miller's Tale." *Speaking of Chaucer* (1970; rpt. New York: W. W. Norton & Company, 1972), pp. 13–29.

All the Canterbury tales that preceded the Parson's are *narrationes* and possessed of plots (even if, as in the case of *Melibee*, thinly so). But it is specifically plotted narrative (that is, fabulation itself and not just Aesopic fable) that the Parson rejects when he refuses to tell "fables and swich wrecchednesse" (X.34).[8] He will instead dispense the pure "whete" of doctrine directly, offering "moralitee and vertuous mateere" in the form of an unplotted *tretys* (X.35–38). And, even before he commences his tale, several conditions that have promoted the rampant narrativity and the stylistic variousness of this discursive community are decisively altered.

Immediately altered is the pilgrims' attitude toward temporality. Until now the pilgrimage itself has—along with the tales the pilgrims tell—unfolded in the temporal realm, in the space of Bakhtin's "historically productive horizontal."[9] An atmosphere congenial to the resolution of narrative conflict in time has, despite occasional openings to the eternal, prevailed. Now we are reminded—rather urgently—that time is at a premium; late afternoon has come and Harry Bailly tells us that his plan is complete for all tales but one and that haste is essential if the Pilgrims are to be fruitful before the setting of the sun. No longer invited to participate in a leisurely temporal unfolding of narrative events, the pilgrims are requested to give "space" (X.64) to the Parson, whose tale will in fact be a spatial rather than a temporal dilatation of various penitential themes. This is not to say that the Parson's tale is brief, which it is most assuredly not, but that its shape will follow the extratemporal demands of the project he sets for himself. The "haste" enjoined by Harry Bailly is a haste to begin his undertaking; once begun, its exposition of a timeless sacrament proceeds without the pressures or interruptions that would signify the passage of worldly time. Its ending in fact is not in temporality at all, but in a timeless vision of a realm of permanent "sikernesse" (X.1077) and in Chaucer's contemplation of Christ reigning in eternity, "per omnia secula."

Also signaled by the Parson's prologue is the end of the *compaignye* of Canterbury pilgrims as a socially varied body of speakers oriented toward pluralistic discourse. Until now the pilgrims have rarely agreed on anything (unless we are to take the sobriety that settles on "every man" at the end of the *Prioress' Tale* as a form of agreement). More often, responses lapse into discord or blatant partiality of understanding, or else apparent unanimity turns out to mask varied response, as at the end of the *Knight's Tale* ("nas ther yong ne oold / That he ne seyde it was a noble storie / . . . And namely the gentils everichon"—I.3110–13). Now, however, we find the audience united in its assent to the Parson's austere intention of telling a moral tale, in prose, emphasizing unmediated doctrine, and redirecting this temporal pilgrimage to an atemporal home in "Jerusalem celestial" (X.51):

8. On *fable* as a narrative with invented plot, see Paul Strohm, "Some Generic Distinctions in the *Canterbury Tales*," *MP* 68 (1971–72): 321–28.
9. "Forms of Time and of the Chronotope in the Novel," *The Dialogic Imagination*, ed. Michael Holquist (Austin: U of Texas P, 1981), p. 157.

> Upon this word we han assented soone,
> For, as it seemed, it was for to doone—
> To enden in som vertuous sentence. (X.61–63)

Harry Bailly has "the wordes for us alle" (X.67) when he gives the Parson free rein and promises audience. For the implication is that the Parson's "sentence" will transcend division and social difference, addressing itself to all Christians without regard to condition, in its awareness of their bondage and need for spiritual repair. The pilgrims are unlikely to slip from this new vantage back into temporality and social dissension. For the *Parson's Tale* would subsume the world of varied temporality into its timeless categories.[1]

The Parson's analytical frame is thoroughly traditional in ways that suggest how far afield Harry Bailly was in judging him a "Lollere" in the canceled endlink to the *Man of Law's Tale*.[2] In marked contrast even to "The Two Ways" by Chaucer's friend Clanvowe, with its reliance on self-regulation, the *Parson's Tale* seeks full submission to church authority as embodied in its injunctions and sacraments. The existence of sin in the world is traced not to erroneous human choice but to failure of full obedience to God (X.338) and to a withdrawal from contemplation of God's timeless blessings into a world of temporal reward. As Chaucer notes, in free adaptation of Augustine: "Deedly synne . . . is whan a man turneth his herte fro God, which that is verray sovereyn bountee, that may nat chaunge, and yeveth his herte to thyng that may chaunge and flitte" (X.367). Chaucer's apparent addition here is the concept of the "sovereyn" nature of God's bounty—an addition that refers mainly to its universal excellence but that also arrays God in the attributes of a supreme ruler from whom beneficence flows and to whom obeisance is due.[3] Running through the *Parson's Tale* is an argumentative and imagistic strain suggesting that the errant Christian has failed to accept God's good lordship, has sought to be a free subject of history and choice who can pursue a variety of temporal options instead of submitting freely to God's singular and permanent sovereignty. This imagery solidifies around the most visible and traditional manifestation of God's eternal order, in the suggestion that the Christian become a vassal of God: the Christian must "yeven his body and al his herte to the service of Jhesu Crist, and therof doon hym hommage" (X.314). The *Parson's Tale* recommends, in effect, a refeudalization of relations, within that sphere of hierarchical transcendence that afforded the original pattern for the descending ideology of high medieval feudalism.

* * *

If the polyphony of the *Canterbury Tales* is a figuration of the variety of the natural state, the monovocality of the Parson's closing treatise is

---

1. Patterson observes that the *Parson's Tale* "cancels out . . . that which precedes." "The Parson's Tale and the Quitting of the Canterbury Tales," *Traditio* 34 (1978): 379.
2. On the orthodox proscription of swearing, see G. R. Owst, *Literature and Pulpit in Medieval England* (Cambridge: Cambridge UP, 1933), pp. 414–25.
3. With respect to Chaucer's source, see Kate Oelzner Peterson, *The Sources of the Parson's Tale* (1901; rpt. New York: AMS Press, 1973), n. to pp. 34–35.

appropriate to the announcement of a more rigid, descending order. The finality of the Parson's utterance is enhanced by its appeal to divine ordinance. Its finality is further enhanced by its status as the last of the tales, told by common consent and followed by the closely associated Retraction, in which Chaucer responds *in propria persona* to the Parson's admonition to repent. And, beyond any of these considerations, the practice of monovocality *itself* aspires to finality. As Bakhtin has observed, "Monologue pretends to be the *ultimate word*. It closes down the represented world and represented persons."[4] In a sense this monologue does close down the *Canterbury Tales*, by denying the autonomy of that natural and varied world of temporality to which the Canterbury pilgrimage offers a literary and stylistic counterpart.

In other important senses, however, the *Canterbury Tales* resists closure, denying to any one pilgrim the finality of utterance to which the voice of the Parson would aspire. One aspect of this denial resides in the manifestly unfinished and fragmentary nature of the *Tales* itself. For an element of the Parson's authority has been our acceptance of his tale's status as the "last word," the concluding utterance of a finished literary work.

His tale does, to be sure, enjoy undoubted status as the last of Chaucer's intended narratives, whether the "thropes ende" (X.12) that the pilgrims are entering as he begins to speak refers to the outskirts of Canterbury (on a "one-way" journey) or London/Southwark (on a "round trip"). But six centuries of scribes, editors, and critics have moved beyond this indisputable fact to a presumption of near-completion that lacks ultimate support in internal evidence. Starting with the activities of the earliest fifteenth-century scribes and editors,[5] this unifying enterprise reached a climax in the middle decades of this century, through a convergence of conclusions derived within two apparently incompatible critical tendencies. Ralph W. Baldwin, accepting the assumptions about organic unity inherent in the "new criticism," launched his argument for the conversion of the *Tales* from a literal to a symbolic journey to "Jerusalem celestial" (X.51).[6] Concurrently, D. W. Robertson and his associates launched their argument for the exegetical unity of the *Tales*, including the rather willful misreading of Chaucer's "this litel tretys or rede" (X.1081) as an application of his Retraction not only to the completed *Parson's Tale* but to the entire work.[7]

Against such claims for Chaucer's final intent must be weighed his own insistence on his work as open, provisional, and unfinished. Our

---

4. *Dostoevsky's Poetics*, p. 293.
5. For a discussion of the activities of the Ellesmere and Hengwrt scribes, with accompanying bibliography, see Derek Pearsall, *The Canterbury Tales* (London: Unwin Critical Library, 1985), pp. 1–23. An interesting account of the "bookish" pretensions of the Ellesmere manuscript has been given by Alan T. Gaylord (unpublished paper, 1982 NCS Congress).
6. Baldwin, *The Unity of the "Canterbury Tales," Anglistica* 5 (Copenhagen, 1955).
7. Robertson's argument that the "litel tretys" of the Retraction is the whole of the *Tales* occurs in *A Preface to Chaucer* (Princeton: Princeton UP, 1962), p. 369. For a corrective, see John W. Clark, " 'This Litel Tretys' Again," *The Chaucer Review* 6 (1971–72): 152–56.

tendency to imagine Chaucer's tales as a "Canterbury book" must, in the first instance, minimize the provisional nature of any arrangement of its inner fragments.[8] Beyond this fact lie other indications of Chaucer's refusal to fix his tales in a definite scheme: his distribution of narratives among many voices, his refusal to invest authority in his often-befuddled narrator or to create a Gowerian genius figure as authoritative interpreter, his minimal interest in devices such as glosses by which Gower and other contemporary authors promoted ultimate monovocality.[9]

Just as Chaucer's text announces its own unfinished nature, so does the evidence of early reception argue for random and piecemeal dissemination. Chaucer's immediate audience would have encountered his work not in presentation volumes, or any volumes at all, or even necessarily in manuscript form.[1] Rather, Chaucer's most immediate and most prized audience must have known his poetry in a discontinuous and segmented way, largely through oral rendition and occasionally, at best, through fragmentary manuscripts. To the extent that we can reconstruct a contemporary response to Chaucer, we must imagine that response less as contemplation of a finished order and more as an awareness of local juxtaposition, of ideas placed side by side, in unresolved contention.

The Parson therefore presents us with a paradox: with a voice that would transcend worldly fragmentation and division, situated in a work that treats fragmentation and division as inevitable aspects of life in the world. Chaucer's own Retraction may offer a partial resolution of this paradox, in its suggestion that the proper response to the Parson's admonitions lies beyond the temporal sphere and beyond works that imitate that sphere—in sacramental time, in "omnia secula." To the limited extent that the Parson's views about hierarchy and transcendence refer back to that temporal and mutivoiced site of personal and ideological contention offered by the *Canterbury Tales*, they must take their chances, among a multitude of contending conceptions.

In situating the Parson's voice at the end of his pilgrimage, Chaucer has shown respect for its special claims. But, at the same time, in *deferring* the Parson's voice to the end of the pilgrimage, Chaucer has

8. Pearsall observes that the text should ideally be presented to modern readers "partly as a bound book (with first and last fragments fixed) and partly as a set of fragments in folders, with the incomplete information as to their nature and placement fully displayed" (*The Canterbury Tales*, p. 23).
9. For arguments that some manuscript glosses may ultimately be authorial, see Daniel S. Silvia, "Glosses to the *Canterbury Tales* from St. Jerome's *Epistola Adversus Jovinianum*," SP 62 (1965): 28–39: Robert E. Lewis, "Glosses to the *Man of Law's Tale* from Pope Innocent III's *De Miseria Humane Conditionis*," SP 64 (1967): 1–16. On the scribal origin of the glosses as an enhancement of the prestige of Chaucer's compilation, see A. I. Doyle and M. B. Parkes, "The Production of Copies of the *Canterbury Tales* and the *Confessio Amantis* in the Early Fifteenth Century," *Medieval Scribes, Manuscripts and Libraries: Essays Presented to N. R. Ker*, ed. Parkes and A. G. Watson (London: Scolar P, 1978), pp. 190–91.
1. Though manuscript circulation of individual tales and fragments prior to Chaucer's death remains a possibility. An argument for the circulation of individual tales in his lifetime, based on independent textual traditions as inferred from textual variants in fifteenth-century manuscripts, is advanced by Charles A. Owen, Jr., "The *Canterbury Tales*: Early Manuscripts and Relative Popularity," *JEGP* 54 (1955): 104–110.

opened a discursive space within which various conceptions of social reality can coexist. The impetus behind the Parson's voice is assertively utopian, in the sense that it would deny division and faction by transcending it. But another, more modestly directed but no less utopian, impulse infuses Chaucer's later poetry as well, in his exploitation of the conciliatory possibilities of literary language to offer his audience a mixed commonwealth of discourse.

Chaucer's commonwealth is implicitly utopian in its accommodation of varied socially and vocationally defined voices and points of view, its opening of existing hierarchies to infiltration by new classes of people and categories of discourse, its treatment of heterogeneity as a normal condition of civic life.[2] A commonwealth so conceived obviously had much to offer Chaucer himself and that new group of fellow gentlepersons "en service" so prominent in his immediate audience. Yet, however densely implicated in its own historical situation and however charged its significance for its original audience, Chaucer's work continues to command the attention of succeeding readers. Its appeal is not that it exists on an aesthetic plane beyond the social fray. Rather, its appeal owes much to its rich situation between contending social models, its subtle poise at the boundaries of rank and class awareness. The comprehensiveness and argumentative energy with which Chaucer's work opens itself to its historical moment allow readers in posterity a continuing opportunity to refresh their own belief in social possibility.

CAROLYN DINSHAW

Eunuch Hermeneutics†

Very early in her *Prologue*, just as she is warming to her theme, the Wife of Bath is interrupted by the Pardoner on the road to Canterbury. He initially bristles at her images of "tribulacion in mariage" (173), but after she orders him to hear her out, he in fact urges her to teach him the tricks of her trade. It might seem as though there couldn't be a more unlikely pair: the Wife, flamboyantly arrayed and ostentatiously heterosexual, "carping" and in good fellowship with the company, and the Pardoner, that defective man, who makes the "gentils" cry out even before he begins his tale. But pilgrims are never only coincidentally brought together in the *Canterbury Tales*, and we begin to sense similarities between these two even on the superficial level of

2. Paul Olson's *The Canterbury Tales and the Good Society* (Princeton: Princeton UP, 1986) also argues for the social significance of Chaucer's literary text. Readers of both studies will note, however, my essential point of difference with Olson's conviction that Chaucer's reconstruction of society depends on a reassertion of hierarchy and a discouragement of pervasively "epicurean" tendencies.

† From *ELH* 55.1 (1988): 27–51. Copyright © The John Hopkins University Press. Reprinted with permission of The Johns Hopkins University Press. We have renumbered the notes and abridged some of them. In revised form this article appears in Professor Dinshaw's *Chaucer's Sexual Poetics* (Madison: U of Wisconsin P, 1989), pp. 156–84.

clothing. The Pardoner is as clothes-conscious as is the Wife of Bath in her "hosen . . . of fyn scarlet reed" (I.456): wearing no hood, with only a cap, "Hym thoughte he rood al of the newe jet" (I.682).[1] The emphasis on the apparel of these two pilgrims leads us to deeper connections between them. As I shall argue, the body is the field on which issues of representation and interpretation are literally and metaphorically played out. The eunuch Pardoner, focusing anxiety about the use of language on the road to Canterbury, embodies a truth about language that explains why the Wife's fantasy of the perfect marriage—analogous, in her *Prologue* and *Tale*, to the perfect glossing of a text—remains but a dream that can never be fully satisfied.

The Wife, so concerned in her *Prologue* with the question of how to read texts, presents in herself a perfect image of a text—a fictional or pagan one, as medieval writers from Macrobius to Richard of Bury imaged it. The fictional text, they write, is like a woman, extravagantly and seductively arrayed. Richard of Bury, for example, writes in his *Philobiblon* that the pagan classics are texts which, like females, appeal to the "wanton minds of men" with their seductive garments, their "masks of pleasure."[2] But the proper way to read such a text is to strip it of those garments, to penetrate to what Richard calls "the naked truth" (*nuda veritas*). I call such an approach to the text a "heterosexual hermeneutic": the text is woman's body, to be stripped and penetrated (or "glossed," from Greek *glossa*, "tongue") by male interpreters.

But this orthodox, "straight" hermeneutic will not work for the Pardoner, that sexually peculiar figure. The Pardoner's fashionable clothes do not, in fact, mask his body: without a hood, his cap reveals his carefully styled but thin and lifeless hair, and that hair, taken with the other details of his appearance, proclaims the unfortunate facts of his anatomy. As critics since W. C. Curry have noted, the Pardoner's "secret" is no secret at all: he appears to be a eunuch, either congenital or castrated.[3] The Pardoner's sense of his own physical lack not only informs his social behavior, but the thematics and narrative strategies of his tale as well. And most important, it represents the nature of language itself. It is not only modern theorists who analyze language as radically fragmentary: medieval writers too were preoccupied with the fundamental incompleteness of human language. The Pardoner enunciates the only possible strategy of using language in a postlapsarian

1. All quotations of Chaucer's poetry are from *The Works of Geoffrey Chaucer*, ed. F. N. Robinson, 2nd ed. (Boston: Houghton Mifflin, 1957). Citations are given parenthetically.
2. Richard of Bury, *Philobiblon*, ed. and trans. Ernest C. Thomas (London: Kegan Paul, Trench, and Co., 1887), 13.180: "Accordingly the wisdom of the ancients devised a remedy by which to entice the wanton minds of men by a kind of pious fraud, the delicate Minerva secretly lurking beneath the mask of pleasure" (trans. Thomas).
3. "The Secret of Chaucer's Pardoner" was W. C. Curry's groundbreaking article in *Journal of English and Germanic Philology* 18 (1919): 593–606, later appearing in his *Chaucer and the Medieval Sciences* (rev. ed., New York: Barnes and Noble, 1960), 54–90. Curry was the first to bring the inference of eunuchry (from the narrator's statement in the *General Prologue*, "I trowe he were a geldyng or a mare") under critical scrutiny, providing evidence from classical and medieval scientific discourse. Curry's particular interpretation of this evidence—his conclusion that the Pardoner is a congenital eunuch, a *eunuchus ex nativitate*—has come under attack, but there has been a broad consensus among Chaucerians that the Pardoner is a eunuch, either congenital or castrated. I address this issue in more detail below, in note 9.

world, cut off from primary wholeness and unity: he acts according to what I call the hermeneutrics of the partial, or, for short, eunuch hermeneutics.

The Pardoner surrounds himself with objects—relics, sealed documents, even language, regarded as a kind of object—that he substitutes for his own lacking parts. But these objects are themselves fragments, and cannot properly fill the lack that hollows the Pardoner's being. To be a eunuch is, as R. P. Miller has demonstrated, a spiritual condition as well as a physical one, and that spiritual condition has a psychological valence which I propose to analyze here: the substitute objects the Pardoner adopts cannot convert his bottomless *cupiditas*, that state of radical wanting, radical desire, into *caritas*, a state of oneness with the Father.[4] Nevertheless, even though the Pardoner knows that his relics, documents, words are defective substitutes—they are fakes, and he tells us so—he holds on to the belief that they can make him whole, part of the body of pilgrims, and of the larger body of Christians. If we express this in terms of the problematics of interpretation, we can say that the eunuch's hermeneutics proceeds by double affirmations, double truths, the incompatible affirmations of knowledge and belief. A heterosexual hermeneutic penetrates and discards fiction for the truth, but the eunuch suggests that the relationship between fiction and truth is not so easy to discern: the eunuch holds on to the fiction, knowing that it is false but wanting to believe that it is true. That desire to believe is everyone's: the eunuch Pardoner, wanting to believe in his own wholeness, plays on his audience's desire to believe in theirs; he exposes everyone's radical longing for completeness.[5]

I

Richard of Bury provides an image for the heterosexual reading act, but he nonetheless associates reading with eunuchs as well. As I have said, he images reading as a seduction by the wanton letter of the text, a penetration to the naked body of woman. But he also—and somewhat contradictorily—emphasizes, with St. Paul, that the reader must leave behind the carnal letter to get to the text's spirit. Thus he suggests elsewhere in the *Philobiblon* that the end of reading is, finally, asexual: he commends Origen as an exemplary reader, one who was not distracted by any improper lusts of the flesh; and he cites the eunuch mentioned by St. Paul in the *Acts* as an example to all those who would learn to read properly: reading the Scriptures without under-

---

4. See Robert P. Miller's classic article, "Chaucer's Pardoner, the Scriptural Eunuch, and the Pardoner's Tale," *Speculum* 30 (1955): 180–99. Augustine's analyses of spiritual conditions are powerful psychological analyses as well, as Donald R. Howard comments in his discussion of the Pardoner in his *Idea of the Canterbury Tales* (Berkeley: U of California, 1976), 355–56. Janet Adelman (" 'That We May Leere Som Wit,' " in *Twentieth-Century Interpretations of the Pardoner*, ed. Dewey R. Faulkner [Englewood Cliffs, N.J.: Prentice-Hall, 1973], 96–106) discusses aesthetic implications of *cupiditas*, seeing in the *Tale's* use of parody and analogy a pattern of false substitution.
5. Here I wish to acknowledge a general indebtedness throughout this essay to R. Howard Bloch, *The Scandal of the Fabliaux* (Chicago: U of Chicago P, 1986).

standing, the eunuch asked Philip to guide him; Philip "preached unto him Jesus" (Acts 8:35), and the eunuch was baptised.[6] To pursue this association of eunuchry with spiritual understanding beyond these citations in Richard of Bury, we need only turn to Abelard, perhaps the most famous of medieval castrati. Abelard built his career as a Christian philosopher upon his castration. He writes in the *Historia calamitatum* that in order to gain spiritual understanding—to read properly—it was necessary not only that he cease reading as he had been with Heloise (a literally heterosexual use of reading), but that he be castrated—although he admits that this was not among the *remedia amoris* he would have chosen—so that he would be freed for the work of the true philosopher. The eunuch, untempted by and discontinuous in the flesh, is the perfect reader.[7]

But Chaucer's eunuch, the Pardoner, is hardly the perfect, "spiritual" reader. There is an extraordinary focus on the body in his portrait, *Prologue*, and *Tale*. He is preoccupied by, chained to, the flesh, never rising out of it to reach the spirit. It is no coincidence that the Pardoner follows the Physician in telling his tale; the Physician is the pilgrim most concerned with the body—he is professionally dependent upon it. The tale the Physician tells, the story of Appius and Virginia, is taken from the *Roman de la rose*, and its narrative position there is significant: the story is told by Raison after her account of Saturn's castration. Raison's point is that justice was lost when Jupiter castrated his father; in the *Roman de la rose*, castration marks the loss of the Golden Age, the loss of an ideal.[8] And it does so, I shall argue, in

6. About the eunuch in the *Acts*, Richard remarks: "Love of his book alone had wholly engrossed this domicile of chastity, under whose guidance he soon deserved to enter the gate of faith" (trans. Thomas). *Philobiblon* 15.203. See also 15.193, for citation of Origen.
7. "Abelard's Letter of Consolation to a Friend," ed. J. T. Muckle, *Medieval Studies* 12 (1950): 182 and passim. For remarks regarding Origen, see letter 4, from Abelard to Heloise, ed. Muckle, *Medieval Studies* 15 (1953): 89–90. R. Howard Bloch's discussion in *Etymologies and Genealogies: A Literary Anthropology of the French Middle Ages* (Chicago: U of Chicago P, 1983), "Philosophy and the Family: Abelard," suggests ways in which castration informs Abelard's theological formulations and his radical break from philosophical tradition.
   Abelard's castration was not voluntary, of course, however salutary he later found it. He notes that Origen acted impetuously and was worthy of blame: "Yet Origen is seriously to be blamed because he sought a remedy for blame in punishment of his body. True, he has zeal for God, but an ill-informed zeal, and the charge of homicide can be proved against him for his self mutilation" (trans. Betty Radice, *The Letters of Abelard and Heloise* [New York: Penguin, 1974], 149). See letter 4, 90. Similarly, John of Salisbury, one of Abelard's students in Paris, commends Origen for his zeal but remarks on his lack of good sense (*Polycraticus* 8.6, in *Patrologia latina* ed. J.-P. Migne, [Paris, 1855], 199: cols. 724D–725D. The idea that self-castration was blameworthy was current throughout the Middle Ages. Voluntary self-castration was not approved of even by the Early Church: opposing Gnostic opinion regarding self-castration, the Council of Nicea (325 A.D.) enunciated the belief that nature should not be mutilated. Aquinas summed up medieval opinion when he stressed that God intended, through nature, that the human body be integral in all its members; see *Summa theologica* 2.2 quaest. 65 ("De mutilatione membrorum"), art i–ii (*Opera omnia* [Parma, 1852–73; reprint, New York: Musurgia, 1948], 3: 244–45). In the *Roman de la rose* (ed. Félix Lecoy, Classiques français du moyen âge, 98 [Paris: Honoré Champion, 1970]), Nature (17022–29) and Genius (20007–52) similarly stress the natural integrity of the body. See John T. Noonan, Jr., *Contraception: A History of Its Treatment by the Catholic Theologians and Canonists* (Cambridge: Harvard UP, 1966), 95, 246, for summary discussion of medieval attitudes toward castration. Richard of Bury does, it is true, acknowledge that Origen's self-castration was a hasty remedy ("repugnant alike to nature and to virtue" in Thomas's emphatic translation), but ends the chapter with his vigorous commendation of the New Testament castrato; the metaphoric charge of Richard's discourse is most important here.
8. *Roman de la rose*, 5505ff.; Genius also explicitly connects castration to the loss of the

the *Canterbury Tales* as well. The Pardoner follows the Physician's redaction of this tale as if to explain the sordid world of the *Physician's Tale*: it's an unjust world, a world cut off from natural justice, natural love—a castrated world.

Harry Bailly's garbled oath in calling for a tale to follow the Physician's ("By corpus bones!" [VI.314]) is a response to both the Physician's occupation and the sense of the corporal that surrounds the Pardoner. But the focus on the body in the Pardoner's portrait, *Prologue*, and *Tale* might more properly be said to be a focus on fragments of the body. First on the list of these fragments is, of course, the Pardoner himself. The narrator expresses some uncertainty about the Pardoner's sexuality in the *General Prologue*—"I trowe he were a geldyng or a mare" (I.691)—but the pieces of information he gives there—thin hair, glaring eyes, high voice, beardlessness—clearly suggest a eunuch, either congenital or castrated.[9] The narrator's uncertainty stems from his perception that something is lacking, either the physical equipment or masculine gender-identification, and, in fact, the categories of eunuchry and other physical and sexual conditions were often conflated in the Middle Ages:[1] As I see it, an enormous lack—the Pardoner's unquenchable *cupiditas*, repeatedly expressed in his Prologue as "I wol . . . I wol . . . I wol"—and a disjunct sexual identity are objectified in his defective, lacking, fragmented physique.

"This fragmented body," writes Jacques Lacan, the modern theorist of the *corps morcelé*, "usually manifests itself in [images] when . . .

Golden Age (20007 ff). For a detailed analysis of the Golden Age in reference to these passages in the *Rose* divergent from the one I will propose here, see John V. Fleming, *Reason and the Lover* (Princeton: Princeton UP, 1984), 97–135.

9. Curry's diagnosis (note 3) has been criticized by Muriel Bowden, *A Commentary on the General Prologue to the Canterbury Tales* (New York: Macmillan, 1957), 274–76; Beryl Rowland, "Chaucer's Idea of the Pardoner," *Chaucer Review* 14 (1979): 140–54; Monica E. McAlpine, "The Pardoner's Homosexuality and How It Matters," *PMLA* 95 (1980): 8–22; and C. David Benson, "Chaucer's Pardoner: His Sexuality and Modern Critics." *Mediaevalia* 8 (1982): 337–49. Curry's conclusion that the Pardoner is a congenital eunuch (rather than a castrated one) is arguable, since he bases this on his own interpretation of the Pardoner's character and not on the medieval physiognomists (according to whom all eunuchs look alike). But, as McAlpine concedes, he reveals that Chaucer does accurately use the physical stereotype of the eunuch in details of the Pardoner's portrait. R. P. Miller (note 4) has provided the Scriptural background that supports the diagnosis *eunuchus*: Chaucer's detailing of the Pardoner's physical condition, as Lee Patterson puts it, renders it meaningful in both realms of science and religious symbol ("Chaucerian Confession: Penitential Literature and the Pardoner," *Medievalia et Humanistica*, n.s., 7 [1976]: 153–73). As I hope to demonstrate, eunuchry has a powerfully determining psychological value as well in the *Prologue* and *Tale*. None of the other suggestions about the Pardoner's sexuality—that he is homosexual (Bowden, McAlpine), or a "testicular pseudo-hermaphrodite of the feminine type" (Rowland, "Animal Imagery and the Pardoner's Abnormality," *Neophilologus* 48 [1964]: 56–60), or a combination pervert (Eric W. Stockton, "The Deadliest Sin in 'The Pardoner's Tale,'" *Tennessee Studies in Literature* 6 [1961], who argues that the Pardoner is "a manic depressive with traces of anal eroticism, and a pervert with a tendency toward alcoholism" [47])—are supported by such a dense pattern of signification on so many levels.

1. The narrator's perception of lack is what Donald R. Howard (note 4) stresses in his reading of the line, "I trowe he were a geldyng or a mare" (343). Howard seeks to restore the sense of the Pardoner's inexplicably strange presence among the pilgrims but accepts, nonetheless, Curry's determination that he is a eunuch. McAlpine (note 9) briefly documents the conflation of sexual categories in the Middle Ages. For more on medieval homosexuality and its conflation with other sexual categories, see John Boswell, *Christianity, Social Tolerance, and Homosexuality: Gay People in Western Europe from the Beginning of the Christian Era to the Fourteenth Century* (Chicago: U of Chicago P, 1980).

analysis encounters a certain level of aggressive disintegration in the individual. It then appears in the form of disjointed limbs."[2] Body parts move grotesquely, almost surrealistically, through the *Prologue* and *Tale*. "Myne handes and my tonge goon so yerne / That it is joye to se my bisynesse" (398–99); "Thanne peyne I me to strecche forth the nekke" (395). "The shorte throte, the tendre mouth" (517) are the loci of gluttony; the "womb, belly, stinking cod" are sites of sin. "Oure blissed Lordes" body (474) is torn, by swearing, into "herte," "nayles," "blood," and "armes" (651–54). Tongues, noses, gullets freely animate the Pardoner's sermon. The Old Man in the exemplum wails that he is nothing but "flessh, and blood, and skyn" (732); his "bones" await their final rest.

But relics are perhaps the things that we remember the best about the Pardoner, even though, as Alfred L. Kellogg has shown, they are not conventional characteristics of abusive pardoners.[3] Relics are holy fragments, scraps and chips of saints, and it is wholly appropriate that the Pardoner claims to have many. He has "a gobet of the seyl / That Seint Peter hadde" (696–97), a jar of "pigges bones," a "shoulder-boon / Which that was of an hooly Jewes sheep" (350–51), a "miteyn" (the shape of a hand), and a "pilwe-beer" (supposed to be Our Lady's veil). I want to consider the nature of sacred fragments for a moment.[4] The Pardoner's relics are not the most fragmentary of medieval relics on record: the relics that would seem to be paradigms of the fragmentary are splinters of the True Cross ("the croys which that Seint Eleyne fond" [951], by which the Host swears in response to the Pardoner). Pilgrims, according to several sources from the early and the high Middle Ages, kissed the Cross and surreptitiously carried the splinters away in their teeth.[5] Other holy monuments, such as tombs and gilded shrines, were broken into bits by pilgrims eager to bring back tokens. Body parts, however, were the medieval relics valued most highly: heads, arms, fingers of saints were severed and boxed in jeweled reliquaries. The efficacy of the whole body of the saint was powerful in these parts: synecdochically, in the divided body grace survived undivided.[6] Interestingly, dismemberment of saints' bodies was not allowed

2. Jacques Lacan, "The mirror stage as formative of the function of the I as revealed in psycho-analytic experience," in his *Ecrits: A Selection*, trans. Alan Sheridan (New York: W. W. Norton & Company, 1977), 4.
3. Alfred L. Kellogg, *Chaucer, Langland, Arthur: Essays in Middle English Literature* (New Brunswick: Rutgers U P, 1972), 212–44.
4. I have found Jonathan Sumption, *Pilgrimage: An Image of Mediaeval Religion* (London: Faber, 1975), especially useful—well documented and lively—on the subject of relics. Other interesting, general treatments I have used include Hippolyte Delehaye, *Les Origines du culte des martyrs*, 2nd ed., rev. (Brussels: Société des Bollandistes, 1933); P. Séjourné, "Reliques," in *Dictionnaire de théologie catholique* (Paris: Librairie Letouzey et Ané, 1937), 13: 2311–75; and Peter Brown, *The Cult of the Saints: Its Rise and Function in Latin Christianity* (Chicago: U of Chicago P, 1981). In the brief discussion that follows, I cite sources from the early through the late Middle Ages; veneration of relics of course varied through the age, but the essential theological idea of relics remained fairly constant: Sumption suggests that the early Church's defenses of relics are echoed in every major apologist of the Middle Ages (23).
5. See A. Frowlow, *La Relique de la vrai croix: recherches sur le développement d'un culte*, Archives de l'orient chrétien, 7 (Paris: Institut français d'études byzantines, 1961), 60–61, 161–65.
6. See Theodoret of Cyrus, *Graecarum affectionum curatio* 8, quoted in Sumption (note 4 above), 28. See also Victricius of Rouen, *De laude sanctorum* 10–11, *Patrologia latina*, 20:

originally by the early Church, but the great demand for relics made more relics necessary: by the eighth century, relics had come to be regarded as requirements for the consecration of a church, and private collectors, from the very early years of Christianity, were greedy for them. In the face of this demand, dismemberment was eventually allowed. (Fortunately, the saints themselves approved of dismemberment, as the story of St. Mammas attests: a finger of that saint detached itself of its own accord when a priest came to the body to collect relics.)[7]

But it was the very practice of fragmentation that led to widespread frauds. Once the bodies were divided into pieces and translated from one church to another, it was impossible to verify their authenticity. And the fragments proliferated: if all the claims were to be believed, there were, by the twelfth century, at least three heads of John the Baptist, innumerable arms and fingers of various saints, five or six foreskins of Christ.[8] Despite growing concern in the late Middle Ages about "multiple" relics—Guibert of Nogent's arguments about the absurdity of some claims to authenticity, very unusual in the twelfth century, began to be echoed by fifteenth-century pilgrims—the cult of relics in itself was not questioned. In *Mandeville's Travels* (c. 1357), for example, the history of John the Baptist's head is carefully recounted (the head was first enclosed in a wall of a church in Sebaste, then translated to Constantinople, where the "hynder partye" remains; the "forpartie" is in Rome, the jaws and platter in Genoa), but then put in question by the claim that the whole head might in fact be at Amiens. But the hesitancy this competing claim provokes is overwhelmed by devotion:

> And summen seyn that the heed of seynt John is at Amyas in Picardye. And other men seyn that it is the heed of seynt John the bysshop; I wot nere, but god knoweth. But in what wyse that men worschipen it the blessed seynt John holt him apayd.[9]

Indeed, there is more than a suggestion that competing claims to the same body part could be believed. A plurality of bodies seems to have been not only plausible, but preferable to a single one in the case of the Blessed Virgin: Our Lady of Coutances was a different entity from Our Lady of Bayeux, and some preferred the former, some the latter.[1]

---

col. 454B, who speaks of saints' bodies, wherein every fragment "is linked by a band to the whole stretch of eternity," as Brown elegantly translates it. See Brown's (note 4 above) discussion of Victricius, 78–79.

7. See Sumption, 28.

8. Guibert of Nogent traces corruption and fraudulent claims to the practice of dismemberment and translation: "All the evil of contention (over relics) originates in the fact that the saints are not permitted the repose of a proper and immutable burial place" (*Gesta Dei per Francos* 1.5, PL 156: col. 695A, my translation). In *De pignoribus sanctorum*, Guibert points to the competing claims of Constantinople and Angeli to the head of the Baptist and remarks: "What, therefore, is more ridiculous than to suppose that this great man had two heads?" (1.3.2, in PL 156: col. 624D; my translation). See Delehaye (note 4 above), 82–83, for a specific history of the head; Sumption summarizes the history of Christ's foreskin (46).

9. *Mandeville's Travels*, ed. from British Museum Ms. Cotton Titus C. XVI by P. Hamelius, Early English Text Society, old series, 153 (London: Kegan Paul, 1919 for 1916), chap. 13, p. 71.

1. See Sumption, 50–51.

And in the case of Christ's foreskins, the multiplicity was perhaps even cultivated, as an index of virility—"humanation," as Leo Steinberg would call it.[2]

But the Pardoner's scraps and chips of saints substitute for his lack of natural virility. As free-floating body parts, they are both reifications of his own fragmentariness and substitutes for his own lacking parts. He can't increase and multiply literally or spiritually, as R. P. Miller stresses.[3] But he uses the proliferating relics as the means by which he unnaturally increases and multiplies: his relics, he claims, will make grain and cattle multiply; he increases the number of believers (even though "that is nat my principal entente" [432]); and he makes his income multiply outrageously.

His other artifacts, those sealed documents from Rome, are closely associated with his own dismemberment as well. I will consider the pardons' more complicated psychological value later, but already we can see the substitution that has been made. We are told in the *General Prologue* that he carries his pardons in his lap: "His walet lay biforn hym in his lappe, / Bretful of pardoun, comen from Rome al hoot" (I.686–87). As rolled-up parchments with seals dangling from them, the Pardoner's documents and bulls, placed conspicuously in his bulging "male" (IV.920), present an iconographic substitute for his own lacking genitals. He emphatically declares that these bulls validate, make potent and unquestionable, his fractured body:

> my bulles shewe I, alle and some.
> Oure lige lordes seel on my patente,
> That shewe I first, my body to warente.
> (336–38)

So written documents and relics both function as body parts for the Pardoner. Historically, they were sometimes assimilated to one another: in the early Middle Ages, a book such as the *Lindisfarne Gospels* was itself a relic and a shrine, because of its association with Saint Cuthbert. Documents were kept along with relics in early treasure stores, and relics, to insure their authenticity, were sometimes sealed with bulls.[4]

Fragmentary and partial themselves, relics and documents also function for the Pardoner as "partial objects," to adapt a psychoanalytic idea to my purposes here. A "partial object," as I shall employ the term, is used by the subject in the attempt to fill the lack brought into being by the loss of an original ideal, an original wholeness and plenitude.[5] In the psychoanalytic economy, the loss of such an ideal of

2. Leo Steinberg, *The Sexuality of Christ in Renaissance Art and in Modern Oblivion* (New York: Pantheon, 1983).
3. Miller (note 4, p. 568), 185–86 and passim.
4. M. T. Clanchy, *From Memory to Written Record: England, 1066–1307* (Cambridge: Harvard UP, 1979), 125. See also Delehaye (note 4, p. 571).
5. My "partial object" is different from Melanie Klein's "part-object." As Harry Guntrip explains, in his *Personality Structure and Human Interaction* (New York: International Universities P, 1961), 226 ff., Klein establishes that in early infancy "all the baby knows or experiences is a breast (a 'part-object') and that it takes time and development for the baby to become aware of the mother in her completeness (a 'whole-object')." The "part-object," to

fullness and plenitude is always associated with castration: the original fullness of continuity with the mother is lost as the child, first perceiving physical differentiation from the mother, fears for the integrity of its own body. With the father's interruption of the mother-child union, the child perceives sexual difference and, specifically, the mother's lack of a penis. According to the Freudian analysis of the male castration complex, when the boy-child perceives the mother's lack, and the lacks of other females around him, he fears his own castration. "If a woman ha[s] been castrated, then his own possession of a penis [is] in danger": this threat of castration puts an end to the boy's Oedipus complex, as he (ideally) detaches himself from the mother and submits to the father.[6] Lacan, reinterpreting Freud, argues that the child not only fears his own castration upon recognition of physical differentiation, but is castrated at this moment, precisely because he is cut off from primary nondifferentiation, primary identification with the mother. In this sense, everyone is castrated, male and female alike; everyone is separated from the realm of primary union and continuity. Law and language, symbolic forms associated with the father, are imposed in the castrated realm of difference: the distance opened up by the entrance of the father creates the distinction between subjects and objects, signifiers and signifieds.[7]

Because of the loss of that ideal, the castrated subject forever seeks the realm of original fullness but must be content with substitutes only partially sufficient. These substitutes by their very nature signify the loss of an ideal, and therefore signify castration, even as they are—

---

the infant, is not partial; it is a whole-object to the baby, and is partial only in the adult's eyes. In my adaptation of the term, the partialness of the object, from the subject's point of view, is important: the object is a substitute for a formerly known whole, and is recognized to be defective in relation to that lost whole. Klein stresses that part-objects remain active as representations of the mother even after the infant has perceived her as a whole, and analysts following Klein have pointed to situations in which older children treat people as part-objects. See, for example, Emilio Rodrigue, "An Analysis of a Three-Year-Old Mute Schizophrenic," in Klein, Heimann, and Money-Kyrle, eds., *New Directions in Psychoanalysis* (New York: Basic Books, 1955), 140–79. It is this afterlife of the Kleinian part-object that led me to the idea that the part has an important function after perception of and loss of the whole: that it is, in fact, fetishized.

6. Sigmund Freud, "Fetishism," in *The Standard Edition of the Works of Sigmund Freud*, ed. and trans. James Strachey (London: Hogarth P, 1953–56), 21:153. See also "The Dissolution of the Oedipus Complex," *Standard Edition*, 19:173–79. The fear of castration, according to Freud, does not apply to the girl-child; she already has been castrated, and her Oedipus complex is the result of her castration. The resolution of the female Oedipus complex remains rather unclear.

7. Lacan, in "The function and field of speech and language in psychoanalysis" (note 2, p. 571, 102–04), reinterprets Freud's analysis of his grandson's game of Fort!/Da!, analyzing the partial object as itself conveying absence: as Anthony Wilden puts it, "The partial object conveys the lack which created the desire for unity from which the movement toward identification springs—since identification is itself dependent upon the discovery of *difference*, itself a kind of absence" (Anthony Wilden, "Lacan and the Discourse of the Other," in Jacques Lacan, *The Language of the Self*, translated and with commentary by Anthony Wilden [Baltimore: Johns Hopkins UP, 1968], 163). The partial object attempts to fill a lack created by a loss of ideal plenitude; Lacan analyzes the restless movement of desire opened up by the loss of the *objet a*, the loss of the relation to an other who is not conceived of as an object. The substitutes will always be partial. This lost object *a* is in particular the mother's body; in Lacan's interpretation of the Oedipal situation, the father interrupts the symbiotic relationship of mother and child; the phallus represents sexual difference and thus is a sign of castration. See "Of the Gaze as *Objet Petit a*," in *Four Fundamental Concepts of Psychoanalysis*, ed. J.-A. Miller, trans. Alan Sheridan (New York: W. W. Norton & Company, 1981), 67–119, esp. 67–77.

because they are—accepted as substitutes for lost genitals. So written documents, as the eunuch Pardoner's partial objects, fill his "male" (I.694) while deceiving no one, and relics provide the means by which he increases and multiplies. That his relics perform this genital role for the Pardoner is made explicit at the end of the *Tale*, when Harry Bailly wishes that he could make the ultimate relic for the Pardoner's collection out of the Pardoner's "coillons" (balls): he would cut them off and enshrine them in a hog's turd. But he can't, for reasons evident to all.

Harry Bailly's response to the Pardoner's invitation to "kiss the re-likes everychon" is surprising in its vehemence: that final moment between the two pilgrims is highly charged with sexual repugnance. But I find Harry's response interesting in another way as well: in its ex-plicit association of relics and balls, it refers to another medieval dis-cussion wherein relics, balls, and writing are all brought together in a discussion of castration. Relics, testicles, and language are not, as far as I know, common bedfellows in medieval literature; we must, there-fore, investigate how and why they are brought together in a passage in the *Roman de la rose*—the text commonly acknowledged to contain, in Faux-Semblant, a source for the characterization of the Pardoner—and from the *Rose* into the *Canterbury Tales*.

II

In the *Roman de la rose*, Raison's narration of the story of Saturn's castration, the event that she identifies as the moment at which the Golden Age, the original ideal community, was lost, leads to a discus-sion of her use of language (6898–7200). Amant quibbles with Rai-son's free naming of "coilles" in her narration. "Balls are not of good repute in the mouth of a courteous lady," he protests, perhaps refer-ring to dirty sex as well as to dirty language.[8] Her language goes against Amors's "clean speech commandment," as John V. Fleming has put it.[9] If such things as balls must be mentioned, Amant insists, Rai-son should at least provide a gloss. The word is dirty, he clearly im-plies, because the thing is dirty.

Raison counters by protesting that neither word nor thing is dirty. Both word and thing are good, and she can name a thing which is good—made by God—openly and by its own name. Her words are proper names of things; they are perfectly adequate to, share in the *propre* of, the things they name. Amant protests further that even if God made the things, he still didn't make the words, which are un-speakably nasty. But Raison goes on to declare that God could have made the words at the time of creation; instead he deputized her to do it at her leisure. Her comment traces language to the time before the Fall: her view here is an essentially prelapsarian view of language, an

8. *Roman de la rose*, 6898–6901).
9. Fleming (note 8, p. 570) 101. Fleming has written the most recent analysis of this scene in his chapter "Words and Things." He identifies Augustine as the most important influence here (the "supertext," to use his term), as I also do; but our conclusions are somewhat differ-ent. My discussion coincides more closely with Bloch, *Etymologies and Genealogies*, 137–41.

Adamic view that words share in the nature of the things they signify.

Raison then goes on to say that if she had called "reliques coilles" and "coilles reliques," Amant would have objected that "reliques" is a base word. Clearly, she implies, "reliques" is a good word because "reliques" are holy things. But even in Raison's suggestion that she could have named "reliques coilles" and vice versa, there is an implication of the arbitrariness of signs: the original relation between word and thing, between *signans* and *signatum*, was, in fact, arbitrary. She could have named the things anything. And her comments on "custom" that follow develop this protonominalist point: names are set by custom, by convention.

These are two distinct and contradictory positions on language: the one "naturalistic," the other "conventional." The issue of the naturalness or conventionality of the relationship between word and thing, sign and signified, had been debated since Plato's *Cratylus*, and both positions are found in medieval writers on language. Medieval writers explicitly adopted Hermogenes' position, asserting that the sign's relation to the signified is determined by convention, but at the same time, their linguistic and analytical habits imply a belief in the natural fitness of signs to things. Socrates too, of course, had it both ways: he judged that there is a natural resemblance between word and thing, but he acknowledged the conventional establishment of meaning as well. This dichotomous or ambivalent position, R. Howard Bloch has suggested, can be seen in writers from the late Latin grammarians (Varro, Priscian) to writers of the high Middle Ages (Abelard, John of Salisbury).[1] Such ambivalence may be very clearly seen in Augustine, whose discussions of sign theory proved fundamental throughout the entire Middle Ages, and whose thought informs this passage in the *Roman de la rose*.

Augustine accepts the anti-Cratylistic notion that the relation between *signans* and *signatum* is conventionally established. Very clearly (even simplistically, as some critics have suggested) he explains in the *De doctrina*:

> the single sign *beta* means a letter among the Greeks but a vegetable among the Latins. When I say *lege*, a Greek understands one thing by these two syllables, a Latin understands another. Therefore just as all of these significations move men's minds in accordance with the consent of their societies, and because their consent varies, they move them differently, nor do men agree upon them because of an innate value, but they have a value because they are agreed upon.[2]

Verbal signs do not have innate referential values. Augustine suggests to Adeodatus in *De magistro* that one cannot even know that a word is

1. Bloch, *Etymologies and Genealogies*, 44–53.
2. St. Augustine, *De doctrine christiana*, ed. J. Martin, Corpus christianorum (hereafter cited as CC), series latina, 32 (Turnholt: Brepols, 1962), 2.24, pp. 59–60. Trans. as *On Christian Doctrine* by D. W. Robertson, Jr. (Indianapolis: Bobbs-Merrill, 1958), 60–61. For a critique of Augustine's position here, see R. A. Markus, "St. Augustine on Signs," in *Augustine: A Collection of Critical Essays*, ed. R. A. Markus (New York: Doubleday Anchor, 1972), 78.

a sign until one knows what it means: the decision to attend to it as a sign is set by convention, as is its meaning.[3] Language is a social phenomenon and there cannot be, according to this position, any constitutive similarity between thing and sign.

Nevertheless, there is in Augustine's writing a deep strain of belief in the natural relation of words and their referents. *De dialectica* includes a chapter on the origins of words: there Augustine argues against the Stoics' claim that *all* words can be traced to their natural origins, but he endorses and practices etymological analysis of many words, tracing them back to find an essential, constitutive similarity between sound and thing.[4] Origins of words are essential to his argument in *De civitate Dei*: the names of the founders of the two cities express the whole program of human history.[5] His fascination with the infant's process of learning language in the *Confessiones* (I.6, 8) suggests a profound desire for verbal signs rooted in the physical, in the body, a language understood by all humans. Even though he is careful, always, to distinguish natural signs from conventional signs and to put language in the latter category, he expresses a definite linguistic nostalgia—a desire for a language in which word and thing are again one.

This nostalgia is a symptom of his desire to escape from the problems that the conventionality of language poses, problems of language's unreliability. For language, established by convention, is radically limited. Augustine's *De magistro* is an extended treatise on the limitations of verbal signs. The conventions that link *signans* to *signatum* can be changed, disregarded, broken. Words are capable only of reminding, not teaching, Augustine says to Adeodatus; they are able to point to the truth but do not possess it. And consequently, all kinds of slips are possible between the speaker, his language, and his audience.[6]

Theologically speaking, the problem of language's defectiveness was

---

3. St. Augustine, *De magistro*, ed. K.-D. Daur, CC, 29 (Turnholt: Brepols, 1970), 11.36, p. 194.

4. *De dialectica* is a work whose authorship has been disputed, but one which has been taken by its most recent translator and by Fleming (note 8, p. 570) as genuinely Augustinian. See the introduction to *De dialectica*, ed. Jan Pinborg, trans. with introduction and notes by B. Darrell Jackson (Boston and Dordrecht, Holland: D. Reidel, 1975). Augustine begins the chapter by suggesting that a word's origin may indeed be a matter of indifference, as long as its meaning is understood; he suggests that the pursuit of the origin of words is a potentially endless task, dependent on the researcher's own ingenuity, and that some words' origins can't ever be accounted for. But he asserts, in the same chapter, that there are many cases of natural resemblance between word and referent: the impressions made on the senses by the sounds of such words as *lene* and *asperitas* are in harmony (*concordarent*) with the impressions made by the referents themselves. Further on, Augustine specifically discusses the *vis* of words—their affective power—suggesting that the sensible qualities of words convey a meaning that is in accord with the referent itself. Sound and referent, physical property of word and physical property of thing, are linked: the word shares the natural property of the thing.

5. Bloch (*Etymologies and Genealogies*, 36) makes this observation and cites *De civitate Dei* 15.17: "Now as Cain, signifying possession, the founder of the earthly city, and his son Enoch, meaning dedication, in whose name it was founded, indicate that this city is earthly both in its beginning and in its end—a city in which nothing more is hoped for than can be seen in this world—so Seth, meaning resurrection, and being the father of generations registered apart from the others, we must consider what this sacred history says of his son." *De civitate Dei*, CC, 47 (Turnholt: Brepols, 1955), 480; trans. M. Dods, in *Basic Writings of Saint Augustine*, ed. Whitney J. Oates (New York: Random House, 1948), 2:300.

6. *De magistro* 13.43 and passim.

solved by the Incarnation. As God took on humanity in a Word made flesh, so can human language express divinity; language is redeemed.[7] The Incarnation restores man to God, the word to the Word: the continuity of language and being, disrupted at the Fall, is reestablished. Nevertheless, the problem of language's defectiveness, exemplified most profoundly by its inability to express the divine, remains. Augustine begins the *Confessiones* by lamenting the poverty of language and asserting the ultimate ineffability of God, and he ends the *De trinitate* similarly—even though it is in this latter treatise that he delineates the mimetic relation of the inner word of the mind to the Word.[8]

So human language is essentially partial. This is why Raison's narration of castration leads to a discussion of language and relics: "coilles," "reliques," "paroles"—all are fragments. A sign itself, Augustine sees, is accurate, but by definition it is only a partial representation of the thing it signifies. The word we speak is only a fragment of what we think (*De magistro* 14.46). And that inner word is only a partial representation of the Word (*De trinitate* 15.10–11). Words are, physically, fragments, one giving way to another in the construction of a whole message (*Confessiones* 4.11). And there is always something left over, unexpressed: language always lags behind the mind (*De catechizandis rudibus*, 2.3).[9] Augustine's awareness of linguistic inadequacy, even as he formulated the idea of a redeemed rhetoric, reflects, as Bloch puts it, an "anguished ambiguity provoked by a deep split between what medieval writers knew about verbal signs and what they desired to believe about them."[1]

The Pardoner, with his "hauteyn speche" (330), missing "coillons," and fake relics, is the focus of anxiety about language in the *Canterbury Tales*. Late-medieval fears about language's instability and unreliability focused, at least in part, on the use of language by self-seeking preachers (especially friars); and the Pardoner is, of course, a false preacher. Fourteenth-century treatises on preaching stress, on the one hand, that preaching is mandated by Christ: it is both necessary and possible with a "redeemed rhetoric" such as Augustine describes, a rhetoric based on the "unity of substance" in the Word, as Robert of Basevorn puts it in his *Forma praedicandi* (1322). Christ preached and ordered his followers to preach; indeed, in so doing, he was following a tradition of preaching that dated from the

---

7. Critical in Augustine's intellectual movement toward Christianity is his understanding of the Incarnation: as Marcia Colish demonstrates, the rhetorician's whole conversion experience can be traced by following this idea of the redemption of language. See Marcia Colish, *The Mirror of Language* (New Haven: Yale UP, 1968), 8–81.
8. *Confessiones* 1.4; see *De trinitate*, ed. W. J. Mountain, CC, 50 (Turnholt: Brepols, 1968), 11 and 15 for the explication of the relationship between word and Word; and 15.28 (Oratio), 533–35, for the final protestation of the ineffability of God and the shortcomings of language: "When the wise man spake of Thee in his book, which is now called by the special name of *Ecclesiasticus*, 'We speak,' he said, 'much, and yet come short; and in sum of words, He is all.' When, therefore, we shall have come to Thee, these very many things that we speak, and yet come short, will cease; and Thou, as One, wilt remain 'all in all.' " Trans. A. W. Haddan, rev. by W. G. T. Shedd, in *Basic Writings of Saint Augustine* (note 5, p. 577), 2:878.
9. St. Augustine, *De catechizandis rudibus*, ed. I. B. Bauer, CC, 46 (Turnholt: Brepols, 1969), 122–23.
1. Bloch, *Etymologies and Genealogies*, 44.

Creation, when, as Robert writes, God first preached to Adam.
Preaching is thus linked to unfallen language.[2] Also associating
preaching with Creation, Humbert of Romans states in his mid-
thirteenth-century treatise on preaching that it functions to "scatter
the word of God like seed."[3]

But on the other hand, language was understood to be partial and
fragmentary; abuses of language in preaching were perceived as not
only possible but rampant. The widespread uneasiness about false
preaching had as its ultimate preoccupation the defective, shifting relationship of the spoken word to the Word. Wycliffe charged again and
again that false preachers—abusive friars—had obfuscated the true
Word.[4] Wycliffe's literalism was extreme and unorthodox, but protests
against friars who "redefined" or altogether discarded the Word to
serve their own ends in sermons were rife: Chaucer's Summoner
paints a perfect portrait of the "glosying" friar; Richard FitzRalph,

2. Robert of Basevorn, *Forma Praedicandi* 6, in *Artes praedicandi*, ed. Th.-M. Charland, O.P.,
   Publications de l'Institut d'Etudes Médiévales d'Ottawa (Paris and Ottawa, 1936): "After
   creating man, God preached (if we extend the word 'preaching'), saying to Adam (Gen.
   2:17): *For in what day soever thou shalt eat of it, thou shalt die the death.* This was the first
   persuasion of which we read in Scripture. . . . And at last He Himself, taking on a human
   soul and body in the unity of substance, came preaching the same theme which his precur-
   sor had preached before, as is seen in Matt. 4:17." Trans. Leopold Krul, O.S.B., in *Three
   Medieval Rhetorical Arts*, ed. James J. Murphy (Berkeley: U of California P, 1971), 126–27.
   See also Thomas Waleys, *De modo componendi sermones cum documentis* 1, in Charland,
   329–41. I have benefitted from the surveys of sermon rhetoric in James J. Murphy, *Rhetoric
   in the Middle Ages: A History of Rhetorical Theory from St. Augustine to the Renaissance*
   (Berkeley and Los Angeles: U of California P, 1974), 269–355; Etienne Gilson, "Michel
   Menot et la technique du sermon médiévale," in his *Les Idées et les lettres*, 2nd ed. (Paris:
   J. Vrin, 1955), 93–154; and Margaret Jennings, C.S.J., "The Ars componendi sermones of
   Ranulph Higden," in *Medieval Eloquence: Studies in the Theory and Practice of Medieval
   Rhetoric*, ed. J. J. Murphy (Berkeley: U of California P, 1978), 112–26.
3. Humbert of Romans, *De eruditione praedicatorum* 1.3, ed. J. J. Berthier (Rome: A. Befani,
   1889), 2:377: "Without preaching, through which the word of God is sown, all the world
   would be sterile and without fruit" (my translation).
4. This accusation is a fundamental one in Wycliffe's continual antifraternal polemic. For
   examples in English, see his vernacular version of his Latin *De officio pastorali* (c. 1377),
   chap. 26:

> thus ther ben many causis that letten goddis word to renne. . . . the fourthe cause is
> bringing in of false freris bi many cuntreys; for, as it is seid bifore, thei letten trewe
> preching to renne and maken curatis bi many weyes to leeue this moost worthy offiss.
> First they robben hem many weyes and maken hem bisy for to lyue, for they deprauen
> hem to ther parischens bi floriyshid wordis that they bringen yn; and no drede they
> shapen ther sermouns by dyuysiouns and othere iapis that they maken moost plese the
> puple. And thus they erren in bileue and maken the puple to trowe to hem that ser-
> mouns ben nought but in ther foorme.

The English Works of Wyclif, Hitherto Unprinted, ed. F. D. Mathew, Early English Text Society, n.v., (London: Trubner, 1880), 445–46. Another example is sermon III, on the Feast of
the Seven Brethren:

> Thes wordis of Crist ben scorned of gramariens and devynes. Gramariens and
> filosophris seien, that Crist knewe not his gendris; and bastard dyvynes seien algatis
> that thes wordis of Crist ben false, and so no wordis of Crist bynden, but to the witt
> that gloseris tellen. But here we seien to thes trowauntis that thei blaiberen thus for de-
> faute of witt. Leeve we thes heretikes as foolis, and seie we sum witt that God hath
> yovon us.

Select English Works of John Wyclif, ed. Thomas Arnold (Oxford: Clarendon P, 1869),
1:375–76. See G. R. Owst, *Preaching in Medieval England: An Introduction to Sermon Manuscripts of the Period, c. 1350–1450* (New York: Russell and Russell, 1965), for a discussion
of fraternal preaching, and *Literature and Pulpit in Medieval England* (Oxford: Basil Blackwell, 1961), 56–109, for literal and allegorical uses of Scripture in sermons. Dom David
Knowles, *The Religious Orders of England* (Cambridge: Cambridge UP, 1957), 2:61–73,
90–115, provides a good discussion of mendicant orders and their critics.

Archbishop of Armagh in the mid-fourteenth century, exclaims against friars who complain of his insistence on textual proof. Such charges against preaching friars as hypocrites point directly to a deep split between the speaker's intention, his spoken word, and the Word.[5]

So false preachers represent not just a threat to language; they represent a truth about language, in fact, language's "double truth." Language is at best a fragment, and, like "coilles" and "reliques," can be cut off altogether from the Significator. Yet people nostalgically believe in it, must believe in it; they necessarily affirm by speaking and listening that the spoken word can adequately express the inner word, and the inner word, the Word. Faux-Semblant, false preacher of the *Roman de la rose*, embodies the uneasy possibility of the breakdown of all coherence and stability in that narrative. As an unfixed, shape-shifting being, putting on clothes without a body beneath, he is a sign without a Significator, a spoken word without a Word. And he is sexually indeterminate: he can adopt both genders, and is neither. If one truth about language associates it with prelapsarian times, a time of perfect sexual relations, gendered but uncorrupted, the other truth cuts it off from perfect sexuality. The breakdown of language and determinate sexuality are of a piece, as it were; and the Pardoner, false preacher, of a broken, corrupted sexuality, is Faux-Semblant's descendant in every way.

III

The Pardoner both exposes and is caught in language's double truth. He uses language as he does his relics and his documents, as a partial object, a substitute for his absent genitals, and for what their absence represents: a lost Golden Age in which there is no differentiation between self and other, signifier and signified—the realm of the Word. His partial objects are flawed; they are inadequate substitutes, and he knows it. In fact he tells the pilgrims again and again that his relics are fakes; he insists that his words and his intentions are discrepant; he admits that Christ's pardon, not his, "is best." Yet he adopts these partial objects in the knowledge of their insufficiency. The psycho-logic of knowingly accepting such faulty substitutes is succinctly expressed by O. Mannoni in his discussion of the fetish: "Je sais bien, mais quand même . . . [I know, but even so . . .]. This is the logic of the eunuch that informs the hermeneutics of the partial.[6]

Mannoni is, of course, following Freud here, who writes that the fetish "is a substitute for the woman's (the mother's) penis that the little boy once believed in, and . . . does not want to give up." The fetish

---

5. Arnold Williams cites a sermon by FitzRalph (British Museum Ms. Lansdowne 393, fol. 108ʳ) in which FitzRalph remarks that "when he challenged the friars to produce one scriptural text commanding poverty or proving that Christ ever begged voluntarily or spontaneously, they complained that he respected only the text of Scripture, not the gloss" ("Chaucer and the Friars," *Speculum* 28 [1953]: 511). Even some friars themselves admitted that they preached sometimes with hatred in their hearts, not with the *caritas* that is the proper significator of all language: see G. R. Owst, *Preaching in Medieval England*, 77.
6. O. Mannoni, *Clefs pour l'imaginaire* (Paris: Seuil, 1969), 9–33.

allows the child to retain the idea of the maternal phallus even after he has perceived sexual difference; it allows him to remain in the realm of nondifferentiation and plenitude (his mother and he are not separate) even after he knows that she doesn't have an organ like his, even after mother and child are cut off from each other by the interruption of the father. But such a substitute is inevitably inadequate; the child *knows* that the mother is separate and other, and anxiously tries to fill that un-fillable emptiness. The fetish is precisely what I have been calling a partial object: it admits the fact of castration even as it refuses to admit it. Thus the fetish is constituted of contrary ideas, of "two mutually in-compatible assertions": the mother has her penis and she has been cas-trated; the child is united with the mother and is cut off from her.[7] The fetishist maintains a conceptual fiction, a fiction of nondifferentiation and plenitude, in the face of perceptual knowledge.[8] "I know, but even so . . . ": the fetish is the first model of all repudiations of reality.[9] Thus the medieval theorists of language know about the fallenness of lan-guage, but hold on to the belief otherwise. Just as the fetishist knows that a foot is just a foot—but even so . . .

The Pardoner, using his partial objects as substitute genitals, is a fetishist. His verbal arts, documents, relics are all entirely transparent substitutes: they are admissions, signs of his lack even as they guard against his acknowledgment of it. He knows that they are only partial, that they are fakes, but even so he uses them—aggressively, desper-ately—in the belief that they can make him whole, somehow part of the body of pilgrims. And his *Tale*, a sample sermon, is a narrative rep-resentation of the fetishist's conflicted psyche. The world of the *Tale* is an Old Testament one, punitive and unredeemed; the "riotoures thre" are dispatched by "Deeth" in a terrifyingly immediate judgment of their sin. Yet the "olde man," embodying mutually incompatible asser-tions, has, along with a knowledge of this implacable "Deeth," a belief in redemption, "even so."[1]

The tavern world of the riotors is the world of the Law. Most of the Pardoner's exempla are drawn from the Old Testament, and he seems in fact to prefer the Old Testament to the New in setting the scene: "Witnesse on Mathew; but in special / Of sweryng seith the hooly Jere-

---

7. Freud (note 6, p. 574), 21:152–53, 157.
8. D. W. Winnicott, "Transitional Objects and Transitional Phenomena: A Study of the First Not-Me Possession," *International Journal of Psycho-Analysis* 34 (1953): 95–96, contrasts the fetish with the transitional object in order to emphasize the abnormality of the fetishist. The fetish, based as it is on a delusion of a maternal phallus, is not a normal phenomenon, whereas the transitional object, based on illusion (an area between primary creativity and objective reality based on reality testing), is healthy and universal. Phyllis Greenacre, "The Fetish and the Transitional object," *Psychoanalytic Study of the Child* 24 (1969): 144–65, also stresses the arrest of development of the fetishist.
9. See Mannoni, 12.
1. Among the many recent critics who have discussed narrative elements of the *Tale* as repre-sentations or projections of the Pardoner himself, see H. Marshall Leicester, Jr., " 'Synne Horrible': The Pardoner's Exegesis of His Tale, and Chaucer's," in *Acts of Interpretation: The Text in Its Contexts, 700–1600,* ed. Mary J. Carruthers and Elizabeth D. Kirk (Norman, Okla.: Pilgrim Books, 1982), 25–50; Alfred David, *The Strumpet Muse* (Bloomington: Indi-ana UP, 1976), 193–204; Patterson (note 9, p. 570), 166–67; and Howard (note 4, p. 568), 357–63.

mye" (634–35). Christ's Redemption is duly acknowledged, but our original corruption and consequent damnation, imposed by an angry God the Father at the Fall, vividly endure in the Pardoner's rhetoric:

> O glotonye, ful of cursednesse!
> O cause first of oure confusioun!
> O original of oure dampnacioun,
> Til Crist hadde boght us with his blood agayn!
> Lo, how deere, shortly for to sayn,
> Aboght was thilke cursed vileynye!
> Corrupt was al this world for glotonye.
>   (498–504)

"Heighe Goddes heestes" (640), the tables of the Law, govern, and sin is inexorably punished: its wages are death. "Deeth," in fact, presides over "this contree"; he has slain "al the peple" (676) and will inevitably prevail over those who seek to slay him. In the emotional economy of the tale, this ineluctable Death is the same force as the Father, "verray God, that is omnipotent" (576). When the Pardoner assigns the three riotors, three stumbling, swearing drunks, to overcome Death, it becomes clear that to his mind redemption from the Law, from this forbidding "verray God," is impossible. " 'Deeth shal be deed!' " the riotors yell, "al dronken in this rage" (710, 705): the three inebriated ruffians are incapable—obviously, lugubriously—of this salvific mission. Death gets them in the end, and there is no thought of salvation.

Indulging in all the sins of which the Pardoner says he is himself guilty, the three riotors are a representation of the Pardoner's belief in the impossibility of atonement with the Father. The "olde man," whom they accost in the search for Death, is another representation of the Pardoner himself: he is an incarnation of the Pardoner's anguished knowledge of his fragmentariness: "Lo how I vanysshe, flessh, and blood, and skyn!" (732). The old man wails for some redemption from his defective and dying corpse, and he expresses this desire not in terms of atonement with the Father but of reunion with his "leeve mooder":

> Thus walke I, lyk a resteless kaityf,
> And on the ground, which is my moodres gate,
> I knokke with my staf, bothe erly and late,
> And seye "Leeve mooder, leet me in!"
>   (728–31)

Between the old man and his "leeve mooder," that lost ideal realm of unity and plenitude, stands "Goddes wille." To be "at reste" in the "ground" with his mother would provide a return to nondifferentiation, a reunion of subject and object, a redemption from the torments of age and separation. Even though he knows of Christ's atonement for the loss of original plenitude—he tells the riotors of it—he remains unredeemed by Him "that boghte agayn mankynde" (766): he walks continually "lyk a restelees kaityf" (728). The old man has an image and a hope of fullness and plenitude—"Deeth" to him is reunion, not separation, and he states that he has not been reunited with his mother "yet"—but the way to this plentitude is not through the Father: "Goddes wille" blocks it.

The figure of the old man in particular articulates the Pardoner's own "incompatible assertions." The Pardoner's world as he imagines it is dominated by a jealous, unforgiving Old Testament God, a castrating Father; Christ's pardon is acknowledged but the Pardoner is still convicted by the image of the forbidding Father, and under the Law there is no redemption, nothing but death as the wages of sin. Cut off, the Pardoner obsessively desires wholeness, and wholeness is what he repeatedly claims his pardons will deliver: he promises his rustic audiences again and again that their cows, calves, sheep will be made "hool" (357, 359), and they themselves will remain a part of the body of Christians (377–88). And he comments to the pilgrims that "Paraventure ther may fallen oon or two / Doun of his hors, and breke his nekke atwo" (935–36), but, he boasts and somehow believes, he is "suffisant" to the task of making them whole again. The Pardoner is an enormous success as a swindler precisely because he truly believes in his own false relics.[2]

So the Pardoner believes in the possibility of the restoration of lost plenitude, and he successfully plays on the fetishism of his audiences as well. His promises of wholeness make him richer by far than any parish priest. And the Pardoner knows that the pilgrims desire wholeness: when he interrupts the Wife of Bath to claim that he was about to wed a wife, when he later proclaims in his *Prologue* that he wants a jolly wench in every town, he is not simply trying to enter the heterosexual world of the pilgrims; he is cannily playing on their desire to believe in the integrity of the body, their desire to believe in the integrity of *his* body, and of their own pilgrim body. He is exploiting their fetishistic ability to admit his oddity even while they refuse the practical consequences of their admission. They know (that he is sexually weird), but even so (they demand a "moral thyng" from him). Their desire for an edifying tale is well described by this fetishistic logic: even out of the mouth of a ribald figure they insist that it will be a "moral thyng"; even though it is fiction, they will find it true. Fiction is not just for "lewed peple" to "holde" onto (438); it is for everyone, a partial object par excellence. Made of flawed language, fiction is not literally true, we know, but it plays on our desire for truth. To paraphrase John of Garland's definition of "realistic fiction" (*argumentum*), "I know that it didn't happen, but even so, it could have . . ."—and we will find the ways in which it can be said to tell the truth.[3]

2. "We have already seen that there are several ways to believe and not to believe" (Mannoni, 24; my translation). The swindler believes, in a certain fashion, in his admittedly false inventions, using the fetishist's belief "even so." Belief is the key to the creation of illusion or of the successful swindle, and as Mannoni suggests, it is the swindler's own belief that makes the job work. "Clearly there is no doubt that disavowal is enough to create magic" (29; my translation).

3. See John of Garland, *Parisiana poetria*, ed. and trans. Traugott Lawler (New Haven: Yale UP, 1974), 5.327–31: "Argumentum est res ficta que tamen fieri potuit, ut contingit in comediis [A Realistic Fiction is a fictitious event which nevertheless could have happened, as is the case in comedies]" (Lawler's translation). This description of *argumentum* was made as early as the *Rhetorica ad herennium* 1.8.13, to which John was indebted. See Ernst Robert Cur-

The particular form of the exemplum is perfectly suited to the Pardoner's, and his audiences', fetishistic purposes. It is not only a lie that tells the truth; it formally demonstrates the psychological stagnation of the fetishist, caught between incompatible affirmations.[4] The exemplum is unnecessary to the logical argument of the sermon; it doesn't develop or complicate a point, but merely demonstrates it. *Radix malorum est cupiditas*: the three riotors are greedy and unscrupulous, and evil befalls them. The wages of sin are death: they set out to find death, and they find it. The plot is nothing but the rigorous working out of what is announced at the outset: how the riotors find death remains to be seen, but that they will find it is certain. The tale itself is, from this standpoint, superfluous—we already know the outcome—and thus it is no coincidence that "superfluytee abhomynable" (471)—drinking, gambling, cursing—motivates the narrative. Yet despite its excessive status there is nothing left over. The admirable neatness of the tale, the clever reification of the *radix malorum* into "under a tree," is a function of its essentially resolved form. Everyone and everything is consumed in the turns of the narrative, either dying or fading out, going "thider as I have to go" (749), as the old man says.

Fetishism is, finally, a conservative behavior: it allows one to maintain a fiction of plenitude even in the face of loss and dislocation. The Pardoner is fixed between knowledge of his fragmentation and belief that he can be made whole; knowledge of Death, God's Law, and judgment, and belief in the possibility of reunion and redemption; knowledge that his pardons are fraudulent, and belief that they can restore him to an original unity. He is neither hopeful nor despairing, but is somewhere between the two. In its stuck quality, this mechanism of disavowal is similar to the cyclical mechanism, as Augustine analyzes it, of sinning that leads to despair that leads to further sinning.[5] But despair is finally destructive, whereas the Pardoner will continue to "go . . . as I have to go," neither destroying himself nor finding redemption.

The Pardoner's coup de grace—or, better, *coupure de grace*—at the end of the tale is the final gesture of the fetishist among his peers: "I have relics and pardon in my male / As fair as any man in Engelond" (920–21), he boasts to the pilgrims. In other words: "I know that they're phony substitutes, but even so, I believe they're 'as fair' as any other man's. And you know that they're frauds, but even so, you want to believe in the grace of absolution. So step right up and kiss them." The Host's threat to castrate the eunuch Pardoner makes sense in this context: "I know that you don't have the balls to be cut off, but even

---

tius, *European Literature and the Latin Middle Ages*, trans. Willard R. Trask (Princeton: Princeton UP, 1953), for the classical background of the distinction among *historia, fabula,* and *argumentum*.

4. Bloch analyzes the psychologically and socially conservative functions of the *fabliau* in similar ways in his *Scandal of the Fabliaux*, 101–28.

5. See Augustine, *Contra Julianum Pelagianum, Patrologia latina,* 44: col. 787: "Thus concupiscence of the flesh . . . is at once sin . . . and punishment of sin . . . and cause of sin" (my translation). Quoted in Kellog (note 3, p. 571), 245–68. See also Howard (note 4, p. 568), 355–57.

so, I posit the fiction to increase the power of my threat." But it is only a fiction: the Host's language, like all language, is itself castrated; it is a partial object, itself a fragment. The Knight's intervention can only return the company to the beginning: "And, as we diden, lat us laughe and pleye" (1967), he exhorts them. As before in Fragment I (856), they again "ryden forth hir weye."

Geoffrey Chaucer: A Chronology†

1327   Reign of Edward III begins.

1337–1453   The Hundred Years War with France.

1340–45   Birth of Geoffrey Chaucer, son of Agnes and John Chaucer, a successful wine-merchant in London.

1348–50   The Black Death. Epidemics of plague recur throughout Chaucer's lifetime.

1357   Chaucer in service as a page in the household of Elizabeth de Burgh, countess of Ulster.

1360   Edward III contributes to Chaucer's ransom after his capture in France. Chaucer carries letters to England from Calais for Lionel, earl of Ulster.

1365–67   Chaucer marries Philippa Roet, a lady-in-waiting to Queen Philippa; they have a son, Thomas, who later becomes a prosperous landholder and respected member of Parliament.

1366   Chaucer in Spain, perhaps on a diplomatic mission.

1367   Edward III grants to Chaucer, his "valet," an annuity of twenty marks for life.

1369   Chaucer in service as an esquire in the royal household. Takes part in John of Gaunt's campaign in northern France.

1370   Chaucer travels on the Continent in the king's service.

1372–73   Chaucer commissioned to establish an English seaport for Genoese trade; to this end and for other matters of the king's business, travels to Genoa and Florence.

1374   Edward III grants Chaucer a pitcher of wine daily. Chaucer leases a house above Aldgate. Appointed Controller of Wool Custom and Subsidy for the Port of London.

1377   Chaucer goes to France and Flanders on the king's secret business. Assists at the negotiations at Montreuil-sur-Mer for peace and in Paris for the marriage of Prince Richard. Reign of Richard II begins.

1378   Chaucer sent to Lombardy on a mission concerning the war.

1381   Chaucer receives a gift of twenty-two pounds from Richard II for his diplomatic service in France. Peasants' Revolt.

1385–86   Chaucer sits as Justice of the Peace for Kent.

1386   Chaucer elected to Parliament as Knight of the Shire

† The principal source for Chaucer's biography is the *Chaucer Life-Records*, ed. Martin M. Crow and Clair C. Olson (Austin: U of Texas P, 1966). The standard biography is Derek Pearsall, *The Life of Geoffrey Chaucer* (Oxford: Blackwell, 1992). A few of these dates are conjectural.

for Kent. Retires as Controller of the Port of London. Richard II's power is weakened.

1389   Richard II regains power. Chaucer appointed Clerk of the King's Works, with responsibility for construction at Westminster, the Tower of London, and several castles and manors.

1390   Chaucer is among those charged with responsibility for the walls, ditches, and other works on the Thames between Woolwich and Greenwich.

1391   Chaucer retires from the clerkship. Appointed deputy forester of the Royal Forest of North Petherton, Somerset.

1393   Richard II awards Chaucer ten pounds for "good service."

1394   Richard II grants Chaucer an annuity of twenty pounds for life.

1397   Richard II's final gift to Chaucer: a "tonel" (252 gallons) of wine a year for life.

1399   Richard II deposed. Henry IV, upon his accession to the throne, renews Richard's gifts to Chaucer and grants him an additional annuity of forty marks. Chaucer leases a residence in the garden of the Lady Chapel of Westminster Abbey.

1400   A sixteenth-century tomb in Westminster Abbey records Chaucer's death as occurring on October 25 of this year.

Selected Bibliography

• indicates works included or excerpted in this Norton Critical Edition.

The amount of published material devoted to Chaucer is enormous, and this selective bibliography is meant only as a starting point for undergraduate and graduate students. We have divided it into some important general areas of Chaucer scholarship and have also listed critical studies of the specific tales included in this Norton Critical Edition. Within each category the arrangement is usually chronological rather than alphabetical. However, if a Chaucer Variorum edition or a Toronto Chaucer Bibliography volume is available for an individual tale, we list that book first, since the publications in these two series provide the most comprehensive surveys of scholarship for that tale.

MODERN EDITIONS AND FACSIMILES

Skeat, W. W., ed. *The Works of Geoffrey Chaucer.* 7 vols. Oxford: Clarendon P, 1894–97.
Manly, John M., and Edith Rickert, eds. *The Text of the Canterbury Tales, Studied on the Basis of All Known Manuscripts.* 8 vols. Chicago: U of Chicago P, 1940.
Robinson, F. N., ed. *The Works of Geoffrey Chaucer.* 2nd ed. Boston: Houghton-Mifflin, 1957.
Baugh, Albert C., ed. *Chaucer's Major Poetry.* New York: Appleton-Century-Crofts, 1963.
Pratt, Robert A., ed. *The Tales of Canterbury.* Boston: Houghton Mifflin, 1974.
Donaldson, E. Talbot, ed. *Chaucer's Poetry: An Anthology for the Modern Reader.* 2nd ed. New York: Ronald Press, 1975.
Fisher, John H., ed. *The Complete Poetry and Prose of Geoffrey Chaucer.* New York: Holt, Rinehart and Winston, 1977. 2nd ed., 1989.
Ruggiers, Paul G., and Donald C. Baker, eds. *The Canterbury Tales: A Facsimile and Transcription of the Hengwrt Manuscript, with Variants from the Ellesmere Manuscript.* Norman: U of Oklahoma P, 1979.
Blake, N. F., ed. *Geoffrey Chaucer: The Canterbury Tales, Edited from the Hengwrt Manuscript.* London: Arnold, 1980.
Benson, Larry D., gen. ed. *The Riverside Chaucer.* 3rd ed. Boston: Houghton Mifflin, 1987.
Hanna, Ralph, III, intro. *The Ellesmere Manuscript of Chaucer's Canterbury Tales: A Working Facsimile.* Rochester, NY: Boydell & Brewer, 1989.
Woodward, Daniel, and Martin Stevens, eds. *The Canterbury Tales by Geoffrey Chaucer: The New Ellesmere Chaucer Facsimile.* San Marino, CA: Huntington Library, 1995. See also Woodward and Stevens, eds., *The Canterbury Tales by Geoffrey Chaucer: The New Ellesmere Chaucer Monochromatic Facsimile.* San Marino, CA: Huntington Library, 1997.

BIBLIOGRAPHIES

Allen, Mark, and Bege K. Bowers, eds. "An Annotated Chaucer Bibliography." *Studies in the Age of Chaucer.* Annual bibliographies begin in volume 1 (1979), offering thorough coverage of work on Chaucer since 1975. They are combined into a single online bibliography at <http://uchaucer.utsa.edu>.
Hammond, Eleanor P. *Chaucer: A Bibliographic Manual.* 1908. New York: Peter Smith, 1933.
Griffith, Dudley D. *Bibliography of Chaucer 1908–1953.* Seattle: U of Washington P, 1955.
Crawford, William R. *Bibliography of Chaucer 1954–63.* Seattle: U of Washington P, 1967.
Baird, Lorrayne Y. *A Bibliography of Chaucer, 1964–73.* Boston: Hall, 1977.
Baird-Lange, Lorrayne Y., and Hildegard Schnuttgen. *A Bibliography of Chaucer, 1974–1985.* Hamden, CT.: Archon, 1988.
Leyerle, John, and Anne Quick. *Chaucer: A Selected Bibliography.* Toronto: U of Toronto P, 1986.

Allen, Mark, and John H. Fisher. *The Essential Chaucer: An Annotated Bibliography of Major Modern Studies*. Boston: G. K. Hall, 1987.

SOURCES AND BACKGROUND MATERIAL

Bryan, W. F., and Germaine Dempster, eds. *Sources and Analogues of Chaucer's Canterbury Tales*. Chicago: U of Chicago P, 1941.

Rickert, Edith. *Chaucer's World*. Ed. Clair C. Olson and Martin M. Crow. New York: Columbia UP, 1948.

Loomis, Roger S. *A Mirror of Chaucer's World*. Princeton: Princeton UP, 1965.

Benson, Larry D., and Theodore M. Andersson, eds. *The Literary Context of Chaucer's Fabliaux*. Indianapolis: Bobbs-Merrill, 1971.

Miller, Robert P., ed. *Chaucer: Sources and Backgrounds*. New York: Oxford UP, 1977.

Besserman, Lawrence. *Chaucer and the Bible: A Critical Review of Research, Indices, and Bibliography*. New York: Garland, 1988.

Blamires, Alcuin, ed., with Karen Pratt and C. W. Marx. *Woman Defamed and Woman Defended: An Anthology of Medieval Texts*. Oxford: Clarendon P, 1992.

Bowers, John M., ed. *The Canterbury Tales: Fifteenth-Century Continuations and Additions*. Kalamazoo: Medieval Institute Publications, 1992.

Correale, Robert M., gen. ed., with Mary Hamel. *Sources and Analogues of the Canterbury Tales*. Vol. I. Cambridge: D. S. Brewer, 2002. Vol. II forthcoming.

LANGUAGE

Tatlock, John S. P., and Arthur G. Kennedy. *A Concordance to the Complete Works of Chaucer and to the Romaunt of the Rose*. 1927. Gloucester: Peter Smith, 1963.

Kökeritz, Helge. *A Guide to Chaucer's Pronunciation*. 1954. Toronto: U of Toronto P, 1978.

Davis, Norman, Douglas Gray, Patricia Ingham, and Anne Wallace-Hadrill. *A Chaucer Glossary*. Oxford: Clarendon P, 1979.

Burnley, David. *A Guide to Chaucer's Language*. Norman: U of Oklahoma P, 1983.

Sandved, Arthur O. *Introduction to Chaucerian English*. Cambridge: D. S. Brewer, 1985.

Oizumi, Akio, ed. Programmed by Kunihiro Miki. *A Complete Concordance to the Works of Geoffrey Chaucer*. 10 vols. New York: Olms-Weidmann, 1991.

Blake, N. F., ed. *The Cambridge History of the English Language: Volume II, 1066–1476*. Cambridge: Cambridge UP, 1992.

Burrow, J. A., and Thorlac Turville-Petre. *A Book of Middle English*. 2d ed. Oxford: Basil Blackwell, 1996.

Fisher, John H. *The Emergence of Standard English*. Lexington: UP of Kentucky, 1996.

Cannon, Christopher. *The Making of Chaucer's English: A Study of Words*. Cambridge: Cambridge UP, 1998.

Trotter, D. A., ed. *Multilingualism in Later Medieval Britain*. Cambridge: D. S. Brewer, 2000.

SPECIAL RESOURCES

The Chaucer Studio Recordings. Audiocassettes of almost all the *Canterbury Tales* read in Middle English, usually one tale per cassette. Not available commercially; for purchases ($5.00 per cassette) or a catalogue contact Professor Paul R. Thomas, Department of English, Brigham Young University, Provo, UT 84602-6218; <paul_thomas@byu.edu>. New recordings and reissues will be on CD.

Ashby, Cristina, Geoff Couldrey, and Susan Dickson. *Chaucer: Life and Times CD-ROM*. Woodbridge, CT.: Primary Source Media, 1995 [provides access to searchable texts, translations, glossary, critical essays, images, and other background information].

Robinson, Peter, ed. *The Wife of Bath's Prologue on CD-ROM*. Cambridge: Cambridge UP, 1996 [digital images and transcriptions of manuscripts and early printed editions, with a user guide, databases, and essays].

Solopova, Elizabeth, ed. *The General Prologue on CD-ROM*. Cambridge: Cambridge UP, 2000 [digital images and transcriptions of manuscripts and early printed editions, with a user guide, databases, and essays].

Stubbs, Estelle, ed. *The Hengwrt Chaucer Digital Facsimile*. Leicester: Scholarly Digital Editions, 2000 [facsimiles and transcriptions of Hengwrt MS and Merthyr fragment of the *Canterbury Tales*, with marginalia].

Abrams, M. H., and Stephen Greenblatt, gen. eds. *Media Companion* on CD-ROM, included free with *The Norton Anthology of English Literature*, 7th ed. New York: W. W. Norton & Company, 2001 [includes readings in Middle English of passages from the *Canterbury Tales* by J. B. Bessinger Jr., Marie Borroff, Alfred David, and V. A. Kolve].

Caxton's Chaucer. London: British Library, 2003. <http://www.bl.uk/treasures/caxton/homepage.html> [facsimiles of William Caxton's 1476 and 1483 editions of the *Canterbury Tales*].

COLLECTIONS OF CRITICAL ESSAYS

Burrow, J. A., ed. *Geoffrey Chaucer: A Critical Anthology*. Baltimore: Penguin, 1969.
Arrathoon, Leigh A., ed. *Chaucer and the Craft of Fiction*. Rochester, MI: Solaris Press, 1986.
Boitani, Piero, and Jill Mann, eds. *The Cambridge Chaucer Companion*. Cambridge: Cambridge UP, 1986. *The Cambridge Companion to Chaucer*, 2nd ed. 2003.
Benson, C. David, and Elizabeth Robertson, eds. *Chaucer's Religious Tales*. Cambridge: D. S. Brewer, 1990.
Andrew, Malcolm, ed. *Critical Essays on Chaucer's Canterbury Tales*. Toronto: U of Toronto P, 1991.
Stevens, Martin, and Daniel Woodward, eds. *The Ellesmere Chaucer: Essays in Interpretation*. San Marino, CA: Huntington Library, 1997.
Beidler, Peter G., ed. *Masculinities in Chaucer: Approaches to Maleness in the* Canterbury Tales *and* Troilus and Criseyde. Cambridge: D. S. Brewer, 1998.
Ellis, Steve, ed. *Chaucer: The Canterbury Tales*. New York: Longman, 1998.
Brown, Peter, ed. *A Companion to Chaucer*. Oxford: Blackwell, 2000.
Koff, Leonard Michael, and Brenda Deen Schildgen, eds. *The Decameron and the Canterbury Tales: New Essays on an Old Question*. Madison, NJ: Fairleigh Dickinson UP, 2000.
Saunders, Corinne, ed. *Chaucer*. Blackwell Guides to Criticism. Oxford: Blackwell, 2000.

GENERAL CRITICAL STUDIES

• Kittredge, George Lyman. *Chaucer and His Poetry*. Cambridge, MA: Harvard UP, 1915, 1970.
Baldwin, Ralph. *The Unity of the* Canterbury Tales. *Anglistica* 5. Copenhagen: Rosenkilde and Bagger, 1955.
Muscatine, Charles. *Chaucer and the French Tradition*. Berkeley: U of California P, 1957.
Robertson, D. W., Jr. *A Preface to Chaucer: Studies in Medieval Perspectives*. Princeton: Princeton UP, 1963.
Jordan, Robert M. *Chaucer and the Shape of Creation: The Aesthetic Possibilities of Inorganic Structure*. Cambridge: Harvard UP, 1967.
Burrow, J. A. *Ricardian Poetry*. New Haven: Yale UP, 1971.
• Du Boulay, F. R. H. "The Historical Chaucer." *Writers and Their Background: Geoffrey Chaucer*. Ed. Derek Brewer. Athens: Ohio UP, 1975. 33–57.
David, Alfred. *The Strumpet Muse: Art and Morals in Chaucer's Poetry*. Bloomington: Indiana UP, 1976.
Howard, Donald R. *The Idea of the* Canterbury Tales. Berkeley: U of California P, 1976.
Brewer, Derek. *Chaucer and His World*. New York: Dodd, Mead, 1977. 2nd ed. 1992.
Owen, Charles A., Jr. *Pilgrimage and Storytelling in the* Canterbury Tales. Norman: U of Oklahoma P, 1977.
Middleton, Anne. "Chaucer's 'New Men' and the Good of Literature in the *Canterbury Tales*." *Literature and Society. Selected Papers from the English Institute*. Ed. Edward W. Said. Baltimore: The Johns Hopkins UP, 1980. 15–56.
Benson, Larry D. "The Order of *The Canterbury Tales*." *Studies in the Age of Chaucer* 3 (1981): 77–120. Rpt. in *Contradictions: From Beowulf to Chaucer: Selected Studies of Larry D. Benson*. Ed. Theodore M. Andersson and Stephen A. Barney. Aldershot, Hants: Scolar, 1995.
Kolve, V. A. *Chaucer and the Imagery of Narrative: The First Five* Canterbury Tales. Stanford: Stanford UP, 1984.
Bowers, John M. "*The Tale of Beryn* and *The Siege of Thebes*: Alternative Ideas of *The Canterbury Tales*." *Studies in the Age of Chaucer* 7 (1985): 23–50.
Ferster, Judith. *Chaucer on Interpretation*. Cambridge: Cambridge UP, 1985.
Pearsall, Derek, *The Canterbury Tales*. London: Allen & Unwin, 1985.
Aers, David. *Chaucer*. Atlantic Highlands, NJ: Humanities Press International, 1986.
Benson, C. David. *Chaucer's Drama of Style: Poetic Variety and Contrast in the* Canterbury Tales. Chapel Hill: U of North Carolina P, 1986.
Ellis, Roger. *Patterns of Religious Narrative in the* Canterbury Tales. Totowa, NJ: Barnes & Noble, 1986.
Knight, Stephen. *Geoffrey Chaucer*. Oxford: Blackwell, 1986:
Olson, Paul A. *The Canterbury Tales and the Good Society*. Princeton: Princeton UP, 1986.
Howard, Donald R. *Chaucer: His Life, His Works, His World*. New York: E. P. Dutton, 1987.
Jordan, Robert M. *Chaucer's Poetics and the Modern Reader*. Berkeley: U of California P, 1987.
Lindahl, Carl. *Earnest Games: Folkloric Patterns in the* Canterbury Tales. Bloomington: Indiana UP, 1987.
Patterson, Lee. *Negotiating the Past: The Historical Understanding of Medieval Literature*. Madison: U of Wisconsin P, 1987.
Kendrick, Laura. *Chaucerian Play: Comedy and Control in the* Canterbury Tales. Berkeley: U of California P, 1988.
Koff, Leonard Michael. *Chaucer and the Art of Storytelling*. Berkeley: U of California P, 1988.
Cooper, Helen. *The Canterbury Tales*. Oxford Guides to Chaucer. New York: Oxford UP, 1989. 2nd ed., 1996.
Dinshaw, Carolyn. *Chaucer's Sexual Poetics*. Madison: U of Wisconsin P, 1989.
• Strohm, Paul. *Social Chaucer*. Cambridge, MA: Harvard UP, 1989.

Wetherbee, Winthrop. *Geoffrey Chaucer: The Canterbury Tales.* Cambridge: Cambridge UP, 1989.

Ganim, John M. *Chaucerian Theatricality.* Princeton: Princeton UP, 1990.

Georgianna, Linda. "The Protestant Chaucer." *Chaucer's Religious Tales.* Ed. C. David Benson and Elizabeth Robertson. Cambridge: D. S. Brewer, 1990. 55–69.

Knapp, Peggy. *Chaucer and the Social Contest.* New York: Routledge, 1990.

Leicester, H. Marshall, Jr. *The Disenchanted Self: Representing the Subject in the* Canterbury Tales. Berkeley: U of California P, 1990.

Brown, Peter, and Andrew Butcher. *The Age of Saturn: Literature and History in the Canterbury Tales.* Oxford: Basil Blackwell, 1991.

Kiser, Lisa J. *Truth and Textuality in Chaucer's Poetry.* Hanover, NH: UP of New England, 1991.

Mann, Jill. *Geoffrey Chaucer: Feminist Readings.* Atlantic Heights, NJ: Humanities Press International, 1991. New ed. *Feminizing Chaucer.* Rochester, NY: D. S. Brewer, 2002.

Patterson, Lee. *Chaucer and the Subject of History.* Madison: U of Wisconsin P, 1991.

Hansen, Elaine Tuttle. *Chaucer and the Fictions of Gender.* Berkeley: U of California P, 1992.

Olson, Glending. "Chaucer's Idea of a Canterbury Game." *The Idea of Medieval Literature: New Essays on Chaucer and Medieval Culture in Honor of Donald R. Howard.* Ed. James M. Dean and Christian Zacher. Newark: U of Delaware P, 1992. 72–90.

Pearsall, Derek. *The Life of Geoffrey Chaucer: A Critical Biography.* Oxford: Basil Blackwell, 1992.

Lerer, Seth. *Chaucer and his Readers: Imagining the Author in Late-Medieval England.* Princeton: Princeton UP, 1993.

Brown, Peter. *Chaucer at Work: The Making of the* Canterbury Tales. New York: Longman, 1994.

Crane, Susan. *Gender and Romance in Chaucer's* Canterbury Tales. Princeton: Princeton UP, 1994.

Wallace, David. *Chaucerian Polity: Absolutist Lineages and Associational Forms in England and Italy.* Stanford: Stanford UP, 1997.

Condren, Edward I. *Chaucer and the Energy of Creation: The Design and Organization of the* Canterbury Tales. Gainesville: UP of Florida, 1999.

Dinshaw, Carolyn. *Getting Medieval: Sexualities and Communities, Pre- and Postmodern.* Durham: Duke UP, 1999.

Olson, Glending. "Geoffrey Chaucer." *The Cambridge History of Medieval English Literature.* Ed. David Wallace. Cambridge: Cambridge UP, 1999. 566–88.

Collette, Carolyn P. *Species, Phantasms, and Images: Vision and Medieval Psychology in The* Canterbury Tales. Ann Arbor: U of Michigan P, 2001.

Trigg, Stephanie. *Congenial Souls: Reading Chaucer from Medieval to Postmodern.* Minneapolis: U of Minnesota P, 2002.

Burger, Glenn. *Chaucer's Queer Nation.* Minneapolis: U of Minnesota P, 2003.

THE GENERAL PROLOGUE

Eckhardt, Caroline D. *Chaucer's* General Prologue *to the* Canterbury Tales: *An Annotated Bibliography, 1900–1984.* Chaucer Bibliographies 3. Toronto: U of Toronto P, 1990.

Andrew, Malcolm; Charles Moorman; Daniel J. Ransom, eds., with Lynne Hunt Levy. *The General Prologue.* 2 vols. The Variorum Chaucer, II:1A and 1B. Norman: U of Oklahoma P, 1993.

Bowden, Muriel. *A Commentary on the General Prologue to the* Canterbury Tales. New York: Macmillan, 1948.

Cunningham, J. V. "The Literary Form of the Prologue to the *Canterbury Tales.*" *Modern Philology* 49 (1952): 172–81.

• Donaldson, E. Talbot. "Chaucer the Pilgrim." *PMLA* 69 (1954): 928–36. Rpt. in *Speaking of Chaucer.* New York: W. W. Norton & Company, 1970. 1–12.

• Hoffman, Arthur W. "Chaucer's Prologue to Pilgrimage: The Two Voices." *ELH: A Journal of English Literary History* 21 (1954): 1–16.

Baldwin, Ralph. "The Prologue." *The Unity of the* Canterbury Tales. Copenhagen: Rosenkilde and Bagger, 1955. 17–64.

Brooks, Harold F. *Chaucer's Pilgrims: The Artistic Order of the Portraits in the* Prologue. London: Methuen, 1962.

Jordan, Robert M. "Chaucer's Sense of Illusion: Roadside Drama Reconsidered." *ELH: A Journal of English Literary History* 29 (1962): 19–33.

Mann, Jill. *Chaucer and Medieval Estates Satire.* Cambridge: Cambridge UP, 1973.

Sumption, Jonathan. *Pilgrimage: An Image of Mediaeval Religion.* Totowa, NJ: Rowman and Littlefield, 1975.

Zacher, Christian K. *Curiosity and Pilgrimage: The Literature of Discovery in Fourteenth-Century England.* Baltimore: The Johns Hopkins UP, 1976.

Leicester, H. Marshall, Jr. "The Art of Impersonation: A General Prologue to the *Canterbury Tales.*" *PMLA* 95 (1980): 213–24.

Eberle, Patricia J. "Commercial Language and the Commercial Outlook in the *General Prologue.*" *Chaucer Review* 18 (1983): 161–74.

• Nolan, Barbara. " 'A Poet Ther Was': Chaucer's Voices in the General Prologue to *The Canterbury Tales.*" *PMLA* 101 (1986): 154–69.

Cooper, Helen. "Langland's and Chaucer's Prologues." *Yearbook of Langland Studies* 1 (1987): 71–81.

Georgianna, Linda. "Love So Dearly Bought: The Terms of Redemption in *The Canterbury Tales*." *Studies in the Age of Chaucer* 12 (1990): 85–116.

Leicester, H. Marshall, Jr. "Structure as Deconstruction: 'Chaucer and Estates Satire' in the *General Prologue*." *Exemplaria* 2 (1990): 241–61.

Stevens, Martin, and Daniel Woodward, eds. *The Ellesmere Chaucer: Essays in Interpretation*. San Marino, CA: Huntington Library, 1997 [essays on pilgrim portraits by Betsy Bowden, Richard K. Emmerson, and Alan T. Gaylord].

Bowers, John M. "Chaucer's Canterbury Tales—Politically Corrected." *Rewriting Chaucer: Culture, Authority, and the Idea of the Authentic Text, 1400–1602*. Ed. Thomas A. Prendergast and Barbara Kline. Columbus: Ohio State UP, 1999. 13–44.

Hodges, Laura F. *Chaucer and Costume: The Secular Pilgrims in the General Prologue*. Cambridge: D. S. Brewer, 2000.

Dyas, Dee. *Pilgrimage in Medieval English Literature 700–1500*. Cambridge: D. S. Brewer, 2001.

THE KNIGHT AND HIS TALE

Frost, William. "An Interpretation of Chaucer's Knight's Tale." *Review of English Studies* 25 (1949): 289–304.

Muscatine, Charles. "Form, Texture, and Meaning in Chaucer's *Knight's Tale*." *PMLA* 65 (1950): 911–29.

Owen, Charles A., Jr. "Chaucer's *Canterbury Tales*: Aesthetic Design in the Stories of the First Day." *English Studies* 35 (1954): 49–56.

Salter, Elizabeth. *Chaucer: The Knight's Tale and the Clerk's Tale*. London: Edward Arnold, 1962.

Hanning, Robert W. " 'The Struggle between Noble Design and Chaos': The Literary Tradition of Chaucer's *Knight's Tale*." *Literary Review* 23 (1980): 519–41.

Jones, Terry. *Chaucer's Knight: The Portrait of a Medieval Mercenary*. 1980; 2nd rev. ed. London: Methuen, 1994.

Minnis, A. J. *Chaucer and Pagan Antiquity*. Woodbridge, Suffolk: Boydell and Brewer, 1982.

Burrow, J. A. "Chaucer's *Knight's Tale* and the Three Ages of Man." *Essays on Medieval Literature*. Oxford: Clarendon P, 1984. 27–48.

Kolve, V. A. "*The Knight's Tale* and Its Settings: The Prison/Garden and the Tournament Amphitheatre." *Chaucer and the Imagery of Narrative*. Stanford: Stanford UP, 1984. 85–157.

Fowler, Elizabeth. "The Afterlife of the Civil Dead: Conquest in the Knight's Tale." *Critical Essays on Geoffrey Chaucer*. Ed. Thomas C. Stillinger. New York: G. K. Hall, 1987. 59–81.

Leicester, H. Marshall, Jr. "The Institution of the Subject: A Reading of the *Knight's Tale*." *The Disenchanted Self: Representing the Subject in the Canterbury Tales*. Berkeley: U of California P, 1990. 219–382.

Wetherbee, Winthrop. "Romance and Epic in Chaucer's *Knight's Tale*." *Exemplaria* 2 (1990): 303–28.

Nolan, Barbara. *Chaucer and the Tradition of the Roman Antique*. Cambridge: Cambridge UP, 1992.

Fradenburg, Louise O. "Sacrificial Desire in Chaucer's *Knight's Tale*." *Journal of Medieval and Early Modern Studies* 27 (1997): 47–75. Rpt. in L. O. Aranye Fradenburg, *Sacrifice Your Love: Psychoanalysis, Historicism, Chaucer*. Minneapolis: U of Minnesota P, 2002. 155–75.

Ingham, Patricia Clare. "Homosociality and Creative Masculinity in the Knight's Tale." *Masculinities in Chaucer: Approaches to Maleness in the Canterbury Tales and Troilus and Criseyde*. Ed. Peter G. Beidler. Cambridge: D. S. Brewer, 1998. 23–35.

Pratt, John H. *Chaucer and War*. Lanham, MD: UP of America, 2000.

Jones, Terry. "The Image of Chaucer's Knight." *Speaking Images: Essays in Honor of V. A. Kolve*. Ed. Robert F. Yeager and Charlotte C. Morse. Asheville, NC: Pegasus Press, 2001. 205–36.

THE MILLER AND HIS TALE

Ross, Thomas W., ed. *The Miller's Tale*. The Variorum Chaucer, II:3. Norman: U of Oklahoma P, 1983.

Burton, T. L., and Rosemary Greentree, eds. *Chaucer's Miller's, Reeve's, and Cook's Tales*. Chaucer Bibliographies 5. Toronto: U of Toronto P, 1997.

Donaldson, E. Talbot. "Idiom of Popular Poetry in the *Miller's Tale*." *English Institute Essays 1950*. Ed. Alan S. Downer. New York: Columbia UP, 1951. 116–40.

Harder, Kelsie B. "Chaucer's Use of the Mystery Plays in the *Miller's Tale*." *Modern Language Quarterly* 17 (1956): 193–98.

Olson, Paul A. "Poetic Justice in the *Miller's Tale*." *Modern Language Quarterly* 24 (1963): 227–36.

Rowland, Beryl. "The Play of the *Miller's Tale*: A Game Within a Game." *Chaucer Review* 5 (1970): 140–46.

Beidler, Peter G. "Art and Scatology in the *Miller's Tale*." *Chaucer Review* 12 (1977): 90–102.

Kolve, V. A. "The Miller's Tale: Nature, Youth, and Nowell's Flood." *Chaucer and the Imagery of Narrative*. Stanford: Stanford UP, 1984. 158–216.

Patterson, Lee. " 'No Man His Reson Herde': Peasant Consciousness, Chaucer's Miller, and the Structure of the *Canterbury Tales.*" *South Atlantic Quarterly* 86 (1987): 457–95. Rpt. as "The *Miller's Tale* and the Politics of Laughter" in *Chaucer and the Subject of History*. Madison: U of Wisconsin P, 1991. 244–79.

Farrell, Thomas J. "Privacy and the Boundaries of Fabliau in the *Miller's Tale.*" *ELH* 56 (1989): 773–95.

Lochrie, Karma. "Women's 'Pryvetees' and Fabliau Politics in the *Miller's Tale.*" *Exemplaria* 6 (1994): 287–304.

Miller, Mark. "Naturalism and Its Discontents in the *Miller's Tale.*" *ELH* 67 (2000): 1–44.

Mann, Jill. "Speaking Images in Chaucer's Miller's Tale.' " *Speaking Images: Essays in Honor of V. A. Kolve*. Ed. Robert F. Yeager and Charlotte C. Morse. Asheville, NC: Pegasus P, 2001. 237–53.

Nolan, Barbara. "Playing Parts : Fragments, Figures and the Mystery of Love in "The Miller's Tale.' " *Speaking Images: Essays in Honor of V. A. Kolve*. Ed. Robert F. Yeager and Charlotte C. Morse. Asheville, NC: Pegasus P, 2001. 255–99.

THE REEVE AND HIS TALE

Burton, T. L., and Rosemary Greentree, eds. *Chaucer's Miller's, Reeve's, and Cook's Tales*. Chaucer Bibliographies 5. Toronto: U of Toronto P, 1997.

Moffett, H. Y. "Oswald the Reeve." *Philological Quarterly* 4 (1925): 208–23.

Tolkien, J. R. R. "Chaucer as a Philologist: *The Reeve's Tale.*" *Transactions of the Philological Society* (1934): 1–70.

Copland, Murray. "*The Reeve's Tale*: Harlotrie or Sermonyng?" *Medium Ævum* 31 (1962): 14–32.

Olson, Paul A. "The *Reeve's Tale*: Chaucer's *Measure for Measure.*" *Studies in Philology* 59 (1962): 1–17.

Delany, Sheila. "Clerks and Quiting in the *Reeve's Tale.*" *Mediaeval Studies* 29 (1967): 351–56.

Friedman, John B. "A Reading of Chaucer's *Reeve's Tale.*" *Chaucer Review* 2 (1967): 8–19.

Brewer, Derek. "The *Reeve's Tale* and the King's Hall, Cambridge." *Chaucer Review* 5 (1971): 311–17.

Olson, Glending. "The *Reeve's Tale* as a Fabliau." *Modern Language Quarterly* 35 (1974): 219–30.

Plummer, John F. " 'Hooly Chirches Blood': Simony and Patrimony in Chaucer's *Reeve's Tale.*" *Chaucer Review* 18 (1983): 49–60.

Kolve, V. A. "The Reeve's Prologue and Tale: Death-as-Tapster and the Horse Unbridled." *Chaucer and the Imagery of Narrative*. Stanford: Stanford UP, 1984. 217–56.

Fein, Susanna Greer. " 'Lat the Children Pleye': The Game Betwixt the Ages in The Reeve's Tale." *Rebels and Rivals: The Contestive Spirit in* The Canterbury Tales. Ed. Susanna Greer Fein, David Raybin, and Peter C. Braeger. Kalamazoo: Medieval Institute Publications, 1991. 73–104.

Harwood, Britton J. "Psychoanalytic Politics: Chaucer and Two Peasants." *ELH* 68 (2000): 1–27.

THE COOK AND HIS TALE

Burton, T. L., and Rosemary Greentree, eds. *Chaucer's Miller's, Reeve's, and Cook's Tales*. Chaucer Bibliographies 5. Toronto: U of Toronto P, 1997.

Stanley, E. G. " 'Of this cokes tale maked Chaucer na moore.' " *Poetica* (Tokyo) 5 (1976): 36–59.

Kolve, V. A. "The Cook's Tale and the Man of Law's Introduction: Crossing the Hengwrt/Ellesmere Gap." *Chaucer and the Imagery of Narrative*. Stanford: Stanford UP, 1984. 257–96.

Scattergood, V. J. "Perkyn Revelour and the *Cook's Tale.*" *Chaucer Review* 19 (1984): 14–23. Rpt. in *Reading the Past: Essays on Medieval and Renaissance Literature*. Portland, OR: Four Courts, 1996. 183–91.

Wallace, David. "Chaucer and the Absent City." *Chaucer's England: Literature in Historical Context*. Ed. Barbara A. Hanawalt. Minneapolis: U of Minnesota P, 1991. 59–90. Rpt. in *Chaucerian Polity* (Stanford: Stanford UP, 1997), chapter 6.

Strohm, Paul. " 'Lad with Revel to Newegate': Chaucerian Narrative and Historical Meta-Narrative." *Art and Context in Late Medieval English Narrative: Essays in Honor of Robert Worth Frank, Jr*. Ed. Robert R. Edwards. Cambridge: D. S. Brewer, 1994. 163–76. Rpt. in *Theory and the Premodern Text*. Minneapolis: U of Minnesota P, 2000. 51–64.

Kang, Ji-Soo. "The (In)completeness of the Cook's Tale." *Medieval English Studies* 5 (1997): 145–70.

THE WIFE OF BATH AND HER TALE

Beidler, Peter G., and Elizabeth M. Biebel. *Chaucer's* Wife of Bath's Prologue and Tale: *An Annotated Bibliography, 1900 to 1995.* Chaucer Bibliographies 6. Toronto: U of Toronto P, 1998.
Shumaker, Wayne. "Alisoun in Wander-land: A Study in Chaucer's Mind and Literary Method." *ELH: A Journal of English Literary History* 18 (1951): 77–89.
Silverstein, Theodore. "The Wife of Bath and the Rhetoric of Enchantment; or, How to Make a Hero See in the Dark." *Modern Philology* 58 (1960–61): 153–73.
Pratt, Robert A. "The Development of the Wife of Bath." *Studies in Medieval Literature.* Ed. MacEdward Leach. Philadelphia: U of Pennsylvania P, 1961. 45–79.
———. "Jankyn's Book of Wikked Wyves: Medieval Antimatrimonial Propaganda in the Universities." *Annuale Mediaevale* 3 (1962): 5–27.
Matthews, William. "The Wife of Bath and All Her Sect." *Viator* 5 (1974): 413–43.
Carruthers, Mary. "The Wife of Bath and the Painting of Lions." *PMLA* 94 (1979): 209–22.
Robertson, D. W., Jr. " 'And For My Land Thus Hastow Mordred Me?': Land Tenure, the Cloth Industry, and the Wife of Bath." *Chaucer Review* 14 (1980): 403–20.
Patterson, Lee. " 'For the Wyves love of Bathe': Feminine Rhetoric and Poetic Resolution in the *Roman de la Rose* and the *Canterbury Tales.*" *Speculum* 58 (1983): 656–95.
Fradenburg, Louise O. "The Wife of Bath's Passing Fancy." *Studies in the Age of Chaucer* 8 (1986): 31–58.
Knapp, Peggy A. "Alisoun Weaves a Text." *Philological Quarterly* 65 (1986): 387–401. Rpt. in *Chaucer and the Social Contest.* New York: Routledge, 1990. 114–28.
Crane, Susan. "Alison's Incapacity and Poetic Instability in the Wife of Bath's Tale." *PMLA* 102 (1987): 20–28.
Hansen, Elaine Tuttle. "The Wife of Bath and the Mark of Adam." *Women's Studies* 15 (1988): 399–416. Rpt. in *Chaucer and the Fictions of Gender.* Berkeley: U of California P, 1992. 26–57.
Blamires, Alcuin. "The Wife of Bath and Lollardy." *Medium Ævum* 58 (1989): 224–42.
Dinshaw, Carolyn. " 'Glose/bele chose': The Wife of Bath and Her Glossators." *Chaucer's Sexual Poetics.* Madison: U of Wisconsin P, 1989. 113–31.
Leicester, H. Marshall, Jr. *The Disenchanted Self: Representing the Subject in the* Canterbury Tales." Berkeley: U of California P, 1990. Chapters 2–5.
Galloway, Andrew. "Marriage Sermons, Polemical Sermons, and *The Wife of Bath's Prologue*: A Generic Excursus." *Studies in the Age of Chaucer* 14 (1992): 3–30.
Strohm, Paul. "Treason in the Household." *Hochon's Arrow: The Social Imagination of Fourteenth-Century Texts*: Princeton: Princeton UP, 1992. 121–44.
Beidler, Peter G., ed. *The Wife of Bath: Complete, Authoritative Text with Biographical and Historical Contexts, Critical History, and Essays from Five Contemporary Critical Perspectives.* Boston: Bedford-St. Martin's, 1996 [critical essays by Laurie Finke, Louise O. Fradenburg, Elaine Tuttle Hansen, H. Marshall Leicester, Jr., and Lee Patterson].

THE FRIAR AND HIS TALE

Birney, Earle. "*After His Ymage*—The Central Ironies of the *Friar's Tale.*" *Mediaeval Studies* 21 (1959): 17–35.
Mroczkowski, Przemyslaw. "The *Friar's Tale* and Its Pulpit Background." *English Studies Today.* Ed. G. A. Bonnard. Berne: Franke, 1961. 107–20.
Richardson, Janette. "Hunter and Prey: Functional Imagery in Chaucer's *Friar's Tale.*" *English Miscellany* 12 (1961): 9–20. Rpt. in *Blameth Nat Me: A Study of Imagery in Chaucer's Fabliaux.* The Hague: Mouton, 1970. 73–85.
Szittya, Penn R. "The Green Yeoman as Loathly Lady: The Friar's Parody of the *Wife of Bath's Tale.*" *PMLA* 90 (1975): 386–94.
Bloomfield, Morton W. "The *Friar's Tale* as a Liminal Tale." *Chaucer Review* 17 (1983): 286–91.
Hahn, Thomas, and Richard W. Kaeuper. "Text and Context: Chaucer's *Friar's Tale.*" *Studies in the Age of Chaucer* 5 (1983): 67–101.
Kolve, V. A. " 'Man in the Middle': Art and Religion in Chaucer's *Friar's Tale.*" *Studies in the Age of Chaucer* 12 (1990): 5–46.
Ridley, Florence H. "The Friar and the Critics." *The Idea of Medieval Literature: New Essays on Chaucer and Medieval Culture in Honor of Donald R. Howard.* Ed. James M. Dean and Christian Zacher. Newark: U of Delaware P, 1992. 160–72.
Wallace, David. "The Powers of the Countryside." *Chaucerian Polity.* Stanford: Stanford UP, 1997. 136–44.
Kline, Daniel T. " 'Myne by Right': Oath Making and Intent in *The Friar's Tale.*" *Philological Quarterly* 77 (1998): 271–93.
Somerset, Fiona. " 'Mark Him Wel for He Is On of Þo' : Training the 'Lewed' Gaze to Discern Hypocrisy." *ELH* 68 (2001): 315–34.

THE SUMMONER AND HIS TALE

Plummer, John F., ed. *The Summoner's Tale.* The Variorum Chaucer, II:7. Norman: U of Oklahoma P, 1995.

Fleming, John V. "The Antifraternalism of the *Summoner's Tale.*" *Journal of English and Germanic Philology* 65 (1966): 688–700.

———. "The Summoner's Prologue: An Iconographic Adjustment." *Chaucer Review* 2 (1967): 95–107.

Levitan, Alan. "The Parody of Pentecost in the *Summoner's Tale.*" *U of Toronto Quarterly* 40 (1971): 236–46.

Szittya, Penn R. "The Friar as False Apostle: Antifraternal Exegesis and the *Summoner's Tale.*" *Studies in Philology* 71 (1974): 19–46. Rpt. in *The Antifraternal Tradition in Medieval Literature.* Princeton: Princeton UP, 1986. 231–46.

Clark, Roy Peter. "Doubting Thomas in Chaucer's *Summoner's Tale.*" *Chaucer Review* 11 (1976): 164–78.

Wentersdorf, Karl P. "The Motif of Exorcism in the *Summoner's Tale.*" *Studies in Short Fiction* 17 (1980): 249–54.

Fleming, John V. "Anticlerical Satire as Theological Essay: Chaucer's *Summoner's Tale.*" *Thalia* 6:1 (1983): 5–22.

Hanning, Robert W. "Roasting a Friar, Mis-taking a Wife, and Other Acts of Textual Harassment in Chaucer's *Canterbury Tales.*" *Studies in the Age of Chaucer* 7 (1985): 3–21.

Mann, Jill. "Anger and 'Glosynge' in the *Canterbury Tales.*" *Proceedings of the British Academy* 76 (1990): 203–23.

Kolve, V. A. "Chaucer's Wheel of False Religion: Theology and Obscenity in the *Summoner's Tale.*" *The Centre and Its Compass: Studies in Medieval Literature in Honor of Professor John Leyerle.* Ed. Robert Taylor, James F. Burke, Patricia J. Eberle, Ian Lancashire, and Brian S. Merrilees. Kalamazoo: Medieval Institute Publications, 1993. 265–96.

Cox, Catherine S. " 'Grope Wel Bihynde': The Subversive Erotics of Chaucer's Summoner." *Exemplaria* 7 (1995): 145–77.

Wallace, David. "The Powers of the Countryside." *Chaucerian Polity.* Stanford: Stanford UP, 1997. 144–52.

Olson, Glending. "The End of *The Summoner's Tale* and the Uses of Pentecost." *Studies in the Age of Chaucer* 21 (1999): 209–45.

Somerset, Fiona. " 'As just as is a squyre': The Politics of 'Lewed Translacion' in Chaucer's *Summoner's Tale.*" *Studies in the Age of Chaucer* 21 (1999): 187–207.

Bowers, John M. "Queering the Summoner: Same-Sex Union in Chaucer's *Canterbury Tales.*" *Speaking Images: Essays in Honor of V. A. Kolve.* Ed. Robert F. Yeager and Charlotte C. Morse. Asheville, NC: Pegasus P, 2001. 301–24.

THE CLERK AND HIS TALE

Sledd, James. "The *Clerk's Tale*: The Monsters and the Critics." *Modern Philology* 51 (1953–54): 73–82.

Salter, Elizabeth. *Chaucer: The Knight's Tale and the Clerk's Tale.* London: Edward Arnold, 1962.

McCall, John P. "The *Clerk's Tale* and the Theme of Obedience." *Modern Language Quarterly* 27 (1966): 260–69.

Utley, Francis Lee. "Five Genres in the *Clerk's Tale.*" *Chaucer Review* 6 (1972): 198–228.

Frese, Dolores W. "Chaucer's *Clerk's Tale*: The Monsters and the Critics Reconsidered." *Chaucer Review* 8 (1973): 133–46.

Johnson, Lynn Staley. "The Prince and His People: A Study of the Two Covenants in the *Clerk's Tale.*" *Chaucer Review* 10 (1975): 17–29.

Middleton, Anne. "The Clerk and his Tale: Some Literary Contexts." *Studies in the Age of Chaucer* 2 (1980): 121–50.

Wimsatt, James I. "The Blessed Virgin and the Two Coronations of Griselda." *Mediaevalia* 6 (1980): 187–207.

Morse, Charlotte C. "The Exemplary Griselda." *Studies in the Age of Chaucer* 7 (1985): 51–86.

Ganim, John M. "Carnival Voices and the Envoy to the *Clerk's Tale.*" *Chaucer Review* 22 (1987): 112–27. Rpt. in *Chaucerian Theatricality.* Princeton: Princeton UP, 1990. 79–91.

Dinshaw, Carolyn. "Griselda Translated." *Chaucer's Sexual Poetics.* Madison: U of Wisconsin P, 1989. 132–55.

Morse, Charlotte C. "Critical Approaches to the 'Clerk's Tale'." *Chaucer's Religious Tales.* Ed. C. David Benson and Elizabeth Robertson. Cambridge: D. S. Brewer, 1990. 71–83.

Wallace, David. " 'Whan She Translated Was': A Chaucerian Critique of the Petrarchan Academy." *Literary Practice and Social Change in Britain, 1380–1530.* Ed. Lee Patterson. Berkeley: U of California P, 1990. 156–215. Rpt. in *Chaucerian Polity.* Stanford: Stanford UP, 1997. 261–98.

Bronfman, Judith. *Chaucer's Clerk's Tale: The Griselda Story Received, Rewritten, Illustrated.* New York: Garland, 1994.

Georgianna, Linda. "The Clerk's Tale and the Grammar of Assent." *Speculum* 70 (1995): 793–821.

Stanbury, Sarah. "Regimes of the Visual in Premodern England: Gaze, Body, and Chaucer's *Clerk's Tale*." *New Literary History* 28 (1997): 261–89.
Morse, Charlotte C. "Griselda Reads Philippa de Coucy." *Speaking Images: Essays in Honor of V. A. Kolve*. Ed. Robert F. Yeager and Charlotte C. Morse. Asheville, NC: Pegasus P, 2001. 347–92.
Olson, Glending. "The Marquis of Saluzzo and the Marquis of Dublin." *Speaking Images: Essays in Honor of V. A. Kolve*. Ed. Robert F. Yeager and Charlotte C. Morse. Asheville, NC: Pegasus P, 2001. 325–45.

THE MERCHANT AND HIS TALE

Burrow, J. A. "Irony in the *Merchant's Tale*." *Anglia* 75 (1957): 199–208.
Olson, Paul A. "Chaucer's Merchant and January's 'hevene in erthe heere,' " *ELH* 28 (1961): 203–14.
Jordan, Robert M. "The Non-Dramatic Disunity of the Merchant's Tale." *PMLA* 78 (1963): 293–99. Rpt. in *Chaucer and the Shape of Creation*. Cambridge, MA: Harvard UP, 1967. 132–51.
Donaldson, E. Talbot. "The Effect of the Merchant's Tale." *Speaking of Chaucer*. New York: W. W. Norton & Company, 1970. 30–45.
Brown, Emerson, Jr. "Chaucer, the Merchant, and Their Tale: Getting Beyond Old Controversies." Parts I and II. *Chaucer Review* 13 (1978–79): 141–56, 247–62.
Wentersdorf, Karl P. "Imagery, Structure, and Theme in Chaucer's *Merchant's Tale*." *Chaucer and the Craft of Fiction*. Ed. Leigh A. Arrathoon. Rochester, MI.: Solaris Press, 1986. 35–62.
Mandel, Jerome. "The Unity of Fragment IV (Group E): The *Clerk's Tale* and the *Merchant's Tale*." *Hebrew University Studies in Literature and the Arts* 16 (1988): 27–50.
Edwards, A. S. G. "*The Merchant's Tale* and Moral Chaucer." *Modern Language Quarterly* 51 (1990): 409–26.
Jager, Eric. "The Carnal Letter in Chaucer's Earthly Paradise." *The Tempter's Voice: Language and the Fall in Medieval Literature*. Ithaca: Cornell UP, 1993. 241–98.
Jost, Jean. "May's Mismarriage of Youth and Elde: The Poetics of Sexual Desire in Chaucer's *Merchant's Tale*." *Feminea Medievalia I: Representations of the Feminine in the Middle Ages*. Ed. Bonnie Wheeler. Cambridge: Academia P, 1993. 117–38.
Rose, Christine. "Women's 'Pryvete,' May, and the Privy: Fissures in the Narrative Voice in the *Merchant's Tale*, 1944–86." *Chaucer Yearbook* 4 (1997): 61–77.
Lucas, Angela M. "The Mirror in the Marketplace: Januarie Through the Looking Glass." *Chaucer Review* 33 (1998): 123–45.

THE FRANKLIN AND HIS TALE

Sledd, James. "Dorigen's Complaint." *Modern Philology* 45 (1947): 36–45.
Blenner-Hassett, Roland. "Autobiographical Aspects of Chaucer's Franklin." *Speculum* 28 (1953): 791–800.
Gaylord, Alan T. "The Promises in *The Franklin's Tale*." *ELH: A Journal of English Literary History* 31 (1964): 331–65.
David, Alfred. "Sentimental Comedy in *The Franklin's Tale*." *Annuale Mediaevale* 6 (1965): 19–27.
Mann, Lindsay A. " 'Gentilesse' and the Franklin's Tale." *Studies in Philology* 63 (1966): 10–29.
Berger, Harry, Jr. "The F-Fragment of the *Canterbury Tales*." *Chaucer Review* 1 (1966–67): 88–102, 135–56.
Peck, Russell. "Sovereignty and the Two Worlds of the *Franklin's Tale*." *Chaucer Review* 1 (1967): 253–71.
Kearney, A. M. "Truth and Illusion in *The Franklin's Tale*," *Essays in Criticism* 19 (1969): 245–53.
Knight, Stephen. "Ideology in *The Franklin's Tale*." *Parergon* 28 (1980): 3–31.
Saul, Nigel. "The Social Status of Chaucer's Franklin: A Reconsideration." *Medium Ævum* 52 (1983): 10–26.
Kolve, V. A. "Rocky Shores and Pleasure Gardens: Poetry vs. Magic in Chaucer's *Franklin's Tale*." *Poetics: Theory and Practice in Medieval English Literature*. Ed. Piero Boitani and Anna Torti. Cambridge: D. S. Brewer, 1991. 165–95.
Riddy, Felicity. "Engendering Pity in the *Franklin's Tale*." *Feminist Readings in Middle English Literature: The Wife of Bath and All Her Sect*. Ed. Ruth Evans and Lesley Johnson. London: Routledge, 1994. 54–71.
Edwards, Robert R. "Source, Context, and Cultural Translation in the *Franklin's Tale*." *Modern Philology* 94 (1996): 141–62.
Green, Richard Firth. "Rash Promises." *A Crisis of Truth: Literature and Law in Ricardian England*. Philadelphia: U of Pennsylvania P, 1999. 293–335.
Lightsey, Scott. "Chaucer's Secular Marvels and the Medieval Economy of Wonder." *Studies in the Age of Chaucer* 23 (2001): 289–316.

THE PARDONER AND HIS TALE

Sutton, Marilyn. *Chaucer's Pardoner's Prologue and Tale: An Annotated Bibliography, 1900 to 1995.* Chaucer Bibliographies 7. Toronto: U of Toronto P, 2000.

Kellogg, Alfred L. "An Augustinian Interpretation of Chaucer's Pardoner." *Speculum* 26 (1951): 465–81.

Miller, Robert P. "Chaucer's Pardoner, the Scriptural Eunuch, and the Pardoner's Tale." *Speculum* 30 (1955): 180–99.

Steadman, John M. "Old Age and *Contemptus Mundi* in *The Pardoner's Tale.*" *Medium Ævum* 33 (1964): 121–30.

Howard, Donald R. "The Pardoner and the Parson." *The Idea of the* Canterbury Tales. Berkeley: U of California P, 1976, 333–87.

Patterson, Lee W. "Chaucerian Confession: Penitential Literature and the Pardoner." *Medievalia et Humanistica* n.s. 7 (1976): 153–73. Rpt. in *Chaucer and the Subject of History.* Madison: U of Wisconsin P, 1991. 367–421.

Minnis, A. J. "Chaucer's Pardoner and the 'Office of Preacher'." *Intellectuals and Writers in Fourteenth-Century Europe.* Ed. Piero Boitani and Anna Torti. Tubingen: Narr; Cambridge: Brewer, 1986. 88–119.

• Dinshaw, Carolyn. "Eunuch Hermeneutics." *ELH* 55 (1988): 27–51.

Leicester, H. Marshall, Jr. *The Disenchanted Self: Representing the Subject in the* Canterbury Tales. Berkeley: U of California P, 1990. Chapters 1, 6, 7.

Burger, Glenn. "Kissing the Pardoner." *PMLA* 107 (1992): 1143–56. Rpt. in *Chaucer's Queer Nation.* Minneapolis: U of Minnesota P, 2003. 140–59.

Frantzen, Allen J. "*The Pardoner's Tale*, the Pervert, and the Price of Order in Chaucer's World." *Class and Gender in Early English Literature: Intersections.* Ed. Britton J. Harwood and Gillian R. Overing. Bloomington: Indiana UP, 1994. 131–48.

Kruger, Steven F. "Claiming the Pardoner: Toward a Gay Reading of Chaucer's *Pardoner's Tale.*" *Exemplaria* 6 (1994): 115–39.

Dinshaw, Carolyn. "Chaucer's Queer Touches / A Queer Touches Chaucer." *Exemplaria* 7 (1995): 75–92. Rpt. in *Getting Medieval: Sexualities and Communities, Pre- and Postmodern.* Durham: Duke UP, 1999. 100–43.

Sturges, Robert S. *Chaucer's Pardoner and Gender Theory: Bodies of Discourse.* New York: St. Martin's P, 2000.

Kelly, Henry Ansgar. "The Pardoner's Voice: Disjunctive Narrative and Modes of Effemination." *Speaking Images: Essays in Honor of V. A. Kolve.* Ed. Robert F. Yeager and Charlotte C. Morse. Asheville, NC: Pegasus P, 2001. 411–44.

Lynch, Kathryn L. "The Pardoner's Digestion: Eating Images in *The Canterbury Tales.*" *Speaking Images: Essays in Honor of V. A. Kolve.* Ed. Robert F. Yeager and Charlotte C. Morse. Asheville, NC: Pegasus P, 2001. 393–409.

Patterson, Lee. "Chaucer's Pardoner on the Couch: Psyche and Clio in Medieval Literary Studies." *Speculum* 76 (2001): 638–80.

THE PRIORESS AND HER TALE

Boyd, Beverly, ed. *The Prioress's Tale.* The Variorum Chaucer, II:20. Norman: U of Oklahoma P, 1987.

Lowes, John Livingston. "Simple and Coy: A Note on Fourteenth-Century Poetic Diction." *Anglia* 33 (1910): 440–51.

Schoeck, Richard J. "Chaucer's Prioress: Mercy and Tender Heart." *The Bridge: Yearbook of Judaeo-Christian Studies* 2 (1956): 239–55.

Beichner, Paul E., C.S.C. "The Grain of Paradise." *Speculum* 36 (1961): 302–307.

Gaylord, Alan T. "The Unconquered Tale of the Prioress." *Papers of the Michigan Academy of Science, Arts, and Letters* 47 (1962): 613–36.

Ridley, Florence H. *The Prioress and the Critics.* University of California English Studies 30. Berkeley and Los Angeles: U of California P, 1965.

Langmuir, Gavin I. "The Knight's Tale of Young Hugh of Lincoln." *Speculum* 47 (1972): 459–82.

Wood, Chauncey. "Chaucer's Use of Signs in His Portrait of the Prioress." *Signs and Symbols in Chaucer's Poetry.* Ed. John P. Hermann and John J. Burke, Jr. University, AL: U of Alabama P, 1981, 81–101.

Frank, Robert Worth, Jr. "Miracles of the Virgin, Medieval Anti-Semitism, and the 'Prioress's Tale.'" *The Wisdom of Poetry: Essays in Early English Literature in Honor of Morton W. Bloomfield.* Ed. Larry D. Benson and Siegfried Wenzel. Kalamazoo: Medieval Institute Publications, 1982. 177–88.

Fradenburg, Louise O. "Criticism, Anti-Semitism and the *Prioress's Tale.*" *Exemplaria* 1 (1989): 69–115.

Ferster, Judith. "'Your Praise is Performed by Men and Children': Language and Gender in the *Prioress's Prologue and Tale.*" *Exemplaria* 2 (1990): 149–68.

Robertson, Elizabeth. "Aspects of Female Piety in the *Prioress's Tale.*" *Chaucer's Religious Tales.* Ed. C. David Benson and Elizabeth Robertson. Cambridge: D. S. Brewer, 1990. 145–60.

Rex, Richard. *"The Sins of Madame Eglentyne" and Other Essays on Chaucer.* Newark: U of Delaware P, 1995.

Kelly, Henry Ansgar. "A Neo-Revisionist Look at Chaucer's Nuns." *Chaucer Review* 31 (1996): 115–32.

Patterson, Lee. " 'The Living Witnesses of Our Redemption': Martyrdom and Imitation in Chaucer's Prioress's Tale." *Journal of Medieval and Early Modern Studies* 31 (2001): 507–60.

CHAUCER'S TALES OF SIR THOPAS AND MELIBEE

Loomis, Laura Hibbard. "Chaucer and the Auchinleck MS: *Thopas and Guy of Warwick.*" *Essays and Studies in Honor of Carleton Brown.* [no editor]. New York: New York UP, 1940. 111–28.

Gaylord, Alan T. "Chaucer's Dainty 'Dogerel': The 'Elvyssh' Prosody of *Sir Thopas.*" *Studies in the Age of Chaucer* 1 (1979): 83–104. Rpt. in *Chaucer's Humor: Critical Essays.* Ed. Jean E. Jost. New York: Garland, 1994. 271–94.

Scattergood, V. J. "Chaucer and the French War: *Sir Thopas* and *Melibee.*" *Court and Poet.* Ed. Glyn S. Burgess et al. Liverpool: Cairns, 1981. 287–96.

Benson, C. David. "Their Telling Difference: Chaucer the Pilgrim and His Two Contrasting Tales." *Chaucer Review* 18 (1983): 61–76. Rpt. *Chaucer's Drama of Style: Poetic Variety and Contrast in the* Canterbury Tales. Chapel Hill: U of North Carolina P, 1986. 26–43.

Gaylord, Alan T. "The 'Miracle' of *Sir Thopas.*" *Studies in the Age of Chaucer* 6 (1984): 65–84.

Askins, William. "*The Tale of Melibee* and the Crisis at Westminster, November, 1387." *Studies in the Age of Chaucer, Proceedings, No. 2 (1986).* Ed. John V. Fleming and Thomas J. Heffernan. Knoxville, TN: New Chaucer Society, 1987. 103–12.

Yeager, R. F. " 'Pax Poetica': On the Pacifism of Chaucer and Gower." *Studies in the Age of Chaucer* 9 (1987): 97–121.

Kempton, Daniel. "Chaucer's *Melibee*: 'A lytel thyng in prose'." *Genre* 21 (1988): 263–78.

Patterson, Lee. " 'What Man Artow?': Authorial Self-Definition in *The Tale of Sir Thopas* and *The Tale of Melibee.*" *Studies in the Age of Chaucer* 11 (1989): 117–75.

Johnson, Lynn Staley. "Inverse Counsel: Contexts for the *Melibee.*" *Studies in Philology* 87 (1990): 137–55. See also David Aers and Lynn Staley. *The Powers of the Holy.* University Park, PA: The Pennsylvania State UP, 1996. 217–33.

Lerer, Seth. " 'Now Holde Youre Mouthe': The Romance of Orality in the *Thopas-Melibee* Section of the *Canterbury Tales,*" *Oral Poetics in Middle English Poetry.* Ed. Mark C. Amodio. New York: Garland, 1994. 181–205.

Burrow, J. A. "Elvish Chaucer." *The Endless Knot: Essays on Old and Middle English in Honor of Marie Borroff.* Ed. M. Teresa Tavormina and R. F. Yeager. Cambridge: D. S. Brewer, 1995. 105–11.

Collette, Carolyn P. "Heeding the Counsel of Prudence: A Context for the *Melibee.*" *Chaucer Review* 29 (1995): 416–33.

Ferster, Judith. "Chaucer's *Tale of Melibee*: Advice to the King and Advice to the King's Advisers." *Fictions of Advice: The Literature and Politics of Counsel in Late Medieval England.* Philadelphia: U of Pennsylvania P, 1996. 89–107.

Blamires, Alcuin. *The Case for Women in Medieval Culture.* Oxford: Clarendon P, 1997.

Wallace, David. "Household Rhetoric: Violence and Eloquence in the *Tale of Melibee.*" *Chaucerian Polity.* Stanford: Stanford UP, 1997. 212–46.

Burger, Glenn. "Mapping a History of Sexuality in Melibee." *Chaucer and Language: Essays in Honour of Douglas Wurtele.* Ed. Robert Myles and David Williams. Montreal: McGill-Queen's UP, 2001. 61–70, 198–203.

THE NUN'S PRIEST AND HIS TALE

Pearsall, Derek, ed. *The Nun's Priest's Tale.* The Variorum Chaucer, II:9. Norman: U of Oklahoma P, 1984.

Curry, Walter Clyde. "Chauntecleer and Pertelote on Dreams." *Englische Studien* 58 (1924): 24–60.

Young, Karl. "Chaucer and Geoffrey of Vinsauf." *Modern Philology* 41 (1943–44): 172–82.

Donovan, Mortimer J. "The *Moralite* of the Nun's Priest's Sermon." *Journal of English and Germanic Philology* 52 (1953): 498–508.

Manning, Stephen. "The Nun's Priest's Morality and the Medieval Attitude toward Fables." *Journal of English and Germanic Philology* 59 (1960): 403–16.

Allen, Judson B. "The Ironic Fruyt: Chauntecleer as Figura." *Studies in Philology* 66 (1969): 25–35.

Pratt, Robert A. "Three Old French Sources of the Nonnes Preestes Tale." *Speculum* 47 (1972): 422–44, 646–68.

Donaldson, E. Talbot. "The Nun's Priest's Tale." *Chaucer's Poetry: An Anthology for the Modern Reader.* 2nd ed. New York: Ronald Press, 1975. 1104–08.

Gallacher, Patrick. "Food, Laxatives, and Catharsis in Chaucer's Nun's Priest's Tale." *Speculum* 51 (1976): 49–68.

Travis, Peter W. "Chaucer's Trivial Fox Chase and the Peasants' Revolt of 1381." *Journal of Medieval and Renaissance Studies* 18 (1988): 195–220.

Scanlon, Larry. "The Authority of Fable: Allegory and Irony in the 'Nun's Priest's Tale.' " *Exemplaria* 1 (1989): 43–68.
McAlpine, Monica E. "The Triumph of Fiction in the Nun's Priest's Tale." *Art and Context in Late Medieval English Narrative: Essays in Honor of Robert Worth Frank, Jr.* Ed. Robert R. Edwards. Cambridge: D. S. Brewer, 1994. 79–92.
Kempton, Daniel. "The Nun's Priest's Festive Doctrine: 'Al That Written Is.' " *Assays* 8 (1995): 101–18.
Wheatley, Edward. "Commentary Displacing Text: 'The Nun's Priest's Tale' and the Scholastic Fable Tradition." *Studies in the Age of Chaucer* 18 (1996): 119–41.
Varty, Kenneth. *Reynard, Renart, Reinaert and Other Foxes in Medieval England: The Iconographic Evidence.* Amsterdam: Amsterdam UP, 1999.

THE MANCIPLE AND HIS TALE

Baker, Donald C., ed. *The Manciple's Tale.* The Variorum Chaucer, II.10. Norman: U of Oklahoma P, 1984.
Shumaker, Wayne. "Chaucer's Manciple's Tale as Part of the Canterbury Group." *University of Toronto Quarterly* 22 (1953): 147–56.
Hazelton, Richard. "The *Manciple's Tale:* Parody and Critique." *Journal of English and Germanic Philology* 62 (1963): 1–31.
Scattergood, V. J. "The Manciple's Manner of Speaking." *Essays in Criticism* 24 (1974): 124–46.
Dean, James. "The Ending of the *Canterbury Tales.*" *Texas Studies in Language and Literature* 21 (1979): 17–33.
Fradenburg, Louise O. "The Manciple's Servant Tongue: Politics and Poetry in The *Canterbury Tales.*" *ELH* 52 (1985): 85–118.
Burrow, J. A. "Chaucer's Canterbury Pilgrimage." *Essays in Criticism* 36 (1986): 97–119.
Allen, Mark. "Penitential Sermons, the Manciple, and the End of *The Canterbury Tales.*" *Studies in the Age of Chaucer* 9 (1987): 77–96.
Grudin, Michaela Paasche. "Chaucer's Manciple's Tale and the Poetics of Guile." *Chaucer Review* 25 (1991): 329–42.
Fisher, John H. "A Gentil Mauneiple Was Ther of a Temple." *Chaucer's Pilgrims: An Historical Guide to the Pilgrims in* The Canterbury Tales. Ed. Laura C. Lambdin and Robert T. Lambdin. Westport, CT.: Greenwood, 1996. 281–87.
Ginsburg, Warren. "Chaucer's Canterbury Poetics: Irony, Allegory, and the *Prologue To The Manciple's Tale.*" *Studies in the Age of Chaucer* 18 (1996): 55–89.
Kensak, Michael. "Apollo Exterminans: The God of Poetry in Chaucer's Manciple's Tale." *Studies in Philology* 98 (2001): 143–57.

THE PARSON'S TALE AND CHAUCER'S RETRACTION

Gordon, James D. "Chaucer's Retraction: A Review of Opinion." *Studies in Medieval Literature in Honor of Professor Albert Croll Baugh.* Ed. MacEdward Leach. Philadelphia. U of Pennsylvania P, 1961. 81–96.
Campbell, A. P. "Chaucer's 'Retraction': Who Retracted What?" *University of Ottawa Quarterly* 35 (1965): 35–53.
Sayce, Olive. "Chaucer's 'Retraction': The Conclusion of the *Canterbury Tales* and Its Place in Literary Tradition." *Medium Ævum* 40 (1971): 230–48.
Allen, Judson Boyce. "The Old Way and the Parson's Way: An Ironic Reading of the *Parson's Tale.*" *Journal of Medieval and Renaissance Studies* 3 (1973): 255–71.
Howard, Donald R. "The Pardoner and the Parson." *The Idea of the* Canterbury Tales. Berkeley: U of California P, 1976. 333–87.
Delasanta, Rodney. "Penance and Poetry in the *Canterbury Tales.*" *PMLA* 93 (1978): 240–47.
• Patterson, Lee. "The *Parson's Tale* and the Quitting of the *Canterbury Tales.*" *Traditio* 34 (1978): 331–80.
Wurtele, Douglas J. "The Penitence of Geoffrey Chaucer." *Viator* 11 (1980): 335–61.
Taylor, Paul Beekman. "The Parson's Amyable Tongue." *English Studies* 64 (1983): 401–09.
McGerr, Rosemarie Potz. "Retraction and Memory: Retrospective Structure in the *Canterbury Tales.*" *Comparative Literature* 37 (1985): 97–113.
Lawton, David. "Chaucer's Two Ways: The Pilgrimage Frame of *The Canterbury Tales.*" *Studies in the Age of Chaucer* 9 (1987): 3–40.
Bestul, Thomas H. "Chaucer's Parson's Tale and the Late-Medieval Tradition of Religious Meditation." *Speculum* 64 (1989): 600–19.
Travis, Peter W. "Deconstructing Chaucer's Retraction." *Exemplaria* 3 (1991): 135–58.
Raybin, David, and Linda Tarte Holley, eds. *Closure in* The Canterbury Tales: *The Role of* The Parson's Tale. Kalamazoo: Medieval Institute Publications, 2000. [Critical essays by Judith Ferster, Charlotte Gross, Holley, Peggy Knapp, Richard Newhauser, Raybin, Gregory Roper, and Siegfried Wenzel; extensive bibliography by Raybin]